The Writing Program Administrator's Resource

A Guide to Reflective Institutional Practice

The Writing Program Administrator's Resource

A Guide to Reflective Institutional Practice

Edited by

Stuart C. Brown
New Mexico State University

Theresa Enos
University of Arizona

Catherine Chaput, Assistant Editor
University of Arizona

2002

LAWRENCE ERLBAUM ASSOCIATES, PUBLISHERS
Mahwah, New Jersey   London

Appendices found at the end of this volume are copyrighted by the
Council of Writing Program Administrators. Reprinted by permission.

Lawrence Erlbaum Associates, Inc., Publishers
10 Industrial Avenue
Mahwah, NJ 07430

Cover design by Kathryn Houghtaling Lacey

Library of Congress Cataloging-in-Publication Data

The writing program administrator's resource : a guide to reflective in-
   stitutional practice / edited by Stuart C. Brown, Theresa Enos,
   Catherine Chaput.
      p. cm.
      Includes bibliographical references and index.
ISBN 0-8058-3826-0 (cloth : alk. paper)
ISBN 0-8058-3827-9 (pbk. : alk. paper)
1. English language—Rhetoric—Study and teaching—United States.
   2. Report writing—Study and teaching (Higher)— United States.
   3. Writing centers—Administration.   I. Brown, Stuart C. (Stuart
   Cameron), 1955– . II. Enos, Theresa. III. Chaput, Catherine.
PE1405.U6 W76 2002
808'.042'071173—dc21   2001051220
                                                                  CIP

Books published by Lawrence Erlbaum Associates are printed on acid-
free paper, and their bindings are chosen for strength and durability.

Printed in the United States of America
10 9 8 7 6 5 4 3 2 1

Contents

꧁ • ꧂

v

Moving Forward: This Foreword

Lynn Z. Bloom
University of Connecticut, Storrs

HANDBOOKS AND THIS HANDBOOK

"Trust yourself. You know more than you think you do," begins Dr. Benjamin Spock's *Baby and Child Care*, with the words that helped make this compendium of useful advice an American classic for half a century. His reassurance continues, "Don't take too seriously all that the neighbors say. Don't be overawed by what the experts say. Don't be afraid to trust your own common sense." In the same soothing vein, he addresses what may be the most complex undertaking of a person's lifetime: "Bringing up your child won't be a complicated job if you take it easy, trust your own instincts, and follow the directions that your doctor gives you" (3). Then follow five hundred pages of very specific directions on How To Do It, proffered by the Expert.

Handbooks of all sorts, whether manuals on how to rear children or repair cars or use standard grammar and mechanics or administer writing programs, are for newcomers—the uncertain, the insecure—as well as the confident who need a ready reference. "It's a good first child book," was Spock's realistic appraisal of his own work. "After that, parents develop confidence and use it primarily to look up specific information in crises." As a novice or prospective writing program administrator, you (I use here the Spockian pronoun) may have had considerable formal education in the subject, and you may be highly sophisticated on an intellectual and theoretical level. You have a good abstract understanding of at least some of the major aspects of the job at hand or you wouldn't have been hired to do it. You may even have served as an apprentice writing program administrator (WPA), in graduate school or in another job. Or perhaps you may, as Polonious observed, have had greatness thrust upon you. In any case, you have never before had the experience of being in charge for the long term. But now here's your own baby, sitting there plump and energetic, right in your lap. What can you do to ensure the appropriate care and feeding of this complex organism, its healthy growth, and its survival over the years—responding to challenges and circumstances that at this point you can't even imagine? And how can you be proactive, providing leadership in a myriad of new areas, new issues rather than providing essentially reactive responses to the hazards on an incendiary turf, putting out fires in one place only to have them break out in another?

The answers to these questions—and many more—are in your hands. Literally. For in the *Writing Program Administrator's Resource,* you can turn for advice to established leaders in the field, scholar-administrators who have not only endured but prevailed, moving the field along even as they have constructed it, with intelligence, authority, and a humane spirit. Because the authors are experts, in the spirit of all handbooks, they straighten out the snarls and offer sensible solutions to the problems; they make even the most complicated of processes seem doable, the most convoluted of conflicts seem manageable. They proffer access, authority, and plans of action. Nevertheless, because these chapters are conceived as a colloquy rather than a compilation of arbitrary pronouncements, neither the authors nor the handbook's editors envision these commentaries as the last—or the only—words on the subject. As readers, you should feel free to enter the conversation, explore the subjects at hand, bring your own experience to bear on the issues, debate; you can adapt and adopt what you read here, modify it, or reject it out of hand and compose your own responses that will take the subject down familiar paths or in entirely new directions. It's up to you.

TITLES AND ROLES: THE VELCRO JOB

Although the *Writing Program Administrator's Resource* abounds in goodwill and good sense, it contains no jokes. To rectify that omission, I offer one that I had to invent, there being a dearth of humorous renderings of the subject: "How many WPAs does it take to change a light bulb?" Or "a student's grade?" Or "a curriculum?" Think about it. In many writing programs, there can be but a single answer: "One"—a single individual responsible for everything, and to whom a plethora of tasks cling as lint to velcro. The titles vary, "Writing Director" (or Coordinator, or Chair), "Director of Freshman Composition," "Writing-across-the-Curriculum Director," "Writing Center Director," "Writing Project Director," "TA Trainer." I have met at least one

"Reflection, Assessment, and Articulation: A Rhetoric of Writing Program Administration"), community outreach (Ann Marie Hall, "Expanding the Community: A Comprehensive Look at Outreach and Articulation"), computing (McAllister and Selfe, identified above), writing centers (Carol Peterson Haviland, "Writing Centers, Writing Programs, and WPAs"), TA training (Daphne Desser and Darin Payne, "WPA Internships"; Edward M. White, "Teaching a Graduate Course in Writing Program Administration"; Meg Morgan, "The GTA Experience"; Amanda Brobbel et al., "GAT Training in Collaborative Teaching ..."), and curricular issues (Yvonne Merrill and Thomas P. Miller, "Making Learning Visible: A Rhetorical Stance on General Education"; and Martha Townsend, "Writing across the Curriculum"). One chapter focuses specifically on community colleges, Victoria Holmsten, "This Site Under Construction: Negotiating Space for WPA Work in the Community College," and another, by Barry Maid, argues for "an independent department of writing."

Political Issues

The administration of writing programs, like other sorts of administration, is seen by the authors of many of these chapters as a political activity—"the science" (or, if you will, art), "of who gets what, when, and why." Dwight D. Eisenhower supplemented this definition with contradictory claims of his own (both made before he was elected president): "Politics is a profession; a serious, complicated and, in its true sense, a noble one" and "Politics ... excites all that is selfish and ambitious in man." WPAs could claim that both are accurate, the former as it applies to their own job, the latter as it applies to those who would tamper with the proper execution of that job—whether conducted by a single individual or a team (see Phelps; Douglas Hesse, "Politics and the WPA"; and Jeanne Gunner, "Collaborative Administration"). Another truism may be found in the claim that "All politics is local"—as the issues are played out, for instance, in the competition for institutional resources: personnel, space, teaching loads, technological support, and more, always more and never enough. But, as *The WPA Resource* makes clear, many of the perspectives are national; they enable the WPA to think globally and to recognize that not only the problems but the solutions—most of which have profound ethical implications—lie in the wider world. Thus Stuart Brown's "Applying Ethics" acknowledges the ethical dimensions of such pervasive matters as "curriculum development, teacher training, intellectual property issues, research methods, data presentation, faculty hiring, evaluation"—and explores the complications that arise when "what seems the right thing to do" conflicts with what seems the easiest (see chap. 10, this volume).

In "Politics and the WPA: Traveling Through and Past Realms of Expertise," Douglas Hesse, who defines politics as "the art of moving people or

- creating insight and communicating forms of experience through artistic works or performance (175–76; qtd. in WPA 9–10).

The WPA's job, continues "Evaluating the Intellectual Work," may be considered intellectual work when it "meets two tests": (a) advancing knowledge, through "production, clarification, connection, reinterpretation, or application," and (b) resulting in "products or activities" that others can evaluate according to their "high level of discipline-related expertise," degree of innovation, ability to be "replicated or elaborated," with results that can be "documented" and "peer-reviewed," and that have "significance or impact" (Diamond and Adam, 14; qtd. in WPA 10). The chapters by Louise Wetherbee Phelps ("Turtles All the Way Down: Educating Academic Leaders"), Theresa Enos ("Reflexive Professional Development: Getting Disciplined in Writing Program Administration"), Gail Stygall ("Certifying the Knowledge of WPAs"), Shirley K. Rose and Irwin Weiser ("WPA as Researcher and Archivist"), and Ken S. McAllister and Cynthia L. Selfe ("Writing Program Administration and Instructional Computing")—among others—offer a wealth of innovative perspectives on ways to think about and enact the WPA's intellectual work. Rose and Weiser, for instance, identify common characteristics of WPA research—its purpose "is to understand program practices in order to improve or retain them"; its participant-subjects are the "program stakeholders—instructional staff, writing students, other faculty and administrators," and the WPA. Its diverse practices and constituencies necessitate "multimethodological" inquiry (see chap. 18, this volume). Chapters such as these are also useful in enabling the WPA to assume a proactive, assertive stance, rather than a beleaguered posture, on occasions when the intellectual dimensions of the WPA's work are under review (as by a promotion/tenure committee) or attack.

Whether these activities are undertaken for the purposes of "instituting change" or "instituting practice" (the handbook's two overarching categories), the handbook offers (in most chapters) a combination of theory and specific information on a wide range of topics that can be translated into institutional scholarship, "the scholarship of administration," in Boyer's term. In these chapters WPAs can find discussions of either institutional practices or research methodology (or both) that will enable them to address local issues and best (possibly worst!) practices from a national perspective. The handbook encourages WPAs to think beyond the confines of their particular institutions in dealing with local administrative issues—such as coexisting with literature faculty and curricula (John Schilb, "The WPA and the Politics of LitComp"), part-timers (Eileen Schell, "Part-time/Adjunct Issues: Working toward Change"), budgeting (Chris Anson, "Figuring It Out: Writing Programs in the Context of University Budgets"), placement (Daniel J. Royer and Roger Gilles, "Placement Issues"), assessment (Christopher Burnham,

- To define, reinterpret, better understand, or reconceive one or more aspects of one's professional role, particularly if it is new or evolving.
- To find intellectual reinforcement (not just in the chapters but in their appended bibliographies), or ethical support for one's current endeavors.
- To find kindred spirits and a sense of community among WPAs, from novices to nabobs.
- To discover new and good ideas, to gain a sense of what works—and how, when, and under what circumstances to try to implement policies and make changes.
- To legitimate one's own inventions, or forays into the institutional unknown. To enable the WPA to go effectively and efficiently where no administrator at one's own school has ever gone before, many of the chapters provide very specific advice to combat the routine deterrent, "It can't be done—we've never done it before." Other WPAs have indeed been there, done that, and this Handbook reflects a variety normative institutional practices around the country.

The Scholarship of Administration

Every chapter of *The Writing Program Administrator's Resource* addresses, directly or indirectly, issues raised in the Council of Writing Program Administrators statement on "Evaluating the Intellectual Work of Writing Administration." This document (see Appendix) offers a "contemporary scholarly paradigm" derived from MLA's "Making Faculty Work Visible." This includes such "projects and enterprises" as:

- creating new questions, problems, information, interpretations, designs, products, frameworks of understanding … through inquiry;
- clarifying, critically examining, weighing, and revising the knowledge claims, beliefs, or understanding of others and oneself;
- connecting knowledge to other knowledge;
- preserving … and reinterpreting past knowledge;
- applying aesthetic, political, and ethical values to make judgments about knowledge and its uses;
- arguing knowledge claims in order to invite criticism and revision;
- making specialized knowledge broadly accessible and usable, e.g., to young learners, to nonspecialists in other disciplines, to the public;
- helping new generations to become active knowers themselves, preparing them for lifelong learning and discovery;
- applying knowledge to practical problems in significant or innovative ways; and

"Convener." In some schools the "Department Chair," perhaps even a "Division Head" or "Dean," administers the writing program along with everything else. In "Writing Program Administration as Preparation for an Administrative Career," David Schwalm, now both a Vice-Provost and Dean, observes, in fact, that "the WPA is usually viewed as a quasi-administrator," trying with difficulty to fulfill the conflicting roles of both faculty and WPA, in contrast to the real administrator, the Dean, whose authority—and salary—reflect genuine institutional power (see chap. 8, this volume).

Any title simplifies the WPA's protean job, which inevitably encompasses a myriad of endeavors from the mundane to the magnificent. Among the numerous roles embedded in the label are policymaker, problem solver, curriculum designer, lobbyist, personnel recruiter and evaluator, teacher, teacher trainer, mentor, judge, community or secondary school liaison, fiscal manager, accountant, fundraiser, computer programmer, test developer, program evaluator, Web designer, scheduler, record keeper, office manager, secretary. More irreverent language might echo the *Chronicle of Higher Education*'s title, "Beggar, Psychologist, Mediator, Maid: The Thankless Job of a Chairman" (March 2, 2001). Add "nurturer," "scold" and "nag"—are we sounding parental yet? Whether these duties combine to give the WPA the status of a CEO—or that of an academic concierge—depends on the nature of the school, the level of support, as well as the personality and aims of the person occupying the job. Louise Wetherbee Phelps summarizes the "wildly divergent self-images of the WPA" that appear in professional narratives: "the exploited worker in the basement, denied tenure; the defiant hero besieged by hostile forces; the clever, manipulative politician; the hapless victim of campus intrigues or arbitrary administrators; the conciliator who mediates ideological conflict; the collaborative colleague who shares power; the radical who seizes writing program administration as an Archimedean lever for transforming society" (see chap. 1, this volume).

Missing from the foregoing discussion are three significant roles—researcher, scholar, and writer—that most likely were for most of us the principal attractions to the academic life, specifically to a career investment in writing. Indeed, for many of the seasoned WPAs who are contributors to this handbook, scholarship and research are of paramount importance, in ways that the next section explains.

DIMENSIONS OF WRITING PROGRAM ADMINISTRATION: SCHOLARSHIP, POLITICS, ETHICS

Ways to Use This Book

Whatever one's title or specific duties as caretakers, inventors, problem solvers (and these are guaranteed to change), there are many reasons to read this handbook, as a source of reference, information, and ammunition:

groups to action on matters that require their assent," offers an astute analysis of how WPAs can negotiate the politics of "time, space, and money" in the departmental, institutional, professional, and public spheres. More specific discussions on some of the more politically freighted issues deal with budgets (Anson), student placement (Daniel J. Royer and Roger Gilles, "Placement Issues"), student performance (Gregory R. Glau, "Hard Work and Hard Data: Using Statistics to Help Your Program"), assessment (Burnham), part-time faculty (Schell); many of these issues are exacerbated when WPAs are token members of a literature-oriented English department (Schilb). David Schwalm ("Writing Program Administration as Preparation for an Administrative Career") and Susan McLeod ("Moving Up the Administrative Ladder") present generally positive views of administrative negotiations and professional advancement. Offering a "nerd hypothesis" of administrative failure, Schwalm identifies the basic social skills necessary for the complex social interactions of academic management: "Faculty tend to be critical, analytical, open-ended, focused, self-centered, and uncompromising; administrators tend to be synthetic, goal oriented, comprehensive in their views, open to compromise—often confused with being wishy washy, valueless, and arbitrary" (see chap. 8, this volume). He offers specific advice on how to shift successfully from faculty member to administrator, which McLeod reinforces with a host of resources—publications, workshops, and mentor—but, she cautions, "be careful what you wish for. University administration is very hard work" (see chap. 7, this volume).

But two chapters are more troubling—some would say three if they are bothered by Sharon Crowley's utopian proposition to make first-year composition elective, in "How the Professional Lives of WPAs Would Change if FYC Were Elective." However, Crowley is discussing what she sees as curricular best practices. The other two chapters deal with worst practices. In chapter 22, Julia Ferganchick's "Contrapower Harassment in Program Administration: Establishing Teacher Authority" reports on her study of "student-to-teacher harassment in writing classrooms." Claiming that neither classroom teachers nor WPAs can completely control "aggressive student behavior," she offers possible solutions through policies on attendance, plagiarism, grading, and conduct. In chapter 9, Veronica Pantoja, Nancy Tribbensee, and Duane Roen raise legal considerations for WPAs: "lines of responsibility/liability," contracts, sexual harassment, copyright, disclosures (of criminal activity, e.g.) by students, disruptive behavior, "hiring practices and personnel evaluations," and recommendation letters. They identify numerous web sites to consult for help, and the protection provided by NCTE's insurance, currently "up to $2,000,000 per claim for a variety of exposures, including 'hiring unqualified persons' and 'failure to educate'" (chap. 9, this volume). Read this terrifying chapter last—but miss it at your peril. Indeed this handbook, like all reference guides, is better read with a specific focus, in small batches, as the need arises. Rebecca Jackson and Patricia Wojahn's "Select Annotated Bibliography" (chap. 30) is a lovely lagniappe.

BACK TO THE FUTURE

As you consult the experts whose advice follows, it's reassuring to remember Dr. Spock's advice in the opening pages of *Baby and Child Care*. "Parents are human," he cautions. "They have needs." "Some children are a lot more difficult than others." "At best, there's lots of hard work and deprivation," but "needless self-sacrifice sours everybody." "Parents should expect something from their children." It is "not humanly possible" for even the best of parents to have "unlimited patience and love for their innocent baby"; parents are "bound to get cross," especially if they "set impossibly high standards for themselves." Admit your "crossness" and "blue feelings," Spock advises, "love for the baby comes gradually." "One trouble with being an inexperienced parent is that part of the time you take the job so seriously that you forget to enjoy it" (4–11).

So, relax. You will find as you read these pages that you do indeed know more than you think you do, for some of the chapters will reify the combination of common sense, formal knowledge, and practical experience that you are bringing to the job of WPA. Other chapters will take you in new directions and stimulate your own thinking and perhaps research. The cutting edge moves ever forward, making any edition of a handbook obsolete within a decade—much sooner in the gargantuan endeavor of writing program administration which has to stay current in order to flourish. With a combination of reflective practice, innovative research, and love of the enterprise, you may become a contributor to the Handbook's next edition.

WORKS CITED

"Evaluating the Intellectual Work of Writing Administration." <http://www.cas.ilstu.edu/English/Hesse/intellec.htm>.
Spock, Benjamin. *Baby and Child Care*. 2nd ed. New York: Pocket, 1957.

Polyvocality and Writing Program Administration: An Introduction

◁╫ • ▷

Stuart C. Brown
New Mexico State University

Theresa Enos
University of Arizona

The genesis for *The Writing Program Administrator's Resource: A Guide to Reflective Institutional Practice* came from the recognition that WPAs wear many, many hats. The nature of writing program administration is inclusive—it comprises people with different talents, backgrounds, and education. It is perhaps *the* single most inclusive position in a modern college or university. The WPA is both administrator and faculty. Unlike department heads who also straddle this divide, the nature of writing program work usually crosses academic boundaries. The WPA necessarily is very much a person with many specialties. To encompass these sometime competing roles requires people of unique character and training.

As good rhetoricians are wont to do, we began this project with a particular audience in mind: the new or aspiring WPA. We sought to develop a collection of articles for this audience that would address fundamental practices and issues encountered by WPAs in their workplace settings. We felt that new WPAs especially need practical, applicable tools to effectively address the many differing, and sometimes competing, roles they find themselves in. But as we worked in shaping the collection, in soliciting various authorities in the

xvii

field, and in working with the authors on their contributions, we came to realize that the book has much to offer not only the new WPA but also the experienced WPA. We found ourselves returning time and again to the recognition that WPAs come in all sizes, shapes, and colors. Formal preparation and training, however, is only now beginning to catch up to the very real needs of not just the new or aspiring WPA but those too who have been making it up as they went along, often for years. We came to realize that the experience represented by the voices here were not simply for the newly initiated but for all of us. We found ourselves rejuvenated in our approaches to our own WPA work.

As the project developed, we also came to realize that WPA work is increasingly specialized *and* professionalized. The list of topics and identities that occur under the umbrella of WPA continues to expand; this did not make the scope of the project any easier. One has only to scan the lists of diverse duties noted in the "Portland Resolution: Guidelines for Writing Program Administrator Positions" adopted by the national Council of Writing Program Administrators (reprinted in Appendix) to become aware of the complex roles WPAs find themselves performing. We became aware that to teach and write in the discipline of rhetoric and composition was in itself a very real and important kind of WPA work. The intellectual work done by WPAs in program creation, curricular design, faculty development, program assessment and evaluation, and program-related textual production is further proof of the viability of writing program administration as a discipline and as a career (see "Evaluating the Intellectual Work of Writing Administration" developed by the Council of Writing Program Administrators and reprinted in the Appendix).

The steady growth of the Council of Writing Program Administrators as an organization, the burgeoning number of graduate programs offering coursework in writing program administration, and the number of publications devoted to writing program administration signal that the profession is maturing. One has only to look at the number of jobs advertised each year that specify writing program administration as a component to note the increasing value placed on the work we do. Writing program administration is now very much a discipline in its own right.

The complexity, multiplicity, and inclusiveness of how we see this discipline—its polyvocality—created problems for us as editors. It was not until we began to write this Introduction that we came upon our final title. The working title, *The WPA Handbook*, sufficed to get us to this point. *Handbook*, however, never felt quite right—too suggestive of brief, alphabetized entries. At various points, we considered calling the book an *encyclopedia* or a *field guide* or a *sourcebook*, given its depth of coverage and comprehensiveness. These genres, however, seemed too prescriptive. In reflecting on the contents of the book, it became clear that both reflection and the idea of WPAs as agents of institutional change and practice are key elements here, thus our subtitle.

Our list of topics quickly outgrew the physical limitations of a book. Organizing the contributions that are here was a challenge in its own right. In these problems, however, we see opportunities. We encourage you to see this book as *praxis*, as an opportunity to reflect on your working life as well as shape its nature. Most of all, however, we envision this book as an essential desk reference, a text as close at hand as the *MLA Handbook* or a dictionary, a resource to consult as the daily complexities of WPA life occur. Hence, *The Writing Program Administrator's Resource: A Guide to Reflective Institutional Practice*.

A note to the new or aspiring WPA: We would like you to consider first and foremost "Why do you want to be a WPA?" To assume a position as a WPA means you are now *It*. You oversee curriculum development, train faculty and graduate students, delegate authority, dole out resources, hire and fire employees, and promote literacy standards. Writing programs are synonymous to many students (and parents and faculty and administrators across campus) with English studies. You deal with problems, some that occur in the classroom and some that occur outside of the classroom. Every day brings challenges in allocating resources, resolving conflicts, and heading off crises. You make *It* work. Your position epitomizes the definition of service. You are a manager, a trainer, sometimes confessor, financial analyst, psychologist, technologist, and mediator. And you likely were trained as a teacher and a scholar. You very likely see yourself as a teacher, researcher, and writer. Very few of your colleagues in your home department, although many will be supportive and sympathetic, fully understand what it is you do. However, you will join a unique cadre of professionals across the country who direct writing programs, writing centers, and writing-across-the-curriculum efforts. This is a collection of their voices, a catalog of their experiences in addressing the complex issues and tasks faced by WPAs.

Working on this collection has been a delight. First, and foremost, the level of professionalism demonstrated by our contributors made the book seem to come together on its own. Second, the work they have provided has truly enriched our understanding of what it means to be a WPA and how to fulfill that role more effectively. The utility and value of this book is very much a result of the inherent hard work, intelligence, and willingness to serve a larger cause exemplified by WPAs everywhere.

We would also like to acknowledge the contribution of Linda Bathgate, our editor at Lawrence Erlbaum, whose confidence in the project made this book possible. Chris Burnham and Larry Evers, department heads at New Mexico State University and the University of Arizona respectively, contributed as only good department heads can in supporting both this particular work and our work as WPAs. We dedicate this book to those WPAs who inspire us by their example, to those WPAs who continue to serve, and, most of all, to those who will follow as the next generation.

I

INSTITUTING CHANGE

1

Turtles All the Way Down: Educating Academic Leaders

⟨❦⟩ • ⟨❦⟩

Louise Wetherbee Phelps
Syracuse University

Leadership education is a neglected goal of faculty development, even in the most enlightened of recent efforts to rethink the career and preparation of the future professoriate. For most academics, leadership is a tacit dimension of service, little noticed or valued as a situated responsibility of institutional life. Few graduate teachers think of leadership in that sense as a faculty competence to be cultivated in doctoral education. As for administration, it is stereotyped as the refuge of those less talented as scholars or past their prime. Narratives by faculty who have become administrators portray it as an accident that befalls an unsuspecting professor, drafted into reluctant duty and entirely naive about what it involves. Administration as intellectual leadership remains, for graduate students and young professors, almost unimaginable as a professional role they might aspire to as part of a faculty career. As a result, most faculty members are woefully unprepared for the complex challenges of program and departmental leadership that many will, sooner or later, take on.

This situation strikes me as very dangerous in the present circumstances of the academy. A tide of cultural and structural change accompanying the global transformation to an information society is rippling through American higher education just as it has other sectors of society. With it comes the breakdown of a century-old paradigm that gave stable meaning and social respect to academic work and faculty roles. No longer trusted to serve the pub-

3

lic good through the autonomous practice of its professional expertise, the professoriate is compelled to renegotiate its compact with society.

Even as higher education tries to reinvent itself for new purposes and realities, American universities are already educating the graduate students who will replace 40 percent of the faculty in the next decade or so. Either these graduates will become a reservoir of leaders whose ideas and energies significantly strengthen the ability of higher education to adapt creatively and thrive; or they will forfeit the opportunity to competitors, including a variety of external policy makers, top-down reformers, and alternate providers of professional credentials and learning options.[1] To become equal partners in reform rather than futile resisters or passive objects of it, faculty themselves must develop thoughtful programs to foster the development of leaders from their own ranks—programs designed to operate seamlessly throughout a faculty career from graduate school to senior leadership roles in higher education.

I would like to advance that work in this essay. Composition and rhetoric is in a unique position to contribute to this goal, since it has pioneered the concept of administration as scholarly and professional work, constituted and certified by its own specialized research, literature, and professional organization. Inevitably, success with this strategy generated the need to credential writing program administrators (WPAs) as professionals through doctoral education. Steps in that direction include the electronic circulation of course plans, recent conference sessions on educating WPAs, and the production of texts for graduate study. Writing program administration is too singular a professional role to provide a universal model for educating faculty leaders, especially at the graduate level. But in focusing here on developing administrative leaders in composition and rhetoric, I hope my analysis can at many points speak more broadly to the challenge that faces all disciplines to help faculty throughout their careers undertake leadership roles as academic citizens and administrators.

The story is told about William James, that after a lecture he was approached by a lady who insisted that the earth is not a round globe circling the sun, but a layer of earth resting on the back of a giant turtle. But, asked James, what does the turtle stand on? "The first turtle stands on the back of another turtle, of course," she replied complacently. "Well, then, what does the second turtle stand on?" The old lady wasn't fazed. "It's no use, Mr. James—it's turtles all the way down!"

---

[1]The most recent issue of the influential series *Policy Perspectives* claims that higher education is ill-served by its present system of choosing leaders, which produces "a managerial talent pool that is neither deep nor broad nor skilled enough" (6), and argues for recruiting senior administrators from outside the academy. Although recognizing there is untapped talent among the faculty, this essay focuses not on developing faculty into leaders but on changing the criteria and methods for selection to favor "those whose training falls outside the traditional box," especially nonacademics ("Inside Out" 8).

When they hear the word *leader*, most people still tend to envision a single, powerful individual dominating activity and decision making from the top down. But, as research and postmodern organizational practice tell us, leadership is understood today as an interdependent function of a dynamic system.[2] Among other things, this means that you can cut through the layers of an academic organization and find leaders all the way down. Unlike the old lady's simple universe, with its turtles stacked like pancakes, a cross section of a college or university reveals a fractal structure, with irregular patterns of leadership repeated at smaller and smaller scales of organization. Any time a group coalesces formally or informally around purposeful activity—a committee, task force, council, senate, research group, or union— leaders emerge because leadership is a necessary function of human enterprises. So leadership is an everyday, if largely invisible, part of belonging to a college faculty. In composition, it is more likely than in most disciplines that this responsibility will rise to a program or departmental level, that it may come early in a faculty career, and that it will require specialized disciplinary expertise in the intellectual work of administration. For that reason, graduate education in rhetoric and composition must incorporate specialized leadership education for prospective WPAs while also providing some level of preparation and opportunities for all students to play leadership roles as academic citizens.

Consider some other implications of the proposition that academic leadership is "turtles all the way down":

- **It applies at all stages of a faculty career.** The opportunity or obligation to be a leader doesn't wait for formal preparation or institutional investment of authority. Students in graduate school (if not before) are already citizens of the academy who may lead in many settings: within student groups and organizations, department and university committees, or a teaching community; in collaborative research projects, conference planning, community outreach, and national professional organizations; even in formal administrative positions (coordinating or supervising the work of others). These early responsibilities are not unique to rhetoric and composition, but they are unusually encouraged and enabled in many of its doctoral programs. Similarly, young compositionists, even when not appointed in positions of formal authority, often take leadership or have

---

[2]For systems views of leadership, see, for example, Berquist; Peeples; Phelps, "Institutional" and "Telling"; and Senge. Similarly, cognition is analyzed in recent theories as socially and culturally "distributed" rather than located in the individual's head (Salomon); and creativity is conceptualized not as a personal attribute, but as a set of relations among person, domain, and field (Csikszentmihalyi). Compare also the view of situated, distributed learning discussed later (Lave and Wenger).

semiadministrative roles in writing programs. But the need for leadership education is not confined to graduate students or those entering major administrative positions as junior faculty (a distinctive feature of writing program administration): It recurs whenever faculty members make the transition to new leadership roles and need professional development to prepare and support them.

• **It means WPAs themselves must teach leadership.** Besides their role as graduate educators, WPAs are responsible for promoting the learning of all workers in the academic environment. If leadership does permeate the system, it is not only right but smart to identify and cultivate leaders among faculty peers, junior faculty, contingent faculty, and staff and to support them through professional development programs, mentoring, access to significant tasks and positions, and other means. Good leadership is, almost by definition, leadership development.

These considerations will lead me to propose an integrated practical model for developing leaders that addresses the full range of needs, settings, and interdependencies implied in a fractal theory of leadership.

EXPERIMENTS IN LEADERSHIP DEVELOPMENT

I recently served again as administrator of my department (an independent writing program) during a transition from one leader to another. This interim position allowed me to experiment with an idea I had been advocating for our newly established PhD program in composition and cultural rhetoric (CCR): offering part-time fellowships in writing program administration, designed to combine opportunities to observe, participate in, study, and discuss administrative and institutional processes.[3] I found some budgeted administrative duties I could assign to four graduate students to replace one or two sections of their teaching assistantships; paired them with staff mentors who normally supervised these tasks; and arranged access to administrative information, functions, and interactions for the "CCR Administrative Fellows." Assignments were matched as closely as possible to students' skills, learning goals, and career aspirations. These opportunistic arrangements, ad hoc as they

---

[3]My ideas are deeply indebted to my own experience in the ACE Fellows Program, an outstanding leadership development program for higher education administrators (see http://www.acenet.edu/programs/fellows/home.cfm). The year-long program triangulates self-directed learning in three sites: placement with an administrative mentor at an institution or educational organization; travel to conferences, institutions, and organizations; and intensive one-week seminars with peer Fellows, balancing observation and participation and blending varied modes of learning. I advocate adapting features of this program to preparing leaders within their institutions at every level of administration and governance, as my experiment imperfectly approximated.

were, provided immediate benefits to graduate students, while allowing coparticipants to develop the concept and demonstrate its viability and value in a pilot program.

Some unique circumstances enabled me to synergize this project with other modes and stages of leadership education. While helping to create a leadership development program for the university's new and continuing department chairs, I had advocated expanding this initiative to include recruiting and educating prospective leaders of programs and departments. Here was a chance to model one approach: a fellowship or special appointment for a junior faculty member to practice and study administration in the local culture, mentored by senior leaders. An advanced assistant professor in our program, Eileen Schell, had been hired in part because of substantial experience as well as scholarship in writing program administration and was a candidate for major administrative roles in the near future. In anticipation of that prospect, I asked Eileen to take a one-year position as a part-time associate director where she could pioneer a practical effort to accomplish such advanced leadership development; her role would combine a major leadership assignment (heading a curriculum task force) with varied opportunities to observe, analyze, teach, supervise, and practice administrative work in our complex environment, working with me and other senior faculty mentors as well as experienced staff. We decided to co-teach a graduate course in writing program administration to coincide with the administrative fellowships. Finally, with leadership changing hands not only in the department but in the college and central administration, I proposed that the Writing Program make administration one of its yearly themes of inquiry. As director, I pledged to renew efforts to make administrative functions, decision making, and their institutional context as transparent as possible for our many constituent groups: graduate students from different degree programs and departments; professional writing instructors; the junior and senior professorial faculty; and staff administrators. These understandings were the fundamental condition for the various ways the program could encourage and enable all these groups to participate as contributors and leaders in governance and collaborative achievements.

This set of interlocking arrangements, combining reflective study, information sharing, participation, mentorship, observation, teaching, and reciprocal learning among students, faculty, staff, and administrators, was a contingent design I improvised instinctively, reflecting my systems orientation to administration and expressing principles of leadership development and learning that I had only partially formulated. As I researched this essay, I began to make those principles explicit and to find theoretical support for them. Although not a formal case study, my analysis relies on insights from several coparticipants in the experiment—Professor Eileen Schell and doctoral students Tracy Hamler Carrick and Tobi Jacobi, drawing on our conversations and interactions, their writings, and taped interviews.[4] Despite a plan crafted from the materials of a unique situation and somewhat ragged in execution, our experiences together as learners and teachers converge here with theories of practical learning to suggest the richness of a multi-modal model of leadership education grounded in active participation and shared reflection among leaders and learners at all levels of the academy.

THE CHANGING LANDSCAPE FOR FACULTY WORK

For over a decade higher education and its critics have engaged in a set of overlapping conversations that interrogate and reconstruct familiar understandings and attitudes toward faculty work. Each frames differently the descriptive, conceptual, and normative grounds for changing (or defending) the current paradigm, but together they are driving serious, consequential reform. In the unstable climate of pressures, conflicts, and conceptual innovation that now surrounds faculty work, professors feel their image, their autonomy, their very jobs to be at risk. These winds of change sculpt a dynamic, changing landscape in which students and faculty make choices about their work and take up professional roles, including writing program administration.

Here's a quick sketch of some of these discourses and the activities they inform and interanimate.[5]

Faculty roles and rewards: an initiative to reform the conventions that define what faculty activities count as professional work—research, teaching,

---

[4]Tracy Hamler Carrick, in her third year, was appointed a program coordinator, with collaborative responsibilities for teaching and supervising new teaching assistants. Tobi Jacobi, then a second year PhD student, worked on professional development planning as a CCR Administrative Fellow (and, when interviewed the following fall, was serving as a program coordinator). As Associate Director, Eileen Schell led a curriculum development initiative, among other responsibilities, and co-taught with me the course in writing program administration taken by Tobi, Tracy, and others. She was subsequently appointed by the new director of the Writing Program as Director of Graduate Studies in Composition and Cultural Rhetoric. I am grateful to my three coparticipants for their contributions to this experiment and for the honesty and perceptiveness with which they talked and wrote about their experiences of composing professional identity as an administrator. With their generous permission, I've drawn on their writings and taped interviews, as well as numerous informal conversations, to construct a kind of experiential subtext for this essay's conceptual analysis and claims. A selective list of the unpublished writings I consulted for this purpose includes Tobi's learning contract for the fellowship (Jacobi); Tracy's reflective essay on her graduate experience, written to qualify for comprehensive exams (Carrick); and an autobiographical document prepared for Eileen's promotion and tenure review (Schell, "Form A"). Space constraints prevent me from analyzing or quoting from these materials here.

[5]The literature on these subjects is too voluminous to cite here, and I will limit citations mainly to parallel conversations or contributions from rhetoric and composition. Web sites for the American Association of Higher Education (AAHE) (http://www.aahe.org); the Carnegie Foundation for the Advancement of Teaching (http://www.carnegiefoundation.org/home.htm), and the Knight Higher Education Collaborative (http://www.irhe.upenn.edu/knight/knight-main.html) are good starting points. AAHE's magazine *Change* and the *Chronicle of Higher Education* track these conversations closely. Contributions to reform by the American Association of Colleges and Universities (AAC&U), at (http://www.aacu-edu.org), are represented in its publication *Liberal Education*.

or service—and assign them relative worth. At issue is how faculty members organize and prioritize their time, how their work is motivated, perceived, and rewarded, and how well the system governing these choices reflects and responds to the changing missions and resources of higher education. Reformers have capitalized on the dissonance many professors feel between work demands, which are various and context-dependent, and what is ultimately valued in their performance. Ernest Boyer's book *Scholarship Reconsidered,* by proposing new terms for differentiating and valuing faculty work (augmenting the scholarship of discovery with "scholarships" of teaching, application, and integration), broadened the discussion beyond revitalizing undergraduate teaching and stimulated enriched descriptions and analyses of the diversity of faculty work and the complexity of the new challenges it faces.[6] Despite impressive progress in reconceptualizing faculty work at a policy level and in some arenas of practice, it has become clear, in light of the deeply conservative nature of the academy and competing discourses of reform, that the future professoriate is the key to long-term internal change, and graduate education a significant lever.

Graduate education: reforms in doctoral programs directed at preparing future professors more adequately and comprehensively for the full range of faculty roles and career paths in higher education. Closely paralleling the roles and rewards project, these efforts address the growing gap between graduate preparation for research careers and the actual experiences and demands on faculty in the heterogeneous workplaces of different types of institutions. They set the stage for a more fundamental, far-reaching reform that recently got underway to re-envision the PhD for the next century, enlisting all sectors of society to ensure it is responsive to their multiple, disparate needs for highly educated professionals.[7]

Professionalism: a discourse featuring competing versions of professionalism pertinent to forming faculty identities—call them the "cynical" or "realist" and the "utopian" interpretations. The first, assuming a perpetual

---

[6]The AAHE launched its "Roles and Rewards" project in 1991 (see also the New Pathways project) and runs an annual conference on the topic; see http://www.aahe.org/FRRR/ffrrnew2.htm. After an initial focus on campuses, urging revisions of promotion and tenure policies, this movement turned to national disciplinary organizations as a crucial lever for change. Most have subsequently produced documents rethinking criteria for defining and evaluating faculty work; in English language and literature, see *Making* from the Modern Language Association. In writing program administration, see "Evaluating" from the Council of Writing Program Administrators. In composition and rhetoric, no comprehensive policy statement has been issued by the national organization (the Conference on College Composition and Communication) or the National Council of Teachers of English; see, however, Gebhardt and Gebhardt for scholarly views.

[7]A seminal research project led by Jody Nyquist, "Re-envisioning the Ph.D.," continues now as a reform initiative; see http://www.grad.washington.edu/envision. Relatedly, two new programs with this purpose have been announced recently: the Carnegie Foundation's project "Rethinking the Doctorate," (http://www.carnegiefoundation.org/doctorate/index.htm); and the Woodrow Wilson Fellowship Foundation's initiative "The Responsive PhD" (http://www.woodrow.org/responsivephd).

hegemony of research over other faculty roles, focuses on "getting ahead" through a high degree of specialization, early and prolific publication, and an orientation to the discipline over the local campus and mission. This ethos of competitive individualism pervades most doctoral programs and advice to junior faculty. The utopian alternative (civic or collegial professionalism) harks back to an older tradition to advocate citizenship, shared governance, and service within a collegial community, emphasizing the institution, its mission, and its social situatedness in a particular location.[8]

Faculty labor: a many-stranded, contentious conversation about faculty jobs that expresses a newly materialist awareness of faculty work as paid labor and the college or university as a workplace, rather than a holding company for individual entrepreneurship. Critics have targeted faculty work and its autonomous individualism for their dissatisfactions with academe's efficiency, productivity, performance, and faculty priorities. Their concerns generated calls for greater accountability, including outcomes assessment and posttenure review; mandates for increasing faculty (teaching) load; attempts to micromanage faculty time and work processes; and attacks on the tenure system. Meanwhile, however, faculty members, especially women, minority, and new faculty, complain about overwork and intense stress. They cite the constant "ratcheting up" of expectations for quality and quantity of their work; conflicts pitting heavy work schedules and tenure clocks against family obligations and personal lives; expanding service duties and new technological and teaching skills to learn; the strains of competing for tenure; and profound fears of being replaced by part-time labor. Meanwhile, contingent faculty, including graduate assistants, have become more activist in trying to improve their status and material conditions.[9]

---

[8]Representative publications on professionalism in composition and rhetoric include Comprone et al.; Gebhardt and Gebhardt; Healy; Olson and Taylor; and Trimbur. This issue is far more salient in composition, especially to WPAs, than in many fields that take professionalization largely for granted; and its take on the topic is complex and multi-dimensional. Besides the professionalization of future faculty in writing studies, debates incorporate the issues of training teaching assistants, many of them not in the field of composition (e.g., Catalano et al.) and providing professional development for contingent faculty (e.g., Hansen; Strenski). Atypically, members of the constituencies being professionalized—graduate students and professional writing instructors—are contributing to the conversation (see, e.g., Leverenz and Goodburn; Schell and Stock). Thus this conversation merges with very specific debates on labor conditions, on the one hand, and, on the other, with the broadest issues of higher education's responsibility for civic engagement.

[9]Labor conditions for teachers of writing, always a major issue for composition and rhetoric, have for some time been growing in importance as a topic for scholarship and activism. Current work is focusing particularly on the contemporary consequences of a gendered, racialized history of part-time and adjunct labor. See Strickland; Schell, *Gypsy;* and Schell and Stock, *Moving,* whose introduction provides a historical account of material conditions for contingent faculty in composition teaching and of activism on this issue. The 2001 Conference on College Composition and Communication had a major strand of scholarly meetings and rallies on the topic. More broadly, the issue of labor in writing studies and teaching was addressed by the 2000 Thomas R. Watson Conference on "Labor, Writing Technologies, and the Shaping of Composition in the Academy" at the University of Louisville; see also Horner.

CATCH-22 FOR THE PROSPECTIVE ADMINISTRATOR

In these widespread attempts to recognize, value, and prepare for a greater range of faculty work, there remains one pointed omission: administration as a faculty role in the spectrum of an academic career.[10] This is more than an oversight. Conceptually, it represents the deliberate exclusion of administration from what counts as the properly "professional" work of academics. Affectively, it expresses faculty attitudes toward administration that range from indifference or skepticism to hostility and alienation. In the case of major administrative roles like writing program administration, faculty members tend to draw a bright line dividing the faculty work categories, even service, from administration as institutionally authorized and formalized leadership.[11]

The core of my concern here in this study is how such concepts and feelings, deeply engrained in academic culture, stand in the way of leadership education. These prejudices apply most severely to officially authorized positions like writing program administration, which are both time-consuming (competing with and displacing traditionally valued faculty work) and suspect for their identification with institutional ideology . Succinctly put, the obstacles to educating administrative leaders represent complex issues of *professionalism* and *power*. As external pressures, they create a difficult climate for those practicing administration that requires analytic understanding and emotional strength to cope with effectively. More important, prospective administrators appropriate these cultural attitudes as both authoritative voices and internally persuasive discourses (Bakhtin 342–49; Prior 216–18), which create intense identity conflicts and instill beliefs that hobble their ability to lead with vigor and confidence.

Even in the most generous expansions and reinterpretations of faculty roles, what qualifies activities as professional is that they flow from the disciplinary expertise inculcated and certified by the research degree. Most faculty do not view administration as a faculty function by this criterion. Despite reform, on most campuses faculty work is still reported and assessed under the

---

[10]The analysis of faculty work from the MLA Commission on Professional Service (*Making*) is a significant exception, reflecting the presence of members (including, from composition, myself and James Slevin) who had major administrative experience as WPAs, department chairs, and graduate directors. This document, drawing on the original (1989) Syracuse Writing Program's promotion and tenure guidelines (see *Policy*), boldly reworks the categories and relationships of research, teaching, and, especially, service (to include the intellectual work of administrative roles) and attempts also to account for administration more directly as cutting across these "sites" of intellectual work and citizenship.

[11]On my own campus, the faculty crafted departmental guidelines for promotion and tenure in the Writing Program in the late nineteen-eighties that introduced administration as a fourth category appropriate for the discipline. After the guidelines had been in use for over a decade, the faculty had to revise them to satisfy objections to this category from members of the College of Arts and Sciences Promotion and Tenure Committee, which was accomplished by folding the work of administration into the three other categories. (See *Policy*.)

three traditional categories and must be explicable in these terms. When faculty members undergo peer evaluation, most leadership activities, including administrative contributions, fall by default under service. However, service itself occupies a very ambiguous position as a component of faculty work; it represents the fault line between two dimensions of professionalism: expertise and citizenship. Service—the vestige of an earlier, more robust ideal of citizenship—is nominally required as a moral obligation of academic professionals, but seldom respected as an arena for intellectual accomplishment (expertise, or "scholarship"). Although powerful arguments have been made for redefining service as a form of knowledge work inherent in practical activity or "application" (Boyer; Lynton), and some even describe administration as an integrative function crossing the categories (*Making; Policy Guidelines*), overwhelmingly, senior faculty still maintain the old sense of service and distinguish it sharply from administration. Their view accurately reflects the fact that the catch-all reductive notion of service becomes absurd when stretched to cover sustained, demanding, consequential leadership. The attempt to straddle this line produces the disastrous splits wherein WPAs are evaluated by administrative supervisors for their performance as leaders, but by peers as faculty members who have substituted mere service for the true faculty work of scholarship.[12]

But in drawing this line, academics are also expressing their sense that organizational leadership is incompatible with a scholarly identity. Full-time administration, or a heavy administrative commitment, subsuming individual autonomy to institutional goals and authority, is equated with abandoning, at least temporarily, faculty status. Conceptually, this is the problem that composition faced in trying to establish writing program administration as a viable professional role within a faculty career.

Culturally and emotionally, too, it is hard for prospective WPAs to cross the bright line between faculty and administration, scholarship and leadership. Many of their peers perceive administration as not merely unscholarly but inherently antithetical to an intellectual vocation because it requires accepting and exercising bureaucratic authority. As an executive function, line administration evokes profound suspicions of institutional power as an infringement on academic freedom. This skepticism is not surprising, given the "insistent individualism" of the academy (Bennett 13–15 passim) and the traditional role of intellectuals as critics of culture and society. But current con-

---

[12]In the converse, equally damaging version of the same split, faculty administrators come to think of their jobs entirely in professionalized terms as intellectual work and see loss of an administrative position as depriving them of academic freedom in their scholarship; however, administrators view them as subject to institutional supervision and choice of leadership, failing to understand their work as intellectual in a disciplinary sense. Neither recognizing the other's framing of this event as simultaneously valid, they talk past one another. This situation exemplifies the clash of coextensive activity systems (discussed later).

ditions exacerbate these fears; administrators become the symbols and putative agents of top-down or externally imposed change. Intellectually, these feelings are reinforced by authoritative critical and cultural theories that characterize power exclusively as ideological oppression, enforcing the dominance of one social group or set of values over others. Read uncritically, these views engender a generalized hostility toward American social institutions, and, specifically, toward the academy as a primary instrument for reproducing such power relations. Many conclude that the only ethical relationship to institutionalized power is resistance—a response to power that defers indefinitely the realities of participating in its responsibilities and temptations.

For graduate students or the young WPA, these persuasive cultural critiques from the academic left, reinforcing pervasive faculty prejudice against administration, turn their own ambitions into a classic Catch-22. Resistance is directed toward the illegitimate or excessive power of others over us and, implicitly, envisions equalizing that situation so that we ourselves can (instead? also?) exercise power. But, upon achieving that result, how are we ethically to regard ourselves—to construct an ethos—as one who "administers" institutional power? Only with great ambivalence. Playing the role imaginatively, or taking up an "office" for the first time, would-be administrators are caught in cross currents of warring feelings about their own leadership and the system that authorizes it. Fearing complicity, she may feel guilt and moral revulsion toward her own authority and desire to "decenter" it. He may fear being held accountable without having the authority necessary to act effectively. She may desire power self-defensively, to escape being marginalized or silenced, or idealistically, to empower the less privileged, or both. He may resent official authority, including administrators to whom he must report, and identify with those who in turn resent his own over them. As suggested by my pronouns, such conflicted feelings are further complicated and magnified by their gender inflections, not only for women administrators, but for men in a "feminized" field.[13]

Such ironies, contradictions, confusions, and self-doubts thread through the discourse of the field: exchanges on the WPA listserv, published narratives of administration, discussions in classes and at conferences. As they read, write, and practice administration, students and faculty try on wildly divergent self-images of the WPA: the exploited worker in the basement, denied tenure;

---

[13]Numerous publications explore the conflicted nexus of authority, power, agency, and writing program administration; for example, see Barr-Ebest; Dickson; Goodburn and Leverenz; Gunner, "Decentering"; Hult, "Politics"; H. Miller; R. Miller, *Learning;* Olson and Moxley; Phelps, "Warrior"; Schell, "Boss"; Strickland; White; Werder). Many of these explore gender as an explicit or implicit theme (conditions for women administrators; the field of composition, or the practice of writing program administration, as historically feminized and disempowered; feminism as a source of a nonhierarchical or collaborative administrative style; choosing between or reconciling "feminist" and "masculinist" ethics of administration; and so on).

the defiant hero besieged by hostile forces; the clever, manipulative politician; the hapless victim of campus intrigues or arbitrary administrators; the conciliator who mediates ideological conflict; the collaborative colleague who shares power; the radical who seizes writing program administration as an Archimedean lever for transforming society. In our experiment, in the persons of Tobi, Tracy, Eileen, and myself, we could observe and experience these motifs at different points of professional maturity. In our and others' talk, reflections, class texts, institutional documents, and published writings, these threads weave autobiographically through the stages of a career in writing program administration, common elements in an ongoing quest to forge a professional identity from disparate images and motives.

LOOKING FOR ANSWERS

Composition has both reason and means to tackle these intersecting problems of professionalism and power in graduate education and academic practice. Whereas most fields simply prepare teachers for individual classrooms, the teaching mission of composition is programmatic. It requires leaders with the skills to build and administer imaginative, conceptually sound, pedagogically and politically effective programs, in complex cross-institutional designs involving multiple constituencies, collaborative partnerships, and nontraditional formats. That is why administration has developed uniquely in rhetoric and composition into a professionalized faculty role (the WPA) requiring specialized disciplinary expertise and preparation. As writing program administration acquired the symbols and instruments of successful professionalization (a journal, professional organization, literature, professors hired and tenured for this work, and now graduate courses and specializations), the Council of Writing Program Administrators codified this role as professional in a policy statement arguing that writing program administration accomplishes intellectual work based on disciplinary (i.e., research-based) knowledge and can be assessed in those terms ("Evaluating"). That move is reinforced by others' arguments for a "scholarship of administration" paralleling Boyer's "scholarship of teaching" and perhaps instantiating his "scholarship of application" (Hult, "Scholarship"; Rose and Weiser).

With this rationale, composition solves in principle the problem of professionalizing the work of writing program administration and has made the case persuasively to many faculty peers in practice. But there are dangers in the prudential strategy that assimilates administration as scholarship to the stretched parameters of an obsolescent roles-and-rewards system that elevates pure thought over action ("application") and devalues local, context-dependent, impermanent knowledge. Despite strenuous efforts to assert that contextualized activity itself embodies inquiry and is intellectually generative ("Evaluating"; *Making*; Rose and Weiser), under the umbrella of the paradigm this radical notion of intellectual work *in* and *through* administration tends to slip constantly toward a more conventional one of researching, theorizing, and publishing *about* administration. Even as writing program administration becomes a viable professional role, educators must do more to analyze and prepare future administrators for the conflicted, unstable context in which WPAs still operate, where traditional concepts and attitudes about faculty work both persist and compete with alternate visions.

The field has been less successful in finding a consensus on the second challenge for practicing and teaching writing program administration: the double bind created by simultaneously holding incompatible views of power as both necessary and illegitimate, forcing the administrator to choose between being ineffectual or unethical. This dilemma shows up in the literature as a double-edged preoccupation with authority, power, and ethos, particularly as they affect untenured faculty and women in WPA roles (see Note 13). Much of this work displays the dilemmas of conscience and confidence I have described. Practically, WPAs demand power as requisite to do their jobs and tell compelling stories of the dire consequences when they lack the authority, resources, or political clout required to meet their responsibilities. Yet ideologically WPAs, viewing leaders' unequal access to power as inherently oppressive, are conflicted over their own. Reflecting this ambivalence, conceptualizations of leadership tend to fall into dichotomous (gender-inflected) choices between hierarchical and collaborative styles, or to search for a middle way to compromise or reconcile them.

The successful argument for professionalizing writing program administration, while rightly emphasizing its intellectual dimension, inadvertently makes it harder for composition to formulate productively the problem of exercising power, because it elides the nature of leadership as consequential action. In the next section, I want to recast the issue of professionalism in terms of participating in an environment—a "profession"—where partly incompatible activity systems overlap and transact. In doing so, I am shifting from the discipline's perspective of justifying administration to an educator's concern with teaching it as a faculty role. Viewed as a learning problem, professionalism becomes for prospective administrators the task of composing and integrating their own personae as participants in and across multiple systems and activities. That process must take into account, and come to terms with, the dimension of leadership within administration, and the use of power as an inescapable, defining feature of leadership. In a learning framework, the converging problems of professionalism and power translate into the challenge of negotiating a professional identity as a WPA. Although identity formation has become increasingly complex for all young faculty in today's environment, and many will eventually reconcile some form of leadership with faculty roles, it poses special issues for WPAs as they recompose their own self-understanding and their place in the academy recurrently throughout their careers.

TRIANGULATING PROFESSIONALISM

At any historical moment when paradigms are unstable, there are not two but many ideas and ideals in play, including both normative and distorted versions of established ideologies and their utopian counterparts. By adopting a strictly dichotomous approach to professionalism and power with graduate students, we misrepresent the complexity of the environment they are entering and predetermine their choice between stereotyped oppositions, instead of encouraging the open-minded inquiry that would develop more nuanced positions and unfold heterogeneous, unforeseen options for participation and identity.

Instead, I propose to understand "professionalizing" as a process of learning to appropriate roles simultaneously in at least three distinct but interpenetrating spheres of sociocultural, historical activity, whose complex coordinations and discords are reflected in the conversations sketched earlier. I will call them the *discipline*, the *collegium*, and the *workplace*.

We could treat these scenic terms as designating alternate models of a single activity system—call it the *profession*. And indeed each functions powerfully as a governing metaphor for competing discourses of academic professionalism, in which different goals, events, roles, relationships, mediating artifacts, and settings are highlighted as perceptible and significant. For instance, in the discourse of disciplinarity the graduate is appointed to a professorship and welcomed into the (international) community of scholars. She performs original intellectual work disseminated through publication to peers whose relations are not primarily face-to-face, but "cosmopolitan"—textual and virtual, spread over time and space. The discipline trumps the institution as her affiliation, since her expertise is transportable easily across institutional and geographical lines (it counts the same everywhere). Success, marked by tenure and rank, is achieved competitively by meeting high, peer-evaluated standards for published scholarship and attaining prominence in disciplinary networks.

The collegium offers a generative term for academic life in proposals for a new or revitalized civic professionalism (Bennett; Rice; Sullivan). Here the graduate joins a campus faculty, becoming a colleague of his professorial fellows. The fellowship of academic life is built on face-to-face relations and networks of reciprocal obligations; as citizen of the department, college, university, and other campus-based collegia, he serves in consultative, legislative, advisory, and mentoring roles—on a continuum from civic participation to informal and formal leadership. Advocates of this model foreground the situated, local nature of collegiality, where students, colleagues, the mission and tradition of the institution, and constituencies in the geographic region constitute one's knowledge and command one's loyalties.

The term *workplace* (although it has broader meaning in activity studies of writing) serves here to evoke the economic, legal, and regulatory commonplaces and labor issues that have come to the fore in higher education and in composition/rhetoric (see Note 9). In this frame, the graduate accepts a job in a particular institution after negotiating about salary, benefits, moving and setup costs, "released time," travel and research funds, and the like. She becomes part of a workforce in a nonprofit sector struggling to survive and thrive in a competitive marketplace through an unstable mix of tuition, federal funding, state or county support, charitable donations, investments, and entrepreneurial partnerships with government, corporate, and other sectors. She may join a union on arrival, or work for better material conditions for contingent faculty, or contest a business model of the university and its consumerist or client image of students. As WPA, she resists being treated as a manager transmitting and executing institutional policy rather than an autonomous professional whose administrative activity is protected intellectual work.

Even in this stereotyped representation, these contrasting vocabularies capture our experience of different visions vying for dominance of the academic profession (with disciplinarity the establishment model, collegiality the utopian choice, and corporatism the dystopian threat). Certainly, leadership or authority means something very different within each of these activity systems. But a monologic image of each discourse masks their internal heterogeneity, while viewing them solely as rivals obscures their complex interpenetrations and interdependencies and exerts constant pressure to reduce and collapse their multiplicity into one. Administration, in fact, is ambiguously defined and ambivalently viewed exactly because it is a product of their borderlines and intersections (hence faculty administrators—department chairs, program heads, even deans—are typically described as mediating figures, traversing worlds). That's why it's useful here to treat each of these discourses as a distinct activity system; both separately and together, they organize or (in Prior's term) "laminate" multiple streams of sociohistoric activity (24 passim). If these systems are currently and (most likely) permanently commingled, it behooves us to explore in research and graduate study the historical dynamics of their confluence in interlocking relations of co-implication, struggle, cooperation, contradiction, and synchrony (remembering that these are not separate from but deeply enmeshed with personal and other, nonacademic activity systems).

This suggestion for conceptualizing professionalism as a "protean institutional form" and "evolving social enterprise" (Sullivan 150, 219) draws on the research tradition of studying work or practice as cultural-historical activity

(Russell and Bazerman), in particular Prior's work on disciplinarity.[14] Prior uses the image of lamination to capture the heterogeneity of any complex, ongoing human enterprise, which features multi-leveled personal and cultural processes of attunement, alignment, conflict, and coordination at the intersection of sociohistoric spheres of activity. Conceived this way, the relations of discipline, collegium, and workplace within professionalism can, indeed, be depicted as a struggle among holistic visions—complexes of habit, attitude, and belief—for exclusivity or dominance. But they can be construed in many other ways: as simultaneous overlays in a concrete situation, one foregrounded and others tacit; as disparate, contradictory strands blended in an activity; as shifting perceptual and linguistic gestalts in which participants frame events; and, internalized, as inconsistent, ambivalent, and labile aspects of our own self-images as professionals. From an individual perspective, the dynamics of complex activities like academic work involve what Prior calls "laminated activity footings," whereby participants form and re-form alignments to themselves and others as they "take up multiple roles and activities, often simultaneously, with some active and others on hold" (144–45). Prior thus pictures acculturation to academic work—what I have called negotiating a professional identity—as a process whereby persons individually and together construct historical trajectories (personal, interpersonal, institutional, and sociocultural) through activities and the systems that organize them (99–134). Such trajectories are the ongoing means whereby "artifacts, practices, institutions, persons, and communities are being produced, reproduced, and transformed in complexly laminated social worlds" (Russell, "Writing" 230)—in this case, mutually forming professionals and professions.

In these terms, the role of WPA may be thought of as a relatively stable ensemble of activity footings whereby the WPA continually reworks his or her relations to the complexly layered systems of professionalism, coordinating and integrating them with one another and with other spheres and histories of personal experience and culture. That identity formation, already problematic for any professional in composition/rhetoric, is further complicated for WPAs by the ways they shiftingly align and attune themselves and their offices to disciplinary, collegial, and/or workplace frames, each shift highlighting certain streams of activities and contested interpretations within them. The evolving products of such negotiations include not only the professional ethos and personal identity of the individual, but also the generic role of WPA, the nature of writing program administration, and all the activi-

---

[14]Russell ("Activity") defines activity system to mean "collectives (often organizations) of people who, over an indefinite period of time, share common purposes (objects and motives) and certain tools used in certain ways.... An activity system is a unit of analysis of social *and* individual behavior, something like a discourse community, but it allows us to think about tools without confining ourselves to discourse and about people who interact purposefully without confining ourselves to the warm and fuzzy notion of community" (81–82).

ties and systems in which each participates. This notion, as we will see, redefines practical learning as a reciprocal, mutually constitutive feature of cultural activity systems and their participants (Lave and Wenger).

AFFORDING PROFESSIONAL IDENTITY AS A WPA: ENERGY IN THE EXECUTIVE

I have argued that without better conceptual resources to imagine principled participation in institutional power one can't self-consistently aspire to an administrative role. To educate leaders and practice writing program administration, composition studies needs to formulate workable concepts of legitimate authority and constructive power that "afford" leadership as a practical-moral relationship to any or all these professional activities and multileveled systems (for a concept of affordance, see Gibson; Prior 183–86 passim). Without invalidating darker interpretations of power as Machiavellian or hegemonic, this approach seeks ways to understand the morality of power, like technology or rhetoric, as not intrinsic but lying in its contextual definition, distribution, and use. What is needed is an ethical ideal that envisions responsible, strong leadership as a conceptual possibility, not an oxymoron. Certainly, leadership can't be explained comprehensively as a function of power (using it, sharing, or giving it up): a vast body of literature, including some of my own writing (Phelps, "Institutional" and "Telling"), explores other dimensions and metaphors for leadership like design, storytelling, invention, and teaching. But here I focus on the intersections of leadership, power, authority, and professionalism as key to conceiving moral agency in administration. The first step in developing these conceptual affordances is to propose a definition of administrative leadership and examine how it presents intertwined problems of efficacy and ethics.

In the view I've developed ("turtles all the way down"), leadership is a function within a dynamic, open historical system of organized practical activity (which, we have recognized, is not autonomous but an intersection of plural systems). Leadership designates a specific relationship to an enterprise: It is that relation, or set of relations, whereby leaders mobilize, orient, and harmonize the efforts of others toward some intellectual, practical, symbolic, or material outcome. Leaders, working from many rhetorical locations inside or outside official channels in an organization, are those participants who take significant responsibility for making multiple streams of human activity effective in terms common to a group and its sustained or emergent purposes. From this perspective, leadership is a centering phenomenon in a multi-nodal network and can't be reduced to a one-dimensional hierarchy.

In the academy, faculty, student, and staff leaders marshal resources, deploy human energies, and catalyze activity and invention in the service of a group's academically relevant enterprise. Examples of the diverse enterprises they might lead (crossing the boundaries of service, teaching, and research) include learning communities, assessments and program evaluations, negotiations of conflicting interests, collaborative research projects, and writing support groups. Such leaders and their functions may or may not be institutionally defined or acknowledged: academic leadership may well involve groups and enterprises at odds with officially sanctioned ones, or interpretations of mission and governance that contest institutional dogma. Relations of such leaders to the institution as a whole may be loose or even adversarial. In contrast, the logic of administrative leadership aligns the leader with the institution, its enterprises, and, broadly, the ideologies that underlie them: Leading academic organizations means (as Bazerman and Paradis say about texts) harnessing social energies to support and advance institutional versions of reality (6). An institutionally defined role like the WPA not only authorizes the administrator to act within the scope of the office, but also provides access to resources: In principle, both powers and resources need to be commensurate with the degree of responsibility for collective accomplishment. The tighter link between leader and organization in administration is captured in this definition, taken from the Syracuse Writing Program's promotion and tenure guidelines:

> [Administration refers to] leadership within an institution that requires taking responsibility for a project or group within the context of the goals of a larger (academic) unit.... It involves making important decisions, developing and articulating policy, directing the tasks and responsibilities of others, reporting to and working closely with institutional administrators, and maintaining communications among individuals and groups, mediating their goals and concerns. (*Policy* 7).

In singularizing one person as responsible for the work of others, the concept of leadership (no matter how qualified or softened by notions of shared power, collaboration, consensus, and servant leadership) inherently posits an unequal relation between the leader and those whose work is orchestrated. Leadership, particularly in executive roles, poses a fundamental ethical question because it appears to involve the leader's using people and their work as instruments for ends other than themselves. (See Phelps, "Constrained.") Bureaucratic discourse suggests this conversion of persons from ends to means in the terms "human resources" or "human capital." Implied is the possibility (or necessity) of doing so through control or coercion, certainly rhetorical influence, which some scholars in both higher education and rhetoric consider inherently violent. The question, therefore, is what in the nature of academic work and organizations (historically and functionally shaped) warrants this relation between a leader and the work of others.

The ethical dilemma, as it emerges distinctively in the context of writing program administration, is two-pronged. The first concern is becoming complicit in institutional power within a culture which holds that academic work should be radically "free" and portrays administrators as purveyors of corporate ideology in institutions that reproduce political, linguistic, and social inequities. The conflicted WPA asks herself, will I be subject to centralized bureaucratic power and become nothing but a conduit for its top-down rules and mandates—in Richard Miller's wonderful phrase, "a petti-fogging, paper-pushing, rule-bound, ring-kissing, social automaton"(*Learning,* 220)? But, conversely, ironically, WPAs also fear the moral backlash of having and using their own personal power to lead. The WPA wonders, will I be morally compromised by having control over others' actions? Will I be drawn into adversarial, competitive power games with other leaders and units of the institution? The institutional position, mission, and gendering of composition exacerbate both concerns. These intense fears of the power relations inherent in organizational leadership—one's own and others'—create a paradox that seems, at least in its acute form, unique to the academic sector.

This was not a theoretical dilemma for me and coparticipants in our experiments with leadership education. Tobi and Tracy, like many graduate students in composition, served on administrative teams responsible for new TA (teaching assistant) teaching that required them to enforce programmatic expectations, communicate relevant rules and regulations, and make administrative reports that could affect decisions about TAs' teaching appointments or future opportunities. They had to balance these obligations (ultimately, to the program's mission of teaching undergraduates) against their responsibilities to support the professional goals and learning of members in their teaching groups (their own peers). Leading a three-part task force representing every constituent group in the Writing Program, Eileen as an associate director, consulting with me (and ultimately subject to faculty vote), had to balance the politics, rules, budget realities, and timing of getting a curriculum proposal approved against unlimited freedom for task force members to invent courses, debate curricular principles, and choose what they would like to teach. As director and department chair, I had to make judgments that affected program members' employment, pedagogical choices, salaries, and access to resources, while handling political disputes with other campus units that required firm defense of the program's authority and principles. Each of us perceived these familiar, everyday activities in writing program administration as shaping our professional ethos in our own and others' perceptions, and discussed them as posing moral choices, often troubling, conflicted, and difficult. These choices are defined that way by the dissonances between activity systems they embody: Among us, we negotiated and reconciled multiple identities as practical learners, researchers, employees, disciplinary colleagues, administrators, student peers, co-teachers, family members, and community activists.

In examining these questions, I will focus primarily on the executive role, keeping in mind the discipline-specific moral issues raised by the authority of many writing program directors over the work of relatively powerless members of the academy (TAs, contingent faculty, untenured faculty, staff administrators, undergraduate employees), as well as the converse problem of having insufficient authority and resources to carry out leadership responsibilities for collective work. WPAs who are not primarily line administrators face less acutely the second prong of the dilemma (their own power), dealing more often with the rhetorical and political issues of lateral consultative and persuasive power relations, which seem ethically if not practically easier (see Werder).

The ethics of administrative leadership are preconditioned on faith in the global potential of higher education institutions to further the public good. It would be impossible to view the academic enterprise itself in moral terms if it were devoted simply to self-aggrandizement: advancing the careers of its participants. Indeed, the contemporary critique of academe is that its institutions have "turned away from their public mission to concentrate narcissistically upon their own inner life and advancing their organizational advantage" (Sullivan 160). But this is a falling away from the "true professional ideal" (Kimball), invented conjointly with the graduate school and the modern university in the late nineteenth and early twentieth centuries (Guillory). In higher education, this ideology developed historically as a complex interplay between technical competence and civic purpose that has many permutations and expressions, including the differentiation of institutions by mission and the role of general education vis-à-vis the disciplinary major. But American academic professionalism has always been defined by the co-presence of these motives, the ideal of their reciprocity, and the history of tensions between them (Bennett; Bender; Sullivan). Whatever the current dysfunctionality of their relationship, the integrative aim of professionalism is

> to organize the conditions of work so that workers can develop and express their individual powers, by engaging them responsibly in ways that assure individual dignity through being recognized as contributing to enterprises of public value. This purpose links expertise, technical innovation, and freedom of enterprise to individual fulfillment through the responsible discharge of socially recognized tasks. (Sullivan 148)

That statement is remarkably like the definitions of leadership and administration offered earlier. Taken together, they suggest that a college or university invests in its administrators and citizen-leaders the responsibility of institutions to create such conditions and, in the ideal, provides the structures and resources needed to mobilize human capacities for "socially attuned work": work that mediates the tensions between freedom and responsibility to achieve personal, professional, and institutional integrity (Sullivan 219–23). In this way, institutions and professions legitimate leadership and, for the administrator as well as for professionals generally, "'moralize' ... the performance of instrumental functions by embedding them in networks of social expectations" (150). The functional ability of institutions to organize and give social meaning to individual professional work as contributions to a common enterprise warrants the administrator in believing it is at least hypothetically possible to make her own efficacy in leadership consistent with moral purpose and moral means.

This, of course, is an ideal, and accounts neither for corruption of that ideal (when expertise becomes radically disconnected from citizenship and the academy from its publics, as reformers claim) nor for vast differences in the way institutions, professionals, and their constituencies interpret the public good and set priorities in missions and activities. As we've observed, that interpretation is exactly what is at stake and under negotiation in today's debates between higher education (itself multivocal) and its many stakeholders at the intersections of discipline, collegium, and workplace. It is the very gaps, overlaps, and conflicts among these systems that give tremendous play for difference between tenure-line professors' views and the commitments of the institutions where they work. Universities, especially, are widely recognized to be loosely coupled enterprises that are often (in their most elite incarnations) anarchic. The disciplinary activity system (with its hallmarks of academic professionalism—tenure and academic freedom) links professors so weakly to local institutions that ideological grounds do not usually weigh heavily in their choosing one place of academic employment over another. Perhaps unrealistically today (considering the lamination of activity systems and changing conditions of labor), academics feel free to pursue their professional work, regardless of institutional setting, in ways compatible with their own views of the public good to be sought through education, research, or service, sometimes in overt disagreement or practical disregard for institutional ideology. (A simple example of such positioning—both its apparent freedom and its ideological limits—is grading.) Tellingly, although they may become leaders in a loyal opposition, it is still possible, by foregrounding disciplinarity, for many professors to live distanced, estranged, or simply indifferent to the central commitments and material situation of the organization they work in, or to insulate themselves from the interests and claims of its many stakeholders.[15]

For WPAs, more tightly bound to the institution and acting in some degree as its representative, it is obviously more difficult to distance their profession-

---

[15]Insofar as ideology matters in applying for and choosing jobs, most applicants discriminate between departments for their views of the discipline, not institutions for their commitments. But this unconcern is becoming more problematic as institutions try to assert more local control, based on mission, over faculty teaching, service obligations, and even research priorities. And, of course, this kind of autonomy from institutional ideology has never applied to the non-tenure-track faculty, including graduate students, who together now constitute over half the teaching faculty in the United States, and an even larger proportion of those teaching writing (Schell and Stock, Introd. 4–5). For recent reports and data on the changing academic workforce, see web sites of the Modern Language Association, http://www.mla.org, and the American Association of University Professors, http://www.aaup.org.

alism ethically from the ideologically saturated structures, processes, conditions, and goals of the organization (and more necessary to consider these in accepting an appointment). At the least, they must accept the institutional character of their own authority and the general framework in which, through their office, they exercise power and deploy resources. Fortunately, heterogeneity in activity systems saves administrators from absolutism in this commitment. Indeed, in a sociocultural activity framework, administrators are participants in producing an evolving institutional culture (including its emergent goals) through its practices, not simply reproducing a static structure and ideology. Even in carrying out instructions from other administrators, much administrative work involves interpreting broad directives or expectations as they apply to concrete circumstances that could not be foreseen in detail (Barnard 181). Faculty administrators who report above the department level or operate cross-institutionally, as many WPAs do, tend to have greater latitude because of the institution's tolerance for diversity in the cultures, practices, and missions of its programs or departments. More important, as members of a cohort of leaders they can gain access and exploit opportunities for principled dissent and argument through coparticipation in highly negotiated, conflictual processes of institution-wide decision making. That potential for collective influence from leaders "all the way down" is both endangered and enhanced by today's situations of crisis, transition, restructuring, and rethinking, which break up frozen power arrangements and reveal hidden information.

Cathy Davidson, after becoming a department chair, wrote that "Power looks monolithic from below; two years ago, before I took this position, I would never have guessed how much of my new life is about compromise, negotiation, consultation, flexibility, rethinking, reversal, and change" (105). In the rhetoric of the humanities

> [a]dministrators are monolithic sources of power, an ominous, foreboding they. Yet to ascribe so much power to them is to forget the precarious role that all of us in higher education play, vis-à-vis the public, state legislators, the federal government, or (for those in private universities) prospective donors and boards of trustees. However beleaguered we are or feel, the binaric language of power—the Foucauldian paradigm of resistance or subversion—serves to make us even more beleaguered. The tired division of us versus them is a binary that ultimately reiterates our position as powerless and thus worthy of disrespect. (98)

She advises "reconceptualizing academic institutions less as binaric and hegemonic structures of power than as conglomerations of power, with elaborate checks and balances, advisory capabilities, democratic glimmerings, and complex levels of reporting and responsibility in which the individual—however minor a figure one cuts or feels like one cuts—has some shaping power" (104–105). (Compare R. Miller, "Intellectual-Bureaucrats.")

Having once accepted the inevitability of institutions as scenes for collective activity, and recognized the spaces their heterogeneity and continuously constructed multiple systems offer leaders for action and for moral choice, WPAs do not need to fear embracing their own authority in a leadership role. The significance of institutional authority is not in making the administrator powerful, but in making it possible to lead with integrity, based on the ethical premise that infuses academic enterprises in their attempt to realize the ideals of professionalism. The institution warrants the administrator's actions (within a circumscribed range), in pursuing the goals of the enterprise, to guide and judge the work of others in those terms. Rather than bringing with it unmitigated "power" in the brute sense of being able to impose one's personal will on others, institutional sanctioning of leadership (through appointment, election, contract, precedent, and practice) confers restrained powers specific to the office that, in principle, if not reliably in practice, closely match its responsibilities. The authority of an administrator is not a personal attribute or possession, despite those who improperly personalize it. The administrator with integrity assimilates personal motives to the social motives of the enterprise, or, as Garry Wills puts it (citing James Madison on the American presidency), "the officeholder's pride and ambition should be merged with the function of his office" (*Federalist Papers*, Introd. xvii; *Federalist Papers*, No. 51, 262). That is the social covenant which enables individuals—faculty professionals, administrators, and US presidents—to advance their own careers and achieve personal success in leadership roles while giving their work public meaning and worth.

One impulse in many theories of writing program administration (as in teaching composition) is to "decenter" authority as a way of empowering others—generally conceptualized, I think, as a subtractive process that beneficially diminishes and transfers the administrator's and institution's power. Although most recognize this as a somewhat futile, self-contradictory, or hypocritical effort, because in the end positional power is inseparable from institutional role, their persistent desire to renounce it arises from having no positive conception of strength as a virtue of the executive. In contrast, the Founding Fathers came to see centered strength or "energy" in the executive as a key requirement of the American presidency. Alexander Hamilton and James Madison proposed to guarantee energy in federal government through the combination of stability (provided by duration in office) and the "unity" achieved by centering strong executive authority in one office, held by one leader (*Federalist Papers*, esp. Nos. 70, 71, and 73 [Hamilton].)[16] Energy in the executive is not a synonym for raw or arbitrary power; as Terry Eastland de-

---

[16]My argument here is for energy in the executive, not single leadership per se. As someone who has proposed and participated in coadministration, I am agnostic on the question of coleadership arrangements, which are argued persuasively by some WPAs who have done them successfully and problematized by others: For varied views, see Gunner, Spec. issue; Cambridge and McClelland. Not all WPA positions are executive roles, and many involve an array of loosely coupled enterprises or highly differentiated duties that co-leaders can divide. Depending on situational factors, collaborative leadership can work in some institutional cultures, but I suspect that stable, long-term successes are as rare in coadministration as in marriage.

tails in his book on the subject, it is demanded and circumscribed by specified powers, responsibilities, and structures in the office that the executive is expected to exercise and defend. These provide the executive with both the duty and the capacity to act energetically, assuring, in Hamilton's words, "vigour and expedition" in action that is held accountable (No. 70, 358). As Eastland puts it, built into the office is both "an ethic of energy *and* an ethic of responsibility" (13).[17]

Gertrude Himmelfarb remarks that contemporary culture emphasizes "caring virtues" like compassion, tolerance, fairness, and decency. But it has neglected and denigrated the heroic "vigorous virtues" that energize accomplishment: "courage, ambition, adventurousness, audacity, creativity" (81). The two are not mutually exclusive, as often assumed, though they do clash in specific situations. WPAs need to learn and practice both—and not treat them as gender-specific. But I'm focusing here on what is missing from our graduate programs and faculty development. Leadership educators need to teach, praise, and analyze the vigorous merits *as* virtuous: not unfortunate, guilt-laden necessities in a tough world, not cynical expressions of overweening personal ambition, but moral correlates and practical requirements of leadership responsibilities.

We must teach, too, that the vigorous, affirmative use of power in administration often legitimately produces or addresses negative situations of conflict and resistance, both within the community of practice being led and between it and external communities. Both kinds of conflict are endemic to writing programs. WPAs need to grasp the nettle of resistance and struggle as part of the realities of multiple activity systems and individuals' mixed relationships to them. In the view developed here, administrative actions and decisions may be unpleasant, difficult, adversarial, or exercise a degree of control over others, yet may be done with integrity.

One reason these kinds of actions seem indefensible to WPAs is the delusion that positional authority constitutes, or confers, an unmediated power over others. In an analysis of how executive (hierarchical) authority actually works in bureaucracies, Chester Barnard defines authority as "the character of a communication ... by which it is accepted by a contributor to or 'member' of the organization as governing the action he contributes; ... determining what he does or is not to do so far as the organization is concerned." In that definition, authority is contextually and concretely determined by the response of those it addresses, and "does not reside in 'persons of authority'" (180).

---

[17]Administration in the academy, of course, is not the same as republican government, no more than it is exactly like corporate management. These two models, though, are relevant to academic leadership, corresponding roughly to the collegium and the workplace, respectively, as activity systems. We can't fully develop a satisfactory theory of leadership in writing programs or departments without addressing the broader problem of college and university governance, which many consider dysfunctional. At the least, the modus vivendi among activity systems that characterized traditional "shared governance" is breaking down under the stresses of current changes, and educators are debating diametrically opposed models of reform. I am interested in ideas and examples from all sectors of society, since the academy seems to be inherently a hybrid form.

Barnard analyzes the specific conditions under which members of the organization accept or reject others' communications as authoritative. Rather than a leader's personal license to command, authority is a process by which, within a certain "zone of indifference," individuals delegate upward in the organization "responsibility for what is an organizational decision—an action which is depersonalized by the fact of its coordinate character" (183–84). Confounding the familiar dichotomy, he reminds us that hierarchy is itself collaborative. And this does not include all the other ways in which organizational power is, as Davidson pointed out, subject to negotiation and mediation at all levels of decision making—in a profession that defines leadership uncertainly at the crossroads of three different activity systems, where the hierarchies and politics of each collide or mesh. Academic culture is traditionally centrifugal, individualistic, and resistant to central direction or unity, as recognized in the cliché that administration is like "herding cats." Far from being ominously powerful figures, Rudolph Weingartner advises, "Academic administrators do not *manage* units composed of faculty or students, however much they may at times dream of doing so." Rather, they must create coherence through "organizational arts" (115). Rhetorical skill and other sources of influence are far more significant to vigorous leadership in the academy than positional authority, even though the powers of the office are essential tools to do the job.

The usual definition of power in organizations as unilateral control or influence over others seems quite inadequate to characterize these indeterminate, negotiated processes, the checks and balances, the reciprocity of codified and informal power relations by which individuals exert and exchange influence within complex social systems. As an administrator, I find it more useful to think of power as a sort of elemental aspect of activity itself, a raw ingredient for agency and effectivity. Bernard Loomer's analysis of power begins with this idea: "If power is roughly defined as the ability to make or establish a claim on life, then ... power is coextensive with life itself. To be alive, in any sense, is to make some claim, large or small. To be alive is to exercise power in some degree" (5).[18] Power *is* activity, the energy of life made efficacious. From a systemic perspective, power is the "distributed" capability of the enterprise and its subsystems to conduct activity, to accomplish things. (See Note 2.) The administrator as an individual "has" or "wields" power only in the sense of tapping into the energies latent in communities of practice (drawing on many sources and modes of access besides holding office). A leader constitutes a node in a multi-dimensional network of power and information flowing in many directions. Each leader is a center that gathers, concentrates, and com-

---

[18]The concept of influence, rooted in life as activity, is common to the two kinds of power that Loomer distinguishes: linear or unilateral power (corresponding roughly to hierarchical models in the theories of writing program administration, and to disciplinarity in critiques of the academy) and relational (corresponding to collaborative models of administration, and to the values of the collegium): See Bennett (16–27). Loomer's concern, like those of Werder and others in writing program administration, is that influence becomes an end in itself and is corrupt if practiced without opening oneself to influence from others. My argument uses his starting point to avoid the dichotomy he constructs.

municates power, tending to harmonize its dissonances and to achieve alignments (Senge 234–36). As leaders, WPAs catalyze, generate, align, and transmit power as it streams through systems of activity.

I found a remarkable iconic representation of this idea in early Turkish carpets as analyzed by the architect Christopher Alexander. In a book of photographs of his carpet collection, he develops and illustrates his theory that beauty is an objective quality of designs whose patterns form complex relationships among centers, each of them "an organization (or field) of other centers" (49). Delightfully for this essay, it turns out, one reconstructed carpet fragment is composed of a lobed turtle shape, which he describes as an archetypal motif that "contains the quality of being to an intense degree" (154). In Alexander's carpets, "turtles" and other motifs form dense, intricate, interleaved patterns "all the way down" to a one-eighth inch (the basic "knot" of weaving): "*Every carpet contains hundreds, in many cases even thousands of centers, strewn, packed, and interlocked throughout its structure*" (36). He explains how the power of any center can enhance the power of others through their patterned relations:

> Every carpet is, at one and the same time, a system of centers, and itself a center. Its goodness depends on the number of centers it contains, and on the number of local symmetries which each of the centers is made of.... To the extent that any given center is itself, made up of further smaller centers, this center is powerful and significant. A given center becomes more and more strong, and more and more significant, to the extent that it is, indeed, a center—and it becomes a center, to the degree that it is composed of other, interacting centers. (49)

Alexander's carpets provide a visual correlate for my premise that leaders' practical efficacy depends on a dense multiplicity of other leaders, whose own creative power is in turn amplified by the ability of a centered leader to attune their contributions to a common enterprise. Such imagery is very far from the idea of power as a finite quantity in a pure zero-sum game, something that can be subtracted, transferred, or shared by dividing it or giving it away. While acknowledging conflict, difference, inequity, fractured purpose, and self-interested motive in the play of activity, we can eschew binaric, static theories of power and instead teach WPAs how to see themselves as vital centers of energy within networks of numerous participants in power. Their efficacy is determined by how they respond to, interact with, and cultivate others as significant decision makers and actors. Such a relational concept of power supports a vision of leaders open to the influence of others but capable of their own integrity and strength. Educators can emphasize that WPAs, to the degree they develop an ethic of power informed by the vigorous virtues, will have greater opportunities to orient social energies toward inventive, constructive accomplishment, rather than simply the defense, protection, and advantage of their units, themselves, or the field. Finally, prospective WPAs can make more sophisticated judgments of prospective positions by analyzing their material, symbolic, and political conditions as more or less hospitable environments—affordances— for energetic and ethically responsible leadership.

AN INTEGRATED MODEL FOR LEADERSHIP EDUCATION

I want to return now to the practical experiment in leadership education that has been a shadowy subtext for this study, implicitly grounding the figures of theory I have been constructing. The intertwining experiences and reflections of its coparticipants come together with a theory of situated learning to argue for a richly integrated model for leadership education, woven together by dense patterns of interconnected learning.

Administration is such a multifaceted, context-dependent activity that it is tempting to conclude it can't be taught at all, only learned. As outlined by the Council of Writing Program Administrators, effective writing program administration calls for a formidable range of knowledge and skills, much of it locally determined and specified for a particular institutional culture ("Evaluating"). As graduate programs in rhetoric and composition begin to construct programmatic emphases or strands in writing program administration, doubts have quickly surfaced. Is it possible, or even desirable, for graduate educators to prepare students for such a complex, highly situated practice? The question incorporates two different concerns. The first (a claim argued by many with respect to another complex activity, writing in the workplace) is that abstract knowledge imparted in formal schooling is relatively useless in preparing people for activities so culturally embedded, contingent, and improvisatory. If, however, advance instruction is in fact useful and needed, another concern arises: The knowledge base required is so comprehensive and diverse that it could overwhelm the graduate curriculum, displacing education in disciplinary content—the very studies of writing, rhetoric, and pedagogy that (so we have argued) give this administrative work its intellectual force.

In order to answer these concerns among educators teaching writing program administration in graduate school, I want to bring them together with other issues that have emerged in this essay: the acculturation of professionals and, in particular, the problems that assail future administrators in composing professional identity; and the reciprocal relations among leaders at different stages of acculturation and identity formation that are implied in my premise of "turtles all the way down." Together, they suggest a matrix model for leadership education in which integrations among learning modes intersect productively with synchronous learning among professionals and leaders of different generations.

In sketching out such a model, we must recognize that graduate programs in rhetoric and composition are more deeply embedded than those of most disciplines in the fields of practice for which its leaders are being educated.

Any writing program (however configured) is itself a site for skills and practices incorporated in administrative leadership and provides a lived example of how disciplinary expertise in writing, rhetoric, literacy education, and administration is being translated for, and transformed by, a particular institutional culture and student body. As noted earlier, for economic and other reasons graduate students in rhetoric and composition typically have access to this culture as responsible practitioners very early on. This situation presents an opportunity for exploring the relations of formal study to practical learning in the context of acculturating newcomers to the profession. The authentic workplace setting of writing programs and departments not only makes practical learning possible for students engaged simultaneously in graduate study, but also brings into play the characteristic processes of continuity and change in communities of practice, wherein learning is not a separate stage of life but indistinguishable from the cogenesis of the culture and its participants. Indeed, I would argue ultimately that these same conditions characterize all education of future faculty (as distinct from professionals preparing for other workplaces), although present ideologies of doctoral education obscure that fact and fail to fully exploit the academy's situational learning potential when they focus primarily on abstract knowledge and on research as the only salient expert practice.

A sharp distinction and disjunction between learning in schools and learning in practice (posited by Dias et al.) reconfigures the old theory/practice dichotomy. That conception fails to account well for the rich variety of learning observed in our experiments, where the transactional relations we deliberately fostered among research, teaching and learning, and programmatic practice produced a spectrum of learning modes that overlap one another and cross the boundaries of their traditional sites and settings (the classroom, the administrative staff meeting, the research project, the graduate colloquium, the policy task force, and so on). Although these modes of leadership education lie along a fuzzy continuum, I've found it useful to group them heuristically into three types: explicit *formal learning* through curricular study and research; *experiential learning,* a convenient term for an array of indirect practical learning modes; and *pragmatic learning* through the direct exercise of leadership in positional administration.

Both experiential learning (as I'm using it narrowly here) and pragmatic learning fit within the broad notion of practical or "situated learning" developed by Jean Lave and Etienne Wenger. Their concept applies here to the process of acculturation whereby students become professionalized in the academy through coparticipation as actors in its multiple activity systems, as locally represented in what the authors call "communities of practice." I am concerned with how administrative roles and aspirations enter into this process and how educators may affect it by staging and synergizing opportunities for learning in different modes. In this application of situated learning, I will make a distinction between learning administration (pragmatically) by doing it, and learning it (experientially) in the course of becoming a member of the community who observes and is affected by administrators and their actions. Although this difference blurs in practice, it is useful for educators in recognizing sites and planning formats for leadership education and meaningful in establishing a continuum between formal and practical learning that is not part of Lave and Wenger's theory. The participants in our experiments, including myself, occupied a named administrative "office" during the year of the experiment (and each of my coparticipants held leadership roles of greater scope or responsibility during the following year, when I interviewed them). I will draw examples of pragmatic learning from their roles and examples of experiential learning from their concurrent opportunities for observing administrative practice.

Lave and Wenger offer a theory of context-based practical learning which initially addresses the liminal situation when would-be practitioners join a community of expert practice, but ultimately expands to view learning as a defining feature of activity itself. Lave and Wenger call it "legitimate peripheral participation" (LPP), a term I will split and modify for my purposes here. Their description of situated learning as co-participation emphasizes learning complex practices by immersion in a community of practice under conditions of (a) authentic (legitimate), responsible participation in activities alongside peers and experts and (b) licensed inexpertise, as newcomers to a community or role, which allows participants to experience genuine but circumscribed agency while slipping in and out of deep engagement in the practice (through nuanced variations and combinations of supervised activity, observation, scaffolded work, independent responsibility, expert contributions, collaborative practices, and so on). Tobi's, Tracy's, and Eileen's administrative practices were constructed very much along the lines of this description: involving authentic responsibilities of a scope and independence commensurate with their different levels of expertise and professionalization, but in each case also delineated as an acculturative experience that made time for reflection, foregrounded teaching and learning relations with others, and invited risk taking and productive error, despite the subordination of learning to accomplishment that characterizes learning within practice. Their agency as administrators included, for Eileen, Tracy, and Tobi, a range in autonomy of action: from independently planning activities and setting agendas as group leaders to engaging in consultative, collaborative decision making with other administrators.

Here, I will borrow the other two parts of Lave and Wenger's phrase to name some special features in our experiment in leadership education. First, legitimation has a different meaning and deeper resonance when applied specifically to practicing leadership rather than professional practice in general. Whereas professionalism is an issue of expertise (and authentic participation in what experts do), administration not only requires specialized knowledge and skills but constructs a different, problematic relationship to others' activities. Legitimating a student or faculty member as an administrator evokes all the ethical and political nuances that we have explored with respect to institutional enterprises, the authority conferred by an office, and the exercise of power. Second, "peripherality" (a rather unsatisfactory term for its original purpose) is extremely apt for the kinds of indirect learning I grouped under the term "experiential." What characterizes this kind of learning is the opportunity to be present at administrative events and interactions as a more or less "peripheral" actor, on a footing ranging from participant-observer affected by (but not responsible for) administrative action to licensed observer (shadower, note taker) to pure researcher (interviewer, ethnographer). At one end of the continuum these footings extend the stance whereby an actor fully engaged in an event modulates her degree of involvement to include moments of analytical distance. On the other end, they merge into research projects and classroom studies. In our experiments, one can trace this critical, inquiring stance among the coparticipants as it modulates seamlessly from reflection closely tied to administrative practice (like discussing the meaning of recent events with mentors) through observations and interviews on campus to the case studies at local institutions conducted for our class.

Our many-layered experiment in leadership development validates Lave and Wenger's insistence on learning complex practices through participation (and illustrates many of the specifics of their analysis), but also contradicts and qualifies its implications for the role of schooling in practical learning. The authors recognize, in passing, the significance of reflective dialogue in practical learning. But they are so intent on equating learning with engaging in a sociocultural practice that they consistently underplay anything resembling deliberate observation or systematic study of that culture. They argue that "a learning curriculum is a field of learning resources in everyday practice *viewed from the perspective of learners*," whereas a teaching curriculum limits learning because it filters access and information through the instructor's intentions and predetermined learning goals (97). Although Lave and Wenger don't analyze school learning in this monograph, scholars of workplace writing have used situated learning theory and their own research to argue that formal preparation for practice, didactic instruction, and even deliberate teaching and learning on the job all make negligible or counterproductive contributions to the kind of acculturation and context-specific learning needed to practice in complex activity systems (Dias et al., 222–235; but compare Blakeslee).

In contrast, experiential learning in our experiments lies on a continuum between learning by practicing (Lave and Wenger's LPP) and explicit learning through formal instruction and inquiry. The experiments deliberately opened up the middle part of the spectrum to the participants by creating roles that juxtaposed genuine administrative responsibilities with invitations (and, where possible, official access) to conduct close observations and systemic analysis. The establishment of mixed positions like administrative fellowships or Eileen's associate role authorizes an ambiguous stance for practitioners to be actor, learner, or both. Making this position public (optionally, depending on the context) privileges the observer, sometimes simply to see and know what participants would not otherwise have access to, sometimes to probe situations with intensive questions (and get candid answers), and sometimes to conduct formal research on site. What links the two ends of the learning spectrum is a stance of inquiry that informs experience, incorporates a distancing and reflective eye into participation, and shades into formal research and study.

Our class on writing program administration was a primary means for making these links or bringing out their presence in each context of learning. The course itself incorporated multiple learning modes and taught them explicitly as forms of inquiry portable to and from administrative practice: Examples include simulation, role playing, contrastive analysis, and metaphoric mapping. The major project of the class, a case study of a regional writing program (planned by my co-teacher Eileen), became a focal point for bringing together and making explicit all the kinds of learning available collectively through one's own practice, indirect access to others' practice, and formalized study. Every issue, inquiry method, set of readings, and type of learning was linked into the students' case studies, using them as a reference point, comparison, and example; observations and discoveries from the cases fed back into previous conceptual learning and transformed those ideas. All of us became aware of how the class leveraged the experiences and practices of its members in other settings to create synergies among one another's learning and generate a greater base of common and individual knowledge.

It became clear in comparing the learning trajectories of all coparticipants during that year and afterwards that the explicit learning afforded in formal study and inquiry (as student, teacher, and researcher) is a dialectic counterpart and catalyst for a scholarly administrative practice. Bridging the two through these overlapping formats of multimodal learning created a dense pattern of multiple connections for every participant in which practice fed questions, problems, and insights into research and motivated writing (for publication, action, and autobiographical reflection), while research habits and scholarly attitudes (study of the literature, systematic information gathering, theorizing data, systemic thinking, perspectival analysis, and so on) carried over pervasively into the contexts of participation and experiential learning and enhanced practitioners' abilities to grasp systems and analyze meanings in events.

Whereas Lave and Wenger don't acknowledge the value of integrating formal ("didactic") learning with practical learning, they are insightful on another kind of integration—the synchrony of learning among different generations of practitioners as they appropriate and negotiate professional identities. For graduate students and faculty alike in our experiments, the overarching issue in leadership education is (re)composing identity in relation to particular professional roles, ideologies, activity systems, and institutions. This ongoing process is foregrounded when critical moments of transition or change call for this articulation. Administrative leadership roles enter into these crises of acculturation and identity formation as one facet of a professional life, often a problematic of these socially embedded negotiations. The process is inseparable, Prior shows (and we confirm) from laminated personal histories, interpersonal relations, and cultural frameworks whose "subjective perspectives" and "evaluative orientations" deeply inform the experience of becoming a member of the profession via a local community of practice (272). As Lave and Wenger note, identities are "long-term living relations between persons and their place and participation in communities of practice" (53). They point out the importance of multi-faceted interdependencies in the concurrent, reciprocal learning of newcomers, relatively experienced practitioners, and old-timers, which belie a limited idea of dyadic mentorship as the primary means of educating practitioners. Though the authors begin by trying to explain how newcomers join complex organizational cultures, this focus expands to cover generational cycles of practical learning as it fashions identities and reproduces communities and culture: In their view, "learning (the historical production of a person) is not generated by abstract macrosocial and historical forces, but by a person's embodied, active, perspectival trajectory through multiple, interpenetrating, internally stratified communities of practice in the world, communities that are themselves dynamic, open, and evolving" (Prior 99). The interweaving and intersections of such trajectories are the means whereby individuals' learning is implicated in processes of cultural continuity and change.

Our experiments in leadership education suggest that these historical paths through activity systems are highly mediated by forms of intersubjective reflection in talk and writing, which simultaneously accomplish and offer accounts of the process of acculturation—its leaps and transformations, its obstacles and struggles, its long historical trajectory. It's not surprising that reflective writing is crucial for identity formation in graduate students, as exemplified by Tobi's learning contract written for the fellowship (Jacobi), and Tracy's reflective essay in preparation for qualifying exams (Carrick). Less noticed is the fact that faculty members write periodic, more or less reflective and analytic autobiographies, ranging from curriculum vitae to elaborate formulations of identity at points of career transition (e.g., Schell, "Form A"). Such summative, projective, reflective articulations of identity at critical moments in professional life become especially powerful and significant when they negotiate activity systems intersubjectively through participants' multiple levels of personal and professional involvement and dialogue.

Most of the time, would-be educators of WPAs lack the resources, time, or perhaps positional authority to institute formal, long-term arrangements for organizing and supporting the wealth of learning modes and the synchronous, intergenerational learning about leadership by graduate students and professors that I have pointed out in our experiment. But one reason I have dwelled on this experiment is precisely that it was hastily constructed, ad hoc, and filled with more or less successful improvisations. Although I would like to see many of its features broadly institutionalized and permanently funded (in fellowships or special appointments for aspiring student or faculty leaders), that is as unlikely at my university as it is elsewhere. My point, though, is that all these elements are already present in everyday practice and—when foregrounded and coordinated—can form the basis for a "learning curriculum" for leaders that relies on the "constitutive role in learning for improvisation, actual cases of interaction, and emergent processes which cannot be reduced to generalized structures" (Lave and Wenger 16). The principles that emerge from this analysis call educators to invent from the conditions and relationships of local situations ad hoc, flexible ways of achieving the matrix I have described, where members of several generations, at different junctures in their own development as professionals and leaders, interact in terms of integrated modes of learning—formal, experiential, pragmatic. These modes operate most intensively and productively at those inflection points in career trajectories where participants reflectively articulate new, complicated forms of their subjectivity. In constructing these opportunities, we must communicate to participants that leaders' education, like the composing of identity, is dynamic, lifelong, inseparable from their scholarly work, teaching, administrative practice, and personal lives, and an intrinsic aspect of the activity, genesis, and reformation of professional culture itself.

WORKS CITED

Alexander, Christopher. *A Foreshadowing of 21st Century Art: The Color and Geometry of Very Early Turkish Carpets.* New York: Oxford UP, 1993.

Bakhtin, M. M. *The Dialogic Imagination: Four Essays.* Ed. Michael Holquist. Trans. Caryl Emerson and Michael Holquist. Austin: U of Texas P, 1981.

Barnard, Chester L. "A Definition of Authority." *Reader in Bureaucracy.* Ed. Robert Merton et al. Glencoe, IL: Free P, 1952. 180–85.

Barr-Ebest, Sally. "Gender Differences in Writing Program Administration." *WPA: Writing Program Administration* 18 (1995): 53–73.

Bazerman, Charles, and James Paradis. "Introduction." *Textual Dynamics of the Professions: Historical and Contemporary Studies of Writing in Professional Communities.* Ed. Charles Bazerman and James Paradis. Madison: U of Wisconsin P, 1991. 3–10.

Bender, Thomas. "Then and Now: The Disciplines and Civic Engagement." *Liberal Education* 87 (2001): 6–17.

Bennett, John B. *College Professionalism: The Academy, Individualism, and the Common Good.* Phoenix: Oryx, 1998.

Bergquist, William. *The Postmodern Organization: Mastering the Art of Irreversible Change*. San Francisco: Jossey-Bass, 1993.

Blakeslee, Ann M. "Activity, Context, Interaction, and Authority." *Journal of Business and Technical Communication* 11 (1997): 125–69.

Boyer, Ernest L. *Scholarship Reconsidered: Priorities of the Professoriate*. Princeton: Carnegie Foundation for the Advancement of Teaching, 1990.

Cambridge, Barbara L., and Ben W. McClelland. "From Icon to Partner: Repositioning the Writing Program Administrator." *Resituating Writing: Constructing and Administering Writing Programs*. Ed. Joseph Janangelo & Kristine Hansen. Portsmouth, NH: Boynton/Cook Heinemann. 151–59.

Carrick, Tracy Hamler. "Literacy Lessons from a Grampasaurus: Theories, Discourses, Actions." Reflective essay, Writing Program, Syracuse U, 2001.

Catalano, Timothy, et al. "TA Training in English: An Annotated Bibliography." *WPA: Writing Program Administration* 19 (1996): 36–54.

Comprone et al. "Watson Conference Oral History #3: The Breadth of Composition Studies: Professionalization and Interdisciplinarity, October 1996." *History, Reflection, and Narrative*. Eds. Mary Rosner, Beth Boehm and Debra Journet. Stamford, CT: Ablex, 1999. 205–23.

Csikszentmihalyi, Mihaly. *Creativity: Flow and the Psychology of Discovery and Invention*. New York: HarperCollins, 1996.

Davidson, Cathy N. "Them Versus Us (and Which One of 'Them' Is Me)?" *Profession 2000*. New York: MLA, 2000. 97–108.

Dias, Patrick, et al. *Worlds Apart: Acting and Writing in Academic and Workplace Contexts*. Mahwah, NJ: Erlbaum, 1999.

Dickson, Marcia. "Directing without Power: Adventures in Constructing a Model of Feminist Writing Program Administration." *Writing Ourselves into the Story: Unheard Voices from Composition Studies*. Ed. Sheryl I. Fontaine and Susan Hunter. Carbondale: Southern Illinois UP, 1993. 140–53.

Eastland, Terry. *Energy in the Executive: The Case for the Strong Presidency*. New York: Free P, 1992.

"Evaluating the Intellectual Work of Writing Program Administration." Statement from the Council of Writing Program Administrators. *WPA: Writing Program Administration* 22 (1998): 85–104.

The Federalist Papers by Alexander Hamilton, James Madison and James Jay. Ed. and intro. Garry Wills. 1787–88. New York: Bantam, 1982.

Gebhardt, Richard C., and Barbara Genelle Smith Gebhardt, eds. *Academic Advancement in Composition Studies: Scholarship, Publication, Promotion, Tenure*. Mahwah, NJ: Erlbaum, 1997.

Gibson, James J. "The Theory of Affordances." *Perceiving, Acting, and Knowing: Toward an Ecological Psychology*. Ed. Robert Shaw and John Bransford. Hillsdale, NJ: Erlbaum, 1977. 67–82.

Goodburn, Amy, and Carrie Shively Leverenz. "Feminist Writing Program Administration: Resisting the Bureaucrat Within." *Feminism and Composition: In Other Words*. Ed. Susan C. Jarratt and Lynn Worsham. New York: MLA, 1998. 276–90.

Guillory, John. "The System of Graduate Education." *PMLA* (2000): 1154–63.

Gunner, Jeanne. "Decentering the WPA." *WPA: Writing Program Administration* 18 (1994): 8–15.

—, ed. Spec. issue of *WPA: Writing Program Administration* 21.2-3 (1998) on collaborative writing program administration. 1–216.

Hansen, Kristine. "Face to Face with Part-Timers: Ethics and the Professionalization of Writing Faculties." Janangelo and Hansen. 23–45.

Healy, Dave. "The Deprofessionalization of the Writing Instructor." *WPA: Writing Program Administration* 16 (1992): 38–49.

Himmelfarb, Gertrude. *One Nation, Two Cultures.* New York: Vintage, 2001.

Horner, Bruce. *Terms of Work for Composition: A Materialist Critique.* Albany: SUNY P, 2000.

Hult, Christine. "Politics Redux: The Organization and Administration of Writing Programs." *WPA: Writing Program Administration* 18.3 (1995): 44–52.

—. "The Scholarship of Administration." Janangelo and Hansen. 119–31.

"Inside Out." *Policy Perspectives* 10 (2001).

Jacobi, Tobi. "Administrative Fellow Learning Contract." Writing Program, Syracuse U, 2000.

Kimball, Bruce. *The "True Professional Ideal" in America.* Cambridge, MA: Blackwell, 1992.

Lave, Jean, and Wenger, Etienne. *Situated Learning: Legitimate Peripheral Participation.* Cambridge, England: Cambridge UP, 1991.

Leverenz, Carrie Shively, and Amy Goodburn. "Professionalizing TA Training: Commitment to Teaching or Rhetorical Response to Market Crisis?" *WPA: Writing Program Administration* 22 (1998): 9–32.

Loomer, Bernard. "Two Kinds of Power." *Process Studies* 6 (1976): 5–32.

Lynton, Ernest. *Making the Case for Professional Service.* Washington, DC: Amer. Assn. for Higher Education, 1995.

Making Faculty Work Visible: Reinterpreting Professional Service, Teaching, and Research in the Fields of Language and Literature. Report of the MLA Commission on Professional Service. New York: MLA, 1996.

Miller, Hildy. "Postmasculinist Directions in Writing Program Administration." *WPA: Writing Program Administration* 20 (1996): 49–61.

Miller, Richard E. *As If Learning Mattered.* Ithaca: Cornell UP, 1998.

—. "Intellectual-Bureaucrats: The Future of Employment in the Twilight of the Professions." Rosner, Boehm, and Journet. 321–31.

Olson, Gary A., and Joseph M. Moxley. "Directing Freshman Composition: The Limits of Authority." *College Composition and Communication* 40 (1989): 51–59.

Olson, Gary, and Todd W. Taylor. *Publishing in Rhetoric and Composition.* Albany: SUNY P, 1997.

Peeples, Tim. "'Seeing' the WPA with/through Postmodern Mapping." *The Writing Program Administrator as Researcher: Inquiry in Action and Reflection.* Ed. Shirley K Rose and Irwin Weiser. Portsmouth, NH: Boynton/Cook Heinemann, 1999. 153–67.

Phelps, Louise Wetherbee. "Becoming a Warrior: Lessons of the Feminist Workplace." *Feminine Principles and Women's Experience in American Composition and Rhetoric.* Ed. Louise Wetherbee Phelps and Janet Emig. Pittsburgh: U of Pittsburgh P, 1995. 289–339.

—. "A Constrained Vision of the Writing Classroom." *ADE Bulletin* 103 (1992): 13–20.

—. "Institutional Invention: (How) Is It Possible?" *New Perspectives on Rhetorical Invention*. Ed. Janet M. Atwill and Janice M. Lauer. Knoxville: U of Tennessee P, forthcoming.

—. "Telling the Writing Program Its Own Story: A Tenth-Anniversary Speech." Rose and Weiser. 168–84.

Policy Guidelines for Promotion and Tenure in the Writing Program. Syracuse: Coll. of Arts and Sciences, Syracuse U, 2000; rev. of *Writing Program Promotion and Tenure Guidelines*, 1989.

Prior, Paul. *Writing/Disciplinarity: A Sociohistoric Account of Literate Activity in the Academy*. Mahwah, NJ: Erlbaum, 1998.

Rice, R. Eugene. *Making a Place for the New American Scholar*. Washington, D.C.: AAHE, 1996.

Rose, Shirley K, and Irwin Weiser, eds. *The Writing Program Administrator as Researcher: Inquiry in Action & Reflection*. Portsmouth, NH: Boynton/Cook Heinemann, 1999.

Russell, David. "Activity Theory and Process Approaches: Writing (Power) in School and Society." *Post-Process Theory*. Ed. Thomas Kent. Carbondale: Southern Illinois P, 1999. 80–95.

—. "Writing and Genre in Higher Education and Workplaces: A Review of Studies That Use Cultural-Historical Activity Theory." *Mind, Culture, and Activity* 4 (1997): 224–37.

Russell, David, and Charles Bazerman, eds. *The Activity of Writing/The Writing of Activity*. Spec. issue of *Mind, Culture, and Activity* 4 (1997).

Salomon, Gavriel, ed. *Distributed Cognitions: Psychological and Educational Considerations*. New York: Cambridge UP, 1993.

Schell, Eileen E. "Form A: A Summary of Professional Activities." Writing Program, Syracuse U, 2000.

—. *Gypsy Academics and Mother-Teachers*. Portsmouth, NH: Boynton/Cook Heinemann, 1998.

—. "Who's the Boss? The Possibilities and Pitfalls of Collaborative Administration for Untenured WPAs." *WPA: Writing Program Administration* 21 (1998): 65–80.

Schell, Eileen E., and Patricia Lambert Stock, eds. *Moving a Mountain: Transforming the Role of Contingent Faculty in Composition Studies and Higher Education*. Urbana, IL: NCTE, 2001.

Senge, Peter M. *The Fifth Discipline: The Art and Practice of the Learning Organization*. New York: Doubleday, 1990.

Strenski, Ellen. "Recruiting and Retraining Experienced Teachers: Balancing Game Plans in an Entrepreneurial Force-Field." Jangelo and Hansen. 82–99.

Strickland, Donna. "Taking Dictation: The Emergence of Writing Programs and the Cultural Contradictions of Composition Teaching." *College English* 63 (2001): 457–79.

Sullivan, William M. *Work and Integrity: The Crisis and Promise of Professionalism in America*. New York: HarperBusiness, 1995.

Trimbur, John. "Writing Instruction and the Politics of Professionalization." *Composition in the Twenty-First Century: Crisis and Change*. Ed. Lynn Z. Bloom. Carbondale: Southern Illinois UP, 1996. 133–45.

Weingartner, Rudolph H. *Fitting Form to Function: A Primer on the Organization of Academic Institutions*. Phoenix: Oryx Press, 1996.

Werder, Carmen. "Rhetorical Agency: Seeing the Ethics of It All." *WPA: Writing Program Administration* 24 (2000): 9–28.

White, Edward M. "Use It or Lose It: Power and the WPA." *WPA: Writing Program Administration* 5 (1991): 3–12.

2

Politics and the WPA: Traveling Through and Past Realms of Expertise

Douglas D. Hesse
Miami University, Ohio

Politics and *rhetoric* share corroded connotations in the popular vocabulary, revealed by the easy way *just* adheres to them: "that's just politics," "just rhetoric." The double doubts are, first, that there is a real world of substance that politicians and rhetoricians only obscure or distort and, second that they do so for narrow personal advancement rather than for broader public good. Steeped in disciplinary histories and theories, writing program administrators (WPAs) reject the poisoned view of rhetoric. However, we tend to be less charitable with politics, which at best seem a necessary evil, at worst a block to programs justified by our professional expertise.

Viewing politics in this fashion is not only naive but also frustrating and ultimately self-defeating. For a good deal of their work, WPAs simply must be politicians—and, of course, rhetoricians. This chapter cannot anticipate all political situations that WPAs might encounter. However, it explains several principles that can make political work more productive, even respectable.

Politics is the art of moving people or groups to action on matters that require their assent. Though WPAs wearing the ermine mantle of composition czar may set the curriculum for a course, they rarely can unilaterally set class sizes or faculty salaries. They need action by individuals with the official power to do so. Because the quality of a writing program depends largely on the conditions in which the program exists, and because the WPA has limited control of those conditions, political action is vital.

To understand academic politics, two propositions are fundamental. First, nonspecialist stakeholders may be little persuaded by specialist knowledge. Expert status accorded WPAs in the pages of a journal may be set aside in the office of a dean. For example, a WPA I know learned one spring by memo that the summer writing placement for incoming freshmen was going to replaced by scores from the ACT. The dean of the general college, who coordinated summer orientation, had decided that a two-hour writing sample took time from more important activities. Besides, it wasn't sufficiently friendly to new students. To convince him that students should actually write, the WPA had to do quite a bit more than flash her credentials in assessment.

Second, the most meaningful political decisions generally involve competition for resources: time, space, and money. This is clearest in terms of class size, faculty lines, salaries, computers, offices, and so on, but even curricular decisions have profound resource dimensions. Determining graduation requirements certainly means debating the nature of the *educated citizen* (or *worker* or *individual*), but it also means contesting for time and space, with resource consequences for departments. I don't mean that all academic politics is material. Deciding whether English 101 should be grounded in classical argument or in cultural studies generally won't affect class sizes or numbers of teachers hired. Still, this chapter foregrounds competition for resources, because the professional training of most WPAs has neglected that way of thinking.

In the sections that follow, I employ these two propositions to analyze political spheres in which WPAs must act: the departmental, the institutional, the professional, and the public. In some, WPA expertise matters more than it does in others. In some, resource considerations predominate while in others they are of small direct consequence. Much of my analysis applies to the range of academic situations, though I should point out that two-year college writing programs differ from four-year in terms of the more hierarchized administrative controls, missions, articulation constraints, and so on; as a result, some of my recommendations make less sense in two-year settings.

THE PROGRAM AND THE DEPARTMENT

Disciplinary expertise counts highly in departmental situations, although these situations vary among schools. WPAs who lead large university composition programs staffed sparsely with tenure-line faculty wield considerable power. Such WPAs can efficiently (even tyrannically, if not wisely) institute pedagogies and policies because they hold a significant power imbalance over usually transitory teachers, and colleagues delight that someone else's expertise absolves them from tending to composition. But expertise even in such situations does not always suffice. The classic example in WPA lore is the University of Minnesota English department decision in 1996 to relieve distinguished composition scholar and teacher Chris Anson from his WPA duties, in favor of an eighteenth-century literature scholar.

WPAs face different circumstances at liberal arts colleges where most tenure-line faculty teach required writing. Although they may have been hired for composition expertise, small-college WPAs (where the position exists at all) tend to be primarily consultative among colleagues used to autonomy. Big-program counterparts may be able to change policies through fiat, if they choose; small-school WPAs depend more on persuasion through a strong ethos.

The issue of WPA power and identity has been much debated within the profession. One perspective would advocate WPAs having considerable autonomy and decision-making power (White). Others encourage more overtly democratic or collaborative arrangements (Gunner). Though it would seem downright anti-American to invite less than full participation in decision making, the matter is actually more complex, reflecting the different spheres in which WPAs work. Within the program, thoroughly involving teachers in deliberative processes ultimately results in strength because there is a broader investment by participants. But beyond the program, especially in academic structures increasingly (and paradoxically) organized hierarchically with a professional managerial administration, WPAs often have to act with a decisiveness that may exceed their democratic sensibilities.

Adopting conventional descriptions of political systems, Christine Hult imagines writing programs ranging from monarchy, dictatorship, and oligarchy to anarchy and constitutional government. Being a monarch or dictator is highly efficient if not always durable, though writing kingdoms are city-states surrounded by the larger institutional empire. A form of oligarchy is possible where a few faculty expert in rhetoric and composition dictate curriculum and policy for masses. Still, some variant of constitutional government obtains most places. Sets of rules and procedures specify how decisions get made and by whom. Deliberations flow through committees, some resulting in actions that are determinative (especially in curricular matters), others in actions that are advisory to specifically charged figures (especially in personnel or fiscal matters) who in effect have veto power. A few principles help negotiate departmental politics:

1. *Know the system.* The point is obvious, but knowing what to know may not be. How do courses get proposed and approved? What about majors and minors? Why does a specific placement practice exist, and might one change it? Who handles course articulation agreements? What are hiring procedures, for adjunct as well as tenure-line positions? What departmental policies exist regarding everything from attendance to plagia-

rism to faculty office hours, and how does one change them? How do faculty get new computers or site-licensed software? How are people nominated for college committees or teaching or research awards? This list is only a starting place, but my point is that making any change requires knowing who is empowered to do so and how.

2. *Develop written policies.* Some programs have extensive handbooks. Others operate with simply an oral history of "the way things have always been done." In the latter case, there are four compelling reasons for creating documents that minimally describe course goals, philosophies, and pedagogies; student rights and responsibilities; grading, evaluation, and assessment practices; credentials for the writing faculty; procedures for handling typical situations such as grade complaints; and the procedures for revising any of these policies. First, formal documents contribute to efficiency by limiting discourse in a given situation. Better for a WPA concerned about a teacher making inappropriate assignments to cite a program handbook than seemingly to construct ad hoc a course rationale. A second advantage is authority. Instead of a colleague or student challenging the person of the WPA, he or she must challenge the rule of law. Of course, any handbook is unavoidably metonymic of the WPA, who curiously both gains stature and protection as someone empowered by yet subject to program documents.

Third, creating documents occasions meaningful faculty development. The stakes in articulating course goals, after all, are high and concrete, and thus carry risks. But the process is an effective opportunity for WPAs to demonstrate professional expertise. Finally, having processes and procedures ensures that things actually get done. Debates about "what we should do" can be exhilarating—and endless. Having to produce an artifact compels discussion toward closure.

3. *Construct an effective ethos.* Though listed here third, an ethos of expertise, competence, sensitivity to local situations, and pursuit of the greater good is essential. Expertise derives from scholarship summarized on a vita but also from the situational ability to ground positions and deploy reasons. Competence is judged by how one sets and achieves goals, deals with immediate situations, or interacts with outside constituents. Sensitivity to local situations is complex, demonstrated by matters as small as knowing when to shut up in department meetings and as large as knowing some local history. Further, faculty cringe at preambles of "The way we did it in my former school …"; and sentences that begin "Theory and research show that …" had best soon show how local circumstances mediate the professional literature. To be perceived as pursuing the greater good, you must consider the conditions of teachers and students in the program with the same care you do course philosophies, and you must strike a

meaningful balance between shutting your door to write book chapters and talking with colleagues in the hallways. A danger well documented among WPAs is too much effacing one's own interests and needs. See, for example, Lynn Bloom's serious spoof, "I Want a Writing Director" or any number of the essays in Diana George's anthology, *Kitchen Cooks, Plate Twirlers, and Troubadours.*

4. *Write strategic reports.* Few things are as effective in a political debate as specific information. Consider the power of having at hand data such as:

- The average GPA across sections of English 101 is....
- The number of conferences in the writing center last semester were....
- The resource costs of decreasing class sizes by two students each or raising them by the same are....
- The number of pages the average student wrote in her WAC courses was....
- What students valued most in their writing courses is....
- The amount of time instructors spend on each writing class is....

Because it's more powerful to have information already available at the point of need than to produce it under crisis, WPAs should analyze the campus climate and schedule strategic reports on some periodic basis. Additionally, a program newsletter or annual report conveys a sense that the program is well-managed. Again, ethos. Accomplishments conveyed through reports frequently are picked up by administrators seeking to document the institution's achievements.

5. *Create processes.* The most important lesson I have learned in fifteen years of administration and leadership is to create structures and timetables for reaching political decisions of any complexity or controversy. I admit that it was a lesson hard learned, since I scoff at practices that seem bureaucratic. However, at the outset of a process, propose (a) who is going to be involved in making the decision, (b) how they are going to be appointed, (c) the charge to the group, (d) a timetable including interim reporting, drafting, or decision stages, (e) the form of the final report, including to whom it will be made, and (f) a description of what will happen after the report is made, including whether it is determinative or advisory. Seek approval or endorsement of this process; it's usually easy to get, and if there are objections, it's better to address them up front. One reason for creating processes is to move always busy academics to make decisions with efficiency—or even at all. The better reason, though, is to invest decisions with the legitimacy people will more likely grant when they believe them made fairly, openly, and under the conditions to which they agreed.

At one level, resource issues within the department are generally uncomplicated, centering on things like how faculty lines are allocated and who teaches what courses or gets what office. Matters heat up when curricular matters like instituting a writing major arise because at stake potentially are student enrollments. But don't discount the cost of "intellectual resources." What is the "cost" to a writing teacher of having to replace certain of her or his conceptions about writing with new ones? What is the psychic cost of replacing one programmatic paradigm with another?

INSTITUTIONAL POLITICS

At the institutional level, arguments grounded in expertise carry less inherent weight. At the same time, resources are more contested. The reasons are fairly obvious: There are lots of campus experts and lots of funding claims. There are a couple of provisos, though: If you are reporting directly to a dean or provost, your expertise counts relatively more than if it's channeled through departments or divisions. And except for moments of crisis or high initiative, academic institutions are relatively conservative; things once in place tend to stay there. To illustrate institutional dynamics, I offer two political situations, one in which I was successful, the other not.

I was directing a large writing program staffed primarily by some eighty-five graduate teaching assistants, about half master's and half doctoral candidates. We had in place a teacher training and support program that had received national recognition (Latterell), and I considered teaching in the program strong. However, the dean of arts and sciences was concerned that so few sections of the writing course were being taught by faculty. Wouldn't it be better, he thought, if we hired a cadre of teachers with master's degrees, gave them 4/4 teaching loads and a 1996 salary of $22,000 plus benefits? Though not tenure line, the lines would be indefinitely renewable, and the teachers' experience would make them better than graduate students necessarily could be.

I thought a second-tier faculty a bad idea. It would reify the lower status of writing, it would cost a successful graduate program assistantships, it would abet agendas to reduce tenure lines, and I wasn't at all sure that we would be able to hire, under these conditions, a faculty able to teach more effectively on the whole than the graduate assistants were teaching.

Yet I did have concerns that each fall, following a week-long teaching orientation and with the benefit of an ongoing three-hour course and a teaching proseminar, we assigned twenty-five to thirty new master's students to sections of English 101. The crunch of beginning graduate studies and teaching for the first time was enormous. That the graduate teaching assistants (GTAs) taught as well as they did was nearly heroic. Would the dean, I asked, support a plan that would ensure all sections of writing had teachers with at least a semester of very highly supervised experience and a completed course in writing theory and pedagogy? We developed a plan, then, whereby we could staff thirty sections of writing by hiring three faculty full-time and one three-quarters, at the same time keeping all the master's students on assistantship during the fall term but assigning them to co-teach a class with veteran GTAs (Sandy). The cost, some $90,000, was covered by funds reallocated through a campuswide general education reform. Political success.

My second example illustrates the opposite. In the early 1990s, Illinois State University began a seven-year process of revising its general education program. During the middle part of this time, I served on the academic senate. At a crucial point in 1995, the senate formed an ad hoc committee to resolve problems raised during campus hearings, then draft a final program structure for a vote. I was appointed to that committee and took responsibility for drafting the pilot implementation procedure. We completed our work about the same time I completed my tenure on the senate. The final vote was scheduled for February 1997.

For years, faculty surveys had revealed a second writing course as a top priority. One component of the new program right from the start was "Language in Context," a writing course focused on how language varied from situation to situation. Our writing program had been offering forty-five sections a semester of a selectively required writing course centered on academic discourses, and making the requirement universal would need about thirty more sections a term.

But a new proposal emerged in December, three months before the final vote, late in the eleventh hour of the seven-year process. Faculty members in foreign languages, history, philosophy, and fine arts believed that the new program shorted the humanities. The English department disagreed, asserting that proposed course categories offered plenty of opportunities. However, two things divided English from the other humanities departments. First, the others were very traditional, largely unvisited by the critical theory debates that had broadened English studies at ISU. Second, with declining numbers of majors, those departments were fretting about resources. Without clearly designated courses in the humanities as they understood them, those departments feared marginalization on campus.

As a result, a group proposed that the category "Language in the Humanities" replace "Language in Context." These courses would emphasize reading and appreciation of important writings, art works, and music. They would include some writing, but limited amounts, because this course would have to rely on "expert" faculty from the disciplines, not teaching assistants, and there were just not enough faculty among these departments. Mass lectures with TA graders were offered as models.

I spoke at hearings on the new proposal, wrote emails, composed a white paper for the senate. I had two main arguments. First, by focusing on the humanities, the new proposal violated the program philosophy by assuming that writing in the humanities would generically transfer to other types of writing. Second, the courses would not be writing courses, even if they might be designated writing intensive. They would not have the production of student texts as their core enterprise. Despite my arguments, "Language in the Humanities" triumphed. Political failure.

Analyzing these two situations, I offer a few maxims important in institutional politics:

1. *Have a place at the table.* In the "Replace the TAs" discussion, I was centrally involved because of my role as WPA. The table was fairly small: the dean, the English department chair, and me. We were not equal in status, certainly, but we were there in formal capacities, which meant that our respective positions got closer attention. It also meant that I could propose alternatives more directly than I could have had this debate been taking place without my involvement.

In the case of the general education program, once I had left the committees I had no formal role and was once removed from deliberative processes. Of course, this doesn't render one powerless; lobbyists influence decisions even though lacking a vote. But I hadn't kept involved, assuming that the inertia of my earlier contributions would somehow carry the proposal to passing. When the revision was finally proposed, then, it caught me more by surprise than it should have. That my continuation on the senate would necessarily have forestalled or defeated the amendment is doubtful. But clearly my not being involved made blocking its passage more difficult, especially when I appeared to be some outsider whose motivations seemed merely to defend disciplinary turf.

The advice, then, is to be involved formally in university committees or processes that may likely affect the writing program. This may mean membership on curriculum, assessment, technology, or other governance committees. The most powerful members of any group are the chair and whoever does the writing. Keeping in mind the risk of spreading yourself too thin, seek one of these roles, at least for the most central committees. Obviously the institution can dangle more opportunities/demands than any WPA can sanely fill. Choosing involvements wisely—or seeking representation through another member of the writing faculty—is vital to your personal well-being.

2. *Know the other participants.* My dean relies strongly on quantitative analyses, framing deliberations with "what is practically doable" rather than "what can be imagined." Knowing this helped pose an alternative to his proposal to replace GTAs. I knew pretty well, too, the faculty and administrators who had been involved over the long run in general education revision. But official members changed, as committees do, and I had paid

little attention to the interests of the humanities faculty until fairly late in the process. Had I known their concerns, I would at least have had the opportunity to explain there were many interesting sites for humanities in the proposed curriculum. It's the old rhetorical principle of knowing your audience—but also the corollary of the audience knowing you. If a WPA's colleagues know her only through a highly exigent position paper, it's easy to assume she acts out of narrow self interest.

3.   *Come to the parties.* Ethos is constructed in formal settings, yes, but also in theatre lobbies, guest lecture halls, readings, student union cafeterias, and halftimes of football games. All these sites provide informal contact with other administrators and faculty. Being known in dimensions other than an administrative role makes it marginally more difficult to have a position dismissed without a hearing. Of course, any WPA's social dance card quickly can fill to bursting, and watching baseball when you have no interest in the game (though your provost's son plays on the team, as does mine) is mercenary, if not silly. My point is that political work is furthered even in places where it officially is not furthered, a legacy as old as the golf course, as new as chaos theory.

4.   *Frame strategies by factoring in the resource climate.* In the second situation described earlier, I too much imagined that right reason would win. If this had been only a philosophical issue, perhaps I'd have been right. But not only did departments perceive their livelihoods to be at stake, central administrators envisioned a problem retrenching faculty members whose training would no longer be in high demand. The cost of staffing thirty more sections of writing a term, even done cheaply through TAs, disturbed a delicate resource balance at both ends, potentially leaving a cadre of faculty with not enough to do. In response to a WPA question about resisting a move to increase class sizes in freshman composition, David Schwalm put the need to understand climates very well:

> [I]nstitutional budgeting is always a zero sum game. Whatever your program gets is always at the expense of someone else's program. And that's true even if you get new funding because everyone's task is open ended, everyone can do better. With new funds, you get to do better at the expense of someone else's doing better.
>
> In this context, it would be very useful—in trying to figure out how to respond to an attempt to raise FYC class sizes—to know what sort of money problem is driving the request. Such information might give you a little better idea of how to respond. If the problem is space, for example, and you want to hold the line on class size, what else can you adjust to help with the space problem? If the problem is reallocation, arguing from average class sizes at peer institutions will have little impact. Depending on your institution, it may be better to argue for the importance of smallish FYC classes to retention and rate of graduation along with the established argument that serving ongoing students is less ex-

pensive than serving and recruiting new students (this is of course tantamount to saying, "Take the money from someone else," but maybe that would be a better way to serve institutional priorities). (Schwalm 2000)

DISCIPLINARY/PROFESSIONAL POLITICS

Disciplinary professional organizations function politically more like departments than like institutions. Expertise is valued so highly here that WPAs may feel more at home at CCCC than on their own campuses. Part of their ease stems from the fact that resource issues are diminished within professional circles. Yes, there are slots on conference programs, elected committees, and tables of contents. But professional organizations transact mainly in ideas, with official position statements or guidelines as the currency.

People join organizations by professing an interest in their purposes and paying dues. In exchange, they receive benefits, including journal subscriptions and invitations to conferences, and rights including to voting and participation. Organizations are led by elected boards and officers. Larger organizations such as NCTE or MLA have a paid professional staff, usually headed by an executive director or secretary. Smaller organizations, such as WPA, do not, relying on board member efforts and volunteers. The distinction between elected leaders and professional staff is important, because the former have authority for determining policies and initiatives for the organization, whereas the latter are simply charged with carrying them out. In point of fact, the comparative longevity and permanency of executive staff means they have considerable power. For example, as director of MLA, Phyllis Franklin has initiated and edited some vital publications, including *Profession*, and she frequently serves as an information clearinghouse, including recommending faculty to government task forces.

These basic structures create considerably more access to an organization's political processes than most people realize or utilize. For example, the CCCC business meeting each spring has trouble drawing a quorum of seventy-five at a conference attended by over three thousand people. Participants at the meeting vote directly on resolutions and can introduce sense-of-the-house motions, both of which compel the CCCC Executive Committee to action. Yet despite guidelines for this political process being faithfully published each year in *College Composition and Communication,* there are rarely resolutions, and only a few caucus groups introduce sense-of-the-house motions. Beyond this business meeting, CCCC forms several ad hoc committees, with members generally appointed, sometimes from lists furnished to the 4C's chair, often from nominations or self-nominations.

Probably one reason relatively few organization members pursue available channels of access available to them is because power exerted by these organizations is seemingly meager. Consider the effects of the Wyoming Resolution on the treatment of nontenured writing teachers, much debated, almost universally embraced as a just cause with reasonable ends, and having ultimately almost no impact on work practices. Professional resolutions or guidelines founder at the level of enforcement, especially when they butt against resource issues.

To illustrate this, consider attempts by the Modern Language Association to address staffing issues within English and foreign language programs. In 1997, the MLA Delegate Assembly called for MLA to define ratios of full- and part-time faculty appropriate to introductory English and foreign language courses. Phyllis Franklin drafted and published a possible set of percentages, then invited comments from individuals and organizations. The Council of Writing Program Administrators Executive Board, among others, sent a letter, and in September 1999, Franklin convened a meeting in New York of representatives from several groups, including CCCC, TYCA, MLA, ADE, ADFL, and WPA, which I represented (Harris and Lovas). While extraordinarily sympathetic to the working conditions of many non-tenure-line faculty, the group ultimately recommended against staffing ratios. Among the concerns, two are worth noting. First, given local variances setting national standards, even by institutional types, proved very nigh impossible. Second, even if those matters could be resolved, there seemed no good enforcement mechanism. The MLA Delegate Assembly had encouraged actions ranging from censure to prohibiting offending departments from advertising in the MLA job list, actions that seemed ineffective and ironic. Staffing ratios would have no weight with accrediting agencies or institutions, especially because the latter could achieve ratios by such other means as dropping course requirements.

Like many political initiatives, this one ultimately met the limits of the professional sphere. However, that is not to say it had no value. Discussions revealed that many departments had generated new tenure-line positions by demonstrating wide faculty commitment to teach the range of the curriculum. As a result the MLA group recommended a strategy—and it may be viewed as a political one—of increasing teaching by permanent faculty in introductory courses to create evidence for hiring more lines.

Advice for Professional Politicking

1. *Be familiar with previous and ongoing political activities.* WPA, CCCC, NCTE, ADE, MLA, and other professional organizations have adopted official statements on everything from the appropriate outcomes of freshman writing, to class sizes, to working conditions for writing teachers. Representing consensus on best practices, such policy statements and guidelines can underpin local arguments. They are helpful, for example, in discussions with a dean who would like to increase English 101 class sizes to twenty-seven students to accommodate an unexpectedly large fresh-

man class. But they are not sufficient to "win" deliberations, because resources generally trump expertise, however lofty the source of that expertise. The NCTE recommendation that "No more than 20 students should be permitted in any writing class" may be entirely unrealistic at a given institution ("Guidelines"). However, citing that statement enhances the WPA's ethos as someone motivated by best professional practice and not personal idiosyncrasy.

WPAs should especially know about the Portland Resolution for defining WPA positions (Hult and the Portland Resolution) and the WPA Statement on "Evaluating the Intellectual Work of Program Administration," both of which provide standards for defining and evaluating WPA positions. When I conduct external tenure reviews of WPAs, I almost always attach a copy of this latter document. Like official statements from other organizations, these are available both in print and on the Web. Knowing ongoing efforts is useful beyond helping in local politics, because it joins you to political efforts that can achieve what someone working singly cannot.

2.   *Become involved in local, regional, and national professional political efforts.* Serving on a task force or helping draft a statement has modest to sometimes negligible direct rewards in terms of tenure and promotion. But in terms of shaping conditions for writing, such work is valuable. How does one get involved? The short answer is to network, persist, and do dependable work.

I have lost as many elections as I have won. There are several lessons in my experience, some of it obvious and sounding like Little Golden Book advice to try, try again. But other aspects of my experience are less apparent. Professional elections don't work like popular ones. Campaigning is bad form, limited to supplying blurbs for ballots and reminding close friends and colleagues to at least look at that ballot. Even more veiled is how one ends up on the ballot in the first place. Most organizations have nominating committees, and although they might invite self-nominations, candidates are generally selected because the nominating committee knows their work. To stand for office, then, you need a scholarly or professional reputation, through publication, personal connections, or professional actions. I benefited considerably from four generous mentors, Susan Lohafer and Carl Klaus, who helped me publish, and Richard Lloyd-Jones and Rick Gebhardt, who introduced me to interesting people in the profession.

A good part of professional life, to paraphrase Woody Allen, is just showing up. I first learned about WPA in 1989 through a conference announcement in the back pages of *PMLA*, and knowing nothing about the group, decided to join. I remember the heady experience of sitting in a circle of a dozen or so people at that first meeting with people like Louise Phelps and David Bartholomae. WPA, then and now, remains a small organization populated by folks doing visible and important work, and connections begun in such meetings carry into less accessible venues such as CCCC. Going to massive publishers parties at those conferences is fun, even productive to a point, but for political involvement, the competing special interest group meetings are more important. At these small sites are places to volunteer for task forces, to work with people from other institutions, to become known as well as involved. This smacks of doing political work for its own ends, to which I simply caution that people should have enough interest in the projects they join to do them well, even when they compete for things like scholarly time.

3. *Seek professional sponsorship for actions.* To bring about a state of affairs, you have two main strategies, one rhetorical and one political (though obviously involving rhetoric). Both are important. The rhetorical approach is to publish a rationale in influential places and hope that as your argument subtly shapes the professional discourse, it helps affect practices. The political approach is to shape practice more directly. Suppose, for example, that one thought small-college concerns underrepresented in the activities of the Council of Writing Program Administrators. One might make the case and its consequences through an article in *Writing Program Administration,* or one might seek to change the WPA constitution to ensure representation from small schools. Although this latter is a more direct action, it is also more difficult.

An important quality of political actions is that their success depends largely on their official endorsement or sponsorship. Consider, for example, the efforts of what became "The Outcomes Group." A number of people on the WPA listserv in 1996 began discussing how it might be useful to have a national statement on the outcomes for freshman writing courses. Some of them decided to meet informally at the upcoming CCCC meeting, literally one of those "I'll be the one wearing a pink carnation in the lobby at 5:00 p.m." kinds of plans. From these early online and in-person discussions, drafts emerged, participants in the project came and went, conference sessions were scheduled, and the group moved toward a final statement. But for it to have any sort of meaningful or lasting effect, the statement needed to be endorsed by a professional organization that could sponsor it. Representatives of the outcomes group approached the Council of Writing Program Administrators, who discussed the draft at one meeting, advocated its publication for comment in the WPA journal, and finally adopted the work in 2000 as an official statement of the organization ("Outcomes Statement"). Given my cautions earlier about the limited power of professional standards, it may seem hollow to pursue official adoption or endorsement. But doing so creates a kind of status and longevity for an effort that it cannot claim for itself.

HIGHER EDUCATION AND THE PUBLIC SPHERE

Provosts, presidents, and boards of trustees go to conferences, too, and have professional organizations replete with journals and books, policy statements, and new ideas to try on your campus. Elsewhere ("Understanding") I have characterized nearly a dozen higher education organizations, most prominently the American Association for Higher Education (AAHE), the American Council on Education (ACE), and the American Association of Colleges and Universities (AAC&U). Browsing their web pages to see the initiatives each is pursing gives some sense of broader higher education agendas, and they may even offer WPAs ways to bolster their programs. Compositionists may believe they invented collaborative work, student-centered classrooms, portfolio assessment, and so on (and indeed can claim being earlier adopters), but when WPAs connect these practices to broad national movements, their efforts gain higher status on campus. There is a downside, too. For example, preparing college teachers has been a central activity for years in writing programs, though it apparently has just dawned on much of the rest of the academy. Existing programs may be seen either as not needing funding to do what they've always been doing or, even, as suspect because they didn't recently originate.

State legislatures and governors have taken increasingly activist roles in higher education. Elected officials have always been directly involved through college budgeting processes, but this involvement has come closer to faculty and curricular interests through agendas increasingly tied to state economics. A spokesman for the National Governors Association explained a three-year study of higher education beginning in 2000 by noting that, "The governors are trying to stay the course on reforming K–12 education, but they realize that if they don't start watching where the universities are going, all that will be for naught" (National A21). Possible directions for these reforms are signaled by pushes to drop "remedial" programs in California, New York, and elsewhere. In Illinois, the governor-appointed State Board of Higher Education has adopted "A Citizens' Agenda for Illinois Higher Education," whose primary goal is that "Higher education will help Illinois business and industry sustain strong economic growth" (1). None of the other five goals mention intellectual, social, or civic development; one focuses on access and the remaining four on issues of productivity, cost-effectiveness, and accountability.

Now, such efforts may seem mere rhetoric at relatively far remove from writing programs and WPA concerns. And though legislative calls for "strong economic growth" may imagine a freshman composition course in business writing as opposed to, say, cultural studies, I do not much worry yet about legislators having a direct say in syllabi for my writing program.

Nonetheless, WPAs should recognize that state politics shape the climates in which writing programs exist. (Lest WPAs at private institutions imagine themselves insulated from external agendas, they might examine the Association of Governing Board's "Statement on Institutional Governance.") As but one example of the implications, consider high-stakes testing. Secondary curricula across the country are directly influenced by exams whose scoring rubrics often privilege a-contextual formalistic theories of writing, rejuvenating pedagogies like five-paragraph-themism under the new guise of "power writing." This year's high school seniors are next year's college freshmen.

Working beyond the department, institution, or discipline is the most difficult and dangerous political activity a WPA can engage, dangerous because the efforts needed to make changes are often extensive and usually unrewarded in tenure and promotion decisions. Yet it is political work too important to ignore. Following are some reasonable means of becoming involved:

1. *Shape public opinion through speaking and writing.* In response to being lambasted during the "theory wars" of the late 1980s and 1990s, the Modern Language Association engaged a public relations firm to improve its image. One thing it learned was that communicating only in response to attack was inherently a weak strategy. In partial response, MLA developed a half-hour radio program, "What's the Word?" that now reaches sixty US markets. On a more modest level, individual WPAs might write proactively about literacy issues for local and state newspapers. Sharing professional expertise with lay audiences ought to figure more substantially in WPAs' professional evaluations (Hesse and Gebhardt).

2. *Form coalitions.* Given the complexities of legislation (just look at the lobbying industry), any WPA imagining he or she can save the world for writing dreams messianic dreams. This is work you cannot go alone. Conversing with WPAs at other institutions, even through informal meetings or listservs, is a forum not only for sharing program ideas but also for sharing information and developing political strategies. Those strategies can be as modest as writing group letters to officials, sharing adjunct salary information and conditions, or putting together press releases. Including high school teachers provides a larger base.

3. *Have a place at the table.* Most state assessment programs have teacher advisory boards. Many legislative efforts involve hearings where public and expert opinions are invited. Occasionally governors or legislatures convene task forces. Sites like these offer relatively more direct ways of influencing state political decisions. Being invited or appointed to them often depends on a recommendation from a recognized group. See Item 2.

Or it depends on being known by an elected official or her staff. See Item 1. Don't be deluded that your participation in these activities will achieve massive change for the good. Though your expertise may be sought, it is but one currency in a complex market. Still, failing to participate makes it easier for unwise views to prevail.

CONCLUSION

How can WPAs prepare for political work? Inescapably, much learning takes place in the position, though a WPA apprenticeship as a graduate student means that the position doesn't have to be the first tenure-line job, with all its high stakes. Also, the growing WPA literature, including volumes like this one, has lots of advice, including valuable anecdotes and case studies. Linda Myers-Breslin's *Administrative Problem-Solving for Writing Programs and Writing Centers* is particularly useful in this regard. However, at some level formal training in the politics of program administration best comes in venues beyond English departments and rhetoric and composition programs. Most universities with extensive colleges of education have graduate courses and sequences in higher education administration, often taught by university deans and vice presidents themselves. Aspiring WPAs might devote a course or two of their doctoral plans of study to this curriculum.

In addition to such course work, graduate students might read in the vast literature of higher education, its politics and administration. Elsewhere ("Understanding") I've described at length some features of this literature, but I simply point out here the importance of such periodicals as the *American Journal of Education, Change, Higher Education Policy, Journal of Higher Education Policy and Management,* and obviously and centrally, the *Chronicle of Higher Education.* Book lists, headed by publishers like Jossey-Bass, cover a vast terrain beyond composition studies. Consider a short list including Bok's *Universities and the Future of America,* Cohen's *The Shaping of American Higher Education: Emergence and Growth of the Contemporary System,* Murphy and Eddy's, *Current Issues in Higher Education: Research and Reforms,* O'Brien's, *All the Essential Half-Truths about Higher Education,* and Tierney's *The Responsive University: Restructuring for High Performance.* I must admit some uneasiness in suggesting that extensive courses and readings should replace some graduate work in composition and English studies or that we ought to add more time to the Ph.D. to include this other work; I believe WPAs' best investment in themselves and their students comes through expertise in matters of reading, writing, and literacy. Still, I suggest these ways of preparing for political work.

Although I have sketched several principles as inhabiting different political spheres, they obviously pertain across boundaries. Creating a compelling ethos and establishing decision processes make sense at levels from the programmatic to the public. To these, I add two last pieces of advice. First, the amount of political work to be done is inexhaustible. WPAs are not. Being effective at the programmatic and institutional levels is key to personal advancement, though it is necessary and not sufficient. To the extent that participating in disciplinary politics enhances your local ethos, it will support your career locally; if done well, it will almost certainly enhance your credentials within the position—though almost never as much as will a good book or set of articles. The best motivation for political work, though, remains the desire to accomplish some good.

Second, WPAs must separate political outcomes from senses of their own worth. Unfavorable outcomes invite WPAs to doubt their abilities. But resources are finite, and expertise is lodged many places in the academy and culture. In a world where even Richard Nixon can be twice reborn, it makes most sense to understand your personae as content expert and as politician to be entwined but ultimately separable, each with endless opportunity for extension and application.

WORKS CITED

Association of Governing Boards of Colleges and Universities. "AGB Statement on Institutional Governance." 8 November 1998. 1 October 2000. <http://www.agb.org/governance.cfm>.

Bloom, Lynn A. "I Want a Writing Director." *College Composition and Communication* 43 (May 1992): 176–78.

Bok, Derek. *Universities and the Future of America.* Durham, NC: Duke UP, 1990.

Cohen, A. M. *The Shaping of American Higher Education: Emergence and Growth of the Contemporary System.* San Francisco: Jossey-Bass, 1998.

Council of Writing Program Administrators. "The WPA Outcomes Statement for First-Year Composition." *WPA: Writing Program Administration* 23 (Fall/Winter 1999): 59–70.

—. "Evaluating the Intellectual Work of Program Administration." *WPA: Writing Program Administration* 22. (Fall/Winter 1999): 85–104.

George, Diana, ed. *Kitchen Cooks, Plate Twirlers, and Troubadours: Writing Program Administrators Tell Their Stories.* Portsmouth, NH: Boynton/Cook, 1999.

Gunner, Jeanne. "Decentering the WPA." *WPA: Writing Program Administration* 18. (Fall/Winter 1994): 8–15.

Harris, Joseph, and John Lovas. "CCCC and MLA Renew Discussions on Staffing Introductory Courses." *College Composition and Communication* 51 (June 2000): 663–64.

Hesse, Douglas. "Understanding Larger Discourses in Higher Education: Practical Advice for WPAs." Allyn & Bacon *Sourcebook for Writing Program Administrators.* Ed. Irene Ward and William Carpenter. Boston: Longman, 2002. 299–314.

Hesse, Douglas, and Barbara Genelle Smith Gebhardt. "Nonacademic Publication as Scholarship." *Academic Advancement in Composition Studies: Scholarship, Publica-*

tion, Promotion, Tenure. Ed. Richard C. Gebhardt and Barbara Genelle Smith Gebhardt. Mahwah, NJ: Lawrence Erlbaum, 1997. 31–42.

Hult, Christine. "Politics Redux: The Organization and Administration of Writing Programs." *WPA: Writing Program Administration* 18 (Spring 1995): 44–52.

Hult, Christine, and the Portland Resolution Committee. "The Portland Resolution." *WPA: Writing Program Administration* 16 (Fall/Winter 1994): 88–94.

Latterell, Catharine G. "Training the Workforce: An Overview of GTA Education Curricula." *WPA: Writing Program Administration* 19 (Spring 1996): 7–23.

Murphy, Stanley D., and John P. Eddy, eds. *Current Issues in Higher Education: Research and Reforms*. Lanham, MD: UP of America, 1998.

Myers-Breslin, Linda. *Administrative Problem-Solving for Writing Programs and Writing Centers*. Urbana, IL: NCTE, 1999.

"National Governors' Association Announces Focus on Higher Education." *Chronicle of Higher Education*. 21 July 2000. A21.

NCTE College Section. "Guidelines for the Workload of the College English Teacher." 1990. 20 September 2000. <http://ncte.org/positions/workload-col.html>.

O'Brien, George Dennis. *All the Essential Half-Truths about Higher Education*. Chicago: U of Chicago P, 1998.

Sandy, Kirsti A. "Learning by Co-Teaching: Mentors and Apprentices in an Intensive Introductory Writing Class." Diss. Illinois State U, 1999.

Schwalm, David. "Re: Average FYW Class Size." <WPA-L@asu.edu>. 21 July 2000 10:19.

State of Illinois Board of Higher Education. "A Citizens' Agenda for Illinois Higher Education." 2 February 1999. 1 October 2000. <http://www.ibhe.state.il.us/Board%20Items/1999/02%20February/1999-02-07.pdf>.

Tierney, William G., ed. *The Responsive University: Restructuring for High Performance*. Baltimore: Johns Hopkins UP, 1998.

White, Edward M. "Use It or Lose It: Power and the WPA." *WPA: Writing Program Administration* 15 (1991): 3–12.

3

Reflexive Professional Development: Getting Disciplined in Writing Program Administration

Theresa Enos
University of Arizona

Although most of us faculty in rhetoric and composition have or will have writing program responsibilities, until recently, few of our doctoral programs offered professional development opportunities as part of their course work. These few have offered credit-bearing courses in professional studies for several years, and now more and more programs are beginning to do so. If you are currently a writing program administrator (WPA), a graduate studies director, or a future WPA or director, how might you integrate professional development into a graduate program curriculum so that students' transcripts reflect such "credentialing" rather than having such work be perceived as part of "service"?

In this chapter I argue for making such work discipline based through the curriculum. First, I synthesize recent critiques of "professionalization" and explore what I mean by *professional development*, a term I consciously use instead of *professionalization* or *professionalism* because it contains both curricular and practical training and experience—instead of self-promotion or just how one "represents" oneself. I next mention some of our discipline's more familiar professional development activities, and then I briefly analyze the present state of the job market in rhet/comp and offer my projection for its future. Finally, I describe my own program's revised core curriculum as one way of getting disciplined in writing program administration through reflexive practice and theory.

CRITIQUE OF PROFESSIONALIZATION

Since 1995 English studies has increasingly focused on graduate students' professional development and more recently has been critiquing it, primarily because of "telescoping" problems. For graduate students in English studies, the term most often used is *professionalization* or *preprofessionalization*, meaning the overall process of legitimizing one's status, or emerging status, in a "profession" (see Sockett). Bourdieu sees professionalization as the primary means of exchange in what Trimbur calls the "currency of credentials" (Bourdieu; Trimbur). The process in English departments, especially in literary studies and because of the current weak job market, has been to forward graduate students' preparation for academic careers—that is, the job search. Thus the emphasis is on publication, conference preparation, a strong teaching portfolio, building and honing a network of contacts—that is, "self-promotion" (see Leverenz and Goodburn). *Professionalism* most often is used in a broader sense, which goes beyond one's preparing to enter the job market through self-promotion (publishing articles, giving conference presentations, and preparing teaching portfolios) by the "professional representation of one's teaching, administrative work, and academic service" (Leverenz and Goodburn 9); rather the term is broader in that it enacts and models the "quality" of practice—much like *praxis* subsuming *practice* because the more inclusive term includes theory.

John Guillory lists some desires of what we mean by *professional*: "desire for security, intellectual work, professional success, prestige, rewards"—nothing wrong with these (92). But what we seem to mean by *professionalization* is the "means by which graduate students internalize a model of professional discourse and behavior" (92). And what we're calling *preprofessionalization* (meaning "premature") is market-driven: Students are "professional" too early—"professional practices" traditionally confined to later stages in a career, such as publication and conference presentations, now pressured to do in graduate school (92). This situation has been compared to the six years usually required for an assistant professor to be promoted and tenured to associate professor. But in the case of the graduate student, the expectations are telescoped and shifting time-wise—to the time as a graduate student rather than one's career as ranked faculty. Preprofessionalization is on-the-job training, where students are encouraged to do everything their professors do. Such activity "inhibits students from developing long-term intellectual projects" (92).

When I attended the MLA meeting of chairs of PhD-granting departments in 1999, professionalization of graduate students elicited more spirited discussion than any other agenda item, with two camps sharply divided: the "antis," who think that efforts to professionalize graduate students are "premature," "too demanding," and that English departments shouldn't be doing it, and the "pros," who say English department faculty "owe" this to their students, that is, that they be "prepared." Some speakers used the term *preprofessionalization;* some called the process "paper professionalization" (this latter term meaning that how one promotes oneself on the *curriculum vitae* [CV] does not necessarily reflect the "real" person). One department chair expressed concern that we were producing "clones"; she said that interviewees are giving the very same answers to questions, that it was increasingly difficult to "get underneath the veneer," that even the CVs looked the same, that graduate students who are going on the job market are getting so overprepared that they are no longer distinguishable from one another. Another problem discussed was the "ratcheting up of expectations," especially in the number of publications. The consensus was that the whole field needs to agree that publications can be fewer and that we need to distinguish between quality and quantity. There was some dismay expressed about an "assembly-line approach" in the time to degree, and there was concern that if this ratcheting-up continues, two books would have to be required for tenure (given the number of publications now "required" for hiring). The meeting consensus was that instead of a constant raising of the bar, English studies needs to set a baseline on what is useful. There was also consensus that the most useful professionalization activities were credit-bearing courses—and that such courses should be required.[1] Perhaps for those in rhet/comp who attended, the remarks seemed somewhat infantile; the majority of department chairs there did not seem to be aware that some graduate programs, though not in literature, had already been addressing this issue for some time, and some offer credit-bearing courses in their curriculum.

Just as scholars and historians are beginning to critique the development of rhetoric and composition studies into a recognized discipline, there are mirror critiques of professionalization having gone too far. Much of what John Trimbur says in "Writing Instruction and the Politics of Professionalization" illuminates the "credentialing" of both the field of study and WPAs. According to Trimbur, "the mission of rhetoric shifted from preparing citizens to participate in public life to training a newly emerging professional-managerial class in composition" (133). And as this "professional-managerial class" became more in demand (it's commonplace to say that administrative work in

---

[1]The MLA Executive Council has set up the Ad Hoc Committee on the Professionalization of PhDs, "with the basic aims of demystifying what we mean by professionalization in our field and trying to determine what hiring departments actually value" (Hutcheon).

rhetoric and composition, unlike other disciplines, comes with the rhet/comp job), the more pressure to professionalize early in a student's graduate studies. One problem that is frequently pointed out is the telescoping of one's graduate studies to more and more narrow interests, to perhaps premature specialization, to an early, forced focus on the dissertation topic, to pressure on publication early on—all this at time when the hiring institutions are more and more demanding their new hires to teach a wide range of courses, to broaden the traditional view of intellectual work, and to actively participate in writing program administration.

GROWTH OF RHET/COMP GRADUATE PROGRAMS/GROWTH OF PROFESSIONAL OPPORTUNITIES

Since the growth of doctoral programs in rhetoric and composition (from thirty-eight in 1987 to seventy-two in 1994) and their current consolidation and stability (sixty-five viable programs in 2000), there have been growth parallels in professional opportunities for graduate students (e.g., administrative duties, first-year composition (FYC) curriculum revision, program committee work). Until very recently, however, there were few writing program administration professional opportunities or training for students that were not student initiated. A 1996 survey by Sally Barr-Ebest showed some formal training in writing program administration being offered: Besides a course in writing program administration offered then at a few universities (Arizona, Purdue, Iowa State, Purdue), other writing program administration experience could be gained through administrative assistantships, such as "assistant-to-the-director" positions, mentors, and various kinds of research assistantships. These noncurricular opportunities and experiences are not part of a student's formal training but, as Ebest points out, depend "primarily on personal initiative and professional foresight," and students "are selected almost completely on the basis of personally initiated requests." Ebest goes on to say that "if graduate students in composition/rhetoric are unaware that a part of their career will probably include writing program administration [and research strongly supports this supposition], it is unlikely that they will receive any training at all" (75).

Now thirteen doctoral programs in rhetoric and composition, according to the response to my WPA listserv query in November 2000, offer a credit-bearing writing program administration course at these universities: Arizona, Illinois, Iowa State, Kansas, New Hampshire, New Mexico State, Northern Illinois, Purdue, Southern Florida, Syracuse, Texas Tech, UC-Santa Barbara, and Washington State. Besides a regularly offered course in writing program administration, Purdue offers a track in writing program administration, described by Shirley Rose:

It's part of our secondary area in writing program administration, a formal plan of study that requires students to take four courses in writing program administration-related studies. The WPA seminar is required in this program; students also must take at least one of (but may take both) an assessment seminar and a seminar in writing across the curriculum; for the fourth course, students can choose from a number of possibilities, including seminars in professional writing, distance education, or several ESL writing courses.

CURRENT JOB MARKET IN RHET/COMP

That there is increasing attention to (formal) training in writing program administration being added to the program curriculum is due in part, especially over the last decade, to the strong job market in rhetoric and composition especially over the last decade. Stygall's research shows that from 1994 to 1998 rhet/comp positions were the "largest share of all advertised jobs in MLA's *Job Information List*" *(JIL)*. Furthermore, tenure-line positions in rhet/comp "for most of the last decade, have represented 25–29 percent" of advertised positions in the *JIL*—the largest number and percentage of positions continue to be rhetoric and composition over the five-year period" ("At the Century's End" 375, 377, 385).

This percentage of rhet/comp positions has held steady overall, since 1982 in fact, although Stygall correctly points out that the biggest change is that nearly all of the current positions advertised in rhet/comp are tenure-line ("At the Century's End" 382). My own research for the *Rhetoric Review* special issue with its updating of rhet/comp doctoral programs showed a very high job placement being reported for 1995–2000, 95 percent of polled institutions reporting 80% to100% placement ("Doctoral"). Information that programs provided shows that twelve doctoral programs in rhet/comp mention writing program administration in their mission statement or program description, thirteen programs list writing program administration work as a faculty specialization, and ten list a writing program administration seminar as part of their curriculum.

Stygall's numbers are convincing: Her conclusion is that we have underproduced, not overproduced (as other specializations in English studies are doing). The job market in rhetoric and composition has remained strong and, I am convinced, will continue to remain strong. The percentage of rhet/comp positions remains between 25 and 29%. The October 2000 *JIL* advertised some one hundred eighty rhet/comp positions, with at least sixty-two (34 percent) mentioning or requiring writing program administration expertise. In addition to the *JIL* there were many—I'd guess as many as thirty or forty—positions (nearly all of them requiring writing program administration experience) posted on the WPA listserv (many of them not having been advertised in the *JIL*).

So what is significant is that all these tenure-line positions do expect, and many require, expertise in the area—and especially for the junior positions, this requires credentialing, or some sort of certification, partially through course work. Furthermore, we know that administrative work in rhet/comp comes with the job. Most new faculty will not be expected to direct a writing program (and I'd hope that none would be, but that's not the case in smaller institutions where the hire in rhet/comp might be the lone rhet/comp person and thus would be in charge of FYC faculty development, TA [teacher assistant] training, and so forth) in their first years of joining the faculty and, preferably, not until being tenured. Indeed, Stygall's figures show that "By 1998 nearly three-quarters of the advertised positions in rhetoric and composition indicated a specialization within the field or an administrative role" (in contrast, fewer than half of the 1994 advertised rhet/comp positions mentioned a specific area; "At the Century's End" 385). Because so many advertised positions for junior faculty mention interest or expertise in writing program administration, the stronger applicants will be those whose academic transcripts reflect some formal certification in the area.

WRITING PROGRAM ADMINISTRATION AS INTELLECTUAL WORK

I think one effect of the WPA Intellectual Work document (see Appendix) is that more graduate students are *choosing* writing program administration as one of their areas of concentration in rhetoric and composition—rather than having it ordained by the job position itself. Our programs are utilizing a range of activities in the areas of research and praxis to help graduate students prepare for their professional lives in academia. Until only recently, writing program administration experience in graduate school has been primarily of a practical nature such as administrative internships and some classroom research. I think another reason is that since about 1989 graduate students have been encouraged to join the national Council of Writing Program Administrators and participate in the Council's work—conferences, workshops, research grants, and so on. In 1989 I invited then graduate student Stuart Brown to attend the WPA breakfast at CCCC with me, the first graduate student to attend this function. I inquired if he were eligible for membership. Certainly, I was told—it seemed that because WPA members historically had been current directors of programs, no one had really thought of graduate students as future WPAs. One reason this was an issue close to my heart is that unlike the other WPA members—I had been a member since 1982—I had never had the official title of "Director," although throughout my career I had engaged in various writing program administrative duties. After that year I was a strong advocate for graduate-student membership and graduate-student rates for both membership and conference participation—and ran on that platform when I was elected to my term as WPA president.

In 1997 I argued that the WPA document, "Evaluating the Intellectual Work of Writing Program Administrators," then still in draft form but since ratified, should be more inclusive, that its focus not be primarily on directors of programs but include "all of us in writing program administration [who] need our administrative work to count more than service in order for it to have some real exchange value" (21). That draft document's main argument, based on the Portland Resolution defining the intellectual work of WPAs, is that "While some of the work we do as WPAs is managerial in nature, the majority of our efforts are conceptually driven by the scholarship and research in composition and rhetoric." This is an important point because it emphasizes that much of our writing program administrative work is discipline based and not managerial (e.g., program design, curricular design, instructional materials and methods, faculty and staff training and supervision, conducting practica for graduate students, TAs, and tutors) and can be disseminated in the form of research and publication.

When graduate students specializing in rhet/comp take advantage of professional development opportunities, serving as assistants to the director (either research or administrative assistants), working in writing centers as coordinators or tutors, developing and piloting curricular changes, and other "discipline-based" administrative work, they enhance their job prospects. But their efforts toward achieving some credible credentials, it seems to me, too often are perceived as "service" rather than intellectual work.

Stygall argues in chapter 4 (this volume) that WPAs' knowledge is more of a professional rather than a management type. She says that "On a larger scale, the rhetoric of professionalism, that of the WPA, competes with the rhetoric of management, that of higher education administration" and, furthermore, "WPAs as a group have not yet attempted to certify the professional knowledge and practices of the WPA, nor have we certified the practices of writing programs themselves." Writing program administration knowledge, she argues, "is specific to our field and can be evaluated as such," whereas WPAs' work includes managing budgets and making personnel decisions; "our principles for doing so are more clearly grounded in the missions associated with the study and teaching of writing." Although Stygall's focus is on going outside the "usual English department way" to developing a "means of displaying expertise" in order to develop a system of certification, she does acknowledge that "traditional academic means of establishing expertise are available" to work with. And it is these "traditional academic means" that I focus on here.

Recognizing that anchoring intellectual work in the curriculum itself, making this large part of the work we do truly discipline based, the doctoral programs that I listed earlier have begun offering course work in writing program administration. Others have indicated their plans for future revision of their curriculum. At my university we made major changes in our rhet/comp doctoral program core requirements to ensure that students' professional development is part of their intellectual work and not relegated to service; that is, we wanted students to get real credit for real work that is so much a part of their field.

A REVISED CURRICULUM

The rhet/comp doctoral program at Arizona revised its core requirements to allow students more flexibility to develop a plan of study that best suits their individual interests. Instead of the more traditional core requirements distributed among categories of history, theory, and pedagogy, we divided our core requirements into three categories: research, theory, and praxis; histories of rhetorics; and professional studies. The broad category of research, theory, and praxis not only reflects our field's commitment to exploring the dynamic overlap of systematic inquiry level but also emphasizes the commonalties among the many important issues currently being pursued by rhetoric and composition scholars rather than assuming research, theory, and praxis are separate domains. The histories of rhetorics courses include surveys in classical, medieval/Renaissance, eighteenth/nineteenth-, and twentieth-century rhetoric, as well as thematic courses in the history of rhetoric.

The professional studies category was, by far, the biggest programmatic change in core requirements. Some of the program's regular offerings fit more neatly into this category than into the previous categories research, theory, and pedagogy: the community literacy practicum,[2] seminars in writing program administration (see chap. 6, this volume), assessment, publishing, and the rhetoric of scholarship. Also included are one- to three-unit courses in the program's professional studies colloquium (a one-hour required course per semester for first-year graduate students in rhet/comp where they are "professionalized" into the field through orientation—of the program itself, stages in graduate studies, how to manage time, preparing for the job market, and so forth[3]), and a regularly offered *Rhetoric Review* internship. The intern-

---

[2]The Community Literacy Practicum gives students the opportunity to learn about community literacy work locally in general and to learn about work in a particular site they select or develop. Each student is to assist a community agency by doing research or other work requested by the agency for six to ten hours each week, write about this experience weekly to examine ideas about literacy, and write a final paper on one aspect of community literacy work. In addition to the aforementioned work, students learn about the history and theory of literacy work by reading assigned texts.

[3]This is our one course in "professionalization," though parts of it are discipline based; all of the other professional studies courses are "professional development," that is, discipline based. The colloquium offers presentations—a number of these by "veteran" students—discussions, and workshops on topics such as program handbook orientation (course work, transfer credits, criteria for satisfactory progress, qualifying and comprehensive examinations, the dissertation, conducting research, mentoring, writing proposals, presenting at conferences, working toward publication, funding opportunities, the going-on-the-market process), important rhet/comp texts, various interdisciplinary theories, rhet/comp faculty research and career interests, grant writing.

ship not only offers students ways to put editing ability and computer and desktop publishing skills into practice but also demystifies publishing and scholarly editing processes.

Students involved in professional development work such as writing center coordinators, the FYC program's *Student's Guide* editors, and administrative assistants to the director of composition[4] can arrange to couple their work to an academic credit-bearing course that would allow them to earn and apply a limited number of units toward course work requirements in the professional studies category. One student, who was working as a writing center coordinator, submitted a proposal to establish satellite writing centers around campus, including residence halls, academic buildings, and the First-Year Student Study Center; such "outposts" would allow writing center consultants to serve students beyond normal working hours and in locations more convenient for students. The proposal was approved and the study undertaken, resulting in a written report to the director of composition and others involved in the university's writing program.

Although much of this work is discipline based, to receive academic credit for these internships requires self-reflexivity on the semester's work. Earning units in this manner foregrounds the reflexive practice that characterizes our program. Thus the basic requirement for earning units in this manner would be a student's reflection on his or her professional work and assigned readings rather than completion of the work itself. A paper connecting research and theory to the professional activity, then, is required for the student to earn academic units that could be applied toward professional studies course work. This reflective paper engages students in self-critical analysis and phenomenology. Through reflexivity students can explore and possibly agree on certain sets of meanings and values that emerge in the process. The paper also encourages students to explore their thinking, or who they were, at the start of the work and through reflexivity to express their thinking, or who they are now, at the end of the work. This kind of cognitive action requires students to handle a number of assumptions and worldviews at the same time, to turn one

---

[4]The writing center coordinators, who report to the writing center director, share equally in the administrative and instructional work of the center. Their responsibilities include some managerial-type work such as supervising undergraduates as they progress through internships to paid positions and helping to select and then train peer tutors. But they also help develop and lead workshops for general education courses, and they are involved in curriculum development. The *Student Guide* editors also "manage" tasks such as late registration and grade appeals, but their discipline-based responsibilities include working with course directors, teaching advisers, and graduate teaching assistants (GTAs) to develop, shape, and edit the writing program's volume that features not only student writing but also program theory-based composition philosophy. The editors are also responsible for the accompanying *Teacher's Guide*. The positions of administrative assistants to the writing program director provide the opportunity for GTAs to work with the Composition Program Director on curriculum, placement, assessment, and transfer issues; to learn about the relationships between the Composition Program and other programs and offices on campus; and to learn about composition programs throughout the state and across the country.

against the other in order to analyze their own assumptions and worldviews pitted against those of others. Through self-reflexivity students critique and thus come to understand their own positionality.

Such credit-bearing credentialing anchors discipline-based writing program administration work to Ernest Boyer's expanded definition of what scholarship should do through a recursive process: create new knowledge, connect knowledge to other knowledge, make specialized knowledge publicly accessible and usable, and communicate experience through the work. These four kinds of scholarship form a mosaic of discovery: integration, application, and teaching. Using Boyer's metaphor of mosaic to help broaden our definition of intellectual work guards us, I think, against moving our administrative work too far toward mere managerial and a tendency to replicate ourselves. Others have questioned whether we are training our graduate students to become "professionals" rather than teachers, at a cost of more opportunities for civic participation, outreach, and community literacy, and whether an emphasis on accountability is moving us too much toward the managerial. In "All Dressed Up and OTM: One ABD's View of the Profession" (1994), Clyde Moneyhun talks about the field's "move" toward the managerial class:

> Developing alongside the growing number of grad assistants and part-timers, but enjoying greater rewards of pay and prestige, has been a managerial class of rhetorical theorists, composition specialists, and writing program administrators. Their primary institutional function is to husband the resources of comp programs and to give vocational training to future rhet/comp managers. (407)

Moneyhun was a graduate student when he wrote these words. In a later article published when he had a been a member of the professoriate for four years, Moneyhun lists a variety of writing program administrative duties that he points out are in addition to a rhet/comp faculty member's expectations to teach a variety of undergraduate and graduate courses, a good number of these being interdisciplinary (see also chap. 5, this volume):

> In addition to a teaching load more varied than anything experienced by our professors, most of us will be called on to perform a bewildering variety of administrative duties, including (still according to the MIA *JILs* I examined) writing program development, TA/part-time instructor recruiting/training/supervision/evaluation, training full-time faculty in writing pedagogy); development of new programs (minor in writing, MA in rhetoric); writing center administration (tutor training/supervision); writing across the curriculum (developing/participating in university-wide writing programs); mentoring/advising undergrads and grads; directing an affiliate of the National Writing Project; participating in campus/public school/community outreach; funding development. ("Still Dressed Up but OTJ" 93)

These duties seem to still fall into what Moneyhun considers the "managerial class" rather than discipline-based intellectual work, but he goes on to ask some important questions about the curriculum in rhet/comp graduate studies:

> How well could any graduate education in rhet/comp prepare students for such a range of duties—prepare us, for example, to develop an entire first-year comp curriculum and sell it to a suspicious faculty? To train and supervise adjunct faculty and graduate assistants? To cooperate with faculty in promoting cutting-edge writing pedagogy across a campus? To manage a budget? To obtain a grant? ("Still Dressed Up but OTJ" 93)

With rhet/comp doctoral programs now integrating into their curriculum courses that are part of the field's intellectual work, and other programs planning to offer such courses, we are beginning to prepare students for these and other duties and responsibilities. Students who choose writing program administration as one of their specializations should have this kind of intellectual work recognized as discipline-based, reflexive professional development.

WORKS CITED

Barr-Ebest, Sally. "The Next Generation of WPAs: A Study of Graduate Students in Composition/Rhetoric." *WPA: Journal of the Council of Writing Program Administrators* 22 (Spring 1999): 65–84.

Bourdieu, Pierre. *Outline of a Theory of Practice.* Trans. Richard Nice. Cambridge, England: Cambridge UP, 1977.

Boyer, Ernest. *Scholarship Reconsidered: Priorities of the Professoriate.* Princeton, NJ: Princeton UP, 1990.

"Doctoral Programs in Rhetoric and Composition." Special Issue. *Rhetoric Review* 18 (Spring 2000).

Enos, Theresa. "The WPA: A Reconsideration, A Redefinition." *WPA: Journal of the Council of Writing Program Administrators* 20 (Spring 1997): 20–22.

Guillory, John. "Preprofessionalism: What Graduate Students Want." *Profession* 1996: 91–99.

Hutcheon, Linda. "Professionalization and Its Discontents." *MLA Newsletter* (Winter 2000): 3–4.

Leverenz, Carrie Shively, and Amy Goodburn. "Professionalizing TA Training: Commitment to Teaching or Rhetorical Resinse to Market Crisis?" *WPA: Writing Program Administration* 22 (Fall/Winter 1998): 9–32.

Moneyhun, Clyde. "All Dressed Up and OTM: One ABD's View of the Profession." *Rhetoric Review* 12 (Spring 1994): 406–12.

—. "Still Dressed Up but OTJ: Beyond the Quest for Perfection in the Rhet/Comp Industry." *College Composition and Communication* 50 (Sept. 1998): 91–95.

Rose, Shirley. E-mail to the author. 15 Nov. 2000.

Sockett, Hugh. *The Moral Base of Teacher Professionalism.* New York: Teachers College P, 1993.

Stygall, Gail. "At the Century's End: The Job Market in Rhetoric and Composition." *Rhetoric Review* 18 (Spring 2000): 375–89.

Trimbur, John. "Writing Instruction and the Politics of Professionalization." *Composition in the Twenty-First Century: Crisis and Change*. Ed. Lynn Z. Bloom, Donald A. Daiker, and Edward M. White. Carbondale: Southern Illinois UP. 133–45.

4

Certifying the Knowledge of WPAs

Gail Stygall
University of Washington

The issue of professional status for contemporary writing program administrators (WPAs) and their relationship to other administrators in higher education is difficult at best. Typically WPAs are faced with the question of how their knowledge of writing program administration can be "certified," or affirmed professionally in meaningful ways. Because our professional knowledge of theoretically sound, best practices is not always well known, some chairs may think anyone in the department could head the writing program, but simply holding the English PhD (or a related degree) does not convey what WPAs know and do. English department chairs, to whom most WPAs report and by whom WPAs are appointed and removed, do not, by and large, have a theory about administering their departments, something much more likely in the repertoire of a WPA. Chairing departments is understood as management of resources, as training on the job, and for many faculty members, as something to be avoided rigorously, and certainly not something about which one would theorize. WPAs, however, either have trained specifically as scholars in rhetoric and composition, or, if originally trained in literature, have retrained along the way. Increasingly, WPAs have also had specific graduate course work in writing program administration or have attended the summer workshop for new WPAs sponsored by the Council of Writing Program Administrators, or both. Thus, although the WPA may have the most direct knowledge—in the department, in the college—about administering an academic program, the WPA's knowledge is professional rather than management knowledge. On a larger scale, the rhetoric of professionalism, that of the WPA, competes with the rhetoric of management, that of higher education administration. Although this competition is focused in this entry on that of WPAs and higher administration, we can anticipate similar problems in any program associated with teaching languages— English-as-a-Second-Language programs and foreign language teaching— where principles of research and scholarship guide program development and practices, rather than cost/benefit and efficiency analysis.

   The certification of the WPA or the writing program itself may provide WPAs with additional resources in arguing not only for professional "respect," but also for better employment conditions of those who staff writing programs with us, better assessment of writing, and better practices on our campuses. Although the Council of Writing Program Administrators' document, "Evaluating the Intellectual Work of Writing Program Administrators" (1996) sets out the standards for judging the administrator's work by those less informed about professional practices within writing programs, WPAs as a group have not yet attempted to either certify the professional knowledge and practices of the WPA, nor have we certified the practices of writing programs themselves. To sketch the context in which WPAs must operate, this entry will examine the history of the professions and the professoriate in this country, the chairing of academic departments, the contemporary corporate climate on our campuses, and options for certifying our academic knowledge.

PROFESSIONS AND THE PROFESSORIATE

Rhetoric and composition comes late to the formation of academic disciplines, unlike that of English, one of the earliest in the United States. The development of most of the traditional academic disciplines took place in the second half of the nineteenth century, though the study of rhetoric, of course, predates by centuries the formation of academic disciplines. Our late development, and our often multi- and interdisciplinary approaches, may put us at some disadvantage in certifying our knowledge, if recognition is based on longevity and pure disciplinarity. An examination of the history of the professions and the professoriate can provide some useful perspective in considering our contemporary position.

   Whereas the PhD degree generally regulates admission to the professoriate, there is typically no further "official" procedure to recognize specialization except through the process of publication. Law and medicine, prototypical professions, currently regulate admissions to practice in quite different ways, in part, because they managed to secure and maintain quasi-governmental regulatory authority for their practitioners. The senior practitioners of these "independent" professions regulate actual entry and procurement of a license to practice. Though the professionalization of law and medicine occurred at approximately the same time in the late 19th century, some of their contemporary practices have diverged. On the one hand, medicine has foregone individualized admission practice, through the use of mass national exams for basic admission to practice. Further examination and certification of their expertise now occurs at the level of specialization, in what is called "board certification" or being a "diplomate" or "fellow" in a medical specialization. This move toward advanced medical specialization originated in the 1920's and has occurred continuously since then. Law, on the other hand, continued until recently to maintain the fiction that all lawyers are fully qualified "general practitioners." For some years, into the 1970s, Supreme Court decisions disallowed stated claims of expertise in attorney advertising, as if any of us would want a tax expert to litigate our divorces or have a probate or estate lawyer litigate our claims against an auto manufacturer for a poorly designed product. Only in the last two decades or so has it been "legal" for lawyers to even advertise (Bates v. State Bar of Arizona, 433 US 350 1977), much less acknowledge specialties (Williams, 573). Some attorneys seeking the mark of specialization have recently opted for the LL.M. degree, an academic degree, a master's, generally awarded after the J.D. degree has been earned. More recently, attorneys have also borrowed the medical model and some area groups, such as that of the American Academy of Matrimonial Lawyers, and are now also producing "diplomates" or "certifications." Both professions also demand continuing education of their members to maintain their certifications.

Much of what people seem to mean when they use the term *profession* is an image of a particular type of independent, unsupervised, client-based practice. This definition would seem to exclude academics from the start, but there are a number of reasons why academics should be considered "professionals." Sociologist Eliot Freidson reviews a wide set of theories about professionals in *Professional Powers,* concluding that education and formal knowledge constitute the key features of being a professional. Earlier Marxist analysis from the Ehrenreichs and Alvin Gouldner and more recent analysis by Pierre Bourdieu focus on the effects professionals produce as well as what they actually do in their work. By these analyses, professionals and the managerial class share similar outlooks and act as a class as a consequence of similar training—higher and postgraduate education to be specific—ultimately producing similar values and of similar class interests. In Bourdieu's analysis one of the critical acquisitions of academics, as a consequence of their educational training, is "cultural capital," and one of the things that they teach to others of their class is "taste" (cf. Bourdieu, *Distinction: A Social Critique of the Judgement of Taste*). By this analysis then, technical professionals—doctors, lawyers, architects, certified public accountants—share similar cultural capital and taste with academics. Although the distribution of "taste" is not limited just to professionals, instead reaching a larger professional class, the shared cultural capital provides a clear basis for similarities between those inside and outside the academy. Moreover, the historical establishment of the contemporary professions and the professoriate is virtually simultaneous in time and in both cases created a kind of monopoly power to certify the entry of members into their respective professional classes.

The formation of departments of modern language, in the late 1860's and 1870's, is followed by the formation of the Modern Language Association in 1883. These developments are concurrent with the beginnings of various educational organizations, such as the American Association for Higher Education, formed in 1870, and of umbrella organizations such as the National Association of State Universities and Land Grant Colleges, formed in 1887. Whereas the precursor of the American Medical Association was visible in New York by 1846, the more substantial certifying power of medicine began to emerge with the creation of the Association of American Medical Colleges in 1876. The American Bar Association was formed in 1878. All of these organizations focused, at least in part, on seeking grants of professional (and thus monopolistic) status, as well as promoting that professional/monopolistic status with legislatures and the larger public.

CHAIRING DEPARTMENTS

Qualifications for academic managers, however, have remained curiously undiscussed and invisible. One of the key reasons why WPAs remain so anomalous is their integration of their professional knowledge with their management role. Scholarly study of the management of academic departments is sparse, and much of it remains in the form of anecdotes. As a recent entry in the Sage series on "Survival Skills for Scholars" *Chairing an Academic Department* begins, "Congratulations! If you have picked up this book you either must want to be or currently are serving as the chair of your department" (1). Considering that in large departments the chair will be managing hundreds of thousands of dollars, this book seems to come a bit late in the process to begin studying for the role. The other primary roles of the chair that authors Walter H. Gmelch and Val D. Miskin identify as financial include managing departmental resources, representing the department to administration, and preparing and proposing budgets. These are also areas for which chairs thought they needed further preparation (79) and Gmelch and Miskin goes as far as calling the role of chair a fiduciary one. Much of their discussion about budgets keeps the focus on "outcomes," measures of "productivity" in terms of students' standardized test scores, student evaluations, placement records, faculty's scholarly production, grants, national recognition, and other "measurable" activity. One area in which the authors strongly urge *not* asking for additional resources are oh-so-familiar to WPAs. They call this the "value-added" method of chairing and two of their examples follow:

> *Problem 1:* Unexpected faculty resignations that leave scheduled courses without instructors.
>
> *Solution 1:* Rather than first looking for new faculty lines, consider additional TA help, added pay for tenured faculty, semester course load tradeoffs, and so on. Then seek opportunities to cancel less-needed courses, shift the teaching/research loads of selected faculty, reallocate resources to program with more demand, and so on.
>
> *Problem 2:* Last-minute request from your dean to teach off-campus or "electronic" classes.
>
> *Solution 2:* Again, your first solution is not more resources. Check for opportunities from any suggestions in Solution 1 as well as special recognition for deserving faculty, new enthusiasm and direction for a less productive faculty member, specialized training to initiate new research streams, private funding opportunity, and so on.

In both cases, in response to requests for additional teaching, the new chair is charged with performing the task without additional resources. As I will discuss in a later section, this is the kind of corporate downsizing endemic in colleges and universities when they adopt corporate management policies which ignore the missions of institutions of higher education. Though WPAs often face similar—and often unrelenting—requests to staff courses for which there are no resources, the presentation of these "solutions" as appropriate to all chairs of departments is a kind of training in the "just say no" theory of academic management. Moreover, both the Gmelch and Miskin and the "classic" Allan Tucker text, *Chairing the Academic Department: Leadership among Peers,* now in its third edition, virtually ignore the financial context in which universities and colleges operate, an intriguing way of separating, even infantilizing the financial planning and resources of department chairs. "Real" budget planning happens elsewhere; chairs manage what they have.

English departments themselves provide another hurdle for WPAs in establishing academic and professional expertise, through the ideology of English departments promoting a kind of "gentlemanly" amateurism in administrative knowledge. This amateurism is itself undermining of power for English academics. This tradition of the gentlemanly amateur as manager has a history which parallels the development of the professional scholar. Early departments of modern languages produced a new focus on a kind of independent practice, that of scholarly research, borrowed from the German universities' model of research in post-baccalaureate education. Gerald Graff's discussion of the emergence of the German model for scholars in English language and literature provides an early vision of the professional status of English professors.

> The new academic professional thought of himself as an "investigator" devoted to advancing the frontiers of knowledge through research and his loyalties were to his "field" rather than to the classroom dedication that had made the older type of college teacher seem a mere schoolmaster. The prototype of the new professional was the German university professor in his lecture room or seminar, a man who supposedly transcended morality and ideology in his disinterested search for the truth.... The new assertion of freedom with respect to the modes of instruction echoed the German academic ideal of *Lehrfreiheit*, which conceived the professor as "a law unto himself," a man who had "but one aim in life: scholarly renown." "Accountable only to himself for his opinions and mode of living." (62)

This conception of the academic professional in English is not as the servant of the state; it is of the same independent professional, affiliated primarily with the profession itself and not with the place of employment. This vision is much more clearly associated with the other professions—law, medicine, architecture, accountancy—than it is civil servants or public school teachers.

From this moment, the power to declare someone a "doctor of philosophy" in English, and to admit new members of the professoriate, was in the hands of current members of the profession. Academics are, as Sheila Slaughter and Larry L. Leslie suggest, "the paramount professionals because they have monopolies on advanced degrees and train and credential all other professionals" in their fields (5). This was so even if the technical power to confer a degree may have been jointly located in the hands of states or institutions, university governing boards, and the faculty as a whole. These changes were visible first at Johns Hopkins, which was the first school to appoint a professorship in English, then Harvard, Yale, and Columbia, and eventually becoming widespread. Even the more recent development of academic expertise in rhetoric and composition, through the appointment of a professoriate specializing in the area, follows the same model of a hundred years earlier. So the claim to professional expertise is certainly made in departments of English and we share historical origins with the practice-based professions.

What doesn't occur is to claim any further specialization, especially as it relates to administration and the relation of administration the area of knowledge, and I locate this resistance to further specialization in an ideology that ultimately undermines the positions of English departments, weakening them in an era of downsizing and reorganization. The ideology I identify here is one of amateurism, or, "we're all English people, trained similarly after all, so, consequently, we all should equally be available to evaluate candidates for admission to the professoriate in any field of English and any one of us can be chair of the department." As we have already seen in the literature of chairing departments, chairs are themselves deprofessionalized. Information about chairing typically is supported by anecdotal evidence of "good" administration and chairing, rather than research or theories of administration strongly linked to disciplinary knowledge. These discussions are marked with the ideology of amateurism—being a good chair is a product of "good communication skills," "an open door," "providing forums for intradisciplinary discussion," "having a good relationship with the dean and provost." These are hardly actions one would describe as powerful. Certainly, the view of the English chair as manager, making small budgets stretch, and "unifying" the English department (surely an impossible task), is the one reported by deans surveyed by Joseph Moxley and Gary Olson. In their survey, deans were decidedly uninterested in their chairs' continuing scholarship, a factor that might help to explain why the scholarship of the WPA continues to seem foreign to deans and chairs. The Moxley–Olson survey matches the general survey conducted of chairs conducted by Gmelch and Miskin. The Gmelch–Miskin survey identifies the top twelve tasks for a department chair as follows:

1. Recruit and select faculty.
2. Represent the department to administration and the field.
3. Evaluate faculty performance.
4. Encourage faculty research and publication.
5. Reduce conflict among faculty.
6. Manage department resources.
7. Encourage professional development of faculty.
8. Develop and initiate long-range department goals.
9. Remain current within academic discipline.
10. Provide informal faculty leadership.
11. Prepare and propose budgets.
12. Solicit ideas to improve the department. (6)

Only Item 9, "remain current within academic discipline," relates the management work of the chair to the discipline of the department. All the rest of the items are financial, personnel, and management endeavors—all to be carried out by amateurs in those very activities, all to be conducted without careful consideration of how the management activities relate to the discipline. Although the WPA would certainly be familiar with most of these tasks, she would pursue theory and practice to a degree unimagined in the preceding list. She would, for example, be likely to design policies on student placement, based on best practices from the research literature, rather than the least costly alternative, such as the ASSET or Criterion tests. Similarly, she might argue for a reduced class size, based on research affirming the importance of smaller classes for intensive writing instruction, rather than accepting the efficiency arguments for larger classes. Perhaps the people who have the most to benefit from more amateurs in academic administration are those who want our programs to be only flexible, cost-efficient, and trouble-free, whose interest is in corporate management rather than academic professionalism.

THE CORPORATE CAMPUS, DOWNSIZING,
AND MANAGING ACADEMIC LABOR

The public discussion of higher education in recent years frequently has been described in terms of the need to make the university more efficient, more accountable, and more fiscally responsible. Yet much of this discussion has little to do with how well resources are managed inside higher education and much to do with the application of corporate management to educational enterprises. Posttenure review has been one of the most visible recent examples. The presentation of this idea to the public has been in terms of making nonproductive faculty perform, which, on the face of it, seems to be a "reasonable" idea. The public is unaware, however, of how the loosening of tenure would also allow college and university management to be more "flexible" in their labor costs. In this view, faculty are simply labor units. As AAUP President James Perley describes it:

> Over the past four years, I have come to realize more and more clearly that all is not what it seems to be. The calls for eliminating tenure were not really about deadwood, and the advocates of punitive post-tenure review understand that there are few nonfunctional faculty members in our colleges and universities, The real issues have been power and control; the driving force behind all of the proposals for change is economic and grows out of concern with the bottom line. (55)

Gary Rhoades and Sheila Slaughter argue that the change to fiscal and management decision making, rather than education-based policies, has been pervasive and accompanied by other serious financial effects. One aspect of the financial context is the change in revenue streams for higher education. As Rhoades and Slaughter indicate, where once public colleges and universities were supported primarily by state taxes, we are currently undergoing a switch to student tuition support and entrepreneurial science and technology. The "usefulness" of what departments produce can become the criterion by which its very existence is determined. As Rhoades and Slaughter comment,

> In recent years, the discourse of executive administrators in higher education has been marked by a corporate "language of alterations." Colleges and universities are (pick your phrase) streamlining, downsizing, repositioning, reengineering, and restructuring. Academic programs are being merged, reduced, and reorganized.... Thus the repeated campus exercises of assessing programs according to their "centrality" ... has replaced merit/quality as the coin of the academic realm. (17)

The "centrality" of a program or department has also been proposed as a measure by which tenure can be revised. If a program is abolished because of its lack of centrality, then so, too, can its faculty be removed, in several of these "centrality" plans. Rather than making decisions then based on a scholarly or educational assessment of the need for departments, programs, or permanent faculty, the new higher education wants to make the decision on management parameters. And to do so, the management needs the flexibility to close programs and departments and de-tenure superfluous faculty members.

Those of us in writing program administration already know what that "flexibility" means. Closer to home for most WPAs is the accelerating shift to part-time instruction, especially in English, in service of management "flexibility." The ever-deepening dependence on part-time instruction for teaching introductory composition courses is pervasive at both four-year institutions with graduate programs and community colleges with part-time instructors. In my home state of Washington, fully 50% of all instruction in both kinds of institutions is conducted by "contingent" faculty, faculty often without benefits, offices, supplies, or institutional resources. Similar numbers can be produced in every state. The recent study by the Coalition on the Academic Workforce finds less than half of all introductory courses are taught by full-time tenure track faculty and notes that "composition programs reported the smallest proportion, with less than 7 percent of the introductory courses being taught by full-time, tenure-track faculty."

Ten years after the Wyoming Resolution, the Modern Language Association produced the "Final Report" of the MLA Committee on Professional Employment in December of 1997, in which a number of recommendations are made relevant to the conditions of work in English departments, in a report that ultimately acquiesces to the inevitability of "contingent workers." Although this report recommends that part-time and adjunct faculty receive adequate compensation and benefits, it makes no recommendation about how that might happen. Though it also recommends that part-time positions be converted to full-time, if not tenurable, positions, in doing so, it accepts the idea that teachers should be paid less than scholars. Moreover, the primary recommendations of the report have more to do with graduate programs and graduate training than with current working conditions for contingent faculty. All of this analysis takes place without the committee's serious consideration of the pervasiveness of these employment conditions across the academy and their presence as a common corporate business practice. Instead, the report recommends that we police our "oversupplying" of graduate students.

PROFESSIONAL PRACTICES, POLITICAL EXIGENCIES

Though traditional academic means of establishing expertise are available, WPAs may need to develop a means of displaying expertise that isn't, strictly speaking, the usual English department way, or even the traditional academic way. Whereas the classical understanding of the term *professional*, when under an economic market analysis, is understood to be an attempt to capture a monopoly on entrance to a field, recent combinations of professionalism and unionization, in the face of large-scale deprofessionalization, may provide us with a more politically stable basis for writing program administration. And this position clearly contradicts the view Marxist James Sledd recently advanced when he said:

> Many of those Leftists belong to the group that I call boss compositionists, comfortable lower managers of a corrupt system, who never tire of denouncing the current traditional or of advertising their own revolution in composition. I maintain ... (4) that by their careerism the boss compositionists have duplicated the wider society's brutal division into have and haven'ts, and (5) that in consequence the deepest lesson of the revolution in composition is the lesson of upward mobility in the polluted main stream, the lesson of going along to get along. ("Composition and Civic Education," 2)

There is no dispute that professionals as a class have been deeply complicit in maintaining social stratification (cf. Macdonald for a discussion of Marxism and the professions), but I believe Sledd's accusation is saturated with streams of "blame the victim," as WPAs clearly lack the administrative power under corporatization of higher education to make the changes Sledd advocates—teaching writing well, demanding fair wages for all composition workers, and resisting social stratification.

The question to ask then is if WPAs can gain the kind of professional power necessary to work for progressive aims. I want to suggest cautiously that a combination of responses might produce this possibility: certifying both the WPA and the writing program itself. Certifying the WPA might begin to give us the "license" to make common cause with our "clientele," the students we teach, the teachers we train, the parents who send their children to our colleges and universities, and the public. With a credential, we might become a more public voice for the teaching of writing at the university level. Second, by certifying programs, we, as a professional group, could provide our various publics with better knowledge of the wide range of contexts for writing programs and an overview of good practices.

How we might go about doing that is what I review next: the various options of admission and specialization that other professions have adopted. Table 4.1 includes the basic outline of admission and specialization available to various occupational classes who have a certification process or licensing procedure. I've contrasted that process to academic administrators above the level of chairs. The categories are not mutually exclusive—some have elements of multiple models—but these in Table 4.1 represent the primary versions of professional practice outside the academy. As I indicated earlier, many of these professional models also require additional training and testing for continuing maintenance of their certificates or licenses.

TABLE 4.1

Professional Certifications versus Academic Administration

Type of Certification	Typical Profession	Function of Certification	Granted or Given by	Entry via	Certifying Body
exclusive right to practice	law / medicine	excludes everyone but those holding the license	state statute	examination, e.g., bar examination	quasi-governmental agency, e.g., a medical licensing board
exclusive right to use name	psychologist / registered nurse / architect / social worker	others doing the same activity cannot use the name; other laws may require government use of "named" source, e.g., architect must approve plans	state statute	statutory requirements, usually requiring specific degrees or training; presentation of credentials; passing examination under some circumstances	usually governmental agency; may be subsection of quasi-governmental agency
license–public certification	teacher	grants right to work in category of public agency	college degree + other state requirements	state boards of education	
license	realtor	grants right to use name	state statute	examination	governmental agency
private certification	financial manager	grants right to use name of organization in practice	professional organization	examination	professional organization

continued on next page

TABLE 4.1 (*continued*)

Type of Certification	Typical Profession	Function of Certification	Granted or Given by	Entry via	Certifying Body
board certification	medicine	grants right to claim membership, use name of organization	professional organization	examination and clinical evaluation	professional organization
fellow college fellow	medicine law	grants professional recognition of advanced training or experience	professional organization	presentation of credentials of training and/or experience	professional organization
academic administrator	dean vice-provost provost president	title while in position	institution	appointment by higher level administrator or board of college or university	membership in professional organization by type of institution

OPTIONS FOR WPAs

Based on these models for other professionals, we need to consider the possibilities. Our work contrasts with upper-level academic administrators, whose professional organizations tend to organize by types of institutions. An academic administrator usually joins these organizations at the level of divisional dean or dean. The career path of an academic administrator tends to remove the administrator from his or her originating discipline, becoming more and more a manager and less a scholar and teacher. While administrators, their daily activities are much more typical of business administrators than those of their fellow academics. Our knowledge as WPAs is specific to our field and can be evaluated as such. Though we also have to manage budgets and make personnel decisions, our principles for doing so are more clearly grounded in the missions associated with the study and teaching of writing. When we opt for a particular approach to teaching writing at a particular location, that decision is based on what is known and what we know about the appropriateness of the program for the context. This is more similar to the judgment of other professionals, rather than the cost-benefit analysis more typically applied in management decisions.

One clear difference between us and many professionals is that many of those professionals hold their license through a relationship with the state. They are written into the law. An architect's approval, for example, may be written in to multiple statutes regarding public planning. And those professions in place by the turn of the century—law and medicine—have their own quasi-governmental agencies that examine candidates and give the license to practice through the state in which the candidate applies. It seems unlikely that this type of license is a viable alternative for WPAs. What does seem plausible, however, is the board certification model from medicine. In that model, candidates after advanced study and/or practice present their credentials to a board of expert examiners. Some specialties do include an examination, but they also typically include a review of clinical practice as well. What that might look like when transferred to the context for a WPA would be the submission of a portfolio to a panel of experts. Those experts—senior, experienced WPAs and scholars in composition and rhetoric—would examine the submitted materials, along the lines suggested by the WPA's Intellectual Work document (see Appendix). Board certification would allow us to declare who may be certified as a WPA and how that certification takes place. Board certification by outside experts is familiar enough in the academic world in its instantiation of tenure and promotion "outside reviews." It might also allow us to address additional "publics," beyond the university, clarifying who is speaking from knowledge of the field and who is speaking from personal opinion. Ultimately, we cannot expect others to respect our expertise unless we ourselves claim it.

Apart from individual professional certification, we might also want to consider extending the scope of the already existing Consultant/Evaluator reviews currently conducted by the National Council of Writing Program Administrators. Already formulated on some of the better accreditation practices—self-study, interviews with a range of participants, review of courses, materials, training, and program teaching practices—a program certification emerging from the Consultant/Evaluator reviews would provide an additional type of professional confirmation (see Appendix for the self-study document).

So what would we have if we were certified professionals or had certified programs? One visible difference would be in the public consequences for substituting a nonexpert in writing program administration for a certified WPA. In the history of the professions, a clear thread of professional activity is the continual and public insistence on qualifications to practice the professional role. Another important difference would be to establish that our administrative principles are located in scholarship in the humanities and social sciences and not in interchangeable management parts. Moreover, it would allow us to speak with a professional "voice" about matters relevant to working conditions in our area. We could become advocates for better solutions for contingent workers, such as proportional pay or "union hall" hiring regionally. And we could provide a counter to "solutions" that ask us to accept that teaching is less worthy of full pay than scholarship.

These solutions may not be apt for the WPA at the community college or in institutions where disciplinary focus is muted. The WPA for a community college may be a rotated assignment among faculty, none of whom specializes just in rhetoric and composition, reflecting the general education mission of many community colleges. Similarly, comprehensive schools with an interdisciplinary framework (my own state's Evergreen State College is an example) may integrate writing so thoroughly with the curriculum that a separate WPA is unimaginable. However, in either of these cases, the need to claim expertise may be equally important. Community colleges, for example, are the single greatest provider of composition instruction out of all institutions of higher education. They are often asked to do this through contingent workers, who may lack basic resources for teaching—adequate wages, offices, phones, email account, and copying. A professionally certified WPA might be in a better position to make a case for more full-time faculty positions and improved working conditions for part-time instructors. Just as with the non-professional department chair, the non-specialist WPA may be profoundly disempowered when offering solutions to continuing problems.

Are we the same as midlevel corporate managers? It would be easy enough to suggest that the rise of writing program administration is concurrent and causally related to the corporatization of higher education. But because the principles of professional writing program administration are located in scholarship and research in writing and writing pedagogy, and because our professional ethics demand that we work against the expansion of the use of "contingent workers," we may be able to better speak on behalf of our work from the position of certified professional or certified program.

When I originally started research on this project, I saw the problem as establishing the expertise of WPAs within English departments. Now I understand the problems to originate in the larger restructuring of colleges and universities toward a management perspective, a perspective that works to deprofessionalize both WPAs and chairs. In some areas, the restructuring is already quite deep. Quite apart from the "managers" of an institution's higher administration, who have never been nor desire to be academics, three other areas stand out: distance learning, outsourcing lower-division instruction, and management programs such as Total Quality Management. To take just one as an example, distance learning, the Provost of the University of Southern California, issued a statement, "Distance Learning: Challenges and Questions" in May of 2000. The statement discusses "unbundl[ing]" the teaching function (3), that is, providing "star" lecturers but only adjuncts to actually respond to student work, market shares, brand value, and competition with private providers. This statement and others like it provide a larger perspective on the community to which those with expertise in writing program administration must speak. Consequently, the reading I suggest here also includes material on the restructuring of higher education.

For further reading on existing support for WPAs' credentialing, see the WPA statement, "Evaluating the Intellectual Work of Writing Program Administration" and the "Self-Study" document administrators prepare for the WPA Consultant-Evaluator visit. Additional information on the Consultant-Evaluator visit is available at http://www.cas.ilstu.edu/English/Hesse/consult.htm. Burton Bledstein's *The Culture of Professionalism: The Middle Class and the Development of Higher Education in America* remains the best general introduction to the establishment of the professions in the United States. Other accounts of professionalization are typically found within particular areas, such as accountancy, specialty medical organizations, and social work, and are too numerous to list here. Peter M. Blau's *The Organization of Academic Work*, originally published in 1973 and reissued in a second edition in 1994, presents a sociological analysis comparing academic organizations with bureaucracies, finding administrative centralization already well in place in the early 1970's. Eliot Freidson provides an update on his thinking about the professions in *Professionalism Reborn: Theory, Prophecy, and Policy* in 1994. Recent work on the profound restructuring the academy is undergoing includes Wesley Shumar's *College for Sale: A Critique of the Commodification of Higher Education*, John Smyth's *Academic Work: The Changing Labour Process in Higher Education*, and Stanley Aronowitz's *The Knowledge Factory: Dismantling the Corporate University and Creating True Higher Learning*.

WORKS CITED

Armstrong, Lloyd. "Distance Learning: Challenges and Questions." Los Angeles, CA: University of Southern California, May 2000.

Aronowitz, Stanley. *The Knowledge Factory: Dismantling the Corporate University and Creating True Higher Learning.* Boston: Beacon, 2000.

Bates v. State Bar of Arizona, 433 U.S. 350 (1977).

Blau, Peter M. *The Organization of Academic Work.* 2nd ed. Brunswick, NJ: Transaction, 1994.

Bledstein, Burton J. *The Culture of Professionalism: The Middle Class and the Development of Higher Education in America.* New York: Norton, 1976.

Bourdieu, Pierre. *Distinction: A Social Critique of the Judgement of Taste.* Trans. Richard Nice. Cambridge, MA: Harvard UP, 1984.

Coalition on the Academic Workforce. "Summary of Data from Surveys by the Coalition Workforce." 2000. <http://www.theaha.org/caw/cawreport.htm>.

Council of Writing Program Administrators. "Evaluating the Intellectual Work of Writing Program Administration." *WPA: Writing Program Administration* 22 (Fall/Winter 1998): 85–104.

Freidson, Eliot. *Professional Powers: A Study of the Institutionalization of Formal Knowledge.* Chicago: U of Chicago P, 1986.

—. *Professionalism Reborn: Theory, Prophecy, and Policy.* Chicago: U of Chicago P, 1994.

Gmelch, Walter H., and Val D. Miskin. *Chairing an Academic Department.* Thousand Oaks, CA: Sage Publications, 1995.

Graff, Gerald. *Professing Literature: An Institutional History.* Chicago: U of Chicago P, 1997.

Macdonald, Keith M. *The Sociology of the Professions.* London: Sage, 1995.

MLA Committee on Professional Employment. "Final Report." New York: MLA, December 1997.

Moxley, Joseph M. and Gary A. Olson. "The English Chair: Scholar or Bureaucrat?" *Thought and Action* 6.1 (Spring 1990): 51–58.

Perley, James E. "Educational Excellence: Presidential Address, 1998 AAUP Annual Meeting." *Academe* 84.6 (Nov.–Dec. 1998): 54–57.

Rhoades, Gary, and Sheila Slaughter. "Academic Capitalism, Managed Professionals, and Supply-Side Higher Education." *Social Text* 51 (Summer 1997): 9–37.

Shumar, Wesley. *College for Sale: A Critique of the Commodification of Higher Education.* London: Falmer, 1997.

Slaughter, Sheila, and Larry L. Leslie. *Academic Capitalism: Politics, Policies, and the Entrepeneurial University.* Baltimore: Johns Hopkins UP, 1997.

Sledd, James. "Composition and Civic Education." Paper presented at the Conference on College Composition and Communication. Milwaukee, WI. March, 1996. ED 403 561.

Smyth, John, ed. *Academic Work: The Changing Labour Process in Higher Education.* Buckingham, England: Society for Research into Higher Education and Open UP, 1995.

Tucker, Allan. *Chairing the Academic Department: Leadership among Peers.* 3rd ed. New York: American Council on Education, 1992.

Williams, Timothy J. "Specialization: Recognizing *De Facto* Specialization and the Fundamental Right of the Attorney to Advertise." *Capital University Law Review* 19 (1990): 573–94.

WPA Executive Committee, with Robert Schwegler, Charles Schuster, Gail Stygall, and Judy Pearce. "Evaluating the Intellectual Work of Writing Program Administrators: A Draft." *WPA: Writing Program Administration.* 20.1-2 (1996): 92–103.

5

Writing Program Administration Internships

Daphne Desser

Darin Payne

The University of Hawaii

In 1997 *College Composition and Communication* published the results of a national survey of graduate students in rhetoric and composition, titled "Present Perfect and Future Imperfect" (S. Miller et al.); those results revealed deep concerns held by students about how well graduate training prepares them for their future careers in academia. Since then many graduate programs in rhetoric and composition have been seriously examining their own practices of professionalizing graduate students, practices that potentially involve empowerment and exploitation. One subject of such reflection is writing program administration internships. By *writing program administration internships*, we mean administrative positions other than grading, teaching, and research assistantships held by graduate students within a writing program. We mean positions that facilitate the running of the program itself: for example, helping to coordinate first-year placement exams or midcareer university-wide writing assessments; serving as assistants to the director of composition; running a writing center, not as tutors but as supervisors and coordinators; working in outreach initiatives with local colleges or high schools on behalf of the university; assisting with the development and/or running of TA-training programs; serving on committees within and beyond the writing program; facilitating innovative projects such as service-learning initiatives and pilot programs involving new technologies; and so on.

In this chapter we discuss some of the strengths and weaknesses of writing program administration internships in general. At their best we see internships providing working models of writing program administration as a form of ethical intellectual work—a form of inquiry that advances knowledge, often amidst difficult labor conditions and unfair political contexts. Internships can empower students by moving them out of student roles and into roles of active participation as they put into practice the theories they learn in course work, implementing their own ideas in real-world academic settings. Internships can also offer students a safe environment in which to discover, at an early stage of their careers, whether they *want* to do such work. Finally internships can improve students' marketability by giving them a breadth of experience upon which to draw before completing their degrees and in preparation for job searches.

Such marketability, however, may come with a price. Assistant professors in rhetoric and composition are routinely expected to be involved in administrative work soon after being hired, which often puts them at a disadvantage in earning tenure and promotion; though internships may aid in initial employment, they may ultimately be of professional disservice in that they enable new assistant professors to take on more than they should. Additionally, even before students have graduated internships may lead to exploitation; students may become overinvolved in programmatic administration, neglecting course work, teaching, or opportunities to develop research agendas and publishing records. Internships may also promote what John Guillory has called "preprofessionalization"—self-promotion rather than intellectual and pedagogical development (91).

For those considering implementing or revising writing program administration internship programs at their own institutions, we offer here some general guidelines that may mitigate some of the aforementioned problems and help administrators configure internships in ways that will benefit their students, their programs, and their institutions. We base those guidelines on the literature we have reviewed and on our own experiences as writing program administration interns during graduate school. The guidelines we offer reflect our general belief that internships need to be implemented carefully, with structured opportunities for critical reflection about the intersections of theory and praxis enabled by the internship and about the political nature of the internship itself. In the following sections, we articulate and offer justifications for guiding principles that will help the reader decide whether offering an internship is appropriate to his or her needs and, if it is, how it may be effectively integrated into an existing writing program. Following those guidelines, we conclude by discussing some pitfalls with internships and by offering some further reading in this area. The guidelines we suggest are as follows: (a) internships should be appropriate to localized conditions of teaching, learning, and writing program administration; (b) internships should extend graduate students' education by enriching their course work and enabling them to apply theories to practice; (c) internships should involve opportunities for students and faculty members to critically evaluate the political circumstances of their work; and (d) faculty members facilitating internships and students taking them need to be compensated appropriately for their work.

INTERNSHIPS SHOULD BE LOCALLY SITUATED AND RESPONSIVE

First and foremost, we believe that internships should be appropriate to local programmatic, departmental, and institutional conditions. An internship in a research-1 university with an extensive composition program will no doubt differ from an internship within an MA-granting institution with one required writing course. Each institution has its own pedagogical and administrative structures that will shape and constrain whatever internship opportunities exist; those structures can also serve as a support system to enable the interns' success. We offer, as one example, our own internship experience at a research-1 university in the Southwest—the University of Arizona. That institution has a first-year composition program that includes basic writing, expository writing, and literary analysis. The university evaluates and places incoming students either through standardized ACT tests combined with a holistically scored timed essay or through an entrance portfolio the students compile in their senior year of high school. The university also has in place a midcareer writing assessment; one that students are asked to take before moving into upper-division course work and one they are required to satisfy before graduating.

Given the size of the institution and the number of students that need to be assessed, such work is handled by the University Composition Board (UCB), a working group comprised of five academic professionals in composition and rhetoric whose duties revolve primarily around large-scale writing assessment, various writing-across-the-curriculum (WAC) projects, and local outreach initiatives. Many of the outreach initiatives performed by the UCB reflect an effort to serve members of the underrepresented Hispanic population situated in the southwest; the UCB provides guidance and instruction in preparing entrance portfolios, for example, to high school students in Nogales, Mexico who are planning to attend the university.

For the academic years of 1997–1999, we had the opportunity to serve as interns for the UCB. We were hired along with three other graduate student interns—one per board member, each of whom acted as a mentor to one intern—to assist in the design and implementation of the First-year Placement Exam, the First-Year Portfolio Placement Project, and the Upper Division Writing Proficiency Exam. We also participated in outreach to high schools in Tucson and Nogales, and we helped host (or presented papers at) various campuswide conferences and teacher-education workshops. Our work in assessment and outreach was thus informed by and situated within a well-established infrastructure that had developed in response to local university needs and commitments.

When we were asked to help retool the university's large-scale assessment instruments, then, we were hardly starting from scratch; before taking on such a task, we were trained in the administering and grading of various large-scale exams, and we were included in meetings between the board and other university representatives, during which we came to know many campuswide concerns surrounding the midcareer assessment and the first-year placement exams. Moreover many of us interns had taken, or were in the process of taking, a graduate course in writing assessment from Edward M. White, a leading scholar in the field. Such courses are not widely available, but they are becoming more common in rhetoric and composition programs. White's course served as a further means of localized support for our internship and contributed to the internship's effectiveness in meeting the remaining guidelines we outline here.

INTERNSHIPS SHOULD EXTEND AND ENRICH GRADUATE STUDENTS' EDUCATION

Internships should not be irrelevant or only marginally connected to graduate-level course work (see chap. 3, this volume). They should instead enable students to apply theory to practice, and they should include opportunities for students to critically reflect on those applications through dialogues, writing assignments, and other structured means. That may seem an obvious point to some, but unless such opportunities—which make both students and teachers/administrators accountable—are created, internships can easily become sites of drudge work in which students do routinized, mundane tasks for which overworked writing professors or program directors have little time. In such cases internships may respond to institutional needs, but they neither enrich nor extend graduate education. Our own internship positions for the UCB concluded each year with our writing an annual report. Reading through such reports in hindsight, we notice explicit connections being made by us between our course work and our internship duties. In one report, for example, one of us wrote, "The work I've done ... has both supplemented and been informed by the education I've been receiving ...; many projects ... have turned out to be 'practical applications' of the theory and pedagogy I have regularly encountered in course work and in research toward the dissertation." Our experience with the UCB afforded us with specific, concrete scenarios through which to re-examine our learning in courses such as White's.

At the same time the experience of White's course gave us an intellectual foundation for enacting UCB policies and procedures. One of us wrote, for instance, about the process of sitting on a committee to extensively revise the Upper Division Writing Proficiency exam: "What I have learned first-hand ... is a working knowledge of just how locally situated assessment practices must be; this was something stressed in the assessment course I took, but I now see with more depth and clarity what 'locally situated' really means." As students we took pleasure in experiencing the immediate applicability of our graduate training, and we felt empowered by our theoretical knowledge of assessment that we brought to bear on the internship. Through that combination we began to feel less like students and more like future colleagues as we were invited to participate in some of the UCB's regular meetings and primary projects.

Our participation in UCB activities also gave us more confidence as emerging scholars and researchers. As one of us wrote in an annual report, "My experience with the portfolio project is a base from which I can write (and hopefully publish) about connections between large-scale assessment and outreach." Thus our hands-on experiences in writing program administration gave us a way into a disciplinary conversation, providing us with a specific site to develop research questions and to make our way among the scholarly discussions we had encountered in our course work. The opportunities we were given to lead workshops and training sessions in writing assessment gave us reasons to reflect upon and to critically investigate our ongoing research and writing projects, providing us with renewed energy and revised perspectives, as one of our reports suggests: "... the [teacher training] workshop I led was a place for me to put into practical application my understanding of collaborative learning—something I have been publishing about and researching since entering the program."

Similarly Carrie Leverenz and Amy Goodburn describe the way in which a writing program administration internship complicated the perspectives that they had developed as graduate students at Ohio State. In "Feminist Writing Program Administration: Resisting the Bureaucrat Within," Leverenz and Goodburn demonstrate how internships enabled them to understand more critically the intellectual work of administration, beyond theoretical applications and imagined enactments. Leverenz and Goodburn entered their internships hoping to practice a model of feminist writing program administration—through shared authority and collaborative decision making, for example. Their actual experiences as interns, however, forced them to take more fully into account working conditions and pervasive models of administration:

> Although we were initially excited by the chance to play important roles in what promised to be a dramatic reform of the writing program, our feminist dream of doing so through non-hierarchical collaboration and shared leadership was often lost sight of in the ensuing struggles for power, authority, ownership, and control. In retrospect we believe that our frustration with the new models of administration we were trying to en-

act reveals the degree to which we had been influenced by bureaucratic models of administration—those that Dixon, Ferguson, and Grundy term patriarchal. (278–79)

What Leverenz and Goodburn's experience demonstrates is that internships can serve as sites of not just practical application, but also critical reflection; they can become places in which students encounter and begin to articulate some of the problems associated with writing program administration—nationally and locally. In this way graduate students gain a level of agency in shaping a significant part of the profession. Important to note, as we indicate in our next section, opportunities for such critical evaluation must be a part of any successful internship program if that program is to legitimately serve the students, their home institutions, and the profession.

INTERNSHIPS SHOULD INVOLVE OPPORTUNITIES FOR STUDENTS AND FACULTY MEMBERS TO CRITICALLY EVALUATE AND RESPOND TO THE POLITICAL CIRCUMSTANCES OF THEIR WORK

As Duane Roen has argued, and as both the Portland Resolution and WPA's "Evaluating the Intellectual Work of Writing Administration" seek to validate, what we normally think of as writing program administration needs to be regarded as both scholarship and teaching; this needs to happen if composition and rhetoric is to improve its academic status and if professors in the discipline are to be granted realistic working conditions for earning tenure and promotion. For those who accept such a premise, the incorporation of writing program administration activities into graduate students' educational experience is not only justifiable but a necessary part of their training. Indeed it is on such grounds that writing program administration courses have recently begun to be offered at universities like Kansas, Purdue, Arizona, and Iowa State; as Sally Barr Ebest reports in a recent survey of composition programs across the country, where such course work is lacking education in administration can occur through internships (75). Complementing Roen, cited earlier, she argues that "If we want future WPAs to avoid the burdens of overwork, understaffing, and insufficient funding which so many of us have experienced, we must ensure that our graduate students learn those skills which will help them run a strong and efficient writing program" (Ebest 76). At least one such skill must be the ability to recognize and respond to difficult working conditions and political circumstances, an ability that can be developed through internships.

Darin Payne and Theresa Enos have in fact written that the greatest contribution to teacher education by the WPA as an organization has been the way in which writing program administration explicitly situates teacher education amidst competing and conflicting political conditions, in the process laying bare those conditions and their impact on intellectual work. In this respect, teacher education itself becomes a participant in the determination of how those conditions impact that work. Payne and Enos write that education that integrates writing program administration "asks TA educators to construct their work at the intersections of theory, practice, and pragmatics, of academic, institutional, and cultural contexts" (14). Internships can do this, and they can embody the kind of explicit situatedness that Payne and Enos describe.

In our work administering writing assessment for the University of Arizona, we regularly came face-to-face with faculty who were disappointed with student writing but who rarely assigned or responded to writing in their courses; moreover, many of these same faculty readily saw writing instruction, along with the gatekeeping function of large-scale assessment, as work to be handled by composition specialists. As interns, we responded by joining a university-wide committee charged with revising the midcareer writing exam. We worked to develop the exam into a junior-level portfolio, one that would require writing from disciplines other than English and writing that would have to be approved by faculty members in those other disciplines. Our revision of the assessment was thus an effort to transform service relegated to composition studies into teaching shared by faculty from across the disciplines. As interns, then, we saw and began to respond to political circumstances that impacted our work and the work of our colleagues. For us the internship became a site a site of ethical, intellectual engagement with those circumstances.

This is not to suggest, of course, that internships are an easy solution to the problems associated with writing program administration. Despite efforts by Roen and others to redefine service, and despite hopes that WPA-related education can help the cause, most WPAs continue to have little power to substantively alter traditionally conceived notions of work that "counts" (Leverenz and Goodburn, "Professionalizing" 24). Indeed strong evidence for the enduring strength of traditional conceptions of valued academic work is exemplified in the experience of Leverenz. Writing (with Goodburn) as an assistant professor at Florida State in 1998, Leverenz says this of her own internship-based graduate school education: "our first response to these calls for increased professionalization might be a smug 'Well, we've been doing this for years'" ("Professionalizing" 10). It is both ironic and sadly appropriate to current academic conditions that Leverenz has since left Florida State because she was denied tenure; her administrative duties took time away from other "more valued" work (143–47). This then leads to our next guideline for integrating writing program administration internships: They need to "count."

FACULTY MEMBERS FACILITATING INTERNSHIPS
AND STUDENTS TAKING THEM SHOULD BE
COMPENSATED APPROPRIATELY FOR THEIR WORK

As Roen's work and documents like the Portland Resolution make clear, writing program administration is intellectual work; it comprises forms of scholarship and teaching that should be recognized as such, especially within institutions that rank those activities above service for promotion and ten-ure—as most do. Leverenz's experience is not uncommon; many of us in rhetoric and composition know at least one colleague who has been denied tenure because his or her administrative work in an English department took time away from research, which—in the end—was all that really mattered to the P&T (promotion and tenure) committee. As interns at the University of Arizona, we were trained not just in administering and evaluating writing as-sessments but also in developing new instruments; such work demands both practical and theoretical knowledge, and the board members who mentored us often did so in modes of research and teaching as well as supervising. Fac-ulty who agree to supervise an internship should attempt to have that work regarded as teaching at the very least and, if possible, as scholarship also. If an internship is to be structured in the ways we are suggesting here, as an inte-gral part of graduate education, the result may be a higher workload for in-volved faculty rather than merely relief from certain administrative duties. With that in mind, those wishing to integrate internships within their writing programs should work toward release-time for participating faculty and ap-propriate credit toward promotion and tenure.

By the same token, students need to be compensated for their work. Al-though the professional experience they gain will certainly serve as a form of capital in career searches, we believe internships should be performed for im-mediate forms of capital: degree units, stipends, or release-time from a teach-ing assistant's normal teaching load. Such compensation can serve as a means to ensure an appropriate level of scholarly investment and production on the part of the student; even more important, however, it acknowledges the sub-stantive work an internship can demand of a graduate student, and it enacts a model of fair treatment that apprentices to this profession need to learn to ex-pect and for which they need to learn to argue.

Such compensation is complemented by less tangible and less direct re-wards that successful internships can provide. Faculty and graduate interns can use their shared experience and research as sites for co-authorship and publication, a means of recognition for both. Internships can further enrich graduate education not just by allowing students to engage theory and praxis, but also by giving students opportunities to perform additional intellectual work that is a substantive part of this profession. As Clyde Moneyhun has noted, graduate students need to know how to write grants, develop curricula, plan budgets, and coordinate administrative projects amidst an array of political conditions (93). Students will be required to do those things as assistant professors, and they can be learned effectively within an internship program. Students become more knowledgeable and, without question, more marketable.

Beyond marketability, students can be rewarded for their work in internships in even more intangible but still significant ways. Our experience as graduate interns in writing program administration empowered us not only as future administrators, but also as teachers and scholars, helping us to redefine and reexamine our professional identities and challenging us to imagine ourselves as future faculty members. Whereas many graduate students feel understandably disempowered by their marginal status in the academy, by their lack of institutional power, and by the their status as contingent, temporary, and underpaid workers, our UCB internship, though not undoing these difficult labor conditions, did provide us with an alternative community—one in which our contributions were valued and we were treated with respect, friendship, and care. It is impossible for us to look back on those years without recognizing the significance of the human relationships that were created. The UCB faculty became our mentors and friends, modeling critical investigations of practice and teaching us the ins and outs of various procedures—celebrating among the five interns two marriage engagements, two weddings, and one baby shower. Thus what comes to mind is not only the professionalizing value of that experience, but also its humanizing value: we were taught how to be active, thoughtful critics of our institution and its practices, while at the same time valuing the unique, creative, thoughtful people who make up our institutions and who are often at work reforming them.

SOME PITFALLS

Despite such potential benefits to students, institutions, and the profession, administrators considering implementing internships need to consider possible pitfalls. The most obvious, of course, is that students may be exploited and faculty may not be appropriately compensated. Still other concerns exist. For example, in "Preprofessionalism: What Graduate Students Want," John Guillory takes issue with the growing pressure on graduate students to be doing the work of assistant professors before completing their degrees, work that includes a broad range of teaching, research, and service—and is likely, therefore, to include internships. Guillory readily acknowledges the market conditions that have led to such pressure, as do the others (Leverenz and Goodburn "Professionalizing"; Moneyhun; S. Miller et al.), but he is concerned that students' professional careers are being "telescoped" into a time period that is ultimately too short (92); the result, he suggests, is that professional development becomes less a form of social and intellectual growth and more a form of self-marketing. The end becomes the job itself rather than the knowledge and experience that will inform that job. In this model an internship's value is that it is a line on a vita rather than an educational opportunity.

Leverenz and Goodburn complement Guillory in arguing that an "overconcern with professional development" in graduate school can lead to an overemphasis on the *representation* of credentials, at the expense of the substance of those credentials ("Professionalizing" 12); that is, when lines on a vita or eloquent articulations of professional work are the primary goals, less attention can be paid to critical self-reflections of professional work. Indeed Leverenz and Goodburn suggest that critical self-reflection may not simply be ignored but may actually be undermined, for asking students to critique their professional development may be asking them to negatively represent themselves in print—a move antithetical to job market preparation ("Professionalizing" 14). Leverenz and Goodburn underscore this danger by valuing professional*ism* over professional*ization*, the former referencing professional development, the latter its representation.

Such professionalism, nevertheless, may even be a problem in and of itself. Professional development—experience Moneyhun references as writing grants, developing curricula, planning budgets, and coordinating administrative projects—may indeed help new assistant professors do their work. But if we really want to help our future colleagues avoid the burdens of overwork, enabling them to be efficient, productive administrators may not be the best way. A cursory look at the 2000 MLA *Job Information List* reveals the growing expectation that rhetoric and composition graduates—far more than graduates of literature programs, for example—demonstrate their abilities to do administrative work "out of the gate." Search committees are able to make such demands, at least in part, because the individuals they are seeking are presenting vitae laden with administrative experience. In other words, the market may be following rather than leading the kind of professional development that internships facilitate. This begs the question: do internships respond to heavily administrative working conditions or help create them? Do internships empower graduate students to negotiate those conditions or disempower students by making them the obvious and easy candidates to take on such work? These are difficult questions about the profession to answer, as can be more localized questions about whether internships are even appropriate to specific political climates or particular institutions. Thus we wish to conclude by offering a summation of our own recommendations and a few suggestions for further reading.

CONCLUSION: SOME FURTHER READING

What has become increasingly clear to us, from our own experience as interns in graduate school, from our work later as assistant professors in PhD-granting institutions, and from disciplinary conversations regarding academic valuations of teaching, research, and service, is that internships cannot be offered in isolation. They cannot become "lines on a vita" removed from critical scholarly discussions about the very working conditions of our profession. By the same token, we do not believe that internships can or should be simply abandoned out of fears that they may be perpetuating a system of unfair working conditions and unequal disciplinary status. For if that system is to be revised, it will need to be so by scholars and teachers—graduate students included—who understand the intellectual and political natures of writing program administration, who can interpret documents like the Portland Resolution and use them to defend challenges to tenure and promotion guidelines or calls for greater institutional support in relation to writing program administration. Our own preference is to structure internships in ways that integrate them effectively into the theoretical and pedagogical education students are receiving. Internships should not only be considered—and implemented accordingly—as part of graduate student learning, but they should also be implemented as explicit responses to localized working conditions.

Some of the sources we have referenced herein inform those suggestions, including especially the works by Leverenz, Leverenz and Goodburn, Guillory, Moneyhun, and Roen. WPA documents, such as "The Portland Resolution" and "Evaluating the Intellectual Work of Writing Administration," have also informed the guidelines we have offered here. For readings on graduate student education relevant to internships and administrative experience, we suggest the following: "Present Perfect and Future Imperfect" by S. Miller et al.; "Community Colleges Train the Professoriate of the Future" by Elder et al.; and "The Next Generation of WPAs: A Study of Graduate Students in Composition/Rhetoric" by Barr-Ebest.

For reading on the need for administrative work to be more valued in higher education, and on the significance of administrative work in composition studies, we suggest Richard E. Miller's *As if Learning Mattered,* in which Miller argues that important educational reforms will only happen when reformers have the administrative ability of the bureaucrat as well as the creative insight of the intellectual. Finally, for those grappling with the myriad issues related to WPA internships, or for those considering implementing or revising such practices, we suggest a healthy perusal of the rest of this book; each chapter illustrates, in one way or another, the complex working conditions that define writing program administration, influence the shape of the profession, and, for better or worse, will soon be in the hands of our students.

WORKS CITED

Barr-Ebest, Sally. "The Next Generation of WPAs: A Study of Graduate Students in Composition/Rhetoric." *WPA: Writing Program Administration* 22.3 (1999): 65–84.

Elder, Dana C., Darin Payne, Stan Lauderbaugh, Bryan West, and Janet Wilbanks. "Community Colleges Train the Professoriate of the Future." *Teaching English in the Two-Year College* 24.2 (1997): 118–25

Guillory, John. "Preprofessionalism: What Graduate Students Want." *Profession 1996.* New York: MLA, 1996. 91–99.

Leverenz, Carrie Shively. "Tenure and Promotion in Rhetoric and Composition." *College Composition and Communication* 52:1 (2000): 143–47.

Leverenz, Carrie Shively, and Amy Goodburn. "Feminist Writing Program Administration: Resisting the Bureaucrat Within." *Feminism and Composition Studies: In Other Words.* Ed. Susan C. Jarratt and Lynn Worsham. New York: MLA, 1998, 276–90.

—. "Professionalizing TA Training: Commitment to Teaching or Rhetorical Response to Market Crisis?" *WPA: Writing Program Administration* 22.1–2 (1998): 9–32.

Miller, Richard E. *As If Learning Mattered: Reforming Higher Education.* Ithaca: Cornell UP, 1998.

Miller, Scott L., Brenda Jo Breuggeman, Dennis Blue, and Deneen M. Shepherd. "Present Perfect and Future Imperfect: Results of a National Survey of Graduate Students in Rhetoric and Composition Programs." *College Composition and Communication* 48 (1997): 329–409.

Moneyhun, Clyde. "Still Dressed Up but OTJ: Beyond the Quest for Perfection in the Rhet/Comp Industry." *College Composition and Communication* 50 (1998): 91–95.

Payne, Darin, and Theresa Enos. "TA Education as Dialogic Response: Furthering the Intellectual Work of the Profession through WPA." *Preparing College Teachers of Writing: Histories, Theories, Programs, and Practices.* Ed. Sarah Liggett and Betty Pytlik. Oxford: Oxford UP, 2001. 50–59.

Roen, Duane H. "Writing Administration as Scholarship and Teaching." *Academic Advancement in Composition Studies.* Ed. Richard C. Gebhardt and Barbara Genelle Smith Gebhardt. Mahwah: Erlbaum, 1997. 43–55.

WPA. "Evaluating the Intellectual Work of Writing Administration." *WPA: Writing Program Administration* 22.1/2 (1998): 85–104.

—. "The Portland Resolution: Guidelines for Writing Program Administrator Positions." *WPA: Writing Program Administration* 16.1-2 (1992): 88–94.

6

Teaching a Graduate Course in Writing Program Administration

Edward M. White
University of Arizona

As Susan McLeod, Theresa Enos, and others point out in this book, most of us who specialize in rhetoric and composition will take our turn in administration. Developed composition programs need not only writing program administrators (WPAs) but also, depending on the program, writing center directors, assessment coordinators, writing-across-the-curriculum directors, faculty writing workshop leaders, graduate program directors, developmental writing coordinators, even deans of writing. Indeed, administrative jobs are so much part of the university composition landscape that it is a surprise to discover that only a few graduate programs are preparing their students for that work. As of this writing, at the opening of our new century, only about a dozen graduate courses concerned with administrative issues are offered in the sixty-five PhD programs in rhetoric and composition. The issue is of substantial importance, in the light of the usual condescending attitudes toward administration that many beginning faculty members seem to have absorbed: Administrators are mindless bureaucrats, our new assistant professors tend to believe, the opponents of creative teachers, agents of an oppressive set of anonymous institutional rulers—in short, the enemy. But that set of attitudes strikes at the functions most of us will undertake. One of the shocks of becoming a WPA is to discover that we are enmeshed in and enforcing the machinery of our institution; we have met the enemy, and, in the words of cartoonist Walt Kelly, "he is us."

This chapter is based on some years of experience offering summer workshops for new (and sometimes experienced) WPAs and on the somewhat different experience of offering a graduate course in writing program administration for PhD candidates. I think that a course in how to be a WPA is appropriate and valuable for our students as they begin their careers and that it can be a creative course to teach. I thank my colleagues, particularly Tilly Warnock, who had previously taught it at the University of Arizona, and Theresa Enos, who wound up at the last minute coteaching it with me, for their creativity and support. And I thank the members of the course, some of whose thoughtful comments about it will follow the discussion herein. Though prospective teachers of such a course are my primary audience, I hope the speculative nature of the chapter will be of wider interest to those concerned about the directions that rhetoric and composition administration will be taking in the twenty-first century.

THEORY AND PRACTICE IN THE WPA COURSE DESIGN

Before I present and discuss the syllabus we used for the course, I must deal with the most difficult pedagogical problem the course presented. In stark contrast to the workshops I had led for active WPAs, this course enrolled graduate students who had never administered a writing program, or, indeed, anything. Well, of course, you might say; that is the nature of graduate education. But this total lack of experience led to much distortion of the material because the students—excellent advanced PhD students to be sure—had to construct the issues and problems we were dealing with from their reading, their imaginations, their slight sense of administration in their undergraduate colleges, and their graduate experience at the University of Arizona, hardly a typical academic environment. For example, during the sixth week of the course, one of the more reflective students said in passing that the complaints he had been noticing in the reading about the status of composition faculty in English departments were of purely historical interest. When I gave a puzzled reply, he responded that because composition and rhetoric faculty now were among the faculty leaders in English departments, recognized and rewarded for their teaching and scholarship, those bad old days were gone forever. I looked at Theresa and she looked back, both of us visualizing harrowing scenes from the recent past; we shook our heads sadly. He was, of course, generalizing from his sense of the situation at UA (and would that it were invariably true there!), and he found it hard to believe that those bad old days were still generally the daily life experience of WPAs in

America. The students were all teaching first-year composition classes, writing dissertations in rhetoric and composition, and far from naive. But the limitations of their experience (not to speak of their blessed idealism) set the boundaries for much of the class discussion.

Thus the text that was most useful in the class was the one I expected to use only as a reference, the Myers-Breslin collection of scenarios relating to writing centers. Each of the scenarios begins with a description of the particular institution, focused on the place of the writing center in relation to the writing program and the interwoven structures of power that influence policy and procedures. The book uses these introductions as settings for the particular problem presented for discussion. But we used them differently. Instead of attending to the problem presented after the background, we were able to focus on the background itself, as an effective way to help the students imagine the variety of academic settings within which WPAs must work. Chris Anson, as I write, is in the final stages of a production of a parallel book of scenarios, with the WPA at the center, and it should be as valuable as the Myers-Breslin one. The next time I teach this class, I will probably use both books to start the course, instead of at the end as the syllabus displayed later has it, as the best substitute for experience available. Those of us who have visited many campuses over many years bring a valuable breadth to a WPA class, a necessary antidote to the unavoidably narrow sense of academia natural to beginners in the field.

I should not have been surprised to encounter the naiveté I have just described; what else could I have expected? But a second limitation of experience was more of a surprise because it revealed a naiveté of my own. The students did not have much of a sense of how colleges operated, how committees functioned, how decisions were made, how money was generated and allocated. Further, they were vague at best about issues of academic freedom, the meaning of tenure, and our professional history. I imagined that I knew these matters, but time and again my knowledge turned out to be far too simple, too much anchored in the institutions I knew best. I had a fund of anecdotes about such matters, based on forty years in academia, including major committees of CCCC, MLA, and WPA. But we could barely touch on such matters, with so much else to do. Everything is complicated in our business, much more complicated than we normally take it to be (including our acronyms: look at how many we have!) and we must be careful to help new WPAs live in the worlds they will be moving to. Perhaps the best advice we could give on this front was to avoid becoming a WPA as long as possible, until after gaining tenure, ideally. Surely, a WPA course needs to concern itself with the contexts within which WPAs function, and these contexts are enormously varied and complicated—often deliberately obscure, as with that magnum mysterium, the university budget (see chap. 15, this volume). We must share our ignorance as well as our knowledge with future WPAs.

A Sample Syllabus

THE UNIVERSITY OF ARIZONA

Writing Program Administration: English 696e-003   Spring 2000

Prof. Edward M. White with Prof. Theresa Enos   W 4:00-6:30 p.m.

E-mail: ewhite@csusb.edu or emwhite@u.arizona.edu   Tel: 520.621.3221

Texts

Required:

> Bloom, Lynn Z., Donald A. Daiker, and Edward M. White. *Composition in the Twenty-First Century: Crisis and Change.* Southern Illinois UP, 1996.
>
> White, Edward M. *Developing Successful College Writing Programs.* Calendar Islands, 1998.
>
> Janangelo, Joseph, and Kristine Hansen. *Resituating Writing: Constructing and Administrating Writing Programs.* Boynton/Cook/Heinemann, 1995.
>
> Bullock, Richard, and John Trimbur. *The Politics of Writing Instruction: Postsecondary.* Boynton/Cook/Heinemann, 1991.
>
> Myers-Breslin, Linda. *Administrative Problem-Solving for Writing Programs and Writing Centers: Scenarios in Effective Program Management.* NCTE, 1999.
>
> WPA: *Writing Program Administration,* Spring 1999 and Fall/Winter 2000. (The WPA journal)
>
> WPA (the organization) official documents:
>
> > The Portland Statement on the role of WPAs
> >
> > The WPA Statement on Administration as Intellectual Work
> >
> > The WPA Guidelines for Self-Study to Precede a Writing Program Evaluation (White 209-19)
> >
> > The First-Year Composition Outcomes Statement
> >
> > WPA-L (the listserv): See Handout on lurking

Recommended Professional Reading:

> Anson, Chris M., et al. *Scenarios for Teaching Writing: Contexts for Discussion and Reflective Practice.* NCTE, 1993.
>
> Hult, Christine, ed. *Evaluating Teachers of Writing.* Urbana, IL: NCTE, 1994.
>
> Rose, Shirley K., and Irwin Weiser, eds. *The Writing Program Administrator as Researcher: Inquiry in Action & Reflection.* Boynton/Cook/Heinemann, 1999.
>
> Straub, Richard, and Ronald F. Lunsford. *12 Readers Reading: Responding to Student Writing.* Cresskill, NH: Hampton, 1995.

Recommended Administrative Reading:

The Chronicle of Higher Education

Change Magazine

The Bulletin of the Association of Departments of English

Goals and Rationale

Every Rhetoric, Composition, and the Teaching of English (RCTE) graduate who plans to teach at an American college or university should expect to serve a term or more as a campus writing program administrator (WPA) at some point–probably sooner than later and probably sooner than is really appropriate. Only recently has the position of WPA become commonly accepted and the demand for WPAs with training for the job is likely to exceed supply for some time to come. The definition and functions of the WPA vary widely from one campus to another, but we can usually assume that the WPA on any campus has the following expressed or implied tasks:

1.   To speak for rhetoric and writing to the English department and to the campus at large: serve on departmental and university committees, make public presentations about writing and writing requirements, and seek to protect and enhance writing programs on campus.

2.   To be responsible for staffing, scheduling, budgets, curriculum, and standards for the first-year writing course (FYC) and perhaps other writing courses.

3.   To engage, sometimes heavily, in assessment activities such as entering student placement, FYC exit criteria, mid-career or graduation writing requirements, and program assessment. The assessment responsibilities may also include assessment of teaching of TAs and other faculty, as a central aspect of hiring and retention decisions.

4.   To oversee or be heavily involved in writing-across-the-curriculum (WAC) programs, writing tutorial centers, teaching assistant and adjunct faculty training programs, and other faculty development programs.

5.   To originate, administer and/or teach in undergraduate writing major or minor programs and graduate programs in rhetoric and composition. (Meanwhile, survival on many campuses still depends on publication of research, as more significant than teaching quality.)

6.   To take responsibility for a range of activities from assisting the English department chair in general to overseeing certain student publications, as defined by campus policies, traditions, or practices.

This course is designed to help prepare RCTE students for these immense challenges. In addition, the course will seek to connect the theories behind rhetoric/composition, administration, and pedagogy to the practices common in American universities.

Requirements

1.   Class attendance, participation, and presentations, demonstrating timely reading as assigned and recommended. There will be regular oral reports on the "question" at the center of each class as well as class listserv discussion. Stay current with issues on the WPA-L so that we can also discuss them. When papers

are due, bring in enough copies so that all members of the seminar can read and discuss your work, or post them in advance to the class listserv or, preferably, both.

2.   Two reports on the work of a particular WPA in relation to his or her program: one local and one via e-mail.

3.   A seminar paper exploring current issues in writing program administration.

4.   A take-home final exam for presentation in class May 12.

Class Schedule

January 12: What is Composition and a Composition Program?

   READ: *Comp 21*, Part 1

      White, Chs. 1, 2, 4

      Janangelo, Foreword, Preface

January 19: What Do/Should We Teach When We Teach Composition?

   READ: White, Chs. 3, 7

      Janangelo, 1

January 26: Who Will Assess Composition and How Will They Assess It?

   READ: *Comp 21*, Part 3

      White, Chs. 5, 6, 10, Appendix A, Appendix B

      Janangelo, Chs. 1, 5, 8, 10

      Bullock, Chs. 13, 18

February 2: What New Issues Will WPAs Confront in the 21st Century?

   READ: *Comp 21*, Part 4

      Bullock, Chs. 9, 14, 15, 16, 17

      Janangelo, Chs. 4, 9, 11

   DUE: Seminar paper problem statement

February 9: Who Should Teach Composition and What Should They Know?

   READ: *Comp 21*, Part 5

      White, Chs. 8, 9

      Janangelo, Chs. 2, 6,

February 16: What Direction Will Composition Take and How Will Research Affect Teaching?

   READ: *Comp 21*, Part 6

   DUE: Seminar paper bibliography

February 23: What Political and Social Issues Will Shape Composition?

READ: *Comp 21,* Parts 7 and 8

Bullock, Chs. 1, 5, 6, 7

DUE: Report 1 (15-minute oral presentation) on a UA or other local WPA ("shadowing")

Determine "long distance" WPA for second report.

March 1: What Have We Learned From the Past and How Can it Shape the Future of Composition?

READ: *Comp 21,* Part 2

Bullock, Chs. 2, 3, 4, 8, 11, 14

Additional readings by David Russell (on WAC), James Berlin and Tom Miller (on the history of composition), and Sharon Crowley (on the "universal requirement")

VISITOR: Tom Miller, former UA WPA: "The WPA at a Large University"

DUE: Seminar paper outline or developed proposal

March 8: How Will Technology and Composition Studies Be Interwoven?

READ: Janangelo, Ch. 3

VISITORS:

Roxanne Mountford: "A New Comp Teacher Becomes a WPA at a Technical University"

Ken McAllister: "A Tech Specialist and Scholar Becomes a New Assistant Professor in RCTE"

March 15: Spring Break

March 22: The Scholarship of Administration and the WPA

READ: Janangelo, Chs. 1, 5, 9, 11

The Portland Resolution

Evaluating the Intellectual Work of the WPA

DUE: Report 2 (15-minute oral presentation), on "long distance" WPA

March 29: WAC, the Writing Center, and Committee Work

READ: Janangelo, Chs. 7, 8

DUE: Seminar paper: Final Draft

April 5: Revision Workshop on Seminar Paper

April 12: CCCC in Minneapolis. WPA Breakfast 7 a.m., April 13.

April 19: Administrative Problem-Solving

READ: Myers-Breslin

REPORTS: On selected chapters of Myers-Breslin

April 26: Nuts and Bolts: Budgets, Grievances, Time Management, etc.

  VISITOR: Tilly Warnock, UA WPA: "Nuts and Bolts for the WPA"

  DUE: Seminar Paper (Presentation/Publication Level)

May 3: The English Department and the WPA

  VISITOR: John Warnock, "A Retrospective and Personal History"

May 10: Final Exam

REFLECTIONS AND LATER THOUGHTS
ON THE SYLLABUS

The Assignments.   The two oral reports worked very well, though a different institution may need to change the first one. The UA writing program is wide-ranging, with a full-scale entry-level placement program, an experimental portfolio project with Tucson high schools, a branch of the national writing project, a well-supported two-course first-year composition program, several writing centers, a professional ESL program, a university midcareer assessment, and an upper-division writing program. There are also several outreach programs and some rudimentary WAC initiatives. So there are plenty of WPA functions to be carried out and a good supply of well-prepared professionals engaged in the work. The students chose a UA person with WPA functions for interviewing and "shadowing" for a day, and their reports showed a surprised and deepened understanding of the complexity of the various jobs they witnessed. This exercise was followed by the second report, on an off-campus WPA. Some students selected their undergraduate campuses, to deal with relatively familiar territory and mentors. Others chose someone who was prominent on the WPA listserv, to discover new ground. As we have come to expect from our colleagues, these busy people made themselves available to the students on e-mail, telephone, and in person at the WPA breakfast at CCCC. Once again, the oral reports showed an expansion of vision, as the students found that different settings required quite different kinds of WPA activities.

The seminar paper was also a great success, in part because of the professionalism of the students, who are eager to begin publishing their work. The syllabus demonstrates the stages of development of the paper, beginning with a "problem statement" in the fourth week of the seventeen-week term. By the time the "final" draft was submitted, the papers were in good shape, ready for the next stage: achievement of presentation level. With over a month to make that move—from a good graduate seminar paper to a paper acceptable for conference presentation or even publication in a good juried journal—many of the students found themselves in a new professional realm, where the professors were allies in achieving common goals.

The Reading.   Here the problems were great, and each year will be greater. Even though the readings for each class session were (barely) manageable for the students, we found it impossible to discuss more than a small fraction of them in the time available. That was a frustrating experience for students and teachers, but superficial treatment of more material in class was an unattractive alternative. *Composition in the Twenty-First Century* was an excellent framing device for the course, because each of its chapters is based on a key question for the field; we used those questions as the core organizing device for the syllabus. But, typically, a sequel to that book will emerge from the 2001 WPA conference (the contracted publication date with SIU press is 2003), with new organizing questions giving rise to new essential essays from leaders of the field—thus effectively doubling the material for that dimension of the course. Again, Irene Ward and William J. Carpenter are editing *The Allyn and Bacon Sourcebook for Writing Program Administration*, due in 2002, and it as well as the volume in which this essay appears will be essential for any WPA course. I feel sure that the number of indispensable books for the course will at least double by the time this volume is printed. The students simply could not keep up with the *Chronicle of Higher Education* (who can?), and they were overextended on the WPA listserv (though we urged them to lurk rather than participate), which they found fascinating. They managed to keep up with the WPA journal, but they, like all of us, felt guilty if they let slide the other crucial journals, such as *CCC, RR, JAC,* and *CE.* "How is it possible for *anyone* to keep up in this field?" one student asked me early in the term. Quite unintentionally, we had gotten one clear message through, I thought, as I said that we all did the best we could and that unremitting guilt was part of WPA baggage.

In light of all that was going on in the class, I began, about halfway through, to highlight the two or three articles or chapters for detailed discussion for the next meeting, to be sure that at least that material would be fresh for class. In addition, I appointed student discussion leaders for specific essays, an exercise that turned out to offer valuable teaching experience and a spur to creativity. Finally, I asked for short response papers to the reading from half the class every other week. I wasn't sure how that would work, but it proved to be successful. One student wrote me that those papers "helped focus our discussions because we could say more about the reading in our papers than time allowed for in discussion. We interacted with the text, articulated responses, and knew our ideas would be heard even if we didn't have time to discuss them.... I appreciated that push."

Those who will be teaching a WPA course in the future will need to decide what to leave out, I hope more effectively than we did. Because the UA program offers a course in writing assessment, we did not attempt to deal with it here; for the same reason, we omitted research issues, historical and rhetorical concerns, and most practical pedagogy. On the other hand, we found ourselves spending substantial time on political concerns, in part because of the excellent essays on the subject in the Bullock and Trimbur book and in part because of the problems airing on the WPA listserv. (This was the term that a WPA in the South started receiving death threats because she finally went public about the routine plagiarism available to the athletes at her institution.) Because coverage of the field is impossible, it would be wise to decide on a focus for a particular syllabus, with full awareness that important, nay essential, matters must be passed by.

The Visitors.   At UA, we are fortunate to have a small but highly qualified faculty in rhetoric and composition, almost all of whom have been WPAs of one sort or another. A highlight of the course was their appearance in class to talk with the students about their experiences. We usually read an article written by the visitor in preparation for the class, but conversations were wide-ranging. These class visitors, along with the oral reports, were essential for maintaining the real-world nature of the course. At institutions with fewer WPAs available, nearby colleges will offer similar resources. One of the students, an experienced high school teacher, focused on the "WPA function" in the middle and high schools, which, he maintained, was split uncomfortably among teachers, principals, district officials, and statewide officers. Wherever there is a writing program, there is a WPA of some kind. We are not shy about sharing our experiences with students, generally warning them about the unexpected tribulations and (more rarely) joys of the function. Students need to see and talk to real people at work in our field.

STUDENT RESPONSES TO THE COURSE

The student evaluations of the course turned out to be extremely positive. As I was preparing this chapter, the term after the course was given, I requested a more discursive response from the students, particularly focusing on what they remembered as most valuable. Here are excerpts from two of them, hasty e-mails both, but capturing the sense of the course both Theresa and I felt as it was going on.

From Ken:

For me, I think several things worked well. First, I liked how you and Theresa shared stories of your experiences. It made the issues and problems we were discussing seem more "real" and concrete. The stories also helped me to recognize the intricacies and subtleties of being a WPA. They also helped to illustrate how highly charged politically WPA positions are and the finesse with which compromise must often be attained. Asking us to consider problems you had already solved was interesting too. It was partially like Monday morning quarterbacking and partially like solving a puzzle. And again, these exercises helped demonstrate how complex the solutions to administrative problems can be; they showed me, time and again, how many layers a seemingly simple problem or situation can have.... Asking us to sign on to the WPA listserv was also a valuable experience for me. Following the online discussions, I was able to glean lots of helpful information, and to get a sense of the difficulties WPAs were currently facing. I found it enlightening to catch glimpses of how differently writing programs operate and how varied their structures and problems are. It was surprising to me to see how many programs seem to be in formative stages and how many programs are dealing with issues I would have expected to have been resolved.

From Shawn:

I still have all my notes from your class and will save them forever so I can hopefully avoid some of the problems we discussed. I loved how you shared problems you encountered and how you resolved them. For example, I found your advice on handling grade grievances to be a potential lifesaver. As a quick reminder: you suggested we should know grade grievances are coming, so we should have a printed set of standards of what the course is trying to achieve.... I can imagine that dealing with an irate student for the first time as a WPA can be very rattling; your advice will be so helpful when I become a WPA.

I found it very valuable to lurk on the WPA-L listserv as a class and discuss interesting posts. It showed us that we have resources, other WPAs, to talk to about problems and successes. Since the people on the WPA list are very generous and supportive, I feel like I know where to go for help. As WPAs shared the scenarios they were dealing with, we could see the dimensions of WPA work and how others have dealt with problems.

Our class discussion with you, Theresa, and Tilly on "questions to ask the interview team for a WPA job" was also extremely valuable. I can imagine being so excited to be considered for a WPA job that I will commit to doing anything without realizing what I'm getting myself into, what resources I will have available to me, or how this decision can affect my future. You suggested we do a rhetorical analysis of the program. I specifically remember you suggesting that we listen carefully to how the department members talk about the program and that we talk to the teachers of the classes and secretaries, and that we find out how willing colleagues are to work with us, how supportive they are, and if they value composition. I appreciate you stressing that we shouldn't take a WPA job without tenure and that we should find out if the department head will be an advocate for us. We also discussed that part of a WPA's job is to educate people on composition so others at the institution can speak for it (who knew that was part of the job?).

The final exam was terrific. Remember how we each applied for a WPA job that we first described. Articulating my proposal and conditions was a terrific end to this course. Best of all, we all presented our responses to the final so we could hear, think about, and discuss other perspectives.

A PERSONAL CONCLUSION

Nobody learns as much from a course as those who teach it. Most important for me was the increased awareness I developed of the complexity of the WPA job. I've been a department chair and a statewide program coordinator for writing programs, but the extraordinary challenges of the WPA job go beyond anything else I have experienced. Some WPAs who have ascended the administrative ladder (and quite a few have) are fond of saying that all they needed to know as provosts (or the like) they learned as WPAs. I wish I had stressed this more in my 1989 book on the subject, which seemed comprehensive to me at the time. A new edition would have to be at least twice the size. The subject is much larger than I thought it was, and the limitations of a single course on it are rather more stringent than I took them to be at the start.

At the same time, as I suggested earlier, I became aware of how much more I should know about the subject. There is an entire literature on administration about which I know little and should know much more. Budgets, I know, are keys to power and I still balance my checkbook each month with considerable effort, alas. The WPA of the future will be dealing with distance education and computer technology for teaching and (the muse preserve us) grading student writing. I don't know nearly as much as I should to teach this course. Nobody really does, of course, but that doesn't make me more comfortable. But I still can't wait for the next time I get to teach it.

7

Moving Up
the Administrative Ladder

❖ • ❖

Susan H. McLeod
University of California, Santa Barbara

Some are born great, some achieve greatness, and some have greatness thrust upon
'em.

—Twelfth Night

If you are now a writing program administrator (WPA), chances are good
that sooner or later you will have an opportunity to move into another administrative position. You may have noticed that a growing number of former
WPAs are now serving as chairs of departments, directors of programs, deans
of colleges, provosts of campuses. This migration to other posts is not entirely
surprising—to be a successful WPA, you need good interpersonal, communication, and problem-solving skills, need to track the details as well as the big
picture, need to function as both manager and leader. Your WPA work is by
its nature interdisciplinary; as Roen et al. note, that fact facilitates a smooth
transition to other administrative positions that require greater investments
in interdisciplinarity. At some point someone may notice that you do your
work well and invite you to apply for another administrative position at your
own or another institution. Why would you want to consider such a move?
What sorts of jobs are available? How can you best prepare yourself if you are
considering moving into another position? This essay will suggest some answers to those questions and offer some advice to those who might want to try
their hand at other sorts of administration, in an effort to help interested

readers understand how they might prepare to achieve, if not greatness, at least success in a new administrative position.

WHY WOULD YOU WANT TO MOVE UP THE ADMINISTRATIVE LADDER?

In the university culture, administration is still regarded by many faculty members as a job it would be unseemly to appear to want—the image of the scholar, dragged reluctantly from the library and the classroom to do the dirty work of the university, is still the image of the ideal administrator for many of us in academe. WPAs are not immune from this view of administration, even when it involves their own jobs. As Richard Bullock points out in his review of two books on writing program administration, often WPAs have not sought their present positions but have had their jobs thrust upon them, being the only person in the department with the disciplinary expertise to run the writing program. Being an administrator was often not in a WPA's career plan (in spite of the fact that a glance at the advertised positions reveals that most of the jobs in composition and rhetoric involve at some point some form of administrative work). Further, WPAs often share their literature colleagues' animosity toward administration (673–74). One WPA friend, in discussing this essay with me, asked me only half in jest, "Why would you want to encourage people to go over to the Dark Side?" If you are an administrator who doesn't like to think of yourself as such, why should you consider another sort of administration, especially a position totally unconnected with your disciplinary grounding?

Before I go into the reasons why I think you should, let me be clear about the fact that I think university administration is an honorable profession. Most of the administrators I have worked for and with are very smart folks, trying their best to make the institution a better place with increasingly limited resources. Because they must think of the institution or the college or their department first, their priorities don't always line up with any single unit of the university (for example, the writing program), and as a result it is easy to critique administrators as not understanding our needs, as unfeeling number crunchers, or other (usually more colorful) descriptors that appear now and again on the WPA listserv. Of course, there are some university administrators who ought not to be in that position, who by virtue of the Peter Principle have reached their level of incompetence or who are more interested in their own careers than in the good of the institution. And of course, administration bashing is a time-honored faculty pastime, something like complaining about your in-laws; a little of it is harmless enough and perhaps to be expected, given the power differential between the critiqued and the critiquers. But if you really feel that *all* administrators are by virtue of their positions difficult, devious and unethical, then certainly you shouldn't considering being one. (If you really feel that way, my guess is that you will also have difficulty working with administrators effectively as a WPA.)

There may be many personal reasons a WPA might decide to move up into another sort of administration (needing a new challenge, seeing the chance to move to another institution, the obvious salary benefits). Those reasons are as different as those considering them. Here I would like to suggest just two reasons to consider university administration that apply to all WPAs:

1. It is good for the institution to have former WPAs in other administrative positions. As Robert Connors points out, work in composition studies reflects "an open and almost ingenuous desire *to do some good in the world* with our study and our teaching" (original emphasis, 237). This desire carries over into our work as WPAs. I don't think it is too broad a generalization to say that as a group, WPAs are student oriented, because they are grounded in a profession that is student oriented. I don't mean to suggest that other administrators are not interested in students, but the fact is that many of them have schedules that don't allow them to teach, and when they do deal with the student population, it's usually with the problem cases. It's easy to develop a jaundiced view of students if the only ones you see are the class disrupter, the binge drinker, or the student with a GPA of 0.00 who wants to be reinstated (and whose dad is a big donor to the football program). As WPAs, we are in a position to know about a wide range of students and can be advocates for making the institution (especially the larger, more bureaucratic institution) more attuned to student needs. We can also serve as advocates for another group on campus we know well—the temporary or non-tenure-track faculty. Although writing programs are not the only units to exploit this group, we are usually the biggest offender on campus. As a WPA you can complain and get on committees trying to improve conditions for temporary faculty, but your main power is rhetorical. If you are a chair or a dean, however, you will have the power of the purse, enabling you to do more to improve working conditions for these faculty.

I think it is also true to say that WPAs as a group are interested in promoting good teaching. For the past several decades, American universities and colleges have been emphasizing research over teaching (see Cuban). Although there have been many efforts to try to shift the focus back toward teaching, most notably the work of Ernest Boyer and the continuation of his efforts in the Boyer Commission Report, it is still true that the faculty reward system in many institutions privileges research over teaching. As an administrator who is higher up in the food chain of the university, you would be in a position to help encourage and reward good teaching as well as good scholarship. One former WPA I know funded a series of popular faculty development seminars to encourage good pedagogy;

another was instrumental in introducing a teaching portfolio as a part of the tenure and promotion process at her university.

2.   It is good for the discipline and for the profession of writing program administration to have former WPAs in other sorts of administration. It wasn't that long ago that the WPA position was simply rotated among the faculty in the English Department, or given to the most junior member as a sort of fraternity initiation activity or because no one else wanted to do it (Corbett). Now we have our own professional organization, our own scholarly journal, a powerful manifesto in the Portland Resolution, a useful guide for us and for other administrators in the WPA document "Evaluating the Intellectual Work of Writing Administration" (both available on the WPA Web site, http://www.cas.ilstu.edu/English/Hesse/aboutwpa.htm), and an increasing number of books (like this one) about what we do and how we do it. But there is always a cultural lag in academe, one we can help counter if we are in positions of more administrative clout. For example, there are institutions where not even English department faculty are aware of CCCC or NCTE, never mind the Council of Writing Program Administrators. You can be much more helpful to our fellow WPAs up for tenure in such departments if you are, say, chair of a department, because that sort of title on an outside letter of evaluation carries considerable weight with college personnel committees and upper administrators. As a chair, you are also in a position to be called upon to evaluate not only WPA colleagues at other institutions, but other English departments. There has been a trend in many financially strapped universities to replace tenured faculty as they retire with temporary/part-time faculty, primarily to teach lower-division classes, including large numbers of writing classes. I was called upon not long ago by such an institution to evaluate a program for a regular internal review. In my report, I made the case to the dean that there were systemic difficulties for writing instruction given the present structure, and argued for more tenure-track appointments in rhetoric and composition as well as more professional treatment of their adjunct writing faculty. We need more administrators doing more of this if we are to have writing instruction seen as we wish it to be seen—as an intellectual endeavor as worthy of respect as other disciplines in the institution.

WHAT SORTS OF JOBS ARE AVAILABLE?

The metaphor of the academic administrative ladder in the title of this essay is an old one, evoking similarities to nineteenth-century corporate management structure. The chair of a department is the front-line manager, the chairs of departments report to a middle manager (the dean), the deans report to a vice-executive of some sort (an academic vice president or provost), the vice presidents report to the chief executive officer (the president), and the president usually reports to a board (of regents or trustees). In large-university systems there is often another layer of administration systemwide, with a central office and a chief executive (chancellor) for all campuses. Those at the top made the decisions, to be implemented by those lower down on the ladder. Not only do those lower down convey decisions to those they manage, but they also are responsible for funneling information from below, through the proper channels, up to the top. It is still true that the usual progression up this ladder of authority is one step at a time, from increasingly responsible administrative slots (like chair and dean) to top executive positions such as vice president or president, vice chancellor or chancellor. The phrase "evidence of increasing levels of authority" is often used in job announcements to indicate that you have satisfactorily served at lower levels before you can climb to higher rungs.

But it is also true that like twenty-first-century corporate managerial structures, university hierarchies are beginning to flatten out (see Kanter), becoming less top-down and, like it or not, more market-driven and entrepreneurial. In the post-industrial university, many new administrative jobs are opening up—the ladder is becoming something that looks more like a web, with decision making not only top-down, but also lateral and bottom-up. Consider these titles, taken from the job ads in the *Chronicle of Higher Education:* Vice Provost for Distance Learning, Director of Interdisciplinary Programs, Dean of the Honors College, Director of General Education, Dean of Instruction, Director of International Education, Vice President for Continuing Education, Dean of Instruction, Director of Community Involvement and Academic Outreach, Vice Provost for Multi-Cultural Affairs, Director of the Freshman Year Experience Program, Dean of the College of Extended Studies, Director of the Center for Teaching and Learning, Director of Service Learning, Dean of the (Branch) Campus. Depending on your interests and background, any of these might be just as appropriate as an up-the-chain-of-command administrative position.[1] It is also true that in these entrepreneurial times, you can sometimes see a need and create your own administrative position. One faculty member of my acquaintance worked for many years on his university's general education committee, trying to achieve some sort of coherent core program for students. He wrote several successful grant proposals, helped build a model program, and created his own present position—Director of General Education. This position is now comparable to a Dean of Undergraduate Studies. Another col-

---

[1] I am assuming that readers of this essay will want to stay on the academic side of the house, in positions where they retain faculty appointments or have retreat rights into their home departments. But there are also administrative positions in other areas, the fastest growing of which is development. Again depending on your background, these too may be of interest to you. I should also point out that my own experience in administration has been entirely in four-year institutions; administrative structures are different at the community college level, so some of what I say here may not apply to two-year institutions. However, I think that the advice offered about preparation is generally applicable to all WPAs, whatever the nature of their institution.

league saw a need for a center for environmental studies, wrote successful grant proposals in concert with various state agencies, and is now director of the center he helped create. The center exists entirely on soft money; thanks to his rhetorical skills, his tireless networking around the state with various environmental groups, and his ability to ferret out what funding opportunities have the highest priority with various governmental agencies, he has been able to keep large grants and contracts coming in routinely. A third colleague got very interested in computer-assisted instruction and web design, and took a few computer classes to hone her skills so that she could be involved in her university's distance-learning initiative. She parlayed her skills into a newly created administrative position at another institution, Associate Dean for Technology and Distance Education.

WHAT SHOULD YOU DO TO PREPARE FOR ANOTHER ADMINISTRATIVE POSITION?

I posted a query on the WPA listserv as I was writing this essay, asking those who had moved into other administrative positions what one piece of advice they would give to a WPA who is contemplating a move like theirs. One of the most common themes in the responses was this: take stock of what you already know and the skills you have already developed. Elaine Maimon, now Provost (Chief Campus Officer) of Arizona State University West, told a gathering of WPAs that she often states that everything she knows about being Provost she learned as a WPA. Here are some of the required qualifications drawn from various administrative job ads: a record of teaching success and scholarly achievement; leadership and administrative experience; excellent organizational, interpersonal, and communication skills; a commitment to collegial governance, broad-based planning, and academic excellence; a capacity for motivating others; skillful management of resources and supervision of staff; ability to interact positively with university faculty and high-level administrators; experience in planning educational programs and curriculum development. It won't take long to develop a list of your present qualifications under many of these headings.

Then you can compare these with the qualifications described in various job announcements, and start researching the areas in which you need to learn more. One area is probably budget. Most WPAs are not in charge of their own budgets, but are subject to them. It's all too easy in such a situation to simply leave the numbers to someone else. Further, many of us in the humanities are not comfortable working with numbers—that's one of the reasons we chose the humanities rather than the sciences as a course of study. But in many administrative positions, you will be in charge of the money, or you will be writing grants that require both creating and administering budgets; you will not only need to be an effective steward, you will also need to justify your budget to others. You will need to understand where the money comes from in university budgets, how it gets allocated, which monies can be used for what purposes, and these days, how to raise money from corporations and private donors. One WPA I know got an MBA in order to prepare herself for administrative work. I don't think a second degree is necessary, but I do recommend that you familiarize yourself with university budgets and how they work. An excellent resource is Dropkin and LaTouche's *The Budget-Building Book for Non-Profits*. If your institution offers a continuing-education program or special breaks for faculty who want to take courses in other departments, consider auditing a finance or an accounting course.

Although you probably already know a good deal about university structure and operation by virtue of being a WPA, there is probably more to learn if you plan to make a move into another sort of administration. Start with your own institution. What does the organizational chart look like? What is the governance structure? What does the mission statement say (and when was it last revised)? What are the key elements of the strategic plan and how are they tied to budgeting? If you don't know complete answers to these questions, you need to start looking around and asking questions. One way to learn more about your own institution is to serve on key committees: e.g., advisory committees to the chair, dean, or provost, and the university or faculty senate committees that handle academic affairs, faculty affairs, and budget. You will broaden your vision of the academic community in which you work, and you will also establish a university-wide network of contacts.

You may also need to broaden your vision nationally, so that you are conversant with not only disciplinary issues but also issues that are being discussed in all areas of higher education. What's going on nationally with distance learning, for example, and why? How should issues of technology be integrated not only into writing instruction, but also into the entire fabric of university life? To learn about these issues and to track the national discussion, a valuable resource is the *Chronicle of Higher Education;* as a subscriber, you can receive the online version of this publication as well, which allows you to search its considerable database. Another valuable resource is *Change Magazine*, published by the American Association on Higher Education. This magazine publishes occasional summary articles on important issues in academe. For example, a recent issue included a piece on the history of efforts over the last two decades to reform teaching in higher education (Lazerson, Wagener, and Shumanis), and another on the fast-developing "parallel universe" of post-secondary IT credentials being offered outside of the usual higher education venues (Adelman). Further important resources are the publications of the Carnegie Foundation for the Advancement of Teaching (e.g., the books of Ernest Boyer and the Boyer Commission Report—see http://www.carnegiefoundation.org/). Even if you decide that you are not interested in university administration, reading some of these publications on a regular basis will help place your local situation as a WPA in a more national perspective, and help you understand the thinking of your dean a little better, because she is reading the same publications.

Search your library and talk to your reference librarian about other periodicals and books related both to general administrative issues and to specific administrative positions that might interest you.[2] Jossey-Bass has a series of books on higher and adult education; for example, a recent book in that series deals with the important issue of higher education and technology (Katz). Within that same series is a sub-series of paperbacks, New Directions in Higher Education. One particularly useful book in this series deals with administration as a profession (Fife and Goodchild); another deals with conflict management (Holton). The American Council on Education in cooperation with Macmillan also publishes a series on higher education, including books on administration; a useful overview is Plante's *Myths and Realities of Academic Administration*. If chair of the English Department looks like a possibility, a good general book is Gmelch and Miskin's *Chairing an Academic Department;* you should also read recent issues of the *ADE Bulletin* to listen in on the professional conversation among English department chairs.

Once you have decided that you want to make your move and have accepted a new position, it is wise to attend one of the workshops or seminars for new administrators. Two are particularly well respected, and require the endorsement of your institution (because the institution usually pays the cost of the seminar). The Bryn Mawr/HERS Summer Institute is a residential program for women sponsored jointly by Bryn Mawr College and Higher Education Resources Services (HERS), Mid-America. This seminar, which has been going for a quarter century, has as its purpose (stated on its Web site, http://www.upenn.edu/penntrex/Institute/home/html):

> ... to improve the status of women in the middle and executive levels of higher education administration, areas in which women traditionally have been under-represented.... The Summer Institute seeks to enrich the leadership of North American higher education by providing its participants with skills and information pertinent to the management and governance of colleges and universities; timely information and perspectives on teaching, research, and service; and a stimulating environment in which to identify and energize career goals.

The Institute focuses on management and leadership, professional development, the academic environment, and finance and budgeting. The Harvard Management Development Program (MDP), also residential, focuses on leadership, fostering innovation and change, planning, financial management, and professional renewal. According to its Web site (http://

---

[2]Here I would like to acknowledge the help of Alice Spitzer, a librarian at Washington State University, who has helped me find elusive references and who is unfailingly helpful and resourceful.

www.gse.harvard.edu/~ppe/programs/mdp/program.htm/), the MDP "is designed for deans, directors, and other administrators who are good at leading their units—and who want to get even better. MDP provides new and useful ideas about critical management issues for mid-level administrators in their first seven years of a responsible leadership position." There are also short but useful workshops for new chairs and deans offered by The American Council on Education (ACE—see http://www.acenet.edu/ for their schedule of workshops), and by the Council of Colleges of Arts and Sciences (CCAS—see http://www.ccas.net/ for the schedules).

Once you have taken the seminars or workshops for new administrators, there are continuing meetings designed to help keep you abreast of national trends and issues. CCAS, mentioned previously, has a yearly meeting for deans of arts and sciences that includes workshops that involve learning from case studies taken from situations at other institutions. The Association of Departments of English (ADE), connected to the Modern Language Association, runs summer seminars each year to discuss issues of importance to the profession and provide opportunities for chairs to get to know one another and talk shop. (If your department is not a member of this valuable organization, you should convince them to join, even if you are not in line to be department chair.) Sometimes schools with similar interests or with regional or other ties (the PAC-10 Deans, for example) organize more local meetings of deans and associate deans to discuss issues of mutual interest and concern. As is the case with our WPA conferences, these meetings are worth attending as much for the contacts you make with your fellow-administrators as for the actual content of the presentations and workshops.

It is also wise find a mentor—an administrator who can answer your questions and point you to useful resources. One time-honored way to be mentored is to serve as an apprentice—as an assistant department chair, associate dean, or vice provost. These are staff rather than line administrative positions, in that they are ones that usually do not involve control of the budget, have faculty reporting to them, or have the power to make independent decisions. But they are invaluable positions in which to learn. Because learning to be an administrator (like learning to be a teacher) is in large part experiential, you can learn much by watching an experienced administrator at work. A good chair, dean, or provost will give you important work to do (such as writing up cases for promotion and tenure), guide you through the process, and keep you from making too many mistakes. A mentor can help you think through other aspects of your preparation. For example, in most administrative career tracks on the academic side of the house, you will need to be a tenured full professor to climb up the career ladder. However, I know two extremely effective vice provosts who are still associate professors; they were spotted early on for their talents at their own institutions, and because they do not intend to leave those universities, their academic rank is less important than their administrative skills and their present title. Mentoring is something that most administrators take seriously, not only because such on-the-job training helps ensure a smooth-running office, it also helps ensure continuity if they themselves are planning to move up the administrative ladder. It is not unusual, for example, for a chair to groom his assistant chair to be his successor.

Likewise, if you are serious about leaving the profession of writing program administration for a different administrative position, you should start to groom your own successor. I sometimes see very capable people who would be superb administrators, but who feel obligated to stay where they are because of what might happen to the writing program if they were no longer running it. Argue for an assistant for your program, or if that fails, look around for someone who could fill in as Interim WPA while a search is conducted. Don't feel that you have to stay if you really want to try something new.

FINAL WORDS OF ADVICE

So far I have focused on the positive aspects of moving into another administrative position. But the epigraph to this essay, taken from the deluded Malvolio in *Twelfth Night*, is a reminder that if you want to achieve another (perhaps higher) position, you should be careful what you wish for. University administration is very hard work. Most administrative positions are twelve-month, allowing you less time for your own research (and for summer vacations). Your schedule is less flexible than that of a faculty member, and more full of (occasionally pointless) meetings. In many ways administrative work is a desk job, and it usually more, sometimes much more, than a forty-hour workweek. It is also crisis oriented and deadline driven; sometimes it is a struggle to remain pro-active in a situation that is more often re-active. You have varied constituencies, and you will find yourself in the middle of competing interests. You will probably also find yourself being asked to do more with less, as university budgets become increasingly tight. You will be expected to be calm and professional at all times, even while you are being loudly accused of nefarious dealing by the inevitable faculty gadfly.

If all that sounds familiar, it should. University administration is a lot like a WPA position writ large; as a WPA, you not only have many of the skills and talents for other kinds of administration, you also are used to the difficulties as well as the rewards of administration. You know already that administration is sometimes a thankless job, but you are in it because you think you can make a difference. You know how necessary and important administrative work is, and you have no doubt found satisfaction in some of the improvements you have made (or some of the disasters you have managed to avert). You can take some pride already in having made your small piece of the institution a better place in some way, and as a good problem solver, where others see difficulties you see—perhaps relish—a new challenge.

So what are you waiting for?

WORKS CITED

Adelman, Chifford. "A Parallel Universe: Certification in the Information Technology Guild." *Change Magazine* 32 (May/June 2000): 20–29.

Boyer, Ernest. *Scholarship Reconsidered*. Lawrenceville, NJ: Princeton UP, 1990.

Boyer Commission on Educating Undergraduates. *Reinventing Undergraduate Education: A Blueprint for America's Research Universities*. New York: State University of New York, Stony Brook for the Carnegie Foundation for the Advancement of Teaching, 1998.

Bullock, Richard. Rev. of *Kitchen Cooks, Plate Twirlers, and Troubadours: Writing Program Administrators Tell Their Stories* and *The Writing Program Administrator as Researcher: Inquiry in Action and Reflection*. *College Composition and Communication* 51 (June 2000): 672–76.

Connors, Robert J. "Rhetorical History as a Component of Composition Studies." Symposium, "What Are We Doing as a Research Community?" *Rhetoric Review* 7 (1989): 230–40.

Corbett, Edward P. J. "A History of Writing Program Administration." *Learning from the Histories of Rhetoric: Essays in Honor of Winifred Bryan Horner*. Ed. Theresa Enos. Carbondale: Southern Illinois UP, 1993. 60–71.

Cuban, Larry. *How Scholars Trumped Teachers: Change without Reform in the University Curriculum, Teaching, and Research, 1890–1999*. New York: Teachers College P, 1999.

Dropkin, Murray, and Bill LaTouche. *The Budget-Building Book for Non-Profits: A Step-by-Step Guide for Managers and Boards*. San Francisco: Jossey-Bass, 1998.

Fife, Jonathan D., and Lester F. Goodchild, eds. *Administration as a Profession*. New Directions for Higher Education 76. San Francisco: Jossey-Bass, 1991.

Gmelch, Walter H., and Val D. Miskin. *Chairing an Academic Department*. Thousand Oaks, CA: Sage, 1995.

Holton, Susan A., ed. *Conflict Management in Higher Education*. New Directions for Higher Education 92. San Francisco: Jossey-Bass, 1995.

Kanter, Rosabeth Moss. *Rosabeth Moss Kanter on the Frontiers of Management*. Boston, MA: Harvard Business School P, 1997.

Katz, Richard N. *Dancing with the Devil: Information Technology and the New Competition in Higher Education*. San Francisco: Jossey-Bass, 1999.

Lazerson, Marvin, Ursula Wagener, and Nichole Shumanis. "What Makes a Revolution? Teaching and Learning in Higher Education, 1980–2000." *Change Magazine* 32 (May/June 2000): 13–19.

Maimon, Elaine. Wrap-up Session, Conference of the Council of Writing Program Administrators. Tucson, AZ: July 19, 1998.

Plante, Patricia R. *Myths and Realities of Academic Administration*. New York : American Council on Education and Macmillan, 1990.

Roen, Duane, Barry M. Maid, Gregory R. Glau, John Rammage, and David Schwalm. "WPA Work Reconsidered and Assessed." *The Writing Program Administrator as Theorist.* Eds. Shirley K. Rose and Irwin Weiser. Portsmouth, NH: Boynton/Cook Hienemann, forthcoming.

8

Writing Program Administration as Preparation for an Administrative Career

David E. Schwalm
Arizona State University East

We had a brief but interesting conversation on the WPA listserv discussion one day about the sense many of us shared that we were total frauds, always a hair's breadth away from being discovered and exposed as the snot-nosed twelve-year-olds we know we really are. One colleague recalled looking in the mirror each morning and saying, "Today's the day they're going to find out," then hurrying off to do what she could to keep the illusion alive for yet another day.

A high level administrator at my university told me that our president is as good as he is because he *really* believes that he is president of the university. But he is *very* unusual, in that he has been a university president somewhere for almost twenty-five years and a university administrator for virtually his entire career.

I'm pretty certain about him, but I'm not so sure about me. For the last 9 years, I have been a vice provost, and I'm trying to figure out why. Certainly, no one starts out in life aspiring to be a vice provost. Most people finish life without even knowing what one is. It's one of those jobs you don't know much about until you've got it. It follows, then, that you have no idea of why you are qualified to have it. Academic affairs administrators usually have been faculty first, and the usual route into administration is through being department chair or occasionally through activity in the faculty senate. My particular route was through being a writing program administrator (WPA). In this chapter, I want to explain why being a WPA is an excellent place to start a career in academic affairs administration—should you choose to do that sort of thing.

First I want to indulge in a bit of personal history that shows how I crept up on administration as a career, as I moved through faculty jobs at four different universities.

For a good part of my career, I was just your regular faculty member, teaching my courses, doing my scholarship, picking up my share of undergraduate advising, and trying to spend some time with my family. I generally knew who the department chair was, but I had no idea where my department was located in the institutional organization, who was dean, who was provost (much less *vice* provost) or who was president of the campus. My first administrative foray started with committee work. I was on the composition committee and became course director of a multi-section advanced comp course. I also got involved in curriculum design as we developed a series of intermediate writing courses that were a bit more clearly defined than "advanced composition." I moved on to direct a master's program in professional writing and rhetoric, a job that included TA (teaching assistant) training. At the same time, I started and directed a National Writing Project site, and I eventually became a WPA. I was then expressly hired to be WPA of the large program at ASU Main in Tempe. I directed that program for 6 years, when I was nominated and subsequently selected for the position of Vice Provost for Academic Programs at ASU West, a comparatively new ASU campus of five thousand students (about the same number as in the comp program) in northwest Phoenix. I served there for four very interesting years, working part-time on ASU *East* planning during the last year at ASU West. I then moved full-time to ASU East as Vice Provost in charge of academic affairs and academic planning for the new campus and was also appointed as founding Dean of East College when that college was created in February of 1997.

Before the ASU West job came along, I had not really thought much beyond being a WPA. Taking on the job as vice provost at ASU West required me to think about what I had done in my career to qualify me for a job in central administration. How people qualify to be central administrators is a puzzle, maybe a paradox. Almost no one is trained for it in the way one becomes a lawyer or doctor. It is not usually a career path one sets out on at the beginning of one's career—at least not in academic affairs administration. In fact, I, like most of us, was trained to be a *faculty member*, the very *antithesis* of an administrator. Becoming an administrator has its attractions, but it requires you to *change:* It requires a commitment to a way of doing and being that is different from what we have been trained for and experienced in and may be orthogonal to some basic faculty values. Thus, I want to talk first about how the typical WPA position helps one to recognize how generally ill-suited faculty are to be administrators. Then I want to discuss how the WPA position, because of its complex nature, can lead to administrative habits that are extraordinarily valuable for central administrators in the contemporary university and can contribute to a positive change in administrative culture.

I'll note, but leave aside, the fact that being a WPA requires you to have an enormous capacity for work without much help and to develop the ability to juggle multiple tasks and roles. Let's start with the important fact that the WPA is usually viewed as a *quasi-administrator*. Although the dean may hold faculty rank and teach an occasional course, there is no question that the dean is an administrator. It's clear on payday if at no other time. The WPA, however, is often viewed by faculty as an administrator and by administrators as a faculty member. WPAs are paid like faculty members, to be sure. As a vice provost and dean, I view myself unequivocally as an administrator, even though I have faculty rank. But, as WPA, I saw myself as both a faculty member and an administrator. I was whining about this to my chair once, and he said, "Get over it. You're management." My ambivalence endured, nonetheless, creating a rather interesting internal conflict that was educational but hard to resolve.

I'm going to offer some sweeping generalizations here in order to make my point. Faculty and administrators are, in many ways, *culturally* antithetical. As a rule, faculty members are not generally *team players*. In fact, they cringe at the term. They are independent thinkers who have consistently been rewarded for intellectual independence, unconventional approaches, intellectual troublemaking. They are generally interested in keeping discussions open rather than bringing them to a close (why else do faculty senate meetings with no agenda last so long?). Their strength lies in analysis and critique, in identifying and complicating problems rather than developing solutions. They tend to be more loyal to the discipline than to the institution—more loyal to the "university of physics" than to ASU, and they are *adamant defenders of academic quality*—especially in their own disciplines and sometimes in self-serving ways. Faculty generally have no interest in "adopting a broader institutional perspective" and they have neither incentives nor opportunities to do so. Increasingly at large institutions, they are unaware both of general graduation requirements and of institutional policies and procedures. They have no idea, for example, of how students register for classes or get financial aid. Faculty, quite properly, are interested in their own work, in their classes, in what goes on in their own disciplines and departments. Who else has these concerns?

Administrators must, of necessity, take an institutional perspective (more or less broad depending on where they are in the hierarchy), reconciling competing interests and demands in ways that are certain to be unsatisfactory to many or most involved. And though administrators are interested in clearly

defined problems, they are also charged with finding solutions—the most satisfactory available—and moving on to the next problem. The fundamental
differences, then, are these: faculty tend to be critical, analytical,
open-ended, focused, self-centered, and uncompromising: administrators
tend to be synthetic, goal oriented, comprehensive in their views, open to
compromise—often confused with being wishy-washy, valueless, and arbitrary. To summarize, see Table 8.1.

As a quasi-administrator, the WPA tries to be both faculty and administrator at once, and it is a very difficult position to be in. It was the faculty member
in me who designed our procedures for evaluating the composition courses of
transfer students. I wanted to be sure that *every* transfer student had composition courses similar to ours. I feared that credentials evaluators across the
campus were not as concerned about the integrity of the composition curriculum as I was, that they would simply take any "English" course as a composition course if the student tried to claim it. As WPA, I set up the kind of
evaluation procedure only a faculty member would create. That is, the key
value of the procedure was "zero tolerance": The composition courses of *every
single transfer student* should undergo very close evaluation. (Keep in mind
that ASU has five thousand freshmen and ten thousand seniors.) All transfer
students had to file a special petition through our office with transcripts and
course descriptions attached, and nearly all of the time of my only assistant
was spent evaluating these equivalency petitions. It did not even occur to me
to measure the impact of this procedure. How many of the courses reviewed
were denied? Did we issue enough denials to justify using scarce resources to
review the petitions, to justify the efforts we required of transfer students to
do a special petition? It was unthinkable to ask how much the specific content
of the students' transferred composition courses affected the likelihood of
their academic success at ASU. I set up a procedure that was designed simply
to enforce close equivalency for every single student without any regard to resources, to efficiency, or to the long range importance of the enterprise. Only

TABLE 8.1

Comparison of Key Traits of Faculty and Administrators

Faculty	Administrators
Critical/analytical	Synthetic
Open-ended/problematizing	Goal oriented
Focused/self-centered	Broader views/institutional perspective
Uncompromising	Open to compromise
Selfish, narrow-minded, rigid	Wishy-washy, valueless, arbitrary

as I became more experienced as an administrator did I begin to view these matters in a larger context, to compromise with my faculty sense of justice and purity—but never without feelings of guilt and reluctance. I just *knew* someone was getting away with a literature course somewhere. Was I selling out, or making reasonable compromises with reality? As a quasi-administrator, the WPA is constantly in this bind. If the WPA can manage to work out this internal cultural dialogue, to preserve important faculty values without becoming immobilized, it is a valuable asset for future work; and it is the first introduction to one of the fundamental changes one most undergo in the faculty-to-administrator metamorphosis—fundamentally a loss of innocence.

A second critical shift in the move from faculty member to administrator is the move from managing time or projects to managing people. A great portion of the WPA's time is spent trying to organize a diverse and often recalcitrant group of instructors around the writing program and its values while addressing their wants and needs and professional development. Another big chunk of time is spent working with students, usually trying to resolve complaints about the program, about instructors, about the general unfairness of life. And, as middle managers or quasi middle managers, WPAs are also *being managed* while they try to manage. They have to learn how to manage and to be managed.

Faculty, in our fields especially, are "independent contractors," not managers or managees. Way too many of the faculty I know, as interesting as they are, either lack or do not display the basic social skills that are necessary for the complex social interactions of academic management. I've got this "nerd hypothesis" of administrative failure. A nerd, whatever virtues or vices he or she may have, is someone who is uncomfortable at a cocktail party with strangers. There are some nerds who are content to be heads-down computer programmers, work in offices by themselves, grow rich, and raise socially adjusted children with perfect teeth. Others who are more resentful pursue the revenge of the nerds by becoming teachers or ministers—specifically because those positions carry with them power over others which the nerd could not win by dint of his or her own personality and social skills. That's bad enough, but Woe unto us all when one of these becomes an academic administrator! Never having had authority and thus not knowing how to use it, they tend to view authority as a weapon for revenge rather than the administrative strategy of last resort. All too many administrative catastrophes can be traced to nerds with authority. Fortunately, most faculty clean up pretty well in fact and have developed moodiness, quirky behavior, and odd manner of dress only by virtue of the company they have been keeping and the lack of regular occasion for polite behavior that does not include cultural one-upsmanship. The fact is that the longer one engages in administration the more one finds it useful to abandon the tonsorial and sartorial norms of faculty colleagues, the personal quirkiness that is endearing in faculty and irritating in deans, and anything that even vaguely resembles a quick temper. You have to compose your *self* with your audience in mind, as opposed to the in-your-face ethos so popular in faculty culture. I have, myself, managed to abandon the style of outlaw biker and have progressed to the Safeway manager look. To summarize, see Table 8.2.

These basic cultural and behavioral moves are essential: you have to give up all your values and adopt the manners of a dancing master. More precisely, you must be willing to recognize and accept the culture of administration and to adopt or revive the social behavior necessary for effective management. If you can or want to do these things, then the *particular* skills you must develop to be successful as a WPA will provide you with remarkable preparation for a career in central administration that can affect the way things get done on your campus.

I mentioned the problem of nerds with authority. Perhaps *the* defining characteristic of the WPA position is "responsibility *without* authority." WPAs usually have responsibility for lots of classes, lots of student, lots of instructors, multiple endeavors (multi-level writing program, writing center, and writing across the curriculum), and all of the complaints generated by this "empire." At the same time, WPAs often do not have control of hiring and firing and of the budget; they do not have direct access to deans; they report to the chair; they have no more control over departmental policy than any other faculty member; they have no official place in the hierarchy; they are quasi-administrators. The litany is familiar. Responsibility without authority. But responsibility without authority—the need to get things done without the wherewithal—can lead to very useful habits of administration. I'm going to discuss five of them:

1. Knowledge Is Power I: There is certain special knowledge that WPAs tend to bring to central administrative positions by virtue of their experience as faculty members and administrators in the field of rhetoric and composition. Composition has been one of the first disciplines to become "learner centered," to develop teaching strategies by looking seriously at how students learn. As WPA, I had responsibilities for training new teachers, and thus I had to learn about teaching and learning writing in particular, about teaching and learning in general. I also had to study

TABLE 8.2

Cultural Norms and Sartorial Outcomes

Faculty	Administrators
Independent contractors	Managers/managees
Blue jeans	Blue blazers

testing and assessment—for placement and for competency. In the process, I had to learn about testing in general, to conduct various kinds of tests, to know about the strengths and weaknesses of various assessment strategies and commercially available instruments, to identify some strategies for evaluating testing strategies that came my way. As director of a program that served thousands of first-year students, it was necessary for me to become familiar with student development literature as a reminder that students have other things on their minds than our courses. This is the stuff that student affairs people read and faculty don't but should. It is an extremely important body of literature that is giving shape to the changes in the way universities are doing things. I have found my ability to talk knowledgeably about learning, assessment, student development, and similar matters to be very rare and thus rather formidable in various administrative forums where other academic administrators from other backgrounds know very little of such things.

2.   Knowledge Is Power II: First-year composition (FYC) is unique in that it is often the only course at many campuses that is required of all students regardless of college or major. The requirement also touches on placement, transfer equivalency, freshman orientation, admissions, records, discipline, counseling, financial aid, graduation requirements, and so on. The "connectedness" of the comp program to virtually all other academic and non-academic units requires the WPA to become knowledgeable about the structure and organization of the institution and to get well beyond his or her own department. In fact, the WPA generally needs a more thoroughgoing knowledge of the campus than the chair does, than *most* other people in the university do. The WPA also needs a broader awareness of university policies, graduation requirements, and many of the subtleties contained in the front pages of the catalog. This broader knowledge of the campus is often enhanced because the WPA is the official campus "writing person" who is called upon whenever the issue of writing comes up on campus anywhere (after the creative writers say, "not us"). This was a critical connection for me when WAC presentations allowed an English department faculty member to look sensible to engineers, and when general studies writing requirements got me on the General Studies Council, which I eventually chaired for about 3 years. My knowledge of various university requirements got me on standards committees, curriculum committees, reengineering groups, and so on. Also, because FYC is the one course articulated with all community colleges, I was immediately immersed in statewide community college articulation matters, statewide general education transfer designs, and all matters of coordination with the community colleges. Not only was I able to have an impact on articulation agreements, but I also know more about university/community college articulation than anyone in Arizona and have a more informed and

thus more positive attitude toward community colleges than most people in the university. I learned how to use the university information systems and how to do certain kinds of institutional analysis on my own. Because I was a WPA, I know my own institution extremely well, and, were I to change institutions, I know what I would have to find out about another institution and whom I would have to get to know.

3.   You Gotta Have Friends: In addition to knowledge, there is another really interesting advantage to the WPA's need to be familiar with the system in which the program is embedded and to be in contact with a broad range of academic and nonacademic units campuswide. *If you don't have power, the next best thing is friends in key places.* When you're a lowly WPA, you don't run with the deans. Instead, you discover a "parallel university" made up of the people who really run the place—the associate deans, assistant registrars, admissions recruiters, advisers, office business managers, and so on. If you really want to get something done, never under estimate the value of one well-disposed assistant registrar. And as WPA, you can make a lot of friends among these master sergeants simply by being friendly and appreciative of how much you have in common (my friends in the registrar's office and admissions office are used to being ignored or treated badly by faculty). You will also meet some very bright, professional, and interesting people. You soon come to appreciate how to get things done in the institution, and you build your network. And this is a network that has subsequently very helpful to me as a central administrator, and I work very hard to maintain it now.

4.   Persuasion: I have found, now that I have a little authority, that it's best to wear it lightly, not to use it just because I have it. As a WPA with responsibility and no authority, I had to learn to get things done without authority. I had to make my case. I had to persuade people—rather than bully them—and I had to lay the groundwork for my proposals ahead of time so that when I brought them forward there was a reasonably receptive audience whose concerns were already addressed because I found out what they were beforehand. Proposals just *slipped* through the system with hardly a sound and with only the slightest friction of opposition. The proposals themselves were much more clearly thought out, better supported with data, more carefully adapted to the situation, more responsive to the needs of all involved. No one was unnecessarily alarmed by a *raw or rash* proposal, the kind of alarm that tends to generate opposition that continues after the real cause is removed. I have found no advantage in abandoning this strategy—which produces better policy and a lot less conflict. (Often, it is a good idea to let others take ownership of your proposals and bring them forward as their own. Ronald Reagan once said that it is amazing how much you can get done if you don't want to take credit. You have

to learn to appreciate the private satisfaction of success.) There is another advantage. Many administrators find that they have to abandon their academic specialties after a few years in full-time administration. *We don't.* We shift the balance from rhetorical theory to rhetorical practice and move into a new scene. Administration is what rhetoric is all about.

5.   You Gotta Have Heart: I have said in the past that a WPA should have a thick skin and a long memory. This could be taken a couple of ways, one more ominous than the other. However, as a WPA, I developed a great deal of fellow feeling for and appreciation of *other* disenfranchised or marginalized members of the academic community. They include the network of professional and classified staff, the master sergeants without whom the university could not run. They include adjunct faculty and non-tenure-track faculty, who carry a lot of weight, do great work, are poorly rewarded, and are generally neglected by the full-time faculty. They include those who are negatively referred to in research universities as "stalled" associate professors, many of whom are stalled because they have decided to put their energies into teaching, and they have often been the staunchest proponents and practitioners of writing across the curriculum. The "marginalized" include graduate students, whose graduate experience tends to be shaped more by the interests of the faculty than by what they really need to succeed in academic careers. The programs that we started with at ASU East—Agribusiness and Engineering Technology—were the marginalized stepchildren of the College of Engineering at ASU Main and have a great deal in common with composition programs. Having been a WPA helps me to understand some of the difficulties these programs have had, the bitterness that most of the faculty are trying now to overcome. And I hope it will help me try to develop a campus that is more inclusive than exclusive and that values the contributions of all members of the campus community.

So, where are we? I have argued that being a WPA taught me about the need to see issues in a larger context, to take broader views, to accept less than 100% solutions, to recognize that although there is a season for deliberation, there is also a season for decisiveness. It has also taught me that the ballroom dancing classes my mother made me attend in junior high were really useful after all and that certain latter day thuggish affectations in dress and manner did not play to standing ovations in all theaters. And, because I had responsibility without situational or statutory authority, I had to find ways to get things done, not through the exercise of raw power of position but through:

- The Power of Knowledge—about education and institutions.
- The Power of Friendships—the elusive strength of networks.

- The Power of Persuasion—in a truly classical sense.
- The Power of Empathy—the power you gain from valuing the work of others.

Let's go back to the thick skin and long memory. WPAs put up with an enormous amount of abuse and insensitivity in the course of their work. Thus there is more than a little temptation—if one moves into central administration (i.e. "real" administration)—to use the opportunity to settle old scores with individuals or with the institution. That's one understanding of having a long memory and one that is delicious to contemplate on some days. But instead, let the content of our long memory be these humane and collaborative sources of authority that helped us to be effective WPAs, that are highly appropriate in academic institutions, and that need to be championed in administrative arenas.

A final anecdote that I think is relevant. Early in my tenure as a dean at ASU East, I got a request from an unhappy student for a full tuition refund long after the refund deadline had passed. I agreed that the student had a good case, so I got on the phone to the master sergeants' network to find out how to do this. One of my friends in the registrar's office explained to me a complex process of back dating withdrawal forms and so on. So I ask, "Who has to approve this?" She says, "*You* have the authority to do this." I think she enjoyed telling me that, and I was glad I hadn't known it. After all, no snot-nosed kid can issue a tuition refund.

Although the comments herein have been drawn from my personal experiences over the last fifteen years, there is, of course, a large body of literature devoted to writing program administration. The following are key articles that discuss the administrative strategies that derive from the common quasi-administrative status of WPAs and could be beneficial to the institution at large if carried forward into central administration. For further reading:

Amorose, Thomas. "WPA Work at the Small College or University: Re-Imaging Power and Making the Small School Visible." *WPA. Writing Program Administration* 23.3 (2000): 85–103.

Dickson, Marcia. "Directing without Power: Adventures in Constructing a Model of Feminist Writing Program Administration." *Writing Ourselves into the Story: Unheard Voices from Composition Studies*. Ed Sheryl I. Fontaine and Susan Hunter. Carbondale, IL: Southern Illinois University Press, 1995, 140–53.

Gunner, Jeanne. "Decentering the WPA." *WPA: Writing Program Administration* 18.3 (Fall/Winter 1994): 8–15.

Hult, Christine. "The Scholarship of Administration." *Resituating Writing: Constructing and Administering Writing Programs*. Ed. Joseph Janangelo and Kristine Hansen. Portsmouth, NH: Heinemann/Boynton-Cook, 1995, 119–31.

White, Edward M. "Use It or Lose It: Power and the WPA." *WPA: Writing Program Administration* 15.1–2 (1991): 3–12.

9

Legal Considerations for Writing Program Administrators

Veronica Pantoja
Nancy Tribbensee
Duane Roen
Arizona State University

In this chapter we offer guidance to assist writing program administrators (WPAs) in identifying legal issues. Julia K. Ferganchick's "Contrapower Harassment" (chap. 22) in this collection provides a unique approach from which to consider the more specific issue of teacher harassment in the writing classroom and also includes additional practical guidance. However, we have used our own experiences and reports published in the *Chronicle of Higher Education* to identify some of the more common legal issues facing administrators in colleges and universities. The issues presented here cover a wide area of administrative duties dealing with personnel and student concerns. These concerns include contracts, sexual harassment, copyright laws, disclosures by students, syllabi, disruptive behavior, student records, plagiarism, hiring practices and personnel evaluations, letters of recommendation, and disability resources.

LINES OF RESPONSIBILITY/LIABILITY

As you ponder the legal issues that we address in this chapter, note that most of them apply to you directly as you perform your duties as WPA. Know, however, you may be held responsible for the actions of others—students, office staff, and teaching staff—who work and study under your supervision. Given your position in the line of responsibility, you may be well served to make certain that staff and students understand their legal rights and responsibilities.

Moreover, faculty and staff should be mindful of procedures to follow and the resources available to them in the event of a lawsuit. The risk management officer or legal counsel for your college or university can tell you whether or not you are covered by the institution's liability insurance. If that coverage is not available to you or is insufficient, you may consider purchasing professional liability insurance. For those of us in English studies, one clearinghouse for this insurance is the National Council of Teachers of English, which currently offers protection up to $2,000,000 per claim for a variety of exposures, including "hiring unqualified persons" and "failure to educate."

Another form of protection is preventative; all who work in higher education must stay informed of major legal developments. The *Chronicle of Higher Education* and the sources listed in this article provide useful information.

Resources

Jones, Larry G. "Institutional Research and Preventative Law: A Partnership." *Preventing Lawsuits: The Role of Institutional Research*. San Francisco: Jossey-Bass, 1997. 71–88.

In addition to providing some practical tools to avoid problematic legal issues, Jones includes an extensive listing of additional sources for college and university administrators.

McKee, Patrick. "Dealing with the Complexities of Higher Education and Law: An Attorney's Perspective." *Preventing Lawsuits: The Role of Institutional Research*. Ed. Larry G. Jones. San Francisco: Jossey-Bass, 1997. 61–69.

Using three hypothetical cases to highlight the complexity of law and education, McKee gives three "simple" principles when dealing with legal intricacies: Stay informed of major legal developments, consult your attorney, and do what is right and prepared to be sued.

The National Council of Teachers of English
1111 W. Kenyon Road
Urbana, IL 61801-1096

Phone: (800) 369-6283; Fax: (217) 328-9645
E-mail: public_info@ncte.org
http://www.ncte.org

Contracts

Before signing any contract or sending any correspondence (including e-mail) that offers or accepts goods or services on behalf of the institution, you must understand the scope of your authority to commit the institution. You should review applicable policies and consult your institution's contract administration office, purchasing office, or legal counsel for clarification of your role. You may discover that as a program-level administrator, you do not have the authority to sign contracts that obligate the institution. If you enter an agreement without the proper authority, you risk being held personally liable for the terms of the contract.

The purchasing officer or contract administrator can assist with contracts for goods or services, such as workshop materials, books, software, guest lectures, and publishing and distribution arrangements. A contract that may appear to be straightforward and innocuous may legally commit you and your institution to obligations that exceed what you understand them to be. For example, you may assume that signing a contract with a custom publisher obligates you to that publisher until you decide you no longer need its services. However, if the contract contains exclusivity language or does not include an end date, you may be legally bound to continue to use this publisher or forced to pay damages. Contract terms that are valid in one state may be inappropriate or illegal in another. Public institutions may have legal constraints not applicable to other parties. Additionally, the contract may not comply with applicable procurement regulations or may conflict with the terms of another institutional contract.

SEXUAL HARASSMENT

Sexual harassment involves unwelcome contact of a sexual nature. Federal law defines two kinds of sexual harassment: (a) quid pro quo and (b) hostile working environment. Both forms of harassment are illegal in the workplace. Quid pro quo sexual harassment conditions an employment decision on the acceptance or rejection of an offer of a sexual nature. This is often what comes to mind when people think of sexual harassment. A hostile working environment, on the other hand, does not require that the employer or the person creating the environment have any malicious intent. The law requires only that the plaintiff show that the conduct has the purpose *or effect* of unreasonably interfering with work performance. The conduct may violate the law even if the person accused of harassment does not intend any harm and the victim does not suffer any economic loss or detrimental job decision.

You should become familiar with your institution's sexual harassment policies by reading them, by attending workshops, and by consulting the institution's general counsel or affirmative action officer. The next step is to make certain that all students and staff are aware of the policies, including the procedures for addressing violations.

As a WPA, you may become aware of or receive reports of harassment by employees, by students, or by an outside consultant or vendor against an employee or student. Your institution may designate different offices to investigate these reports. Harassment can occur in a variety of contexts, including classroom or learning activities, the workplace, over the phone, or electronically by e-mail or on a Web site. As WPA, you are not charged with evaluating whether or not an allegation constitutes illegal harassment. You are responsible for promptly forwarding any report you receive to the appropriate office. Failure to take appropriate supervisory action in suspected cases may create additional liability for you and the institution.

Immediately upon receipt or notice of a complaint, contact the office at your institution responsible for investigating that complaint; do not undertake any investigation or other action without the advice of that office. Institutions need to know when someone is engaging in a pattern of harassing behavior because both the severity and duration are important criteria for appropriately addressing the harassment. The office designated to respond for the institution needs prompt notice to advise the person making the report of the limited timelines for filing a complaint with an outside agency.

If someone reports possible sexual harassment to you but asks that you keep the report confidential, explain that you need to discuss the matter with the individual designated by the institution to receive the report. That official will determine to what extent a request for confidentiality can be honored while developing an appropriate institutional response.

Resources

20 United States Code §§ 1681–83 (1980). <http://www4.law.cornell.edu/uscode/20/1681.html>.

42 United States Code § 2000e (1980). <http://www4.law.cornell.edu/uscode/42/2000e.html>.

Kaplan, Bill, and Gary Pavela. "Rick's Revenge: A Case Study on Cyberspace Speech and Peer Harassment at State University." *College Administration Publications, Inc. Homepage.* <http://www.collegepubs.com/ref/SfxCseStdyRicksRevenge.shtml>.

A case study of online harassment by a student using university resources and how administrators can resolve such a situation. The case study cites recent legal guidelines and cases.

National Education Association. "Stop Student Sexual Harassment Now." *National Education Association Homepage.* 21 August 2000. <http://www.nea.org/bt/6-association/harass.pdf>.

This publication from the National Education Association includes a FAQ about sexual harassment on school campuses as well as an explanation of Title IX.

US Department of Education Office for Civil Rights and National Association for the Attorneys General. *Protecting Students from Harassment and Hate Crimes: A Guide for Schools. US Department of Education Homepage.* January 1999. <Http://www.ed.gov/pubs/Harassment/>.

Available both online and in portable document format, this guide provides school administrators information to create policies to help protect students from all forms of harassment.

US Department of Education Office for Civil Rights. "Revised Sexual Harassment Guidance: Harassment of Students by School Employees, Other Students, or Third Parties." *US Department of Education Office of Civil Rights Homepage.* 16 January 2001. <http://www.ed.gov/offices/OCR/shguide/index.html>.

This link provides information for educational institutions to investigate and resolve claims of sexual harassment of students. (See also "Resources for Addressing Sexual Harassment" and "Products and Publications" at http://www.ed.gov/offices/OCR/sexharassresources.html for more information.)

COPYRIGHT

Copyright law allows the author of a copyrightable work to control the reproduction of the work. It also gives the author the right to control the production of derivative works (for example, translating the work into another language or changing it to an electronic format) and the public performance or display of the work (such as showing a video or using a work on a Web site). Damages for copyright infringement can be extensive. Courts can award substantial statutory damages even for "innocent" infringement and each separate act of willful infringement may result in an award of up to $100,000. Before your faculty or staff uses copyrighted works in the classroom, in publications, in multimedia presentations or on a Web site, we urge you as WPA to seek copyright guidance from your institution's office of general counsel or copyright administrator to inform your staff.

Even with firewalls, constructing course web pages makes course materials readily available to a wider range of people, including those who may own the copyright on some materials that will be placed on a Web site. To guard against possible infringement, you might suggest the following to faculty and staff: (a) using passwords or other security to allow access only by students currently enrolled in the class and (b) obtaining permission before using any copyrighted video, music, graphic, or text material.

Given the growing market for online courses, faculty are often intimately involved in the development of these courses for their institutions. Before getting started, you should review with your teaching staff your institutional policies regarding intellectual property, distance/distributed learning, and outside consulting. If you are not sure whether the policy covers what you intend to do or if you want to vary from the policy, work with the department chair and legal counsel to negotiate and document any mutually acceptable variation.

Student works are protected under copyright law to the extent they are original works. Before making a student's work available to others, faculty and staff need to get the student's voluntary written consent. The consent form must be in writing, but it need not be elaborate. It should clearly describe the work (by title and date), identify any coauthors, indicate how the work is to be used and for how long. For example, an instructor may request the right to use the work in any media, in perpetuity, for noncommercial educational use. The consent form may also indicate that the student's identity will not be disclosed except as required by law if the student wants such protection. If faculty or staff enlists the assistance of students in developing a web page or publication, they will need a written agreement with each student getting permission to use the work, describing each party's ownership interest in the completed work and the relevant components, and perhaps assigning ownership of the work to the institution.

Many academics incorrectly assume that if they are using a copyrighted work for an educational purpose, they fall within the "fair use" exception and do not need to seek permission. Educational and nonprofit uses can be infringing uses. For an excellent discussion of the fair-use doctrine and other copyright issues, we recommend the Copyright Crash Course on the University of Texas Web site (address in next subsection).

Resources

Copyright Crash Course.
        http://www.utsystem.edu/ogc/intellectualproperty/cprtindx.htm
        Copyright Clearance Center

222 Rosewood Drive
Danvers, MA 01923
Phone: (978) 750-8400
Fax: (978) 750-4470
E-mail: info@copyright.com
http://www.copyright.com/

An easy way to get permission to use copyrighted materials to facilitate compliance with US copyright law. The company currently manages rights relating to over 1.75 million works and represents more than 9,600 publishers.

United States Copyright Office
Library of Congress
101 Independence Ave. SE
Washington, DC 20559-6000
E-mail: copyinfo@loc.gov
http://lcweb.loc.gov/copyright/

Site that's updated daily with news and information about copyright and copyright legislation.

DISCLOSURES BY STUDENTS

If a teacher discovers—through class discussion or through a student's writing, for example—that a student has perpetrated or has knowledge of an unadjudicated crime, the teacher may be legally obligated to report that crime. For example, many states have laws that require reporting of suspected abuse of a child or an elderly person. These laws typically provide protection from liability (for the report) for individuals who file a report in good faith. If a student discloses anything that suggests a violent crime, abuse or neglect, contact the department chair and legal counsel to determine your obligations under the laws of your state. You may also wish to contact your institution's student counseling center or student affairs office if a student makes disclosures that reveal inappropriate campus conduct or raise concerns about student welfare. You may wish to provide notice to students in the syllabus that you are under no obligation to keep confidential any disclosures they make in class.

SYLLABUS

The class syllabus should provide information for students about the instructor, course, program, department, and university expectations for learning and how that learning is to occur. From a pedagogical perspective, an effective syllabus is another tool for guiding students as they learn. From a classroom-management perspective, an effective syllabus also promotes learning by helping members of the class understand their roles as learners and colearners. From a legal perspective, a well-constructed syllabus can provide notice to students of applicable policies and conditions of class attendance. As program administrator, you may wish to suggest language appropriate to add to each syllabus used in the program. For example, each syllabus should include a reference to relevant institutional policies, such as those on academic honesty and student conduct. You might also consider identifying the campus office responsible for evaluating requests for disability accommodation.

In addition to the basic contents of a syllabus, (policies and procedures about how the class will be conducted), the syllabus should also include guidelines for class discussions (whatever forms those discussions may take). Additional issues to address include attendance, make-up assignments, and the teacher's grading system. You might also consider using the syllabus to notify students of course content that some may deem objectionable.

DISRUPTIVE BEHAVIOR

One disruptive student in a classroom can alter the classroom experience for the instructor and the other students. This is why you must make certain that each instructor understands how to encourage and promote civil behavior. For example, the syllabus can provide information about the protocol for classroom discussion (e.g., participants are not permitted to interrupt a speaker, a speaker must yield to the next speaker upon the request of the instructor, everyone must remain seated during the discussion, yelling and badgering are not permitted).

In addition, you can promote civil behavior in the classroom by asking that instructors not tolerate disruptive behavior. The first step here is for instructors to identify to the student the behavior he or she needs to do or change. This can be stated briefly in class and reinforced in a private conversation after class or in a scheduled meeting. If the student is particularly difficult, an instructor may provide you with a notice in writing or by e-mail. Unless the student poses a physical threat, ideally the student should receive an opportunity to demonstrate the appropriate behavior after having been put on notice of unacceptable past behavior. If the student poses a threat, however, the instructor may need to contact the department chair, police, or conduct officer to pursue removal of the student from the class.

STUDENT RECORDS

The Family Educational Rights and Privacy Act (FERPA) of 1974—also known as the Buckley Amendment—establishes requirements for protecting current and former students' educational records. FERPA defines an educational record as any record about a student that is constructed and maintained by the institution or any person working for the institution. Such records include academic, advising, financial, residential, and medical documents. E-mail messages and memoranda you send about a student are part of the student's educational record, and the student is entitled to review them.

FERPA requires that students have access to their own educational records and that students have privacy rights. Those who have legitimate access to a student's records include the student, anyone granted access by the student, and university officials who have a legitimate educational interest in the record.

Once a student attends a post secondary institution, the student holds the rights of access and privacy under FERPA. It does not matter that the student may be a minor or that the parent(s) may be funding the student's education. Although you need a student's permission to discuss his or her individual performance with parents, you do not need permission to describe university, college, department, program, or course requirements, policies, practices, or procedures that may apply to the student. A student's parent(s) may gain access in one of two ways: (a) The student consents in writing to allow access or, (b) the parent(s) of the student files an Affidavit of Dependency, along with a photocopy of the most recent federal 1040 IRS form, with the institution. This second option, by the way, must be repeated annually. You should direct parents to the Office of the Registrar for information about the availability of this option.

Here are some other considerations when releasing information about a student's performance. First, don't release confidential information to a student over the phone unless you recognize that student's voice. You should be even more cautious about releasing information about a student over e-mail, unless you are using a secure server. If officers of the law request to see a student's records, they must have a subpoena to do so and your institution, through its legal counsel, may have a procedure in place for responding to a subpoena or court order.

Resources

Family Policy Compliance Office
    US Department of Education
    400 Maryland Ave. SW
    Washington, DC 20202-4605
    E-mail: om@ed.gov
    http://www.ed.gov/offices/OM/ferpa.html
    Presents basic information about FERPA.

FERPA (from the Council on Law in Higher Education).
    http://clhe.org/ferpa

Includes FERPA regulation explanations. See also Records Management and Data Analysis Legislation and Regulations at http://clhe.org/issues/records.htm.

Council on Law in Higher Education
    1551 Forum Place, Bldgs. 200–400
    West Palm Beach, FL 33401
    Phone: (561) 640-5762
    Fax: (561) 640-6030
    E-mail: info@clhe.org
    http://clhe.org/ferpa

Organization involved in improving the understanding of higher education law for educators and administrators to further compliance and avoid legal risks.

PLAGIARISM

Because writing courses require writing, you will soon or later encounter cases of plagiarism. To help avoid such cases, of course, you can advocate certain pedagogical practices that can reduce the likelihood of some forms of plagiarism. Even then, though, a few cases are likely to occur. From an educational perspective, consider ways of handling plagiarism that encourage students to achieve the learning goals of the course and the program. Make certain that students and teachers understand and follow your institution's policies and procedures for addressing suspected cases. No instructor should accuse a student of plagiarism in the absence of evidence of such dishonesty. Before any punitive action is taken, the student should be advised of the allegation or suspicion and allowed to respond.

A recent survey found that a majority of students don't feel that plagiarism is serious; one in three students felt that copying a few lines from a source without citing the source was serious (McCabe). The Internet is spurring a new debate about plagiarism, with students sometimes not realizing the breach of academic integrity. Students and faculty need to understand appropriate rules of attribution and citation. They also need to know the consequences of plagiarism at your institution.

Resources

McCabe, Donald. "New Research on Academic Integrity: The Success of 'Modified' Honor Codes." *College Administration Publications, Inc. Homepage.* <http://www.collegepubs.com/ref/SFX000515.shtml>.

McCabe reports on his ten-year survey of fourteen thousand students in sixty colleges and universities about academic integrity and cheating on campus.

Pavela, Gary. "John and Metad, Part II: A Case Study on Academic Integrity." *College Administration Publications, Inc. Homepage.* <http://www.collegepubs.com/ref/SfxCseStdyOnAcademicIntegrity.shtml>.

This case study highlights the legal implications that can arise when a faculty member suspects students of cheating.

HIRING PRACTICES AND PERSONNEL EVALUATIONS

Because writing programs are large at many postsecondary institutions, WPAs frequently participate in hiring full-time or part-time faculty. To ensure that hiring is fair and to project your institution and yourself, contact your school's equal opportunity/affirmative action officer. At most schools EO/AA officers regularly conduct workshops for faculty and administrators who participate in hiring. Participate in those workshops before the beginning of the hiring season and attend them at least every two years—to keep your knowledge current.

WPAs can inadvertently commit the institution to hiring unqualified part-time or full-time faculty by writing job advertisements that don't accurately describe the duties, the "required" qualifications, and "desired" qualifications for a faculty position. We cannot overstate how important it is to write job ads carefully because once an ad is approved and published, it constitutes the legally binding criteria for evaluating applicants. By including too many "required" qualifications, you may be forced to exclude applicants who are very well equipped to do the job. By including too few "required" qualifications, you may be legally compelled to hire faculty who are really unqualified to teach composition. To avoid such problems, work closely with colleagues, other administrators, and your EO/AA officer to write any job ad.

When you begin screening applicants, you must treat all applicants equally. Equally apply the criteria implied by the job ad as you read and evaluate application materials. If your hiring process involves a campus visit, make certain that colleagues participating in sessions during the visit know what questions are inappropriate and illegal. (The *MLA Job Information List* includes a list of such topics.)

If you are responsible for evaluating staff or instructors, you should review your institutional policies. These policies (or the appropriate administrative offices) should explain how often the evaluations should occur, the content, the rating system, and the appropriate level of participation by the person being evaluated. Don't overlook the evaluation as an opportunity to address and document difficult issues or persistent complaints. If you fail to document a concern or problem, you may later be unable to take appropriate steps to discipline or replace the employee in a timely way.

Resources

MLA Job Information List.
   Http://www.mla.org/main_jil.htm

United States Equal Employment Opportunity Commission
   1801 L Street, NW
   Washington, DC 20507
   Phone: (202) 663-4900; TTY: (202) 663-4494
   http://www.eeoc.gov/

LETTERS OF RECOMMENDATION

A common complaint with letters of recommendation is that they too often are hyperbolic. A candidate may be described as "the best student ever to go through English 101" or someone's latest genius. Other recommendations are vague and don't give valid, adequate information about a candidate. Describing a candidate as "showing considerable progress" doesn't explain from what point he or she has progressed or where the candidate is now. With the weight and importance placed on letters for both students and job applicants, writing letters of recommendation is a serious issue that can have legal implications. For instance, an author's failing to disclose abuse or malfeasance on the job by the candidate could have legal consequences if the new employer relies on the misleading letter and the candidate repeats the abuse or malfeasance in the new position.

You may decide to decline to write a letter of recommendation for someone whom you cannot fully support. You should not agree to write any letter unless you believe you can be truthful. If you are contacted by a third party for a reference, always obtain the candidate's consent to discuss his or her circumstances or to write a letter. For each statement in the letter, if it is your opinion, it should be clearly labeled as such; if you believe you are stating a fact, be prepared to offer factual support. False or malicious statements may create legal liability for you and your institution. You may also wish to contact your legal counsel to understand state law that may provide guidance in preparing letters of reference.

DISABILITY RESOURCES

You and everyone who teaches in your program should become familiar with campus resources for persons with disabilities. If possible, ask that office to conduct a workshops for teachers in your program. Also, find out how that office prefers to work with both students and faculty.

For a student to be eligible for accommodation, he or she may first have to be registered with your campus office of disability resources. Each teacher should include in the syllabus a sentence or two describing the procedure for students to request appropriate accommodation. You should also ask your teachers to make an announcement in class about the accommodation procedures outlined in the syllabus. If a student asks the teacher for an accommodation, the teacher should direct the student to the office designated by the institution to review these requests. That office (not the instructor) may ask the student for documentation to support the request. If you are uncertain how to offer appropriate accommodation, call the campus office for guidance.

You can also facilitate the process by asking teachers to have course materials and class handouts selected as early as possible. This will allow the disabilities resources office to acquire nonprint versions (e.g., audiotapes, Braille) of materials before the semester begins.

Resources

The Individuals with Disabilities Education Act (IDEA)
http://www.ed.gov/offices/OSERS/IDEA/geninfo.html

Provides an overview and questions and answers about IDEA. Also with links to training modules.

US Department of Justice Americans with Disabilities Act Homepage
http://www.usdoj.gov/crt/ada/adahom1.htm

Includes a link for *Enforcing the ADA: Looking Back on a Decade of Progress*, a tenth anniversary status report from the Department of Justice.

GENERAL RESOURCES

Books

Breslin-Myers, Linda, ed. *Administrative Problem-Solving for Writing Programs and Writing Centers: Scenarios in Effective Program Management*. Urbana: NCTE, 1999.

A collection of works dealing with how to prepare for WPA work, including selections on selection and training, program development and departmental authority, and professional development.

Hollander, Patricia A., D. Parker Young, and Donald D. Gehring. *A Practical Guide to Legal Issues Affecting College Teachers*. Asheville, NC: College

Administration Publications, 1995. Purchase at
<http://www.collegepubs.com/descrip/9.shtml>.

Revised edition provides an overview of the legal rights and responsibilities
that all faculty need to know.

Jones, Larry G., ed. *Preventing Lawsuits: The Role of Institutional Research.* San
Francisco: Jossey-Bass, 1997.

Useful collection of essays describing the ways in which higher education administrators can avoid some possible legal risks.

Kaplin, William A., and Barbara A. Lee. *The Law of Higher Education: A
Comprehensive Guide To Legal Implications of Administrative Decision
Making.* 3rd ed. San Francisco: Jossey-Bass, 1995.

The basic legal reference guide, with case index.

Leap, Terry L. *Tenure, Discrimination, and the Courts.* Ithaca: Cornell UP,
1995.

Based on a fifteen-year study, this book provides legal guidance for dealing
with issues of promotion, tenure, reappointment, contract negotiations, and
other personnel practices. Also explores the rationale behind recent court
cases involving personnel issues.

Olivas, Michael A. *The Law and Higher Education: Cases and Materials on
Colleges and Court.* 2nd ed. Durham: Carolina Academic, 1997.

An extensive casebook dealing with a number of themes including academic
freedom, the law and faculty, students and the law, and affirmative action,
with summaries of each case. Intended for classroom use and general legal
reference.

Smith, Michael Clay, and Richard Fossey. *Crime on Campus: Legal Issues and
Campus Administration.* Phoenix: Oryx, 1995.

Includes many court cases as examples of campus crime and what administrators and decision makers can do about it.

Toma, J. Douglas, and Richard L. Palm. *The Academic Instructor and the Law:
What Every Dean and Department Chair Needs to Know.* ASHE-ERIC
Higher Education Report Volume 26, No. 5. Washington, DC: George
Washington, Graduate School of Education and Human Develop-
ment, 1999.

Designed for deans and chairs who direct academic programs in higher education, this book includes specific information on different types of legal situations for different types of institutions. Includes extensive reference list.

Organizations

American Association of School Administrators
1801 North Moore Street
Arlington, VA 22209
Phone: (703) 528-0700; Fax: (703) 841-1543
E-mail: Info@aasa.org
http://www.aasa.org

American Association of University Administrators
17103 Preston Road, LB 107, Suite 250
Dallas, TX 75248-1332
Phone: (972) 248-3957; Fax: (972) 713-8209
http://www.aaua.org

American Association of University Professors
1012 Fourteenth Street NW Suite 500
Washington, DC 20005-3465
Phone: (202) 737-5900; Fax (202) 737-5526
E-mail: aaup@aaup.org
http://www.aaup.org

American College Personnel Association
One Dupont Circle, Suite 300
Washington, DC 20036
Phone: (202) 835-2272
Fax: (202) 296-3286
E-mail: info@acpa.nche.edu
http://www.acpa.nche.edu/

Council on Law in Higher Education
1551 Forum Place, Bldgs. 200-400
West Palm Beach, FL 33401
Phone: (561) 640-5762 ; Fax: (561) 640-6030
E-mail: info@clhe.org
http://www.clhe.org/

Education Law Association
Mail Drop 0528
300 College Park

Dayton, OH 45469
Phone: (937) 229-3589; Fax: (937)229-3845
E-mail: ela@udayton.edu
http://www.educationlaw.org

National Association of College and University Attorneys
One Dupont Circle, Suite 620
Washington, DC 20036
Phone: (202) 833-8390
Fax: (202) 296-8379
E-mail: nacua@nacua.org
http://www.nacua.org/

National Association of Student Personnel Administrators
NASPA, Student Affairs Administrators in Higher Education
1875 Connecticut Avenue, NW, Suite 418
Washington, DC_ 20009
Phone: (202) 265-7500; Fax: (202) 797-1157
Email: office@naspa.org
http://www.naspa.org/

National Organization on Legal Problems in Education
Southwest Plaza Building
3601 SW, 29th Street, Suite 223
Topeka, KS, 66614
Phone: (913) 273-3550; Fax: (913) 273-2001

US Department of Education Office of Postsecondary Education Department of Education
Office of Postsecondary Education
1990 K Street, NW
Washington, DC 20006
E-mail: ope_www@ed.gov
http://www.ed.gov/offices/OPE/

Electronic Resources

Campus Administration Publications, Inc.
http://www.collegepubs.com/

Click on electronic bulletin for other news and events. A thorough site for additional resources on a variety of topics in law and higher education.

Campus Mediation Resources
http://www.mtds.wayne.edu/campus.htm

Maintained by Wayne State University, this site's main focus is conflict resolution and mediation, yet it does include sources for diversity on campus and other law-related resources.

Computers and Academic Freedom Project
http://www.eff.org/CAF/

A site that critiques and explains various computer use policies in place in universities all over the country. Also includes links for brief descriptions of specific cases dealing with online rights and responsibilities.

Findlaw
http://www.findlaw.com/

An immense search engine dealing specifically with legal issues and reference.

Conferences and Seminars

Higher Education and the Law
Annual conference sponsored by the Institute of Higher Education at the University of Georgia, Athens.
http://www.uga.edu/ihe/

Law and Policy in Higher Education
Annual seminar from College Administration Publications.
http://www.collegepubs.com/seminars.shtml

Journals

The Journal Of College and University Law. Washington, DC: National Association of College and University Attorneys.

The Yearbook of Education Law. Topeka: National Organization on Legal Problems of Education.

10

Applying Ethics: A Decision-Making Heuristic for Writing Program Administrators

❦ • ❧

Stuart C. Brown
New Mexico State University

A young woman sits across the desk from me. She has a two-week old infant in her lap. We are six weeks into the spring semester. The Dean has brought to my attention that a graduate student instructor—as well as three faculty in other departments—purportedly told the student at the semester's beginning that she could bring the infant to class provided she would leave if the baby became disruptive. Day care is not an option, as none will take the child until he is at least six weeks old. The student is new to town, she knows no one she can leave the baby with, and her husband's work schedule precludes her changing sections to an evening or weekend class. She has to be registered for and satisfactorily complete at least twelve credit hours to maintain financial aid; this means she can neither drop the class nor fail it. University policy and the *Student Handbook,* however, expressly prohibit anyone not registered for a class to attend on a regular basis. Further, university policy—which both the instructor and student ought to be aware of—allows children to be brought to work or class only in "emergency" situations, and never on a regular basis. The student's history professor is going to "home school" her independently of class. The other faculty, in another college, are allowing her to bring the child. Why is there a problem with her bringing the child to her rhetoric and composition class? Especially after the graduate assistant, herself four months pregnant, had already told the student that it would be fine?

I'm mildly exasperated. I want to keep this student in school. I want to honor the graduate student's generous impulse, mistaken as it was. I want to keep the Dean happy, but I also don't want twenty other students distracted by a two-week-old infant. I am also concerned that if the student is allowed this dispensation, others may expect it as well.

I spot our required text for the first-semester course in the photocopy request basket. Curious, I note the request for twenty-nine copies of two of the text's chapters. Students in that section should have this book. Our first writing course is closely "scripted" with a standardized syllabus, assignments, and required readings. I know the instructor; he had been through our semester-long course on composition pedagogy a year before and had taught in Bulgaria for the Peace Corp. He is experienced, rigorous, creative, and enthusiastic. Student evaluations indicate he is doing a fine job. He admits that he did not have the students buy the book because he was "not using it much," but bringing in alternative materials. He does not want students to have the expense of a book that they will not be using, though it occurs to him belatedly that the Department is footing the bill for the photocopying.

I do not want to cut off this teacher's investment in the course nor the innovations he brings. I remember chafing under similar constraints. I do, however, want his students to have close to the same curriculum eleven hundred other students are experiencing this semester in this course. I have assured the University's General Education Committee that the Writing Program strives for consistency. For this instructor to "do it his way" means everyone else has to pay.

I've just received funding to open three more sections of our required first year composition course. Already scheduled sections have been full since the second summer student orientation. Enrollment is up 8 percent over last year at this time.

I have a stack of résumés on my desk. This has grown over the summer, and now includes recent graduates of our program, partners of graduate students and faculty, people newly retired and interested in a second career, and attorneys and public school teachers looking to supplement their incomes. These are the new ones. I already have a dozen or so I hire nearly every semester. My program pays significantly better than the competing schools in the area, provides office space with computers and phones, and offers an interesting variety of courses to teach. We do not have health or retirement benefits associated with these positions, hire only on a semester-by-semester basis, and pay a per credit hour wage that makes these hires cheaper than graduate students. I've already hired everyone I'm certain is an excellent teacher.

I have concerns in filling these new sections. Do I offer additional sections to the already hired teachers (thereby restricting the pool of experienced teachers for future semesters) or do I take a chance on unknown teachers whom I will not be able to evaluate until the end of the semester? How culpable am I in perpetuating the use of part-time faculty? Do I create a backlog of students needing these courses to graduate? Do I risk increased class sizes to avert that backlog? Classes start tomorrow.

These *stories* provide a small sample of the daily mediations required of writing program administrators (WPAs). I suggest here that a useful mode for constructing these "interventions" is to cast them within an ethical frame. Particularly for contemporary WPAs, ethical conflicts dominate our professional lives. Curriculum development, teacher training, intellectual property issues, research methods, data presentation, faculty hiring, evaluation practices, and fiscal responsibilities all have their ethical dimensions. Haswell and Lu's collection *Comp Tales* and George's collection *Kitchen Cooks, Plate Twirlers, and Troubadours: Writing Program Administrators Tell Their Stories* could easily serve as collections of ethical case studies for WPAs.

As a result of shifting focus from *techné* to *praxis* (see Crowley; Miller; Phelps; Porter, "Developing"), the new rhetorics of the twentieth century have brought renewed attention to ethics. And this shift in emphasis "leads us to inquiries about the relationship between rhetoric and politics/power (i.e., how knowledge is used) and, eventually, ethics (i.e., the aims of that use of knowledge)" (Porter, "Developing" 208). I suspect that the twenty-first century will heighten this attention as competing ideologies and interests further complicate the WPA's professional life.

A burgeoning number of guides, frameworks, and worksheets on the World Wide Web suggest a great deal of attention is being directed toward ethical or moral decision making (see MacDonald; McDonald; Velasquez et al;). Especially useful are three Web sites devoted to applied ethics: Centre for Applied Ethics at the University of British Columbia (http://www.eth-ics.ubc.ca), Ethics Update (edited by Lawrence M. Hinman, http://eth-ics.acusd.edu), and Markkula Center for Applied Ethics at Santa Clara University (http://www.scu.edu/SCU/Centers/Ethics). More specific to rhetorical interests are Dombrowski; Johannesen; Katz; Kinneavy, all of whom provide indispensable background reading in the history and theory of communication ethics.

Moral dilemmas often arise when conflict occurs between what seems the *right* thing to do and what seems the *easiest* thing to do. Personal values often obscure the problem as well. However, given the positions of power and responsibility that WPAs occupy, we would be well served to consider ourselves moral agents. Most of us consider ourselves ethical beings attempting to act for the general good. A more demanding step would be to position ourselves as *actively* engaged in the development and reflection upon the moral and ethical assumptions implicit in our roles as agents and arbiters. Over the past few years as an administrator I've developed a somewhat idiosyncratic model of what I call a "moral heuristic," a device I use to help sift the ethical morass of much of a WPA's decision making. I offer this heuristic as an aid for developing an ethical framework for WPA decision making, a kind of template for the design of sound conflict resolution.

A MORAL HEURISTIC

What follows is not terribly sophisticated, nor is it intended to be a precise model for complicated ethical reasoning. However, as Strike, Haller, and Soltis point out "people engage in ethical reflection all the time" (3). At the risk of oversimplification, the goal here is to "sensitize you to the kinds of moral issues that arise in the normal activities of administrative life" (3) and then allow you to build your own framework to aid in your work as a WPA.

Much of my WPA life consists of resolving conflicts. These conflicts—or what I term *ethical tensions*—usually result from competing claims for resources, boundary disputes between or about agency and power, or uncertainties over obligations. The self-interest of the various parties and institutions is usually a factor. I use my particular heuristic to identify stakeholders and separate their respective claims. The stories I've cited here represent the most common stakeholders I encounter in my WPA role: institution, instructor, curriculum, student, and myself. I find if I can take the time to sort out the competing nature of these stakeholders' interests, I usually arrive at a decision I feel reasonably resolves the conflict. Using this heuristic makes it possible for me to articulate or justify my decision more clearly to the participants as well. I also do better when I recognize my own conflation of con*duct* and *con*duct, of authority and courtesy, and of responsibility and vulnerability. As a WPA, I have power—limited, but there nonetheless (for perspectives on the nature of WPAs and power, see Dickson; Olson and Moxley; White; see also chap. 1, this volume). If I can conceive of using that power while maintaining my own character or ethos, I'll feel better about assuming—and using—that power.

A growing ethics literature is tied directly to the daily lives of WPAs. Buranen and Roy's collection on plagiarism is an invaluable guide to intellectual property issues. "Guidelines for the Ethical Treatment of Students and Student Writing in Composition Studies" has been recently issued by The CCC Ad Hoc Committee on the Ethical Use of Students and Student Writing in Composition Studies (guidelines such as these or "codes of ethics" can be useful heuristics for developing policy or having stakeholders preempt potential disputes, but they can also create problems—see Brown; Johannesen). Hansen's "Face to Face with Part-Timers: Ethics and the Professionalization of Writing Faculties" focuses attention on a crucial issue facing the profession. Two recent collections, Fontaine and Hunter's *Foregrounding Ethical Awareness in Composition and English Studies* and Pemberton's *The Ethics of Writing*

Instruction: Issues in Theory and Practice, are rich resources. See also Bamberg; Morgan; Porter, "Legal Realities ..."; Werder.

As WPAs, our decisions usually combine personal and professional values. The various stakeholders in a dispute, however, may not share these values. You may not even recognize either your values at play in a particular situation or the values others have brought to the issues at hand. I find that my own values, and their origin, can take on strange nuances when I have to articulate them. As a consequence, I have devised the following heuristic to help me respond to a situation confounded by ethical tensions. It is divided into two parts: matters of fact, which involves identifying what can be known about the participants and the issue at hand; and matters of consequence, which is more speculative. As a demonstration, I'll work through my decision-making process using the first case; essential elements are noted in bold.

AN ETHICS-BASED DECISION-MAPPING PROCESS

Matters of Fact

1. *Where does **agency** reside? Who is the best person to resolve this issue or make the decision?* Ideally, the instructor and the student are the best people to resolve this because it is their issue. However, I have been directed to intervene by a higher authority, the Dean. At a certain point, I will cease being a factor here beyond determining and informing the student and the instructor of policy and of options. The key decisions will be between the student and the instructor.

How much of a role does expediency or time pressure play in resolving the dispute? When exactly does a decision need to be made and in what form (memo, letter, report, discussion)? What other circumstances are going on that require attention and therefore distract my attention from the matter at hand? Given that we are past the drop date, timing is somewhat at issue here, though it's not critical. Fall scheduling, outcomes assessment, and revising the business communication course curriculum are occupying my time. But, once I recognize these other pressures, I can balance them against the need to decide to be judicious and evenhanded.

2. *Who are the **stakeholders**? What stake does each have in this dispute? How does each want the situation to be resolved? Have all of the stakeholders had an opportunity to present their side of the issue?* The stakeholders include the university (its policy is at stake here), the student (who has enrolled in classes with the understanding that bringing her child to class would not be a problem), the instructor (who made a promise and who is sympathetic to the student's plight), the other members of the class (who are entitled to a classroom situation equal to that of other sections of the same course), and me (whose job at this point is to sort it all out).

3. *What is the central* **issue** *or problem? Based on your values, how is it an ethical or moral one?* The first problem is that the student would be in violation of university policy by bringing the infant to class. The second problem is that the other students in the class are being subjected to unequal conditions by having a two-week-old infant in their midst. A third problem would be the establishment of precedent.

4. *What is the* **relationship** *among the various stakeholders? What possibility is there for effective mediation?* The situation is rife with power issues: teacher/student; administrator/WPA; WPA/instructor; WPA/student; individual/group. Everyone, up to this point, is on good terms, recognizing that there is a problem that needs to be addressed and maintaining their civility in addressing it.

5. *What* **values** *are involved?* We must assume trust is established among the participants in that all of us are aware that the others are sincere in their attempt to find a fair solution. Each of the participants also has a degree of autonomy in the issue at hand, although the ultimate decision may not be to everyone's liking. Every effort is being made to arrive at a decision as equitable and beneficial to all of the stakeholders as it can be.

6. *What is my* **duty** *as WPA to each of the stakeholders?* I have an obligation to administer university policy; an obligation to the student to treat her as fairly as I would any other student; an obligation to the instructor to help her sort the circumstances out for her, for this student, and for her other students; and I have an obligation to the other students in the class (and in all other sections of the course) to provide them with as equal an experience in the course as they would have in another section.

Matters of Consequence

1. *How is the decision affected by the exigency of the situation?* The student cannot continue to bring the infant to class, but is constrained by other factors from attending the class without the child. She is missing class and falling behind in her work for the class.

2. *How do my institution's interests affect the decision?* I have a duty to fulfill, an obligation to make the best possible decision based on my assigned role and to assume responsibility for that decision.

3. *How do my own interests determine the decision?* I want to keep the Dean happy; I want the instructor to be satisfied with the outcome; I want the other students in the class not to have to experience a two-week old infant; I want this situation resolved.

4. *What decision will provide the greatest benefit (or least harm) for the greatest number?* The decision not to allow the student to bring the infant

to class is the most likely to result in the least amount of distractions for everyone.

5. *What decision demonstrates genuine concern for those who need the most help?* The student is in need of the most help here, but allowing her to bring her child is not in the class's best interest nor hers, as it would be quite difficult for her to be fully engaged in the class and still responsive to her child.

6. *What harm will result from my action?* The decision to prohibit the student from bringing her child to class puts the student at the greatest risk in that she will likely not be able to maintain her financial aid and will most likely, as her husband informed me, never be back.

7. *Based on my own personal values, can I live with my decision? How can I reflect upon this particular situation and decision?* The aforementioned is an attempt to represent my use of this heuristic both as a tool for decision making and as a means for reflecting about decisions. It works best when I have the time and patience to work through a set of responses, to map out the stakeholders and relationships at play. In all honesty, that rarely happens. Usually, reflection is only possible after decisions have been made. On those rare occasions when I have the time to revisit the situation and use the model to examine the situation, its stakeholders, and the consequences, I find it useful. It is by no means completely worked out in my own mind. Yet I can envision eventually using this heuristic as an effective training tool, one that provides an analytic frame for approaching case study. At some point, I could see casting it as a decision tree.

Regardless of how this heuristic is or is not used, my essential aim here is to underscore and integrate the awareness of ethics in the WPA role. Bringing an ethical or moral dimension to decision making as a WPA enriches those decisions. WPAs are very much agents of change. Our leadership position establishes the imperative to act ethically (see chap. 1, this volume). On some days, I can even lay claim to aspirations toward becoming a virtuous person, one attentive to his ethos. If, as rhetoricians, we choose to uphold the classical dictum of a "good person speaking well," then attention to our "good" character seems as necessary as our attention to our rhetorical practice.

In that spirit, I leave you with a scenario to "resolve":

A graduate assistant sits across the desk from you. She is in a panic about a student in her sophomore-level technical writing class. She has brought you a writing sample. It contains no verbs. The student has successfully transferred the first semester composition course prerequisite in from another institution, Gaudellet University. The student is deaf and his primary language is American Sign; he will bring an interpreter to class. The university's ADA officer is on the phone; you have just read her the writing sample and she found it quite *moving*. In fact the writing *is* quite moving, like a tone poem; but it is unlike any writing sample you have ever seen in response to a technical writing assignment, and it does not fulfill the assignment's specific requirements. The instructor is in her third semester of teaching and her first semester of teaching this class. She has no idea how to begin working with this kind of student. And neither do you.

The ADA officer wants to keep the student in class. The student wants to stay in class at this particular time and will not consider moving to a more experienced instructor. The student has met the prerequisites established by the department and the university; he needs this class for his major and for his degree, because it is a general education requirement.

WORKS CITED

Bamberg, Betty. "Conflicts between Teaching and Assessing Writing: Using Program-Based Research to Resolve Pedagogical and Ethical Dilemmas." *The Writing Program Administrator as Researcher: Inquiry in Action and Reflection*. Ed. Shirley K Rose and Irwin Weiser. Portsmouth, NH: Boynton/Cook, 1999. 28–39.

Brown, Stuart C. "Rhetoric, Ethical Codes, and the Revival of *Ethos* in Publications Management." *Publications Management: Essays for Professional Communicators*. Ed. O. Jane Allen and Lynn H. Deming. Amityville, NY: Baywood, 1994. 189–200.

Buranen, Lise and Alice M. Roy, eds. *Perspectives on Plagiarism and Intellectual Property in a Postmodern World*. Albany, NY: State U of New York P, 1999.

Crowley, Sharon. "Composition's Ethic of Service, the Universal Requirement, and the Discourse of Human Need." *Composition in the University: Historical and Polemical Essays*. Pittsburgh: U of Pittsburgh P, 1998.

——. "A Plea for the Revival of Sophistry." *Rhetoric Review* 7 (Spring 1989): 318–34.

Dickson, Marcia. "Directing without Power: Adventures in Constructing a Model of Feminist Writing Programs Administration." *Writing Ourselves into the Story: Unheard Voices from Composition Studies*. Ed. Sheryl I. Fontaine and Susan Hunter. Carbondale: Southern Illinois UP, 1993. 140–53.

Dombrowski, Paul. *Ethics in Technical Communication*. Needham Heights, MA: Allyn & Bacon, 2000.

Fontaine, Sheryl I., and Susan M. Hunter. *Foregrounding Ethical Awareness in Composition and English Studies*. Portsmouth, NH: Boynton/Cook, 1998.

"Guidelines for the Ethical Treatment of Students and Student Writing in Composition Studies." *College Composition and Communication* 52.3 (February 2001): 485–90.

George, Diana, ed. *Kitchen Cooks, Plate Twirlers, and Troubadours: Writing Program Administrators Tell Their Stories*. Portsmouth, NH: Boynton/Cook, 1999.

Hansen, Kristine. "Face to Face with Part-Timers: Ethics and the Professionalization of Writing Faculties." *Resituating Writing: Constructing and Administering Writing Programs*. Ed. Joseph Janangelo and Kristine Hansen. Portsmouth, NH: Boynton/Cook, 1995. 23–45

Haswell, Richard H., and Min-Zhan Lu, eds. *Comp Tales*. New York: Longman, 2000.

Johannessen, Richard L. "Ethics." *Encyclopedia of Rhetoric and Composition: Communication from Ancient Times to the Information Age*. Ed. Theresa Enos. New York: Garland, 1996, 235–40.

—. *Ethics in Human Communication*. 4th ed. Prospect Heights, IL: Waveland P, 1996.

Katz, Steven B. "Aristotle's Rhetoric, Hitler's Program, and the Ideological Problem of Praxis, Power, and Professional Discourse." *Journal of Business and Technical Communication* 7 (1992): 37–62.

—. "The Ethic of Expediency: Classical Rhetoric, Technology, and the Holocaust." *College English* 54 (1992): 255–75.

Kinneavy, James L. "Writing about Ethical or Political Issues: How to Be Moral without Being Dogmatic." *Teaching Composition in the 90s: Sites of Contention*. Ed. Christina G. Russell and Robert L. McDonald. New York: HarperCollins, 1994. 33–52.

MacDonald, Chris. "A Guide to Moral Decision Making." <http://www.ethics.ubc.ca/chrismac/publications/moral.decision.html>.

McDonald, Michael. "A Framework for Ethical Decision-Making: Version 4 Ethics Shareware." <http://www.ethics.ubc.ca/mcdonald/decisions.html>.

Miller, Carolyn R. "What's Practical about Technical Writing." *Technical Writing: Theory and Practice*. Ed. B. E. Fearing and W. K. Sparrow. New York: MLA, 1989. 14–24.

Morgan, Dan. "Ethical Issues Raised by Students' Personal Writing." *College English* 60 (1998): 318–25.

Olson, Gary A., and Joseph M. Moxley. "Directing Freshman Composition: The Limits of Authority." *College Composition and Communication* 40 (1989): 51–60.

Pemberton, Michael A, ed. *The Ethics of Writing Instruction: Issues in Theory and Practice*. Greenwich, CT: Ablex, 2000.

Phelps, Louise Wetherbee. *Composition as a Human Science: Contributions to the Self-Understanding of a Discipline*. New York: Oxford UP, 1988.

Porter, James E. "Developing a Postmodern Ethics of Rhetoric and Composition." *Defining the New Rhetorics*. Ed. Theresa Enos and Stuart C. Brown. Newbury Park, CA: Sage, 1994. 207–26.

—. "Legal Realities and Ethical Hyperrealities: A Critical Approach toward Cyberwriting." *Computers and Technical Communication: Pedagogical and Programmatic Perspectives*. Ed. Stuart A. Selber. Greenwich, CT: Ablex, 1997. 45–73.

Strike, Kenneth A., Emil J. Haller, and Jonas F. Soltis. *The Ethics of School Administration*. 2nd ed. New York: Teachers College P, 1998.

Velasquez, Manuel, Claire Andre, Thomas Shanks, S.J., and Michael J. Meyer. "Thinking Ethically: A Framework for Moral Decision Making." <http://www.scu.edu/SCU/Centers/Ethics/practicing/decision/>.

Werder, Carmen. "Rhetorical Agency: Seeing the Ethics of It All." *Writing Program Administrator* 24 (2000): 9–28.

White, Edward M. "Power and the WPA: A Devil's Bargain for New Faculty." *Teaching Composition in the 90s: Sites of Contention*. Ed. Christina G. Russell and Robert L. McDonald. New York: HarperCollins, 1994. 151–63.

11

The WPA and the Politics of LitComp

John Schilb
Indiana University, Bloomington

This summer, once again I became a writing program director. Having assumed the role twice before at another university, I thought I knew what to expect. My first duty, I figured, would be to train new teachers of my university's required composition course. Yet early on I found myself immersed in a different task: getting better offices. For the last several years, the program's headquarters had been an assortment of small, separate rooms, hardly an ideal base of operations. Moving proved difficult, though. I wound up in prolonged negotiations with the department's chair, associate chair, and other program directors, all of whom were staking claims to particular territories. I am glad to report that after several tense conversations, we all did obtain good homes. I write these words in a nice, large office that was formerly the department's chief meeting room and the site of our debates over space.

Our wrangling over physical turf reminded me of two things about writing program administration. Though I always knew that I would have to engage in diplomacy, I grew newly aware that one aim is decent facilities. The whole experience underscored for me, too, English departments' traditional marginalizing of composition. I doubt that I would have had to fight for adequate physical space if my department had given composition adequate conceptual space—that is, seen composition as a central part of "English." To be fair, at no time in our debates over offices did the participants mock composition. Everyone realized the writing program deserved better rooms. Still, that the program was poorly housed in the first place suggests its skewed ideological positioning.

Ironically, the office I now occupy was, in its previous incarnation, known as the William Riley Parker Library. Parker was a revered chair of our department, and we intend to keep honoring his local contributions by finding another room to name for him. But within the discipline of English at large, perhaps he is best known for his 1967 *College English* article "Where Do English Departments Come From?" As I sat in what was then the Parker Library arguing over where my program would go, inevitably I thought of his article, for it detailed early conditions of English bound to leave composition unsettled.

In the article, Parker argues against the notion that literature and composition naturally belong together. He points out that their copresence in English departments resulted less from a smooth, Hegelian evolution of ideas than from various bureaucratic maneuvers, especially in response to the great expansion of the college population in the late 1800s. As he concludes his piece, Parker emphasizes that written composition "has always had the most tenuous connection with the academic study of language and literature" (14). Nevertheless, he observes, English departments have long clung to composition out of self-interest. Even when they doubt composition's intellectual worth, they see that it helps them perpetuate English as a discipline. Among composition's practical advantages for literature faculty, Parker tartly declares, is that it permits "the frugal subsidizing of countless graduate students who cannot wait to escape it" (14).

Unfortunately, Parker does not proceed to recommend that English departments do more to justify including composition in their curriculum. Nor does he propose that writing programs secede from English. Instead, he ends by suggesting that English departments build stronger bridges to speech, linguistics, and foreign languages. In effect, he leaves the relation between literary studies and composition studies as "tenuous" as ever.

The fragility of their bond is indicated by the fact that not every English department has a writing program director. Some English departments, such as Northwestern's and the University of Chicago's, have always been overwhelmingly departments of literature, with writing instruction carried out by another unit at their school. In recent years, certain writing programs such as Syracuse's have conspicuously separated from English. Meanwhile, English departments at many small liberal arts colleges teach courses in writing but without an official program. Many of them, such as Williams and Kenyon, have never searched for a specialist in composition. Their refusal to do so reflects their long commitment to a belles-lettristic notion of culture, which they more or less assume would be soiled by the crass practicality that "composition" evokes for them.

The discipline of English at large has also been slow to acknowledge that composition belongs alongside literature. Only after many years did the Modern Language Association establish a Division on the Teaching of Writing. Only recently has MLA devoted a book series to the subject, or regularly sent its chief officers to composition's national conference. Only now is there a prospect of composition's finally being covered in the annual MLA bibliography. And though MLA has begun to address the poor working climate of many adjunct writing instructors, this move does not mean the organization has come to cherish composition as a field. MLA's new regard for composition's adjuncts stems from another fact: that several of these teachers actually specialize in literature, though a dearth of tenure-track jobs for them has left them "stuck" teaching writing.

If you direct a writing program in an English department, you may have to deal with the sordid aspects of this vexed disciplinary history. At the very least, I suspect, you will have colleagues who tend to ignore composition even if their graduate students are busy teaching it. In my experience, only rarely do literature specialists feel moved to declare the two subjects intellectually akin. One such occasion is when people in charge of the writing program talk of making it independent. At a moment like this, English departments with graduate students fear that losing the writing program will mean losing assistantships; hence, literature specialists suddenly proclaim themselves composition's ally. Recently, a related type of circumstance prompted similar declarations in my department. Like writing programs at several schools, ours has increasingly faced attempts by other departments to establish their own versions of first-year writing, whether or not these departments really know how to teach composition. At a meeting of English faculty, several teachers of literature criticized this encroachment. Moreover, they resolved to treat composition as a real partner to their enterprise. Yet, though I found their words sincere and inspiring, I knew why they had to speak in the first place. Until then, composition's role in their department had been peripheral for them at best.

Plenty of writing program directors report that literature colleagues have blatantly abused them. In her now-legendary keynote address at the 1985 meeting of the Conference on College Composition and Communication, Maxine Hairston alluded to these complaints and urged writing instructors to liberate themselves from literary studies. According to her, most literature faculty are unwilling even to listen to those who teach writing. Therefore, composition specialists need to detach themselves psychologically from their colleagues in English. Going much further than Parker, Hairston raised the prospect of writing programs' even becoming separate departments.

Elsewhere, I have expressed reservations about her proposal (*Between* 66). Here I will simply note that it has proven hard to enact. For one thing, composition specialists and literature specialists share at least some concerns. Always, both camps have thought much about the properties of texts. Lately, both have attended much to social contexts, especially the ways that authors are influenced by characteristics such as gender, race, and class. Indeed, for the last several years, both composition studies and literary studies have been markedly social-constructionist in bent, studying how the very notions of truth, identity, knowledge, and value are shaped by discourse as well as material circumstance. If the literary canon still consists mostly of fiction, poetry, and drama, specialists in literature have increasingly turned to other kinds of texts and even other media, whereas composition specialists remain concerned with various discourses including their students'. Understandably, then, specialists in writing have come to admire many of the same theorists that their colleagues in literature do. The influence of such people as Stanley Fish, Michel Foucault, and Judith Butler cuts across both fields. In her 1985 speech and on later occasions, Hairston tried to bolster her call for autonomy by scorning thinkers like these, but her attacks were too sketchy and ill-informed to succeed. True, the traffic in theory has been deplorably one way: If many compositionists are familiar with Fish, Foucault, and Butler, few literature faculty have bothered to read the likes of Susan Miller or James Berlin. Thus, hopes for a grand unification of English remain utopian. But enough of a common theoretical pantheon exists to undercut Hairston's call for a split.

Besides, though composition studies has become, if anything, hyperprofessionalized, most graduate programs in the field still make their students take some courses in literature. Quite a few of us who currently direct writing programs have a substantial literary background. Actually, many of us continue to teach literature on occasion. Moreover, we contribute to or appreciate scholarship philosophically linking it with composition, even as we see English departments leaving the connections purely theoretical.

Hairston deserves credit for underscoring a situation that Parker merely intimated. The typical English department continues to privilege literature, at composition's expense. It's a situation to which the word *politics* easily applies. In any sense of the term, *politics* refers to struggles for rights, resources, and recognition. When literature faculty refer to "politics," however, usually they are thinking of civic conflicts, especially clashes involving historically oppressed groups. Ironically, Hairston is now notorious in composition for arguing in a 1992 article that writing curricula should steer clear of this latter political realm. For many years, though, writing instructors have related the word *politics* to yet another, more local set of conflicts: their struggles with their department's literary-minded majority. Significantly, the award-winning 1991 collection *The Politics of Writing Instruction: Post-Secondary* focuses mostly on this institutional scene.

As Richard Ohmann points out in his introduction to the *Politics* volume, focusing on departmental inequities does risk obscuring oppression in the wider world. Yet composition's marginality in English departments can be hard for writing instructors to forget. Especially vexing are instances when literature faculty celebrated for protesting social injustice prove content with the low status of their department's composition adjuncts. I have known, for example, more than one feminist literary critic who shunned female part-timers teaching composition just down the hall. For someone who administers an English department's writing program, this politics of the periphery is often as plain as gravity.

The very term *writing program director* is, as they say in linguistics, marked. Hardly any English department has a literature program director; after all, would that not be a redundant term for the chair? By virtue of your position, then, you may spend a lot of time brooding about how your concerns fit into a department centered on literature. Of course, composition has plenty of affinities, real or potential, with fields other than literary studies. Over the last few decades, composition scholarship has drawn on psychology and the social sciences at least as much. More conspicuously, first-year writing courses aim to help students meet the demands of various disciplines. Also, by now many colleges have instituted writing across the curriculum programs that formally link English composition to other departments. Still, because composition programs are usually in close proximity to programs in literature, the relations between the two are most apt to occupy a WPA's (writing program administrator) mind. Unofficially, we even become "directors of composition/literature relations," for we more than anyone have to figure out ways of making the two subjects coexist.

Relating them, I find, is not a matter of formulating some ideal synthesis that will persuade and inspire all parties. How you as a WPA refer to composition or literature, let alone to their possible links, may shift with context. When I give a paper at CCCC, for example, I feel able to criticize certain aspects of composition studies, for I am among people fundamentally committed to it. When I discuss the field with literary colleagues, however, I tend not to mention its internal disputes; rather, I portray writing specialists as a unified collective devoted to good. Similarly, whereas at CCCC I rarely mention that my dissertation was on Henry James, in literature circles I often bring up this fact. After all, at CCCC few might care about and many might be irked by my literature background, whereas in the second instance it might boost my credibility. In general, relating composition and literature is a fluid, unstable process that requires a WPA to decide what's appropriate for the moment. It involves, to use a classic rhetorical term, the WPA's sense of *kairos*. Of course, to bring up such a term at all is to acknowledge that relating the two subjects is fundamentally a rhetorical enterprise, perpetually demanding the WPA be sensitive to situation and audience.

Even an audience composed mostly of literature specialists may be far from hostile. In my experience, rarely do literature faculty declare open war on writing programs and on composition in general. True, they tend to imply that "English" is the study of literature, with the exception of creative writing. But when called upon to acknowledge composition's role in their department,

most of my colleagues in literature have endorsed its presence, if only by re-
fraining from explicit criticism. Surely one reason for their stance is pragmatic: Not only do graduate assistantships depend on the writing program's
need for labor, but the department benefits materially from the horde of students who take first-year composition. Reinforcing literature faculty's support for composition is, I would guess, professional awareness: A glance at any
MLA *Job Information List* reveals that positions in composition greatly exceed
those available in any one literary field. Also at work, conceivably, is the sheer
force of tradition. Most literature faculty probably find hard to imagine English without composition, whatever the degree of their personal interest in it.

In fact, they are capable of feeling embarrassed by their limited acquaintance with the field. As I have discussed elsewhere (*Between* 9), a number of
my colleagues in literature have shamefacedly confessed to me, "I don't know
anything about composition!" Unfortunately, they seem able to live with
their embarrassment, whereas they would never wish to appear unacquainted
with Shakespeare's plays, Keats's odes, or George Eliot's novels. As I have
suggested (*Between* 9), their ignorance of composition can be seen as strategic: that is, as a willful if unconscious effort to keep writing courses present but
marginal. Whatever their motives, they may leave you as WPA having to explain—perhaps over and over—what it means to treat composition as more
than just an auxiliary "service" to the college at large.

We composition directors could spend a great deal of time monitoring and
responding to literature faculty's slights. Yet obviously our work should entail
action much more than reaction. Just as we risk being consumed by the brush
fires, the daily crises, that beset writing programs, so too may we lapse into
paranoia and melancholy due to our colleagues' indifference. In the matter of
litcomp politics, as with our other concerns, we need to cultivate in ourselves
a feeling of agency. However limited our power, we need to *direct*, in that
term's best sense. Recall Parker's account of how the coexistence of literature
and composition resulted from historical contingency rather than metaphysi-
cal fate. Even today, the two subjects' relations with each other are always, to
use a current phrase, socially constructed, whether the faculty and administrators doing the constructing admit their influence or not. Writing program
directors in English departments cannot afford to forget that they, too, shape
their field's relationship to literature, if only on their local level. And the best
way to engage in social construction is through active effort, not sullen acqui-
escence in the status quo.

Here, I want to identify some ways in which we WPAs can try to confront
productively the politics of litcomp. I concede immediately that what I have
to say may apply more to universities and four-year colleges than to community colleges. The latter type of institution has, in many respects, its own particular dynamics; also, it is a sector with which I am only modestly familiar.
Still, I hope at least some of the following observations and suggestions will be

relevant to community colleges as well as to the kinds of schools I know better. First, I will deal with basic decisions that writing program directors must make. Then, I will turn to ways of educating literature faculty about composition, so that whatever decisions *they* make about the program are both well informed and fair. Because they can be woefully insensitive when writing program directors come up for tenure, I will devote a particular section to this subject. In a coda, I will discuss how litcomp politics are being played out in the academic labor struggles currently preoccupying many in the discipline of English.

BASIC DECISIONS

Immediately upon assuming the role of WPA, you need to decide certain things about your program's relation to literature. For instance, you must determine what part, if any, literature will play in your first-year writing courses. By now this issue has spawned a considerable body of scholarship, including a notable debate in which Gary Tate advocated a literature-based writing curriculum and Erika Lindemann argued against it. Personally, much as I like to read and teach literature, I tend to side with Lindemann. Allowing literature in writing courses does enable their instructors to draw upon the kinds of texts they probably know best, and often literature spurs more nuanced thinking than does many a piece of expository prose. But students need to practice writing about a range of subjects, not just literature, if they are to handle the variety of assignments they will get throughout their college careers. Besides, most students have already written about literature a lot in high school; at this stage, they ought to branch out. Just as crucial is attending now to their own composing, a priority that teachers may jettison in favor of explicating the literary work at hand. To be sure, granting literature egress in is less risky if it is confined to the second or third course of a sequence. At any rate, if you are a WPA in an English department, you may face considerable pressure to let literature utterly pervade first-year composition or to look away when some teachers smuggle it in. Graduate students may be especially eager to incorporate texts that are the focus of their dissertations or the content of their seminars. But you need to ask yourself whether literature will benefit your program's students instead of merely satisfying your staff's own disciplinary tastes.

Admittedly, skills of close reading developed from a background in literature can serve a writing instructor well. The question then becomes what sort of composition curriculum enables teachers to draw on these skills while preparing students to write in realms beyond literary studies. Lately, in fact, both literary studies and composition studies have newly resolved to look outward. Among other things, they now express interest in producing public intellectuals, writers who can engage a broad audience and shape its views on civic issues. To assign a curriculum this goal is to connect with politics in its larger sense. Even then, however, a composition course may have all kinds of content, and so you must still decide exactly what sort of political education your program will promote.

Within literary studies, plenty of faculty still dwell on stories, poems, and plays, though now focusing on their ideological elements. Furthermore, I would argue, several composition programs—guided by certain textbooks—still privilege a literary sensibility by calling for students to read and write personal essays that are basically exercises in identity politics. Even the textbook our program uses, Maasik and Solomon's *Signs of Life in the USA,* shows signs of this trend by including in its new edition Melissa Algranati's "Being an Other," a piece that begins as follows: "Throughout my whole life, people have mistaken me for other ethnic backgrounds rather than for what I really am. I learned early on that there are not too many Puerto Rican, Egyptian Jews out there" (570). I suspect that literary-minded writing instructors are drawn to an essay like Algranati's because of its novelistic emphasis on the expression of individual subjectivity. Often enough, though, such recitals of personal demographics, no matter how articulate and poignant, hinder the coalition building needed for social change. Just as unfortunate, this kind of writing implies that *any* civic involvement must be preceded by self-histories couched in eloquent anguish.

To be sure, problems can arise when a composition program focuses squarely on political argument, a practice also encouraged by several textbooks. In such a curriculum, often the topics become wearily familiar even to the students. They, too, can grow tired of debating gun control, euthanasia, and the death penalty. Besides, writing on these subjects can easily lapse into ranting.

A composition program can, I think, address politics while navigating between the Scylla and Charybdis of belles-lettristic memoir and didactic harangue. One possible approach is that taken by my own department's first-year writing course, largely designed by Christine Farris. The course's writing assignments ask for rhetorical and ideological analyses of images in popular culture, especially representations related to systemic power arrangements based on gender and race. As students move through a sequence focused in turn on clothes, packages, stores, ads, and films, they are encouraged to complicate their views of artifacts they have taken for granted. Meanwhile, their teachers make use of exegetical methods they themselves learned in literature classes. Nevertheless, the course's objects of study include more than printed texts; in particular, the teachers find visual imagery a departure from their usual academic province. Overall, the aim is to teach strategies of analysis that students can apply to a wide range of discourse, not just literature alone.

Even if your composition program steers clear of literature, as its administrator you will have to decide whether to award transfer credit for literature-based writing courses that students have taken elsewhere. When I first became a WPA, little did I know that I would be spending much of my time ruling on students' requests for exemption from the school's composition requirement. If anything, I thought, I would be helping students learn from the composition course I supervised, not helping them avoid it. But soon I found that exemption petitions are a major fact of a WPA's life. In some sense, actually, they are the dirty little secret lurking within guides to writing program administration. And often enough, a WPA whose program excludes literature is asked to accept composition courses that focus on it. Yet the concept of writing that these courses put forth—their aims, methods, and objects of study—may differ significantly from the program's own. At the very least, you as director need to be cautious about deeming literary criticism equivalent to whatever kinds of writing your program exalts.

Litcomp relations come into play, too, when you decide who your instructors should be in the first place. Almost invariably, the new WPA encounters a program whose staffing arrangements are rather entrenched, whether they involve tenure-stream faculty, adjunct staff, graduate teaching assistants, or a combination thereof. Yet current arrangements may not be the best, and as composition director you would do well to leave open the prospect of overhauling or fine-tuning them. For one thing, you need to make clear that having a background or interest in literature does not guarantee a person's ability to teach writing. Back in the early 1980s, at the liberal arts college where I then taught, the English department did not care whether job applicants had composition experience, though writing courses would be half their load. In the department's view, people with impressive credentials in literature were surely "smart" enough to teach writing as well. Although this attitude has not vanished, it seems much less common now. The spread of graduate programs in our field signifies that writing instruction is a professional enterprise, requiring real preparation rather than just sheer brains. When recruiting adjuncts, you may still have to hire some literature specialists who have never or rarely taught writing. But even then, departments are less apt than before to assume that such people are versatile. Rather, the WPA accepts the task of retooling them.

The situation with graduate students is roughly similar. At many universities, the composition staff is packed with master's and doctoral candidates fulfilling assistantships they won as promising scholars of literature or as budding creative writers. The "hiring" is done by the English department's graduate admissions committee, the majority of whom specialize in literature. Seldom does the committee believe that the applicants chosen will automatically teach composition well; instead, the idea is that the writing program director will train them. And many of these graduate teaching assistants do turn out to be excellent writing instructors. Unlike the hiring of adjuncts, however, the process of awarding assistantships may rob you of crucial authority. Plenty of us have been left out of the committee's deliberations, learning only later who will teach for us next fall. Furthermore, often we have little recourse if someone picked for an assistantship ultimately flops as a writing instructor. If you lack an ex-officio role in the selection process, you should campaign for one. After getting a seat at the table, you may fail to block some troubling candidates or to procure some you like, but having a voice in the process is still better than being silenced. Just as important, you need procedures available to you for removing any dismal teacher already on your staff.

OUTREACH

Decisions about curriculum and personnel are unavoidable matters in a WPA's life. But you can be apathetic or energetic about otherwise reaching out to literature faculty. I know of several writing programs that have not seceded from the English department and yet maintain themselves as a virtual fortress within it, striving to keep the literati distant and refusing to hire writing instructors familiar with stories, poems, or plays. Yet, not surprisingly, the keepers of the fort often wind up feeling more alienated than ever. Their posture can especially backfire when they must get the whole department to authorize a new hire or to tenure one of their present crew. As thorny as the literature wing can be, raising its consciousness of composition has to be on the WPA's permanent agenda.

In particular, as a WPA you must do all you can to remind the department that your program thrives intellectually, not just administratively. Working toward this goal means holding several well-publicized departmental gatherings where the program's staff discuss writing instruction. Even a workshop on marking papers, limited though this topic may be, can certify the program as a fount of issues and ideas. In fact, the writing program may be the catalyst for most of the department's discussions of pedagogy. Although many literature faculty care about teaching and seek ways to do it better, their field denies teaching the scholarly cachet it has long enjoyed in composition, thus making them more timid about organizing meetings on the subject. Even now, relatively few universities have programs that prepare graduate students to teach literature, and those programs usually take the composition staff's training as a model.

Especially worth your time and effort are workshops that touch on writing's role in literature classes. Obviously a subject like this increases the chance that literature faculty will come, especially because many of them would appreciate suggestions for teaching students how to write papers on literature. Indeed, many graduate students in literature have told me they wish their seminars would spend more time addressing their own writing and the rhetoric of literary criticism in general. Even at this late stage in their education, they feel they need to learn more strategies for making their arguments persuasive, including strategies more or less specific to their field. In particular, many of them would love to develop more skill in wielding the discourse of theory, which they were barely aware of as undergraduates. Ironically or not, few literature textbooks beyond the freshman and sophomore level offer genuinely useful advice for writing about literature. They leave the door open for composition specialists to shed light on the practice.

A similar opportunity can arise if writing programs offer workshops on new information technology. Composition faculty might even collaborate on these events with literature colleagues well versed in the subject. Joint consideration of how to use the Internet and the Web obviously has the value of bringing disparate wings of an English department physically together. But another benefit emerges as literature and writing instructors collectively explore how to create Web sites and contribute to conversations in cyberspace. These inquiries tend to blend analysis, the traditional domain of literary studies, with production, the perennial concern of compositionists, so that intellectual barriers between the two fields may weaken.

So far, I have mentioned rather formal outreach activities. But most of a WPA's encounters with literature faculty occur through everyday conversation in hallways. These, too, are opportunities for you to heighten awareness of your writing program. Even if the chitchat sticks with small matters of teaching, scholarship, or management, it can be part of your ongoing effort to inform literature-oriented colleagues about composition. Of course, no faculty member enjoys hearing lecture after lecture about another's bailiwick. On most occasions of small talk, any "lessons" that you provide may need to be brief, subtle, casual, and respectful, offered in a spirit of exchange rather than in a fit of sermonizing. Anecdotes about teaching and studying literature may have to be part of the chatter. Still, with a modicum of rhetorical maneuvering, the talk can turn to the writing program's current issues and projects.

Underlying all these remarks about outreach is one basic premise. Even if the department's literature specialists seem enlightened about composition, a writing program director should never assume they are. Almost certainly, their knowledge of the field will have gaps, which can harm the program if not anticipated and addressed. Even my own department, which is fairly congenial to composition, remains capable of holding a meeting where I had to remind my colleagues that "English" is not synonymous with "literature." We were reviewing a committee's proposal for a course designed to help M.A. students connect our discipline to various careers. Writing studies can be highly relevant to fields cited in the proposal, such as law, politics, and advertising. Yet the proposal failed to mention composition at all, and the person in charge of presenting it referred to literature alone. The neglect did not seem a devious, calculated ploy. Still, I felt compelled to raise my hand and point out how, despite its supposedly wide scope, the proposal excluded my program's concerns.

THE MATTER OF TENURE

That I felt able to raise my hand attests to the security I enjoy as a writing program director who is tenured. If you are without the security of tenure, you may want to stay mute in department and committee meetings, even when composition is disregarded or scorned. The untenured's temptation to keep silent is understandable. When others have the power to punish you for your views, speaking out carries risks, especially when you represent the peripheral. Ironically, literary studies now resembles composition and rhetoric in that all three fields have grown keenly interested in how differences in power shape writers' interactions with audiences. The same attention could be paid to the conversational dynamics of English department meetings.

It is a truth universally acknowledged among compositionists that one should never direct a writing program before tenure. Unfortunately, the principle is often violated. For many composition specialists, directing is all or part of their first academic job. The most important difference, perhaps, between their field and literary studies is that so many junior people in composition must direct writing programs while the average literature specialist turns to administration later or never. This difference in role means a difference in available time. Even with a course release, usually the duties of a WPA consume far more hours than do those of a literature instructor. Meanwhile, whereas junior faculty in literature are rarely obliged to speak for institutions greater than themselves, junior-level WPAs are supposed to advocate for their program despite their limited clout.

It would be easy for me to say that whenever writing programs face challenges, their directors should speak up whether tenured or not. But this advice seems glib, especially when the director's continued employment is at stake. I know that as a tenured WPA, I speak much more freely than I did years ago when I directed another writing program without tenure. To be sure, speaking freely does not mean speaking rudely. If a colleague's remark slights composition, my response is more often a gentle wisecrack than a fierce protest. Any anger I feel, I tend to share with composition colleagues backstage. In the long run, whatever our faculty rank, we WPAs probably gain more from tact than from tirades. Nevertheless, untenured WPA s are bound to face moments when even modest demurral sees risky. At such times, they have to decide on their own whether opening their mouths is imperative. Of course, speaking is easier for all composition directors when they can count on some people reinforcing them, so cultivating allies beforehand is important. Potentially these include some colleagues in literature, whose voices may resonate whatever the size of their chorus.

When a WPA ultimately does come up for tenure in an English department, all members of it may feel nervous. In reviewing the candidate, the faculty as a whole find themselves having to re-evaluate their own basic notions about their discipline. The process is well captured, I think, in Clifford Geertz's analysis of the Balinese cockfight:

> What sets the cockfight [the English department meeting about tenure, promotion, or hiring] apart from the ordinary course of life, lifts it from the realm of everyday practical affairs, and surrounds it with an aura of enlarged importance is not, as functionalist sociology would have it, that it reinforces status discriminations (such reinforcement is hardly necessary in a society where every act proclaims them), but that it provides a metasocial commentary upon the whole matter of assorting human beings into fixed hierarchical ranks and then organizing the major part of collective existence around that assortment. Its function, if you want to call it that, is interpretive: it is a Balinese [English faculty] reading of Balinese [English faculty] experience, a story they tell themselves about themselves. (448)

In the story that literature faculty tell themselves about themselves, composition is merely a subplot. If they taught writing back in graduate school, they now see their professional life as a *bildungsroman* in which they have soared to a better plane. Thus, when asked to let a composition specialist permanently join them, they may feel they are being pushed to concoct a new tale about their own histories. When considering in particular the candidacy of a WPA, they may be slow to perceive how this person's endeavors suit a career in English. Most likely they will be hazy about the nature and worth of writing program administration, just as they are apt to be unfamiliar with composition studies in general. When they say "I don't know anything about composition!," we have every reason to think they really mean it.

For instance, probably most literature faculty will not know the reputation of particular books, journals, and conferences within the world of composition. If you are coming up for tenure having published an article in *College Composition and Communication,* your literature colleagues will need to be told about that venue's prestige. Similarly, they will need help figuring out how your record should be divided into research, teaching, and service. For one thing, much composition scholarship focuses on pedagogy, whereas literary research has tended to leave teaching out of its intellectual inquiries. Thus, whether directing a program or not, a composition specialist may already be producing material that deconstructs the traditional three categories. Furthermore, someone who does direct composition may do many things in the name of service that involve research and teaching, too. The process of educating colleagues about this boundary-troubling work has to begin well in advance of a tenure or promotion decision. Even if you are a senior-level WPA, you ought to report program developments regularly to the chair and other key faculty, as well as keep them informed of events and trends in composition studies at large.

If you are a writing program director who has yet to come up for tenure, try to maintain a portfolio in which you note most everything you do. At tenure time, you need to be able to rely on more than just your own vague memories of your various accomplishments in the job. A detailed record of your actions will exert greater rhetorical force. Your log should include even those mundane activities that you yourself may be tempted to label "mere service," such as your handling of exemption requests and your observations of staff members' classes. Granted, record keeping can be tedious. Worse, on plenty of days writing program administration seems an endless immersion in files. Nevertheless, a file very much worth maintaining is the one that will document for literature faculty the nature and range of your work.

Many departments rely on outside evaluators when faculty eventually come up for tenure or promotion. If such is your situation, the best external judges of your work will be those good at explaining the composition world to the literature one. Unfortunately, not every leading composition scholar cares about this audience or excels at addressing it. But the realities of working in English departments have led many veterans of composition to develop skills of translation that they never thought to possess and yet are now willing to exercise, if only to spare others in their field the cruelties of ignorance. Once tenured as a WPA, you yourself can expect to be tapped for this mission.

CODA

Earlier, I noted that a considerable number of literature specialists are currently working as composition adjuncts rather than achieving the tenure-track job of their dreams. I want to conclude by returning to this issue of labor, for it may soon become the most-discussed aspect of relations between composition and literature. Already the MLA Delegate Assembly has approved several resolutions that, in one way or another, protest the academy's increasing reliance on part-time, limited-term hires. Even writing program directors who do not employ many adjuncts need to realize that this situation is stirring widespread concern.

When I emerged from graduate school in the late 1970s, I switched from modern fiction to composition partly because tenure-track jobs in literature were few even then. But academe assumed the dearth reflected a temporary recession. Supposedly, things would improve for literature specialists once the country's fortunes revived and all the faculty hired in the boom of the 1960s retired. Yet in general the job market in literary studies remains tight. One reason, as John Guillory has argued, is that the new information economy leads many students to think that courses in writing will yield more cultural capital than courses in literature will. Another reason is that, like various sectors of the postmodern order, the academy has chosen to limit costs by downsizing, by outsourcing, and by denying its workers steady employment. True, the last few years have seen marked growth of tenure-track jobs in composition, traceable to that field's increased professionalization as well as society's burgeoning need for information managers. Nevertheless, writing programs depend more than ever on adjuncts, many of whom hope for jobs in literature but are toiling long in the composition reserves.

Within MLA, the situation has sparked various responses. They include talk of unionization, proposals for steering graduate students toward nonacademic jobs, vague musings about increasing the number of humanities post-docs, and calls for censuring any department that is now little more than a temp agency. Whatever the feasibility of these ideas, the employment prospects of literature specialists are not likely to brighten soon. Nor, for that matter, are tenure-track jobs for composition specialists likely to keep growing. We cannot even be sure that the number of positions in literature or composition will remain stable. Most certainly, large segments of both fields will still teach writing on a contingency basis.

If, as a composition director, you supervise faculty of this sort, most likely you strive to ensure a good climate for them. Simultaneously, though, you ought not to settle for a contingency staff. Rather, the goal should be better positions, jobs that are full-fledged and truly secure. Meanwhile, you may have to combat the view that composition is merely a literature specialist's purgatory. You can sympathize with people yet to ascend to the job of their dreams, but explain to them that meanwhile, writing instruction has value. Its right to conceptual space needs to be recognized, whatever the ultimate politics of litcomp.

WORKS CITED

Algranati, Melissa. "Being an Other." *Signs of Life in the USA*. Ed. Sonia Maasik and Jack Solomon. 3rd ed. Boston: Bedford/St. Martin's, 2000. 570–75.

Bullock, Richard and John Trimbur, eds. *The Politics of Writing Instruction: Postsecondary*. Portsmouth, NH: Boynton/Cook, 1991.

Geertz, Clifford. *The Interpretation of Cultures*. New York: Basic, 1973.

Guillory, John. *Cultural Capital: The Problem of Literary Canon Formation*. Chicago: U of Chicago P, 1993.

Hairston, Maxine. "Breaking Our Bonds and Affirming Our Connections." *College Composition and Communication* 36 (Oct. 1985): 272–82.

—. "Diversity, Ideology, and Teaching Writing." *College Composition and Communication* 43 (May 1992): 179–93.

Lindemann, Erika. "Freshman Composition: No Place for Literature." *College English* 55 (Mar. 1993): 311–16.

Ohmann, Richard. "Foreword." Bullock and Trimbur, ix–xvi.

Parker, William Riley. "Where Do English Departments Come From?" *College English* 28 (Feb. 1967): 339–51. Rpt. in *The Writing Teacher's Sourcebook*. Ed. Gary Tate and Edward P. J. Corbett. 2nd ed. New York: Oxford UP, 1988. 3–15.

Schilb, John. *Between the Lines: Relating Composition Theory and Literary Theory*. Portsmouth, NH: Boynton/Cook, 1996.

Tate, Gary. "A Place for Literature in Freshman Composition." *College English* 55 (Mar.1993): 317–21.

12

Part-Time/Adjunct Issues: Working Toward Change

Eileen E. Schell
Syracuse University

The importance of the conditions of teaching personnel is the utmost because those are also the learning conditions of the students. —*Karen Thompson* (qtd. in Cox A12)

According to a survey by the Coalition on the Academic Workforce (CAW), a group of twenty-five disciplinary associations, part-time and non-tenure-track faculty comprise a large percentage of those responsible for first-year writing instruction. In the CAW/Modern Language Association "Survey," nearly one third (32 percent) of those who teach introductory writing courses situated in English departments are part-time faculty. An additional one tenth (9.5 percent) are full-time, non-tenure-track faculty, and 22.2 percent are graduate student teaching assistants ("MLA Survey," Table 2). Thus, in English departments only one third of all instructional staff who teach writing courses are full-time, tenured, or tenure-track faculty (36.3 percent). In the CAW/CCCC survey of freestanding writing programs, those that constitute a department with a separate budget and instructional lines from English departments, approximately one fifth (18.2 percent) of first-year writing courses are taught by full-time, non-tenure-track faculty, one third (32.5 percent) are taught by part-time faculty, and almost half (42.5 percent) by graduate teaching assistants. Only 6.9 percent of introductory writing courses are staffed by tenured and tenure-track faculty (Cox A13–14). Clearly, part-time and non-tenure-track faculty comprise a significant percentage of those responsible for teaching general education writing requirements.

Although the CAW statistics on the labor distribution of first-year composition courses are new, the story of the overuse and exploitation of part-time and non-tenure-track faculty is not. In "Overwork and Underpay: Labor and Status in Writing Instruction Since 1880," Robert Connors finds that writing instructors working off the tenure track historically have been ill paid, overworked, unsure of their continued employment, and ill regarded by their colleagues (108). Unfortunately, the same abysmal working conditions often exist today. Part-time and non-tenure-track faculty often earn piece-rate salaries equivalent to those of fast-food workers. In the Modern Language Association report on the CAW survey, the average annual salary for part-time faculty was $2,428 per course for 572 of the reporting English departments. Broken out by institutional type, the average annual salary per course was $3,492 for doctoral-granting departments; $1,715 for English departments granting an Associate's degree ("MLA Survey," Table 5). In the MLA Survey, only 16.9 percent of the per-course paid part-time faculty qualify for a health plan paid by themselves and the school. Only 15.7 percent qualify for the retirement plan; 9.4 percent for life insurance. For 69.4 percent of these faculty positions, no benefits are offered. Thus, many part-time faculty are forced to "get by" without health insurance for themselves and their families. Equally problematic is the fact that part-time faculty are often hired and let go at the last minute. Last-minute contracts often make it impossible to prepare courses in advance. Whereas full-time, non-tenure-track faculty (91.8 percent) are likely to have six weeks' notice of their teaching assignments, roughly one third (33.1 percent) of all part-time faculty in English do not (MLA Survey). In addition, part-time faculty, full-time non-tenure-track faculty and graduate students are frequently thrust into distance education where they often face oversize classes and minimal training and support (DeVoss, Hayden, Selfe, and Selfe 261). In addition, many part-time and full-time, non-tenure-track faculty are involved in administration and service activities: TA (teacher assistant) training and writing program administrative work, for instance.

The overuse and exploitation of part-time and non-tenure-track faculty affects tenure-track faculty workloads as well. Part-time faculty across the disciplines now outnumber full-time, tenure-track faculty, which often means that tenure-track and tenured faculty face increasing pressure to take on more advising and committee assignments. In addition, at many colleges and universities, tenured and tenure-track faculty face speed-up and productivity pressures to publish more, teach more, and do more service. With so many faculty working off the tenure track, the academic governance system is compromised, because academic freedom and job security are not assured to part-time and non-tenure-track faculty. As many labor scholars and historians of higher education have argued, the rise of part-time and non-tenure-track employment is part and parcel of the post-Fordist corporate academy (see Nelson). The overuse and exploitation of contingent faculty has serious ramifications for those of us who teach in and direct first-year composition programs.

In this chapter I examine how writing program administrators (WPAs) and others in our field have taken action to address part-time and non-tenure-track writing faculty's working conditions. My point in doing so is to share with new and experienced WPAs alike, strategies for making writing programs a place where part-time and non-tenure-track, or "contingent," faculty can do their best teaching. Although writing faculty continue to have a history of exploitive working conditions, our field has made a number of attempts to change those working conditions. The CCCC's widely endorsed and cited "Wyoming Resolution" (see Robertson, Crowley, and Lentricchia) and the more controversial CCCC "Statement of Principles and Standards for the Postsecondary Teaching of Writing" (see CCCC Executive Committee), along with the "Statement from the Conference on the Growing Use of Part-Time/Adjunct Faculty" (endorsed by NCTE, CCCC, and MLA), are indicative of our field's ongoing concern over part-time and non-tenure-track faculty's working conditions. In addition to these policy statements, we have a growing number of narratives and case studies of WPAs, department chairs, and deans working to effect change in part-time and non-tenure-track faculty's working conditions (see Anson and Jewell; Enos; Hansen; Maid; Ronald; Schell and Stock). Often, WPAs have served at the forefront of these efforts, working as "change agents" (McLeod 108), recognizing that quality writing instruction cannot happen when part-time and non-tenure-track faculty do not have quality working conditions.

WPAs AND THE POLITICS OF LOCATION

Though WPAs can serve as change agents, we also face a number of structural and political challenges that affect our ability to initiate changes in labor practices. As Sharon Crowley argues, WPAs are often hindered by their *own* working conditions:

> In colleges and universities that employ part-time teachers of composition, program directors often do not hire the people who teach the courses they are supposed to supervise; in large programs, directors may never even meet all the members of the composition staff. In addition, there is no built-in institutional assurance that people hired to teach composition know anything about it or how to teach it. Many part-time teachers of composition train to teach literature or creative writing and find, when they have finished their degrees, that no work is available in these fields. Hence they become part-time teachers of the required introductory composition courses, by default. All in all directors of composition programs are expected to take moral and legal responsibility for workers they did not hire and who may or may not know enough or

care enough about the work they do in order to perform it well. Given these circumstances, it is remarkable, to say the least, that the quality of instruction in required
first-year composition is as good as it often is. (6)

How should WPAs go about changing working conditions if they are not in
charge of hiring decisions, do not control budgets, and when they uphold a
universal requirement that at its base presents serious problems of labor, staffing, and curricular quality and consistency? What can and should WPAs do
when their institution and department's employment practices are such that
they obstruct quality writing instruction? In addition, what can and should
WPAs do about these working conditions when they are untenured and are
overworked, undercompensated, and concerned about their own jobs, let
alone that of part-time and non-tenure-track faculty teaching in their programs? Sally Barr-Ebest's analysis of women WPAs' struggles to gain tenure
serves as a reminder that most WPAs can hardly claim the status of "boss
compositionists." In addition, some WPAs *are* part-time and non-tenure-track faculty. A quick glance at the MLA *Joblist* or job ads in the *Chronicle of Higher Education* reveals that non-tenure-track faculty are often asked
to take positions that include administrative responsibilities.

Obviously, the WPA's power base (or lack thereof) and politics of location
will affect his or her ability to address part-time and non-tenure-track faculty's working conditions. The presence of a union or a professional association is also a deciding factor. Because every writing program and every college
and university has a complex set of economic and political circumstances, I
will not offer a one-size-fits-all set of solutions that a WPA should take to address part-time and non-tenure-track faculty's issues; rather I will suggest basic organizing principles and strategies, offering an analysis of the strategies
WPAs, department chairs, and activists have utilized and can utilize to address part-time and non-tenure-track faculty's working conditions. The key
in any effort to address working conditions, however, is to build coalitions.
The figure of the solitary WPA hero/heroine is often favored in our tales of institutional reform. Though individual WPAs can make a difference in addressing problematic working conditions, a WPA acting in concert with a
like-minded group of colleagues, a departmental or university-wide committee on part-time and non-tenure-track concerns, or a faculty union stands a
better change of achieving lasting changes. Before attempting reforms, however, a WPA should consider how he or she will work with others to make the
case for improved working conditions. What rhetorical strategies and what
actions will bring about change?

RHETORICS OF CHANGE

Many academics make ethical appeals for improvements in working conditions, grounding their arguments in the discourses on worker rights, employ-

ment equity, and social justice. Ethical arguments, though important, are ultimately not as compelling as appeals made to employment equity as it relates to students' learning conditions. An analysis of a comment made by a university president will illustrate my point. In response to the statistics on part-time faculty pay rates publicized in the recently released Coalition on the Academic Work Force survey, David Adamany, former President of Temple University, stated in a *Chronicle of Higher Education* interview that:

> This [the CAW survey] describes who does the teaching but not whether that has any effect upon students or not.... It may well be that part-time teachers are as effective or even more effective in introductory courses than full-time faculty, but we don't know that. This report gives us useful information but doesn't answer the fundamental question of whether the growing use of part-time faculty has any effect whatsoever on education. (qtd. in Cox A14)

Adamany's response reveals several key assumptions representative of the administrative logics behind the employment of part-time faculty. Though he is correct that there has not been any *hard data* (quantitative studies) that show the effect on undergraduate education, part-time faculty and WPAs alike know that problematic working conditions often compromise a teacher's ability to prepare courses in advance, spend quality time with students, and internalize a deep understanding of a curriculum. As Helen O'Grady, a part-time instructor who taught at multiple colleges in the Northeast, argues in "Trafficking in Freeway Flyers: (Re)Viewing Literacy, Working Conditions, and Quality Writing Instruction":

> [T]eaching more than sixty students a semester [and here she refers to the CCCC "Statement's" Guidelines about class loads per semester] did cut down on the amount of time I could conference with individual students and the numbers of drafts per assignment to which I could respond. Also, I think it is important to distinguish between applying the sixty-student guideline within one institution as opposed to more than one institution. Teaching sixty students full-time in one place is not the same as teaching them part time in more than one place. For example, multiple preparation with multiple appointments multiplies time spent negotiating different institutional philosophies and different student demographics, not to mention the time driving from one place to another. It's just not the same. (137)

O'Grady's comments about the effects of "interinstitutional" teaching provide an important glimpse into the day-to-day realities of contingent work. Seconding O'Grady's views, Walter Jacobsohn, an adjunct faculty member and union activist in the New York City area, argues that contingent faculty members do not have the time they need to reflect on their teaching and to contribute to a much-needed dialogue about higher education's changing student demographics:

> Unfortunately, the sense we [part-time and non-tenure-track faculty] make of our experiences too often goes undocumented and unpublished because we lack the luxury

of time and the venues to make connections among the theories of professional practice developed by established faculty. Our personal experiences, our common experience, and the lessons we have learned often go unheard and unrecognized. Nor do we
find time to introduce, conduct, and sustain a desperately needed dialogue with tenure-track faculty about the changes that are taking place in higher education under
our eyes [as teachers of service courses and extension courses], but without our acknowledgment. (160)

As O'Grady and Jacobsohn contend, those who are responsible for a large
share of undergraduate literacy instruction often do not have the time or the
compensation they need to prepare courses, comment on student work, meet
with students, and participate in curricular conversations because they are
teaching at multiple campuses. And what happens to contingent faculty
when they use uncompensated time to meet the demands of the job? The unfortunate answer is that many good teachers end up burning themselves out,
leaving the profession, or cutting corners to survive the demands on them.
The result is a seriously corrupt employment system and often second-rate
instruction created by second-rate wages and fueled by full-time faculty and
administrators who look the other way.

Even if the proof is there that the use of contingent labor affects the quality
of higher education, many administrators will say that there is no money to
hire more full-timers. The usual argument is that economic determinism, not
economic choices made by institutions and their leaders, has created the situation: inflation, rising costs, shifting student demographics, a convenient
oversupply of English MAs and PhDs willing to do this work. David
Adamany, former president of Temple University, concedes in the *Chronicle of
Higher Education* interview that contingent faculty pay rates are low, yet he
questions where the "money for raises might come from," arguing that
"[I]nstitutions don't have the resources to hire more full-timers … when the
full-time professors they already have are winning reduced teaching loads
and avoiding teaching introductory courses" (qtd. in Cox A14). Adamany's
response sidesteps the issue, passing the buck on to tenure-track faculty. His
tacit assumption is that full-time faculty avoid lower-division teaching because it is distasteful to them. This assumption may encompass some full-time
faculty's reasons for avoiding lower-division teaching, but there are institutional and economic reasons for this avoidance. The tenure system, especially
at research universities like Temple University, tends to reward and recognize
faculty for teaching upper-division specialized undergraduate and graduate
courses, not undergraduate writing instruction. In addition, Adamany's
sweeping comments do not address the teaching loads of tenure-track faculty
at community colleges, private liberal arts colleges, and comprehensive state
universities. At many of these institutions, teaching general education writing courses is a often a regular part of full-time, tenure-track faculty's work
loads and counts in tenure and promotion decisions.

Adamany is right that improving working conditions for existing part-time and non-tenure-track positions and hiring more full-time, tenure-track faculty will be an expensive proposition. Accomplishing this goal at nonunionized campuses will mean taking a hard look at how monies are allocated within college and university budgets. To improve working conditions, instructional needs must be balanced against other programs and student services the university provides. Educational dollars will need to be reallocated to instructional budgets, and the proliferation of managerial and staff positions must be reexamined as they relate to a potential decrease in instructional budgets. In addition, correcting the overuse and exploitation of contingent faculty will require increased public funding for higher education, not less, along with cultivation of new sources of revenue for funding higher education. In addition, we must not overlook organized labor as a major force in addressing employment equity issues in higher education. Growing numbers of graduate students and contingent faculty are unionizing. Coalitions of academics, students, and a range of university workers, including staff, cafeteria, and physical plant workers have in some cases worked together and, in other cases, separately, to launch labor campaigns: Fair Wage initiatives, campaigns against sweatshops, prison labor, and contingent labor issues. Together these campus, municipal, state-wide, and national organizing efforts are creating the momentum for a revitalized academic labor movement.

Whether one works at a unionized campus or in a "right to work" state where unionization is a far-off possibility, the most effective arguments for change are those that address how contingent faculty's working conditions may inhibit them from providing quality instruction. Chief administrative officers can ignore pleas for social justice, citing financial exigency as a prohibitive factor. When confronted with arguments from students and teachers that the provision of quality education is hampered by instructors' exploitive working conditions, institutions may think twice about exploiting part-time and non-tenure-track faculty. They may also think twice when their labor practices and their effects on quality instruction are held up to close scrutiny by accrediting agencies, coalitions of taxpayers, faculty, students, and other interested parties.

STRATEGIES FOR CHANGE

Within proactive—as opposed to reactive—administrative cultures, there have been a wide range of strategies for providing part-time and non-tenure-track faculty with quality working conditions. A WPA armed with the CAW statistics and with relevant information from professional statements and scholarship in the field can begin to take informed action and begin to build coalitions. In *Gypsy Academics and Mother-Teachers: Gender, Contingent Labor, and Writing Instruction*, I identify four strategies for addressing part-time and non-tenure-track faculty's working conditions: the conversionist (converting part-time positions into full-time, tenure-track lines), reformist (improving existing working conditions of part-time and non-tenure-track positions), unionist/collectivist (addressing work conditions through unionization, collective bargaining, and community organizing), and abolitionist strategies (abolishing the first-year writing requirement and reforming labor conditions). In the following sections I discuss the possibilities and limitations of each strategy, showing how WPAs, contingent faculty, and others have worked within and around the constraints of their institutions to implement these strategies.

The Conversionist Strategy

Those who favor the conversionist strategy advocate the conversion of part-time and non-tenure-track lines into tenure-track lines to protect academic freedom and tenure. This was the stance advocated in the CCCC "Statement of Principles and Standards for Postsecondary Writing Instruction," which argued that no more than 10 percent of introductory writing courses should be staffed by part-time faculty (CCCC Executive Committee 333). The conversionist strategy is also part of the American Association of University Professors' Committee G "Statement" on part-time employment, which puts the proper departmental ratio of full-time, tenure-track faculty to part-time faculty at 75/25 percent (44). The conversionist stance, although widely endorsed by faculty and their professional associations, has proved challenging to implement because of one simple fact: the price tag. Reversing reliance on contingent faculty will decrease institutional "flexibility" and cost savings. Because higher education leaders have increasingly embraced a business-oriented model of instructional delivery and because many sectors of the public do not regard the funding of higher education as a significant priority, the wide-scale conversion of part-time and non-tenure-track positions to full-time, tenure-track positions will be a costly and slow process; however, it will be a worthwhile one if we have any hope of saving tenure in our public institutions.

There are a few examples of departments who have pursued the conversion of non-tenure-track positions and TAships into tenure-track faculty lines. Reed Way Dasenbrock describes an effort at New Mexico State University to convert three TA lines per year into one tenure-track position over a span of four years, thus cutting back on the overproduction of TA positions and restructuring tenure-track faculty's workloads to include the teaching of general education requirements such as composition (41). Other institutions have begun to create full-time tenure-track positions devoted exclusively to teaching first-year writing courses. For instance, the University of Southern Connecticut recently hired seven tenure-track writing faculty with PhDs in rhetoric and composition to teach mostly first-year writing courses (Crawford). In many ways, the positions at University of Southern Connecticut are a realization of Eugene Rice's and Ernest Boyer's arguments for teaching-intensive positions that acknowledge that teaching is a form of knowledge making.

Legislative action also offers an arena in which to launch conversionist efforts. John Lovas, a tenured faculty member at DeAnza College, argues that "[e]ffective state legislation establishes a framework for addressing these issues but requires funding mechanisms to support such improvements" (199). Legislation about full-time/part-time faculty ratios has been in existence in the state of California for over a decade. In California in 1988, AB 1725, the community college reform act, was introduced. The bill specifies that the ratio of full-time to part-time faculty instructional hours should be 75/25 percent in California Community Colleges (213). As Lovas reports, "the initial legislation provided incentive funding for districts to move toward that ratio. For three years, real improvements were made. Then, a California recession dried up funding, but the colleges kept hiring part-time faculty" (213). Despite the legal mandate, the employment situation is still dire in California community colleges, and organized action is needed, argues Lovas: "Governors, legislators, and trustees must be made aware of the significant threats to quality in this massive shift to part-time teachers. Campaigns must be mounted among students, parents, and business leaders to support significant new funding to improve the quality of undergraduate teaching" (214–15). Taxpayers, contends Lovas, must "be convinced that the quality of higher education depends on maintaining a full-time professoriate" (199). The only way to achieve that goal is for faculty to organize and bring this issue to the attention of the public. Ultimately, the conversionist stance is highly dependent on the unionist/collectivist stance, for without unions, professional associations, faculty coalitions, and other concerned parties working together to address problems of funding and employment, the conversionist strategy will likely remain a set of ratios not a reality.

The Reformist Strategy

Many WPAs have worked tirelessly to reform part-time and non-tenure-track faculty's working conditions. In many cases reform efforts have been focused on local efforts to consolidate part-time writing instructorships into full-time, non-tenure-track positions—career-track instructorships—with improved salaries, health benefits, support for professional development, and often peer review procedures. A series of case studies published in recent years detail the development of such full-time, non-tenure-track positions at the University of Nevada, Reno (Ronald), Louisiana State University (Killingsworth, Langford, and Crider), New Mexico State University

(Dasenbrock), the University of Arkansas–Little Rock (Maid), and the University of Wyoming (Brumberger). Generally speaking, such positions offer renewable, long-term contracts, rank advancement, and salary increases. Although these positions enable important gains in salaries and contracts, they do not address the overall problem of job security and the erosion of the tenure system. Even though highly professionalized and often excellent teachers, non-tenure-track faculty can be laid off without the due process afforded tenured or tenure-track faculty. In addition, these positions constitute separate classes of faculty and separate and unequal systems in the faculty reward system. In her examination of career-track instructorships at the University of Wyoming, Eva Brumberger argues that "[c]reating a separate track of instructors to teach primarily writing courses in many ways makes this struggle for equity more difficult rather than less so" (105). Teaching-intensive, off-the-tenure-track writing instructorships are an improvement on semester-to-semester part-time contracts with piece-rate salaries, but they are not enough. As Schell and Stock note, "While a step toward achieving better working conditions, professionalized writing instructorships do not adequately address more fundamental questions about the weight and value assigned to undergraduate literacy instruction in the faculty reward system" (33). Ultimately, we have to examine the larger question of how our institutions reward undergraduate instruction and teaching-intensive positions.

Whereas there has been considerable attention paid to full-time career-track instructorships, less attention has been paid to creating well-paying, stable part-time teaching positions for those who want them, especially women or men seeking career flexibility for family reasons (see Enos; Schell). Tenure-track part-time positions have often been cited in the literature on part-time employment as a viable career option, especially for academics who wish to raise families while holding down an academic career. Most part-time faculty who want stable part-time work at better wages are not given tenured part-time work or job-sharing as an option. The 1993 AAUP "Report: The Status of Non-tenure-Track Faculty" reported that a minor fraction of institutions (6 percent) offer the option of tenure to part-time faculty. For the most part, though, these are not positions offered to existing part-time faculty but positions created for already tenured faculty who have retired, who have family responsibilities, or whose health makes it necessary for them to work part time (44). Elizabeth Wallace reported in her 1984 study of part-time faculty that institutions that offer tenure to part-time faculty tend to be private colleges and universities like Bryn Mawr College, Carleton College, Colgate University, Columbia University, Cornell University, and others; these institutions, she contends, can afford such positions (51). Along with part-time, tenured positions, job sharing has been heralded as a viable strategy for improving part-time faculty working conditions. In a job-share situation, two part-time faculty can share a full-time job and split the benefits; however, job sharing has not lived up to its promise for part-time faculty. Like part-time tenure-track positions, job-sharing situations are usually held by full-time, tenure-track and tenured faculty with PhDs who seek out such positions to solve a commuter marriage or to make time to devote to raising a family. Even as feminist scholars and activists have made many strides toward opening the academy for women, many women and now increasing numbers of men, especially since the humanities job crisis in the 1990s, are working in low-paying, part-time teaching positions.

One way to cope with these continuing problems, argues WPA Kristine Hansen in "Face to Face with Part-Timers: Ethics and the Professionalization of Writing Faculties," is through professionalization. Professionalizing part-time faculty is "the best route to pursue for the WPA who wants to respond ethically to the problem of the two-tiered faculty" (32). Hansen contends that professional standards documents like the CCCC "Statement," although useful, do not create the ethical imperative necessary to convince academic administrators to act. This ethical imperative to act comes from "face-to-face" relations where part-time faculty's needs and contributions are made visible and pressing (37). Inspired by her reading of Emmanuel Levinas's and Nel Noddings's theories of ethical relations, Hansen describes a four-step approach she undertook to professionalize part-time writing faculty's working conditions at her institution: (a) a memo writing campaign to raise administrators' and faculty's awareness of part-time faculty's working conditions and needed actions, (b) the initiation of face-to-face conversations with part-time faculty and higher-level administrators about part-time faculty's working conditions, (c) the undertaking of a peer institution survey to measure working conditions in comparison to other institutions, and (d) a week-long summer seminar on composition theory and practice, subscriptions to professional journals, and follow-up symposia in which part-time faculty presented papers on their teaching and continued discussions (36–40). These steps, then, led the associate academic vice president at her institution to form a committee of part-time faculty, which authored a report arguing for improvements regarding working conditions. However, the associate academic vice president's recommendations were stalemated when there was turnover in that position. Part-time salaries remained per-course-section rates rather than pro rata compensation and contracts continued on a semester-to-semester basis (41). Eventually, salary increases were made available to part-time faculty in the English department, although Hansen acknowledges that working conditions fell far short of the CCCC "Statement's" recommendations. Hansen's insightful case study poses the problem of sustainability. If improvements are going to outlive the whims of changing administrative positions, they must include a sustained organizing effort on the part of contingent faculty and other faculty groups to ensure adequate compensation and contractual stability and safeguards and protections to ensure their continuation. Those wishing to initiate reforms need a structure and process for doing so, a committee, professional association, union or other group, and they need a vision of how those reforms are linked to a national agenda on fair employment for college and university teachers.

The Unionist/Collectivist Strategy

A third strategy of change is the unionist/collectivist strategy, which is a multipronged strategy being broadly applied at a number of colleges and universities where part-time and non-tenure-track faculty have formed unions or professional associations. The unionization of part-time faculty (whether in a bargaining unit with full-timers or forming a separate part-time unit) is increasingly a path many part-time faculty and graduate students are taking. Part-time faculty like Karen Thompson, who helped found a union at Rutgers University, and Walter Jacobsohn, a former union officer at Long Island University Brooklyn, have experienced benefits and increased political solidarity through unionization. Thompson is the president of the Rutgers University AAUP part-time faculty union (193), and Jacobsohn was a union officer and member of a combined full-time/part-time faculty unit at Long Island University–Brooklyn (162–66). Such unions can often be strengthened through statewide coalition-building efforts on the part of unionized faculty. Statewide coalitions of community college faculty in California, the California Part-Time Faculty Association, and Washington, the Washington State Part-Time Faculty Association, have led to successful statewide organizing campaigns to improve part-time faculty salaries and health benefits. The California Part-Time Faculty Association, newly revived in 1998, promotes "professional equity for all faculty in the California Community College System by ending the exploitation of part-time faculty" (Brasket 1). The CPFA's goal is threefold: (a) to foster communication and resource sharing among part-time faculty, (b) to educate multiple publics about part-time faculty issues, and (c) to work to improve the quality of education through improving part-time faculty working conditions (Brasket 1). The CPFA, banding together with unions, professional associations, and local activists, sponsored "Part-Time Faculty Equity Week" (Action Coalition 2000 or A2K) in April 2000. A2K activists engaged in a petition drive campaigning around "Equal Pay for Equal Work," urging the state to set aside funds ($75 million) for improving part-time faculty salaries, which equal approximately one third the compensation a full-time faculty member makes for teaching a course (Baringer 1). California Governor Gray Davis recently earmarked $62 million for improving part-time faculty salaries, a significant victory (Leatherman, "Part-Time" A13). Washington State has seen similar gains. Keith Hoeller, a part-time adjunct philosophy professor at Green River Community College and cofounder of the Washington Part-Time Faculty Association, which represents the needs and concerns of part-time faculty statewide, has used the courts, petition drives, lobbying efforts, and organized action to get the issues of contingent faculty's wages and benefits on the statewide agenda (Leatherman, "Do Accreditors" A12). The CPFA and WPFA are two key examples of broad-based coalitions among staff and graduate and undergraduate students as well as those outside the academy.

Recently, the labor organizing of part-time and non-tenure-track faculty has moved into a national arena. A group known as the Coalition on Contingent Academic Labor (COCAL) has galvanized part-time faculty unions, professional associations, full-time faculty advocates, undergraduate students, and community activists to take up the issue of contingent employment, employment equity, and quality education. COCAL, a "national network of activists seeking to improve the work lives of the growing ranks of part-time and nontenure-line faculty and graduate teaching and research assistants," was formed as a result of three academic conferences held in 1997–1999 ("Adjuncts Unite!" 1). In 2001 the fourth annual COCAL Conference brought together adjunct activists, union organizers, full-timers, scholars, and others to address working conditions and to create a national agenda. COCAL "pledged to hold a national Equity Week in the Fall," organizing teach-ins, petitions, protests, and other actions to call attention to the overuse and exploitation of contingent faculty (Leatherman, "Do Accreditors" A12). As a result, Campus Equity Week will be held October 29–November 3, 2001.

One of the more successful COCAL campaigns, and perhaps a model applicable to the national agenda, has been conducted in the greater Boston area where in 1998, part-time faculty activists spearheaded an organizing campaign at the University of Massachusetts–Boston, which resulted in numerous gains: "half time status; full medical, dental, and pension benefits; and a floor of $4,000 per course" (Boston Coalition on Contingent Academic Labor 1). After winning these gains, the University of Massachusetts–Boston adjunct activists joined forces with professional associations, other union members and leaders to form the Boston chapter of COCAL. Cosponsored by the AAUP, local labor organizations, and undergraduate students, the Boston COCAL activists have conducted informational pickets at target colleges with problematic labor practices, held meetings to organize part-time faculty at area colleges (both public and private), and are working to help graduate students as well as contingent faculty organize (1–2). COCAL's "10 point program" connects quality working conditions to quality learning conditions:

- Equal pay for equal work at the appropriate academic rank.
- Full medical, dental, and retirement benefits for those teaching two or more courses per term. Pro-rated benefits for those teaching fewer. Tuition remission for family members.

- Job security. No one terminated without just cause and due process.
- Adequate office space and facilities.
- Full participation in department and college or university governance.
- Opportunities for professional development, including financial support for research and creative work.
- Promotion of part-time faculty to full-time positions.
- Narrowing of salary disparities within the faculty.
- Full protection of free-speech rights and all other forms of academic freedom.
- Recognition and respect as vital members of the academic community. (1)

As these examples should make clear, broad-based coalitions of academic workers are on the rise, often fueled by the organizing efforts of teaching assistants, part-time faculty organizations, and undergraduate students organizing against sweatshops. These broad-based coalitions are promising because they move the conversation from a local, discipline-specific discourse to the more broadly conceived discourses of labor organizing, worker rights, and quality instruction. Key to the success of such organizing efforts will be making the link between quality working conditions and quality learning conditions and convincing the American public that these issues matter.

The Abolitionist Strategy

Last but not least is the abolitionist strategy, whose chief proponent has been Sharon Crowley. Crowley, a former WPA and former chair of the CCCC Committee on Professional Standards as well as one of the prime forces behind the "Wyoming Resolution," has been a strong advocate for improving part-time and non-tenure-track faculty's working conditions. One way to achieve improvements in working conditions, she argues, is to address the root cause of exploitation: the problematic status and uncertain value of the first-year composition course. Instead of remaining in voluntary or involuntary servitude to the first-year requirement and all of its attendant ills with assessment, staffing, and curricular incoherence, we, Crowley argues, should abolish the requirement, not the course, and should institute an elective system. Abolishing the requirement will give us control of our labor, contends Crowley:

> Departments adopting the modest proposal will be in control of course enrollments, offering only the number of sections that can be responsibly staffed and supported. And, since such departments will know how many sections of the introductory course they plan to staff, far in advance of any given semester or quarter, they can redesign their hiring practices to meet professional standards as well as the needs of teachers of writing who reside nearby. They will be able to staff sections of the elective course with

trained and enthusiastic teachers; they can pay teachers in accordance with their skills and experience; they can hire them well in advance of their scheduled teaching assignments. I hope it is not utopian to imagine that in some schools these practices might lead to others: promoting teachers of writing based on the work that they do, and offering them security of employment in accordance with the standards that are used for all faculty at that institution. (245)

Crowley's plan is one for putting ourselves out of the business of exploitation; it is also a plan that asks for serious reinvention of the material base of composition. It is, indeed, a radical plan because it calls for the fundamental material and psychological reconstruction of our field. Perhaps the biggest prohibitive factor is the loss of jobs. Plain and simple: The first-year composition industry with its host of TAs and part-time faculty would be compromised; graduate programs built on supply-demand for writing program leaders, graduate professorships, and writing program administration jobs would have to be restructured or reconfigured. Crowley is aware of the possibilities and risks her plan carries with it. She recognizes that:

[F]aculty and administration at some universities will read the modest proposal as an invitation to eliminate or reduce the number of part-time and graduate student teaching positions at their schools, rather than engaging in the hard work and planning that are necessary to upgrade teaching positions, institute meaningful professional development, and write curricula for new elective composition courses. I leave it to my readers to decide whether the risk entailed in adopting the modest proposal ought to be undertaken at their schools. (246)

Responding to Crowley's plan, Charles Bazerman make an argument that the abolitionist strategy could turn composition professionals into an endangered species:

If there were no first-year writing courses to be taught and overseen, how many writing professionals would most English departments support? If there were not first-year writing courses, how many of the now-autonomous writing programs could avoid being folded back into other units? It there were not strong first-year writing program, how many writing across the curriculum programs could resist the drift of loosely monitored writing intensive requirements and the habit of disciplines to make their rhetoric invisible in the service of epistemic authority? (259)

Bazerman asks an important question: What happens when first-year writing ceases to be our material base? What new structures and arrangements would be brought on by the abolitionist argument? Crowley makes a compelling argument that there would still be demand for writing courses, arguing that "in documented cases where the requirement has been lifted, high numbers of students have continued to enroll in an elective introductory courses" (246). Crowley's plan has been discussed and publicized (Petraglia), although as of yet not widely implemented. For a number of writing professionals, the abolitionist strategy has become a way to radically reimagine our modes of practice and ways of operating (see Crowley, chap. 14, this volume).

THE CCCCs: COMPENSATION, CONTRACTS, CONDITIONS, AND COALITION BUILDING

I recite this litany of strategies to indicate the sheer variety of approaches to initiating change in exploitive working conditions. Although these strategies each take a different path, they all have a common goal: the achievement of better working conditions for part-time and non-tenure-track faculty. Regardless of the approach, a WPA, whether a tenure-track faculty member or non-tenure-track faculty member, needs to pay attention to the CCCC, the four elements part-time and non-tenure-track faculty need in order to teach successfully: compensation, contracts, conditions that enable quality teaching, and coalition building (Schell, "What's" 331–32).

Compensation

- Part-time faculty should be paid on a pro rata basis, their pay based on a percentage of full-time pay and paid out as a salary rather than a section rate. Rather than allowing for piece-rate part-time positions, full-time positions (non-tenure track or tenure-track) or regularized part-time positions should be favored.

Contracts

- As a general principle, an employing department should work to undertake a multipronged strategy to avoid ad hoc, short-term staffing plans that compromise quality education. Part-time and non-tenure-track faculty must be awarded year-long renewable and multiple-year rather than semester-to-semester contracts. Programs should consolidate part-time positions into full-time, non-tenure-track ones with reasonable salaries and benefits. At the same time, departments should lobby to create more full-time tenure-track positions, preserving some stable, well-paid part-time positions for those who wish to work part time.
- New and returning part-time and non-tenure-track faculty must have professional support: orientation and training for their teaching responsibilities, mentoring, access to technology, and professional development. Every writing program should have an ongoing program of professional development for part-time and non-tenure-track faculty and should provide opportunities for these faculty to obtain travel funds, instructional grants, and other forms of support for teaching and for research.
- Peer review and fair, consistent, multileveled evaluation practices should be implemented rather than ad-hoc arrangements (see Schwalm; Strenski).

- The CCCC "Statement" guidelines on class size should be followed, and basic components must be met: access to office space, computers, secretarial support, and xeroxing. Above all, professional support must enable part-time and non-tenure-track faculty to give their students the sort of quality instruction they require in order to succeed.
- The concept of collegiality must be extended to part-time and non-tenure-track faculty as well as full-time faculty. Teaching-intensive positions must be valued, rewarded, supported, and recognized by colleagues whose teaching responsibilities are different or whose research and administrative responsibilities are greater. Recognizing a common vision of higher education and a renewed understanding of the value of teaching is at the center of an expanded vision of collegiality.
- The movement to embrace a scholarship of teaching (see Stock et al.) is one promising arena for change that our field needs to continue to investigate and implement.

Coalition Building

How these elements will be achieved will depend on the strategies adopted, whether conversionist, reformist, unionist/collectivist, or abolitionist. As the narratives and case studies show in Schell and Stock's *Moving a Mountain*, the "organizing strategies that will work best [toward achieving that goal] must be adaptive and multiple" (337) and will involve coalition building (Schell, "What's"). WPAs can play a significant role in this movement for change, especially if we use our considerable critical and rhetorical skills to call attention to the link between employment equity and quality literacy instruction. A number of ways to begin this work are possible:

- First a WPA working with a composition committee or other departmental committee should study the available statistics and reports on the growth of part-time and non-tenure-track faculty, for instance, the data available from the Coalition on the Academic Workforce survey on English Departments. He or she can draw on the guidelines for equitable employment from the "Wyoming Resolution" and the CCCC "Statement" and can begin to create guidelines for employment practices that are suitable to the institution.
- Next, those statistics can be used to compare local conditions, to undertake local surveys, and to begin building coalitions with other faculty and students to call attention to needed changes.
- On unionized campuses, part-time faculty and full-time faculty can make use of the union's committee structures and can strengthen existing coalitions to bring part-time issues to the fore in the collective bargaining process. Increasing attention to part-time work issues on the part of the American Federation of Teachers and the National Educa-

tion Association bodes well for organizing and raising awareness about the importance of part-time faculty issues. As Karen Thompson argues, the UPS Teamster's strike taught us what is possible when part-time and full-time workers band together: "The combination of high participation by part-timers in the strike and the full-timers' willingness to fight for part-time worker's concerns was key to the strikers' victory" (192). Coalition building between part-time and full-time faculty is key to improving working conditions in academe as well.

- At nonunionized and unionized campuses, students can become an important group of advocates for employment equity issues. In "Same Struggle, Same Fight," Elana Peled et al. detail a "lay-off" of composition instructors that incited undergraduate students to action and coalition building with faculty at San Francisco State University. Peled et al. conclude that when students "recognize the kinship that exists between their own precarious social positions and the precarious positions of faculty, particularly composition faculty who teach a course in which they received individual instruction, they will be willing to join our fight" (242–43).
- Accrediting agencies, legislative action, and state and national coalition building also can be utilized to build public awareness of the issues (see Perley; Lovas; Schell, "What's").

CONCLUSION

Like James Slevin, I believe there can be no revolution in the teaching of writing until we alleviate the exploitation of writing teachers. We can propose and build innovative curricula, syllabi, and assignments; we can add on tenure-track positions and offer PhDs in rhetoric and composition, but until we make the working conditions of the majority of the field's practitioners a priority, we are shortchanging quality literacy instruction for our students. WPAs and the professional organizations that support them must be advocates for improving part-time and non-tenure-track faculty's working conditions. Why? The answer is simple, although the actions we must take to realize it are not: Teachers' working conditions are students' learning conditions.

WORKS CITED

AAUP Committee G on Part-Time and Non-Tenure-Track Appointments. 1993. "Report: The Status of Non-Tenure-Track Faculty." *Academe* 79.4 (July–Aug. 1993): 39–46.

Anson, Chris M., and Richard Jewell. "Shadows of the Mountain." Schell and Stock, 47–75.

Baringer, Sandra. "Kudos to the A2K Coalition: Over 40,000 Petition Signatures Gathered, and a Nationwide A2K II on the Horizon." *California Part-Time Faculty Association Pro-News*. 3.1 (Fall 2000): 1, 12.

Barr-Ebest, Sally. "Gender Differences in Writing Program Administration." *WPA: Writing Program Administration* 18 (Spring 1995): 53–72.

Bazerman, Charles. "Responses: Curricular Responsibilities and Professional Definition." *Reconceiving Writing, Rethinking Writing Instruction*. Ed. Joseph Petraglia. Hillsdale, NJ: Erlbaum, 1995. 249–59.

Boston Coalition on Contingent Academic Labor. "Adjuncts Unite! Newsletter." 1–2.

Boyer, Ernest. *Scholarship Reconsidered: Priorities of the Professoriate*. Princeton, NJ: Carnegie Foundation for the Advancement of Teaching, 1990.

Brasket, Deborah. "Welcome to CPFA PRO-NEWS!" *California Part-Time Faculty Association* 3 (Fall 2000): 1.

Brumberger, Eva. "The Best of Times, the Worst of Times: One Version of the 'Humane' Lectureship." Schell and Stock, 91–106.

CCCC Executive Committee. "Statement of Principles and Standards for the Postsecondary Teaching of Writing." *College Composition and Communication* 40 (Oct. 1989): 329–36.

Connors, Robert. "Overwork/Underpay: Labor and Status of Composition Teachers Since 1880." *Rhetoric Review* 9 (Fall 1990): 108–26.

Crawford, Ilene. E-mail post to Writing Program Administration WPA-L@ASU.EDU, September 4, 2000.

Crowley, Sharon. *Composition in the University: Historical and Polemical Essays*. Pittsburgh: U of Pittsburgh P, 1998.

Cox, Ana Marie. "Study Shows Colleges' Dependence on Their Part-Time Instructors." *Chronicle of Higher Education* 1 Dec., 2000: A 12–14.

Dasenbrock, Reed Way. "The Crisis in the Job Market: Beyond Scapegoating." *ADE Bulletin* 114 (Fall 1996): 39–43.

DeVoss, Danielle, Dawn Hayden, Cynthia L. Selfe, and Richard J. Selfe, Jr. "Distance Education: Political and Professional Agency for Adjunct and Part-Time Faculty and GTAs." Schell and Stock, 261–86.

Enos, Theresa. *Gender Roles and Faculty Lives in Rhetoric and Composition*. Carbondale: Southern Illinois UP, 1996.

Hansen, Kristine. "Face to Face with Part-Timers: Ethics and the Professionalization of Writing Faculties." *Resituating Writing: Constructing and Administering Writing Programs*. Ed. Joseph Janangelo and Kristine Hansen. Portsmouth, NH: Heinemann-Boynton/Cook, 1995. 23–45.

Jacobsohn, Walter. "The Real Scandal in Higher Education." Schell and Stock, 159–84.

Killingsworth, M. J., T. Langford, and R. Crider. "Short-Term Faculty Members: A National Dilemma and a Local Solution." *ADE Bulletin* 94 (Winter 1988): 33–39.

Leatherman, Courtney. "Do Accreditors Look the Other Way When Colleges Rely on Part-Timers?" *Chronicle of Higher Education* 7 Nov. 1997: A12.

—. "Part-Time Faculty Members Try to Organize Nationally." *Chronicle of Higher Education* 26 Jan. 2001: A12–13.

Lovas, John. "How Did We Get in This Fix?: A Personal Account of the Shift to a Part-Time Faculty in a Leading Two-Year College District." Schell and Stock, 196–217.

Maid, Barry. "Non-Tenure-Track Instructors at UALR: Breaking Rules, Splitting Departments." Schell and Stock, 76–90.

McLeod, Susan. "The Foreigner: WAC Directors as Agents of Change." *Resituating Writing: Constructing and Administering Writing Programs*. Ed. Joseph Janangelo and Kristine Hansen. Portsmouth, NH: Heinemann-Boynton/Cook, 1995. 108–16.

Modern Language Association. "MLA Survey of Staffing in English and Foreign Language Departments, Fall 1999." New York: MLA, 1999.

Nelson, Cary, ed. *Will Teach for Food: Academic Labor in Crisis*. Minneapolis: U of Minnesota P, 1997.

O'Grady, Helen. "Trafficking in Freeway Flyers: (Re)Viewing Literacy, Working Conditions, and Quality Instruction." Schell and Stock, 132–55.

Peled, Elana, Diana Hines, Michael John Martin, Anne Stafford, Brian Strang, Mary Winegarden, and Melanie Wise. "Same Struggle, Same Fight: A Case Study of University Students and Faculty United in Labor Activism." Schell and Stock, 233–44.

Perley, James. "Educational Excellence: Presidential Address." *Academe* 84.6 (Nov.–Dec. 1998): 54–57.

Petraglia, Joseph, ed. *Reconceiving Writing, Rethinking Writing Instruction*. Hillsdale, NJ: Erlbaum, 1995.

Rice, Eugene. "The Academic Profession in Transition: Toward a New Social Fiction." *Teaching Sociology* 14.1 (Jan. 1986): 12–23.

Robertson, Linda, Sharon Crowley, and Frank Lentricchia. "Opinion: The Wyoming Conference Resolution: Opposing Unfair Salaries and Working Conditions for Postsecondary Teachers of Writing." *College English* 49 (Mar. 1989): 274–80.

Ronald, Ann. "Separate but (Sort of) Equal: Permanent Non-Tenure-Track Faculty Members in the Composition Program." *ADE Bulletin* 95 (1990): 33–37.

Schell, Eileen E. *Gypsy Academics and Mother-Teachers: Gender, Contingent Labor, and Writing Instruction*. Portsmouth, NH: Boynton/Cook-Heinemann, 1998.

—. "What's the Bottom-Line: Literacy and Quality Education in the Twenty-First Century." Schell and Stock, 324–40.

Schell, Eileen E., and Patricia Lambert Stock. *Moving a Mountain: Transforming the Role of Contingent Faculty in Composition Studies and Higher Education*. Urbana, IL: NCTE, 2001.

Schwalm, David. "Evaluating Adjunct Faculty." *Evaluating Teachers of Writing*. Ed. Christine Hult. Urbana, IL: NCTE, 1994. 123–32.

Slevin, James. "Depoliticizing and Politicizing Composition Studies." *The Politics of Writing Instruction: Postsecondary*. Ed. Richard Bullock and John Trimbur. Portsmouth, NH: Boynton/Cook, 1991. 1–21.

"Statement from the Conference on the Growing Use of Part-Time and Adjunct Faculty." *ADE Bulletin* 119 (Spring 1998): 19–26.

Stock, Patricia Lambert, Amanda Brown, David Franke, and John Starkweather. "The Scholarship of Teaching: Contributions from Contingent Faculty." Schell and Stock, 287–323.

Strenski, Ellen. "Peer Review of Writing Faculty." *Evaluating Teachers of Writing.* Ed. Christine Hult. Urbana, IL: NCTE, 1994, 55–72.

Thompson, Karen. "Faculty at the Crossroads: Making the Part-Time Problem a Full-Time Focus." Schell and Stock, 185–95.

Wallace, Elizabeth, ed. *Part-Time Academic Employment in the Humanities.* New York: MLA, 1984.

13

Making Learning Visible: A Rhetorical Stance on General Education

Yvonne Merrill
Thomas P. Miller
University of Arizona

Imagine yourself in this situation, which actually occurred at the University of Arizona a few years ago. It is midsummer, and you are moving into your new office as the just appointed administrator of a comprehensive writing program. You receive a phone call from the provost. He would like you to give a presentation to his ad hoc curriculum committee on how writing across the curriculum can replace required first-year composition courses. About eight thousand students take first-year composition courses in your program each year. The program administrator you are replacing is out of town for the summer, and the chair of the English department is out of the country. You do a little research and find out that this group of deans and senior professors has been meeting over the summer outside regular planning structures and will make a proposal to overhaul general education at summer's end. What do you do?

This is the sort of situation that can confront a writing program administrator (WPA) as a result of nationwide reforms in general education. Administrators often want to take a public stand to improve undergraduate education, and writing instruction can appear to be the place to make a stand because there is nothing more general and nothing more generally criticized.

We responded to the provost's invitation by politely pumping his staff on the committee's deliberations, explaining that we would be better able to speak to their concerns if we knew what they had read and discussed. The group was reading articles from *Change* magazine and the *Chronicle of Higher Education* (the two most used sources at such junctures). We learned that the provost was imagining a core curriculum where composition requirements (and resources) would be dispersed into a writing-across-the-curriculum program. The group was looking at a core curriculum model from a University of California campus where writing was taught by an interdisciplinary "team of faculty" (actually graduate student graders overseen by an adjunct lecturer working for several "content" professors). By getting a better sense of the group's thinking, we were prepared to help them think differently. Their basic idea about how to improve the first-year experience was to require all students to take the same courses, which would be based on standardized syllabi. The provost discouraged talk about how five thousand entering students could be accommodated or how faculty from varied disciplines could be expected to teach from common syllabi. We were to think in new ways about general education, "outside the box" as it were. In this and other ways, this "visionary" approach failed to focus on the institutional pragmatics that would determine the curricular changes that were actually made after the two years of meetings that followed the provost's summer brainstorm.

By the time all the dust had settled, the provost, the vice provost, and other proponents of the reforms had moved on to other institutions or positions. As elsewhere, the envisioned reforms generated intense faculty resistance as soon as they were publicized, in part because the provost took a top-down approach to organizational change. He blamed declining public support on the faculty's inattention to general education, and he did not grasp how standardizing syllabi would be an anathema to faculty. We responded to the ensuing debate by becoming involved in all the committees that were set up to develop the new curriculum. As the committees got down to the actual work of developing courses and requirements, we succeeded in persuading people that first-year composition courses helped students to synthesize, reflect, and develop cross-curricular aptitudes, and were thus precisely what were needed to advance the interdisciplinary purposes of the core curriculum. Through our involvement, we came to know more about the institutional work that was going on than many central administrators did. We orchestrated our collaborations to make practical sense of the process in ways that were quite useful as the committees became mired in the rhetorical process of translating ambitious ideals into actual programs.

Here as elsewhere, reforms of general education targeted the writing program for several obvious reasons. Writing skills may be seen as a problem that composition programs have failed to fix. Unlike most major funding commitments, the budget of a composition program can be redistributed to support reforms because funds for adjuncts and graduate assistants can be reallocated whereas salaries for tenure-line faculty cannot, at least not without a high political cost. To develop convincing arguments for preserving such support for literacy work, we WPAs need to understand how our colleagues think about writing instruction. Proposals to redistribute "temporary" funding from writing programs can be reinforced by perceptions that students do not write well because composition courses do not teach the "basics," that writing is better taught in courses with "content," and that composition requirements serve to support bloated PhD programs in English producing unemployable graduates. Such tacitly accepted assumptions have explicitly been argued within our own field by "abolitionists" who favor eliminating first-year requirements, and such arguments can gain broader currency when general education comes up for debate if WPAs have not worked to publicize what composition courses do. The politics of general education demonstrate just how important it is to articulate the public mission of writing and writing instruction. Such articulations can be enriched through a critical reassessment of the civic tradition in rhetoric.

Taking a rhetorical stance on writing can enable us to see writing "problems" as an opportunity for collaborative deliberations on shared needs. As rhetoricians, we understand that controversies arise where established assumptions are called into question against changing needs. We should thus welcome intensifying arguments about general education as an opportunity to articulate how writing makes learning visible. We have all seen how students' writing can make learning visible in ways that can disorient "content" faculty. When confronted with students' writing, faculty members are often jolted because they can no longer assume that what they teach is what students learn. Once they recognize that courses are co-authored with students, faculty can begin attending more effectively to students' learning. Outside the classroom as well, work on student writing makes learning visible. Assessment programs generally focus on writing not simply because it has value but because it can be evaluated. Writing often comes to the fore in faculty development, learning centers, and teaching with technology programs because people readily see it as a shared concern. But the student-support networks that tend to converge around writing instruction, assessment, and general education often remain invisible to faculty. Such structures can appear peripheral to research faculty, who tend to map out a university around their own fields of study. General education programs tend to be built upon such maps, unless writing teachers and administrators can establish strategic collaborations that help faculty see the primacy of students' learning and learning programs.

These basic processes and structures can be better understood when viewed historically from a rhetorical stance concerned with the pragmatics of how knowledge is acquired and used in institutions of public learning. In this essay we will outline such a perspective by sketching out a broader historical context for assessing the institutional and intellectual issues that converge on reforms of general education. A civic sense of rhetoric provides a guiding vision that WPAs can use to help faculty recognize that writing makes learning visible in ways that reveal how disciplines work. When writing is viewed not as an isolated skill but as a means of negotiating situational constraints to achieve shared purposes, then work with writing can be situated at the center of debates over how shared expectations and experiences become codified in the conventions that constitute domains of inquiry. Such discussions can enable students, faculty and administrators to see collaborations on curricular reform as opportunities for reflecting upon shared purposes and broader public needs. Rhetoric has much to add to such reflections, for it has traditionally been the art of translating deliberative inquiries into collaborative action. As such, rhetoric provides an important philosophical and practical resource for publicizing the work that writing programs do.

WHAT'S GENERAL IN HIGHER EDUCATION?

Rhetoric began to lose its interdisciplinary presence as the liberal arts were reformulated into general education programs a century ago. At the end of the nineteenth century, university-wide programs of oratorical exercises on civic themes were replaced by first-year composition courses as the curriculum expanded to include diverse fields of specialized research. Many accounts have examined how these new composition requirements were set up to discipline the rising numbers of less prepared students, but this gate-keeping function was but one part of the general transition from a scribal to a print information economy within higher education. *Russell's Writing in the Academic Disciplines, 1870–1990* (1991) provides perhaps the best account for assessing how writing instruction was transformed by print in the first modern general education programs (see also Connors; Crowley; and Brereton). As classes expanded, student recitations became overwhelmingly time consuming. In the classroom as elsewhere, more work was done in writing, and standardized exams, textbooks, and courses on the mechanics of writing were instituted to cope with an expanding student population that did not plan on going into the oratorical professions of "the pulpit, the senate, and the bar" (Russell 3–5). Departing from classical models for oratorical education, universities often quit emphasizing speaking and did not teach writing well, in part because the research emphasis tended to equate learning with the transmission of specialized forms of knowledge. The teaching of literacy was subordinated to literary studies by those who set the humanities in opposition to expanding specialization, whereas "Progressive" administrators supported disciplinary diversification to improve efficiency and expand choices. Commonality was supposed to be sustained amidst diversity through a shared sense of the cooperative enterprise of advancing knowledge, but neither model really gave the needed attention to how to collaborate on teaching, learning and writing.

Caught between diverging domains of knowledge and the diversification of the student body, writing appeared to be a skill always and already in need of remediation—a prerequisite for professional knowledge that should have been mastered elsewhere. A student who failed to learn was personally inadequate and unprofessional, rather than unfamiliar with the complex rhetorical conventions of varied fields of inquiry—none of which treated teaching as professional work. Responsibility for writing instruction was downloaded into basic "service" courses to remediate students deemed to be deficient in basic skills, giving rise to the drill-the-skill mentality that still persists among many otherwise sophisticated scholars, even those with a strategic understanding of how to negotiate disciplinary conventions. Such practical understanding tends to remain tacit and unrelated to thinking about how such conventions are learned because academics have not been rewarded for making academic discourses accessible. Access generally tends to be subordinated to excellence within professional disciplines, humanistic as well as scientific and technical (see Russell). Students' failure to achieve mastery is seen as a result of their personal inability to learn a natural skill, rather than as the disciplines' failure to articulate its work to more public audiences. As a result, professionals, including professional educators, often fail to translate their tacit knowledge of rhetorical conventions into a practical understanding of learning to write, writing to learn, and the strategies involved in negotiating unfamiliar rhetorical situations.

The history of recent educational reforms can be traced back through the "culture wars" and "open admissions" to the waves of students who came to college after World War II and the wars in Korea and Viet Nam. Confronted with such "nontraditional" students, general education programs often tried to accommodate differences while maintaining conventional core curricula in the arts and sciences. Liberal arts models lost coherence with the proliferation of disciplines and the diversification of the student body, raising basic question about general skills and generally educated people (see Petraglia). General education often ended up being ill-defined catalogues of departmental offerings, often quite specialized and rarely oriented to the common needs of learners. In the 1980s the communication technologies of the information economy made writing seen less natural, and literacy began to be seen as a disciplinary construct rather than just a personal need. General education reforms intensified as Cold War research funding declined, and students became seen as "customers" needing to be prepared for a service economy. Reassessments of such needs have figured prominently in general education reforms. A wide range of college catalogues was surveyed in 1991 by Hurtado, Astin and Dey, who concluded that many different structures had emerged to serve the common goal of bringing coherence to the undergraduate experience while improving basic skills (see Higginbottom133–34). Increased attention to assessment and student learning has also been noted as guiding concerns by Jerry G. Gaff's *New Life for the College Curriculum*, which identifies a range of related innovations: Requirements have become more highly structured, sometimes into specific interdisciplinary or thematic clusters that combine arts and sciences materials with a more interdisciplinary attention to cultural diversity, ethical concerns, and global themes. Standards are better defined as a result of an increased emphasis on assessing learning outcomes. Basic skills are taught through more "student-centered" and active modes of learning, with collaborative learning and teaching programs often implemented to give more cohesion to the first years of college.

These varied institutional models often turn on efforts to redefine what it means to be generally educated. For example, this statement of guiding assumptions was established for the general education that was eventually instituted here at the University of Arizona:

> General education programs provide breadth of knowledge as a balance and complement to the depth provided by the major. General education is designed to accomplish several goals: first, to afford students the opportunity to learn how different disciplines define, acquire, and organize knowledge; second, to provide a basis for an examination of values; third, to develop analytic, synthetic, linguistic and computational skills useful in lifelong learning; and finally, to provide a common foundation for wide-ranging dialogue with peers on issues of significance. Taken together, the experiences of general education encourage the student to develop a critical and inquiring attitude, an appreciation of complexity and ambiguity, a tolerance for and empathy with persons of different backgrounds or values, and a deepened sense of self. In short, the goal of the general education program is to prepare students to respond more fully and effectively to an increasingly complex world. ("University-Wide")

Here as elsewhere, general education reformers attempted to balance specialized skills and knowledge with broader and more synthetic modes of inquiry concerned with learning by doing.

Many such efforts converge on basic questions about how to prepare lifelong learners with the skills needed to solve problems and communicate solutions. A model for the generally educated person who can negotiate differences is sketched out by Richard Clewett. Drawing upon theories of identity and society by Rorty, Gergen, Gilligan, Benhabib, and Habermas, Clewett argues that general education programs need to help students become "flexible and adaptable," with "a sense of self" as a work under construction. Clewett acknowledges that such a model can be criticized from the right for being relativist and from the left for being conformist. According to Clewett, we cannot sustain the Ciceronian ideal of "preparing the individual to take a place in society that gives sufficient attention to the individual's own temperament or individual nature" because we no longer believe in the autonomy of the individual self, though such humanistic models continue to challenge us to think holistically about learning (265). Clewett aptly articulates how many general education programs attempt to "enable the development of attitudes, values, knowledge, and skills" needed to be "morally and practically successful" citizens (269). This civic perspective gives new value to such "basic" skills as listening to others and negotiating the contingencies of differing rhetorical situations and value systems. It values composing a situated sense of self, not just in writing and speaking, but also in interpersonal negotiations where individuals have to determine whether to defend a position or compromise with others (275). To learn such practical skills, according to Clewett, general education must foster "thoughtfulness" by providing opportunities to solve problems, make value judgments, and work collaboratively on projects that foster cognitive and emotional development. Students thereby come to understand "the extent to which our ideas, values, [and] self-concepts ... are much more matters of local history and much less a matter of universal necessity than we usually think" (Clewett 274). Such generally educated people can effectively negotiate change because they value the differences that enable groups to imagine alternatives.

The civic dimensions of these models can be enriched by a rhetorical stance on the work with experiential learning, collaborative inquiry, and deliberative problem solving that is done in composition courses. When articulated from such a stance, first-year courses in rhetoric and composition provide models for reforms of general education. Learning by doing has long been a mainstay of composition courses taught as writing workshops, and compositionists are often involved in expanding the "undergraduate experience" to include community-based research and service learning. These efforts have the potential to transform general education because they challenge the hierarchy of research, teaching, and service that has constrained academic inquiry and marginalized the outreach and articulation efforts of comprehensive writing programs. The "service" mission of composition takes on broader possibilities in debates of the general education mission of institutions of public learning. Composition courses' lack of disciplinary standing can actually become an asset when administrators and faculty are considering models and support structures for the creation of "learning communities" in which students, and occasionally faculty, participate in interdisciplinary collaborations that reach beyond the confines of particular courses. If composition programs can help faculty understand writing from a rhetorical stance grounded in experiential and collaborative work, administrators and faculty can be persuaded to see composition classes as sites to synthesize and reflect on general education, rather than as adjuncts to "content" courses.

Comprehensive composition programs are often strategically situated to help university teachers and students learn to use the arts of rhetoric to enrich literacy and citizenship. While varied institutional contexts have produced varied structures for teaching and administering writing, a rhetorical perspective can help writing personnel play a vital role in general education, whether they teach required first-year courses, collaborate with faculty on teaching writing in other disciplines, or administer learning centers or assessment programs. First-year composition courses can play a "foundational" role in acquiring basic aptitudes, including not just basic writing skills but a rhetorical awareness of how shared experiences give rise to expectations that become codified in generic conventions. Courses that teach reading and writing through rhetorical analysis can help students think critically about disciplinary conventions and the political hierarchies they embody. Such awareness can be fostered throughout the curriculum by working with faculty to treat writing as a mode of collaborative inquiry concerned with negotiating new knowledge and shared values. Collaborating with assessment programs, student-support structures, and peer-tutoring centers, composition programs can help faculty and students develop the rhetorical awareness needed to assess how the beliefs and experiences of an interpretive community provide it with resources to understand its changing needs. First-year and capstone courses in varied disciplines can help students reflect upon, interpret, and synthesize their experiences inside and across disciplines. Rhetorical analyses of how audiences, situations and purposes are negotiated can foster the sort of metacognitive awareness that includes the emotionally engaging modes of understanding fostered by humanistic studies such as literature, and rhetoric can help students apply such modes of interpretation and identification to practical action.

WHAT'S RHETORICAL IN GENERAL EDUCATION?

Our history provides many examples of how rhetorical studies become enmeshed in formalism as formal categories become ends in themselves divorced from changing needs and purposes. When taught well, students can benefit from formal instruction in the conventions of academic discourses, but students also need to learn how to make use of the dialectical interplay of experiences, expectations, and purposes that constitute such conventions. As teachers of writing, we know that traditional didactic forms of instruction need to be combined with "hands-on" modes of learning to foster critical reflection through social interaction. Cross-disciplinary inquiries of the sort common in composition courses juxtapose varied disciplinary projects in order to make the rhetorical dynamics of academic discourses visible. At such interdisciplinary junctures, students can see knowledge making at work in different settings. Through the study of rhetoric, students can learn to assess how disciplines develop shared expectations about how practical situations are to be negotiated, and how these expectations and experiences then become codified into the generic conventions that constitute the work of the field. Through such study, students can reflect upon how disciplines establish shared expectations for texts, objects of study, credentialing processes, and the other conventions that determine what can be said and who gets to say it.

One way that such studies can be related to introductory courses in other disciplines is to focus instruction on heuristics that address the situational dynamics between texts and contexts. Just as other courses in general education provide students with the vocabulary to talk about fundamental principles and processes, a rhetorical perspective on composition can provide students with categories for analyzing how audiences, situations and purposes shape individual texts and the general construction of knowledge in disciplines. Collaborative, student-centered courses in composition can provide the experiential base for fostering a practical understanding of such concepts in action and interaction, while an attention to ideological critique and community-based learning can expand the frame of reference to the arts of citizenship that have made the study of rhetoric the bridge between academic inquiry and public needs.

Like traditional deliberative, forensic, and ceremonial domains of rhetoric, academic discourses are generally suasory, concerned as they are with convincing people to represent and solve problems in particular ways. As part of its attention to how to use received beliefs to address shared purposes, rhetoric has a long tradition of "ethnographic" study concerned with the practical art of developing persuasive accounts of experiences and values. This civic tradition can help students make sense of how knowledge is composed in academic disciplines and other discursive domains. Rhetoric can help students think critically about the generic strategies involved in:

- Observations and descriptions that use specialized terms for field-specific concepts.
- Analyses that deploy disciplinary categories to define particular objects of study.
- Syntheses of categories and concepts that form general interpretive schemata.
- Applications of such schemata to unfamiliar cases.
- Inventions of multiple and sometimes novel interpretations of those cases.

Faculty generally agree that such skills are the learning outcomes they value when explicitly asked about them in workshops and rating sessions, but such basic modes of inquiry are rarely defined in accessible and systematic ways, even in general education courses. Students have few opportunities to consider how a "hard" scientist's modes of observation, analysis, synthesis, and interpretation differ from those of a visual artist, humanist, or social scientist. Can a "common rhetoric" be derived for such problem-solving strategies, as

Donna Gessell claimed at the Fourth Annual Writing Across the Curriculum Conference? Gessell argued that such familiar categories as *assertion, evidence,* and *evaluation* are the rhetorical modalities common to academic discourses. Such formal processes can be better understood by drawing on traditional rhetorical heuristics for investigating the controversies that constitute disciplines, as for example in the case of *stasis* theory, which categorizes controversies according to whether they turn on debates about facts, definitions, evaluations, or procedures. Rhetoric has a wide repertoire of such heuristics for examining how public issues are transformed into disciplinary *topoi* in specialized discourses.

As general education reformers continue to try to make sense of disciplinary differences, rhetoric and composition courses can foster coherence and integration by providing students and teachers with ways to talk about negotiations of generic conventions. Although the easiest way to make disciplinary writing accessible to students is to have faculty share their own writing, faculty themselves often need to be taught how to talk about the strategies they use to negotiate situational contingencies in writing. Faculty sometimes perceive writing in rhetorical ways that assume that the specialized conventions of their area are appropriate for all situations. From her study of student definitions of "good" writing, Hildegard Hoeller has concluded that students often place a high value on what Clifford Geertz calls "common sense" thinking—thinking that appears natural, transparent, and logical, and not as a socio-institutional construction. Experts may compound the confusion for students by discussing writing in commonsensical ways as "clear, logical, and concise," rather than critically evaluating their own disciplinary methods. But such terms do not convey the same meaning to students or explain what modes of inquiry are at issue in their learning and writing. In fact, as Hoeller points out, academic discourses can seem unclear, disconnected and verbose to novices precisely because "to construct new knowledge or refine methodologies, received assumptions must be challenged and reframed." Faced with such disparities between what is expected and what is explained, students often find academic writing to be so alienating that they resist the academic texts they are expected to imitate. Though faculty may themselves fall back upon the commonsense virtue of clarity in discussing student writing, the faculty we have worked with in workshops will often go on to discuss how they expect students to "question authorities," "problematize received knowledge," "derive original interpretations," and "critique others' logic." Students who do not have an adequate vocabulary to represent such rhetorical demands may themselves revert to commonsensical modes of expression that seem formulaic, generalized, and lacking in the sorts of specific modes of evidence that seem self-evident to an expert in a particular field. When conventional discursive negotiations are made visible to students, they can be learned more effectively. A rhetorical stance can help both experts and novices assess their differing expectations and the ways those expectations arise out of different domains of experience that have become codified in the conventions that distinguish between them.

By active participation in general education reforms, composition programs can help institutions develop more productive ways to talk about writing to learn and learning to write. Compositionists tend to volunteer for a wide range of university committees because such service provides us with opportunities to articulate strategies for teaching, assessing, and supporting writing. At the University of Arizona, we have expanded such collaborations by setting up an advisory council of leaders from local businesses and agencies to help us consider how writing can be taught in ways that make sense beyond the academy, and we also work with community literacy centers and service learning programs to help students see that writing is about more than jobs. To make the work of our teachers and students more visible, we publish our own textbooks, which serve to strengthen the coherence and cohesion of our curriculum. We give our anthology of our students' writing to teachers in local schools and to faculty across the university to help them see how we teach students to write. We also publish an anthology of writings by faculty from across the University of Arizona to help our students and our colleagues see the university as a community of writers at work on issues of public significance. We also treat matters such as assessment as collaborative processes. Entering students from local high schools can submit portfolios of their high school writings (including an essay from outside English) to be placed into one of our composition sequences, and the portfolios are evaluated by local teachers along with college instructors. We are currently in the process of revising our midcareer assessment program that brings faculty from across the university together to share their responses to students' writing. This program has taken on new value as the only existing assessment of undergraduate education, but dealing with the overwhelming numbers involved threatens to swamp our other outreach and articulation efforts. All of our undergraduates are also supposed to have capstone courses that emphasize writing, and we would like to extend attention to rhetorical analysis to such courses. As in other comprehensive writing programs across the county, such possibilities challenge us to reflect upon how we can make writing and learning more visible as rhetorical processes that are fundamental to the work of universities as institutions of public learning.

HOW CAN WE GENERALIZE ABOUT COLLEGE WRITING?

Though David Russell's *Writing in the Academic Disciplines, 1870–1990* may be the best study of the historical development of general education and writing, it is certainly the most critical of first-year composition courses that profess to teach academic discourse. There is no "Academic Esperanto" according to Russell, for writing can be learned only by working within the generic conventions that constitute particular disciplines, professions, and public spheres. Russell maintains that composition courses are too marginalized and lacking in rigor to achieve the impossible goals set for them, and they should thus be replaced with writing-across-the-curriculum programs and "liberal arts" courses "*about* writing" ("Activity Theory" 74). Russell's research figures prominently in calls to abolish first-year requirements. Though we are glad that our provost did not read his work, every WPA should, along with the writings of Sharon Crowley and other "abolitionists" (see Petraglia). Abolishing first-year requirements may make sense in some institutions, but in others first-year courses are integral parts of comprehensive programs that offer unparalleled support for learning. We believe that the best courses about writing are composition courses grounded in the rhetorical concerns that we have examined in this essay, and from our experience, composition provides unparalleled support for student learning, not just in "student-centered" courses, but in writing centers, student-support programs and the bridge programs that are essential to recruiting and retaining students from traditionally under-represented backgrounds (see Thomas Miller).

When our provost recommended their abolition, we defended our first-year rhetoric and composition courses not simply because that is what we do, but also because all that our program does would have been weakened by cutting the courses that come closest to the models advanced by Russell and by many other advocates of general education reform. Though composition courses have often been reduced to the formal conventions of academic discourse, an emphasis on rhetorical analysis foregrounds the practical strategies involved in negotiating varied disciplinary conventions. Although there may be no generic academic discourse that can be taught in a formulaic form, the rhetorical strategies involved in mediating genres of discourse can be learned, formally as well as experientially, and the cross-disciplinary position of introductory composition courses provides a strategic site for such learning to begin. In first-year courses *and* across the curriculum, a rhetorical perspective on writing makes learning visible in the classroom, in the institution, and in other discursive domains. As they learn to attend to situational constraints, guiding purposes, and established conventions, students can develop a strategic sense of how to address the power differentials that limit access and determine who can say what. From the first year through graduation, rhetorical analysis is critical to work with literacy for citizenship. The distinction between functional and critical literacy turns on the ability to critique texts against contexts in order to assess the purposes that are served by the ways the issues are represented. Rhetoric's traditional emphasis on situation, audience and purpose helps students to see writing as a collaborative process of negotiating situational exigencies to deliberate upon what is and what ought to be.

At our institution and many others, administrators and senior faculty often fail to see writing and learning as collaborative processes. As a result, vitally needed reforms can be badly articulated. Unfortunately, many writing programs are simply too overwhelmed to develop the strategic collaborations needed to publicize the teaching of writing. In such collaborations as elsewhere, the rhetoric we use defines us and the work that we do. Rhetoric can help us foster a shared understanding of how writing makes learning visible. Reforms of general education present opportunities for WPAs to use rhetorical analyses to make learning assessable in order to gain increased support for the teaching of writing. Nothing is more important for WPAs to be doing if we are to confront the basic fact that although the teaching of writing may have considerable value, teachers of writing are among the worst paid and most overworked teachers in higher education. Reforms of general education will be of limited value unless we can persuade the powers that be to change that basic fact.

On this and other points, national trends in general education present opportunities for us to explain the value of what we do to broader audiences. Our interdisciplinary standpoint provides us with a vantage point of considerable power, especially if we treat our administrative work as a form of scholarly inquiry and do the needed research on the issues involved in reforms of general education. Too often taskforces and ad hoc committees make major institutional changes without bothering to do the sort of research that is required in any other form of scholarly activity. Considerable power can be garnered in debates over proposed reforms by ensuring that one is well informed on the issues involved. Looking beyond scholarship in our own area of study, groups such as the Association of American Colleges have published reports on how to begin curricular revisions with systematic assessments of learning incomes and then develop an inclusive process to avoid the sort of problems that occur when administrators revamp the curriculum behind closed doors. The Jossey-Bass Higher and Adult Education Series includes numerous related volumes such as Jerry Gaff's *New Life for the College Curriculum*. Works such as Gardiner's *Redesigning Higher Education* and Gary Miller's *The Meaning of General Education* position current reforms within broader historical and social trends in ways that complement research on the history of rhetoric and composition. The civic perspective that we have developed from such research can be supplemented by readings in such interdisciplinary journals as *Liberal Education,* including such articles as Cronon's "'Only Connect': The Goals of a Liberal Education" that can help reformers of general education to negotiate the strategic ground between abstract goals and existing course offerings. Research on interdisciplinarity such as the work of Julie Klein can help people working in composition to strengthen their curricular position by identifying their work with the national movement to redress the historical tendency toward hyperspecialization by establishing synthetic cross-disciplinary studies grounded on practical projects that involve issues that reach beyond the classroom, including service learning projects (on the latter, see Devitis, Johns and Simpson).

Much of the broader research on general education examines "innovations" that are well-established parts of work in composition, and a WPA who can position our work within these broader trends can gain considerable authority in discussions of general education reforms. For example, works such as Hutchings's *Behind Outcomes* and Hutchings, Marchese, and Wright's *Using Assessment to Strengthen General Education* provide a broader sense of the increasing importance of learning outcomes in reforms of general education (see also Palomba, and Banta). Similarly, those familiar with research on portfolios within composition studies can make broader claims for their usefulness by becoming familiar with works such as Sunstein and Lovell's *The Portfolio Standard*. Broader interdisciplinary trends such as the critical thinking movement provide broadly persuasive grounds for discussing reforms of general education, and work with writing can be given increased value by proponents who can articulate how a workshop approach to the teaching of rhetoric and composition can help students develop "skills" in collaborative thinking, critical analysis and public problem solving (see, for example, Paul and Binker's collection *Critical Thinking: What Every Person Needs to Survive in a Rapidly Changing World*). Such interdisciplinary discussions provide WPAs with lines of argument that can be used to move debates over general education offerings into more substantive and strategic directions. As such, they provide resources that WPAs can use to publicize and thereby give increased value to the work of composition and rhetoric.

WORKS CITED

Association of American Colleges. Task Group on General Education. *A New Vitality in General Education: Planning, Teaching, and Supporting Effective Liberal Learning.* Washington, DC: Association of American Colleges, 1988.

Brereton, John C., ed. *The Origins of Composition Studies in the American College, 1875–1925: A Documentary History.* Pittsburgh: U of Pittsburgh P, 1995.

Clewett, Richard M. Jr. "A General Education Focus for the Coming Years." *The Journal of General Education* 47 (1998): 265–81.

Connors, Robert J. *Composition-Rhetoric: Backgrounds, Theory, and Pedagogy.* Pittsburgh: U of Pittsburgh P, 1997.

Cronon, William. "'Only Connect': The Goals of a Liberal Education." *Liberal Education* 85 (1999): 6–12.

Crowley, Sharon. *Composition in the University: Historical and Polemical Essays.* Pittsburgh: U of Pittsburgh P, 1998.

DeVitis, Joseph L., Robert W. Johns, and Douglas J. Simpson, eds. *To Serve and Learn: The Spirit of Community in Liberal Education. Counterpoints: Studies in the Postmodern Theory of Education.* Vol. 37. New York: Peter Lang Publishing, 1998.

Gaff, Jerry G. *New Life for the College Curriculum: Assessing Achievements and Furthering Progress in the Reform of General Education.* San Francisco: Jossey-Bass, 1991.

Gardiner, Lion F. *Redesigning Higher Education: Producing Dramatic Gains in Student Learning.* Washington, DC: Graduate School of Education and Human Development, George Washington University, 1994.

Geertz, Clifford. *Local Knowledge: Further Essays in Interpretive Anthropology.* New York: Basic, 1983.

Gesell, Donna. "Assertion, Evidence, and Evaluation: A Common Rhetoric for Writing Across the Curriculum." Fourth National Writing Across the Curriculum Conference. Cornell University, Ithaca, NY. 4 June 1999.

Higginbottom, George. "Concluding Remarks." *New Directions for Community Colleges* 92 (Winter 1995): 89–95.

Hoeller, Hildegard. "The ABC of Academic Thinking." Fourth National Writing Across the Curriculum Conference. Cornell University, Ithaca, NY. 4 June 1999.

Hutchings, Pat. *Behind Outcomes: Contexts and Questions.* AAHE Assessment Forum. Washington, DC: AAHE, 1989.

Hutchings, Pat, Ted Marchese, and Barbara Wright. *Using Assessment to Strengthen General Education.* AAHE Assessment Forum. Washington, DC: AAHE, 1991.

Klein, Julie Thompson. "The Discourse of Interdisciplinarity: Perspectives from the 'Handbook of the Undergraduate Curriculum.'" *Liberal Education* 84 (1998): 4–11.

—. *Mapping Interdisciplinary Studies. The Academy in Transition.* Washington, DC: AACU, 1999.

Miller, Gary E. *The Meaning of General Education: The Emergence of a Curricular Paradigm.* New York: Teachers College P, 1988.

Miller, Thomas P. "Rhetoric within and without Composition: Reimagining the Civic." *Coming of Age: Rhetoric and Writing in the English Major.* Ed. Linda Shamoon et al. Portsmouth, NH: Boynton-Cook/Heinemann, 2000. 32–41.

Palomba, Catherine A., and Trudy W. Banta. *Assessment Essentials: Planning, Implementing, and Improving Assessment in Higher Education.* Jossey-Bass Higher and Adult Education Series. San Francisco: Jossey-Bass, 1999.

Paul, Richard W., and A. J. A. Binker, eds. *Critical Thinking: What Every Person Needs to Survive in a Rapidly Changing World.* Rohnert Park, CA: Sonoma State University Center for Critical Thinking and Moral Critique, 1990.

Petraglia, Joseph, ed. *Reconceiving Writing, Rethinking Writing Instruction.* Hillsdale, NJ: Erlbaum, 1995.

Russell, David R. "Activity Theory and Its Implications for Writing Instruction." Petraglia. 51–77.

—. *Writing in the Academic Disciplines, 1987–1990.* Carbondale: Southern Illinois UP, 1991.

Sunstein, Bonnie S., and Jonathan H. Lovell, eds. *The Portfolio Standard: How Students Can Show Us What They Know and Are Able to Do.* Portsmouth, NH: Heineman, 2000.

University of Arizona University-Wide General Education Committee. "The University-Wide General Education Structure in a Nutshell." <http://w3.arizona.edu/~uge/gened/nutshell.htm#TIER>.

14

How the Professional Lives of WPAs Would Change if FYC Were Elective

Sharon Crowley
Arizona State University

The editors of this collection assigned me the task of explaining how the lives of writing program administrators (WPAs) would change if there were no universal requirement in first-year composition (FYC). In 1991 I proposed that writing teachers and WPAs consider the possibility of dropping the universal requirement. My proposal has met with a chilly reception, to say the least. I hope to show here that the professional lives of WPAs and writing teachers would improve if FYC were made elective, and hence to make the proposal more attractive to those who may be hesitant to consider it.

The chief difficulty presented by the universal requirement, it seems to me, is that it ties scheduling to enrollments, and hence staffing in FYC is driven by the numbers of students who show up every semester. As WPAs know only too well, this makes planning nearly impossible. If the course were not universally required WPAs could control enrollment by limiting the numbers of sections offered each semester, thus ensuring not only that every section has a teacher and a suitable classroom but that every teacher in every section is adequately trained to teach FYC. A transfer of authority over enrollments would increase the quality of instruction in the first-year courses because WPAs care much more about the quality of first-year writing programs than do administrators further removed from the course who are more concerned with the bottom line. WPAs garner a second important advantage by dropping the requirement: relieved of the administrative burden it imposes, they would literally have time to think. In large schools that have a universal requirement, WPAs assume responsibility for the welfare of as many people as does the mayor of a small town—around fifteen thousand souls a semester at my university, for example. Because the WPA runs this large and complex operation without the resources that are available to a mayor—a comptroller, a bursar, a chaplain, a school board, a hospital, a police force, a librarian, and a fire department, to name only a few—she must take on their duties herself. Because of the enormous size of the programs they supervise, WPAs spend their work days responding to emergencies rather than planning for the future. And so time to think and plan is a precious commodity. Without the requirement, planning could be done according to the WPA's schedule, not the registrar's. And with time made available for thinking and planning, WPAs could begin to work toward installing writing instruction throughout the curriculum, toward strengthening and expanding writing centers, toward establishing departments of writing in institutions where that is appropriate, and toward offering writing courses outside of the academy where that is appropriate.

SCENARIO

Let's chart a bit of the professional life of a hypothetical WPA—call her Gertrude Buck—whose university has dropped its universal requirement. Professor Buck is WPA and associate professor of English at MyState University, a land-grant four-year public university somewhere west of the Poconos.[1] MyState enrolls about thirty thousand undergraduates and about five thousand graduate students. It has good professional schools in business, engineering, and communications that attract undergraduates locally and from nearby states. MyState has no medical or law schools, but it does offer a number of MAs, chiefly in professional programs such as Public Policy and Justice Studies although students can also earn MA degrees in the arts, sciences, and fine arts. MyState has only two PhD programs, both in the sciences.

Before MyState dropped its universal requirement in FYC, Professor Buck spent much of every spring semester trying to convince the vice president's office that she would need additional writing teachers hired, trained, and in place before the fall semester began. Every semester she was able to give the vice president the exact number of additional teachers required to meet demand because she had carefully studied enrollment patterns at MyState, and she knew to within one or two sections how many students would enroll in FYC in a given fall semester. The vice president's office nearly always rejected

---

[1] I do not consider the impact of my proposal on community colleges because staffing and funding policies in those institutions differ from those used in four-year colleges and universities.

her springtime requests, and as a result she spent the months of August and September frantically trying to hire (never mind train) people to teach sections of the first-year course—usually the exact number of sections she predicted in the previous spring—using soft money that the vice president finally freed up when he began to get calls from angry parents whose children were unable to find seats in a course required of them for graduation.

But no more. Five years ago, Professor Buck and her colleagues convinced the university administration that FYC should be made elective. They convinced university administrators to adopt their plan by arguing that an elective vertical writing curriculum would still make money for the university (though not of course in the stunning amounts garnered through the requirement), because it could be run more efficiently than a required first-year program. For one thing, the elective program could retain a quasi-permanent staff, thus reducing the expense of continually searching for, hiring, and training new teachers. For another, the student drop-out rate—which hovered around 25 to 30 percent of initial enrollment under the requirement—would be much reduced in an elective program, thus reducing the need for teachers to grade early on the work of students who would later drop the course. Obviously, an elective writing program could not be run as cheaply as a requirement that relied on exploited labor; but Professor Buck and her colleagues convinced MyState's administration that exploitative hiring practices were so costly to faculty morale and the university's reputation that they should be abandoned. They also pointed out that the ill will and student complaints that were a constant feature of the requirement would simply evaporate were the course made elective.

The writing faculty phased in the elective program over a three-year period. To date, then, two new first-year classes have been permitted to elect FYC. If things go according to plan, this year the university will approve implementation of the series of courses in professional and technical writing and in writing theory that Professor Buck and her staff designed during the past three summer sessions, supported by a combination of grant money and soft money garnered from the same vice president who used to be so reluctant to take her calls. These summer sessions are pure professional pleasure for Professor Buck, who loves curriculum development because it calls on both her knowledge of the field and her years of experience as a composition teacher. She works with a cadre of colleagues who have been teaching in the writing program for several years. All are highly qualified and experienced teachers, and they know each other fairly well—certainly much better than they did before the program became elective, when there was a certain uneasiness in the relation between Professor Buck and her staff because instant layoffs were always a possibility.

While the new elective system was being negotiated, Professor Buck convinced the relevant deans and provosts to upgrade the positions of people who teach in her program on the ground that better working conditions would attract better teachers who would stay longer and require less on-the-job training. As a result, her colleagues now work in contracted lines in which their employment is renewed every five years, and they have full health and retirement benefits. They teach three to four sections a semester depending on whether they wish to do research, undertake administrative duties, or simply teach. Their teaching schedules will soon become much richer than they were under the requirement, when everyone taught the same course. Once the new array of courses is in place, teachers will have a choice of assignments, working with courses that they helped design. But even now they are articulating unforeseen benefits of lifting the requirement. For example, they point out that teachers now have more time to plan classes and grade papers in part because they don't have to keep records of attendance, which was mandatory under the requirement. Teachers also report that because the introductory course is no longer required, students undertake the work assigned in it more seriously and energetically.

Professor Buck also has more time available this fall because she no longer has to administer the local placement exam developed by a previous WPA who was frustrated by the limitations of standardized exams used for this purpose. Without the requirement, there is no need for placement exams. About 5 percent of the sections of the introductory course are designated honors, and students identified with that college compete to enroll in those sections. Another 10 percent of the sections are designated ESL and developmental. At registration students whose test scores and/or high school grades suggest that they should enroll in any of these sections are strongly advised to do so. Among other things, they are shown a history of retention rates that Professor Buck developed for just this purpose. The study demonstrates that students who are advised into developmental courses and who stick with them also stay in school and finish their degrees. Professor Buck and her staff were surprised at the ease with which students slipped into this new way of doing things—whereas students were reluctant at first to elect developmental course work, more have been doing so in the years following the implementation of the elective program as they become aware that no one is forcing them to undertake the extra work that will help them succeed.

This fall, instead of scrambling to find teachers to fill sections created at the last minute to meet student demand, Professor Buck is developing a proposal for extending the writing center. Now that the need for this facility is much more apparent to faculty campuswide, she has been able to secure full-time lines for its administration. The capable person who now runs the center is very much interested in extending the center's services into a full-blown WID (writing-in-the-disciplines) program, and the grant proposal Professor Buck is writing will provide seed money to get started on that project. Later that day she will meet with the chairs of the biology and geology departments to explain the benefits of her proposal to their instructional programs and she hopes to get their support for it. Later in the week she will meet with teachers who are already piloting WID programs in engineering and business. These teachers are former colleagues and TAs (teaching assistants), so she looks forward to the meeting. Now, though, she is interrupted briefly by the composition staff person, who needs a signature. Professor Buck reflects that her staff person's demeanor has greatly improved because he no longer has to deal with angry transfer students whose first-year courses at other universities were deemed not to meet the terms of MyState's composition requirement. The headache of transfer evaluation simply disappeared along with the requirement.

Professor Buck steps into the outer office to refill her coffee cup, and while there she chats briefly with a new TA she met during the TA workshop held the week before classes began. She and her teaching staff will visit this TA's classes several times during the semester, and she is interested in his scholarly work as well. She wonders if she should write him into the proposal she is working on, because he is doing research on WID programs. They chat briefly about an assignment he has designed, and she returns to her office, making a note to be sure the new TAs are told in their weekly workshop about the teaching opportunities that will be available to them once the new curriculum is in place. Before she resumes work on the proposal, Professor Buck sips her coffee and reflects on the way life was when FYC was required of every student who matriculated at My State, when her time was literally consumed with student and faculty complaints, transfer evaluation, textbook selection, updating course policies, rewriting the standard syllabus, and justifying the requirement to parents and the coaches of MyState's athletic teams, when her professional time seemed to be devoted to issues that mattered to everyone but herself and her staff.

EFFECTS ON EMPLOYMENT

My proposal to drop the requirement has been in circulation for over ten years now. I first forwarded it out of desperation, hoping that my or anyone's taking such an outrageous position might draw attention to the important issue—the appalling working conditions that face teachers of FYC. In the aftermath of CCCC's adoption of the Wyoming Resolution in 1988, I thought that if we could just get rid of the requirement, we might be able to bring some sanity and compassion to the hiring of the people who teach FYC. That was before I was confronted with the immense sticking power of the required first-year course, as I have since been, or with the intense resistance the proposal has received from WPAs and from the very people I am trying to help—marginally employed composition teachers.

Obviously, the proposal has been negatively received in part because WPAs and composition teachers fear that if the universal requirement is

abandoned, they will lose their jobs. This reaction is common, and it is born of
the fear and powerlessness inflicted on teachers of the first-year course by current hiring practices. But there are two major reasons why across-the-board
loss of jobs and positions need not necessarily result from dropping the requirement.

First, students will elect good writing courses in well-run writing programs.
In the few times and places where the requirement has been abandoned, students have continued to enroll in FYC courses (Brannon, Hoover). Evidence
also suggests that FYC enjoys good word-of-mouth among students; for example, my university interviews graduating seniors who regularly report that FYC
was good for them in some way. I suspect that other schools report similar findings. I acknowledge that some, perhaps many, entering students will not elect
FYC if they are not required to take it. However, I expect that those who duck
writing courses early in their academic careers will elect them later on when
their more advanced course work impresses upon them the importance of
learning to write well. Other departments with reputations for rigor and hard
work—mathematics, philosophy, and history, for example—all continue to
prosper under the elective system, and I see no reason why composition could
not do so as well. If the worst does happen and students flee composition in
droves once it is no longer required, the size of composition programs and of
English departments will shrink. Those who fear such a development might
want to ask themselves if they wish to continue professing a field whose study
and practice must be forced upon undergraduates. I understand that my proposal entails disciplinary consequences, insofar as many people discover the
"joys" of composition because they are forced by the universal requirement either to teach or to study it. If the first-year course were not required, this argument goes, far fewer people would be attracted into composition studies as
teachers and researchers. Despite the empirical persuasiveness of this argument, I worry about the ethics of maintaining the sheer size of a field by requiring its study of all who wish to pursue a college degree.

Second, job loss can be avoided with careful planning and by virtue of natural rates of attrition among composition teachers. At most schools it would
take time to implement the proposal fully—perhaps two to five years—and in
that time careful planning must be done in order to insure that the number of
teachers who move away, get full-time jobs, and/or finish degrees at a given location matches the declining numbers of composition sections offered. I assume that universities would beef up writing centers and WAC/WID
(writing-across-the-curriculum/writing-in-the-disciplines) programs where
appropriate and that composition specialists would put a vertical elective
composition curriculum in place at the same time as they phase out the requirement. However the requirement is phased out, the point not to be lost is
that in an elective curriculum the size of the composition program is under
the control of its WPA rather than the admissions office, as is now the case.

Elective composition courses would mean, of course, that composition studies would have to sell its courses just as any other discipline does. This should not be difficult, given the reputed importance of FYC to students' professional lives.

Last, and let's be honest here, composition programs can afford to lose some positions—I refer to those very temporary positions that WPAs scramble to fill every fall as an extra one hundred or one thousand freshmen show up on the university's doorstep, expecting to be accommodated in a section of the universally-required course. Many of these latecomer freshmen disappear by spring semester, and so do their teachers' jobs. As matters now stand, then, those last-hired first-fired positions offer little in the way of compensation or status, and nothing at all in the way of benefits or security of employment.

Now that I've put the issue of job loss on the table, I feel that I must announce once again my utter sympathy with those who must teach in marginal positions in order to feed their families. I greatly respect the continuing high quality of their teaching under conditions that systematically disinvite excellence. I admire their resourcefulness, resilience, serenity, and patience. My sympathy and admiration for composition teachers do not entail, however, that I must respect their conditions of employment. I simply cannot accept the argument that FYC must remain required in order to employ everyone who wants a teaching position in the university. Far too many people are still being admitted to graduate work in English solely in order to maintain the size and specialized nature of graduate programs in literary studies and creative writing, at a time when there are precious few tenure-stream full-time jobs available in these fields. In other words, full-time faculty in creative writing and literary studies create the pool of unemployed teachers whose thwarted expectations are exploited by universities. I refuse to endorse a scam that benefits full-time faculty at the same time as it oppresses graduate students, marginally employed teachers of composition, and millions of freshmen. The implementation of an elective first-year writing program whose staffing was under the direct control of a WPA would discourage English departments from persisting in this unethical practice.

TENURE AND TEACHING

If I were now permitted to modify my original proposal, I would abandon its defense of tenure. I inherited this position from discussions of the Committee on Professional Standards, the group charged by CCCC to implement the Wyoming Resolution. In the report issued to the profession in 1991, the committee hung onto the concept of tenure because at that time tenure looked like the best available ground from which to assail the increasing use of marginally employed teachers ("Report"). The defense of tenure also allowed the committee to argue that all postsecondary writing teachers who present the

appropriate qualifications and who are hired under appropriate circumstances are entitled to the same academic benefits enjoyed by any other college teacher, including and especially academic freedom. Provision of this
benefit, in other words, was as compelling for composition teachers as it was
for literary scholars, political scientists, or biologists. Representatives of marginally employed teachers were quick to point out to committee members
that this argument supports composition's claim to disciplinarity, whereas
any aid or comfort it might offer to marginally employed teachers depends on
the possibility of their becoming researchers rather than teachers. Nonetheless, the argument that tenure protects academic freedom still seems compelling to me, particularly given the relative lack of academic freedom entailed
in current staffing practices in FYC, where teachers are often forbidden by
program policies to create their own assignments, choose their own textbooks, or design their own syllabi. Marginally employed writing teachers understand perfectly that their conditions of employment deny them academic
freedom, and hence they are careful never to seem to be rocking the boat, uncomfortable as the boat may be.

Today, however, I am convinced that tenure will eventually be awarded to
so few people that its effects on curriculum and planning will become negligible. When I first proposed abandonment of the universal requirement I did
not fully realize the extent to which universities had changed between about
1975 and 1990. During that time, universities got incorporated—by which
term I mean that they began to be run like corporations—to make money, to
turn out more (always more) and better "product" more efficiently and ever
more cheaply. As state legislatures and private donors decreased their support
of universities during the relatively hard times of the 1970s and early 1980s,
large numbers of full-time faculty were retired or retrenched and, when students kept on coming to college (as they tend to do in economic hard times)
the vacant faculty lines were filled by part-time workers. When administrators realized that this temporary measure was a moneymaker, they made it a
permanent feature of their hiring practices. At the same time, universities began to hire more (and more expensive) administrators to run programs and
offices that have little to do with delivery of instruction and much to do with
maintaining their images and jollying potential donors. It does not stretch the
term too far to say that downsizing of instructional staff and reallocation of
salaries away from faculty lines toward administration (and technology) has
resulted in the outsourcing of lower-division undergraduate education. For
the foreseeable future, I believe, tenure will continue to be confined (as it
now is) to about one third of faculty positions (Nelson/Watt 25). From the
point of view of the people who now manage them, universities simply do not
need tenured faculty members (Aronowitz 76). Tenured faculty have a degree of autonomy that unsettles corporate planning. In addition their presence in appreciable numbers reduces the flexibility with which administrators

can respond to fluctuations in enrollment, both in the university as a whole and among disciplines as their relative importance to the job market shifts.

So I now think that those of us who are concerned about the future of composition studies should try to establish respectable, well-paid, infinitely renewable teaching positions that will make professional life bearable, even satisfactory, for those who occupy them.[2] We should make sure that these positions are as secure as they can be made to be, particularly in states where workers are not protected either by state law or by union affiliation. People who teach composition should enjoy benefits, salaries, and working conditions commensurate with their contributions to the university and they should teach a wide range of exciting courses developed to function within a vertical elective composition program. Whether or not they do research is a question that should be negotiated by each employee. I imagine a college teaching career which is secure and throughout which teachers may do some teaching-related or administrative research, for which they are rewarded with higher salaries and/or promotion. People who want to do research in addition to teaching, I would hope, would still look to the tenure track for positions.

THE VELCRO PROFESSOR

As matters now stand, the WPA at most colleges and universities is "the velcro professor."[3] All the negative effects of the requirement stick to her though she gets little credit or reward for holding it all together. The position of WPA is unique in the university: the person who holds it has enormous responsibility and almost no power, serving as she does at the pleasure of a chair of an English department whose scholarly interests and pedagogical commitments often lie elsewhere than with rhetoric and composition. At many universities the staff and students in the FYC program outnumber those of other departments and colleges, and yet WPAs are paid far less than chairs and deans. Upper-level administrators want the first-year writing program to run smoothly, with no uproar, and yet the small interactive classrooms that typify contemporary writing instruction invite confrontation between teacher and students or among students in a way that is simply not available in the large lecture sections in which other kinds of introductory instruction are delivered. Parents assure WPAs that the universal requirement is a necessary part of undergraduate education, until it is their child who has been unable to escape it. Coaches promise that they will get their athletes to class and that ath-

---

[2]Michael Murphy has recently argued that the picture I paint here is largely a myth and that part-timers are treated better these days. If this is true that part-timers now have better benefits, salaries, and other working conditions, I attribute this development to the current high rate of unemployment. When the economy worsens and more workers are available to fill low-end jobs, I hope that these gains are not washed away.

[3]Apparently, Lynn Bloom is to be credited with coinage of this term. I thank Katherine Heenan, Maureen Goggin, and Janice Norton for their help during the drafting of this essay.

letes will write their own papers—until it is the star setter or quarterback who fails the class for non-attendance or non-participation. Even though the WPA may seem to her staff to own great institutional power, from the point of view of her supervisors she is eminently expendable if she refuses to accede to the desires of powerful faculty or higher-level administrators—as WPAs at major universities have discovered in recent years.

I think that dropping the universal requirement would effect change for the better in the professional lives of WPAs. Making the first-year course elective would also eliminate the corrosive and harmful hiring practices that now typify staffing in FYC. Students would benefit from electivity insofar as they might enjoy the introductory course more were they to select it rather than having it imposed on them; in addition they might feel less inclined to plagiarize than they now do if they had convinced themselves of the worth of the course. Electivity would also stimulate curriculum development and composition research. If WPAs, composition specialists, and writing teachers were not saddled with a universal requirement in FYC, they could devote more of their time to the development of vertical elective curricula in writing, composing theory, and rhetoric. A variety of courses could be offered at the introductory level, and/or, if the introductory writing program remains large, WPAs might feel more comfortable than they now do in allowing teachers to devise and implement new curricula or courses, because both hiring practices and professional development should improve in an elective program. The relative permanence of the staff should improve curricular planning as well.

Even as I write, I realize that much of this sounds like pie in the sky. That realization testifies to the weight exerted on my professional imagination by a required FYC program. Faculty in most other disciplines long ago established vertical curricula on both the undergraduate and graduate levels whereas we in composition have just begun to develop upper-division undergraduate curricula. And even now we often establish non-introductory courses not from a desire to define and practice a discipline but in response to students' request for more specialized work in technical or professional writing or administrators' desire to make more profit. This, too, is a legacy of the universal requirement. And there is one further legacy of the requirement that is even more insidious: its curriculum and staffing may no longer belong to us. I have assumed throughout this discussion that WPAs and writing teachers still own enough curricular authority over the first-year course that they can drop the universal requirement if they choose to do so, but at least one former WPA doubts that this is any longer the case; On September 1, 2000, Irwin Weiser posted the following message to the WPA listserv:

> WPAs don't usually have much control over the requirement. That is, since the course is required by our institutions in one way or another (gen. ed. requirement, graduation requirement for specific schools, majors, programs, etc.), a WPA or an English department would probably find it very difficult to "abolish" the requirement. We could argue

against it, we could offer fewer sections when we couldn't staff them appropriately (though I interpret the comments of many on the list to indicate that the pressure to staff courses in order to allow students to meet the requirement is severe), but I doubt we could unilaterally make it go away.

If Weiser is right, the universal requirement looms much larger in the academy than whatever professional authority WPAs and writing teachers may have acquired in the last thirty years. That is to say, our academic freedom may already have disappeared into the maw of the universal requirement, as have so many other of our professional attainments.

SOME THINGS TO READ

The editors of this collection asked me to append a list of "key publications" that center around the topics I address here. My proposal to drop the requirement originally appeared in a 1991 issue of *PRE/TEXT*, and I made a more elaborate set of arguments for the proposal in *Composition in the University* (1998). (Full citations for all of the work mentioned in this paragraph are given in the list of works cited attached to this essay). Robert J. Connors's useful history of "abolitionism" (a term he coined) distinguishes between current discussions about lifting the universal requirement and older calls to abolish Freshman English altogether, and see also Goggin/Miller for a useful commentary on such proposals. Several negative reactions to my proposal have been published. Two thoughtful examples, written by Michael Murphy and Joseph Harris, appeared in the September 2000 issue of *CCC*. Of course anyone who is interested in the issue of labor in FYC and the complicity of full-time faculty with these practices must read James Sledd on the sins committed by "boss compositionists." A large body of literature attends the issues of working conditions in required composition and marginal employment in the academy at large. For a good description of the lives of marginally employed teachers and strategies to alter employment conditions in FYC, see Eileen Schell's masterful *Gypsy Academics and Mother-Teachers* (1998). Judith Gappa and David Leslie's *The Invisible Faculty* (1993), though dated, is still a good introduction to the issues surrounding the use of marginally employed teachers in the academy at large. A useful bibliography of literature about academic working conditions appears in Schell and Stock (2001). Cary Nelson has written a number of books and articles about the effect of the dwindling number of full-time faculty positions on graduate study in English. The most useful of his reflections on these issues can be found in the third section of his *Manifesto of a Tenured Radical* (1997), but see also the relevant entries in Nelson and Watt's *Academic Keywords*. Nelson also edited an issue of *Social Text* containing accounts of the graduate student strike over working conditions at Yale in 1995–1996; the essays published therein have since appeared as *Will Teach for Food*, edited by Nelson (1997). Stanley Aronowitz reflects on the institutional effects of the increasing reliance in universities upon marginally employed faculty in *The Knowledge Factory* (2000), and Bill Reddings also addresses this issue in *The University in Ruins* (1996).

WORKS CITED

Aronowitz, Stanley. *The Knowledge Factory: Dismantling the Corporate University and Creating True Higher Learning*. Boston: Beacon, 2000.

Brannon, Lil. "(Dis)Missing Compulsory First-Year Composition." *Reconceiving Writing, Rethinking Writing Instruction*. Ed. Joseph Petraglia. Hillsdale, NJ: Erlbaum, 1995. 239–48.

Connors, Robert J. "The Abolition Debate in Composition: A Short History." *Composition in the Twenty-First Century: Crisis and Change*. Ed. Lynn Z. Bloom, Don Daiker, and Ed White. Carbondale: Southern Illinois UP, 1996. 47–63.

Crowley, Sharon. *Composition in the University: Historical and Polemical Essays*. Pittsburgh: Pittsburgh UP, 1998.

Crowley, Sharon. "A Personal Essay on Freshman English." *PRE/TEXT* 12: (Fall/Winter 1991): 156–76.

Gappa, Judith M., and David W. Leslie. *The Invisible Faculty: Improving the Status of Part-Timers in Higher Education*. San Francisco: Jossey-Bass, 1993.

Goggin, Maureen, and Susan Kay Miller. "What Is New about the 'New Abolitionists': Continuities and Discontinuities in the Great Debate." *Composition Studies* 28.2 (2000): 85–112.

Harris, Joseph. "Meet the New Boss, Same as the Old Boss: Class Consciousness in Composition." *College Composition and Communication* 52 (September 2000): 43–68.

Hoover, Regina. "Taps for Freshman English?" *College Composition and Communication* 25 (May 1974): 149–54.

Murphy, Michael. "New Faculty for a New University: Toward a Full-Time Teaching-Intensive Faculty Track in Composition." *College Composition and Communication* 51 (Sept. 2000): 14–42.

Nelson, Cary. *Manifesto of a Tenured Radical*. New York: New York UP, 1997.

—, ed. *Will Teach for Food: Academic Labor in Crisis*. Minneapolis: Minnesota UP, 1997.

Nelson, Cary, and Stephen Watt. *Academic Keywords: A Devil's Dictionary for Higher Education*. New York: Routledge, 1999.

Reddings, Bill. *The University in Ruins*. Cambridge, MA: Harvard UP, 1996.

Report to the Profession from the Committee on Professional Standards. *College Composition and Communication* 42 (1991): 330–44.

Schell, Eileen. *Gypsy Academics and Mother-Teachers: Gender, Contingent Labor, and Writing Instruction*. Portsmouth, NH: Boynton-Cook, 1998.

Schell, Eileen, and Patricia Lambert Stock, eds. *Moving a Mountain: Transforming the Role of Contingent Faculty in Composition Studies and Higher Education*. Urbana, IL: NCTE, 2001.

Sledd, James. "Why the Wyoming Resolution Had to Be Emasculated: A History and a Quixotism." *Journal of Advanced Composition* 11 (1991): 269–81.

Weiser, Irwin. Online posting. 1 Sept. 2000 WPA-L. <http://lists.asu.edu/archives/wpa-l.html>.

II

INSTITUTING PRACTICE

15

Figuring It Out: Writing Programs in the Context of University Budgets

Chris M. Anson
North Carolina State University

Working with money can be challenging for those of us who were not especially attracted to the subject of finance in our own scholarly training or, for that matter, in our personal lives. Even financially-minded faculty who take on the management of a program or department can feel bewildered by university budgeting, especially on large and complex campuses. Yet, as vexing or unappealing as the subject of money may be to many of us, no writing program can run without a budget, and no administrator can ignore the effects of finances on the principles and delivery of writing instruction.

The need to understand the nature of a program budget in the context of wider institutional practice is as important for experienced writing program administrators (WPAs) making career changes as it is for newly appointed WPAs. Someone who has administered a writing program for several years at an institution where he or she had little control over the program's budget may be newly faced with the management of a complex budget in a more autonomous program. Even a seasoned WPA who has accepted a position at another university will need to learn about many new idiosyncrasies of the budgeting process.

No essay can hope to offer specific advice about how to work with a writing program budget that experiences the influence of operational history, the vagaries of institutional practice, and the politics of local administration.[1] Some publications, such as chapter 6 ("Managing the Program's Budget") of Hilgers and Marsella's *Making Your Writing Program Work* offer useful general advice for the newly appointed WPA. Case descriptions of actual programs, such as those in Connolly and Vilardi's *New Methods in College Writing Programs*, provide examples of writing program operation. But understanding a program budget in the context of a complex administrative and institutional structure is not like trying to maintain your car by reading about engine lubrication systems or the nature of fuel injection. Nor is it like looking at a few other cars from different manufacturers. Without a national chain of maintenance centers for writing programs, every WPA must become a self-taught budget expert in a specific context, gaining the critical expertise required for responsible financial management.

Because situated learning is largely experiential, the WPA is perhaps better served by questions and new perspectives than avuncular advice. To that end, this essay describes the heuristic process of *mapping* as one technique for understanding and working with a program's budget. Mapping, or creating visual representations of ideas, is a useful way to understand the budgeting process because budgeting is by its very nature categorical, with funds being allocated from various sources and for specific kinds of expenses. Managing a budget means thinking in these categories and discovering possible relationships among them. Mapping also creates bridges between numbers and operations, between the abstractions of math and the material, educational, and human elements of a writing program. These visually displayed relationships can reveal inequities in funding, gaps in our knowledge, and areas where, in our capacity as WPAs locally and nationally, we can improve the role of our research and instruction in university education.

In recommending such a heuristic process, I borrow from Tim Peeples's essay, "'Seeing' the WPA with/through Postmodern Mapping." Peeples offers postmodern mapping as a research method which "enables WPAs to investigate their own positioning in institutions as well as to investigate and analyze a variety of relationships among various institutional spaces within and outside the writing program" (154). My use of mapping begins somewhat more simply than Peeples's case application, less to describe social and organizational space than to reveal the relationship between social processes and the "material structures" of finance. The pragmatic goal of understanding a budget soon yields more sophisticated kinds of mapping that relate money to other dimensions of the social and organizational space of

---

[1]Financial operations also vary considerably by institutional type. Many community colleges, for example, are organizationally structured so that money flows in and out of composition instruction in quite different ways than it does in a four-year liberal arts college or a major land-grant university.

the WPA, such as resources, constituencies, reporting lines, and organizational type or size (Peeples 156).

FIGURING IT IN: WHAT'S IN THE BUDGET?

During a roundtable discussion at a recent WPA conference, several WPAs who had held their positions for more than two years admitted to incomplete knowledge of their own programs' budgets. Because most budget decisions were made for them, they worked under a kind of allowance system within their departments, trying hard not to make too many photocopies or request extra tutorial hours in the writing center, but not really knowing what funding was available to them, where it came from, or how it could be used for different needs.

Although it may be possible to manage a writing program well in such a system, financial details should not be a mystery. Certain possibilities and creative ideas open up from a full knowledge of how money flows into and out of a program. Even WPAs who do have considerable control over their finances may not have a complete picture of their budgets. Understanding a budget means being able to create categories for all of the program's current expenses and then considering how these relate to each other and to potential but as-yet-unrealized categories.

Mapping Expenses.   Create a web or map of every category of *spending* in your budget. At first broad categories will come to mind: teacher salaries or stipends, supplies, operating expenses; these may match certain categories or codes used at your institution. As you work, try extending your categories by including specific items within them. Include any items about which you're unsure. If your program's budget sheets pull all expenses apart, consolidate them into categories, using budget codes if necessary. The process of creating a categorical map can often help to simplify a complicated budget and give a conceptual orientation to a mass of figures.

A preliminary expense map (see Fig. 15.1) offers a picture of the main spending categories for a typical writing program at a midsize, state-supported institution, Cowling State University.[2] This particular program is located within an English Department. Jodi Purcell, the Director of Composition, is an associate professor of English whose area of specialization is composition studies. Jodi has included in this map the salary lines for teach-

---

[2]The extended example in this essay describes a fictitious program, WPA, and university; however, it represents a composite of several actual programs whose directors provided information about their budgets through maps, interviews, and numerical data. Most of the numbers and detailed information in the composite are real, as are the issues that emerge in the subsequent maps.

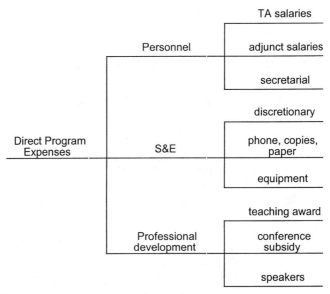

FIG. 15.1.   A preliminary categorical map of expenses.

ers and other personnel; supplies and equipment; and professional development. As she continues to map out the main categories, Jodi decides to
include figures to give her a clearer picture of the budget.[3] Fig. 15.2 shows further detail in the category of personnel.

At Cowling State, teaching assistants are appointed at a 50 percent teaching load, which is equivalent to two sections of composition per semester. Included in their stipends is some modest health insurance coverage, which
provides for clinical and outpatient services at the student health center and
a more comprehensive plan with a local HMO. Although teaching assistants
(TAs) teach for nine months, their insurance covers the summer months as
long as they are in residence during the spring semester.

As Jodi continues to learn about her budget, she realizes that there is a category of expense for TAs that does not come into the budget to be "spent" but is
still technically debited: partial tuition remission. At some universities, graduate tuition coverage is provided to teaching assistants as part of their contracts
but is "counted" only at a higher level, within a collegiate or university budget;
the costs are indirect because the faculty are already teaching graduate courses

---

[3]It is important to realize that mapping a budget is not an orthodox way of working with numbers. For
example, full-time adjunct pay will be included in a typical budget spreadsheet as lump-sum salaries; the
"cost per section" has to be worked out separately. Mapping helps us to conceptualize these numbers in our
own, no less accurate ways, allowing us to learn the budget more thoroughly and revealing useful patterns
and relationships.

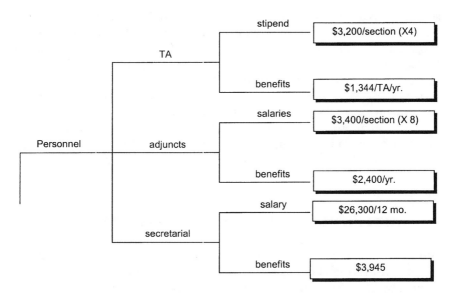

FIG. 15.2.   Personnel detail.

and it's assumed that a percentage of TAs would not otherwise matriculate if they had not received a teaching assistantship. At Cowling State, however, the figure is charged to departments to give them an accounting of the indirect costs they are incurring. (Other aspects of indirect costs will figure into Jodi's budget later on.) Jodi elaborates the TA category in Fig. 15.3.

Cowling State also has a small, independent extension division which offers nondegree programs as well as degrees in business, accounting, and occupational therapy. Extension Services pays the Composition Program enough to offer six sections of introductory and eight sections of advanced composition per year for Extension students. For historical reasons involving equity with sections of other Extension courses, the pay per section has always been a little higher than for regular daytime sections of the same courses. (Exten-

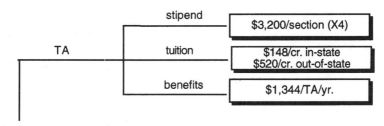

FIG. 15.3.   TA costs with tuition benefits.

sion sections are assigned to TAs and adjuncts on the basis of seniority.) Extension has a simple pay-per-section relationship with the Composition Program, and therefore incurs no costs for benefits. Jodi therefore elaborates her personnel map to include the Extension details (see Fig. 15.4).

At this point, Jodi doesn't include any further categories in her expense map; nor does she cost out these categories based on the numbers of in-state and out-of-state TAs in her program, the number of adjuncts, and so on. Later, for other purposes, she will extend the indirect costs to include a portion of her own and other salary lines and begin to look at the overall budget picture of her program. Even at this more general level, however, it is interesting to compare the costs for TA lines (both in-state and out-of-state) with those for adjuncts.

WHO FIGURES IN THE BUDGET: SOURCES OF INCOME

Writing programs get their funding from a wide range of sources, depending on their institution's financial processes. Many programs' budgets are part of a larger budget within an English department, whose chair or head allocates funds to the WPA. Other programs may be funded more directly from a college- or university-level source. Some programs receive funding from a variety of sources: Perhaps costs for the writing center are paid by Student

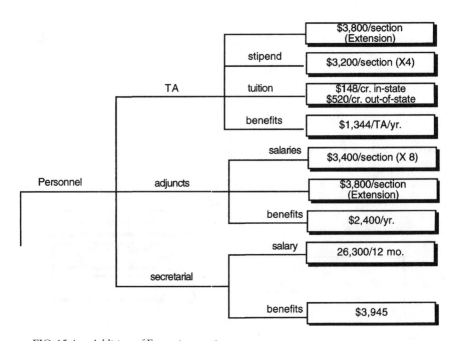

FIG. 15.4.   Addition of Extension sections.

Services; perhaps certain divisions or colleges on campus chip in for special sections of courses for their students; perhaps the Honors Program underwrites sections of advanced composition open only to honors students. Knowing both the present and potential sources of funding for a program can enhance a WPA's ability to plan strategically for nourishing and developing a writing program.

Mapping Sources of Income.   Create a web or map of every *source of funds* in your budget. It helps to use the main or second-level headings you generated in the expenses map to show who provides funds for what. In some cases your map may be quite simple: everything comes from the English department chair, or the dean of your college. In other cases, your program may be receiving funds, directly or indirectly, from a variety of sources, and some expense categories may be funded jointly.

Jodi's budget includes five sources of funds: the English department (which allocates part of its overall budget to the Composition Program); the dean of the college; the Honors Program; Student Services; and the Extension Division (see Fig. 15.5). Every year the director asks the dean for modest discretionary funds which, for historical reasons, bypass the English department. Jodi learns to include the discretionary funds as a separate category in her budget because, under state law, no state-allocated funds at the university may be used for food or entertainment. If a department wants to pay for a social gathering, it must find and use money from other sources—a grant, private donors, the foundation, and so on. The dean's office, which has access to such funds, has agreed to provide the Composition Program with $500 a year in discretionary funds, which Jodi has used to pay for refreshments (coffee and bagels) at the weeklong pre-fall-orientation seminars for instructors. The

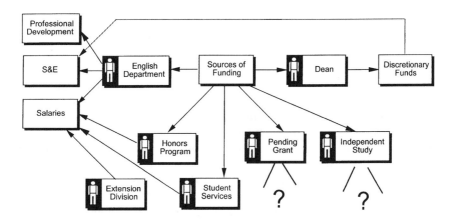

FIG. 15.5.   Sources of funds.

balance subsidizes some of the costs of coffee in the instructors' lounge for the year, and whatever is left over pays for soft drinks and supplies at the year-end potluck party. Notice that Jodi has attached this to the supplies-and-equipment category; technically, these funds are in a different budget category so that there is no room for spending errors.

Complicating Jodi's budget somewhat are two agreements the Composition Program has with Student Services and the Honors Program. Honors subsidizes eight special sections of the first-year composition course (four per semester) by paying for the equivalent of two sections of the regular course. In exchange, the Composition Program cuts the enrollment in the honors sections by five students, from twenty to fifteen. The payment covers the lost seats (forty per year). Although the dean could simply pay for this arrangement directly, Cowling State prefers to have all such arrangements specified in the budgets of each unit, no matter how small its budget may be. The other arrangement involves some cost sharing between Composition and Student Services for "The Writing Place," a tutorial center for undergraduates. Usage data have suggested that most students who visit The Writing Place do so for help in their composition courses. The rest come from courses across the university. Student Services pays for the equivalent of one regular TA to cover the noncomposition students. (As Cowling State begins the expansion of its fledgling writing-across-the-curriculum [WAC] program, Jodi knows that this support could increase if the data show a rise in usage by non-Composition students.)

In both these arrangements, it's important to realize that certain indirect costs (preparing the TAs to teach the special honors sections, training the additional tutor in The Writing Place, paying for the photocopying or supplies used by these additional instructors) are borne by the program. Such facts become important in calculating equity in the areas of supply budgets, for example.

Finally, Jodi has included two potential sources of income: an external grant for which she and a colleague have applied to pilot a program of special composition courses linked to subject-matter courses, and the possible development of correspondence courses for the Independent Study division. The grant would provide money for teacher development, extra supplies and equipment, one or two visits by outside consultant/speakers, and release time in the personnel category (i.e., the hiring of TAs or adjuncts to replace sections of composition and English courses ordinarily taught by Jodi and fellow grantwriter Seth Cunnien). Although the source of funding is "irregular" and the spending is primarily for the grant, Jodi knows that her program will realize certain benefits from the grant, such as the opportunity for all instructors to attend the sessions of guest speakers. At this point, she is not ready to map out the budgetary implications of either the grant or the Independent Study option (which will be described later).

It is helpful to note that the English department allocates funds to the Composition Program in the category of "professional development." In her spending map, Jodi had divided this category into "teaching award," "conference subsidy," and "speakers." During the annual departmental celebration and award ceremony, the Composition Program gives a "teacher of the year" award to one instructor in the program, who receives a plaque and a $250 check. Another $1000 goes to subsidize up to five composition instructors (at $200 each) to give papers at regional or national conferences. The balance, which ranges from $250 to $500 each year, pays for a composition-related presentation. Because this amount is insufficient to bring in speakers of national renown, the money has sometimes reverted to the English department. Twice it was used to increase the instructor travel subsidy. On one occasion it added to the stipend of a speaker who had been brought in by another department, and the Program was able to offer a presentation at relatively low cost without incurring travel and hotel expenses.

By filling in the total allocation from each funding source (see Fig. 15.6), Jodi can elaborate her map to give her a rough profile of her program's expenses.

Working with the Figures: Problems and Budget Management

Every administrator must face budgetary problems small and large as a routine part of the job. In one case, a WPA was approving expenses on behalf of a colleague who had received a substantial federal grant that was administered through the writing program. Some of these expenses were for small pieces of equipment such as a $75 digital photo card reader and a $375 digital camera. Unfortunately, the WPA did not know that the equipment had to be used ex-

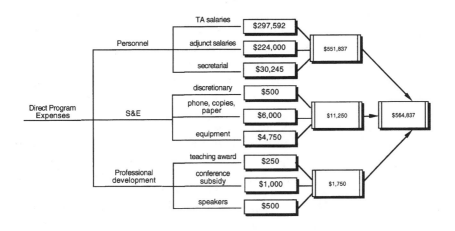

FIG. 15.6.   Expense profile of the program.

clusively for the grant project and also came below an expense threshold for the purchase of equipment. The WPA faced the possibility of having to reimburse the project budget for over $1,000 from funds that had not been allocated for program-related equipment purchases.

But budgetary problems need not involve unforeseen glitches like these. Longer term and more systemic problems, such as low pay or poor benefits for teachers, hang like a cloud over many writing programs (see, for example, Schell and Stock). Because these problems appear to be so insurmountable, many WPAs focus on their daily operations and expenses, leaving larger concerns about funding unconsidered and unresolved.

Mapping Problems. What are your biggest budgetary concerns? When it comes to thinking about money, funding, and spending, what parts of your program are you most worried about? Try listing these out randomly; don't get concerned about their degree of severity or their relative importance in the overall budget of your program. (Worrying about paying for the coffee in the main office may pale next to keeping class size low in the face of a budget retrenchment, but it's still part of the overall financial picture of your program and should be included. Finding solutions to the small problems can also open up new strategies for tackling the larger ones.) Then look for ways to group or cluster the concerns, perhaps from most to least important or from those that are in different domains of funding. Making all your concerns visual can help you to put them into perspective and show their relationship to each other and to wider institutional issues.

In Fig. 15.7, Jodi has identified several major budget-related concerns. The assistant director, usually an experienced adjunct, is given only a quarter-time release from his or her teaching load (one course per semester) which is built into the program's budget as a line item equivalent to the cost of replacing the courses with a TA (two sections plus one half the cost of tuition and benefits). As noted previously, state-allocated funds can't be used for food at Cowling, so Jodi relies on the dean to pay for some refreshments. The supply budget is too restrictive for the needs of the instructors. Final budget notifications occur late in the year, which makes it difficult for Jodi to complete the hiring process in a timely way. She is also concerned about the rules on the use of a petty cash account.

Further mapping helps Jodi to place the problem of instructor pay high on her list of budget issues. As she analyzes the cost of instruction in her program, for example, she compares the salaries of adjuncts and teaching assistants. The cost of a TA who receives an in-state tuition remission for a full course load (nine credit hours) and teaches four semester courses of first-year composition is only $169 more per section than the cost per section for an adjunct instructor (see Fig. 15.8). About a third of Jodi's thirty TAs do not have state residency, however, which increases their cost to $1,006 per section

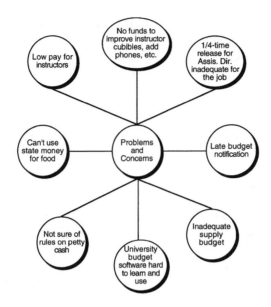

FIG. 15.7.   A map of Jodi's budget concerns.

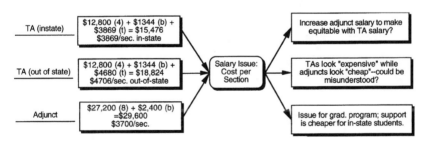

FIG. 15.8.   Map comparing cost per section for TAs and adjuncts.

more than the cost of an adjunct teaching the same section. For these out-of-state TAs, the program is spending almost $20,000 more than it would cost to staff the same sections with adjuncts.

The upper administration at Cowling State is ambivalent about reliance on full- and part-time non-tenure-track faculty to teach basic courses. Though mindful of the national concern about this topic, they know that there is also a good market for such instructors in the area, and the financial benefits to the institution are obvious. Although Jodi might be able to use her comparisons to support an argument for higher adjunct pay, the same data could be interpreted by her administration as a good reason to keep a cap on the number of TAs while continuing to advocate the hiring of adjuncts at high section loads. Clearly, Jodi's budget is not just about dollars, it's about ideology and the politics of education. In working towards equity for adjuncts, she will need to consider the larger budgetary picture of her program in relation to the rest of the university, a subject we'll return to later.

Jodi is also concerned about the different pay scale for sections of the same composition courses taught for Extension Services. Her first idea, which she explores in a map (see Fig. 15.9), considers the possibility of using increased funds from Extension to help with administration. In one scenario, she would pursue the idea of maintaining the per-section funding (from Extension) at $3800 but paying for those sections at the same rate as non-Extension sections. This would provide her program with $8,000 of additional funds that would cover increased administrative assistance. (Reducing the pay for Extension sections could lead to some protests among a few instructors, but these sections have always been understood as "special.") In another scenario, she would request additional funds from Extension for the indirect costs and keep the higher pay per section; depending on who is appointed to teach the sections, the extra funds could amount to between $5,000 and

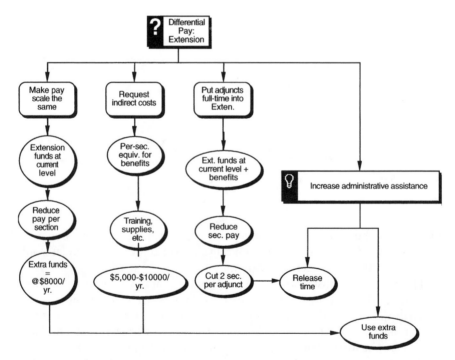

FIG. 15.9.   A map of possible schemes to fund administrative assistance.

$10,000 per year or more. A third option would be to concentrate two full-time adjuncts into the Extension courses, reduce their pay to the regular level, and reduce their section loads by one course per semester to involve them in administration. The extra salary money from Extension would buy the adjuncts out of one course each, allowing Jodi to have two additional administrative assistants. Under this plan, she could also argue that Extension needs to pick up the cost of benefits.

Note here that Jodi's mapping process allows her to reach an important insight. She is seeing one problem (the differential pay scales) as an opportunity to solve another problem (lack of sufficient administrative support). She might just as well use the pay scale problem to argue for increased pay in non-Extension courses in order to create greater equity. Her decisions come from an understanding of her most immediate needs and what courses of action have the greatest chance for success at her institution.

Some other concerns in Jodi's problem map (Fig. 15.7) suggest simpler solutions. A brief meeting with her college budget officer might give her the information she needs regarding petty cash. In the absence of any reform in the timing of budgetary information, careful planning and consultation can help in her hiring process. For example, a preliminary assurance from a dean that a certain number of sections of composition courses will definitely be offered will allow her to send out appointment letters to many or most of her teachers, with a "subject to final budget approval" clause. Other problems, such as the annual discretionary fund request, suggest longer term strategies, such as consulting a fund-raising officer on campus to explore the possibilities of seeking small gifts from potential donors to help the program. (Regardless of the strategies Jodi develops to solve the problem of food costs, the very presence of these state regulations suggests an area for Jodi to learn more about, because university budgeting is often constrained by such legal and legislative dictates.) Still other problems, such as the insufficient supplies and equipment budget, will require a case to be made and presented to those in charge of allocating funds to the program.

RECONFIGURING: ANTICIPATING CHANGES IN THE BUDGETING PROCESS

Like most aspects of administration, a budget never stands still. Money is flowing in and out of accounts in certain planned ways, but broader changes in finance are happening beyond the budget and will affect it during or after the fiscal year. Aside from those very rare occasions when a WPA has more money in the budget than he or she knows what to do with, the best we can usually hope for is that the financial part of our operation runs smoothly. Unforeseen problems will inevitably arise because there are people behind our budget figures, and peoples' lives are unpredictable. For example, the previous year, an instructor in Jodi's program took a maternity leave (which is provided for in the adjunct contract) three weeks earlier than expected. In order to cover the teacher's sections, Jodi slightly reduced the walk-in hours in The Writing Place and appointed one of the regular tutors to take over the unstaffed sections. Her creative handling of the problem and its effect on her budget was noted favorably by her dean.

It is also not uncommon for administrators to propose possible reductions in an annual budget and ask chairs or unit coordinators to describe what they might do if faced with such a reduction. In a more dramatic scenario, administrators may simply cut a budget and expect that departments and programs will figure out a way to manage. Of course, budget surprises may also be good ones, such as state-mandated pay increases or an influx of technology funds to buy new computers for instructors or for a writing center. Whatever the case, however, it's sometimes necessary to respond quickly and wisely to fluctuations in funding.

In recent years, some universities have even overhauled their entire financial management systems. One popular trend is based on the assumption that every unit on a campus is a "responsibility center," charged with generating income and spending it wisely. In some departments, millions of dollars may be generated by large grants; in others, almost all revenues come from student tuition. A "responsibility center" must spend in proportion to what it earns. For example, a Department of Asian Language Studies may have eight tenured faculty and no TAs at a cost, with overheads, of $492,000 per year to the institution. Graduate courses in this department enroll a handful of students each; the average class size in the undergraduate curriculum is fourteen. Tuition revenues from this department total about $239,500, from approximately 32 graduate students and 360 undergraduates (calculated on the basis of both in-state and out-of-state tuition). The faculty course load is 2/2 with releases for the chair and undergraduate coordinator. Consequently, this department drains $252,000 per year from the university's budget, not including the additional costs for infrastructure (buildings, power and heat, maintenance, student services, etc.). In contrast, an undergraduate foreign-language program teaching required courses in French, German, and Italian may use many TAs and part-time instructors and end up generating a million dollars in profit for the institution after all expenses. Traditionally, this has not been seen as "profit" because it simply offsets the expenses from less financially productive units.

Under a system of "responsibility center management," each of these units would need to figure out how to use its money wisely.[4] The former would face difficult questions about retrenchment, mergers with other units, the use of

---

[4]For more information on this funding scheme, see the very informative information, especially the page "What is RCM?" at: <http://weathertop.bry.indiana.edu/mas/rcm/>.

TAs, or other ways to balance costs and revenues. The latter would need to decide how to spend the income it generates, a portion of which would now come directly back to the unit as "income." In such a system, it is easy to see how lucrative many composition programs are to their institutions, often because of deplorable pay rates and poor working conditions. When such programs have independent status, there is also the risk that other units, such as the English department, may want to gain control of them to garner their revenues. At a time of considerable volatility in higher education financing, it is important for all WPAs to keep abreast of major changes in financial planning and management that could have serious effects on the nature, delivery, and administrative control of writing instruction.

A somewhat more local issue has come before Jodi's program in recent months. Cowling State has a fledging but growing independent-study initiative which is part of the Extension Division. Independent Study, or IS, has been commissioning faculty and graduate students to write Web-based and desktop-published manuals for online correspondence courses that their surveys suggest will be popular among students. Recently, IS representatives met with Jodi to talk about the possibilities of offering the first-year composition sequence as a correspondence course.

Jodi is philosophically opposed to correspondence courses in composition, which, she believes, take away the important elements of collaboration and community from the learning of writing. But she agrees to consider the IS proposal to see what budgetary implications it might yield. After meeting with the coordinators of IS courses, she creates the following map outlining the effects on her budget (see Fig. 15.10).

The arrangement proposed by IS involves two sources of income for Jodi's program: work-for-hire funds to create Web-based independent study manuals, and stipends for reader/graders of the material submitted electronically by students in the IS courses. The former involves individual contracts with authors; the latter, correspondence contracts with teachers on a per-student basis. Jodi knows that IS will want to keep their instructional costs low, but she also guesses that a new program will need to show success. By using IS's enrollment projections (initially, forty students per year), she calculates a certain level of "administration" required to manage the additional IS system. If IS agrees to her plan, Jodi will need to decide whether taking on this additional responsibility will be a good thing for her program; it will certainly generate more work, but will it yield new opportunities for growth, development, and teamwork? Could she use the funds for the manuals to create a team of writers who would simultaneously improve the larger writing curriculum? Could she make a case for some new, high-end computer equipment for the program? Realizing considerable financial gain, will IS be willing to provide additional funds that could further enhance training and development? Jodi has projected such funds at the equivalent of one half of a course release for a

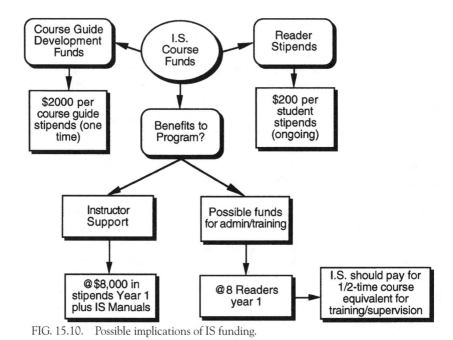

FIG. 15.10.   Possible implications of IS funding.

faculty member. Could this help her to involve another department member in her program? Could such involvement benefit Jodi's program in some developmental way, perhaps by providing a new "first" stage for TAs—or are these opportunities diminished by the theoretical limitations of IS courses in composition? Clearly, Jodi's options for exploiting a new source of income depend on the philosophy of education and management that she is trying to establish for her program.

IT FIGURES, BUT ... EQUALITY WITH DIPLOMACY

Few issues in the administration of writing programs create as much tension as money and budgets, perhaps with the exception of outsiders deciding curriculum for WPAs. Many a WPA has been incensed by a proposal or action of a dean, provost, or other higher administrator which seems to counter the WPA's strongest convictions about good, theoretically informed pedagogy. Defending an existing budget or arguing for increases in funding can easily lead a WPA beyond reserve and into emotional response. Much is at stake: teachers whose lives depend on consistent employment; TAs who count on reappointments to pay themselves through graduate school; enough support to prepare instructors adequately to teach large numbers of students in required courses.

When advocating on behalf of a program's budget, clearly presented facts and information often speak far more strongly to higher administrators than does emotional or contestatory language. An administrative decision about funding class sections of composition, for example, will be more effectively influenced by enrollment data showing a need for some number of first-year writing sections than by an emotional appeal based on the financial needs of yet-to-be-hired instructors. No higher administrator will want to force students to delay taking a required first-year course. That point could make a more compelling case for full funding than focusing on the needs of TAs.

In this sense, it helps to separate the immediate budgetary issues facing a program from the broader problems of inequity or insufficient support. Jodi wants to increase support for her TAs and adjuncts, whose pay is very low relative to the cost of living in the local area of Cowling. But her dean has just asked her to consider increasing her section size in composition courses from twenty-three to twenty-six in order to cut costs. As she thinks about this request, she knows that working strategically and methodically on the problem may be more effective than turning it into a scandal. First, Jodi needs to know her program's budget at least as well as any other administrator. Beyond that knowledge, it will help her to work out different scenarios to solve the problem at hand or offer counterproposals to solutions already broached.

Because Jodi's budget is already so lean, she doesn't have much room to explore various options to her dean's suggestion. She can argue against the suggestion based on the effects of increased class size on the quality of instruction, using various national position statements as support. She can prepare a comparative analysis of pay rates for composition at some of Cowling's peer institutions (and she knows anecdotally that Cowling will come in low). Or she might explore some creative way to exempt a small percentage of students from the upper-level composition course requirement based on the submission of a writing portfolio, and try to keep section size the same as a result.

Jodi also decides to develop a back-up strategy, a more general "point" to make about the Program's budget should her ideas be met with skepticism. She has a hunch that her program generates income for Cowling State; after all, her instructors are paid poorly, and her entire operation receives little financial support. But she needs some basis for using this point in advocating for her program. She decides to work out a general index of her program's profitability to Cowling State.

To do this, she needs to calculate every expense incurred by her program, including her own time and other indirect costs. Then she needs to figure out how much revenue her program generates—not how much she is allocated in her budget, but how much the operation of her program brings in to the university. In this case, almost all the revenue comes from student tuition.

A few calls to her Department of Planning and Analysis and the Registrar give Jodi some precise information on the number of students (both in-state and out-of-state) who enrolled in Composition courses. Note that her own records may be suspect: registered students can drop courses, for example, and receive full or partial tuition refunds.

During the previous academic year, her program generated $2,221,048 in tuition revenues from over 150 sections of composition courses (Jodi will not be concerned with the effects of scholarships or other federal and state tuition payment programs in her calculations; she also ignores both the revenues and the costs of Extension courses because of the somewhat independent status of that unit). From these revenues she subtracts all the costs of operating her program (as previously mapped in Fig. 15.6) for the prior year. She also adds to this amount some indirect costs she had not included in the original expenses map. First she includes half of her own salary and benefits in her capacity as Director (or 50% of $56,500). Three tenured faculty in the English Department also teach sections of composition courses, and she needs to figure this effort into her expenses.[5] She does this by taking each of their total salaries and benefits, calculating the cost per section for each and then multiplying by the number of composition sections each teaches (either one or two per year), yielding a total of $64,635 for their contributions of five sections. She does not include the cost of funding tutors for The Writing Place, nor the release time given to instructors who help with administration: these costs have already been included in the salary estimates as full course loads for those instructors. (See Fig. 15.11.)

Jodi's calculations show that her program generates about $1.5 million in revenue for Cowling State University after expenses. Of course, there are still further indirect costs that need to be subtracted in any pure analysis of her

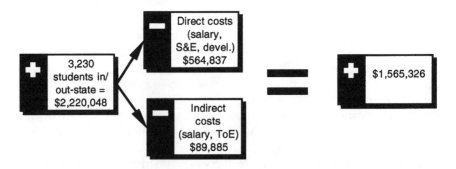

FIG. 15.11.   Index of the Program's tuition revenues after expenses.

---

[5]In some universities, faculty in other departments may teach composition sections in exchange for the cost of replacing one of their courses, usually a "service" course, with a lecturer or TA. This is a relatively inexpensive way to bring in tenured faculty. In other situations, the cost may be calculated by dividing the faculty member's salary and benefits by the number of sections of composition he or she teaches.

program's profitability; the costs of actually running the institution must be taken into account, and this will include many other non-revenue-producing units such as Registration and Records, the upper administration, student services, and the like. Because so many Composition students use classroom space and account for a portion of all the other institutional resources, these cannot be ignored. But they are also seen as a percentage of the costs generated by the entire university. The question Jodi needs to ask is whether her unit is, in comparison with other departments, financially contributing to the university or draining its resources. Comparing her revenue calculations with those of other departments could help her to answer this question. If Cowling State is like many other universities, her program is likely to fare well in such comparisons.

For Jodi to use such an analysis, first she has to be sure it is accurate, and that means checking her calculations out with budgetary personnel and others. Second, she needs to anticipate the reaction to her analysis: How will the chairs of other departments respond to a cost comparison with Composition? How will her dean or other higher administrators feel about her analysis—that she is thinking creatively? that she is being a responsible steward of her program? or that she is overstepping her bounds and making trouble? Finally—and related to the question of audience—she needs to decide just how much of her analysis she wants to share. Suggesting to a dean that her program generates lots of revenue and that some thought should be given to increasing the salaries of instructors is not quite the same as sending the dean a detailed financial analysis attached to a formal request for a pay increase. Few areas of administration require as careful a rhetorical strategy as arguing for more money; the key to this analysis lies in a keen understanding of the audiences to which that argument is being directed.[6]

Regardless of what use Jodi could put such an analysis to at Cowling, it has additional value more broadly, in the profession and beyond. That a program is forced to pays its teachers less than the full-time salary at the fast-food restaurant in the student union, and that it is unable to buy a new computer or provide donuts and coffee at its teacher-development meetings even though it is generating hundreds of thousands of dollars in net revenues is a sad commentary on the way in which an essential part of college-level instruction is viewed by those who govern our higher education institutions. Jodi's analysis, done carefully and disinterestedly, can contribute much more effectively to the mobilization of forces against such continued exploitation than will unsupported assertions, anecdotes, or the sort of victim mentality that leads to a begrudging acceptance of the status quo.

---

[6]Becoming acquainted with administrators in the context of less volatile concerns can help the WPA to craft a way to present certain requests, recommendations, or data when the issue is more serious.

CONCLUSION

Of all that is most rewarding about managing a writing program, overseeing the budget process probably ranks fairly low on most WPAs' lists. In part this is because working with budgets takes us into domains of accounting and financial management that were not what attracted us to jobs in higher education. But there is no reason for us not to manage our budgets and finances as creatively and energetically as we develop our teachers, design our curriculum, and work with our students. As Lynn Bloom has put it, the administration of writing programs represents a balance between "bureaucracy and creativity, the preordained, the pragmatic, and the precedent-setting." Because WPAs are "among the chronically fiscally challenged," budgets and budget choices fall into the least attractive our responsibilities. Yet taking a creative view of these processes can, Bloom argues, "transform a routine endeavor into a creative enterprise with enormous benefits for students, faculty, institutions—even the entire profession" (73).

In this essay, I have described and illustrated a potentially creative way to work with budgets using various kinds of maps and visual representations of budget categories and financial statistics. This method offers us a way to make budgets our own—to transform what may be alien-looking spreadsheets and bewildering numbers into texts that we can understand and, as we work with them, turn into a creative process of management and reform. Of course, no method will work uniformly well in every program at all institutions. Nor does mapping substitute for the kind of financial preparation that a WPA might gain from participating in campus or local workshops and seminars or meeting with college-level financial officers. The flexibility of mapping, however, will allow most WPAs to explore their budgets in ways that make sense to them, even if they begin the process doodling on a piece of scratch paper in one of those increasingly rare reflective moments during the busy workday.

WORKS CITED

Bloom, Lynn Z. "Making a Difference: Writing Program Administration as a Creative Process." *Resituating Writing: Constructing and Administering Writing Programs.* Ed. Joseph Janangelo and Kristine Hansen. Portsmouth, NH: Heinemann, 1995. 73–81.

Connolly, Paul, and Teresa Vilardi, eds. *New Methods in College Writing Programs.* New York: MLA, 1986.

Hilgers, Thomas L., and Joy Marsella. *Making Your Writing Program Work: A Guide to Good Practices.* Newbury Park, CA: Sage, 1992.

Peeples, Tim. "'Seeing' the WPA with/through Postmodern Mapping." *The Writing Program Administrator as Researcher: Inquiry in Action and Reflection.* Ed. Shirley K. Rose and Irwin Weiser. Portsmouth, NH: Heinemann, 1999. 153–67.

Schell, Eileen E., and Patricia Lambert Stock, eds. *Moving a Mountain: Transforming the Role of Contingent Faculty in Composition Studies and Higher Education.* Urbana, IL: NCTE, 2001.

16

Collaborative Administration

Jeanne Gunner
Santa Clara University

> [T]he only productive way to direct a writing program is to acknowledge that no one person can or should have ultimate control; faculties should collaboratively direct the writing program themselves. —*Dickson* (140)

When you become a writing program administrator (WPA), one of the first and most critical tasks you face is defining your leadership style. In all likelihood, a default definition was awaiting you when you accepted your job, and also likely is that that definition reflects a traditional model of authority/subordinates—a "centered" WPA who reports to a chair and who directs an often-marginalized faculty and staff. Institutionally, the WPA is often pushed into a synecdochic relationship with the program he or she directs: it quickly becomes "your program" in institutional discourse and soon "my program" in the WPA's own speech, perpetuating the traditional model of a sole authority. What can get lost within such a structure is the WPA's sense of the complex of cultural, institutional, professional, and personal forces that continually affect a program—forces that both keep its direction out of the WPA's full control and challenge the very model of total authority. An alternative to the authority model can be found in the theory of collaborative administration, an administrative model in which authority is shared among the members of a writing program.

Because the citations provided in this essay include many case studies in collaborative administration, I won't attempt to construct artificial examples, which inevitably lack the real-world contexts that a WPA must consider in all administrative planning and decisions. What you will find here are the varied definitions and historical origins of collaborative administration, a taxonomy of collaborative structures derived from actual collaboratively-run programs, and a detailed discussion of the factors that show why collaborative program structure is not an administrative panacea or theoretical ideal. In attempting to develop my own administrative flexibility and pragmatic leadership, I've had to shift from an earlier, idealistic attitude toward democratic program structure—the kind of strong claim Marcia Dickson makes in this essay's opening quotation—to a recognition that the WPA needs a repertoire of possible administrative responses as he or she faces continually changing local program conditions. This essay maps out one such response.

DEFINITIONS: FROM HIERARCHY TO SHARED AUTHORITY

Collaborative writing program administration, an idea that came to national attention in the 1990s, is an administrative structural plan that in varied forms has become fairly well entrenched in a range of institutions over the past decade. Although not directly connected to collaborative pedagogical theory, collaborative administration does share in its theoretical foundation some of the values and goals of decentered teaching and learning. Because collaborative writing program administration is more an idea than a single structure, plan, or model that can be described, assessed, and adopted, its definition is necessarily unstable. It is as much a political concept as it is an organizational design. It is not a single practice but a shifting, fluid approach to the flux of conditions in and surrounding a writing program, its administrators, and its faculty. What might be fairly claimed is that, consciously or not, collaborative administration entails ideological critique, a restructuring of institutional power, and, in practice, a sharing of authority. As an idea and often in practice, collaborative administration challenges the traditional model of program administration as a defined hierarchy, with a WPA reporting to a chair and department and directing faculty (often a marginalized one, either by adjunct appointment or graduate student status), and exercising concentrated authority over curriculum and program policies. In place of the traditional model, collaborative structures emphasize community, shared responsibility, and open exchange of information, ideas, and criticism.

In the professional literature on collaborative administration, the working organization has been called "collectivism," "rule by committee," "federalism," "codirecting," "comentoring," "constitutional government"—and "chaos." It has also been seen more pragmatically as an administrative "solution" to some of the typical challenges a program faces—heavy workloads, graduate training, and balancing administration and scholarship, particularly for untenured WPAs. Collaborative administration might best be defined as one possible program response to a particular institutional setting.

In applied form collaborative organizational structures tend to show what has been called a "flattened hierarchy," with areas of program responsibility broken into specific tasks, each assigned to an individual program member, with these members often being of differing rank. A collaborative writing program structure, in one incarnation, might consist of two or more colleagues who have agreed, often within the confines of the program rather than as a department-driven decision, to share the work of administering the writing program. Charted, the division of labor might seem clear-cut—job titles might include WPA, Director of Placement, TA Coordinator, and so on—but often job charts refer more to the work of a program than the actual individual duties of its administrators; and in practice labor, authority, and responsibility are shared, shifting, and intermixed. In another form a collaborative structure might consist of senior colleagues who occupy program positions by rotation—each takes on the freshman program duties for a three-year period, for example, and then moves out of administration or shifts to another administrative position—from WPA to head of graduate studies, perhaps. Where such senior compositionists exist, the collaborative structure often includes administrative positions designed for graduate-student training; graduate students develop on-the-job WPA skills by heading up placement or the teaching practicum, or by serving as administrative assistants to the senior WPA. In general terms where labor and responsibility are shared, where administrators have some degree of authority over their particular duties, and where the various "heads" meet to consider the program as a whole rather than individually reporting "up" to a single person in charge (or where such concentrated authority is redelegated to writing faculty committees), we can say a collaborative program structure exists.

HISTORICAL, DISCIPLINARY, AND THEORETICAL ORIGINS

In its earliest form, collaborative administration was the product of writing-across-the-curriculum (WAC) programs. This form of collaborative structure should be differentiated from writing program collaborative structures, because WAC programs typically have organizational ties to departments and administrative offices outside the writing program or English department and are themselves often organized as separate academic units not under departmental aegis. (I should add, however, that this division is quite an oversimplification; WAC programs are very often part of a larger writing program, administered by the WPA or a program faculty member, and they involve the program in complex extradepartmental relations and politics that complicate collaborative program structures; an extensive body of literature exists on WAC collaboration, which I will not attempt to detail here.) The original English Composition Board at the University of Michigan, founded in 1978, is probably the best-known collaborative structure of the extradepartmental type and perhaps best illustrates the goals and conflicts in such a system (for a critique of the University of Michigan experience, see Quiroz). The historical forces behind WAC and collaborative administrative efforts are multiple: The rise of rhetoric-composition as a research area and the increasing disciplinary specialization in higher education overall, combined with the continued perceived literacy crisis and a strong economy, created an environment conducive to program expansion and cross-disciplinary cooperation. In campuswide collaborative structures, faculty from a range of disciplines and staff from related offices (i.e., libraries, writing centers, AAP programs) are appointed to help oversee such areas as composition curriculum, program policies, and evaluation/assessment; the range of areas of responsibilities and degree of oversight varies—as does the degree of success in supporting the teaching of writing. A current and successful model of campuswide collaborative structures can be seen in the Composition Board at the University of Arizona's English department web site (http://w3fp.arizona.edu/ucb).

The viability of campuswide collaborative programs may well be determined by the presence or absence of a strong graduate program in rhetoric-composition and accompanying senior positions in the field. The politics of administration of any sort are intensified when some of the participants have more institutional status and influence than others, and, especially in the 1980s, composition faculty were typically neither tenured nor perceived as having scholarly credentials. Campuswide collaborative structures seem to have been the most successful where there is a balance of powers based on disciplinary claims. For a discussion of such political relations, see Wingate on the challenges faced by writing centers, themselves typically highly collaborative in structure and philosophical orientation.

Interest in collaborative administrative models within writing programs, not surprisingly, followed in the years after rhetoric-composition's rise, as writing teachers became increasingly sophisticated in the theory of the field and as the professionalization of it developed. Seeking improved working conditions, increased authority over curricular plans and program practices, and an equitable distribution of labor, especially for those entering administrative work on the tenure track, and inspired by a growing array of theoretical critiques of institutional power (especially feminist, critical, and collaborative pedagogical theories; see Miller; Phelps; Lunsford and Ede), writing program faculty at schools where some program autonomy existed reformulated their program structures to be less hierarchical, more cooperative, and, idealistically, more efficient, democratic, and responsive to faculty and student needs. For early discussions of collaborative administrative change, see Howard; Dickson; Gunner; Cambridge and McClelland; and Gere; for political models and characteristics of democratic organizational structures, see Dickson; Wingate; Hult; Cambridge and McClelland; and Phelps, "Telling."

Thus collaborative administration was and is a response to traditional configurations of power. As I have argued in "Decentering the WPA" and elsewhere, writing programs, at least through the 1980s, were often identified with their directors, and this WPA often wielded total authority over faculty, curriculum, and program policies. He or she also set the terms of the position's duration; a system of change or rotation was not commonly in practice. Faculty, often in marginalized positions, were cut off from decision making or had strictly advisory roles. The composition-literature split gave writing program authority to those outside of the field because departments were typically and in terms of power unequally divided by disciplinary lines. The Wyoming Resolution, CCCC Statement on Principles and Standards, and the Portland Resolution helped advance the professionalizing of the field and its faculty. Added to this rising sense of professional identity were emerging theories of feminist and liberatory principles, providing new constructions of cooperative leadership that rejected binary structures, hierarchies, and competitive, adversarial, "masculinist" models of professional power. Freirean critical pedagogical theory provided the rationale for resisting oppressive social practices, questioning received "knowledge," and accepting institutional control of social relations. Rhetoricians and compositionists led the struggle to have collaborative writing recognized not only as valid professional production but as integral to all rhetorical situations. The theory and means to critique, in other words, were now available, and traditional administrative practices soon came under critical scrutiny, and then came in for material change. It was after this first wave of critique of the traditional institutional practices in writing programs that critique of the "solution"—collaborative administration—became possible.

A TAXONOMY OF CURRENT COLLABORATIVE STRUCTURES

We can formulate a taxonomy of collaborative structures; such constructs, however, are not meant to be prescriptive but rather to provide some heuristic for developing collaborative structures that address a program's current local needs and values. Although the term *program* suggests a fixed set of stable practices, a program exists in social and institutional contexts that are themselves in flux; thus a "program" acts and is acted upon in ways that impose or require change. Over time program models decay: The recognition of the need for change, or the agency to bring it about, may be lacking, and as conditions change (a new dean comes in, the freshman enrollment increases or decreases, a writing major is proposed, GE requirements are introduced, writing requirements are voted in or out, the ratio of full-time to part-time faculty changes), the structure that is in place becomes increasingly out of synch with the program's context and interconnections. Because collaborative structures typically involve intensified communication among program directors, each of whom is able to see and share perceptions about the varied program connections to the institution and its own constituents, they are often more responsive to shifting conditions and can adjust to new realities. The actual degree of collaboration might change; for instance, a program resisting some external pressure might for a time need a strong, senior "front," or, in order to support a junior colleague seeking tenure, responsibilities might be increasingly shared out. And types of collaborative structures in actual material forms are unlikely to be "pure"; a program may have several different collaborative strands.

The following are common types of collaborative structures:

"Flattened" Hierarchies. This is the "textbook" type of collaborative structure in which individual faculty members take on individual duties, sharing the work and consulting as a group to direct the program. One person may be designated as the WPA, or a program may name codirectors; these are the individuals who represent the program to administrators and departments beyond the program's bounds (i.e., meeting with chairs and/or deans). See Howard for one of the earlier models of this type; Harrington, Fox, and Hogue for a charted description of a collaborative structure; and Schell for a codirecting model.

Professional Training Tracks. Two very different program structures are most likely to employ graduate teaching assistants as part-time administrators, and not all such programs can be considered actually collaborative—they may be completely hierarchical, with the graduate WPA overseeing already-established policies and acting as a manager of particular tasks, reporting back to a senior WPA. Programs within departments that offer graduate degrees in rhetoric, perhaps because they are more often sites of theoretical study of writing program administration, may have more truly collaborative graduate administrative positions. Graduate students may work in teams to design and teach/facilitate practica, working with less experienced peers on pedagogy and curriculum for freshman writing courses, or they may run the writing center. The Purdue, Rutgers, and University of Arizona programs offer models of collaborative graduate administrative work. We now have a multitude of articles describing the role of graduate WPAs written by current and former graduate administrators (often, these are critiques as well as descriptive pieces); for sample descriptions of graduate student administrative roles, see Thomas; Meeks and Hult; Powell, Mach, O'Neill, and Huot; and Gray-Rosendale and Cahill.

Rotational Collaboration. Sharing the established program positions by having faculty routinely rotate through them is another form of collaborative administration. The arguments for such a system include preventing

WPA "burn out," allowing for change through change of directors, helping administrators balance scholarly and administrative work, and enhancing a sense of shared responsibility for program design. Like many collaborative models, the rotational model may be official or unofficial. The Purdue program, for example, has an established policy of rotation, whereas Aronson and Hansen describe a de facto rotational policy.

IDEOLOGICAL AND EXPERIENCE-BASED CRITIQUES

In 1998, Eileen Schell charged that "[t]he scholarship on collaborative writing program administration … has, for the most part, remained strangely silent about the tensions and conflicts that accompany collaborative leadership efforts, often painting collaborative administration as a utopian or progressive, non-hierarchical practice" (77). Her words were entirely accurate at the time, though the special issue of WPA: *Writing Program Administration* in which they appeared did include some of the first critical studies of collaborative administration, her article an important one of them. Since that time, more critiques have been published, many of them, interestingly, written by graduate student WPAs. For explorations of the conflicts and limits of graduate WPA collaborative administration, see Long, Holberg, and Taylor; Anson and Rutz; Jukuri and Williamson; and Keller, Lee, McClelland, and Robertson.

A second line of critique emerged from tenure-track faculty, who voice concerns about the implications of collaborative administration for professional "credit" in tenure reviews and who deconstruct the role gender plays in collaborative administration (see Schell; Aronson and Hansen). Several articles, Schell's most prominently, take up the charge that early versions of collaborative administration were naive and idealistic. Harrington, Fox, and Hogue detail the problems they encountered in a "flattened hierarchy" and argue that "[a] collaborative administrative structure will not automatically promote pluralism. Without an agreement to converse and a willingness to explore disagreements, shared administration can degenerate into a front, masking the will to power of some dominant person or group" (61). Amid hopes that collaborative programs could ease work loads, foster inclusiveness, and allow for better work/life or administration/scholarship balance, we have had reports on how communication problems, gender bias, power differentials, and increasing time demands continue to plague even the best-designed collaborative structures. WPA "burn out" remains a major affliction. Writing programs are sites of contention, exacerbated by their "gatekeeper" status in many institutions, vulnerable to budget cuts due to faculty size, often powerless in the face of higher administrative decisions, and responsible for an overwhelming number of "service" tasks—placement, assessment, remediation, TA training, faculty development, WAC administration, program development, all of these frequently contested practices, within and beyond the writing program. No structure can "automatically" transform program administration into a completely sane and equitable process. In considering some of the theoretical grounds advocating for collaborative administration, we can also see the inherent conflicts mitigating against realization of its (perhaps idealized) goals. John Trimbur's 1989 *College English* article critiquing collaborative learning applies to collaborative administration as well. He examines claims that "consensus" can become an oppressive force, leading to "parochialism, demagoguery, narrow appeals to common sense, an urge to reach noncontroversial consensus without considering alternatives" (603), and he argues that dissensus is necessary if collaborative forms are to avoid conformity and allow for democratic exchange and if they are to respond to more than purely local conditions. In collaborative administration the reality of unequal power relations needs continual surfacing, acknowledgment, and negotiation.

Pragmatic uses of collaborative administration as a solution to administrative pressures have also had less than ideal results. Program growth in the 1980s—WAC, technical communication, ESL, basic writing programs and writing centers—required increased numbers of administrators, even as increased numbers of tenure-track jobs created a tension between administrative work and scholarly production. Many junior faculty found themselves exploited for six years, only to face a negative tenure vote. For female WPAs this pattern often followed a larger cultural script of women as caretakers and service workers, roles antithetical to a "scholarly" profile. And if these women worked from feminist grounds, their collaborative work often served to further this cultural bias.

Gender bias, communication breakdowns, promotion credit, a clash between collaborative program and hierarchical institutional structures, resistance to change, exploitation of labor, and power differentials: All of these forces affect collaborative programs and may hinder their structural success. But all of these forces exist in social relations, so it is not possible to draw a causative connection to explain success or failure; we can only observe that a program's structural form will be affected by institutional settings. A truism in writing program theory is that local conditions need always inform program form and policies, and the same wisdom applies to collaborative administration.

Collaborative administration remains a statement about power relations, a statement that has serious implications for the lives of administrators, faculty, and students—and note that these are not exclusive roles; a single individual may occupy all three. As a strategy for sharing authority, collaborative structures, whether resistant, transgressive, and democratic or pragmatic, efficient, and vocational, are appealing in ideal form and effective in practice, in certain places, for certain times.

WORKS CITED

Anson, Chris M., and Carol Rutz. "Graduate Students, Writing Programs, and Consensus-Based Management: Collaboration in the Face of Disciplinary Ideology." *WPA: Writing Program Administration* 21 (Spring 1998): 106–120.

Aronson, Ann, and Craig T. Hansen. "Doubling Our Chances: Co-Directing a Writing Program." *WPA: Writing Program Administration* 21 (Spring 1998): 23–32.

Cambridge, Barbara L., and Ben W. McClelland. "From Icon to Partner: Repositioning the Writing Program Administrator." *Resituating Writing: Constructing and Administering Writing Programs.* Ed. Joseph Janangelo and Kristine Hansen. Portsmouth, NH: Boynton/Cook Heinemann, 1995. 151–59.

Dickson, Marcia. "Directing without Power: Adventures in Constructing a Model of Feminist Writing Program Administration." *Writing Ourselves into the Story: Unheard Voices from Composition Studies.* Carbondale: Southern Illinois UP, 1993. 140–53.

Gere, Anne Ruggles. "The Long Revolution in Composition." *Composition in the Twenty-First Century: Crisis and Change.* Ed. Lynn Z. Bloom, Donald A. Daiker, and Edward M. White. Carbondale: Southern Illinois UP, 1996. 119–32.

Gray-Rosendale, Laura, and Lisa Cahill. "Power, Knowledge, and the Nature of Graduate Student Expertise in WAC/WID Administration." *Dialogue: A Journal for Writing Specialists* 6 (Spring 2000): 111–44.

Gunner, Jeanne. "Decentering the WPA." *WPA: Writing Program Administration* 18 (Fall–Winter 1994): 8–15.

Harrington, Susanmarie, Steve Fox, and Tere Molinder Hogue. "Power, Partnership, and Negotiations: The Limits of Collaboration." *WPA: Writing Program Administration* 21 (Spring 1998): 52–64.

Howard, Rebecca Moore. "Power Revisited: Or, How We Became a Department." *WPA: Writing Program Administration* 16 (Spring 1993): 37–49.

Hult, Christine. "Politics Redux: The Organization and Administration of Writing Programs." *WPA: Writing Program Administration* 18 (Spring 1995): 44–52.

Jukuri, Stephen Davenport, and W. J. Williamson. "How to Be a Wishy-Washy Graduate Student WPA, or Undefined but Overdetermined: The Positioning of Graduate Student WPAs." *Kitchen Cooks, Plate Twirlers, and Troubadours: Writing Program Administrators Tell Their Stories.* Ed. Diana George. Portsmouth, NH: Boynton/Cook Heinemann, 1999. 105–19.

Keller, Katherine L., Jennie Lee, Ben W. McClelland, and Brenda Robertson. "Reconstituting Authority: Four Perspectives on a Team Approach to Writing Program Administration." *WPA: Writing Program Administration* 21 (Spring 1998): 33–51.

Long, Mark C., Jennifer H. Holberg, and Marcy M. Taylor. "Beyond Apprenticeship: Graduate Students, Professional Development Programs and the Future(s) of English Studies." *WPA: Writing Program Administration* 20 (Fall/Winter 1996): 66–78.

Lunsford, Andrea A., and Lisa Ede. *Singular Texts/Plural Authors: Perspectives on Collaborative Writing.* Carbondale: Southern Illinois UP, 1990.

Meeks, Lynn, and Christine Hult. "A Co-Mentoring Model of Administration." *WPA: Writing Program Administration* 21 (Spring 1998): 9–22.

Miller, Hildy. "Postmasculinist Directions in Writing Program Administration." *WPA: Writing Program Administration* 20 (Fall-Winter 1996): 49–61.

Phelps, Louise Wetherbee. "The Institutional Logic of Writing Programs: Catalyst, Laboratory, and Pattern for Change." *The Politics of Writing Instruction: Postsecondary*. Ed. Richard Bullock and John Trimbur. Portsmouth, NH: Boynton/Cook Heinemann, 1991. 155–70.

—. "Telling a Writing Program Its Own Story: A Tenth Anniversary Speech." *The Writing Program Administrator as Researcher*. Ed. Shirley K Rose and Irwin Weiser. Portsmouth, NH: Boynton/Cook Heinemann, 1999. 168–84.

Powell, Katrina M., Cassandra Mach, Peggy O'Neill, and Brian Huot. "Graduate Students Negotiating Multiple Literacies as Writing Program Administrators: An Example of Collaborative Reflection." *Dialogue: A Journal for Writing Specialists* 6 (Spring 2000): 82–110.

Quiroz, Sharon. "Collaborating at the ECB: A Reflection." *WPA: Writing Program Administration* 21 (Spring 1998): 81–91.

Schell, Eileen. "Who's the Boss? The Possibilities and Pitfalls of Collaborative Administration for Untenured WPAs." *WPA: Writing Program Administration* 21 (Spring 1998): 65–80.

Thomas, Trudelle. "The Graduate Student as Apprentice WPA: Experiencing the Future." *WPA: Writing Program Administration* 14 (Spring 1991): 41–51.

Trimbur, John. "Consensus and Difference in Collaborative Learning." *College English* 51 (Oct. 1989): 602–16.

Wingate, Molly. "The Politics of Collaboration: Writing Centers within Their Institution." *Resituating Writing: Constructing and Administering Writing Programs*. Ed. Joseph Janangelo and Kristine Hansen. Portsmouth, NH: Boynton Cook Heinemann, 1995. 100–07.

17

Placement Issues

Daniel J. Royer
Roger Gilles
Grand Valley State University

Placement has always been an issue in our field. As Robert Connors has pointed out, college-level composition began as a course designed for students who demonstrated through a written placement examination that their writing abilities were substandard (128-29). At Harvard in 1874, over half the incoming class was "placed" into freshman composition. Given the perception that so many students needed college-level writing instruction, it didn't take long for Harvard and other schools to institute a required composition course for *all* students. This shifted the placement effort to students deemed unprepared for the standard course. Many schools added "honors" composition to the mix, or exemption from the requirement altogether. So for most of the twentieth century, institutions faced the potential of placing students into one of three or more categories.

With the creation of open-admissions policies in the 1960s and the dramatic increase in college enrollments in the years since, remedial or developmental writing—usually called basic writing—itself has divided into several levels, and it is not uncommon for schools to place students into one of two or more courses at the prestandard level. In his 1991–1992 survey of writing placement practices, Brian Huot found that at least three fourths of all colleges and universities offered some kind of basic writing program, and about half offered some kind of honors program ("Survey" 52). Virtually all made some kind of placement decision with students entering their programs (54).

Most writing program administrators (WPAs), then, accept the need for placement as a given and indeed as a major part of the job.

It is important, however, for you to consider the placement needs of your *own* institution before adopting models from other schools. One of the more important developments in writing placement over the past three decades has been the growing recognition of the context-specific institutional variables affecting all placement decisions. Throughout his important 1989 book, *Developing Successful College Writing Programs*, Edward M. White emphasized the need to consider the particular needs of students and faculty within a particular institution when establishing and developing all aspects of a college writing program. Context-specific theories of writing assessment have been further articulated by Roberta Camp, William L. Smith, Brian Huot, Richard Haswell and Susan Wyche-Smith, and Liz Hamp-Lyons and William Condon, among others. Smith, for example, insists that the "scale" with which we rate student writing for purposes of placement is not a universal scale, or even a scale determined by that year's pool of entering students, but a scale determined by "... the curriculum, the assumptions about composition, and the purposes of each course" (149).

As a WPA seeking to develop or revise your placement methods, you face three central issues:

1. Is there a need at your institution for more than one "entry course" for incoming students? If so, how exactly should the various entry courses differ?
2. What kind of placement method should be used? That is, what is the most valid and reliable way to ensure that students at your institution begin with the course that is right for them?
3. How can you gain institutional support to implement and sustain the appropriate curriculum and placement method?

ESTABLISHING THE NEED FOR PLACEMENT

Most of the theorists mentioned earlier assume that some kind of placement is needed at most or all schools. In fact, placement is so common that it is as if colleges and universities have established a bell curve of placement, with something like 20 percent of the students being placed into basic writing, 10 percent of the students being placed into honors composition, and 70 percent of the students being placed in the standard first-year course. The numbers may vary, but as White says, "several levels of composition instruction are necessary at almost all institutions" (141). This may be true, but our first suggestion is for you to resist accepting this assumption without thinking seriously about the real needs of your students and faculty.

There are only two reasons to place students into different first-year writing courses: one is to give under-prepared or otherwise disadvantaged students a better chance to succeed in your program, and the other is to separate students of differing abilities so that teachers can design reading and writing activities for students of roughly equal abilities. So before committing to any kind of placement system, you need to ask yourself these two sets of questions:

1. What does it mean to succeed in your writing program? If it means passing the required course or courses, are you sure that a significant number of your students will fail without a course or two of developmental work?
2. How great is the range of writing ability in your first-year students? Given that range, does the pedagogy of your program demand the segregation of students into groups of similar abilities?

We all want our students to do well, but most universities demand only that students do passing work—or perhaps "C" level work—to satisfy the writing requirement. In a very literal way, then, enforced placement into basic writing courses is justifiable only for students with very little chance of passing the standard first-semester writing course, however that course happens to define passing. And what constitutes "passing" will of course vary from school to school.

Placing students in a basic writing course to help them get a B+ instead of a C+ in the regular course is a whole different matter, and we should condemn that practice as both patronizing and self-serving. If a C+ is in fact not good enough, it should not be a C+. And if we insist that students take an extra course when in fact they can earn a passing grade in the required one, we are creating extra requirements for students who already have too many—and we may be propping up a basic writing curriculum that only we think is necessary.

Mixing students who are all capable of at least passing a course in one semester is neither unreasonable nor unmanageable. The course should be designed to "work" for exactly these students—that is, students who are capable of distinguishing themselves with "A" work; students who are capable in a single semester of achieving "B" work, but probably no better; and students who, with diligence and helpful guidance, are capable of reaching the basic level of competence demanded of "C" work. College writing teachers will undoubtedly recognize that this represents quite a range of ability, but this is the range of ability that the grading system demands that a program group together. One programmatic goal is to design a first-semester course or sequence that addresses the needs of all three of these student groups.

Matters of pedagogy are addressed in other parts of this volume, but let us say in general that taking a process-based approach to writing instruction allows for productive work to be done with students with a relatively wide range of abilities. At our own institution, we advocate a workshoplike classroom setting involving reading and writing for ideas, drafting, and revising within a community of writers working toward the shared goals of the program. The point of the class is to become familiar with the basic forms of academic writing—and to improve from beginning to end. Mixing writers of varying abilities does not strike us as a problem.

Of course, most schools have some entering students who, for whatever reason, are simply not capable of achieving "C" work (as defined by that institution) in a given semester. These are the students for whom a basic writing program needs to be designed. We suggest that you begin by asking the teachers of your standard first-semester course about the students who fail. Who fails the course, and why? Likewise, there will be some students whose writing abilities on entrance to the school already match or exceed the exit requirements of the first-year writing program. For these students, honors classes or exemptions are certainly in order. But again, it is only for this outer range of students that we need to design placement mechanisms.

Some, like Rhonda Grego and Nancy Thompson, and Mary Soliday have advocated for an elimination of placement altogether in favor of mainstreaming students of all abilities into the same required course or courses. Their goal is not to give underprepared and disadvantaged students no chance to succeed, of course; rather, they call on us to integrate "basic writers" into our regular courses and provide support for their development in the form of supplemental writing studios and other forms of attention and assistance. In addition, we feel that we should make use of the great strides colleges and universities have made over the past thirty years in the general academic support available to students with special needs. Student support systems unheard of thirty years ago—from writing centers and library guides to Learning-Disability Offices and At-Risk Student Services—challenge the assumption that we must rely on the first-year writing program alone to ensure the success of underprepared and disadvantaged students. We've come a long way since the early 1960s. Maybe now it's time just to get back to the job of teaching writing.

DESIGNING AN EFFECTIVE PLACEMENT METHOD

If your school has some entering students who are not capable of achieving "C" work, then through some form of placement, they must be channeled into a course or program that will give them the extra support they need to do passing work in the required course.

Effective placement must be understood as "effective" for a particular program at a particular institution. Effective means students who need extra support are receiving it, and those who do not need it are not being given such support whether they like it or not. There are many ways to channel students into different courses. In brief, some schools use an external, indirect indicator such as SAT/ACT score, the TSWE, and/or high school grade point average (GPA). Some schools use a diagnostic essay and/or a portfolio of writing from high school. Some schools are now using directed self-placement—explaining the differences among the available courses and guiding students in their decisions about which course to take.

WPAs have always juggled the twin concerns of *validity* and *reliability* in adopting or designing placement methods. Broadly speaking, validity has to do with the appropriateness of a particular assessment, and reliability has to do with the consistency of results (see Maurice Scharton for a good discussion of these two terms). In terms of placement methods, WPAs are usually most concerned with three kinds of validity:

- **Content validity**—the relationship between the placement method and the curriculum into which students are being placed. Most assessment theorists agree that a placement method should be derived from the curriculum itself in order to increase its validity.
- **Predictive validity**—the relationship between placement results and student success in the curriculum. Again, the literal goal of any placement method is to intervene when it appears that a student is heading for trouble. So some way of predicting trouble—or success—is desirable.
- **Systemic validity**—the relationship between the placement method, the curriculum, and the rest of the students' academic lives. Placement should be seen in the context of the entire institution and the consequences that it creates for students of different abilities.

Whereas validity has to do with the substance of a placement device, reliability has to do with the consistency of its results. Objective tests are very reliable in that they provide right and wrong answers, with precise results figured down to the decimal point. And a student taking an objective test one day will probably score very similarly the next day. The results are reliable.

The struggle has long been to find more valid ways of measuring writing ability while retaining a respectable amount of reliability. As far back as 1966, the CCCC's "Committee on Testing" acknowledged this struggle: "Under present circumstances," the committee concluded, "the use of objective tests for English placement seems inevitable, since essay tests are expensive, or unreliable—often both" (272). Though most good measures of writing are still relatively expensive, the last three decades have seen tremendous progress in improving the reliability of direct writing assessment (see Cherry and Meyer, for example, for an overview of the reliability of holistic assessment of writing). It is now quite possible to justify various forms of direct writing assessment as reliable. The main questions continue to have to do with validity and—as much today as in 1966—expense.

But as we say, placement cannot be separated from the program we are seeking to place students into. Designing a placement program without thinking hard about what we are placing students into is to think as an essentialist, that is, to think that basic writers are born basic writers, and to view basic writers as a category of people that exist apart from our curricula. In short, placement apart from the complex context that we are placing students into is a meaningless concept. Placement degrades to mere labeling or to an essentialist, static view of writers when we insist, quite apart from the programs that placement serves, that we can sort students for placement by using some universal standard of good writing. The point is, placement should be *future* directed: it is a judgment about what someone could do, might be able to do, not a judgment about what they have already done. Thinking backward to what students have done is essentialist labeling; thinking forward to what they might be able to do in a given curriculum gives a pragmatic meaning to the term *basic writer* and thus energizes the entire placement process with live consequences.

To the extent that what students have done in the past is an indicator of what they will do in the future, past performance is a place to begin thinking about placement with students. But when, as program directors, we look at SAT/ACT scores or a sample of student writing, we are trying to extrapolate from what has been done to what could be done in the courses we are offering. Because test scores and GPA are very general indices of academic ability (and their validity as an index varies a great deal), these scores can only estimate, in very general ways, the students' future abilities. Obviously, in moving from high school to college, students change very much, and their performance as students may follow suit or it may not.

Because these static scores have only the most general predictive value (perhaps they help to sort the very best writers and the very worst), most schools in search of more valid procedures have tried to adopt some sort of direct writing assessment in order to pin down more specifically a student's writing ability. By taking a sample of student writing at orientation, the theory has it that trained readers can determine who needs extra help in order to pass the regular course and who does not. Although this method can pick out static samples of good writing and of poor writing, unfortunately these samples may not be valid indicators of which students with some effort could achieve a C or better in the regular course and those who could not and thus need a basic writing course. We might infer that someone who can write well in a one-shot timed-writing situation would consequently have all the confidence, study habits, research skills, and preparation necessary to pass the regular first-year writing course, but such an inference is understandably a stretch, especially for those students in the "average" category. How much can one glean about the prospects of a student's success in a fifteen-week course from a single piece of writing?

In search of greater content validity and in an effort to achieve greater predictive accuracy, some colleges have asked students to present a portfolio of writing. The portfolio represents writing produced under circumstances more like the ones students will encounter in a college course (i.e., it is not timed and has undergone revision). Thus, it tends to have more content validity than a timed essay, indicating more accurately how well a student can write in circumstances like what our courses will present to them. With portfolios, the thinking is that because the writing is produced in realistic circumstances, then the writing portfolio is a better indication of how well one can write. This may be true as far as it goes, but how well one has written in high school or how well a student can polish a portfolio may or may not have better predictive validity than a timed essay. We are unaware of any research indicating that portfolios are better predictors of future success in a course than is a timed writing sample, although on the face of it, the content validity has increased. Again, the intuitive sense that the portfolio reveals more than a timed essay about what a writer is capable of doing with effort and revision seems reasonable and accurate. But this is not exactly the knowledge that placement is seeking. We want to know how well a student might do in our curriculum, not how well a student has done in a high school curriculum. In other words, that same intuition also tells us that in itself, a portfolio does not indicate that a student will revise, that a student can repeat these past performances with similar polish and motivation, or that a student is comfortable producing similar finished products in the new, and very different, college environment.

Of course, such portfolios are valuable and should factor into a student's decision-making process about which course to take in college. The content validity of portfolio placement sends a message to students about what is important in the curriculum, and it provides a more valid picture of how students write than does a standardized achievement test or GPA. In this way, portfolios can be said to possess more systemic, or consequential, validity than other forms of placement. But as we have said, placement gets much of its meaning when we also factor in what it is we are placing students into and why. Portfolios are thicker indicators of what a student is capable of writing than are test scores or timed essays, but are they better predictors of a student's future success in a course? These are related but different questions. The former question asks what kind of writer a student *is*, thus allowing us to group students with similar writing abilities; the latter asks what kind of a writer a student could become in our curriculum, thus allowing us to place students in a course that best matches their own personal goals with regard to the promises of our curriculum.

However, predicting how well a student might do in a course opens a complex web of issues. First of all, success for some may be just passing the course, and for others the prospect of a high B or an A is counted as success. Second, how hard is a student willing to work, and how much extra help is the student willing to get? There are personal, social, and psychological factors that make gauging the prospects of "success" very difficult. Such factors are certainly not revealed in a timed essay or in a portfolio of writing. If, however, SAT/ACT scores (or for that matter timed essays and portfolio placements) correlate to some predictive value of success in a course, what they fail to do is measure that success by anything other than mere retention; and they ignore the student's subjective aim as he or she participates in the educational process. Direct writing assessment moved many of us away from bare-bones predictors of success precisely because they ignored everything but the statistical probability of retention. Portfolios and timed essays are more valid and thus do a better job of orienting students toward the purposes of our placement and help us to put students in courses that match the written products they show us. Yet we may still talk of the student "self" that is sacrificed at our insistence on making the decision for the student. It has been said about placement, "Tests don't have validity; *decisions* have validity" (Williamson).

Because placement as a future-directed decision is such a complex issue, and because the decision itself is one that gains or loses validity as it is informed by the student's own purposes and expectations, some schools have adopted directed self-placement (DSP). DSP requires that we explain the program course options, including the kind of work that is expected of students in each course. It requires that we offer guidance to students about what skills and preparation are implicit prerequisites for each course. And it requires that we direct students through a personal decision-making process that takes into account their own skills and preparation as well as their psychological and social readiness for tasks laid out before them as clearly and as honestly as we can.

We argue in "Directed Self-Placement: An Attitude of Orientation" and in "Pragmatism and Directed Self-Placement at Grand Valley State University" that DSP, more than any other placement method, integrates the student into an important educational process—fostering instead of sacrificing the student self—and at once trumping problems of reliability and validity by asking students themselves to take responsibility for their own educational lives as they survey our curriculum and its demands. The reliability (would they make the same decision from one day to the next?) of DSP is measured by the student's own self-understanding. The validity of DSP (does their decision have meaningful consequences?) is measured by the student's own sense that he or she is taking on an appropriate level of course of study that corresponds to his or her subjective aims and commitments. Again, these decisions are not made alone but under the guidance and *direction* of faculty and staff who have experience with the curriculum and past experience with students facing the same decision.

But most important, all the validity and reliability that we can attribute to any placement method means nothing if our curriculum itself does not reflect a reliable and valid program. If each section of first-year composition does not share goals or outcomes across the program; if each section presents the students with the task of figuring out what the teacher wants instead of what the program wants, then all our efforts at valid placement are wasted. DSP in particular depends on a consistent curriculum and on delivering that curriculum as advertised. DSP pushes the focus of our placement efforts back on to the question of what does it mean to succeed in a given program. So much of what vexes WPAs with regard to placement has to do with the tension between predictive and content validity. Would we rather have a disembodied number that predicts success in college or would we rather have several pieces of writing that tell us what kind of writing someone can produce in circumstances prior to their knowing our curriculum or course expectations? DSP offers something more like systemic validity: integrity of placement method, curriculum, and the students' academic life. When placement is seen in the context of the writing program and entire institutional culture and the consequences that it creates for students of different abilities, then we finally begin to talk about meaningful placement.

The best placement method directs our attention not to the conflict between content and predictive validity but to the curriculum we offer. Placement should force us to ask how well our students are finding their way into appropriate courses and succeeding in ways that meet at least our minimal expectations and also the students' own subjective purposes staked out in advance. Good placement is about placement *into* a program, so we first need a coherent program. Building a good program should be the first order of business, and finally this is much more important than placement because it is what in fact makes placement meaningful.

GAINING INSTITUTIONAL SUPPORT
FOR YOUR PLACEMENT PROGRAM

Gaining institutional support for your program begins with establishing an ethos of responsibility and demonstrating a willingness to respond to concerns of faculty and administrators. A first-year writing program is typically a *university* requirement, not a department requirement, and if support for a program is forthcoming, it will begin when we foreground this fact in our discussions with others. When we release our grip as "sole authority" on writing matters and present ourselves as writing experts in stewardship of a university program seeking to respond to university needs, we begin to take possession of the great weight of responsibility that a writing program has in a university community. If, on the other hand, as program directors we present our first-year writing program as an English department program, or as a program with aims that can only be understood by specialists in rhetoric and composition, we risk cutting ourselves off from our biggest supporters, the university community. At GVSU, we have found that the disciplinary diversity of the university community is a much stronger ally than a literature-dominated English department with narrow and sometimes doctrinaire strictures. Finding your program beholden to a university curriculum committee representing the common sense of faculty around the university can liberate your program from niggling turf concerns and the idiosyncrasies of faculty who "have been teaching composition for twenty-five years"—or not at all.

Those of us trained in composition and rhetoric traffic in a technical language and ideological set we bring with us from graduate school and develop in our professional associations. We talk about discourse communities and expressivist, social, and postprocess theories of composing. We are sometimes reactive to labels like *service course* or *remedial writing*. Often our colleagues around the university, however, are quite indifferent to our doctrinal concerns, and in practice we are often in much closer agreement with innocent common sense than our jargon would suggest. Everyone wants students to write well.

Naturally administrators are hesitant to put money into programs when they believe there is nothing to be gained, or if they believe that they have no say-so in what goes on in the program. In the early 1990s, the usual complaints about low standards and inconsistency across sections of first-year composition circulated widely at our own institution. Together with other colleagues, we refocused the first-year writing courses and added a junior-level WID (writing-in-the-disciplines) course to the program. We initiated team-graded course portfolios and published a formal student's guide featuring course goals, sample assignments, grading criteria, and student papers. From the early to the late 1990s, the GPA in the required first-year writing course dropped from 3.1 to 2.7—and it has held there for four years running. Non-English faculty and administrators realized that the writing faculty were taking their concerns seriously. Now, a new proposal or a further revision to the curriculum is likely to be met with trust and approval, in large part because we were willing to give our academic community what it was looking for: a sense of rigor and consistency. It's important to us, however, to emphasize that we have maintained what we believe to be sound pedagogical practices and course goals; we simply found ways to work those into a frame that made sense to the larger community.

The idea of seeking out ways to create a context of accountability and responsibility may sound like a hazardous practice. In fact, it may be if finally your program can't deliver the goods. But a program that does not see itself in service to the university's curriculum and that does not understand its importance vis-à-vis admissions, WAC (writing across the curriculum), and other programs loses all its political and practical leverage. When we initiated DSP at GVSU, we did so with a record of activity that had demonstrated we shared the concerns of the administration and university community. Nobody feared our motives might have to do with building a stronger fortress around our program. Discussions we had with provosts and admissions directors in prior months and years about grading standards and program goals made it much easier for us to talk with them about DSP. Of course we emphasized that DSP would make the admission process much smoother, but allowing administrators to participate in initiatives that improve pedagogy and university climate is part of the sharing of responsibility we think is important to promote.

FURTHER READING

WPAs new to the assessment literature should become familiar with several key books: Charles R. Cooper and Lee Odell's *Evaluating Writing;* the books of Edward M. White, including his latest, *Teaching and Assessing Writing;* Willa Wolcott and Sue M. Legg's *An Overview of Writing Assessment;* Laurel Black, Donald A. Daiker, Jeffrey Sommers, and Gail Stygall's *New Directions in Portfolio Assessment;* and Pat Belanoff and Marcia *Dickson's Portfolios: Process and Product.* We can also recommend several articles published in *College Composition and Communication:* Sandra Murphy and Ed Nolte's "Report to the CCCC Executive Committee: Survey of Postsecondary Writing Assessment Practices," the CCCC Committee on Assessment's "Writing Assessment: A Position Statement," and Richard Haswell and Susan Wyche-Smith's "Adventuring into Writing Assessment." Finally, we also recommend several articles published in *Assessing Writing:* Karen L. Greenberg's "Validity and Reliability Issues in the Direct Assessment of Writing," Susanmarie Harrington's "New Visions of Authority in Placement Test Rating," and Sandra Murphy's "Portfolios and Curriculum Reform: Patterns in Practice."

WORKS CITED

Camp, Roberta. "Changing the Model for Direct Assessment of Writing." *Validating Holistic Scoring for Writing Assessment: Theoretical and Empirical Foundations.* Ed. Michael M. Williamson and Brian A. Huot. Cresskill, NJ: Hampton, 1993. 45–78.

Cherry, Roger D., and Paul R. Meyer. "Reliability Issues in Holistic Assessment." *Validating Holistic Scoring for Writing Assessment: Theoretical and Empirical Foundations.* Ed. Michael M. Williamson and Brian A. Huot. Cresskill, NJ: Hampton, 1993. 109–41.

Committee on Testing. "Terminal Report." *College Composition and Communication* 17 (1966): 269–72.

Connors, Robert J. *Composition-Rhetoric: Backgrounds, Theory, and Pedagogy.* Pittsburgh: U of Pittsburgh P, 1997.

Grego, Rhonda, and Nancy Thompson. "Repositioning Remediation: Negotiating Composition's Work in the Academy." *College Composition and Communication* 47 (1996): 62–84.

Hamp-Lyons, Liz, and William Condon. *Assessing the Portfolio: Principles for Practice, Theory, and Research.* Cresskill, NJ: Hampton, 2000.

Haswell, Richard, and Susan Wyche-Smith. "Adventuring into Writing Assessment." *College Composition and Communication* 45 (1994): 220–36.

Huot, Brian. "A Survey of College and University Writing Placement Practices."
    WPA: Writing Program Administration 17.3 (1994): 49–65.
—. "Toward a New Theory of Writing Assessment." *College Composition and Commu-
    nication* 47 (1996): 549–66.
Royer, Daniel J., and Roger Gilles. "Directed Self-Placement: An Attitude of Orien-
    tation." *College Composition and Communication* 50 (1998): 54–70.
—. "Pragmatism and Directed Self-Placement at Grand Valley State University." *Di-
    rected Self-Placement: Principles and Practices.* Ed. Daniel J. Royer and Roger Gilles.
    Cresskill, NJ: Hampton, 2002, in press.
Scharton, Maurice. "The Politics of Validity." *Assessment of Writing: Politics, Policies,
    Practices.* Eds. Edward M. White, William D. Lutz, and Sandra Kamusikiri. New
    York: MLA, 1996. 53–75.
Smith, William L. "Assessing the Reliability and Adequacy of Using Holistic Scoring
    of Essays as a College Placement Technique." *Validating Holistic Scoring for Writing
    Assessment: Theoretical and Empirical Foundations.* Ed. Michael M. Williamson and
    Brian A. Huot. Cresskill, NJ: Hampton, 1993. 142–205.
Soliday, Mary. "From the Margins to the Mainstream: Reconceiving Remediation."
    College Composition and Communication 47 (1996): 85–100.
White, Edward M. *Developing Successful College Writing Programs.* San Francisco:
    Jossey-Bass, 1989.
Williamson, Michael. "Assessing Students, Assessing Ourselves." Presented at the
    Fifty-First Annual Conference on College Composition and Communication.
    April 12, 2000. Minneapolis, MN.

18

The WPA as Researcher and Archivist

◆❦ • ❦◆

Shirley K. Rose
Irwin Weiser
Purdue University

When writing program administrators (WPAs) describe their work, what do they say it entails? Certainly, most WPAs would include curriculum development, staffing and staff development, and assessment. Many would include budgeting, establishing interdisciplinary relationships, and representing the writing program on various committees. All would mention the day-to-day troubleshooting and problem solving that makes it often impossible to anticipate what one will accomplish at the office on a particular day. But too often programmatic research and the development of program archives are not activities that WPAs consider as integral to their positions. We believe that WPAs who do not include these activities as conscious parts of their jobs are underestimating the value of their work and perhaps making that work harder and less satisfying than it might otherwise be.

We understand why some WPAs may not think of program research and the development of program archives as essential. After all, writing program administration is very much a job based on dealing with the immediate: the immediate need to hire someone to teach, the immediate need to complete a required report or a budget request, the immediate need to address a student complaint or an instructor's problem. Research, on the other hand, is often thought to be a contemplative activity, demanding, above all, large chunks of time that WPAs typically can't find. And research is not typically as schedule-bound as other work WPAs do. If a report isn't submitted on time, problems may arise. If, on the other hand, the WPA lets work on an article about her program sit ignored for two months, the consequences are less immediately apparent. Similarly, archiving does not impose its own schedule; instead, archiving requires a long view, one that anticipates the future of the writing program—and the program's future administrators.

In this chapter we will argue that *writing program research and writing program records management are essential and interdependent responsibilities* of every WPA. WPAs may feel that they don't have the time to do either or that neither is appropriate to their administrative roles. Systematic research may seem impossible for a WPA immersed in the daily flow of program administration. Managing program records may be seen as a clerical task, and a program archive may seem like a luxury appropriate only to programs with excess staff and space. Yet we believe that the WPA who develops a strategy for establishing program archives and for thinking about those archives as the sources of data for research makes significant contributions to her ability to administer her program effectively, adds to the field's knowledge of administrative practices, and establishes a rich source of data for future research. Equally important, the research conducted by and the archives established by WPAs document their work in ways that transcend their programs or their discipline. Such documentation is often valuable in presenting the accomplishments and needs of the writing program to administrators who are unlikely to have detailed knowledge of it, but who may have a great deal to say about its funding, growth, and status.

THE RESEARCHER/ARCHIVIST MIND-SET

WPAs who assume the researcher/archivist mind-set do so in addition to their other ways of thinking about themselves and their work. They must think of themselves not only as administrators, curriculum designers, and preparers of teachers of writing but also as researchers and archivists. To assume the researcher/archivist mind-set, WPAs must consciously conceive of their administrative work and their programs as generative of data. Such a mind-set requires a different orientation to the work of program administration. WPAs define their work relationally whereas conventional conceptions of "researcher" and "archivist" construct these professionals as relatively autonomous and independent. WPAs who develop a researcher/archivist frame of mind have, for example, a different orientation to time. We must step out of the immediacy of the daily administrative flow, where the time we devote to an issue is often dictated by the situation and, for the purposes of research and archival work, take a longer view. Researchers and archivists plan their work and impose their schedules; they exercise control over the time they spend on such activities.

Not only does the research/archivist mind-set require a different orientation to time, it also has a different orientation to information. WPAs who include research and archiving in their conception of their work think about the information they generate or that crosses their desks not simply in terms of its immediate purpose, but also as data to be systematically collected, reviewed, and interpreted. Further, the researcher/archivist mind-set allows WPAs to pose and define problems and questions for themselves in addition to solving problems identified or created by others. It relies on abstract, studied, contemplative, even meditative thinking rather than the adept, expeditious, multitasking that is also required to administer a writing program successfully.

The researcher/archivist mind-set is thus purposeful, requiring planning. It requires the WPA to look into the future and speculate about what information will be needed and how it might be used before making decisions about what documents or data need to be generated, collected, or retained. Writing program records do not become an archive or data simply because they are old or they have not been discarded. Records become an archive and thus a potential resource for research when intellectual control has been exercised over them; that is, they must be organized and accessible to use. Thus, archiving, like research, is a deliberate activity, one requiring the exercise of agency.

WHY WPAs SHOULD BE RESEARCHERS[1]

In the past several years, composition studies has begun to give increasing attention to acknowledging, describing, and valuing/evaluating the intellectual work of writing program administration, recognizing that WPAs play a critical role in the development as well as application of knowledge in the field. This attention is reflected in the reception the profession has given the Council of Writing Program Administrators' document describing the intellectual work of program administration. Yet, WPAs' work as researchers is not well understood outside the profession or by new WPAs, and even experienced WPAs need to learn additional ways to identify the opportunities for doing significant intellectual work in the context of their programs.

Several shared features and qualities characterize WPA research. First, the *purpose* of WPAs' research is to understand program practices in order to improve or retain them. Thus, the *site of this inquiry* is those writing program practices—curriculum development, faculty development, and program evaluation. The *participant-subjects* in the research projects at these sites are the program stakeholders—instructional staff, writing students, other faculty and administrators, as well as the WPA himself or herself. Because these pro-

---

[1]This section is based on the introductory chapter of our collection *The Writing Program Administrator as Researcher.*

gram practices, sites, and stakeholders are diverse, the *inquiry is multimethodological*, drawing on historical/archival, theoretical, empirical, and hermeneutic inquiry processes.

These features suggest that WPA research is guided by the following values: It is motivated by a desire to improve writing program practices; it is responsible to the field of writing program administration by answering or contributing to answers for shared questions; and it is ethical in its involvement of participants. Thus good research in writing program administration has the following qualities:

- It is informed by current theory and previous research in composition and rhetoric, literacy studies, education, and other related and contributing fields and in turn has a potential to inform future theorizing and research in these fields.
- It invokes, corresponds to, and acknowledges values shared by the professional community of WPAs at the same time it shapes, constructs, or calls into question these values.
- It is worthwhile and ethical.
- It is rigorous and systematic and does not squander human or material resources of time, energy, and money.
- It responds to or answers the questions that prompted it or generates new, better questions.
- It can withstand review by peers (even if not subjected to their review).
- It is documented in program records.
- It is circulated at the institutional site through documents and presentations to administrators and teachers and through application of its conclusions in program practices, and it may be circulated beyond the immediate institutional context through electronic or print publication to WPAs and other composition studies researchers in other contexts.
- Its conclusions enable WPAs to justify strategic plans to implement program change where appropriate or to justify decisions to preserve program practices where appropriate.

These nine features together suggest an overarching criterion for WPA research: It must require and develop the WPA's agency by deploying his or her expertise and energies in responsive and responsible ways and by satisfying his or her need to gain understanding and insight into the culture and practices of the writing program and the broader institutional context.

As we hope is clear, the ways in which WPAs conduct research and the kinds of expertise their research requires are not categorically different from other research in rhetoric and writing studies. WPA research differs because of the institutional role of the WPA. Because the WPA is held responsible for the writing program, research on that program is in the WPA's own interest.

Thus, the WPA cannot pose as a seeker of knowledge for its own sake but must acknowledge that the outcome of her inquiry may have an immediate, obvious impact on many teachers and students. Her interested-ness does not, however, diminish the WPA's desire to understand, her intellectual engagement with the issues her research projects address, or her obligation and commitment to conduct principled inquiry and circulate its conclusions.

These characteristics, features, and criteria suggest the following definition of WPAs' research: *Research in writing program administration is theoretically-informed, systematic, principled inquiry for the purpose of developing, sustaining, and leading a sound, yet dynamic, writing program.*[2]

WHY WPAs SHOULD BE ARCHIVISTS

The research that WPAs conduct generally depends on the collection, organization, and interpretation of documents found in program records, and those records, when managed and maintained deliberately, constitute the program archive. Thus program research and program archiving are interdependent activities with the former ensuring the generation of records that will constitute a useable archive of documents and the latter ensuring that the product of the research will not be lost. As Duane Roen has pointed out and as all WPAs know, WPAs and writing programs generate and receive enormous volumes of documents—program descriptions, syllabi, instructors' applications and files, course evaluations, reports, and a myriad of correspondence, memos, and so forth. Though it may be tempting, particularly in the age of electronic communication, to simply save everything, such unreflective saving cannot provide a *useful* archive.[3] Establishing an archive is not merely an act of accumulating and filing documents; they must also be evaluated. Determining the value of program records requires informed and careful analysis, for archivists must be able to evaluate the significance of the records' source, their informational content, uniqueness, usability, and relationship to other records (Schellenberg, "Appraisal" 61). Thus, making judgments about the archival significance of writing program records draws on WPAs' professional expertise. Even if the WPA is not directly managing the archive, she must be involved in developing the documentation strategy on which it is based.

Evaluating the archival significance of writing program records requires an understanding of rhetorical principles and writing theory, an understanding of administrative practices and principles gained through experience as WPAs, and an understanding of the research interests of the field of composi-

---

[2]This is an elaboration of Christine Hult's definition in "The Scholarship of Administration."

[3]And we caution against relying on digitally stored documents because the long-term stability of disks and other media is questionable, and the formats of data storage media change rapidly: How many of us can read documents stored on 5¼" floppy disks or created on computers using CPM as their operating system?

tion studies in general. This expertise is necessary to determine both the primary values of archives (the values for the originating agency, for administrative, fiscal, legal, and operating purposes) and the secondary values of archival materials, including evidential value (evidence of the organization and functioning of the agency that produced the records) and informational value (their value for information on persons, places, subjects, and things other than the organization that created them).[4]

Elliott lists several "understandings" necessary to archivists that are shared by writing theorists and researchers: understanding of document–event relations (360), understanding that a document can have different functions at different times for different audiences (362), and understanding that the form of a text is determined by the conversant's need to express something *within a particular situation* (363). WPAs' immersion in writing theory disposes them to agree that, as Samuels explains, "the integrated nature of society's institutions and its recorded documentation must be reflected in archivists' efforts to document those institutions" (112). WPAs need to work with professional archivists in their institutions in order to coordinate efforts and benefit from their expertise in such areas as archival principles and standard practices. Professional archivists can advise us on when and how to apply traditional archival principles and concepts such as original order, provenance, the life cycle of a document, and authority control. Professional archivists also can help us understand and apply relevant information systems theory and assist us in applying organization theory to development of our records management and archival practices for our writing programs.

But we can't depend on already overburdened and underfunded professional archivists at our institutions. Even in the most ideal of circumstances for qualified staffing and funding of program archives, WPAs need to participate actively in critical decision making about developing and maintaining their programs' archives. The extent to which we are involved in creating, developing, and maintaining our own archives determines the degree of intellectual control (as well as physical control) we will have over the record of our work. As archivists for our own programs, our knowledge of what records are in our collection, where they came from, and how they relate to one another gives us intellectual control of our program archives. Our knowledge of the location of materials and of how they can be retrieved gives us physical control. Given our intimate knowledge of our writing programs, we are optimally situated to meet the three primary objectives of archival programs identified by Kesner: identifying and selecting or collecting records for preservation, arranging and preserving these records, and ensuring the records' accessibility by providing finding aids and reference services (101).

---

[4]These definitions of *primary, secondary, evidential,* and *informational values* for archives have been taken from Schellenberg (*Management*).

As O'Toole has suggested, anyone who works as an archivist must understand the reasons for recording information in the first place, the reasons for saving information for long periods, the technology that supports records creation, and the characteristics and uses of recorded information (10). Given our overview of most of the activities of our programs, WPAs are well situated to become archivists for the writing programs. As the original creators of many of our programs' records, we know why and how they were developed, why they took the form they did, and what their continuing significance is likely to be. As creators and users of our programs' records, we can make informed judgments about the strengths, weaknesses, and potential future uses of records and analyze their long-term value (Schellenberg, "Appraisal" 59). In these ways, the work of establishing and maintaining a writing program archive is an intellectual task that draws on a WPA's professional experience and engagement in disciplinary practices.

DOCUMENTATION STRATEGIES
FOR DEVELOPING ARCHIVES

The term *documentation strategy* refers to a proactive approach to records management and creating an archive, one that is particularly appropriate for writing programs. Originally developed by Helen Willa Samuels, a theorist of archive practices, a documentation strategy is a plan for establishing a usable archive of an aspect of society or culture that is of significance and interest. In the specific case of a writing program, a documentation strategy is a plan for archiving the program's practices: its development, its procedures, and its participants. The strategy is designed, promoted, and implemented by the mutual efforts of document creators, record managers, archivists, users, other experts, and beneficiaries and other interested parties. It is regularly refined or revised in response to changing conditions. Following are specific characteristics of a documentation strategy:

1. **How is a documentation strategy different from a conventional archival program?** Documentation strategies depend on cooperation between records creators and records managers in a variety of institutional positions; a conventional archival program, focusing on the activities of a single institution or unit, operates more independently and autonomously. Documentation strategies focus on *interactions* among individuals and organizations; collections typically focus on actions of central figures of importance whose papers have been preserved. A conventional archival program *collects*; implementers of a documentation strategy do not necessarily collect—that is, assume physical custody—of all records, but *take steps to ensure retention of records* in various institutions and departments. A traditional archival program only collects records already generated and

saved; a documentation strategy plans for creation and retention of some records that might not otherwise have existed.

2. **How are documentation strategies developed?** The first step in developing a documentation strategy for a writing program is to *draft a statement of the strategy*—that is, to create a document. To do this, participants, including representatives from as many of the program's constituents or stakeholders as possible, draw on a variety of information. They develop a profile of the way in which records are created, used, and administered by the groups and individuals participating in the program or project being documented; they develop data on records already included in the program's active records and archive; and they develop data on the use of archival and related documentation by persons other than the records creators.

This information is analyzed in order to address the following questions: What kinds of records are archival quality because they are vital to the future needs of the creators? What kinds of records are archival because they are important to the interests of others? What types of archival records lend themselves to sampling, through the selection either of certain records or of certain records creators, and what selection approaches seem most feasible, effective, and efficient? Who are the key groups and individuals who can most persuasively convince records creators, administrators, archival repositories, and others to consider the recommendations of the documentation strategy statement? How can these groups and individuals be persuaded to assist in implementing the strategy? What information is needed to improve future analysis of documentation conditions and needs and how might this be obtained? What needs of records creators and others presently are not being met because certain types of records are not being created at all? How might records creators be persuaded to create such records?

To *implement the documentation strategy*, records creators and records managers take measures to ensure that the appropriate documents are generated, circulated to the appropriate audience, and retained in an efficient filing system. Records creators take measures to adequately format and identify the records they generate.

The focus of *the documentation strategy is regularly reviewed and reconsidered* to determine whether its scope is clear and appropriate, and what revisions might be needed.

3. **Why are documentation strategies needed for writing programs?** As must be clear from the outline of the steps involved in a documentation strategy, developing, implementing, and reviewing a writing program's documentation strategy is a complex intellectual task that requires (a) an intimate knowledge of a writing program's practices and those

of the larger institution in which it is located, (b) a sophisticated theoretical understanding of written discourse, and (c) considerable rhetorical skill, in addition to a significant amount of time and energy—and it uses a lot of paper and space.

DOCUMENTATION STRATEGIES AND WPA RESEARCH

Writing program research and writing program documentation strategies can be strategically integrated. A well-designed and maintained documentation strategy for a specific element or activity of a writing program can develop a data bank for research projects related to that aspect of the program. For example, at Purdue we have developed a documentation strategy for a revision of the first-year composition curriculum, and we are developing a documentation strategy for our nationally recognized teaching assistant mentoring program. A more general documentation strategy for a writing program can ensure that basic program data such as enrollment and staffing profiles and program policies and procedures are available in anticipation of a variety of possible future uses of the information. The individual WPA can use the data to make strategic decisions for program development. The data can also be useful beyond the program for what it can contribute to research that develops our collective understanding of writing program administration. The data also have traditional historical research value for their potential contribution to the construction of narratives of writing program development, evolution of administrative practices, and the development of composition studies more generally.

In each of these integrations of documentation strategies and research, the WPA-archivist anticipates the interpretive work the WPA-researcher will do in the future. Recognizing that program records are not transparent, but rather wholly rhetorical representations of information, the WPA-archivist acknowledges and speculates about their potential strategic use. The WPA-archivist also recognizes that her or his choices about what records to generate will determine which aspects of the writing program are made visible and which are erased over time, what is remembered and what is forgotten. In addition, the archives a WPA establishes provide the opportunity for program continuity because they establish a history for subsequent WPAs to refer to. In this way the WPA-archivist makes decisions about what can be known to researchers.

GUIDELINES FOR INTEGRATING DOCUMENTATION STRATEGIES AND PROGRAM RESEARCH

The integration of documentation strategies and program research requires that the WPA think of archival development as a multiple-step process:

1. First the WPA needs to develop a general documentation strategy for the writing program that will ensure the development and maintenance of basic, general information about the status of program activities and practices. This "information" is not, of course, transparent; the documents that comprise it are, as we have indicated earlier, collected based on principles developed by the WPA and other stakeholders in the writing program and serve as the source of specific data about the program for research—principles that are ideologically, culturally, and politically determined.

2. Reviewing and interpreting this general information will enable the WPA to identify specific areas of the program that may require systematic research—either to determine whether a problem exists or to explore possible solutions to an acknowledged problem or aspect of the program in need of change. Thus this information can generate research questions or enable the WPA to refine research questions that may initially be quite broad. For each specific research project, the WPA develops an appropriate documentation strategy to collect relevant data. For these documentation strategies, choices made about types of documents to generate and collect are critical because they will determine the outcome of the research project.

3. If the outcome of such a research project leads the WPA to undertake a change in program practices, a strategy for documenting that change should be developed as well in order to provide a record of the processes and decisions underlying the change. The specific focus of this documentation strategy will be determined in part by the WPA's particular interests and expertise, and it may evolve as the WPA reviews and reflects on the information gathered. In developing this documentation strategy, the WPA anticipates possible future research projects that will draw on the information. These documentation strategies may not immediately or directly affect the writing program's daily practices; that is, they yield archives that are records of a particular development in the program that may become research sources for the longer term.

Once the research questions are articulated, the WPA can determine what records/data are needed to adequately document the program area's activities and practices in order to answer them. At this stage of research, then, WPAs need to answer the following three questions:

1. What records are already routinely generated?
2. Which of these records need to be preserved?
3. What additional records need to be created?

Archival records may thus play a recursive role in WPA research: An examination of records may yield research questions, and the records may also provide partial answers to those questions.

At the outset, and throughout the implementation of the documentation strategy, it is important to establish consistent practices for identifying, collecting, and organizing the records/data. The following guidelines should be observed:

1. Establish consistent formats for created documents (indicating names of originators, dates, titles, page numbers, etc.).
2. Add the aforementioned information on documents generated by others if it does not appear.
3. Establish one collection point for records, to avoid duplication or efforts.
4. Determine a system for filing/organizing records, and follow it consistently.
5. Document all of the above decisions and provide a rationale for them.

Throughout the implementation of the documentation strategy, it is necessary to analyze and interpret the records and data generated and collected in order to determine whether and how well they address the research questions. A documentation strategy is not static. Though it is important to plan for the collection of documents as carefully as possible prior to beginning research, to anticipate as much as possible what kinds of documents will need to be collected, created, or located, it is also important to realize that during the course of research, it may be necessary to revise the documentation strategy to include additional kinds of records.

CONCLUSION

These guidelines for integrating writing program research and documentation strategies may seem obvious; but what is not self-evident is that WPAs need to adopt the researcher/archivist mind-set so they consciously view the documents they generate and review as data for program research. As we indicated earlier, it is easy for busy WPAs to focus on the immediate demands of their work. But in doing so, they may limit themselves to the managerial aspects of program administration. We want to urge WPAs to take as comprehensive a view of program administration as possible, to see their administrative work as consistent with and contributing to their work as researchers and scholars. And we believe that thinking of themselves as archivists and researchers who produce work that merits documentation, preservation and subsequent investigation enables them to do so.

WORKS CITED

Council of Writing Program Administrators. "Evaluating the Intellectual Work of Writing Program Administration." *WPA: Writing Program Administration* 22.1/2 (1998): 85–104.

Elliott, Clark. "Communications and Events in History: Toward a Theory for Documenting the Past." *American Archivist* 48 (1985): 357–68.

Hult, Christine. "The Scholarship of Administration." *Resituating Writing: Constructing and Administering Writing Programs*. Ed. Joseph Janangelo and Kristine Hansen. Portsmouth, NH: Boynton/Cook, 1995. 119–31.

Kesner, Richard M. "Archival Collection Development: Building a Successful Acquisitions Program." *Midwestern Archivist* 5.2 (1981): 101–12.

O'Toole, James M. *Understanding Archives and Manuscripts*. Archival Fundamentals Series. Chicago: Society of American Archivists, 1990.

Roen, Duane H. "Writing Administration as Scholarship and Teaching." *Scholarship, Promotion, and Tenure in Composition Studies*. Ed. Richard C. Gebhardt and Barbara Gebhardt. Mahwah, NJ: Erlbaum, 1996. 43–55.

Rose, Shirley K, and Irwin Weiser. "Introduction." *The Writing Program Administrator as Researcher: Inquiry in Action and Reflection*. Portsmouth, NH: Heinemann-Boynton/Cook, 1999. v–xi.

Samuels, Helen W. "Who Controls the Past?" *American Archivist* 49 (1986): 109–24.

Schellenberg, T. R. "The Appraisal of Modern Public Records." National Archives Bulletin No. 8. Washington, DC: National Archives Records Services, 1956.

—. *The Management of Archives*. New York: Columbia UP, 1965.

SELECT RESOURCES FOR WRITING PROGRAM ARCHIVISTS/RESEARCHERS

Archival Theory

Atherton, Jay. "From Life Cycle to Continuum: Some Thoughts on the Records Management-Archives Relationship." *Archivaria* 21 (Winter 1985–86): 43–51.

Boles, Frank, and Julia Marks Young. "Exploring the Black Box: The Appraisal of University Administrative Records." *American Archivist* 48 (Spring 1985): 121–40.

Cox, Richard J., and Helen W. Samuels. "The Archivist's First Responsibility: A Research Agenda to Improve the Identification and Retention of Records of Enduring Value." *American Archivist* 51 (Winter–Spring 1988): 28–46 (includes "Commentary" by Frank Boles 43–46).

Elliott, Clark A. "Communication and Events in History: Toward a Theory for Documenting the Past." *American Archivist* 48 (Fall 1985): 357–68.

Hackman, Larry J., and Joan Warnow-Blewett. "The Documentation Strategy Process: A Model and a Case Study." *American Archivist* 50 (Winter 1987): 12–47.

Ham, F. Gerald. "Archival Choices: Managing the Historical Records in an Age of Abundance." *American Archivist* 47 (Winter 1984): 11–22.

Heald, Carolyn. "Is There Room for Archives in the Postmodern World?" *American Archivist* 59 (Winter 1996): 88–101.

Kuhn, Clifford M. "A Historian's Perspective on Archives and the Documentary Process." *American Archivist* 59 (Summer 1996): 312–20.

Lutzker, Michael A. "Max Weber and the Analysis of Modern Bureaucratic Organization: Notes toward a Theory of Appraisal." *American Archivist* 45 (Spring 1982): 119–30.

Samuels, Helen Willa. "Improving Our Disposition: Documentation Strategy." *Archivaria* 33 (Winter 1991–92): 125–40.

Samuels, Helen Willa. "Who Controls the Past." *American Archivist* 49 (Spring 1986): 109–24.

Archiving Guidelines and Handbooks

Bellardo, Lewis J., and Lynn Lady Bellardo. *A Glossary for Archivists, Manuscript Curators and Records Managers*. SSA Archival Fundamentals Series. Chicago: Society of American Archivists, 1992.

Ham, F. Gerald. *Selecting and Appraising Archives and Manuscripts*. SSA Archival Fundamentals Series. Chicago: Society of American Archivists, 1993

Hunter, Gregory S. *Developing and Maintaining Practical Archives: A How-To-Do-It Manual*. Neal-Schuman, 1996.

Miller, Frederic. *Arranging and Describing Archives and Manuscripts*. SSA Archival Fundamentals Series. Chicago: Society of American Archivists, 1990.

O'Toole, James M. *Understanding Archives and Manuscripts*. SSA Archival Fundamentals Series. Chicago: Society of American Archivists, 1993.

Pugh, Mary Jo. *Providing Reference Services for Archives and Manuscripts*. SSA Archival Fundamentals Series. Chicago: Society of American Archivists, 1992.

Ritzenthaler, Mary Lynn. *Preserving Archives and Manuscripts*. SSA Archival Fundamentals Series. Chicago: Society of American Archivists, 1993.

Wilsted, Thomas, and William Nolte. *Managing Archival and Manuscript Repositories*. SSA Archival Fundamentals Series. Chicago: Society of American Archivists, 1991.

Archival Theory and Historiography in Rhetoric and Composition Studies

Brereton, John. "Rethinking Our Archive: A Beginning." *College English* 61 (May 1999): 574–76.

Connors, Robert. "Historical Inquiry in Composition Studies." *The Writing Instructor* 3 (Summer 1984): 157–67.

Ferreira-Buckley, Linda. "Rescuing the Archives from Foucault." *College English* 61 (May 1999): 577–83.

Mailloux, Steven. "Reading Typos, Reading Archives." *College English* 61 (May 1999): 584–90.

Miller, Susan. "Is There a Text in This Class?" *Freshman English News* 11 (Spring 1982): 20–24.

Miller, Thomas P., and Melody Bowdon. "A Rhetorical Stance on the Archives of Civic Action." *College English* 61 (May 1999): 591–98.

WPA as Researcher/Archivist

Mirtz, Ruth M. "WPAs as Historians: Discovering a First Year Writing Program by Researching Its Past." *The Writing Program Administrator as Researcher: Inquiry in Action and Reflection.* Ed. Shirley K Rose and Irwin Weiser. Portsmouth, NH: Heinemann-Boynton/Cook, 1999. 119–30.

Rose, Shirley K. "Discovering and Preserving Our Histories of Institutional Change: The WPA's Intellectual Work in the Writing Program Archives." *The Writing Program Administrator as Researcher: Inquiry in Action and Reflection.* Ed. Shirley K Rose and Irwin Weiser. Portsmouth, NH: Heinemann-Boynton/Cook, 1999. 107–18.

WPA Research

Clegg, Stewart R., Cynthia Hardy, and Walter R. Nord, eds. *Handbook of Organization Studies.* Thousand Oaks, CA: Sage, 1996.

Cook, Thomas D., and William R. Shadish. "Program Evaluation: The Worldly Science." *Annual Review of Psychology* 37 (1986): 93–292.

Daiker, Donald, and Max Morenberg, eds. *The Writing Teacher as Researcher: Essays in the Theory and Practice of Class-Based Research.* Portsmouth, NH: Boynton/Cook, 1990.

Denzin, Norman, and Yvonna S. Lincoln, eds. *Handbook of Qualitative Research.* Thousand Oaks, CA: Sage, 1994.

Farris, Christine, and Chris M. Anson, eds. *Under Construction: Working at the Intersections of Composition Theory, Research, and Practice.* Logan: Utah State UP, 1998.

Goodlad, John. *Curriculum Inquiry: The Study of Curriculum Practice.* New York: McGraw-Hill, 1979.

Guba, Egon, and Yvonne Lincoln. *Effective Evaluation.* San Francisco: Jossey-Bass, 1982.

Hillocks, George. *Research on Written Composition.* Urbana, IL: NCTE, 1986.

Kirsch, Gesa, and Patricia A. Sullivan, eds. *Methods and Methodology in Composition Research.* Carbondale: Southern Illinois UP, 1992.

Lauer, Janice, and J. William Asher. *Composition Research: Empirical Designs.* New York: Oxford UP, 1988.

McClelland, Ben W., and Timothy R. Donovan, eds. *Perspectives on Research and Scholarship in Composition.* New York: MLA, 1985.

McKernan, James. *Curriculum Action Research: A Handbook of Methods and Resources for the Reflective Practitioner.* London: Kogan Page, 1991.

North, Stephen M. *The Making of Knowledge in Composition: Portrait of an Emerging Field.* Upper Montclair, NJ: Boynton/Cook, 1987.

Ray, Ruth E. *The Practice of Theory: Teacher Research in Composition.* Urbana, IL: NCTE, 1993.

Rose, Shirley K, and Irwin Weiser, eds. *The Writing Program Administrator as Researcher: Inquiry in Action and Reflection.* Portsmouth, NH: Boynton/Cook Heinemann, 1999.

Schön, Donald A. *Educating the Reflective Practitioner: Toward a New Design for Teaching and Learning in the Professions.* San Francisco: Jossey-Bass, 1987.

—. *The Reflective Practitioner: How Professionals Think in Action.* New York: Basic, 1983.

Sullivan, Patricia A., and James E. Porter. *Opening Spaces: Writing Technologies and Critical Research Practices.* Norwood, NJ: Ablex/Computers and Composition, 1997.

White, Edward. *Teaching and Assessing Writing: Recent Advances in Understanding, Evaluating, and Improving Student Performance.* 2nd ed. San Francisco: Jossey-Bass. 1994.

Witte, Stephen P., and Lester Faigley. *Evaluating College Writing Programs.* Carbondale: Southern Illinois UP, 1983.

WPA Executive Committee with primary contributions from Robert Schwegler, Charles Schuster, Gail Stygall, and Judy Pearce. "Evaluating the Intellectual Work of Writing Program Administrators." *WPA: Writing Program Administration* 20 (Fall/Winter 1996): 92–103.

Bibliographies

O'Toole, James M. *Understanding Archives and Manuscripts.* Chicago: Society of American Archivists, 1990. "Bibliographical Note." 71–75.

Yankel, Elizabeth. *Starting an Archives.* Metuchen, NJ: Society of American Archivists, 1994. "Bibliographical Essay." 66–79.

Web Resources

Society of American Archivists <http://www.archivists.org>. "A Code of Ethics for Archivists with Commentary." Society of American Archivists. <http://www.archivists.org/governance/handbook/app_ethics.html>.

"A Guide to Deeds of Gift." <http://www.archivists.org/catalog/deed_of_gift.html>.

"A Guide to Donating Your Organizational Records to a Repository." Society of American Archivists. <http://www.archivists.org/catalog/donating-orgrecs.html>.

"A Guide to Donating Your Personal or Family Papers to a Repository." <http://www.archivists.org/catalog/donating-familyrecs.html>.

"Guidelines for College and University Archives." <http://archivist.org/goverance/cu_guidelines.html>.

ARCHIVES listserv archives (also subscribe to the listserv at this URL) <http://listserv.muohio.edu/archives/archives.html>.

Association of Records Managers and Administrators, Inc. <http://www.arma.org>.

Conservation Resources International. <http://www.conservationresources.com/>.

COOL Conservation Online: Resources for Conservation Specialists. <http://paimpsest.stanford.edu/>.

Midwest Archives Conference. <http://www.midwestarchives.org/index.htm>.

National Archives and Records Administration. <http://www.nara.gov>.

Melody Blowdon's Web links for "On-Line Archival Research." <http://www.ncte.org/ce/may99/archivelinks/>.

Repositories of Primary Sources. <http://www.uidaho.edu/special-collec-
tions/Other.Repositories.html>.
EAD (Encoded Archival Description) Tag Library. <http://www.loc.gov/ead/>.
Basic RAD (Rules for Archival Description). <http://www.lrb74123.usask.ca/
scaa/rad>.
Navigating Finding Aids in Panorama. <http://www.loc.gov/rr/ead/pano.html>.

19

Hard Work and Hard Data: Using Statistics to Help Your Program[1]

Gregory R. Glau
Arizona State University

- At a faulty meeting, one of your colleagues—a full professor—comments that the "student writing in my American Literature class gets worse every year." She turns to you and asks, "Are our first-year students less well prepared than they used to be? Is their writing getting worse?"
- A reporter from the campus newspaper calls and says, "I'm doing a story on student retention, and I understand that we lose a lot of students between their first and second semesters. Can you tell me the percentage of students who take ENG 101 in the fall who register for ENG 102 the next spring? Can you tell me if that rate is improving?"
- At an informal gathering in the dean's office, an assistant dean mentions, "I was glancing over the data from last semester, and it looks to me like the pass rate in first-year composition has gotten worse. Do you know why?"
- The director of your college's Office for Minority Affairs calls and asks, "How are students from underrepresented groups doing in your composition classes? I have the sense that many just aren't making it."

---

[1]This chapter grew out of a presentation I made at the 1999 CCCC. It also draws on suggestions from Terry Collins's presentation at the 1998 CCCC.

Though such queries aren't necessarily a writing program administrator's (WPA's) worst nightmare, questions like these often come out of the blue, usually demand our immediate attention, and always seem to carry several implied accusations: that our pass rates are low and that they should be improving, that some percentage of our students are not succeeding and their lack of success is the writing program's fault, that the university's retention rate is somehow the total responsibility of the composition program, and so on.

Worse, we in the humanities generally are not trained to collect useful statistical information, nor are we prone to "blowing our own horns" in terms of seeking favorable publicity for our writing programs. And as Julia Ferganchick-Neufang reminds us, we are all so busy running our writing programs that we "have difficulty juggling the additional workload of a research project that is unrelated" to our day-to-day responsibilities (21).

However, if we consider such questions as providing a potential teaching moment rather than as a challenge, perhaps we can "take the lemons we're given and make lemonade." Instead of attempting to deflect the queries we receive, let's instead use them to further our own purposes, to put a positive light on the work we do.

One thing we WPAs *are* generally good at is seeing things rhetorically, so consider how we might respond to the questions we get from a rhetorical perspective: what's the situation, who's our audience, and so on?

- Our *occasion* for writing is that we've been asked for information (as in some of the questions that open this chapter) or that we want to be proactive in presenting the success of our writing program.
- Our *purpose* is to explain and present what we do in the most effective manner; in most cases, it is to persuade our audience that what we do, works.
- Our *audience* is usually clear: we're composing a report for a dean, we're writing a brief column for the local newspaper, we're answering someone's question about our writing program. As with any writing situation, we need to really think about what this particular audience needs to know and how we can best explain the information.
- Our *topic* is the information we collect, our program's data (some of this might be statistical, other may be anecdotal, perhaps there are surveys or evaluations we already collect, and so on). Note that some of the information we compile may not be useful, or it might not correlate to other data as we hoped it would. For example, we might examine how our students who come from underrepresented groups are doing in terms of pass rates and then learn that they, on average, don't do quite as well as others. That isn't necessarily data we'd want to publicize, but information we can use internally to try to learn why and to then try to improve the situation.

Thinking rhetorically, as Ed White puts it so clearly, asks us to consider, "What kind of evidence will be accepted as real, as convincing, for the particular audience examining our program?" ("The Rhetorical Problem" 132). Once we frame the questions we receive as a rhetorical situation, we can then conceptualize how to answer those questions in a way we're accustomed to.

Although there are a number of approaches (and problems) associated with accessing an entire writing program (see DeGenaro and White; Gleason; White, *Developing* and "The Rhetorical Problem"; White, Lutz, and Kamusikiri; Witte; Yancey), I want to suggest that there are useful and powerful smaller bits of information readily available to us if we know where to look. This is not to say that programmatic assessment doesn't need to be done; rather, I'm suggesting that we can often answer some of the data queries we receive with solid statistical information about our writing programs. Fellow ASU professor John Ramage calls these factual pieces of information "nuggets," and he is exactly right. But for our nuggets to be effective, we can't get by with, "well, most of our students continue from ENG 101 into ENG 102." Instead, we need to be able to say, "Last academic year 83 percent of our students took ENG 102 in the spring, following ENG 101 in the fall. And, that retention and continuation rate has improved over the past three years. Would you like those numbers?"

Busy administrators, too, often unfamiliar with the work we do, more easily grasp "nuggets of information" than ten-page reports (for more on how to talk with administrative types, see Kinkead and Simpson; Rhodes). What this means is that we don't always need to provide a lengthy explanation of how our entire program is functioning but instead can (at least sometimes) tightly focus on specific statistical data that shows how effective our work really is.

FINDING USEFUL INFORMATION

Before we can even start thinking about audience or presentation, we have to find out what information is available. Someone at every college probably already collects statistical information on its student population; these offices are often called Institutional Analysis or Institutional Data, so our first step is to learn who on campus might have statistical information about our students and program.

Consider your own situation: Does your college have a student database you or your office staff can access? Many have several: one that contains "live" or current information and another into which they "dump" the live data at various times. Often the latter kind of system has a query program available through which you can gather statistical data, and many can download the information into an Excel spreadsheet. Once the data is in the spreadsheet, you can sort it, filter it, chart it, and so on.

Does your writing program now conduct surveys or other data-collection instruments that you might "mine" for useful data? If not, can you implement such a survey?

As with the invention activities we ask our students to work through, your first step is simply to get started, to learn what information is available and how you can access it. There's no need to worry at this point about what you might learn, for this is *inventio* in its best sense: start with some questions and try to find answers to them.

An effective rubric is to think of the questions that a college newspaper reporter might ask. To provide some sense of the kind of answers we might come up with, and what follow-up questions such answers always lead to, I've also listed some brief examples from what we do at Arizona State University:

- *Who* attends our classes? What is their ethnic mix? Average age? Test scores? Educational background? Attitudes toward writing? Toward college? What are their goals? How does writing fit into those goals? How do we know? What do our students have to say about our writing classes? *Example:* In the basic writing program I've supervised (ASU's "Stretch Program"), we ask for the typical end-of-semester departmental evaluations, but we also conduct an anonymous survey, requiring narrative responses to questions such as "Did this class help improve your writing? If so, how? If not, why not?" This gives us an anecdotal database with actual student comments and suggestions. It also allows us to say, "of the students who completed our anonymous surveys, 87 percent say the program helped their writing" (Glau 87). That's the kind of statistic that administrators and parents understand and listen to.
- *What* kinds of things are done in our classes to help students succeed? That is, what are our pedagogical approaches and what goals does our writing program have and in what ways are they articulated and are we meeting those goals? How can we tell? *Example:* Our ENG 101 pass rate increased dramatically when our writing program moved from a more product-oriented pedagogy to one that rewarded process. We can argue over whether or not this is a good thing (have we aided grade inflation?), but we need to know what the data is before we can have such a discussion.
- *When* do students succeed and when do they fail? Why? If we have some students working in computer-mediated classrooms, do they perform better in some way? Why? Is there one group of our teachers who consistently pass more of their students or receive higher evaluations than another group? Why? Is there any correlation between SAT or ACT scores and student success? *Example:* For the past several years, about a quarter of our basic writing and our ENG 102 classes have been held in computer-mediated class-

rooms, but we haven't yet looked at pass or student satisfaction rates for those classes. We also are currently piloting what we call "hybrid" online classes: Students meet one day a week in the classroom and the other day online. Will students in such an environment pass at a higher rate? Will student satisfaction with the classes increase or decrease? Will students achieve the goals and objectives we have for all of our writing classes? How will we know?

- *Why* do our students succeed or fail? That is, do we lose students because they stop coming (what percentage?) or because they actually fail (what percentage?) and are those rates changing? Is there a group of students that do better or worse than others? Does the time of day matter? Class size?
  Example: Once we learned that many of those students who fail our basic writing sequence fail because they stop coming to class, we started calling those who were close to the absence limit, noting that they'd missed a number of classes and asking if we can help. There is no way we can do the same for our ENG 101 students (about three thousand five hundred in fall semesters), but we can for the smaller number of basic writing students.

- *Where* do our students come from? Do they perform better (in what way?) if they live on campus or if they commute? What is their educational background?
  Example: Our students traditionally have been commuter students, but that's changing (we're building more dorms and in the last five years have doubled the size of our first-year class), and each student is now required to get an e-mail account. So, our students should be more accessible and we should be able to contact them easier; will the shift increase pass rates?

- *How* well do our students perform? What's the pass rate for the classes we offer? Is it improving or getting worse? How accurate is our placement process? How can we tell? Does our writing program aid retention (and should it)? In what ways?
  Example: As noted earlier, our ENG 101 pass rate has been improving, since we changed our pedagogical approach. At the same time, we've been giving more A grades and fewer C grades; is that an improvement?

It makes sense, then, for a WPA to think about what information might help support the writing program and then to collect the kind of data that will help to effectively answer some of those problematic questions. Better yet, if we arm ourselves with the right kind(s) of information and learn to use that data in a proactive manner, we can present our programs in their best light—and thus shortstop some of the questions we get about student success, retention, and so on. That is, once we're "armed" with good information, we can use statistics to publicize and to showcase our writing program.

PRESENTING YOUR DATA

I want now to move to suggestions on how to most effectively present that data to various audiences. As Chris Anson and Robert Brown, Jr., put it, such data "are not only important but may be the material products on which the survival of the WPA or the entire writing program depends" (141). As in any rhetorical situation, it's critical to understand who our audience is and what they need to know to be convinced, and I want to suggest that John Ramage's notion (personal communication) of "nuggets of information" serves us well here. That is, once we've learned something about our program—to answer that dean's question, or to publicize the program—we should try to condense the data down into a real "nugget."

So, some suggestions: Put statistical data into simple terms, make sure that tables of that data are easy to read and understand, and when possible, present data in a graphical form. Presenting data in a chart format is especially important for time-series information (changes in pass rates over the last few years, for instance), as such data is difficult to grasp in other formats.

Here's a brief example: Let's say for the past few fall semesters you've collected enrollment data for your ENG 101 students.[2] Table 19.1 presents your information.

Though it is clear that the size of your ENG 101 class dipped a couple of times, overall it's been growing. What might this information tell you?

First, you might be able to track the *funding* your program has received, knowing that (at least at my institution) funding *lags* enrollment. That is, when enrollment increases, you don't necessarily receive more funding until the following year. For the data in Table 19.1, that means you probably got more funding in the fall of 1998 because of the growth in students from 1996 to 1997 (2,751 to 3,277), but that you were hurting in the fall of 1999, since your fall 1998 enrollment *dropped*.

Second, though you understand the increased work the greater number of students require, it might be useful to point out to the dean and others in higher administration that because your ENG 101 class size has increased from 2,649 students in the fall of 1994 to 3,524 students in the fall of 1999, the

TABLE 19.1

ENG 101 Enrollment, Fall Semesters 1994–1999

Fall 1994	Fall 1995	Fall 1996	Fall 1997	Fall 1998	Fall 1999
2,649	2,631	2,751	3,277	3,132	3,524

[2]These data are all real statistics, from ASU records.

number of problems and issues (student complaints, for example) also will have increased *at the same rate*. That is, from 1994 to 1999 on a percentage basis, your ENG 101 class increased by 875 students, and 875/2,649 = a 33 percent increase—the number of students with problems or issues or grade appeals also will have increased by about one third. You therefore can make a good case that you need more administrative staff to handle the increased workload. Putting the same information into a chart often makes it even clearer; Fig. 19.1 presents your enrollment data as a chart, which makes changes over time easier to understand.

Once you have some basic information like this, you can start working with it in various ways. For example, to dramatize the growth in enrollment, you might change the scale of your chart. The image in Fig. 19.1 has a scale that starts at zero; Fig. 19.2 changes the scale to start at 2,500 students registered in ENG 101, so the growth is more dramatic.

To indicate even more the *trend* of your ENG 101 enrollment, you might add a simple trend line, and let this trend line project out for, say, two more fall semesters. That is, you use your historical information to project future enrollment levels. Figure 19.3 tells you that you probably can expect more students in your ENG 101 class for the next two fall semesters.[3]

Such information, presented in this fashion to your dean, might just help you get more faculty lines (you're going to need more people to teach all of the incoming students), more office and classroom space, more staff, and so on.

Let's move from enrollment growth to pass rates: how many of your students pass your classes? Is the trend increasing or decreasing? Does it matter? Which direction would you like it to head? Along the same line, are your teachers giving out more A– grades then they used to? Why? Is that a good or bad thing?

ENG 101 fall enrollment

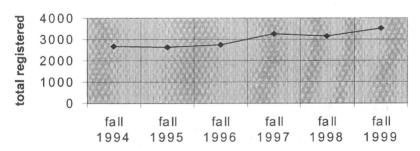

FIG. 19.1.   Chart of ENG 101 enrollment, fall semester 1994–1999.

[3]This simple trend line predicted almost exactly the number of ENG 101 students ASU registered in the 2000 fall semester—3,789 as of 9/11/2000.

ENG 101 fall enrollment

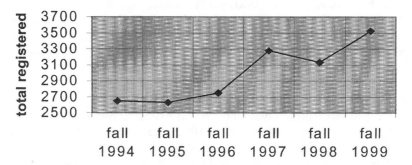

FIG. 19.2.   New Scale: ENG 101 enrollment, fall semester 1994–1999.

ENG 101 fall enrollment

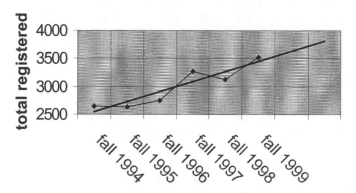

FIG. 19.3.   ENG 101 enrollment, fall semesters 1994–1999, with trend line.

There are no right or wrong answers to questions like these because everything is local: What is right for your program and your specific situation isn't necessarily the best answer for another college or university. Let's consider how you might present pass rate information for, say, an ENG 301 (Business and Professional Writing) class.

As shown in Table 19.2, about 42 percent of the students received an A, a third received a B, and so on. Eighty-two percent passed the class. Because these data are different than the continuation rate (in Figs. 19.1–19.3), you don't want to present this information in a line graph, for there is no time series involved. Instead, a column or bar graph best shows the differences in the categories.

TABLE 19.2

Grand Distribution Data and Percentage

Grade	# Receiving	Percentage	Cumulative %
A	771	41.68 %	41.68%
B	625	33.78	75.46
C	124	6.70	82.16 total pass rate
D	15	.81	82.97
E	73	3.95	86.92
I (Incomplete)	16	.86	87.78
W (Withdraw)	223	12.05	99.84
Other	3	.16	100.00

Figure 19.4 is a visual representation of the data for ENG 301. In addition to about a 75 percent A– or B– grade rate, you might wonder why more than 10 percent of these students chose to withdraw from the class. This image, in other words, might give you a sense of what other information to look for, what other comparisons you might make (do more than 10 percent of the students usually withdraw from this class? Is this the norm for upper-division classes? Is the rate changing?).

In addition, then, to giving the WPA useful information she might use to work toward more faculty lines, statistical data also can serve as warning flags. For example, what might the picture in Figure 19.5 tell you?

Is Figure 19.5 a picture of grade inflation? Would such an image concern you? What other information might you want to compare this to?

In addition to single-item data and graphs, you can use the statistical information you collect to make comparisons. In my own work with our basic-writing program, I've found it especially helpful to use data to show how "Stretch" students (who have an extra semester of guided writing experience) pass ENG 101 at a higher rate than do "regular" ENG 101 students, and I present the information as shown in Figure 19.6.

Here I've compared pass rates for "regular" ENG 101 students to those who've had a previous extra semester of guided writing experience (the "Stretch Program"). An image such as this makes it easy to see and to understand that "Stretch" students pass ENG 101 at a higher rate than do "regular" ENG 101 students. It also might make us question why the Stretch students' pass rate dropped from the 1997–1998 academic year to the 1998–1999 period.

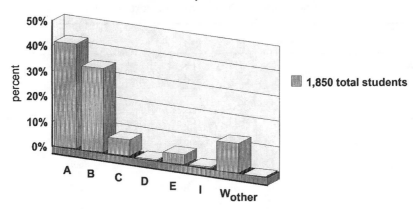

FIG.19.4.   Grade distribution column chart, ENG 301.

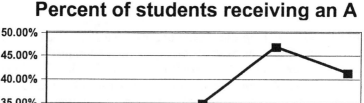

FIG. 19.5.   Students earning an A, fall semester 1995–1999.

I provide these data not only to upper administrators but also to "Stretch Program" students, so they can see what the program can help them achieve ("Stretch Program Statistics + Information").

A FINAL NOTE

To help you get started at finding the "nuggets of information" to present your own program in the most effective manner, try to move outside of your writing program, to come at it as if *you* were evaluating it. What hard questions

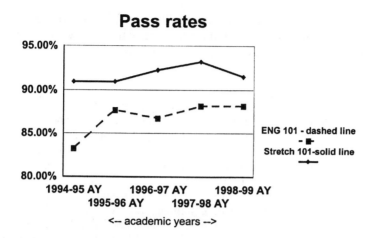

FIG. 19.6.   Pass rates, stretch students compared to ENG 101 students.

might you ask? What would you like answers to? What data might raise some red flags about potential future problems (a continual decrease in pass rates, for example)? What statistical information would convince *you* that the program was doing a good job? If you were applying for a WPA position at your own college or university, what information would you like to know about its writing program?

Another way to think about the questions to ask is to narrow down your focus from your entire writing program to its component parts:

- Do you have an English as a Second Language (ESL) program and, if so, how are those students performing? What is their retention rate and is it improving and how well do they perform in other classes?
- Maybe you have some of your writing class in computer-mediated classrooms, or offer entirely online classes. What is the student population for these courses? How do items like pass rates or instructor evaluations or student comments compare to those classes held in standard classrooms?
- Perhaps you offer special classes (or as we do, a particular sequence of classes) for students identified as basic writers. Who are these students? How are they identified? How might you tell if your placement process is working? How do these students perform in subsequent classes? It will come of no surprise to anyone that basic-writing programs are under attack, and have been for some time—so they're the ones that have been forced to justify what they do based on hard, statistical evidence (see Collins; DeGenaro and White; Freeman, Gum, and Blackburn; Glau; Gleason; "Student Racial/Ethnic Diversity").

There are any number of questions you'll get as WPA—as those at the start of this essay— want to suggest that most if not all have answers in the form of solid, factual data you can obtain, with a bit of work.

WORKS CITED

Anson, Chris M., and Robert L. Brown, Jr. "Subject to Interpretation." *The Writing Program Administrator as Researcher.* Ed. Shirley K. Rose and Irwin Weiser. Portsmouth, NH: Boynton/Cook Heinemann, 1999. 141–52.

Collins, Terence. "Basic Writing Programs and Access Allies: Finding and Maintaining Your Support Network." 1998 Conference on College Composition and Communication. Chicago. 1 Apr. 1998.

DeGenaro, William, and Edward M. White. "Going Around in Circles: Methodological Issues in Basic Writing Research." *Journal of Basic Writing* 19 (2000): 22–35.

Ferganchick-Neufang, Julia. "Research (Im)Possibilities." *The Writing Program Administrator as Researcher.* Ed. Shirley K. Rose and Irwin Weiser. Portsmouth, NH: Boynton/Cook Heinemann, 1999. 18–27.

Freeman, G., M. Gum, and J. M. Blackburn. "Proactive Approaches to Improving Outcomes for At-Risk Students." ERIC document ED 430948, 1999.

Glau, Gregory R. "Hard Work and Hard Data: Getting Our Message Out." 1999 CCCC Convention. Atlanta. March 1999. ERIC document ED 430229, 2000.

—. "The 'Stretch Program': Arizona State University's New Model of University-Level Basic Writing Instruction." *WPA: Writing Program Administration* 20 (1996): 79–91.

Gleason, Barbara. "Evaluating Writing Programs in Real Time: The Politics of Remediation." *College Composition and Communication* 51 (Feb. 2000): 560–88.

Kinkead, Joyce, and Jeanne Simpson. "The Administrative Audience: A Rhetorical Problem." *WPA: Writing Program Administration* 23.3 (Spring 2000): 71–84.

Rhodes, Keith. "Marketing Composition for the 21st Century." *WPA: Writing Program Administration* 23.3 (Spring 2000): 51–69.

"Stretch Program Statistics + Information." 13 Dec. 2000. <http://www.asu.edu/clas/english/composition/cbw/stretch.htm>.

"Student Racial/Ethnic Diversity: Trends in Enrollment, Graduation, and Retention." ERIC document ED 430467, 1999.

White, Edward. *Developing Successful Writing College Writing Programs.* San Francisco: Jossey-Bass, 1989.

—. "The Rhetorical Problem of Program Evaluation and the WPA." *Resituating Writing.* Ed. Joseph Janangelo and Kristine Hansen. Portsmouth, NH: Boynton/Cook Heinemann, 1995. 132–50.

White, Edward M., William D. Lutz, and Sandra Kamusikiri, ed. *Assessment of Writing: Politics, Policies, Practices.* New York: MLA, 1996.

Witte, Stephen, and Lester Faigley. *Evaluating College Writing Programs.* Carbondale: Southern Illinois UP, 1983.

Yancey, Kathleen Blake. "Outcomes Assessment and Basic Writing: What, Why, and How?" *BWe: Basic Writing e-Journal* 1 (1999). 11 Sept. 2000. <http://www.asu.edu/clas/english/composition/cbw/bwe_summer1999.htm>.

20

Reflection, Assessment, and Articulation: A Rhetoric of Writing Program Administration

Christopher Burnham
New Mexico State University

Assessment is arguably the greatest challenge a writing program administrator (WPA) confronts. Assessment pervades our work as teachers, mentors and trainers, teacher and program evaluators, and researchers and scholars. Accrediting boards have placed outcomes assessment and other accountability measures at the center of their evaluation and certification schemes, calling even more attention to the importance of assessment. Thus and correctly, work in assessment should figure prominently in a WPA's professional formation.

This has not always been the case. I speak as an experienced WPA, an old hand, who has wrestled with assessment in its various forms, from basic skills and proficiency testing in the 1970s and 1980s to program evaluation and student outcomes assessment in the 1990s. Rather than battle tales, though, I'd like to share an epiphany: Assessment is central to my work, is the unifying theme in my professional life. WPAs of my generation should pass on our wisdom and knowledge about assessment. It is our legacy. Such is my aim in this essay.

What do I mean by assessment? I contrast assessment with evaluation. Evaluation is the less complex of the two. Evaluation is assigning value. Though we speak of formative and summative evaluation, the former is more correctly labeled assessment. More than assigning value, assessment ascertains the nature of something. Assessment is linked etymologically to both *assay* and *essay*. *Assay* is to determine the composition of something as in to assay ore to determine its purity. *Essay* is to attempt or try. A personal essay is an attempt to describe oneself, to articulate one's motive and purpose in thinking or acting. *Essay* also carries an older sense: to "try," a process through which something is rendered in its purist form. Whalers on deck the Pequod light the night with fires under the try pots, rendering whale blubber into pure oil. When I invoke assessment I am speaking of more than assigning a grade to a paper or determining whether a teacher has been effective enough to be rehired. To me assessment means more than determining how many of our stated objectives are achieved in a course or a program or determining what ought to be listed in a strategic plan. When I invoke assessment I mean looking closely at what we do, the many things we do, to get to the essence, to examine what we do and why, and how we might do it better. Outcomes assessment involves determining not only whether students are learning what we claim to be teaching, but also determining whether what we are teaching is worth teaching or the best approach to helping students become writers and learners. We may not want to admit this level of complexity, but I believe to approach our professional roles in any other way trivializes our work.

Assessment became the unifying strand in the web of my professional life when I began to view assessment as reflection, at both the personal and professional levels. I see the connection as analogous to Edward O. Wilson's consilience. Wilson argues that the current age suffers from overspecialization that obstructs seeing the fundamental connectedness of all knowledge. Consilience occurs when connections are made across the boundaries, when the borders between the sciences, social sciences, and humanities dissolve, signaling a genuine insight. Making such connections allows seeing the world as it really is: "Only fluency across the boundaries will provide a clear view of the world as it really is, not as seen through the lens of ideologies and religious dogmas or commanded by myopic response to immediate need" (13). Joining assessment and professional reflection allows us to glimpse connectedness.

Reflection and assessment are intrinsically related, like process and product, interdependent. Moreover, they are rhetorical phenomena, or should be considered so. They must be purposeful and audience aware. Ironically, we teachers of rhetoric are not as rhetorically aware as we ought to be.

As a rhetorical act, assessment is completed only when results are articulated to various audiences to achieve specific ends. That assessment implies or requires articulation is not widely understood or appreciated. Effective articulation requires boundary crossing by engaging various audiences in conversation to validate an assessment and apply its findings by confirming or revising practice and/or reconciling policy with assessment findings. The circle closes: reflection critiques individual and institutional practice; assessment examines questions framed through reflection as an act of public inquiry; and articulation presents the findings of the inquiry and culminates in application. For WPAs, the sequence of reflection, assessment, articulation, and application constitutes a rhetoric, a system through which people act to achieve certain ends.

WPAs serve along the borders where the profession, the academy, and its stakeholders intersect. Work by WPAs over the last twenty-five years has examined these boundaries, providing commentary and direction for navigating the hazards of our work, especially assessment. Through this work we have earned disciplinary legitimacy and professionalized composition studies. Having a disciplinary identity, we can claim voice and agency. Because assessment plays so central a role in higher education, and because WPAs lead assessment projects, assessment offers us the opportunity to project a credible voice, a voice that must be attended to, especially when we have acquired interdisciplinary knowledge and political wiles. Assessment, then, offers WPAs the opportunity to act as change agents across the borders they work. We see evidence of this in the recent "WPA Outcomes Statement for First-Year Composition," a professional position statement advocating change across borders.

Viewing assessment as an opportunity to facilitate consilience and writing program administration as a rhetorical system involving an organic sequence of reflection, assessment, and articulation enables WPAs to assert influence and serve as powerful agents of change. This is how I ask WPAs to view themselves. This is our ethos. WPAs are uniquely positioned to mediate conflicts between the audiences inhabiting our world, including students, fellow faculty, managers and administrators, policymakers, legislators, and the taxpayers who underwrite the entire project. We have the opportunity to help them see beyond disciplinary ideologies and immediate needs and join in creating a world of mutual respect that encourages participation by all to the benefit of all.

ASSESSMENT AS PROFESSIONAL REFLECTION

To explore assessment as professional reflection, I turn to Donald Schön. Schön's professional reflection is a subspecies of reflective thinking, a concept that has been important in American intellectual history at least since Emerson, especially in "Experience," "Self Reliance," and "Compensation." John Dewey embraces Emerson's concept, arguing that reflecting on experience is how we learn. Reflection is as central to Dewey's cognitive theory and educational philosophy as experience is. Dewey's *How We Think* offers his theory in an accessible form. Reading *How We Think* also demonstrates the debt much current thinking on reflection and learning owes to Dewey.

George Hillocks, Jr.'s *Teaching Writing as Reflective Practice* and Kathleen Blake Yancey's *Reflection in the Writing Classroom* carry Dewey through Schön to composition studies. Both focus on reflective thinking but in the immediate context of writing and teaching writing. WPAs-in-training need to be familiar with both books. Hillocks and Yancey work from the perspective of teachers instructing student/learners or teachers in training. They do not consider assessment and how it can function for WPAs working along the boundaries of composition studies. Yancey, however, is mindful of rhetoric and its potential. Summarizing the strands she has woven into her book's whole cloth, she asserts "that reflection is both individual and social; as such, reflection is always rhetorical" (201). Taking her cue, I will focus on the rhetorical nature of the WPA's work with assessment, especially in relation to the current accountability movement.

WPAs must view themselves as professionals. The professional's advantage, Donald Schön argues throughout *Educating the Reflective Practitioner*, is "reflection-in-practice," a repertoire of behaviors grown from long and focused practice and an elaborate though tacit "theory-in-action" informing that practice. A professional welcomes the unexpected as a surprise, an opportunity to experience what Dewey, Schön's primary source, describes as the opportunity to "stop and think," to join "observation and memory" and enter the "heart of reflection" (*Democracy and Education*, 64). Recognizing an anomaly in the routine, the professional refocuses attention, reflects to frame a different or additional question to guide performance, and, in an analytical and critical act, devises an experiment enacting a new plan. The professional carefully attends to outcomes to evaluate whether the problem is solved, further complicated, or unaffected. And this experience is assimilated into the tacit theory-of-practice that will guide subsequent action (26–28).

The professional carries the whole repertoire of learning from experience from one situation to the next. The reflective practitioner sees a problem as lying within a set of problems but sufficiently distinct to require drawing on the *art* of practice by following the pattern of anomaly detecting and problem framing, treatment adjusting, testing, evaluating, and cycling back into the problem or generalizing from the problem. The process never really ceases because this experience becomes part of a knowledge and experience base that will be invoked once another problem is encountered. Reflection-in-practice resembles problem solving, inquiry, and scientific reasoning. A process, it links observation and problem defining (reflection), devising and testing a solution (assessing), and applying the results (articulating and adjusting practice and/or negotiating policy changes). This is what we want to teach our students. It is how we live our professional lives.

According to Schön, reflection-in-action, the "artistry" (13) of practice resists direct teaching (17). He argues that reflection-in-action can be modeled and encouraged through a reflective practicum that places professionals and novices in relation to one another under circumstances closely resembling the studio of the architect or musician, the clinic or office of the psychoanalyst or counselor, or the encounter between consultant and client—each a locus where professional problems are posed, analyzed, and solved. Working with the professional as coach, consultant, and supervisor, novices can begin to learn the artistry of practice. I counter that the analytic frame provided by a rhetorical perspective that places purpose, audience, and action at the center of professional work allows, even encourages, conscious learning and direct teaching of reflection-in-action. I join reflection, assessment, and articulation as stages in the process which is reflection-in-action.

INTELLECTUAL WORK: AN ISSUE OF VALUE

Viewing assessment as professional reflection legitimizes its role in our work. But it is work that has historically been undervalued within English studies. We must revalue assessment both in our immediate circle of composition studies and in our larger community of English studies. James Slevin's "Engaging Intellectual Work: The Faculty's Role in Assessment," challenges faculty attitudes, characterized too often by disinterest or disdain, towards outcomes assessment. He argues that assessment constitutes the primary intellectual work of the academy. But to make this argument, Slevin must first constitute us as a community. Once constituted, we can get to work.

Outcomes assessment has been controlled by administrators and policy managers, not faculty, and characterized as service. "What really concerns me is a process that seems to be taking the faculty out of the picture of higher education or putting us to the side, or putting us aside" (292). The consequence is "reducing the intellectual work of faculty and students to the parameters of an 'instructional program' [and substituting] managerial efficiency for educational seriousness. Values are upside down; indeed, the goal should be just the reverse" (293). Slevin argues that faculty should control assessment because assessment is intrinsically linked to teaching. If faculty accept assessment as service, then they have accepted a diminished role for teaching. Faculty reject trivializing teaching as service. Slevin shows how faculty can reclaim assessment as significant intellectual work different in kind but equal in value to research and publication.

In fairness, we should acknowledge alternative views that portray outcomes assessment in more positive terms, as a vital collaboration within the entire higher education community. The American Association for Higher Education (AAHE) Assessment Forum provides this perspective in *Learning through Assessment: A Resource Guide for Higher Education*. AAHE describes outcomes assessment as an information loop through which all the constituents of an institution cooperate respectfully to discover and affirm the value of their work and strive toward continuous quality improvement. The quality model, borrowed from industry, may not speak to English faculty, but many of the audiences WPAs face find it familiar and persuasive. Catherine A. Palomba and Trudy W. Banta, associates in the AAHE, have created a manual for outcomes assessment that faculty and administration can use to assure assessment efforts are productive from the perspective of accrediting bodies and policymakers. *Assessment Essentials: Planning, Implementing, and Improving Assessment in Higher Education* defines terms, describes programs, highlights best practices, and provides an extensive annotated bibliography. WPAs working in assessment are well served to become familiar with these resources. They describe the state of the art from an administrative perspective.

What distinguishes Slevin's English faculty perspective from the AAHE perspective is a question of value. The first lesson of rhetoric is that language shapes attitudes and provides access to or limits power. Slevin shifts the language of assessment to empower faculty, not administrators and central policymakers, to theorize assessment and, as teacher researchers, to document the value of their work. His language defines assessment as intellectual work. In so doing, he exemplifies how rhetorical awareness can use language to refocus assessment in ways that empower faculty.

Slevin begins with a critique of current writing about outcomes assessment, offering a close examination of the language of assessment as developed by AAHE, in particular by a senior spokesperson, Catherine Wehlburg. She describes outcomes assessment in the language of educational managers and policy wonks. Outcomes assessment is "a tool for accountability" and a way of getting "information about student outcomes." Slevin criticizes the narrow vision implicit in such technocratic jargon. "This narrowness is troubling, but perhaps less troubling than the fact that, again, assessment is envisioned as *service*, specifically to 'the students, the institution, state boards, policy makers, and accreditors.' Those served include faculty members only to the degree that faculty members identify themselves as unnamed but presumably implied part 'of the institution'" (291).

Having defined the problem, he proposes a solution. Slevin assails existing faculty evaluation schemes based on function categories, such as research, teaching, and service. Such systems encourage post facto assessments of productivity in ways similar to the learning-outcomes-based quality model. Not only outcomes assessment, the entire academic evaluation system is suspect.

Slevin's alternative evaluation scheme values intellectual work above function and shifts attention from products such as articles and student-credit-hour production to the sites where intellectual work occurs, especially program administration and evaluation. Himself a WPA, Slevin is concerned with first-year writing's role in the academy. The first-year course, he argues, rather than "foundation, preparation, and anticipation" of the real work of the institution must be *organic with* the rest of the curriculum; it should not ground but *enact* the intellectual work of the university; it should not anticipate but *begin* the students' education. (288): "[W]e should take the work of writing programs not as prelude to the work of higher education, but rather as the epitome of what is most important about higher education" (299).

Such a shift in value makes the interaction between faculty and students of central value. But value cannot merely be asserted. That value had been claimed but not documented caused the current problem. Faculty must demonstrate their value: "The quality of the faculty's study and review of student learning becomes a factor in program review, and faculty should demonstrate that they have developed sound professional practices for informing students about the quality of their work and the progress of their educations" (303). Faculty must abandon systems that measure quality by units of publication and student credit hours and adopt a new ethic that values student learning and collaboration between students and faculty and among faculty: "Efforts to understand and judge the quality of programs should focus on the study and review of how the program creates a spirit of collegiality devoted to critical inquiry—the producing and testing of knowledge" (303).

Slevin's rhetoric shifts the focus to purpose and action, and he returns agency to faculty. In the end, however, he retreats from truly communal action by claiming a role for faculty that, in its extreme, absolves them from responsibility to articulate the results of assessment to all stakeholders in ways open to scrutiny and dialogical validation. He becomes a victim of his own faculty-centered ideology. His final gesture frustrates rather than advances the conversation about assessment, reestablishing faculty as the sole mediators of value: "[T]he evaluation of students (i.e., the study and review of student work) is the sole province of the faculty member who teaches them" (304). Finally, he limits the discussion to the faculty club. Doing so he forgets that the power of the WPA comes from working across boundaries.

CROSS-DISCIPLINARITY, VOICE, AND AGENCY

Ed White's "The Opening of the Modern Era of Writing Assessment: A Narrative," examines English studies' historical relation to assessment from a participant's perspective. He attends to the issue of faculty authority over curriculum, especially to the process through which WPAs can find voice and claim power. White tells the story of his own formation as a rhetor, how he gained power through struggles with administrators and test makers by engaging in conversation and learning to use the terms of art appropriate to each of the communities along boundaries he worked. His story counters Slevin's exclusionary gesture. Rather than being subject to psychometricians, administrators, state boards and legislators, White demonstrates how WPAs can educate themselves to claim the power needed to mediate the conflicting perspectives of stakeholders, engaging all as participants, coming to respect each participant's perspective by understanding that it is formed by specific needs and purposes. The success of the negotiation depends on the WPA's knowledge and skills, as well as the rhetorical and political strategies used to accomplish specific purposes.

White recounts conflicts between English faculty, the California State University (CSU) central administration, and Educational Testing Service (ETS) concerning the nature of the first-year writing sequence and its purpose and position in the university curriculum. In 1971, in California and elsewhere, English faculty interest in the first-year sequence went little beyond accepting such requirements as service that funded English programs and provided work for graduate students. Little attention was paid to the substance of the sequence as evidenced in the wide variation in standards for placement and exit certification across the system. This disinterest ultimately resulted in a loss of voice.

Confronting tight budgets, growing demand, and increased interest in accountability, CSU's central administration saw proficiency testing as it had recently been developed and marketed by ETS in the College-Level Examination Program (CLEP), a set of multiple-choice subject-area exams designed by ETS in consultation with a committee of subject-area faculty "experts," as an expedient solution to a pressing problem. Students could take CLEP tests to establish proficiency and "test out" of a course or requirement. CSU's central administration was most attracted to the CLEP program for its economic efficiency. The institution could charge fees and assign credit without paying for teaching, resulting in quicker progress through degree programs. Moreover, given generally negative attitudes towards English requirements, CSU central administration also saw their testing solution as politically innocuous. University faculty, tweedy English faculty in particular, did not enjoy a reputation for activism. Central administration did not expect a challenge.

Two constraints compromised the CLEP test in English composition, expedience and scope. Used for placement, results had to be quickly available. Though brief impromptu writing was included in some versions of these exams, reading and scoring student writing took time. The multiple-choice questions could be quickly and accurately scored by clerks, and placement derived by using either ETS-determined national norms or locally developed ones. Placement and exemption were not based on a direct measure of student writing. Now, after decades of work on portfolios, such a practice would not be tolerated. Additionally, because the CLEP program was national in scope, test content could only be general, limited to error recognition and editing skills, never getting at writing process or the sophisticated reading and critical thinking needed to write well. The information provided by such proficiency testing did not serve programs whose students had special language or learning needs resulting from local social, economic, or dialect conditions. Now specialized information about a student's local dialect and language communities is deemed crucial. The linguistic knowledge students bring with them becomes part of the curriculum, groundwork they can use to learn academic and professional dialects.

Faculty, however, were generally ignorant of such testing issues. CSU central administration expected little resistance, so they moved forward with proficiency testing. This is where White's story begins. A subset of the English faculty in the CSU system recognized that the plan was not in the best interest of either students or faculty. This led to the formation of the CSU English Council, a collection of department chairs and writing program directors. The group resisted the plan, ultimately designing a legitimate and useful testing and placement system that served as the model for the nation for quite some time, although this model has now been superseded by portfolio assessment. In fact, White suggests that the work of the CSU English Council paved the way for subsequent work in assessment:

> The CSU system faculty senate, the central chancellor's office, the legislature, the governor, and the state funding agencies all in turn were persuaded to follow the lead of the English faculties, a situation as astonishing as it was unprecedented. This is what I mean by the "modern era" of writing assessment: a time in which because responsible academics and scholars somehow gained actual power over the assessment of writing, the developed assessment that took place embodied current writing theory, writing research, and writing pedagogy (309).

White was one of the leaders of this group, and he describes how faculty "somehow gained actual power." His story focuses on the problem of constituting a community with authority and power sufficient to make its voice be heard. Claiming agency required the group to become sufficiently expert in the technical business of testing and evaluation so that they could claim equal status to the ETS experts. Once this authority was established, faculty could claim additional power from their context-specific expertise as teachers who, unlike the ETS experts, worked daily helping students become writers. Ultimately, faculty are more knowledgeable than testing experts. White offers the information and expertise needed to become authoritative about testing and evaluation to WPAs and teachers of writing in two books: *Assigning, Responding, Evaluating: A Writing Teacher's Guide* and *Teaching and Assessing Writing: Recent Advances in Understanding, Evaluating, and Improving Student Performance*. Both are basic reading for WPAs and WPAs-in-training.

Like Slevin, White describes the CSU English Council's dilemma as a political problem. English faculty were subject to the decisions of an ambitious centralized administration because they had not defined the work of the first-year sequence in terms of outcomes that made writing central in the university's curriculum. Their work was defined for them. Administration labeled first-year writing remedial, mere preparation for the real work of a college education. The English faculty's traditional gatekeeping role was reframed as an obstacle blocking the progress of burgeoning numbers of talented students wanting access to higher education.

The English Council had to assert its power to define and control curriculum. It had to define the role of the English sequence in relation to the whole curriculum, and it could do this only by paying close attention to the testing programs used to place students in the writing sequence. White distills the lessons learned, so that they can be applied today:

> Writing as the center of the liberal arts, as a means of understanding who we are and how we think, as a critical means of learning itself, is under attack by a merely utilitarian view of writing as simple communication in the service of business interests. We cannot tell what the future will bring, but we need not sit passively by and wring our hands in frustration at the forces swirling about us. We know that we can gather together and collectively influence that future.... Assessment, with its appeal to professionalism, certification, and standards (all ambiguous criteria to be sure), has given us a way to reassert the value of our field and its ethical power. (319)

White celebrates the power claimed by faculty as some kind of lucky accident when it really had to do with rhetorical awareness and skill. White overlooks the rhetorical nature of the WPA's work. He narrates a struggle, but he fails to define the problem as a rhetorical one. Rather, he opts for soft social theory, invoking the tendency of groups to recognize only their own perspectives and not those of others. He talks about faculty solipsism:

> For instance, we will all approve resolutions on writing assessment that the *only* reason to assess student writing is to assess student learning—a position that seems obviously right and appropriate to us as teachers. But we should recognize that position is an expression of a particular point of view, as a special interest perspective that is likely to be dismissed by other interest groups (316).

In fact, recognizing that the work of WPAs entails the whole sequence of reflection, assessment, articulation, and application, as I have argued it should, allows us the best access to power in service to our various stakeholders. From White we can distill three prerequisites for agency: a sense of value rooted in our commitment to the project of teaching writing as a central activity of the university; membership in a community that can articulate its own mission and value; and authority that originates in professionalism and disciplinary knowledge equal to or greater than that of the various audiences with whom we work.

ACHIEVING RHETORICAL POWER: WPA OUTCOMES STATEMENT

Whereas White describes the origins of the modern era of assessment, "The WPA Outcomes Statement for First-Year Composition" documents state-of-the-art practice. Outcomes are detailed in four areas: rhetorical knowledge; critical thinking, reading, and writing; processes; and knowledge of conventions. Each area includes specific statements about what students should be able to do and how faculty can help students master specific knowledge, dispositions, and skills. In this, the WPA statement fulfills White's promise by distilling the profession's best theoretical and pedagogical practices and balancing what we have discovered students need to be able to do to succeed in the academy against the equally important need for faculty to determine how this is to be done and demonstrated in their immediate context. The WPA statement makes clear the values that underlie it, and they reflect the lessons learned through history and personal and institutional struggles documented in CE: "[O]ur purpose was curricular. In calling the document an 'Outcomes' Statement, however, we achieved two rhetorical advantages. We could focus on expectations, on what we want students to know, to do, to understand. And we could assign to individual campuses the appropriate authority for standards; they may determine how well these expectations will be met—should they choose to adopt the outcomes at all" (323).

I propose viewing assessment as rhetorical activity involving the sequence of reflection, assessment, articulation, and application as a liberatory move that will enable WPAs to make good arguments justifying our value as teachers of writing and WPAs. In addition, this approach demonstrates our roles as mediators and negotiators of conflict, as potential agents of change across boundaries.

With power comes responsibility, perhaps more than we are willing to bear, or more than we are strong enough to carry. In the tradition of rhetoric we must learn all the available means of persuasion in every instance. We must ourselves be sufficiently familiar with assessment practices and issues to make authoritative arguments concerning methodology and interpretation. For our stakeholders, we must create a credible and authoritative ethos by showing that we understand their values and contexts and are responding to their needs. We must understand students' increasingly complex dilemmas and faculty conflicts as they balance the humanistic ideals instilled in them by their training against the reality of poorly prepared and sometimes purposeless students. We must be aware of the empirical paradigms of the educationists, psychometricians, and industry-trained policymakers and use the limitations of their approach in defense of our alternatives. We have models, including Slevin, White, and the committee that wrote the WPA Statement on Assessment, on whose backs we can stand. And increasingly at conferences and in the growing literature on outcomes assessment, we have examples of assessment projects that have tried to meet the challenge of mediating the many conflicting agendas of our stakeholders.

WORKS CITED

Dewey, John. *Democracy and Education*. 1916. New York: Free P, 1967.
—. *How We Think*. (1933). Lexington: Heath, 1960.

Gardner, Lion F., Caitlin Anderson, and Barbara L. Cambridge. *Learning through Assessment: A Resource Guide for Higher Education.* Washington, DC: American Association for Higher Education, 1997.

Hillocks, George, Jr. *Teaching Writing as Reflective Practice.* New York: Teachers College P, 1995.

Palomba, Catherine A., and Trudy W. Banta, eds. *Assessment Essentials: Planning, Implementing, and Improving Assessment in Higher Education.* San Francisco: Jossey-Bass, 1999.

Schön, Donald. *Educating the Reflective Practitioner.* San Francisco: Jossey-Bass, 1987.

Slevin, James. "Engaging Intellectual Work: The Faculty's Role in Assessment," *College English* 63 (2001): 288–307.

White, Edward. *Assigning, Responding, Evaluating: A Writing Teacher's Guide.* 3rd ed. New York: St. Martin's, 1999.

—. "The Opening of the Modern Era of Writing Assessment: A Narrative." *College English* 63 (2001): 306–20.

—. *Teaching and Assessing Writing: Recent Advances in Understanding, Evaluating, and Improving Student Performance.* San Francisco: Jossey-Bass, 1994.

WPA Outcomes Committee. "WPA Outcomes Statement for First-Year Composition." *College English* 63, (2001): 321–25.

Wilson, Edward O. *Consilience: The Unity of Knowledge.* New York: Knopf, 1998.

Yancey, Kathleene Blake. *Reflection in the Writing Classroom.* Logan, UT: Utah State UP, 1998.

21

Expanding the Community: A Comprehensive Look at Outreach and Articulation

Anne-Marie Hall
University of Arizona

Mere instruction that is not accompanied with direct participation in school affairs upon a genuine community basis will not go far....
—John Dewey (*Democracy in Education*, 1916)

Miriam T. Chaplin writes that the "English profession cannot be of the world and not in the world" (168). This speaks in compelling terms for recognizing the interdependence between higher education and the larger community. Indeed, Donald Daiker exclaims that "the most exciting things are happening outside and away from the college classroom" (2). Yet sites of learning have become increasingly separated both spatially and symbolically from the tasks of everyday life, argues Kurt Spellmeyer. What qualifies as "knowledge" is "almost always removed from experience at the local or personal level" ("Inventing" 42). Knowledge, then, in a Cartesian fashion, becomes "disembodied" from its context. In the academy we bow down at the altar of the universal at the expense of the particulars. Local knowledge is somehow "less than" and never "equal to." Spellmeyer challenges us to recognize nonspecialists as genuine collaborators in the making of knowledge ("Inventing" 44).

This chapter will give advice to writing program administrators (WPAs) who are interested in building an outreach program; in particular, I will focus on school–college outreach and articulation. The notion of reaching out (*university* derives from *universe*, a turning into one) has its origins in the mission of land-grant colleges, those first uniquely American colleges based on the new (and American) idea of bringing the finest minds of each state to the service of its people to assist agriculture and industry. At The University of Arizona, a land-grant university, outreach is defined as "a part of our mission that involves generating, delivering, applying, and preserving knowledge in order to address state, national, and international societal needs" (http://www.arizona.edu).

Typically, outreach involving school–college collaborations work together in one of three ways: to facilitate movement of students from one educational level to the next, to improve the quality of teaching and learning in secondary schools through curriculum development, and to establish stronger professional ties between high school and college teachers (Fortune xii).

Before considering what kind of outreach program you might want, it will be helpful to understand both the macro and the micro perspectives. I will offer brief arguments in favor of outreach, talk about changes in outreach in recent years, showcase some model programs, and conclude with considerations and practical relationships WPAs in colleges and universities should contemplate in designing outreach programs.

WHY OUTREACH?

Understanding Our Students

One of the great benefits of having university–school collaborative programs between higher education and public schools is that they help us understand what students bring with them to the composition classroom. This in turn helps you with curriculum development and revision, pedagogy in composition courses, assessment of writing, research, and technology expectations/expertise of entering students. We should be focusing not only on whether our students are ready for college writing tasks but on what *we can do* in higher education to get ready for these students.

Coherent Curriculum

We live in a postmodern world of fragmentation. Dale Coye talks about the world of college as the world of "disconnects"—those lost connections or areas where linkages ought to exist but do not, such as the tension between what high school students are taught and what colleges expect, between academic and social lives of students, between the campus and the outside world (21). Recognizing that there are few unifying experiences in college, making connections smoother and more explicit between the high school curriculum and the college curriculum can bring coherence.

Preparing WPAs of the Future

Easing graduate students into the discipline—what James Slevin calls the "disciplining of students" ("Disciplining" 153)—includes modeling how things ought to be. We must expose graduate students to a wider range of responsibilities, helping them break out of what Slevin calls the "culture of silence" of graduate schools (163). As future WPAs, our graduate students will oversee the work of teaching and learning that takes place in writing programs and classrooms. Indeed, the curriculum of the future may be what Ann Ruggles Gere calls the extracurricular of composition, "all the life that happens outside of us, beyond us" (80–91).

Another way that outreach shapes the mind-set of future WPAs is in what Foucault calls an "insurrection of subjugated knowledge" (81), those disciplinary ways of knowing, seen as in conflict with popular knowledge that is disqualified as naive and unscientific. In the process of filtering the disciplinarity of composition, we may be transformed into someone who can no longer hear the countervoices or counterknowledge, especially if those voices don't fit with existing professional practices. By not listening, these knowledges are not eliminated but rather "driven underground—tugging at the margins of professional experience" (Trimbur 143).

A final argument for linking college and public school classrooms is that we are helping graduate students imagine an institution of higher education where effective teaching matters. By forming coalitions with teachers who teach more than we do, Erika Lindemann's "over there" (K–12) becomes "here" (179). Good teaching must be defined publicly and it must be defined by many voices (Lindemann 179).

Research

The possibilities of redefining what research can be, of truly letting practice inform theory and not just the opposite, is a major benefit of collaborating with public school teachers as well as the community. Coordinating teacher research and university research helps us negotiate meaning between different groups and broadens the process.

Building Alliances

Composition is a contact zone to foster articulation programs. Contact zones are to Mary Louise Pratt "social spaces where cultures meet, clash, and grapple with each other, often in contexts of highly asymmetrical relations of power" (34). Because writing is always about something else, the curriculum and the students lean into and engage in more collaborations than in other college courses. As Linda Flower says, "Composition courses reflect our public vision of literacy, and once again, that vision is under reconstruction" (249). It is a site of learning with endless possibilities for articulation with public schools and the wider community. And it is intellectual work that can make higher education more visible to the community.

The MLA Commission of Professional Service's report, "Making Faculty Work Visible: Reinterpreting Professional Service, Teaching, and Research in the Fields of Language and Literature," has a very inclusive list of items comprising intellectual work. Especially apt is their recommendation that we make "specialized knowledge broadly accessible and usable ... to young learners, to nonspecialists in other disciplines, to the public" (16).

Service Learning

As a methodology, service learning emphasizes connections between education and community by having students engage in community service and then reflect on their experiences through writing. Students become not just learners but citizens and community members. Hailing back to John Dewey, service learning has its roots in experiential learning—students learn by doing. And in composition courses, students learn to make connections between writing and action. Often students produce texts that benefit the community they are at once a part of and working with (i.e., grants, brochures, Web sites). There is also a link between reflection and action; this kind of writing helps students recognize the intersections between people and ideas. Finally, on an institutional level, service learning programs challenge the university to take seriously its commitment to the communities within which they exist. Partnerships are forged between educational institutions and community organizations and in so doing, the partners give and receive different kinds of knowledge and resources to and from each other.

Let's look briefly at the evolution of outreach. To give a full history of outreach is beyond the scope of this chapter. But it might be helpful to recognize some of the patterns that are emerging in contemporary outreach.

CHANGES IN OUTREACH

Outreach has gone through many phases, but in recent years, it has become more integral to writing programs. Courses abound in service learning, and graduate programs recognize the need for students to have more diverse learning experiences. In addition, graduate students today frequently insist on academic work that is meaningful and relevant to everyday life.

The tone of outreach has changed as well. Programs (thus knowledge itself) are defined more collaboratively as boundaries are crossed, expanded, or broken down entirely. As outreach grows to take on sociocultural and sociopolitical dimensions, it often includes community programs as well as public school articulations. It could be considered "traditional" work in the framework that Bruce Horner argues for, namely a transgression of:

> the limits of formal representations of knowledge, rejecting the claims and class status of professional expertise, sharing responsibility for any work accomplished as widely as possible, including sharing responsibility with students and the public, and turning institutional structures to ends alternative to those officially prescribed. (381)

As WPAs, you are well aware that composition programs are already burdened with responsibilities—from textbook selection to training of graduate students, from placement and testing to issues of funding, from curricular design to defending programs to administrators and the community. Outreach might seem like yet one more thing placed on the broad shoulders of WPAs. Ernest Boyer writes, however, that the "complexity of modern life requires more, not less, information, more, not less, participation" (77).

In sum, characteristics of contemporary outreach programs include using multiple forums, mediums, and audiences to get messages across; conceiving of writing as beyond the curriculum that allows us to bring dichotomies together; braiding more projects into existing programs/goals; seeing the making of knowledge as one with the conveying of it; and a greater spirit of cooperation between communities and schools.

MODELS OF OUTREACH

Perhaps the single most telling feature of school–college outreach and articulation programs is this: They are short-lived but brilliant. In researching seventeen programs across the United States that were thriving in the 1980s, I found only seven still in existence. They may have morphed or been consolidated into something else, but I found no trace. The following programs are representative of long-lasting programs that have met the many challenges to outreach programs.

Writing Projects

The success is well documented since the founding of the National Writing Project in 1974. This is the quintessential model of higher education collaborating with K–12 teachers: bringing exemplary teachers from all grade levels and subject areas together to teach them the latest theory in the teaching of writing, enabling them to teach their own best practices to each other, and developing them as writers so that they might become better teachers of writing. Federal funds have been available to sites from the United States Department of Education since 1991. Today, the National Writing Project has 167 affiliated sites in 49 states. The basic premises of the Project are that:

- Universities and schools must work together as partners in coopera-tive-collaborative efforts to solve writing problems.
- Successful teachers of writing can be identified and brought together in summer institutes to be trained to teach other teachers of writing in fol-low-up school year programs.
- Teachers themselves are the best teachers of other teachers.
- Summer institutes must include teachers of all levels and subject areas.
- Teachers of writing must write themselves.
- Real change in the classroom happens over time so effective staff devel-opment programs must be ongoing and systematic.
- Knowledge about the teaching of writing comes not only from research but from the practice of those who teach writing. (Gray 38–39)

This type of university collaboration is not top-down—the university pro-vides resources and current research on the teaching and learning of writing but the leaders of writing projects are local teachers (Brinkley and Hall 10-11). Mature writing project sites have developed additional smaller pro-grams: young writers' camps, teacher research institutes, school year semi-nars, writing retreats, sustained writing groups, partnerships with museums and community organizations.

Central to writing projects are five points: the idea of a partnership be-tween college and schools must be believed; there must be an early and mu-tual recognition that knowledge from both levels can contribute and must be tapped; that follow-up programs to the summer institutes must be offered; that all workshops must be voluntary; and that school–university cooperative programs must be planned as success models, putting a premium on what works rather than on deficit models. Put simply, celebrate good teachers, good teaching (Gray 45).

Graduate Seminars and Institutes

Although these come and go in different institutions, they generally oper-ate similarly. A college or university gets a small grant, often funded by the National Endowment for the Humanities, to support a seminar in which high school teachers and college teachers can collaborate. One model di-vides each semester into five workshops. Fall semester workshops focus on teaching (what works) and a particular content such as humanities or rhet-oric (what we teach and why we teach this subject). Spring semester work-shops might focus on developing curricular materials for class and for wider distribution. Perhaps a publication will come out of this such as "Writing in the Disciplines" or "Writing in the Humanities" that will be distributed to local teachers and even be available nationally (Slevin, "Georgetown Uni-versity" 1–7).

Another version is the summer seminar, again focusing on a particular need such as writing in the disciplines. This might involve five English professors, five non-English professors, and thirty or more high school and community college teachers. For example, in a two-and-a-half week summer workshop, public school and college teachers might plan a new, discipline-specific writing course, make an existing course more writing intensive, or add writing components to an existing course. Usually there are school year follow-up sessions with these kinds of summer intensive programs (Boshoff 120–26).

One of the long-running and stable programs is the Institute for Writing and Thinking at Bard College. Funded with grants from Booth Ferris, Ford, and, later, Exxon foundations, these institutes provide workshops for high school and college teachers who want to improve interactive instruction in critical reading, creative thinking, and clear writing in all courses. Because all activities are experiential, teachers do not "talk at" colleagues but give them many opportunities to write, reflect, listen, and examine their practices. Like any long-lasting program in writing, this institute resists recipes and gimmicks, looking at writing as "an object to think with" (Connolly 8–13).

Bridge Programs

These programs ease the adjustment of high school students into college and improve articulation between curriculum in high school and college with the hope of improving the writing ability of incoming students. A portfolio placement project is one type of bridge program. A variation of this is an assessment program that intervenes at the junior level of high school to improve writing before attending college. Bridge programs might include computer-linked classrooms where first-year composition students talk to and collaborate with high school students on a particular assignment or project, or summer programs for high school students on college campuses that focus on preprofessional careers like premed or general topics like "writing your way into the university." Three programs that have lasted close to a decade or more are outlined here.

Miami University's EECAP (Early English Composition Assessment Program). This is a partnership between the Ohio Writing Project and the composition program at Miami University for the purpose of assessing student writing in the junior year of high school. Students submit a piece of writing that is evaluated in an ETS-like holistic grading session. Individual evaluations are computer generated for each student. In addition, summary profiles are sent to participating schools and districts. Suggestions are made to the students for improving their writing in senior year and districts receive specific directives about composition areas they can focus on to improve writing instruction. Finally, four inservice workshops are planned for each district in the following year (Fuller and Morenberg 46–51).

Miami University Portfolio Project.   In 1990 Miami University (Ohio) became the first college to award credit and advanced placement in composition through the use of portfolios in the belief that multiple samples of writing gave a more complete picture of the reading and writing abilities of entering students than did a timed, impromptu writing sample. The Miami Portfolio consists of a reflective letter, a narrative or short story, explanatory, exploratory, or persuasive essay, and a response to a text. As a small institution, they are able to use the placement portfolio as a way of allowing students to "test out" of a composition course. Their Web site has examples of student portfolios, directions about submission, and advice from the scorers. Resource: http://www.muohio.edu/portfolio/.

The University of Arizona Portfolio Placement Project.   The UA's Portfolio Placement Project, inspired and modeled on the Miami University Portfolio Project, offers a nice contrast between managing a bridge program in a large, public university versus a smaller private university. Since 1992 the UA portfolio has been used as an option for placement, not as an exemption or award of credit as at Miami. In reality, it is more an outreach tool than a placement instrument because it involves University and high school English teachers collaborating on the four selections of best high school writing to be included, taking care to support the kind of writing that students *actually do* in high school while considering the kinds of writing students *need to do* in college. The four selections include expressive writing, a literary analysis, expository writing from a discipline other than English, and a reflective letter. During the school year, students and teachers receive *Portfolio Guides*. In the student's *Guide* there are sample portfolios with comments from readers to help students understand both the genres of each selections and the criteria for evaluating and scoring the portfolio; in the teacher's *Guide,* the teachers receive tips for teaching the selections and advice from participating high school teachers. Finally, workshops on teaching the selections are offered for local high school teachers and tutorials are scheduled to assist students in selecting pieces for the portfolio. This kind of regular exchange helps keep misinformation about composition at the University to a minimum.

Two special features of the University of Arizona's Portfolio Placement Project are the inclusion of high school teachers in the holistic scoring sessions, and the production of two handwritten comments to each student. The inclusion of high school teachers in the project has resulted in the interpenetration of values between the university and the schools. Additionally, as we develop a common language with which to discuss student writing, our students find standards about writing demystified. Finally, because this is a small project (five hundred portfolios a year), we are able to attend to the local and particular concerns about writing that characterize one university and its feeder schools. The entire process serves to calibrate community standards about writing, driving curriculum from both levels. Resource: http://w3.arizona.edu/~writprog/student_info/portfolio.htm.

Young Writers Programs

These programs involve a celebration of writing, a collaboration between local schools and the university, and last anywhere from one to three days. One successful model, the English Festival at Youngstown State University, offers two separate tracks during the day, one for students and one for teachers, designed and led by university and school teachers, resource: www.ysu.edu (access the English Festival from the English Department link).

Students read seven carefully chosen books on an annual festival booklist in order to attend a talk by a nationally recognized author on campus, take a book quiz to determine if they've read the seven books and choose from a variety of concurrent activities such as impromptu writing contests; writing games; prose, poetry, journalism workshops; writing labs in computer classrooms; and more. The culmination of the day is an awards ceremony for achievements in the various competitions.

Teachers follow a different schedule for the day. They hear the guest author and attend a follow-up session with the author. Later they hear specialists talk about a problem of interest to teachers, parents, librarians; participate in a holistic and primary-trait scoring session (to enable them to judge the products from the students' activities prior to the awards sessions); and attend any of the student activities in order to learn new teaching strategies.

Funding for Young Writers Festivals can include gifts from local businesses, book stores, banks, and contributions from the schools and university. The problems with most of these programs are that they become too successful (too many want to participate) and they are extremely time-consuming (Brothers, Gay, Murphy, and Salvern 45–60).

Cooperative Teaching Programs

These programs often begin out of necessity—a need to staff composition courses. Nonetheless, there are several models that creatively use high school teachers to solve a teaching shortage while building a strong articulation program at the same time. One design is to pair a small number of high school teachers (who might be working on Masters of Arts degrees) with university teachers to team-teach sections of composition. Usually there are funds to offer the high school teachers scholarships (Slevin, "Georgetown University" 1–7).

Another variation is to find school districts that offer sabbaticals of one year to teachers to forge stronger articulation with the university. These are usually half-pay leaves and require that the university pay the other half of the salary. The high school teachers teach a full load of composition courses, attend the orientation and training with the new graduate student teaching assistants, are given teaching advisors, enroll in a professional seminar on the theory of teaching composition, and write short papers or give oral presentations on the theory and practice of teaching writing (Shuman 880–85).

Yet another model has high school and community college teachers team-teaching with university teachers in their various contexts. They study current research together. In the fall the high school/community college teachers team teach at the university; in the spring semester, they reverse the site and university teachers go to the high schools and community colleges and team teach. The culmination of this model is a summer curriculum-planning workshop and an evaluation of the program (Fortune and Neuleib 111–19).

Carnegie Mellon University's Center for University Outreach

One of the more comprehensive outreach programs in the nation is at Carnegie Mellon where the focus is on urban education, communication technology, and collaborative problem solving. Carnegie Mellon's Web site has information on student opportunities, resources for creating community-based courses, interactive programs inviting participation in dialogues and educational activities, and a comprehensive list of every outreach program on campus. Resource: http://English.cmu.edu (click on Center for University Outreach).

CONSIDERATIONS, PRACTICAL MATTERS, CHALLENGES

When you are designing outreach, you should consider three main problems—maintaining focus, gathering support, and building alliances—and keep in mind the following:

1. Define your own role and choose your own path. Material conditions mediate what kind of outreach programs you can have. The differences in the provision of outreach will be based on the type of educational institution. Or as Ernest Boyer writes about research (equally applicable to outreach): What is appropriate for some institutions if adopted by all, creates a shadow over the entire enterprise, thus becoming "the" yardstick by which all institutions would be measured (12). We need to "relate the work of the academy more directly to the realities of contemporary life" (Boyer 13). We can't impose a single model of outreach.

2. Build outreach programs that are organic. You should begin with local concerns addressing the particulars of a narrow context. These concerns may even be top-down (like a portfolio placement project), but they should always have bottom-up effects. There must be grassroots support and there must be institutional structures designed for bringing communities together. Sometimes integrating outreach into the fabric of the university is the biggest challenge (Parks and Goldblatt 588, 594). Begin by investigating what programs your university currently offers. Then ask yourself, what is my relationship with the local schools? A good place to start is by assembling a list of department chairs or contact persons in each English Department in your area. Or contact the nearest writing project as a resource for teachers' names.

3. Be patient. Change is slow. Focus on long-term cooperation and remember that schools change slowly.

4. Investigate the different roles your institution designates for the training of teachers. Teacher education is often situated in Colleges of Education whereas composition is situated in Colleges of Arts and Sciences. There can be problems in bringing two faculties together when one unit controls the training and educating of secondary teachers and the other unit focuses on teaching undergraduates and educating future college teachers.

5. Focus on consistent leadership and stability. The key characteristic of outreach programs is their lack of duration. First, do not rely on one leader for everything; the key word these days is *cross-train*. Engage as many people as possible to head programs and create opportunities for them to share information frequently. Second, in considering the burn-out factor, you should develop programs that are flexible enough in how they define the role and the work of the directors or they will become exhausted emotionally and intellectually. Directors need to figure out what they need to run a program and then learn how to disperse authority. If that's impossible (no one else is willing or able to help from either the schools or the university), then that *is* the message. One person cannot sustain a program (Brinkley and Hall 10–11).

6. Look for multiple sources for funding. Adequate resources are always a problem. Many outreach programs begin with a short grant and then fizzle when the monies run out. Finding diverse sources for funding (internal and external) is always the best way to go. If you do get a small start-up grant, begin thinking about building capacity from the get go. How will you sustain this program? Often seed money enables you to make a program visible. Then if it is successful, it becomes easier to raise monies to continue. Again, think long term. This is a nice segue into evaluation of programs. If you build an assessment structure into the program from the beginning, it will also be easier to sustain funding.

7.   Define clear goals, produce results, present them, and offer critique. In other words, build assessment into outreach from the ground up. There is a need to produce outcomes that are valued by both the academy and the community. You must be able to evaluate the quality of the project in terms of its significance, its attention to context, its internal and external impact, and its scholarship (Sandman, Foster-Fishman, Lloyd, Rauhe, and Rosaen 45–52). For example, get an umbrella question before the project gets under way (an overarching goal) and then balance university goals with the need to be flexible. In terms of context, it's important that you realize collaboration is time consuming, but it also provides opportunities for thinking critically about our work. Also, the processes of outreach can be as important as the product. When you do produce a product, it needs to have different forms for different audiences. For example, the university values peer-reviewed articles, presentations at conferences, theses, and dissertations whereas schools or community organizations may want guides, training programs, curricular materials, evaluation designs, briefing papers, fact sheets, literature reviews, best practices, or case reports. It is important, though, to perceive these products as concurrent from the outset. Finally, scholarship must be built into outreach from the beginning. Obviously that includes a final product, an opportunity to share that product with colleagues, and a way to critique your program (Sandman, Foster-Fishman, Lloyd, Rauhe, and Rosaen 49–51).

8.   Recognize the challenges in applying the most recent and sophisticated theory to secondary classrooms (Parks and Goldblatt 594). This is where teacher exchanges and team-teaching situations that are reciprocal are crucial.

9.   Make graduate student internships integral to the mission of the department and the outreach program. Internships in outreach are often available to graduate students, but you need to build structures for the graduate students to reflect, evaluate, and give oral and written presentations. In other words, their experiences in outreach must be brought back to campus for reflection and connection to the core curriculum.

WORK THAT MATTERS

I have become convinced that we will not make a difference in the teaching and learning of writing unless we collaborate at all levels with K–12 teachers and students. There's an ethical aspect to this for many of us involved in outreach. For example, though I treasure time alone with the latest literature on the teaching of composition, I also value the collaborative knowledge making that occurs when working with K–12 teachers. It's work that matters. Making a difference in the lives of teachers is work that should be valued. Kurt Spellmeyer says this kind of work will help us become ethnographers of experience—"scholar/teachers who find out how people actually feel." Thus the "search for basic grammars of emotional life may give us the future that we have never had, a future beyond the university" ("After Theory" 911).

Fortunately, the exchange value of this kind of work has increased in recent years. In 1990 Ernest Boyer set the standard for how service needed to be conceptualized:

> To be considered scholarship, service activities must be tied directly to one's special field of knowledge and relate to, and flow directly out of, this professional activity. Such service is serious, demanding work, requiring the rigor—and the accountability—traditionally associated with research activities. (22)

Further, the MLA Commission on Professional Service argues that how we identify our work (as research, teaching, or service) carries powerful positive or negative value. We should question the status quo, they argue. Work needs to be valued based on the "quality, significance, and impact of work on knowledge enterprises or in support of institutions" (20).

Make no mistake. Whether coordinating a portfolio project that places high school teachers on equal footing with university teachers or directing a writing project, this kind of work subverts hierarchies. These programs make university teachers bridge the theory–practice gap. And it is stealthlike work, especially if you are in an institution where research and publication are defined and valued in narrow or traditional ways. The key is to make the work bend to the shape you want.

Composition itself occupies a marginal position in the academy (Horner 394). That puts outreach, then, on the margins of the margins. But that may not be so bad. As bell hooks writes, "To be in the margin is to be part of the whole but outside the main body" (341). She sees these margins not as sites of deprivation but as sites of "radical possibility." In other words, working in the margins is something we should cling to because it helps us with perspective, offering the possibility to see and create alternatives (341).

Finally, when setting up any outreach program, the questions to ask are these: Do you have adequate resources? Are there learning opportunities for the students? Is there the potential to produce scholarly outcomes? Is this a priority to your university or college? Department? Self? Does this project fit with your research and teaching agenda? Is it a good investment of your time? (Sandman, Foster-Fishman, Lloyd, Rauhe, and Rosaen 46).

There are several good books that will help you in setting up and evaluating an outreach program. However, because of the constant changes in most outreach programs, I find that Web sites are the most current source for information. Following are some good references to get you started:

Boyer, Ernest. *Scholarship Reconsidered: Priorities of the Professoriate*. Princeton, NJ: Carnegie Foundation for the Advancement of Teaching, 1990.

Michigan State University. *Points of Distinction: A Guidebook for Planning and Evaluating Quality Outreach.* Rev ed. East Lansing, MI: Michigan State University, 1996.

Modern Language Association. *School-College Collaborative Programs in English.* Ed. Ron Fortune. New York: MLA, 1986.

Sandmann, Lorilee R., Pennie G. Foster-Fishman, James Lloyd, Warren Rauhe, & Cheryl Rosaen. "Managing Critical Tensions: How to Strengthen the Scholarship Component of Outreach." *Change* (Jan.-Feb. 2000): 45–52.

Zlotkowski, Ed, ed. *Successful Service-Learning Programs: New Models of Excellence in Higher Education.* Boston: Anker, 1998.

Web sites:

Carnegie Mellon University (click on Center for University Outreach): <http://English.cmu.edu>.

Bard College (click on Institutes and Publications, then click on Institute For Writing and Thinking): <http://www.bard.edu>.

Miami University: <http://www.muohio.edu/portfolios/>.

National Endowment for the Humanities (click on Teaching): <http://www.neh.fed.us>.

National Writing Project: <http://writingproject.org>.

WORKS CITED

Boshoff, Philip P. "Skidmore College: Cooperative Program in Cross-Curricular Writing." Ed. Ron Fortune. *School-College Collaborative Programs in English.* New York: MLA, 1986. 120–26.

Boyer, Ernest L. *Scholarship Reconsidered: Priorities of the Professoriate.* Princeton, NJ: Carnegie Foundation for the Advancement of Teaching, 1990.

Brinkley, Ellen, and Anne-Marie Hall. "Tapping the Potential: Building Teacher Leadership While Rethinking Your Site." *The Voice* 5.1 (2000): 10–11.

Brothers, Barbara, Carol Gay, Gratia Murphy, and Gary Salvern. "Youngstown State University: The English Festival and Project ARETE." Ed. Ron Fortune. *School-College Collaborative Programs in English.* New York: MLA, 1986. 52–60.

Chaplin, Miriam T. "National Standards and College Composition: Are They Kissing Cousins or Natural Siblings." *Composition in the Twenty-First Century: Crisis and Change.* Ed. Lynn Bloom, Donald A. Daiker, and Edward M. White. Carbondale: Southern Illinois UP, 1996. 166–76.

Connolly, Paul. "Bard College: Institute for Writing and Thinking." Ed. Ron Fortune. *School-College Collaborative Programs in English.* New York: MLA, 1986. 8–13.

Coye, Dale. "Ernest Boyer and the New American College: Connecting the 'Disconnects.'" *Change,* May/June 1997: 21–29.

Daiker, Donald A. "Introduction: The New Geography of Composition." *Composition in the Twenty-First Century: Crisis and Change.* Ed. Lynn Bloom, Donald A. Daiker, and Edward M. White. Carbondale: Southern Illinois UP, 1996. 1–7.

Dewey, John. *Democracy and Education.* New York: Macmillan, 1916.

Flower, Linda. "Literate Action." *Composition in the Twenty-First Century: Crisis and Change.* Ed. Lynn Bloom, Donald A. Daiker, and Edward M. White. Carbondale: Southern Illinois UP, 1996. 249–60.

Fortune, Ron. "Introduction." *School-College Collaborative Programs in English.* New York: MLA, 1986. vii–xxii.

Fortune, Ron, and Janice Neuleib. "Illinois State University: The Cooperative Teaching Program." Ed. Ron Fortune. *School-College Collaborative Programs in English.* New York: MLA, 1986. 111–19.

Foucault, Michel. *Power/Knowledge: Selected Interviews and Other Writings, 1972–1977.* Ed. Colin Gordon. New York: Pantheon, 1980.

Fuller, Mary, and Max Morenberg. "Miami University (Ohio): The Ohio Writing Project—Early English Composition Assessment Program." Ed. Ron Fortune. *School-College Collaborative Programs in English.* New York: MLA, 1986. 46–51.

Gere, Ann Ruggles. "Kitchen Tables and Rented Rooms: The Extracurriculum of Composition." *College Composition and Communication* 45 (Feb. 1994): 75–92.

Gray, James. "University of California, Berkeley: The Bay Area Writing Project and the National Writing Project." Ed. Ron Fortune. *School-College Collaborative Programs in English.* New York: MLA, 1986. 35–45.

hooks, bell. "marginality as site of resistance." *Out There: Marginalization and Contemporary Cultures.* Ed. Russell Ferguson, Martha Gever, Trinh T. Minh-ha, and Cornel West. New York: New Museum of Contemporary Art; Cambridge, MA: MIT P, 1990. 341–43.

Horner, Bruce. "Traditions and Professionalization: Reconceiving Work in Composition." *College English* 51 (Feb. 2000): 366–98.

Lindemann, Erika. "Enlarging the Community." *Composition in the Twenty-First Century: Crisis and Change.* Ed. Lynn Bloom, Donald A. Daiker, and Edward M. White. Carbondale: Southern Illinois UP, 1996. 177–80.

Modern Language Association Commission on Professional Service. Making Faculty Work Visible: Reinterpreting Professional Service, Teaching, and Research in the Fields of Language and Literature. New York: MLA, December 1996.

Parks, Steve, and Eli Goldblatt. "Writing beyond the Curriculum: Fostering New Collaborations in Literacy." *College English* 62 (May 2000): 584–606.

Pratt, Mary Louse. "Arts of the Contact Zone." *Profession 91.* New York: MLA, 1991. 33–40.

Sandman, Lorilee R., Pennie G. Foster-Fishman, James Lloyd, Warren Rauhe, and Cheryl Rosaen. "Managing Critical Tensions: How to Strength the Scholarship Component of Outreach." *Change,* Jan./Feb. 2000: 45–52.

Shuman, R. Baird. "University of Illinois, Urbana-Champaign: University Associates in Rhetoric Program." Ed. Ron Fortune. *School-College Collaborative Programs in English.* New York: MLA, 1986. 880–85.

Slevin, James. "Disciplining Students: Whom Should Composition Teach and What Should They Know?" *Composition in the Twenty-First Century: Crisis and Change.* Ed. Lynn Bloom, Donald A. Daiker, and Edward M. White. Carbondale: Southern Illinois UP, 1996. 153–65.

—. "Georgetown University: The Articulation Program and Related Projects." Ed. Ron Fortune. *School-College Collaborative Programs in English.* New York: MLA, 1986. 1–7.

Spellmeyer, Kurt. "After Theory: From Textuality to Attunement with the World." *College English* 58 (Dec. 1996): 893–913.

—. "Inventing the University Student." *Composition in the Twenty-First Century: Crisis and Change.* Ed. Lynn Bloom, Donald A. Daiker, and Edward M. White. Carbondale: Southern Illinois UP, 1996. 39–44.

Trimbur, John. "Writing Instruction and the Politics of Professionalization." *Composition in the Twenty-First Century: Crisis and Change.* Ed. Lynn Bloom, Donald A. Daiker, and Edward M. White. Carbondale: Southern Illinois UP, 1996. 133–45.

22

Contrapower Harassment in Program Administration: Establishing Teacher Authority

Julia K. Ferganchick
University of Arizona

The trend to decenter authority in the composition classroom affects teachers of writing at every level, and the questioning of teacher authority has touched nearly every aspect of our scholarship, changing the way we theorize about, research, and practice the teaching of writing. Although teacher authority has been at the center of our discussions in teacher training, workshops, conventions, and publications, little attention has been paid to the different social and cultural positions of men and women. As a community, we have taken for granted a stable and single definition of teacher authority that does not account for gender, racial, cultural, or other differences. I am certainly not arguing here that these various movements to alter our conceptions of teacher authority are invalid, but I do think we have missed a crucial aspect of this conversation. Particularly in a field where the majority of practitioners are women, we should be taking these differences into account when we discuss issues of teacher authority.

In this chapter I will first introduce contrapower harassment and trace some of the research that provides both contexts and examples of student-to-teacher harassment in writing classrooms. I will then suggest strategies for dealing with these issues within the context of writing program administration.

In 1995 Tilly Warnock, Julie Jung, and I began to address this problem when we surveyed nine hundred female teachers of college composition across the United States about student-to-teacher harassment (see Ferganchick-Neufang for the preliminary results of this study). We received 235 responses; of those, 137 (60 percent) said they had experienced gender-specific problems in the classroom; 132 (56 percent) replied "yes" when asked if they thought "many" women in their program face these same problems; and 146 (62 percent) said their awareness of gender-specific problems affects how they teach. The problems women who responded to our survey describe range from disruptive behavior in class to physical assault. Following is a brief sample of those stories:

I had a very driven Asian male student in my class. He received a B+ on his research paper. During exam week he came to my office, which was deserted except for us. He demanded to know why he had a B+ for the course. We went back and forth for nearly an hour. He said, "Well, why is it that in my other classes (math and science related courses) I'm getting Cs and Ds but I'm not angry with those instructors?" I answered that possibly it was because he saw those courses as more objective than [this one], but thinking it over later I wondered whether it was because his other instructors were male, but I don't know. At this point the student appeared very agitated and angry and I felt it best to move to a standing position because of the way he was hovering almost threateningly over me.... [As he was leaving, the student] said, "One of these days I'm going to come back and I'm going to kill you."

A very large male student was unhappy with his grade on a paper; he stood very close to me, bent down close to my face, and proceeded to speak (yell) loudly and threateningly. I very firmly told him that I would not discuss his paper grade until the next class day when he had had a chance to think about the paper and my comments. When he came to my office hours after the next class day, he very firmly closed my office door (I usually leave it open) then pulled his chair up close to mine. He was angry and attempting to blame me for his grade—"you said you wanted ...," etc.

A male student tried to get me to change a grade on his essay by shouting, insulting, and physically intimidating me by standing too close, leaning towards me, and waving his arms. When I reported him to my supervisor and the professor (male) spoke to the student, the student exhibited none of the above behavior.

I've had one clear cut case of harassment from a male student who openly resented the course content (we critiqued sexism in advertising, for example) and announced his resentment of women. In a private conference with me, he described his hatred of his mother, on whom he blamed all his problems, and as he described his feelings he invaded my personal space, raised his voice, and claimed he was so angry with me he could slap me.

I was teaching basic writing, an average class. I ran into a colleague who was younger, shorter, quieter than myself. She said she had this student in her class who was thoroughly obnoxious and sexist to her. She was going to have him moved. The university moves students in these situations at the student's convenience to another class at the same time. He ended up in my class. I thought, I'm older, taller, more experienced, have a louder voice. I will deal w/ him better than she could. Boy, was I wrong. From day one this guy was belligerent and obnoxious. His fellow students learned quickly to dislike him—that was a mercy. He created in instant community in my class. I spoke to the composition coordinator. He sent a male faculty member to speak to this guy before my class one day. We both decided he needed to be called on the carpet by someone other than me. He ignored my authority, so we sent someone we thought he wouldn't ignore. It didn't help. I was ill one day and my husband took my classes. This guy had the gall to make all sorts of sexual remarks and jokes about me in class that day, until my husband announced that he was my husband. Then this guy apologized profusely. What made things worse was that he never turned in any work. He would come to my office and act like he had been a bad son and beg my forgiveness—this lasted for 3 weeks, until he realized that I wasn't buying it. Then he became more belligerent in class. Finally, I had a conference with him and I told him I was dropping him from the class because he could only fail if he remained. The following morning before class, he showed up at my office and begged my forgiveness. When I refused, he got angry and threatened me. A teacher next door called the police and then came out and announced that the police were on their way. He left. The police suggested that they accompany me to class. They did. He was there. They removed him. In a subsequent interview w/ the dean, he complained that I hated men. The dean commiserated w/ him and explained that the university was full of angry women, so he'd better keep his head down. There, that's my story.

A male student called me "stupid" in class and told me, in front of other students, that he only comes to class because I am pretty. The semester culminated when he described an attack/rape of his English teacher.

A male student came to my office hours more frequently than I was comfortable with. He also made some remarks in class to the effect he would like to "lay me" on the table.

A group of young men continually gossiped together at the back of the class. When I asked them to share it with the class, they laughed raucously. After class, a female student told me they regularly discussed what I looked like under my dress.

A student wrote and handed in a journal entry that was sexually explicit and directed specifically toward me (detailed what he would like to do with/to various parts of my anatomy).

Whereas 60 percent of the female teachers who responded to our survey described experiences with student-to-teacher harassment such as the ones listed previously, many other respondents said that they didn't believe student-to-teacher harassment could happen because teachers had more "power" than students.

Taking a brief look at the official definition of sexual harassment, we can see why some may hold to the perspective that those in a lower position of institutional authority have no power to harass. Sexual harassment is legally defined as:

any unwelcome sexual advance, behavior, or conduct in any aspect of employment, housing, or academia that creates an intimidating or hostile environment. There are two types of sexual harassment: "Quid-pro-quo" (this-for-that), and "hostile environment." The law recognizes three scenarios for the workplace:

(a) Submission to sexual conduct or demand is, directly or indirectly, a condition of employment.

(b) Submission to sexual conduct or demand is, directly or indirectly, a condition for employment decisions such as promotion or a raise.

(c) Submission to such conduct results in interference with work performance or creates a hostile or intimidating work environment.

Notice, that the bulk of this definition relates to situations in which the person who claims harassment must necessarily be in a position of less institutional authority than her or his aggressor. An employer, for example, cannot be dependent on an employee for conditions of employment, nor can an employer be dependent on an employee for promotions and raises. When applied to an educational setting, these first two conditions clearly cannot be applied to student-to-teacher harassment, for students have, theoretically, no control over a teacher's conditions for employment, promotion, or financial rewards (except, of course, in the case of student evaluations). In fact, most of the women in our survey who denied the possibility of student-to-teacher harassment did so on the basis of power differences between students and teachers. Teachers, they argue, have power over students, and therefore students cannot harass teachers.

The third condition for defining sexual harassment, however, does allow for situations in which the harassed person is in a position of higher institutional authority than that of his or her aggressor. It is possible, for example, for an employee to create a hostile working environment for an employer; it is also possible—as many of us know from personal experience—for a student to create a hostile working environment for an instructor. But this third clause has not publicly been applied to these conditions. Every public case of sexual harassment that has been extensively covered by the media involves an employee's accusations of an employer. Those who have followed sexual harassment discussions in the media—ranging from "Nightline" to "Ricki Lake"—will have seen that the issue of institutional authority of the aggressor in such cases is always taken for granted.

However, some researchers have acknowledged the reality of what Katherine Benson terms "contrapower" sexual harassment. In a 1984 comment on Phyllis Crocker's analysis of university definitions of sexual harassment, Benson points out that "There is a general lack of awareness of [sexual harassment of women professors by their men students] not only in Crocker's work and in the official definitions but also in other research on sexual harassment within educational institutions" (516). In her short analysis of this issue, Benson suggests that future research address questions about contrapower harassment, as very little data is available on this issue. Since that time, few have acknowledged this need.

Kathleen McKinney, in her 1990 empirical study of sexual harassment in universities, includes a discussion of contrapower harassment. Her results suggest that the definition of "harassment" has a significant impact on the reports of such incidents. Because we fail to define student-to-teacher aggression as harassment, such problems go unreported and unexamined. Elizabeth Grauerholz's 1989 study focuses specifically on the harassment of women professors by students. Her questionnaire, sent to all female professors at Purdue University, asked respondents to report whether or not they had ex-

perienced specific incidents of contrapower harassment such as sexist comments, remarks about dress or body, comments about sexual behavior or
values, physical advances, and sexual bribery. Grauerholz's study, though limited in scope, suggests that contrapower harassment does exist, and her data
emphasize the need for more research in this area.

When surveying gender research in discourse analysis, Evlynn Ashton-Jones explains that in professional situations, a woman who is a more
powerful position, a position with more institutional authority, is often still at
a disadvantage in mixed-sex conversations:

> While it seems reasonable to speculate that these conversation patterns [of male dom-
> inance] might be subverted or reversed in situations where a woman clearly holds
> power—for example, a female employer conversing with a male employee or a female
> doctor talking to a male patient—this does not seem to be the case. Candace West, for
> instance, finds that female physicians use language that minimizes status differences,
> whereas their male counterparts use language that emphasizes the physician-patient
> hierarchy—in both cases, regardless of the patient's gender. More to the point, how-
> ever, Helena Leet-Pellegrini's examination of gender and expertise as covariables in
> mixed-sex conversation shows that, even when women hold positions of power, the
> conversational advantage that men enjoy is not eliminated. In fact, possessing a higher
> level of expertise than men did simply reinforced women's supportive work in
> mixed-sex conversation. (15)

Women, then, can be at an authoritative disadvantage, even when attaining a position of authority such as that of a college instructor. Women who responded to our survey reported numerous incidents of student aggression
that include written attacks, such as the student who turned in an essay de-
tailing the rape of an English teacher; verbal threats, such as the student who
threatened to pull a gun on his instructor if she failed him from the course for
excessive absences; and physical violence, such as the student who, angry
with the grade he earned on his essay, picked up a desk and hurled it across the
room. These are the most striking examples. Most were more subtle: students
commenting on a teacher's appearance, asking inappropriate questions
about a teacher's personal life, demanding excessive attention from female
teachers, and disrupting class with irrelevant and/or inappropriate remarks.

The study supports previous research results: Student-to-teacher harassment is a very real problem for many female instructors in the traditional
classroom. Given the gravity of this issue, what can writing program administrators (WPAs) do? Obviously, more research and discussion is needed to
both define the problem of contrapower harassment, how it affects the teachers in our programs, and what can be done about it. However, over the past
few years and in collaboration with numerous colleagues in our field, I have
developed some practical approaches to student–teacher conflict that WPAs
can use in their own programs. I outline these approaches in the next section,
but I begin with a strong word of caution: Suggesting that either WPAs or

teachers can themselves control aggressive student behavior would be both untrue and potentially dangerous. If, for example, a teacher could (or, worse, should) control student behavior, then that teacher, rather than the aggressive student, could be held accountable for any conflict that arose. This, as we know, is simply not the case. Thus, in discussing ways to deal with contrapower harassment, we must remember that our ability to control any given situation is limited. We can certainly take steps to protect ourselves as teachers, but we cannot hold accountable those who become victims of student aggression. And I urge WPAs to make this fact known to their staff within any discussion of student–teacher conflicts.

This leads us to my first suggestion: bring the issue of contrapower harassment out into the open in department and/or program discussions of pedagogy and classroom procedure. Teacher assistant (TA) training and other forms of faculty development workshops are ideal places to begin discussions of teacher–student relationships including the issue of aggressive student behavior.

The remaining approaches to student–teacher conflict I classify into indirect and direct categories. The indirect approaches may, at first glance, seem unrelated to the issue at hand, but, as the aforementioned research shows, are in fact relevant.

INDIRECT APPROACHES
TO AGGRESSIVE STUDENT BEHAVIOR

Attendance

One of the primary points of contention between students and teachers is that of attendance. Students, as we all know, will often go to extreme measures to get out of going to class. Composition classes, being primarily workshop in nature, usually require attendance as a condition of enrollment. Conflict can arise when neither teacher nor student is perfectly clear about attendance requirements and repercussions for not meeting those requirements. Therefore, one of the more basic steps WPAs can take to help alleviate student–teacher conflict is the design of a clear attendance policy such as this one: "You are expected to be present and prepared for each class meeting. More than three absences will result in a lowering of your final grade; more than four absences will result in a no-credit for the course." Notice that in this policy there is not distinction between "excused" and "unexcused" absences, a distinction that can cause quite a bit of confusion. What exactly is an excused absence, anyway? Leaving out any mention of excused absence creates a policy that can be enforced regardless of the reason for the absence. However, it does not exclude the possibility that the teacher can excuse any absence he or she sees fit. The other quality that makes the aforementioned policy useful is that it clearly states the requirement and the consequences for not meeting that requirement.

Plagiarism

Another site of potential conflict between teachers and students in the composition classroom is plagiarism. The following policy can be an effective deterrent to disagreements about this academic affliction:

> Plagiarism is a serious offense, one that can result in the failure of an assignment and the course. "Plagiarism" means taking credit for another's work, using another's words without attributing them, or using another's ideas or research without proper documentation. Always cite such use of language, ideas, or research. Papers turned in without proper documentation will receive **no** credit. See the Student Code of Conduct for details.

Cases of plagiarism that can be clearly proved normally fall under a university's student code of conduct, to which the aforementioned policy refers such cases. Those blurry cases that cannot be proved, however, can cause problems for teachers. The aforementioned policy does two things to promote accord: First, it defines plagiarism in simple terms that students can understand, and second, it offers a broad category, "proper documentation," for which a student can be held accountable, thus moving the debate from the topic of "right and wrong" on the part of the student to that of quality of work. The policy leaves intact traditional avenues of dealing with blatant and provable plagiarism, while also providing teachers a way of dealing with the more common and more complicated varieties. Also, the aforementioned policy clearly states the consequences for turning in work that is not properly documented.

Grading

The evaluation of student work is admittedly a difficult topic, one that has attracted much debate in our field and one that has generated much argument between students and teachers, as anyone who has taught even one writing course will quickly attest to. Thus an analysis of grading criteria, methods, and standards is beyond the scope of this essay. I would be remise, however, in not mentioning it here, as disagreements about grades generate much student–teacher conflict (see Ferganchick-Neufang). And the following list provides some suggestions for WPAs and teachers when considering grading in relation to contrapower harassment:

1. Clearly outline assignments, assignment requirements, and point distribution in course syllabi.

2. Clearly state consequences for late or incomplete assignments.
3. Include numeric descriptions for each grade.
4. Use grids or grading charts to help students understand grading criteria.

DIRECT APPROACHES
TO AGGRESSIVE STUDENT BEHAVIOR

Conduct Policy

Most institutions have in place a student code of conduct that will address, to some extent, issues of appropriate student behavior. These documents, though certainly valuable, are often vague and, for reasons mentioned earlier, may omit any mention of contrapower harassment. I have found it useful, therefore, both to remind students of the relevant section of their code of conduct and to elaborate on it, as the following example shows:

> Code of Conduct: All students are responsible for upholding the Code of Conduct, available through the Office of the Dean of Students. Section XX states that the following conduct is subject to disciplinary action: "Engaging in harassment or unlawful discriminatory activities on the basis of age, gender, handicapped condition, national origin, race, religion, sexual orientation or veteran status, or violating university rules governing harassment or discrimination...."

> In this class you are expected to participate in discussions and limit comments to those related to discussion topics. You are expected to treat each other and your instructor with respect and courtesy. If your behavior does not meet these guidelines, you will be given a warning—two warnings and you will be asked to leave class, obtaining an absence for that day. If you are asked to leave class twice, or if the offenses are severe, you will be reported to the dean of students and may be removed from class with a failing grade.

Paper Trail

Despite careful preparation and well-designed policies, we cannot prevent contrapower harassment in the classroom. Thus we must prepare teachers in our programs to deal with such problems in the event they do arise. The most important information to give teachers is that if they feel threatened or believe a student in their classroom is in any danger at any time, they should immediately call for help. The following list provides some suggestions for dealing with more subtle problems:

- Keep a clear record of attendance and grades.
- Maintain a log of inappropriate or aggressive student behavior; include names, dates, and descriptions.
- Provide a written warning to any student whose behavior is disruptive or disturbing.

- When appealing to a supervisor for assistance in dealing with an aggressive student, put your complaint in writing and provide supporting documentation such as records, logs, and written communication with the student.

Regardless of what policies a teacher chooses to adopt for his or her classroom, WPAs can help ensure those policies are effective for establishing positive student–teacher relationships by keeping the following in mind:

1. Syllabi should be clearly written and easily accessible for students; this will help alleviate any miscommunication between teacher and student.
2. All policies should clearly descripe those issues involved (such as attendance) and include a statement of consequences for not abiding by that policy.
3. When possible, classroom policies such as those for attendance, plagiarism, grading, and conduct should be adopted program- or department-wide; this adds validity to the policies.

As I said earlier, the best-laid plans for avoiding student–teacher conflict can be for naught in some situations. As WPAs and teachers, we simply cannot control the behavior of our students, and our culture is becoming an increasingly violent one. What we can do is educate ourselves and our students about university policies and create an environment in our writing programs that fosters open communication between administrators and teachers. This is by the far the most effective tool for negotiating student–teacher conflict.

WORKS CITED

Ashton-Jones, Evelyn. "Collaboration, Conversation, and the Politics of Gender." *Feminine Principles and Women's Experience in American Composition and Rhetoric.* Ed. Louise Wetherbee Phelps and Janet Emig. Pitt Series in Composition, Literacy, and Culture. Pittsburgh: U of Pittsburgh P, 1995. 5–26.

Benson, Katherine. "Comment on Crocker's 'An Analysis of University Definitions of Sexual Harassment.'" *Signs* 9 (1984): 516–19.

Ferganchick-Neufang, Julia. "Breaking the Silence: A Study of Gender-Specific Problems in the Writing Classroom." *Composition Forum* 7.1 (1996): 17–30.

Grauerholz, Elizabeth. "Sexual Harassment of Women Professors by Students: Exploring the Dynamics of Power, Authority, and Gender in a University Setting." *Sex Roles* 21 (1989): 789–801.

McKinney, Kathleen. "Sexual Harassment of University Faculty by Colleagues and Students." *Sex Roles* 23 (1990): 421–38.

23

Writing Program Administration and Instructional Computing

Ken S. McAllister
University of Arizona

Cynthia L. Selfe
Michigan Technological University

In the contested and complex intellectual landscape of world-order changes resulting from shifting political economies and, in highly industrialized countries, made manifest in the volatile exchange values that define the importance of "information," few territories are more unstable and uncharted—and, conversely, more promising and vigorous—than the one encompassing the intersection of computing and literacy.

For this reason, it is an impossible task to anticipate *all* of the contemporary challenges writing program administrators (WPAs) are likely to encounter when dealing with computers. In many programs around the country, WPAs are asked to integrate computers into writing curricula in meaningful ways: negotiate the changes—personal, instructional, and economic—associated with increasing computer use in writing programs; design, administer, and sustain departmental computer-supported writing facilities; make decisions for teaching assistants (TAs), instructors, lecturers, and faculty about computer upgrades and maintenance; manage technology budgets and staff; and educate faculty and graduate students about teaching effectively with technology.

The unsettled nature of this landscape, however, also makes it a particularly productive arena for identifying new perspectives on the teaching of writing and literacy. And for many WPAs—especially those who enjoy the intellectual work of thinking critically about the teaching of writing and literacy, and the labor involved in shaping material reality so that it reflects this critique—this fact is particularly appealing.

Our goal in this chapter is to lay a foundation for planning and reflection that will help WPAs discover some new ways of imagining the problems and possibilities of instructional computing, and of transforming those imaginings into workable strategies for writing and literacy programs.

SOME BACKGROUND: WHY WPAs SHOULD PAY ATTENTION TO TECHNOLOGY

In part, WPAs must attend to technology for pragmatic reasons. Decisions need to be made about the use of computers in writing programs, and WPAs are often the people involved in making these decisions.

But there are also intellectual and pedagogical reasons for attending to technology. Faculty and TAs who are interested in teaching writing in computer-rich environments often share a commitment to the educational spaces of classrooms, writing centers, and literacy programs, as well as to language studies. These teacher/scholars are often interested in the teaching of reading and composing (in the broadest sense of these terms and, increasingly often, in contexts that are not limited to alphabetic representation)—and in the dynamic nature of language as it unfolds in new computer-based environments. Those who work in this area also frequently share an interest in exploring the relationships between humans and machines, as well as the social issues—agency, identity, humanity, responsibility—that those relationships throw into such sharp relief.

WPAs who choose to foreground technology-use issues in their programmatic and instructional discussions with other teachers may also find that faculty and TAs are interested in—and engaged with—such discussions because they build on shared intellectual ground. Among the landmarks characterizing this territory are the following:

- An interest not only in language studies, but also in rhetorical and social theory. Given the fact that technology serves as a nexus of power, money, ideology, and political influence, it is not surprising that many teacher/scholars interested in technology issues feel the theoretical narratives of rhetoric (Berlin, *Rhetoric and Reality*; Faigley, "Study"; Vitanza, "Concerning," "Open Letters," "Three"), Marxism and cultural studies (Berlin, "English"; Harkin & Schilb; Sosnoski; "Notes," "Postmodern"), ideology (Berlin, *Rhetoric*; Eagleton), and feminism (Balsamo; Caywood & Overing; Haraway, "Manifesto," *Simians*, "Situated"; Turkle, "Computational," *Life, Second Self;* Turkle and Papert) possess great explanatory power. In addition, given the ways in which the recent rise of technological systems have both shaped, and been shaped by, conditions associated with postmodernism, those interested in using computers to teach composition may also share interest in the work of Baudrillard; Berlin ("Postmodernism," "Poststructuralism"); Castells (*End, Power, Rise*); Faigley (*Fragments*); Jameson; Lyotard.

- A belief in social justice and the ability and responsibility of teachers to enact productive social change—even if only temporary, partial, and fragmentary—that will make the lives of certain groups of people (particularly people of color, people labeled *illiterate, underprepared,* or *basic writers;* underrepresented groups or groups who may hold positions counter to the dominant systems of power, particularly women, the lesbian, gay, biaffectionate, and transgendered community, speakers of English as a foreign language; and people who are poor) and, thus, the lives of people at large, better, more just, more equitable. This work is often informed by theorists like Giddens, deCerteau, Deleuze & Guattari, Laclau and Mouffe, and Ohmann. Associated with this belief is an emerging understanding of the many difficulties associated with achieving social justice and enacting change and the tendential forces associated with stasis.

- A commitment to educational settings (including classrooms, schools and institutions, writing centers, educational sites in workplaces, and community literacy programs) as potential venues for enacting productive social change. Paradoxically, this commitment is often shaped by a sense of hope and optimistic pragmatism, even while it is tempered by skepticism. Influencing the latter is the work of critical pedagogists such as Berlin ("English," "Postmodernism"), Cooper ("Ecology," "Postmodern"), Faigley (*Fragments*, "Literacy," "Material"), Giroux (*Border,* "Modernism," *Resisting*), Knoblauch and Brannon, Ohmann, and Snyder and Joyce—who understand the contributory role that educational systems and settings play in reproducing inequities along the related axes of race, class, gender, and orientation.

- An understanding of technology and technological systems as both a possible vector for enacting productive change, and a powerful force for resisting such change and continuing inequity. This belief often rests on two understandings: first, that technology consists not only of machines—of computers, for instance—but also of a complexly articulated set of social formations and, second, that, given these formations, technology and power and literacy practices are linked at fundamental levels (Faigley, "Literacy," "Material"; Feenberg, *Alternative, Critical, Questioning;* Marcuse; McLuhan, *Gutenberg, Understanding;* Mumford; Ohmann; Selfe; Turkle, *Life;* Winner; Wise; Zuboff).

Given such vigorous intellectual contexts, teachers who experiment with new technologies are often motivated to re-examine their own teaching practices from new perspectives. WPAs may find these teachers willing to study, design, and exploit the productive potential of various forms of computer technology (e.g., systems, networks, the Web, individual machines, MOOs, listservs, word-processing packages, computer-based classrooms) as possible vectors for critically-informed pedagogical approaches or critically-informed social action within the settings of classrooms, writing centers, and writing programs.

The contested possibilities of computer-based learning environments may also encourage teachers who seek increasingly egalitarian contexts for communicative exchanges (Castner; Gomez; Romano; Whitaker and Hill); more complicated understandings of discursive effective agency in feminist and multicultural contexts (LeCourt; Selfe & Selfe); the productive exercises of responsibility (Cooper, "Postmodern"; Janangelo); or an appreciation for difference along the related axes of race, class (Bennet & Walsh; Taylor), physical and mental challenges (Buckley; Retish and Reiter), orientation (DeWitt; Janangelo; Woodland, "I Plan," "Queer"), and writing skill level (Crafton).

It is this kind of intellectual and pedagogical vigor that WPAs are often able to draw upon when they foreground issues of technology use in their programmatic discussions and work with faculty and TAs.

ENGAGING COMPUTING:
FIVE MOMENTS FOR WPA ACTION

Recognizing the variety of intellectual and pedagogical issues at play in the landscape of technology-use issues, how are WPAs to decide where to begin? A pragmatic assessment of one's current situation vis-à-vis instructional computing is usually a helpful place to start.

Most WPAs, for example, no longer have the luxury of planning their instructional computing initiatives from scratch. Most institutions now have minimal instructional computing projects under way: Computers in the writing center, e-mail exchanges among students and teachers, and rhetorical analyses of Web sites are among the most common and least expensive of such initiatives. Wealthier schools have launched massive and technologically sophisticated "Computers in Composition" programs, some of which use interactive Web sites, streaming audio and video, and even virtual reality.

Given this context of computer use as a project-in-progress for most departments, most WPAs begin working with technology *in medias res*. With this in mind, in the remainder of this essay we try to avoid suggestions that smack of "just start over, but do it right this time." Instead, we focus on five key moments when WPAs are likely to be confronted with certain types of computer-use challenges and issues, and we suggest how WPAs might respond to these moments.

We have arranged our discussion of these five moments in an order that we hope is conducive to critical reflection, and to the hermeneutic relationship among practice, theory, reflection, and praxis. We expect, however, that most readers will locate their particular situations or concerns among the five moments and imagine new possibilities from there. Regardless of where you begin, however, we urge you to consider all five moments in relation to your particular program—we believe that the development of a critical consciousness about the relationship between technology and literacy often begins with the example and initiatives established by careful, thoughtful WPAs.

We should note, early in this discussion, that the five moments we identify share an expectation that approaches to writing pedagogy and administration should always be informed by critique. Toward this end, we also suggest two basic sets of questions that can be useful to WPAs as they read through the material that follows and attempt to apply the precepts of this chapter to their own situations:

- What are the instructional goals of the writing program? How can these goals be made to drive a computer-based program/course/activity/facility/decision?
- Who is being served by these goals and the computer-based instruction that is derived from them? Who is not?

These two questions will not always lead directly to a practical answer, nor are they meant to. Instead, we hope that they help keep WPAs focused primarily on their writing program's basic sense of mission and pedagogical ethic, and only secondarily on computing.

Moment #1: Focusing on Programmatic and Curricular Goals

Certainly one moment in which WPAs can productively address the relationship between computing and the teaching of composition occurs during discussions of programmatic and curricular goals. WPAs can use these opportunities to make sure that pedagogical and intellectual goals remain the primary driving forces of curricula in writing programs, and that technology use remains a secondary consideration, one that continues to be shaped by—and motivated by—the primary goals of instruction.

This rule, of course, is not always easy to follow, and WPAs will recognize that each teacher must situate this relationship in the context of his or her own professional practices and circumstances. For example, many WPAs recognize that computer-based projects represent a large proportion of the limited funding opportunities available to graduate student teachers and adjuncts in English Departments. Administrators interested in establishing the technological credentials of their unit, for example, often seem more will-ing and able to produce money for computer-based projects involving dy-namic Web-based learning environments, educational MOOs, or collaborative software applications than they are for more mundane—albeit no less important or necessary—projects of a more conventional stripe.

Nor are administrators the only people persuaded to let technology drive educational efforts. TAs often seem bent on integrating computer-based as-signments into their classrooms, not because they think such assignments will do a better job of accomplishing their stated pedagogical goals, but rather, be-cause they want to take advantage of students' personal interest in MOOs and MUDs, listservs, or the World Wide Web. Junior faculty thinking about tenure and senior faculty looking for ways to beat salary compression are also susceptible to technological flash and can allow their courses to be driven by technology instead of teaching. In such circumstances, WPAs can often serve most effectively by insisting that a careful examination of programmatic and pedagogical goals precede discussions of—or decisions about—technology. In this effort, WPAs can help teachers who are often overworked and under-paid to think carefully and act responsibly before taking on the demanding additional tasks of learning to teach with computers.

Of course, WPAs can also anticipate and plan to avoid such situations, us-ing programmatic and pedagogical goals as a focal point around which to de-sign and implement professional development programs for teachers who want to use technology. Such programs need to begin with a concentrated fo-cus on pedagogical or programmatic goals and proceed to computer-oriented approaches only after this important groundwork has been laid. If designed carefully, these sessions can help faculty and TAs develop the important habit of using clearly articulated curricular and pedagogical goals to drive decisions about technology.

This kind of professional development program can also help teachers re-alize that the mechanical skills of keyboarding, storing information, and re-trieving it—although obviously part of technological literacy—do not comprise its whole. And they can provide instructors with strategies for teaching not only technical skills (e.g. how to teach writing with word-pro-cessing programs), but also critical skills (e.g., what behaviors are being en-couraged—intentionally and unintentionally—by teaching writing with word processing). At the root of such professional development programs or workshops can be the recognition that technology use, even when well inten-tioned, is also less than complete if it simply encourages the habitual use of computers as communication devices—an unthinking dependence on com-puter-based word processing to complete assignments for papers, on com-puter networks for collaborative responses, on the World Wide Web for writing research papers, to name just a few.

Such workshops can also help teachers understand the linkages between technology and literacy, the social contexts for computer-based discourse and communication, and the products and practices of technological communication—all of which go into a robust cultural and historical understanding of what it means to be technologically literate. With such professional development opportunities, teachers can help students understand how values are designed into computers as manufactured artifacts; who has and does not have access to electronic environments; how technology relates to and helps shape the cultural formations of science, education, poverty, racism, sexism; how the skills of technological literacy are taught and learned in this country; how access to and use of technology benefit citizens differentially according to power, race, gender, and socio-economic status; and why technological systems are constructed and distributed as they are within this country and around the world.

Another way for WPAs to facilitate principle-driven pedagogy is by establishing a set of technology-related outcomes for computer-enhanced writing classes that include equal emphasis on students' use of technology and their understanding of technology's complex social and cultural relationship with literacy values and practices. Although the task of assessing these outcomes would be challenging, they would be no more difficult to assess than more traditional performance outcomes such as "organization" and "clarity." This is to say, of course, that the effort would be very difficult indeed, but probably worth the effort.

Finally, WPAs can use all professional development opportunities and discussions of instructional goals—and the technology-based instruction that derives from these—as occasions to think about the populations being well served by their programs and those not being so well served. With computing especially, this activity is crucial. In the United States, technology use is now inextricably linked to literacy—by the time individuals graduate from high school and college, they are no longer considered "literate" unless they know how to communicate in computer-supported environments (Selfe; *Standards* 25). Yet, not all students currently have equitable opportunities to develop such literacies. It is a fact that poor students and students of color are less likely to have had access to a technology-rich education at all levels than are wealthy students and White students, and thus less likely to be prepared to work in technology-rich environments in college settings (Coley, Crandler, & Engle; Hoffman & Novak; "Americans"; Selfe).

Moment #2: Focusing on Issues of Access

The challenges associated with who has access to computers and under what conditions are so imposing that many WPAs find them easier to ignore than to face. Charles Moran eloquently critiques this tendency—especially common among administrators and teachers—in his essay "Access: The 'A' Word in Technology Studies." We will not rehearse his argument here, but will confirm its truth and encourage all WPAs to consider Moran's observations and arguments in light of their particular programs. Most WPAs who take this challenge seriously will quickly learn that access cannot be reduced simply to a question of who owns a computer and who doesn't. Access also turns on the more complex points of degree and quality.

WPAs who explore how access issues affect their writing programs may find it useful to ask, and answer, the following questions:

- What is the saturation level of computers and computer support in a community?
- Is access to computers genuine or theoretical for teachers and students?
- Is existing computer equipment sufficient and appropriate for the particular activities of composing and communicating? And are they adequate to meet the other curricular needs of the writing program?
- Is there adequate technical support for computer-using teachers and students?
- Are there groups of students/faculty for whom access is more difficult than others?

The first consideration for WPAs thinking about computer access in their program involves the saturation levels of technology resources on a campus or in a department. It is not necessary for all teachers and students to *own* computers in order to have a responsible computer-supported writing program, but WPAs do need to make sure that teachers have an appropriate level of access to technology, to appropriately sophisticated technology, to professional development opportunities, and to technical support systems—*before* they are asked to teach computer-intensive courses or create online course materials. All of these factors constitute the saturation level of technology resources in a community, and WPAs are often in a position to speak to departmental and university administrators about ensuring a responsible level of technology saturation before allowing computer-use efforts to change from experimental projects to broader curricular requirements. Similarly, WPAs can help individual teachers understand the importance of making sure that an adequate saturation level exists to support the projects they ask students to do in courses. If only some teachers or some students have sufficient access to computers, to adequate training, and/or to technical support, then either allowances or exceptions must be made for those who do not, or resources must be obtained for those in need.

A second area of concern for WPAs thinking about issues of access also has to do with the pragmatics of institutional conditions. WPAs who rely solely on statistics about computers on campus will find it easy to misjudge the extent to which teachers and students have genuine access to technological environments for writing. On a given campus, for example, six of "eight multimedia computer labs" may be open only from 8:00 a.m. to 5:30 p.m., thus making plans to hold evening classes in these spaces much more difficult. Similarly, some computer classrooms may be reserved for special purposes on particular days; some may have only old machines, have no network connections, or may be in the process of being remodeled or moved. In other words, there is usually a difference between *theoretical* and *genuine* access to computers. *Theoretical access* is based on a simple count of all computers on a campus, regardless of age, available software, and access restrictions on various populations. *Genuine access* takes all salient factors into consideration for a given population. Often theoretical access counts include computers used by support staff, computers that have not yet been removed from the institution's formal inventory record, and/or computers with unlicensed software. Similarly, theoretical access figures for home or dorm machines may erroneously extrapolate from incoming first-year student surveys to describe the entire student body. Such figures may also be based on average counts that mask the differential distribution of computers among under-represented populations. In this latter case, statistically-driven oversights can generate a host of classist, racist, and sexist problems which, if left unattended, necessarily become embedded in the curricula of computer-enhanced courses and in the mission of the writing program itself.

Genuine access is determined not only by the number and kind of computers to which individuals have access, but also by the numbers of people who must share these resources. Although the efficient use of available computer time is generally considered less a priority than it was twenty or more years ago, the sharing of computers still regularly occurs in most departments and on most campuses and can sometimes create problems for both teachers and students. For example, teachers who must share their desk computers with office mates or their home computers with family members have restricted access to computer resources. Similarly, students who have to share a computer with other family members or roommates may also be at a disadvantage.

Open-access computer labs, though usually a boon to resource-hungry students and teachers, should also be considered in terms of both theoretical and genuine access. Such dense collections of computers can easily give the impression that computer resources are abundant. A WPA who reads that there are "over three hundred public access computers" available in open-access labs, for example, can be overly impressed with numbers until she does the basic math. If three hundred computers must be shared among three thousand students, the genuine level of access is 1:10, one computer for every ten people. This might seem like an acceptable figure, at first glance, but when WPAs consider the fact that all ten people may be likely to want to use that one computer during peak hours of 10:00 a.m.–3:00 p.m. and 7:00–10:00 p.m., it quickly becomes clear that lines of waiting students will be forming out the door of the computer lab and down the hallway. This situation can be exacerbated at midterm and final-exam time when students and teachers alike need to work extra hours to produce and evaluate computer-based projects. Levels of genuine access may also depend on time limits imposed on the use of open-lab computers, for example, when labs are reserved for class use or for certain majors.

Most WPAs can obtain information about the factors influencing levels of genuine access from their institutions' computer centers or through their own field research. Knowing the answers to these kinds of questions will help WPAs understand the limits of the available resources and allow them to design more effective training and curriculum strategies for their programs.

A third area of concern for WPAs considering issues of access has to do with the extent to which an institution's computer environments support the particular activities of composing and communicating, and the other more specific pedagogical objectives associated with writing courses. WPAs will want to know, for example, whether computers are fast enough, have enough memory, and contain the software and peripherals needed for multimedia composition or the graphics-intensive, Web-based research that many teachers now include in advanced writing courses. If a writing program has the objective of teaching first-year composition students to analyze Web sites from a rhetorical perspective, WPAs need to know if the network infrastructure underlying the department's computer classroom is capable of supporting twenty-five, fifty, or one hundred fifty students as they simultaneously browse Web sites. Similarly, WPAs will want to be able to advise instructors who plan to put class readings online and scan print articles into digital formats. Such documents may require special viewing programs that need to be downloaded from the Web, and they may be very large because of the way they are processed. Teachers will need help planning appropriately for their technology use so that students will be able to read and access such documents easily.

These access problems are not insurmountable, and they should not necessarily deter an instructor or WPA from using such technologies. Our point is that these kinds of problems need to be recognized and addressed before they are unintentionally designed into writing program strategies. And though we do not want to suggest that WPAs be technology experts, they should know where to go for expert information and technological support.

A fourth area of concern for WPAs considering access issues for their program has to do with the availability of appropriate technical support. Any teacher with experience using computers in a course will be able to tell stories about computer malfunctions that stop otherwise engaging classes dead in their tracks: a network gone down, a projector with faulty settings, software upgraded overnight or without warning. For novice computer-using teachers, these problems can be both frustrating and defeating. Moreover, though more experienced computer-using teachers should know enough to have Plan B ready to go in such situations, a certain hubris can kick in, motivating these teachers to spend an unwise amount of class time trying to fix them.

For these reasons, adequate and appropriate technical support is crucial for computer-supported composition programs, no matter what technical skill level instructors may have. Teachers need to focus on teaching, not troubleshooting computers. WPAs, therefore, need to be diligent about obtaining consistent and high-quality technical support for the computer classrooms their teachers use, and vigilant in countering proposals for minimal salaries for technical support personnel in a department or on a campus. In composition classes, technical support personnel can do more than just fix computer problems when they arise; with a teacher's help, they can also be expert at sizing up technical situations that negatively affect pedagogical goals. WPAs need to be aware of this expertise, support its presence on a campus or within a department, and encourage teachers to draw upon it.

Indeed, WPAs can avoid a number of access problems simply by understanding the relationship between the available technical support resources and writing programs and formulating well-publicized guidelines that help teachers and students understand this relationship as well. Such guidelines can help clarify, for example, what a teacher's responsibility is if a home computer goes down while a student is working on a class project. Such guidelines can not only list available technical support resources on campus, but also outline an extension policy for computer-intensive classes. Although some teachers will be concerned that such a procedure will invite student fraud (e.g., "the computer ate my file"), all but the most cynical will recognize that technological glitches happen—often through no fault of students or teachers. And both teachers and students alike will benefit from having such a policy in place so that when such mishaps do occur, instructors are able to respond fairly, calmly, and without an excessive amount of suspicion. At the institutional level, teachers and WPAs alike ought to know to whom to turn for timely help if there's a problem with a school's server, or a computer-supported classroom, or a desktop computer.

A final question for WPAs to ask about technology access has to do with equity: Is access to computers (and to the instruction needed to use computers effectively) more difficult to obtain for some groups than for others? And, if so, why? The specific answers to these questions—which will depend on institutional populations, constraints, and locations—can help WPAs identify equity problems that negatively affect teaching and learning performance. Examining the answers to such questions early and often may help WPAs avoid more complicated problems and complaints down the road.

Moment #3: Focusing on Issues of Administration

The third kind of moment during which WPAs may find opportunities to address issues of computer use occurs during the performance of routine administrative duties associated with assessment, classroom scheduling and course assignments, and the design of computer-supported teaching spaces. Each of these areas can generate both possibilities and problems for WPAs and the people with whom they work.

Assessment.   We start with writing assessment because—even *without* computers—it is so notoriously difficult. Few WPAs are content with the system of entrance and exit exams, performance tests, or portfolio examinations that shape their programs. Writing instruction, after all, remains a messy and complicated undertaking. It is not carried out under controlled laboratory conditions that allow us to determine the effects of specific instructional activities, or to fully understand the pedagogical implications of students' approaches to thinking about writing and understanding themselves as writers. When we add computer-based instruction to the mix, the complexity of assessment factors that must be considered only increases.

Despite this difficult situation, however, WPAs are still regularly asked to justify the work their teachers and students do within computer-supported composing and communication environments. It is not unusual, for example, for WPAs to be asked to provide evidence that limited institutional funds are being used to provide a positive return on a technological investment or to justify expensive pedagogical decisions within increasingly corporatized and competitive institutions. Nor is every attempt to assess computer-supported writing programs wrong-headed. Computer-based writing curricula are sometimes assessed for the same reasons that writing programs in general are sometimes assessed—in an honest attempt to determine if students are learning what teachers want them to learn.

What kinds of assessment are most worth pursuing? We suggest that WPAs avoid spending their time on the question "Should we be teaching with computers?" In cultures that are increasingly dependent on computer-supported environments for communicating and in an educational system in which literacy and technology have become inextricably related, this question is moot. If we do not prepare students to communicate in—and especially to think critically about—computer-supported environments, we are abrogating our responsibility to prepare them for the world they will face after leaving the classroom. WPAs who still find it necessary to argue this point can turn, among other sources, to President Clinton's Technology Literacy Challenge, to the Goals 2000 initiative, or to the English/Language Arts Standards of the National Council of Teachers of English to argue that individuals must know how to read, write, research, and communicate within computer-supported environments in order to be considered "literate" citizens in the twenty-first century (cf. *Getting America's Students; Goals 2000; Standards*). WPAs can also turn to the sources of employment data that now emphasize the importance of computer skills in high-tech workplaces (cf. Meares and Sargent; *Futurework*).

We also suggest that WPAs avoid spending their time trying to assess questions such as "Does the use of computer-supported word processing improve overall writing quality?" In numerous studies on this question conducted from the early 1980s to the early 1990s (cf. Hawisher, "Research," "Studies"; Bruce and Rubin), no systematic evidence emerged to indicate that computers improve the overall quality of students' writing. To a great extent, the mixed results of these studies were a result of the fact that they were classroom-based investigations—given the differences that characterize instructional settings, investigators who conducted these studies ended up considering different factors and operating under different conditions. The inherent messiness of classroom teaching meant that there could be no strict controls that could isolate one treatment variable. Each of these studies was conducted by different investigators, looking at students working in different conditions and on different computer systems, working with different teachers who used different methods of approaching composition studies. Hence, no single set of findings emerged as definitive. And, in addition to these inconclusive findings is the simple fact that, at least in industrialized societies, the cultural dependence on computers has become so great that the question of word processing's beneficial and detrimental effects on student writing is immaterial. Many students today have never written papers and reports with anything *other* than a computer, a trend that is likely to continue and expand.

One question that WPAs might productively explore in terms of large-scale, programmatic evaluations, we believe, is "How might computers be used most productively to support curricular goals in this department's/university's writing program?" Such large-scale assessments, however, are time consuming because they involve so many people, instructional settings, goals, and situations. WPAs undertaking such-large-scale assessments of computer use in a writing program should make sure to include a range of stakeholders (e.g., students, teachers, technical staff, administrators, parents, equipment vendors) in the initial identification of assessment goals, in the design of the assessment effort, and in the implementation of the overall assessment project. Moreover, given the complexity of most programs' computer-use efforts (e.g., some classes use computers only as word-processing support and never meet in computer classrooms, other classes meet regularly in computer classrooms and are built around advanced multimedia composition, and still other classes occasionally meet in computer classrooms and use the WWW as a research medium), we also suggest that WPAs seek—and use—multiple sources of information, empirical data and interpretive commentary and narratives from teachers, students, administrators, and technical support staff. We also suggest that they provide for both formative and summative assessment, and count on a long-term effort if they hope to construct a complex understanding of the multiple ways in which computer use relates to curricular goals. Finally, we believe that WPAs should pay

serious attention to both functional technological literacy and critical technological literacy, and pay special care to identifying those individuals and
groups who may *not* be benefitting fully from computer use in a program—gathering specific information on the relationships between computer use and students of color, students trapped in poverty, and
under-prepared students. These relationships can be usefully examined by investigating students' pre-college exposure and access to computers, their
ability to pay computer fees, and their access to ongoing computer support
and training.

These suggestions reveal a bias that we have in assessment matters: we believe WPAs should focus not only on assessing student or teacher performance,
but also on assessing those resources allocated to computer-use efforts that directly or indirectly affect such performance. Assessment efforts that focus only
on what students are able to *do* with computers, can discourage institutions
from paying attention to the larger ecological systems of which technological
literacy is only a part (Bruce & Hogan). They can allow us to ignore the very
real material conditions necessary for teaching and learning, and the continuing, intergenerational linkage between class, race, illiteracy, and technology.
When WPAs focus only on student performance, they are much less likely to
fix some proportion of responsibility more broadly, where it appropriately belongs, and much less likely to acknowledge that courses, institutions, or society
itself may have failed to provide an adequate environment within which students can learn such functional and critical skills.

Finally, we suggest that WPAs encourage individual faculty and staff to
conduct small-scale assessment efforts of technology use that are self-spon-
sored, formative, and ongoing. Such efforts often grow out of questions that
teachers have about their own classrooms or that technical staff members
have about the computer-supported facilities within which they work. As a
result, they are more locally situated and can reflect on the efficacy of computer use in a particular course or classroom, with a smaller population of students. Teachers who use computers in their classes, for example, can be
encouraged to begin their classes by having students identify their incoming
level of technological literacy (see Appendix A). The details gleaned from
such activities will provide information that teachers can use in determining
the appropriateness of assignments, availability of readings, and fairness of
course policies. Teachers in computer-enhanced classrooms should also be
encouraged to make an early effort to assess their students' critical abilities—for example, their understanding of how to evaluate the relative authority of Web sites, their knowledge of intellectual property issues, and their
ability to identify the socio-political interests of authors and designers.

Scheduling.   Scheduling classrooms and assigning courses are additional administrative duties that can provide WPAs with the opportunity to

wrestle with formidable technology challenges—answering a demand for computer-based classrooms that is greater than the available supply of such spaces, addressing the need to assign computer-based classrooms to teachers willing to take advantage of electronic resources, reconciling the demands of graduate teaching assistants who want experience teaching computer-intensive courses with those of faculty who claim seniority in teaching the same courses, coping with institutional databases that don't readily allow for the identification of computerized sections or for split schedules (e.g. 50% in computer classroom, 50% in traditional classroom), tracking courses that are computer-intensive when taught by some teachers but not when they are taught by others. And though it is impossible to provide advice that fits every single situation that WPAs will encounter, we can suggest the benefits of careful planning, a long lead time, and a good relationship with faculty and the institution's room-scheduling office.

In trying to cope with the challenges of scheduling computer-supported classrooms, the best tool that WPAs can have is a timeline of the general scheduling process. Using this document, WPAs can plan far enough in advance to work productively with the individuals who need information at critical junctures throughout the university. Often, for example, a departmental scheduling representative will be assigned to modify the previous year's report, resubmit it to the scheduling office, receive and proof a revised draft a couple of weeks later, proof it, then resubmit a final copy. Cooperation with this scheduling representative and a careful analysis of the process he or she needs to follow can help WPAs identify the deadlines that must be met in order to make special requests, for example, using a "C" to designate all sections taught in computer classrooms. Often, it is useful for WPAs to make and maintain a scheduling diagram that identifies all of the major stages and events involved in university scheduling, including precise deadlines of when information is needed. This tool can help WPAs see and sort out scheduling problems before they occur, and has the added advantage of being useful for new staff people. We would also encourage WPAs to make a list of contact people across campus who are involved in scheduling computer classrooms. Such a list may be most useful when a WPA is trying to take maximum advantage of computer-supported teaching spaces.

We can also suggest two principles that can make the task of assigning computer-supported courses to faculty and TAs a bit easier, although no set of principles can completely ameliorate the tensions generated by a limited number of computer classrooms. First, we suggest that writing programs avoid the practice of mandating large-scale computer use across multiple-section courses such as first-year English unless the WPA is absolutely sure that sufficient numbers of faculty and TAs are *willing* and *prepared* to teach such courses, and that adequately supported computer classrooms are available for all of these instructors at times when they are available for teaching. We have seen too many programs in which faculty members, lecturers, or TAs are required to teach in computer classrooms, regardless of their willingness and preparedness, with the result being a program plagued by resentment and hostility. These programs often fail to produce the desired result of better instruction. Instead, they produce instructors who resent technology, as well as the burdens of extra planning, and work involved in computer-intensive classes. Given this situation, they provide less than enthusiastic instruction to students and make a bad use of computer-supported classrooms. The programs we have seen succeed best are those that treat computer-supported sections and computer-intensive courses as privileges for teachers who want to assume additional challenges and who are committed to making their instruction succeed in such environments.

Second, we suggest that all teachers assigned to computer-intensive sections or courses should be specially prepared do so—either by academic credentials, experience and self-education, or by a more formal process of professional development within the university, the department, or the writing program. This principle may provide WPAs with another difficult set of policy decisions to make (e.g., coming up with guidelines for determining when teachers are adequately prepared for such duties), but it recognizes, rightly we believe, that sending untrained teachers into such environments is unfair both to them and to students, and is often a waste of resources. Teaching is challenging enough as it is, and in a computer classroom, it is often more so because additional technical and pedagogical skills are required.

This principle also, however, commits WPAs to identifying ways of supporting the professional development of TAs, faculty, and lecturers who do not have computer-based teaching skills but may want to develop them. Some departments find it easiest to answer this need by offering an ongoing series of optional teaching-with-technology seminars that cover a range of topics and are taught by volunteers who already teach in computer-intensive environments (see Appendix B). Other departments have the advantage of having access to a faculty technology support person attached to their own graduate or undergraduate programs or who is accessible through a teaching-innovation center or a centralized computing-resources group. These staff members often provide faculty one-on-one support for planning and implementing computer-supported courses or sections and offer help during their first terms in computer-intensive environments. Still other programs build technology training into TA preparation, or designate specific courses at the undergraduate or graduate level—or intensive summer institutes—that interested faculty can take to prepare themselves for teaching effectively in computer-intensive environments. The best departments, of course, provide a range of such support systems.

Computer-Classroom Design.   WPAs may also find productive opportunities to address computer-use issues when they are asked to participate in the design of computer-supported composition classrooms. At the end of this chapter, we provide several bibliographic resources for WPAs who find themselves invited to participate in such an activity. These resources will help WPAs think about some of the technical and pedagogical issues involved in designing and operating computer-supported classrooms, including reasons to arrange such classrooms in rows or pods (and what shape of pod), what hardware and software to purchase, the advantages and disadvantages of projection systems, the benefits of raised floors, the issues associated with security, the options of staffing such facilities, and the various kinds of lab fee arrangements that some schools implement.

The primary focus for WPAs to maintain during all stages of computer-classroom design here, however, has to do with the kinds of composing and language-exploration activities that the space will ultimately need to support. Keeping this focus clearly in mind—and involving a range of stakeholders (e.g., faculty, students, technical staff, university facility representatives) in thinking about how best to design a space that can support such activities in rich and innovative ways—can help yield classrooms that are both functional and well used. Finally, given the continuing problems associated with the digital divide in the United States and other parts of the world (cf. *Americans;* Castells, *End, Power, Rise;* Selfe), we also suggest that WPAs work to make sure that questions of equity are foregrounded at all stages of computer-classroom design, asking which groups of students and community members are and are not being served by the various design decisions being made.

Moment #4: Issues of Professional Development and Support

WPAs responsible for the professional development of faculty and TAs often find that their efforts in this area will overlap in substantial ways with computer-use issues. Most WPAs take the responsibility of teacher education very seriously, for example, and provide an ongoing series of seminars and/or classroom visitations for TAs or instructors who are in the process of developing their teaching skills within writing programs. Increasingly, however, WPAs involved in such efforts are discovering the need to provide specific help for teachers working in computer-supported classrooms as well. Teachers who are offered no training in teaching with computers frequently become frustrated, defensive, and impatient in the classroom—not because they're bad teachers (which, unfortunately, their student evaluations will suggest), but because they have not learned a rudimentary set of skills that they need in order to be effective in computer-supported teaching and learning environments. Such problems are bound to make it back to WPAs, along with the evaluations of disgruntled students. WPAs need to accept responsibility for making sure that teachers are adequately educated about techniques and strategies that work well in computer-supported classrooms, and can get ongoing advice about how to integrate computers effectively into their various courses.

We suggest that WPAs will need to provide teachers with both *technical* and *critical* resources as part of their professional development. Teachers, for example, will need to be provided with technical assistance in learning how to use a basic suite of composition-focused software programs in effective ways: among them, word-processing packages, page layout and design packages, graphics generation and photographic manipulation software, and course-authoring packages. Many teachers will also want to be introduced to the WWW, and learn specific techniques for using browsers and a range of search engines, including the comparative strengths and weaknesses of each engine. Many teachers will also want to know how to download Web-based materials, make PDF files, design and create web pages, and use HTML editing software. Teachers may also want to have specific help in learning about electronic portfolios, the use of synchronous and asynchronous chat programs, ways to set up and moderate online conferences and listservs, the use of e-mail to supplement classroom discussion, and the best ways to employ graphically-based MOOs as instructional environments. Teachers with specific assignments, such as technical communication, for example, may need additional instruction—in presentation software, table and chart design software, web page and online help development, or database applications. Teachers who work with physically challenged students need to know how to find and set up computer applications that will help provide reasonable accommodations for students who need them.

Setting up such a wide range of technical-training opportunities is not an insignificant task. We suggest that WPAs just beginning such efforts explore multiple options, among them:

- Providing release time for the most able computer-classroom instructor in exchange for a series of computer-based instruction workshops.
- Organizing skilled TAs and faculty as volunteer seminar leaders to teach their most effective strategies for computer-supported environments (see Appendix B).
- Asking the campus center for teaching innovation or the central computing group to offer a specific series of computer-based education seminars to writing program faculty and TAs.
- Hiring an instructional computing specialist—or finding a faculty member who could serve in such a role in exchange for release time—to work with both faculty and TAs in developing effective computer-based instruction.
- Providing travel funds and registration fees for faculty and TAs interested in attending off-campus workshops focusing on instructional computing if these individuals agree to lead a series of on-campus workshops when they return.

When setting up such technical education seminars, WPAs need to be sure that all instructors begin with an examination of program and course goals to make sure that these instructional foci shape technology use in thoughtful and meaningful ways.

In addition to providing faculty the opportunity to develop their technical skills, WPAs will also want to provide them opportunities to develop critical understandings of technology issues: to make connections between various theoretical understandings of language or literacy and the technical environments best suited to modeling such instruction; to read and discuss scholarship and research in the field of computers and composition; to learn about intellectual property and privacy issues and the case law that is currently shaping such issues; to explore parameters of the digital divide as it is made manifest in a particular state or on a particular campus; or to share reports on books that deal with technology criticism and the use of new media for instruction.

To help teachers develop a critical understanding of technology issues, WPAs may want to try some of the following approaches:

- Organize reading groups of faculty and TAs who want to explore technology criticism or computers and composition research on a regular basis.
- Circulate readings that provide a critical understanding of the ways in which computers are affecting intellectual property and copyright issues, privacy issues, literacy and illiteracy, the gap between rich and poor Americans, globalization, tenure and promotion criteria, communication patterns, career prospects, and economic prosperity (see Appendix C).
- Organize a speaker series in which faculty, TAs, and technical support staff present papers on topics related to critical understandings of technology.
- Provide faculty and TAs reading lists of books and articles that might be helpful in developing a critical understanding of technology issues (see Appendix C).
- Offer faculty and TAs travel money and registration fees to attend conferences or institutes that focus on critical understandings of technology if they agree to offer or participate in a series of workshops upon their return (see Appendix D).
- Compile and share the URLs of Web sites that can help teachers develop critical understandings of technology (see Appendix E).

WPAs may also want to encourage the formation of informal support teams for computer classroom teachers who use technology and who want to explore technology issues regularly. Even with the best of professional devel-

opment opportunities, teaching in—and dealing with—the unpredictable
environments of computer classrooms and of electronic space can be perplex-
ing and stressful for teachers. Regular informal meetings of computer-using
teachers can provide a venue for exploring common experiences and serve as
a place where ideas, advice, wisdom, humor, and warnings can be shared.

Moment #5: Issues of Funding

The proper funding of writing programs is among the most contentious issues
that WPAs have to address, and computers seldom serve to make things
better. WPAs must now argue not only for more funded sections, lower enrollment caps, higher salaries for TAs, more equitable benefits for part-time
teachers, and more positions for support staff, but also for the return of computer lab fees to departmental budgets, for updated computers on the desks
of writing teachers, for software upgrades and hardware maintenance in
computer-supported writing classrooms, for new projection systems and
equipment repair contracts. Clearly, with all of these contending needs,
WPAs never worry about a surplus of funds.

How can WPAs balance funding needs appropriately—especially in connection to technology? We can offer several suggestions in this area.

First, know the *real* cost of technology. By "real cost," we refer to not only
the initial cost of the equipment itself (e.g., computers, printers, and peripherals), which is where most people stop, but also to the cost of other initial ex-
penditures related to the machines (e.g., software, installation fees, shipping
and handling charges, new office network connections, furniture to put the
computer user in and the computer on). Add to these initial equipment costs,
the ongoing costs of maintaining a machine (e.g., the cost of repair and maintenance contracts or the cost of using university repair services, the amortized
costs of replacing machines in three to five years depending on your departmental computer plan, the cost of yearly or biannual software upgrades; the
monthly costs of office computer connections) and the costs associated with
personnel who make the technology usable (e.g., salaries of technical support
people in the department, professional development costs, salaries of staff
members or TAs who support departmental computer rooms and efforts).
Add all of these costs and calculate an annual budget that shows all of these
costs, subtract any income from returned lab fees or monies that the university provides departments for computer support. Divide the final figure by the
number of machines that the writing program is responsible for, and you will
have the real cost, per year and per machine. It will be clear from this exercise
that the initial cost of the computer equipment is a relatively minor cost—a
fact that most faculty do not realize.

Second, educate administrators, faculty, staff, and students about the *real*
cost of technology. Take the time to let department chairs, deans, and faculty

know how much it really costs to maintain technology within the department. Pass along the budget you have worked out. Discuss both the sources of income (e.g., lab fees, university monies, departmental contributions) and the expenses (e.g., initial costs, ongoing costs). These activities keep all stakeholders honest about the real costs of instructional computing.

Third, never seek money for technology without seeking money for the people who make it usable. The budgeting exercise that we recommended earlier should convince most WPAs that the cost of computers alone is the least of their concerns. Computers don't work for long and don't work well without human support. Hence, whenever you make requests for equipment—in grants, university funding proposals, foundation projects—make sure to include adequate funding for the personnel who will keep the machines running, that will support faculty and TAs as they learn to integrate technology into their courses in effective and meaningful ways, and will pay for the staff necessary for overseeing computer-supported labs and classrooms.

Fourth, understand that technology costs are related to equity issues. The costs associated with computing are among the greatest factors in creating the digital divide in wealthy nations, and such costs often unfairly affect individuals from under-represented and oppressed groups. Examine the fee policies for computer use in your university and department and try to determine which groups are well served and which groups are not being well served. Consider forming endowment funds for TAs, students, or faculty who cannot afford departmental or university computer costs. Also consider affirmative action hirings for technology support positions for which you have some say.

Fifth, volunteer to serve on university computer committees. It is in these committees (e.g., technology policy committees, lab fee committees, computer-use committees, distance-education committees) that policy for technology is often set. By serving on these committees, WPAs can often affect funding procedures for departments and make sure that equity issues continue to be raised and discussed.

Sixth, help teachers and students use their minds creatively when computer resources are not available. Encourage them to be political as well: let business communications classes write letters to administrators proposing policy changes that would help get them more access to campus computer resources and monies for technology support personnel; let first-year composition students write technology autobiographies in which they investigate their own relationships to technology and consider the ways in which they describe how their technological literacies have been nurtured or constrained; let learning and physically disabled students articulate the ways in which computer resources and support staff members could help them within the institution. Such activities draw on the resource of human talents by which every WPA is surrounded. And this resource has a remarkable characteristic— the more it is used, the more it grows.

CONCLUSION

It is not easy to escape the consumerist mentality that pervades even our schools these days, but the fact is that the latest and greatest technologies are rarely necessary to accomplish the pedagogical goals most writing programs have established. The attraction toward faster, newer, more sophisticated computer resources—virtual reality, streaming video and audio, digital paper—is powerful. As a result, even faculty who have little interest in teaching with computers are often seduced—or shamed—into doing so. But innovative—or even simply effective—computer-supported writing programs do not result from simple tendential force.

Rather, the best of such programs are crafted carefully by knowledgeable people, often WPAs. They are usually established slowly, and they rest on a broad and solid foundation of thoughtful, committed community. By "broad," we mean that the people in such a group represent the full diversity of a writing program—those who are serving and those being served. Among this community are faculty, staff, graduate and undergraduate students, administrators, artists, engineers, people of color, people who speak multiple languages, people with learning and physical challenges—everyone who will add a unique voice to the planning and a careful hand to the work that needs doing. By "solid," we mean that the people in the project can be trusted to be honest, thoughtful, diligent, caring, and curious in their work. It means that they understand a range of technology issues, and, even more important, they are committed to the principle of making sure that technology decisions are always shaped by the needs of human beings and the goals of writing instruction.

We do not make this recommendation naively, and in fact know this to be among the most difficult responsibilities we have proposed for WPAs yet. To build a community such as this will be trying at times; when principles are at stake, the work is never easy. Over time, all writing programs change. And that's why keeping this principle at the forefront of the community is such an important responsibility of WPAs.

WORKS CITED

"Americans in the Information Age: Falling through the Net." Web page sponsored by the National Telecommunications and Information Office. 29 December 2000. <http://www.ntia.doc.gov/ntiahome/digitaldivide/index.html>.

Balsamo, Anne. *Technologies of the Gendered Body: Reading Cyborg Women*. Durham, NC: Duke UP, 1996.

Baudrillard, Jean. *Simulations*. Trans. Paul Foss, Paul Patton, and Philip Beitchman. New York: Semiotext(e), 1983.

Bennett, Michael, and Kathleen Walsh. "Desperately Seeking Diversity: Going Online to Achieve a Racially Balanced Classroom." *Computers and Composition* 14.2 (1997): 217–228.

—. "English Studies, Work, and Politics in the New Economy." *Composition in the Twenty-First Century: Crisis and Change*. Ed. Lynn Z. Bloom, Donald A. Daiker, and Edward M. White. Carbondale: Southern Illinois UP, 1996. 215–25.

—. "Postmodernism, the College Curriculum, and Composition." *Composition in Context*. Ed. W. Ross Winterowd and Vincent Gillespie. Carbondale: Southern Illinois UP, 1994. 46–61.

Berlin, James A. "Postmodernism, Politics, and Histories of Rhetorics." *PRE/TEXT* 11. 3–4.

—. "Poststructuralism, Cultural Studies, and the Composition Classroom." *Rhetoric Review* (Fall 1992): 16–33. Rpt. *Professing the New Rhetoric*. Ed. Theresa Enos and Stuart C. Brown. Englewood Cliffs, NJ: Prentice Hall, 1994. 461–80.

—. "Rhetoric and Ideology in the Writing Class." *College English* 50 (1988): 477–94.

—. *Rhetoric and Reality: Writing Instruction in American Colleges, 1900–1985*. Carbondale: Southern Illinois UP, 1987.

Bruce, Bertram, and Andee Rubin. *Electronic Quills: A Situated Evaluation of Using Computers for Writing in Classrooms*. Hillsdale, NJ: Erlbaum, 1993.

Bruce, Bertram, and Maureen P. Hogan. "The Disappearance of Technology: Toward an Ecological Model of Literacy." *Handbook of Literacy and Technology: Transformations in a Post-Typographic World*. Ed. David Reinking et al. Mahwah, NJ: Erlbaum, 1998. 269–81.

Buckley, Joanne. "The Invisible Audience and the Disembodied Voice: Online Teaching and the Loss of Body Image." *Computers and Composition* 14.2 (1997): 179–88.

Castells, Manuel. *End of the Millennium*. Malden, MA: Blackwell, 1998. Vol. 3 of *The Information Age: Economy, Society, and Culture*.

—. *The Power of Identity*. Malden, MA: Blackwell, 1997. Vol. 2 of *The Information Age: Economy, Society, and Culture*.

—. *The Rise of the Network Society*. Malden, MA: Blackwell, 1996. Vol. 1 of *The Information Age: Economy, Society, and Culture*.

Castner, Joanna. "The Clash of Social Categories: What Can We Do to Encourage Egalitarianism in Networked Writing Classrooms?" *Computers and Composition* 14.2 (1997): 257–63.

Caywood, Cynthia L., and Gilian R. Overing. *Teaching Writing: Pedagogy, Gender, and Equity*. Albany: State U of New York P, 1987.

Coley, R. J., J. Crandler, and P. Engle. *Computers and Classrooms: The Status of Technology in U.S. Schools*. Educational Testing Service, Policy Information Center. Princeton, NJ: ETS, 1997.

Cooper, Marilyn M. "The Ecology of Writing." *College English* 48 (1986): 364–75.

—. "Postmodern Pedagogy in Electronic Conversations." *Passions, Pedagogies, and 21st Century Technologies*. Ed. Gail Hawisher and Cynthia Selfe. Logan, UT: Utah State UP, 1999. 140–60.

Crafton, Robert E. "Promises, Promises: Computer-Assisted Revision and Basic Writers." *Computers and Composition* 13.3 (1996): 317–26.

deCerteau, Michel. *The Practice of Everyday Life*. Trans. S. Randall Berkeley: U of California P, 1984.

Deleuze, Gilles, and Felix Guattari. *A Thousand Plateaus: Capitalism and Schizophrenia*. 1980. Trans. B. Massumi. Minneapolis: U of Minnesota P, 1987.

DeWitt, Scott Lloyd. "Out There on the Web: Pedagogy and Identity in the Face of Opposition." *Computers and Composition* 14.2 (1997): 229–44.

Eagleton, Terry. *An Introduction to Ideology*. London: Verso, 1991.

Faigley, Lester. "The Study of Writing and the Study of Language." *Rhetoric Review* 7 (1989): 240–56.

—. *Fragments of Rationality: Postmodernity and the Subject of Composition*. Pittsburgh: U of Pittsburgh P, 1992.

—. "Literacy after the Revolution." *College Composition and Communication* v. 48 n.1 (1997): 30–43.

—. "Material Literacy and Visual Design." *Rhetorical Bodies: Toward a Material Rhetoric*. Ed. Jack Selzer and Sharon Crowley. Madison: U of Wisconsin P, 1999. 171–201.

Feenberg, Andrew. *Alternative Modernity: The Technical Turn in Philosophy and Social Theory*. Berkeley: U of California P, 1995.

—. *Critical Theory of Technology*. New York: Oxford UP, 1991.

—. *Questioning Technology*. New York: Routledge, 1999.

Giddens, Anthony. *The Constitution of Society: Outline of a Theory of Structuration*. Berkeley: U of California P, 1984.

Giroux, Henry A. *Border Crossings: Cultural Workers and the Politics of Education*. New York: Routledge, 1992.

—. "Modernism, Postmodernism, and Feminism: Rethinking the Boundaries of Educational Discourse." *Postmodernism, Feminism, and Cultural Politics: Redrawing Educational Boundaries*. Ed. Henry A. Giroux. Albany: State U of New York P, 1991. 1–59.

—. "Resisting Difference: Cultural Studies and the Discourse of Critical Pedagogy." *Cultural Studies*. Ed. Lawrence Grossberg, Cary Nelson, and Paula Treichler. New York: Routledge, 1992. 199–212.

Gomez, Mary Louise. "The Equitable Teaching of Composition." *Evolving Perspectives on Computers and Composition Studies*. Ed. G. E. Hawisher and C. L. Selfe. Urbana, IL: NCTE; Houghton, MI: Computers and Composition Press, 1991. 318–35.

Haraway, Donna. "A Manifesto for Cyborgs: Science, Technology, and Socialist Feminism." *Feminism/Postmodernism*. Ed. L. J. Nicholson. London: Routledge, Chapman & Hall, 1990. 190–233.

—. *Simians, Cyborgs, and Women: The Reinvention of Nature*. New York: Routledge, 1991.

—. "Situated Knowledges: The Science Question in Feminism and the Privilege of Partial Perspective." *Simians, Cyborgs, and Women: The Reinvention of Nature*. New York: Routledge, 1991. 183–201.

Harkin, Patricia, and John Schilb, eds. *Contending with Words: Composition and Rhetoric in a Postmodern Age*. New York: MLA, 1991.

Hawisher, Gail. "Studies in Word Processing." *Computers and Composition* 4.1 (1986): 6–31.

—. "Research and Recommendations for Computers and Composition." *Critical Perspectives on Computers and Composition Instruction*. Ed. G. E. Hawisher and C. L. Selfe. New York: Teachers College P, 1989. 44–69.

Hoffman, Donna L., and Thomas P. Novak. "Bridging the Racial Divide on the Internet." *Science* 280 (17 Apr. 1998): 390–91.

Jameson, Frederic. *Postmodernism or the Cultural Logic of Late Capitalism.* Durham, NC: Duke UP, 1991.

Janangelo, Joseph. "Technopower and Technoppression: Some Abuses of Power and Control in Computer-Assisted Writing Environments." *Computers and Composition* 9.1 (1991): 47–64.

Knoblauch, C. H., and Lil Brannon. *Critical Teaching and the Idea of Literacy.* Portsmouth, NH: Boynton/Cook, 1993.

Laclau, Ernesto, and Chantal Mouffe. *Hegemony and Socialist Strategy: Toward a Radical Democratic Politics.* London: Verso, 1985.

LeCourt, Donna. "Critical Pedagogy in the Computer Classroom: Politicizing the Writing Space." *Computers and Composition* 15.3 (1997): 275–96.

Lyotard, Jean-François. *The Postmodern Condition: A Report on Knowledge.* Trans. Geoff Bennington and Brian Massumi. Minneapolis, MN: U of Minnesota P, 1993.

Marcuse, Herbert. *One-Dimensional Man.* New York: Beacon Press, 1966.

McLuhan, Marshall. *The Gutenberg Galaxy: The Making of Typographic Man.* Toronto: U of Toronto P, 1962.

—. *Understanding Media: The Extensions of Man.* Cambridge: MIT P, 1964.

Meares, Carol Ann, and John F. Sargent princ. auth. *The Digital Workforce: Building Infotech Skills at the Speed of Innovation.* US Dept. of Commerce, Office of Technology Policy. Wash: GPO, 1999.

Moran, Charles. "Access—The 'A' Word in Technology Studies." *Passions, Pedagogies, and 21st Century Technologies.* Ed. Gail Hawisher and Cynthia Selfe. Logan: Utah State UP, 1999. 205–20.

Mumford, Lewis. *Technics and Civilization.* New York: Harcourt, 1963.

Ohmann, R. (1985). Literacy, Technology, and Monopoly Capitalism. *College English* 47.7 (1985): 675–89.

Retish, Paul, and Shunit Reiter. *Adults with Disabilities: International Perspectives in the Community.* Mahwah, NJ: Erlbaum, 1999.

Romano, Susan. "The Egalitarianism Narrative: Whose Story? Which Yardstick?" *Computers and Composition* 10.3 (1993): 5–28.

Selfe, Cynthia L. *Technology and Literacy in the Twenty-First Century: The Perils of Not Paying Attention.* Carbondale: Southern Illinois UP, 1999.

Selfe, Cynthia L., and Selfe, Richard J. "The Politics of the Interface: Power and Its Exercise in Electronic Contact Zones," *College Composition and Communication* 45.4 (1994): 480–504.

Snyder, Illana, and Michael Joyce, eds. *Page to Screen: Taking Literacy into the Electronic Era.* New York: Routledge, 1998.

Sosnoski, James J. "Notes On Postmodern Double Agency and the Arts of Lurking." *College Composition and Communication* 47.2 (1996): 288–92.

—. "Postmodern Teachers in Their Postmodern Classrooms: Socrates Begone!" *Contending with Words: Composition and Rhetoric in a Postmodern Age.* Ed. Patricia Harkin & John Schib. New York: MLA, 1991. 198–219.

Standards for the English Language Arts. Newark, DE: IRA; Urbana IL: NCTE, 1996.

Taylor, Todd. "The Persistence of Difference in Networked Classrooms: Non-Negotiable Difference and the African American Student." *Computers and Composition* 14.2 (1997): 169–78.

Turkle, Sherry. "Computational reticence: Why women fear the intimate machine." *Technology and Women's Voices: Keeping in Touch.* Ed. Cheris Kramarae. London: Routledge, 1988.

—. *Life on the Screen: Identity in the Age of the Internet.* New York: Simon, 1995.

—. *The Second Self: Computers and the Human Spirit.* London: Granada, 1984.

Turkle, Sherry, and S. Papert. "Epistemological Pluralism: Styles and Voices within the Computer Culture." *Signs: Journal of Women in Culture and Society* 16.11 (1990): 128–57.

United States. Dept. of Labor. *Futurework: Trends and Challenges for Work in the 21st Century.* Washington, DC: GPO, 1999.

—. Dept. of Education. *Getting America's Students Ready for the 21st Century: Meeting the Technology Literacy Challenge, A Report to the Nation on Technology and Education.* Washington, DC: GPO, 1996.

United States. *Goals 2000: Educate America Act.* 103rd Cong., 2nd ses. 25 Jan. 1994. 29 Dec. 2000. <http://www.ed.gov/legislation/GOALS2000/TheAct>.

Vitanza, Victor. "Concerning a Postclassical Ethos as Para/Rhetorical Ethics, the 'Selphs,' and the Excluded Third." *Ethos: New Essays in Rhetorical and Critical Theory.* Ed. James S. Baumolin and Tita French Baumlin. Dallas: Southern Methodist UP, 1994. 380–431.

—. "An Open Letter to My 'colligs': On Paraethics, Pararhetorics, and the Hysterical Turn." *PRE/TEXT* 11 (1990): 237–87.

—. "Three Countertheses: Or, a Critical In(ter)vention into Composition Theories and Pedagogies." *Contending with Words: Composition and Rhetoric in a Postmodern Age.* Ed. Patricia Harkin & John Schilb. New York: MLA 1991. 139–72.

Whitaker, Elaine, and Elaine N. Hill. "Virtual Voices in 'Letters across Cultures': Listening for Race, Class, and Gender." *Computers and Composition* 15.3 (1998): 331–46.

Winner, Langdon. *The Whale and the Reactor: A Search for Limits in an Age of High Technology.* Chicago: The U of Chicago P, 1986.

Wise, J. Mcgregor. *Exploring Technology and Social Space.* Thousand Oaks, CA: Sage, 1997.

Woodland, Randall. "'I Plan to Be a 10': Online Literacy and Lesbian, Gay, Bisexual, and Transgender Students." *Computers and Composition* 16.1 (1999): 73–88.

—. "Queer Spaces, Modem Boys and Pagan Statues: Gay/Lesbian Identity and the Construction of Cyberspace." *Works and Days* 13.1/2 (1995): 221–40.

Zuboff, S. *In the Age of the Smart Machine: The Future of Work and Power.* New York: Basic, 1988.

APPENDIX A
TECHNOLOGICAL LITERACY DIAGNOSTIC

Dickie Selfe
Michigan Technological University

➤ What were your earliest experiences with technological devices or artifacts? What were they? What do you remember about using them?

➤ What gadgets were popular in your house while you were growing up?

➤ Who do you identify as being technologically "literate" in your life? Do they tend to be one gender or another? One race or another? What does it mean to be technologically literate? How do you measure up?

➤ What technologies are in your work area at home? What technological devices are you carrying now? What's on your technological "wish list"?

➤ How do your experiences differ from those of your brothers and sisters, your parents, your grandparents? (You may wish to interview older members of your family to learn about their technological memories.)

➤ How do you see technology as a force in the future, either in your career or personal life?

➤ What are your technological strengths? What technology outside of class do you have access to that might be useful in this course? How willing are you to incorporate teaching into the course requirements of the class, that is, take on the job of being the technical expert for novices in the class?

➤ What image best represents a computer or computer network to you (other than the computer itself)?

> "A computer is like a _____."

> "A computer is a _____."

Please elaborate: Why do you say this? In what specific ways is it true? Please sketch your favorite image below.

APPENDIX B
SELECTED TEACHING WITH TECHNOLOGY WORKSHOPS

Michigan Technological University

N.B. All presenters are volunteers. All attendance is voluntary.

- Plagiarism, Intellectual Property, and the Web
- Making Course Materials Available to Students Online
- Spanish in an Online Classroom: Teaching, Planning, and Support
- Promotion and Tenure When You're a Geek
- Introduction to Javascripting
- University-Wide Support System for WebCT
- State of the Field in Computers and Composition
- Flash Demonstration
- Workshop on Research Agendas in Computers and Composition (and Rhetoric and …)
- Assessment and Technology
- Creating Adobe PDF Files
- 30 Lines of Code to Password Protect a Site
- WebCT/FirstClass/Blackboard and other Webbed Course Development Tools
- The NorthWoodsMOO Project (an online professional development site)
- Chat and Web-Forum Software to Link to Class Web Sites
- Efficient Telecommuting
- Effective Search Strategies on the Web and in the Library
- HTML

University of Arizona

N.B. Some presenters received honoraria. Some attendees were required to come for programmatic credentialing.

- Grading and the Internet
- Teaching ESL in Computer-Enhanced Classrooms
- Research Methodologies in Computer-Related Humanities Projects
- Second Language Acquisition and Teaching with Electronic Media
- Emerging Instructional Technologies
- Teaching with the World Wide Web
- Say Goodbye to Textbooks: Putting Course Readings Online
- Building Interactive Course Materials with Director
- Teaching and Learning on the MOO
- Synchronous Discussion Technologies in the Classroom

- Secrets of the Search Engines
- Virtual Reality: Problems and Possibilities
- XML
- Introduction to Computer-Based Graphic Design
- Duke Nukem Comes to Class: Teaching Composition with Computer Games
- Audio Effects as Course Material
- Don't Forget about the Internet: Exploring the World beyond the WWW

APPENDIX C
SELECTED BIBLIOGRAPHY: CRITICAL PERSPECTIVES
ON TECHNOLOGICAL LITERACY

"Americans in the Information Age: Falling through the Net." Web page sponsored by the National Telecommunications and Information Office. 29 December 2000. <http://www.ntia.doc.gov/ntiahome/digitaldivide/index.html>.

Apple, Michael. "The New Technology: Is It Part of the Solution or Part of the Problem in Education?" *Computers in the Schools* v.8 n.½/3 (1991): 59–77.

Banks, Sandy, and Lucille Renwick. "Technology Remains Promise, Not Panacea—Education: Schools Have Invested Heavily, but with Little Academic Results. More Teacher Training Is Urged." *Los Angeles Times* 8 June 1997: A1.

Barron, Nancy Guerra. "Egalitarian Moments: Computer Mediated Communications in a Chicano Studies (ChS 111) Course." Master's Thesis, California State U, Los Angeles, 1998.

Bennehum, David S., Brook S. Riggs, Paulina Borsook, Marissa Rowe, Simson Garfinkle, Steve Johnson, Douglas Rushkoff, Andrew Shapiro, David Shonk, Steve Silberman, Mark Stahlman, and Stefanie Syman. "Get Real! A Manifesto from a New Generation of Cultural Critics: Technorealism." *The Nation* v.266 n.12 (1998): 19–20.

Borgman, Albert. *Technology and the Character of Contemporary Life*. Chicago: U of Chicago P, 1984.

Bruce, Bertram, and Maureen P. Hogan. "The Disappearance of Technology: Toward an Ecological Model of Literacy." *Handbook of Literacy and Technology: Transformations in a Post-Typographic World*. Ed. David Reinking et al. Mahwah, NJ: Erlbaum, 1998. 269–81.

"CCCC Promotion and Tenure Guidelines for Work with Technology." Online discussion. 4 Apr. 1998. 29 December 2000. <http://www.ncte.org/ccc/12/sub/state8.html>.

Casey, James, Randy Ross, and Marcia Warren. *Native Networking: Telecommunications and Information Technology in Indian County*. Ed. Jean Smith. Washington, DC: Benton Foundation, 1999. 29 Dec. 2000. <http://www.benton.org/Library/Native/>.

Castells, Manuel. *The Rise of the Network Society*. Malden, MA: Blackwell, 1996. Vol. 1 of *The Information Age: Economy, Society, and Culture*.

—. *The Power of Identity*. Malden, MA: Blackwell, 1997. Vol 2 of *The Information Age: Economy, Society, and Culture*.

—. *End of the Millennium*. Malden, MA: Blackwell, 1998. Vol. 3 of *The Information Age: Economy, Society, and Culture*.

Closing the Gap for U.S. Hispanic Youth: Public/Private Strategies. Washington, DC: Hispanic Policy Development Project, 1988.

Cole, Michael, and Peg Griffin. *Contextual Factors in Education: Improving Science and Mathematics Education for Minorities and Women*. Madison: Wisconsin Center for Education Research, University of Wisconsin, 1987.

Coley, R. J., J. Crandler, and P. Engle. *Computers and Classrooms: The Status of Technology in U.S. Schools*. Educational Testing Service, Policy Information Center. Princeton, NJ: ETS, 1997.

The Condition of Education 1997. NCES 97-388. Washington, DC: US Department of Education, Office of Educational Research and Improvement, National Center for Education Statistics, 1997.

The Condition of Education 1998. NCES 98-013. Washington, DC: US Department of Education, Office of Educational Research and Improvement, National Center for Education Statistics, 1998.

Cooper, Mark. *Disconnected, Disadvantaged, and Disenfranchised: Explorations in the Digital Divide*. A report sponsored by the Consumer Federation of America and the Consumers' Union, 2000. 29 Dec. 2000. <Http://www.conumer.org/pdf/disonnect.pdf>.

Copeland, Regina. "Identifying Barriers to Computer-Supported Instruction." Diss. West Virginia U, 1997.

Digest of Education Statistics 1996. NCES 96-133. Washington, DC: US Department of Education, Office of Educational Research and Improvement, National Center for Educational Statistics, 1996.

Digest of Education Statistics 1987. Washington, DC: US Department of Education, Office of Educational Research and Improvement, National Center for Educational Statistics, 1987.

Eagleton, Terry. *Ideology: An Introduction*. London: Verso, 1991.

Ellul, Jacques. *The Technological Society*. New York: Vintage, 1954. English trans. 1964.

Faigley, Lester. "Literacy After the Revolution." *College Composition and Communication* v.48 n.1 (1997): 30–43.

Feenberg, Andrew. *Critical Theory of Technology*. New York: Oxford UP, 1991.

Gee, James. *Social Linguistics and Literacies: Ideology in Discourses*. Brighton, England: Falmer P, 1990.

Gerver, Elizabeth. "Computers and Gender." *Computers in the Human Context: Information Technology, Productivity, and People*. Ed. T. Forester. Cambridge: MIT P, 1989. 481–501.

Giddens, Anthony. *The Constitution of Society: Outline of a Theory of Structuration*. Berkeley: U of California P, 1984.

Glaser, Rob. "Universal Service Does Matter." *Wired* v.3 n.1 (Jan. 1995): 96–98.

Glennan, T. K., and A. Melmed. *Fostering the Use of Educational Technology: Elements of a National Strategy.* Washington, DC: RAND, 1996.

Gomez, Mary Louise. "The Equitable Teaching of Composition." *Evolving Perspectives on Computers and Composition Studies.* Ed. G. E. Hawisher and C. L. Selfe. Urbana, IL: NCTE; Houghton, MI: Computers and Composition Press, 1991. 318–35.

Goslee, Susan. "Losing Ground Bit by Bit: Low-Income Communities in the Information Age." Washington, DC: Benton Foundation, 1998. 29 Dec. 2000. <http://www.benton.org/Library/Low-Income>.

Graff, H. J. *The Legacy of Literacy: Continuities and Contradictions in Western Culture and Society.* Bloomington: Indiana UP, 1987.

Haraway, Donna. "Situated Knowledges: The Science Question in Feminism and the Privilege of Partial Perspective." *Technology and the Politics of Knowledge.* Ed. Andrew Feenberg and Alastair Hannay. Bloomington: Indiana UP, 1995.

Hawisher, Gail E., Paul LeBlanc, Charles Moran, and Cynthia L. Selfe. *Computers and the Teaching of Writing in American Higher Education, 1979–1984: A History.* Norwood, NJ: Ablex, 1996.

Hawisher, Gail E., and Cynthia L. Selfe, eds. *Global Literacies and the World-Wide Web.* London: Routledge, 2000.

—. *Passions, Pedagogies, and 21st Century Technologies.* Logan: Utah State UP, 1999.

—. "Tradition and Change in Computer-Supported Writing Environments: A Call for Action." *Theoretical and Critical Perspectives on Teacher Change.* Ed. P. Kahaney, J. Janangelo, and L. A. M. Perry. Norwood, NJ: Ablex, 1993. 155–86.

—. "The Rhetoric of Technology and the Electronic Writing Class." *College Composition and Communication* v.42 n.1 (1991): 55–65.

Hawisher, Gail, and Patricia Sullivan. "Fleeting Images: Women Visually Writing the Web." *Passions, Pedagogies, and 21st Century Technologies.* Ed. G. Hawisher and C. Selfe. Logan: Utah State UP, 1999. 268–91.

Hawkins, J. "Computers and Girls: Rethinking the Issues." *Sex Roles* 13 (1985): 165–80.

Heidegger, Martin. *The Question Concerning Technology.* New York: Harper, 1977.

Hoffman, Donna L., and Thomas P. Novak. "Bridging the Racial Divide on the Internet." *Science* 280 (17 Apr. 1998): 390–91.

Illich, Ivan. *Tools for Conviviality.* New York: Harper, 1973.

Jessup, Emily. "Feminism and Computers in Composition Instruction." *Evolving Perspectives on Computers and Composition Studies: Questions for the 1990s.* Ed. G. E. Hawisher and C. L. Selfe. Urbana, IL: NCTE; Houghton, MI: Computers and Composition Press, 1991. 336–55.

Knoblauch, C. H. "Literacy and the Practice of Education." *The Right to Literacy.* Ed. Andrea A. Lunsford, Helen Moglen, and James Slevin. New York: MLA, 1990. 74–80.

LeBlanc, Paul. "Competing Ideologies in Software Design for Computer-Aided Composition." *Computers and Composition* v.7 n.2 (1990): 8–19.

Livingstone, David, ed. *Critical Pedagogy and Cultural Power.* South Hadley, MA: Bergin and Garvey, 1987.

McAllister, Ken S. "The TICTOC (Teaching in Cyberspace through Online Courses) Manifesto." *Works and Days* 29/30 v. 15, n.½ (1997). 327–31.

Means, B., ed. *Technology and Education Reform: The Reality Behind the Promise*. San Francisco: Jossey-Bass, 1994.

Ohmann, R. "Literacy, Technology, and Monopoly Capitalism." *College English* v.47 n.7 (1985): 675–89.

Olson, C. Paul. "Who Computes?" *Critical Pedagogy and Cultural Power*. Ed. David Livingstone. South Hadley, MA: Bergin and Garvey, 1987. 179–204.

Oppenheimer, T. "The Computer Delusion." *The Atlantic Monthly* v.280 n.1 (1997): 45–62.

Riess, Donna, Dickie Selfe, and Art Young. *Electronic Communication across the Curriculum*. Urbana, IL: NCTE, 1998.

Rose, Mike. *Lives on the Boundary: The Struggles and Achievements of America's Underprepared*. New York: Free P, 1989.

Selfe, Cynthia L. *Technology and Literacy in the Twenty-First Century: The Perils of Not Paying Attention*. Carbondale: Southern Illinois UP, 1999.

Selfe, Cynthia L., and Richard J. Selfe. "The Politics of the Interface: Power and Its Exercise in Electronic Contact Zones." *College Composition and Communication* v.45 n.4 (1994): 480–504.

Shor, Ira. *Critical Teaching and Everyday Life*. Chicago: U of Chicago P, 1987.

Spooner, Tom, and Lee Rainie. *African Americans and the Internet*. A Pew Online Life Report. 22 Oct. 2000. 29 Dec. 2000. <http://www.pewinternet.org/reports/toc.asp?Report=25>.

Standards for the English Language Arts. Newark, DE: IRA; Urbana, IL: NCTE, 1996.

Street, B. V. *Social Literacies: Critical Approaches to Literacy in Development, Ethnography, and Education*. London: Longman, 1995.

Stuckey, Elspeth. *The Violence of Literacy*. Portsmouth, NH: Boynton Cook/Heinemann, 1991.

Talbott, Stephan. *The Future Does Not Compute—Transcending the Machines in Our Midst*. Sebastopol, CA: O'Reilly and Assoc., 1995.

Thompson, William, ed. *Controlling Technology—Contemporary Issues*. Buffalo: Prometheus, 1991.

United States. Dept. of Commerce. Information Infrastructure Task Force. *The National Information Infrastructure: Agenda for Action*. 15 Sept. 1993. Washington, DC: GPO, 1993.

United States. Dept. of Education. *Getting America's Students Ready for the 21st Century: Meeting the Technology Literacy Challenge, A Report to the Nation on Technology and Education*. Washington, DC: GPO, 1996.

Zimmer, JoAnn. "The Continuing Challenge: Computers and Writing." *Computers and Composition* v.2 n.3 (1985): 4–6.

APPENDIX D
INSTITUTES AND ORGANIZATIONS WITH A CRITICAL
APPROACH TO TECHNOLOGY

Computers in Writing-Intensive Classrooms (CIWIC): An institute held each summer during the last two weeks of June in Houghton, Michigan, at Michigan Technological University. CIWIC offers teachers from all levels (e.g., college, secondary, and elementary) a variety of opportunities to learn about integrating computers into writing classrooms, to explore new media, and to work on individual projects. Participants in this institute have twenty-four-hour access to a computer-supported communication facility, and they learn how to lead technology-integration efforts within writing programs. Attention is given to helping participants develop both critical understandings of technology and functional technology skills. See <http://www.hu.mtu.edu/ciwic>.

Computers in Composition Working Group (CICWG): A research group at the University of Arizona that studies instructional technology particularly within writing classrooms. Members of CICWG are faculty, staff, students, and meet regularly to examine and critique both established and new technologies that are being used to teach writing. Special interest groups within CICWG concentrate on (a) critical theories of technology, (b) pedagogical applications of technology, and (c) departmental policy issues concerning instructional technology. See <http://www.coh.arizona.edu/comp/cic/index.html>.

Alternative Educational Environments (AEE): A not-for-profit organization devoted to the simultaneous development and critique of instructional technologies. AEE helps support a variety of ongoing projects, including Virtual Harlem, a digital and interactive virtual reality environment modeled after Harlem in the 1920s and 1930s; the Computer Enhanced Writing and Learning Project, a database-driven interactive Web site for writing teachers who use computers in their classes; and the Narrative Visualization Initiative, which is working to develop an easy-to-use three-dimensional modeling application for teachers to use to build their own virtual worlds. See <http://www.caee.net>.

APPENDIX E
URLs FOR CRITICAL PERSPECTIVES ON TECHNOLOGY

"Americans in the Information Age: Falling through the Net." A Web page sponsored by the National Telecommunications and Information Office. Accessed 29 Dec. 2000 at <http://www.ntia.doc.gov/ntiahome/digitaldivide/index.html>.

"Apropos the 'Digital Divide'." A Web page contributed by Art McGee. Accessed 29 Dec. 2000 at <http://www.macbowen.org/p2/id/digital_divide_links.htm>.

Brown, Danika, and Anne Bartlett. "The MOO Made Us Do It: Utilizing a Critical Theory of Technology to Enact Critical Pedagogy: A Collaborative Analysis of MOO Technology in a Composition Classroom." Accessed 29 Dec. 2000 at <http://www.u.arizona.edu/~danika/brown-bartlett.htm>.

Button, Graham, and Paul Dourish. "Technomethodology: Paradoxes and Possibilities." *CHI '96 Proceedings*. Accessed 29 Dec. 2000 at <http://www.acm.org/sigchi/chi96/proceedings/papers/Button/jpd_txt.htm>.

"Center for Democracy and Technology." A Web page of the Center for Democracy and Technology. Accessed 29 Dec. 2000 at <http://www.cdt.org>.

"Digital Divide Series." A web page sponsored by the Public Broadcasting System. Accessed 29 Dec. 2000 at <http://www.pbs.org/digitaldivide/index.html>.

"Digital Future Coalition." A Web page of the DFC. Accessed 29 Dec. 2000 at <http://www.dfc.org>.

Dyson, E., G. Gilder, G. Keyworth, and A. Toffler. "Cyberspace and the American Dream: A Magna Carta for the Knowledge Age." A Web page sponsored by the Progress and Freedom Foundations. Accessed 29 Dec. 2000 at <http://www.pff.org/position.html>.

"EASI: Equal Access to Software and Information." A Web site that advocates for students and professionals with disabilities. Sponsored in part by the National Science Foundation. Accessed 29 Dec. 2000 at <http://www.rit.edu/~easi/>.

"Electronic Frontier Foundation: Protecting Rights and Promoting Freedom in the Electronic Frontier." A Web page of the Electronic Frontier Foundation. Accessed 29 Dec. 2000 at <http://www.eff.org/>.

"Technology and Equity." A Web page sponsored by the Mid-Atlantic Equity Consortium (MAEC) containing links to sites related to technology and racial, ethnic, class, gender, and cultural equity. Accessed 27 Sept. 2001 at <http://www.maec.org/techeq.html>.

Greco, Diane. "Hypertext with Consequences: Recovering a Politics of Hypertext." *Hypertext '96: Proceedings of the Seventh ACM Conference on Hypertext*. New York: ACM Press, 1996. 85–92. 29 Dec. 2000. <http://65.107.211.207/ht/greco1.html>.

"Human Development Report 1999: Reducing the Gap between the Knows and Know Nots." A Web page for the 1999 Human Development Report sponsored by the United Nations Development Programme. Accessed 30 Oct. 2000 at <http://www.undp.org/hdro/E3.html>.

The Loka Institute. A Web site for a nonprofit research and advocacy organization concerned with the social, political, and environmental repercussions of research, science, and technology. Accessed 30 Oct. 2000 at <http://www.loka.org>.

"Losing Ground Bit by Bit: Low-Income Communities in the Information Age." A Web page sponsored by the Benton Foundation. Accessed 29 Dec. 2000 at <http://www.benton.org/Library/Low-Income/low-income.pdf>.

Observatory of the Information Society. A Web site sponsored by UNESCO that reports on "[e]thical, legal & societal challenges of the Information Society." Accessed 29 Dec. 2000 at <http://www.unesco.org/webworld/observatory/index.shtml>.

Oppenheimer, Todd. "The Computer Delusion." *The Atlantic Monthly* July 1997. 29 Dec. 2000. <http://www.theatlantic.com/issues/97jul/computer.htm>.

Noble, David F. "Digital Diploma Mills: The Automation of Higher Education." *First Monday* v.3 n. 1 (1998). Accessed 29 Dec. 2000 at <http://www.firstmonday.dk/issues/issue3_1/noble>.

"Race and Class in Cyberspace Links." A Web page posted by Janedoe. Accessed 29 Dec. 2000 at <http://www.echonyc.com/~janedoe/links/raceclasslinks.htm>.

Rammert, Werner. "Relations that Constitute Technology and Media That Make a Difference: Toward a Social Pragmatic Theory of Technicization." *Techne: The Journal for the Society of Philosophy and Technology* v.4 n.3 (1999). Accessed 29 Dec. 2000 at <http://scholar.lib.vt.edu/ejournals/SPT/v4_n3html/RAMMERT.html>.

Reeves, Thomas C. "The Impact of Media and Technology in Schools: A Research Report Prepared for The Bertelsmann Foundation." 1998. Accessed 29 Dec. 2000 at <http://www.athensacademy.org/instruct/media_tech/reeves0.html>.

24

Writing Centers, Writing Programs, and WPAs: Roles by Any Other Names?

❦ • ❦

Carol Peterson Haviland
California State University, San Bernardino

Denise Stephenson
Grand Valley State University

The relationships between writing centers and writing program administrators (WPAs) vary significantly. For example, some campuses designate a single person as the WPA to whom all other writing program directors report; this WPA may direct first-year composition (FYC), the writing center, writing across the curriculum (WAC), or other writing programs. In contrast, other campuses have several faculty and staff who direct a number of loosely connected writing programs, each reporting to a different department chair, academic dean, academic vice president, student services dean, or provost. Thus writing center directors may have direct, indirect, or nonexistent relationships with other campus WPAs, or they may be the chief or sole WPA. These configurations grow out of composition theory as well as campuses' specific histories and cultures, some of them open to change and others not. However, as this book complicates our views of WPAs as more than schedulers of FYC and of the different ways writing program directors are positioned both by themselves and in relationships with others, it offers greater understanding of the terrain. The WPA roles that writing center directors play as they shape programs, educate staff, and secure budgets is one piece of this complicated whole, the piece that this chapter will explore.

LOCAL AND GLOBAL ROLES

Labels are one aspect of role definition. *Writing center* is the most common designation for the spaces in which peer and professional writing consultants offer their services to writers. However, such centers also are called writing labs, centers for teaching and learning excellence, reading and writing centers, or learning centers. The WPAs who direct these centers are most often called directors or coordinators; those who are staff may carry additional titles, and those who are faculty may also carry the appropriate professor rank. Other writing center staff include consultants, often known as tutors, writing fellows, peers, or readers. Although the most common or at least the most recognized title is *tutor,* in this chapter we will use the term *consultant.* Certainly this is not the only good choice, but it is helpful in turning both students' and faculty members' perceptions from a focus on remediation to one that includes a full range of writing done by undergraduate and graduate students as well as faculty, staff, and administrators across all disciplines.

The theoretical underpinnings of writing center directors and many other WPAs commit them to working collaboratively and respectfully even when the terrain does not encourage connection and cooperation. Thus we set the stage for this discussion of WPA/writing center director roles by sketching two contrasting scenes that highlight a central role issue for writing center directors, especially those who happen to be staff rather than faculty: the issue of exclusion.

Writing center directors may be appointed to staff positions because of institutional structure, because of historical circumstances, because they are not eligible for faculty appointment, because their writing centers are seen as remedial and their directors thereby less important, or simply "because." However, this exclusion is compounded when writing center directors are not perceived as WPAs on their campuses and particularly when it occurs within writing center or WPA organizations. During the past year, Denise has felt this exclusion on several occasions. It has not affected her writing center work directly, but it has led to heated debates in a number of areas.

Several events have made Denise aware of how important labels can be, whether that label is "faculty" or "WPA." Although Denise has a PhD, at the time of her hire many faculty around the country were not getting tenure in such positions, so her institution created a staff position for the writing center director. For five years, this has been ideal on her campus; she has been able to run a successful writing center and to organize many faculty development workshops for the WAC program. Last year, at the urging of her dean, she offered to take over the WAC program from a faculty member who was stepping down. Suddenly, the English department chair registered concern because the WPA guidelines stated that only faculty should hold such positions. Nevertheless, the university curriculum committee agreed that a staff person as qualified as Denise could "do the job."

A few months later at a WPA summer workshop, one of the presenters voiced her public agreement with the English chair that such positions should be filled by faculty. In both of these instances, location seemed to matter more to WPA constituents than did credentials, ability to do the job, or campus organization structures. A few days later at the WPA conference, Denise had a similar encounter with someone who was trying to organize a WPA meeting in her state. Denise felt again excluded, this time dismissed as not being a WPA because she ran a writing center rather than a composition program. Even after Denise stated twice that she ran a writing center and a WAC program, the person continued to ask for the WPA's name on her campus. These are small moments in time, but they raise important questions about what constitutes a WPA, about the status of various WPAs, and about WPAs' relationships among themselves and with other colleagues.

Carol's situation raises other issues. She began her writing center work as a new English faculty member with half of her time assigned to directing the writing center, an arrangement that functioned well. Several years later, however, as a tenured associate professor fully engaged in her department's activities and directing a center that had doubled its size, she recognized that she could not, even if she worked very hard, do all of the work she had taken on at a satisfying level. The undergraduate-division dean to whom the writing center reported urged her to drop her English department responsibilities and become a full-time writing center director. However, Carol was reluctant to make this move because it would not allow her to teach her present mix of undergraduate and graduate composition courses, would cut her off from her academic home, and would increase her administrative commitments. The English department was reluctant to lose her participation in its activities, particularly because its composition faculty, as on most campuses, are already stretched thin with assignments to composition committees, graduate programs, and other comp-related projects. Thus, she resisted the dean's request that she be assigned full time to the writing center and negotiated the shifting of two graduate assistants to staff positions where they coordinate scheduling, data collection, and online tutoring.

Creating these new positions allowed three things to happen: Carol was able to continue her directing/teaching combination and to expand the writing center's WAC collaborations, two excellent graduate assistant writing consultants who had just completed their MA programs moved into professional positions, and the writing center was able to build a collaborative directorship rather than consolidate authority in a single position. To support faculty positions configured such as hers, Carol notes the importance of audience awareness and rhetorical flexibility as directors describe their work to review committees. She emphasizes the need to help reviewers see nonclassroom teaching as teaching rather than administration or service. For example, much director-consultant interaction is collaborative teaching, not administration, as consultants use composition theory to interrogate their writing center practices. Also, in-class WAC workshops help students develop as writers and faculty develop as teachers who interact collaboratively over texts and who are better predictors of the problems students encounter in their assignments. In contrasting ways, both Denise's and Carol's situations illustrate the in-the-middle positions that writing center directors occupy as they negotiate a mix of formal and informal teaching, research, and service.

PHILOSOPHICAL/THEORETICAL POSITIONING

Like other writing programs, writing center staff draw on composition theories to shape their practices, working at the heart of "the cultural conflicts embedded in literacy" (Grimm, "Rearticulating," 530). Many position themselves somewhere along the continuum Lunsford describes as storehouses (top-down information transfers), garrets (private searches for Truth), and Burkean Parlours (collaborative communities) and then incorporate and embroider some features of each as they construct their work. Postmodern concepts such context, instability, conflict, dialogism, collaboration, and agency figure prominently in writing center work as the differently situated participants negotiate being "in-the-middle" of liminal spaces (Sunstein). For example, consultants occupy this middle space as they help writers use others' ideas yet retain control of their own texts and as they explain intellectual property to faculty who struggle to reconcile their desires for both "perfect" and "original" student writing. Feminist theories too lead many writing center staff to listen carefully to previously silenced voices, to interrogate institutional and rhetorical boundaries that may exclude participants, to see difference as a source of richness rather than as a deficit.

Thus, like other writing programs, writing centers have a history of moving between their institutions' margins and centers. On the one hand, they like to have adequate and stable funding and accessible, well-lighted spaces, preferably with windows—all hallmarks of being in the center. Also, they do not want to shortchange students by placing their own desires to resist ahead of students' requests to understand existing academic arenas (Delpit). On the other hand, being on the margin offers desirable freedoms. For example, the margins are spaces where play can occur; it can occur with conventions, with pedagogies, with roles, even with toys that make language more visible and tangible. Margins allow the freedom to take risks—to write drafts filled with errors but also with good ideas, drafts that later can be groomed for publication. These marginal philosophies extend to physical spaces so that writing centers look more like homes than classrooms, furnished with cushioned castoffs and decorated with student writing and art. At their best, writing centers can use their intensely collaborative work to make traditional university borders more permeable than can other more firmly fixed programs (Ede and Lunsford 34).

However, life on the margins can be perilous. Students who challenge traditions, particularly first-generation or multilingual students, basic writers, and those with disabilities, are frequently reminded that they don't fit in the university, at least not easily, and writing centers that welcome these students can be labeled *unfit* as well, causing other writers to stay away. The margins can also be dangerous professionally. Faculty directors are challenged to describe their unconventional work in conventional terms as they move toward promotion and tenure, and directors who are not tenure track faculty may feel marginalized because of their lack of faculty status, even though they may be positioned thoughtfully within a university's structure. Thus, negotiating spaces in the continuum between the regulatory function that produces and sustains institutional discourses and the resistance function that shifts authority from institutions to students is an ongoing struggle (Grimm, "Regulatory," 6; Boquet 466). As Brannon and North urge, writing centers "need to stay institutionally nimble without being institutionally naive" (11).

Because this chapter cannot cover the full range of roles writing center directors play in different configurations and concerns, it will focus on two areas: writing center-based work and links between writing centers and other campus programs, which may help new as well as experienced writing center directors and other WPAs locate themselves among writing colleagues on their campuses.

WRITING CENTER-BASED WORK

At the core of writing center work are one-to-one tutoring conferences in which consultants and writers work on specific writing projects. One frequent configuration is that of student writers and peer consultants working on assignments for undergraduate composition courses. However, the variables are multiple. Consultants may be faculty or staff members, graduate or undergraduate students, and writers may be lower- or upper-division students writing in chemistry, marketing, art, sociology, or English courses; graduate students writing theses and dissertations; faculty members designing student writing projects or writing for publication; or staff writing grant proposals. Until fairly recently, most consultations were conducted face-to-face; however, increasing numbers of centers have added online consultations, some that are synchronous audio-video, others using synchronous text only, and still others with asynchronous text exchanges.

In addition to one-to-one writing conferences, consultants often conduct workshops for both students and faculty on issues such as understanding disciplinary genre, writing summaries and abstracts, writing application materials for graduate schools or for jobs, handling MLA or APA citations, or using punctuation. They also offer conversation groups in which multilingual students work with native speakers on oral communication. Some centers feature readings of student and professional writers of essays, poetry, and fiction or serve as sites for service learning. Consultants also work outside their centers, working directly with composition instructors, conferencing with students writing in computer labs, and leading in-class draft workshops, often as part of larger WAC projects.

Location

For all of these activities, space is essential. The location of the space isn't everything, but it is important. Because space shapes the roles any composition program can play as well as the images it constructs of itself (Reynolds 18), material spaces have political edges that are costly if ignored (Colby, Fye, and Haviland). Just as tortilla chip vendors invest in expensive end-of-the-aisle displays in supermarkets, and CEOs choose corner window offices rather than behind-the-stairwell nooks, writing centers thrive in accessible, commodious spaces. Space creates atmosphere and affiliations; proximity increases use. Indeed, getting and keeping good space is one of the writing center functions that can help a director become a visible WPA, and doing so means knowing how universities work and understanding the culture of writing on individual campuses. It means remembering that the success of even the most theoretically elegant administrative and physical locations or programmatic links hinge on the people who inhabit those structures. For example, a writing center located in "just the right place" during one administration may be plagued by frustration when that administration changes—as administrations frequently do. It also means speaking out for writing center theories and values and making connections across boundaries. In short, being a writing center WPA means setting aside the comfort of staying small and insular and working to see/know/create contexts for writing programs on specific campuses.

Staff Education

Writing center staff prepare for their work in a variety of ways. They commonly have backgrounds in English and graduate work in rhetoric and composition; however, where writing centers are centered in WAC programs, they may be based in a variety of disciplines. Student consultants are usually recommended because they are themselves capable writers who interact well with others; on some campuses they come chiefly from English departments and on others from across the disciplines. They engage in a variety of educational ventures, ranging from quarter- or semester-long courses, to intensive preterm seminars, to short orientations, most of which are accompanied by weekly or monthly staff development sessions. Some programs make the consultants' writing central, helping students develop a metacognitive approach to both writing and tutoring; many use newsletters, Web sites, bulletin boards, and listservs as well as print texts to create discussion forums. Common to all of these configurations is a combination of formal and informal writing, theory, pedagogy, observation, reflection, and role playing so that consultants are not simply trained to respond to specific situations but rather are encouraged to practice what Mary Catherine Bateson calls theorized improvisation (1–14). That is, they study collaborative reading and writing practices to develop consulting theories that can anchor a variety of consultant-writer situations.

Many writing centers are quick to reject "fix-it shop" or "grammar garage" designations, focusing on their roles in writer development rather than paper repair. Consultants talk with writers about the meaning of assignments, about invention, about rhetorical and citation conventions, and about the relationship between gender inclusiveness and pronoun agreement; they also pose counterarguments, remind writers to support assertions with evidence, and encourage them to use but expand on disciplinary traditions. Sometimes these theoretical commitments frustrate both students who visit the writing center and their faculty, because students often leave conferences with less than "perfect" papers. Consultants focus on keeping students in charge of their learning rather than on becoming gatekeepers.

Directors support this investment in long-term writing and learning processes by encouraging consultants to begin with higher order concerns, such as focus and support, before turning to sentence structure and documentation details—whether students are basic writers, international students, or native speakers writing dissertations. First, they note that learning requires engagement in process, not simply handing over correct answers. Second, they recognize that they cannot supply all of the answers because, given the complexity of language, even punctuation changes meaning; therefore, consultants cannot edit without knowing the meaning a writer intends. Third, they point to the ethics of collaboration that require consultants to make certain that writers maintain ownership of their own papers. Thus, as students sometimes comment, writing centers sound more like talking centers than writing centers. They are noisy places in which consultants take on Socratic or dialogic roles, asking questions, offering choices, and turning to textual, consultant, and online resources. Rather than writing for students, consultants talk and write with them, modeling positive writer behaviors as they collaborate.

The multilingual students and students with disabilities who use writing centers challenge writing center staff to reconsider what they mean by collaboration, especially how to maintain their collaborative pedagogies without taking over inappropriately. Some of these students need very specific help with idioms, plurals, articles, prepositions, and spelling or with the physical acts of reading and writing—help that can be easily supplied with prescriptive answers. In fact, writing consultants often ask this question directly: "Shall we give them prepositions?" In some cases, this may mean that consultants may begin with lower order concerns, enmeshing them with higher order concerns, but it need not mean shifting from consulting, modeling, and guiding to lecturing and fixing. Consultants can make the accommodations necessary without resorting to doing the writing themselves. Consultants who do not try to address all questions in a single session, who listen carefully to students' descriptions of their needs, and who consult with linguists, TESOL specialists, and counselors for international and disabled students can extend their own understandings of collaboration.

Credit Courses

Writing centers sometimes offer credit bearing writing courses to the general student population, usually through English departments though occasionally as linked components of writing intensive courses in the disciplines. Because these courses are often supplemental to other courses, they commonly generate one or two credits. Faculty are always involved in these courses, whether they are assigned solely to the writing center or on-loan from various departments. Sometimes the faculty work in conjunction with peer consultants and sometimes not, but the writing center environment tends to model instruction on one-to-one conferencing that provides immediate feedback and allows for self-paced study. These courses are particularly important features at open-admissions, community college, and vocational-technical institutions.

Online Centers

Writing centers, like most educational ventures, work to balance administrative demands for large-scale technology-supported distance learning with the very real contributions that technology can make to writing center work, both within centers and at a distance. Indeed, one of the first budget negotiations new directors can expect is with administrators who anticipate rooms full of computers instead of well-paid consultants; like most thoughtful education, writing center work is labor intensive—and that labor is at its richest when it is human. However, most writing centers do use technology that supports their theoretical commitments, and many now offer online resources, some of their own design and some through links with long established Web sites such as Purdue's online writing lab (OWL). Online writing conferences are, of course, particularly appealing to students who live far from campus or attend evening classes after full workdays, and a number of writing centers are conducting interesting research comparing online and face-to-face conferencing. Two of the most important early findings note the importance of seeing these two as quite different, even as they share some features. They suggest that online consultants not simply try to replicate face-to-face conferences online, and they point out that, not surprisingly, online conferencing is more not less expensive than face-to-face conferencing. Therefore, online conferences may contribute in important ways to writing center work, not because they cut costs but because they extend both writing center services and scholarship.

Data Collection

Record keeping is critical for writing centers, for data help directors not only justify to administrators their existences in terms of budgets, staff, and space but also shape programs, communicate with faculty, and conduct research. Relatively simple spreadsheets can provide basic aggregate data; however, many directors use packaged or locally developed databases, often integrated with other campus programs that track multiple student activities. Almost all centers track student use; many keep files on individual students, which allows the consultants to see patterns that might illuminate their practices. Some centers track special populations and prepare reports for various support programs, such as federally sponsored TRIO programs or locally funded disabled students or second language programs. Many centers notify faculty of students who wish to report their writing center conferences; most do this only with student consent. These data help directors show how their work contributes to retention and graduation rates as well as more general student satisfaction (Lerner). In addition, some centers play central roles in campus writing assessment and thus both keep records and gather an assortment of assessment data (Johnson-Shull, Wyche, and Griffith). It is important that directors monitor data use carefully, not only to make certain that correlation is not misrepresented as causation but also to protect student and faculty anonymity.

Research

Some writing center research draws on databases assembled for record keeping and assessment purposes. However, many other very interesting studies grow out of work with faculty and student writers and with writing assignments. Each year, staff and consultants generate a number of very rich studies of genre, disciplinary discourse, pedagogy, culture, power, agency, and intellectual property from their writing center work. Staff find the site a particularly rich space for extended ethnographic studies, and graduate students find that writing center TAships help them interrogate the perceived hierarchies that often exist in traditional classrooms. Indeed, writing centers have become such an attractive research site that directors feel an increasing imperative to protect students from researchers on the hunt for subjects. Students who are experimenting with new composing processes, for instance, may shut down if they find themselves pinned under the gaze of even a well-intentioned scholar. Nevertheless, it is important that WPAs not limit writing centers to a service function but recognize them as richly situated sites of teaching and research. (See "Resources.")

WRITING CENTER LINKS WITH OTHER PROGRAMS

Directors may opt for freestanding locations, following Jeanne Simpson's advice to position themselves as close to funding sources as possible because each authority layer siphons off more money, vetoes requests, and reorders priorities. Yet they also create links that support their theoretical and programmatic commitments. Some of the most common include those with English departments, WAC programs, and learning centers.

Links with English Departments

Many writing centers are attached to English departments simply because staff are most commonly prepared in English, rhetoric, and composition programs. However, this attachment may be disadvantageous if it cements other disciplinary faculty members' preferences that writing be an English department "problem" while reinforcing expectations that all students who have passed FYC courses "write logically and put the commas where they belong." Also, the attachment can take an even uglier turn. Indeed, some writing center directors have fought to escape English departments that expected them to provide the grammar and mechanical assistance for which faculty eschewed responsibility. Such departments may treat directors with the same disrespect as they do the students "condemned" to the writing center. However, healthy English department links can generate reciprocal richness. Writing center directors who are also English faculty can benefit from easy interaction with an extended group of academic peers, writing center theory and pedagogy can inform teaching and scholarship, and English majors who become writing consultants can see a more complete picture of rhetoric and composition. Thus, very rich possibilities exist when writing center directors have cordial interaction with English departments but are situated under larger university umbrellas where they can orchestrate strong campuswide writing programs.

Links with WAC/WID

The relationships between writing centers and WAC or writing-in-the-disciplines (WID) programs create rich spaces for writing and research

(Haviland; Waldo). On campuses where writing centers precede WAC programs, writing center staff typically lead faculty development workshops, providing faculty with research and consultant support for using writing in disciplinary courses. On campuses where WAC programs predate writing centers, WAC directors more commonly plan this work with faculty, and then, with their writing centers, orchestrate ongoing writing consultancy for students in WAC courses. On campuses with active faculty teaching and learning centers, writing center and WAC directors can often work collaboratively by becoming part of faculty development programs.

WAC links stimulate one current debate in writing centers—are students best served by generalist or discipline-specific consultants? On the one hand, collaboration is at its best when each participant brings a different expertise to the table: the generalist consultant comes as expert reader, the writer brings disciplinary expertise, and together they negotiate meaning for yet a third reader. Discipline specific consultants, on the other hand, know their disciplines' expectations for style, tone, and structures, which helps students not only revise specific papers but also build disciplinary expertise of their own. However, it may be economically and logistically difficult to provide rhetorically sophisticated, discipline-based consultants for all writers, which is where the collaborative underpinnings of writing centers are helpful—consultants do not have to know everything if they are willing to use print, online, and peer resources. Susan McLeod and Elaine Maimon's perspective is useful here: rather than seeing WAC and WID as two very different approaches, they see them as intertwined, complementary ways of thinking about generalist and discipline based writing.

Another way that writing centers interact with WAC is by preparing consultants to work directly with faculty in their classes. Following Brown University's writing fellows model, consultants read course materials and meet with the faculty to learn about their expectations for both the course and the consultations. Consultants may work with the whole class, in small groups, or with individuals—inside or outside of the classroom.

Links with Learning Centers

When writing centers are located outside of English departments, they often are part of larger learning centers that provide tutoring in many subjects. If learning centers and writing centers share common goals, these marriages may be happy—even fruitful—as they encourage cross-disciplinary consultant interactions (Colby, Fye, and Haviland). Although having working partnerships with learning centers may not be crucial for writing centers that are located outside of learning centers, it is useful for them to work in complementary ways, and proactive WPAs can facilitate these associations so that they support rather than compete with or contradict each other.

Links with Service Learning and Professional Writing

The relationships between WAC and service learning are enacted in at least two ways in writing centers. Because of their cross-curricular WAC affiliations, many writing centers already have developed working relationships with potential service learning sites. For example, students enrolled in tutor preparation courses may do some of their tutorial internships in local schools, whereas writing centers may also offer online writing conferences to K–12 schools. Also, through their work with students in a variety of disciplines, writing centers make connections with community-based organizations, offering a center for service learning sites. Although some of these extensions to professional writing and service learning are fairly new, writing centers are emerging as potential service learning clearinghouses as well as engaging in service-learning training for faculty and students.

Like most WPAs, writing center directors occupy variously orchestrated roles that are shaped by their professional theories and affiliations and by local culture. These often unstable and in-the-middle elements contribute to their positions' many rewards as well as its frustrations. Daily, directors negotiate their own positions along with those of their centers and their students; whether as sole WPAs or as members of a group, writing center directors must strike a balance among many constituencies.

RECOMMENDATIONS

Writing center director roles have evolved in many of the same ways that other WPA roles have evolved, mushrooming from starting up small, tidily-boxed, single programs to working with large, not-so-tidily categorized, intersecting programs. They have evolved within their own walls as well as within their campus structures. We would like to recommend that, because they share so much theoretically and ideologically, writing center directors and other WPAs explore their intersections as carefully as they observe their differences. This will require initiatives on the parts of all participants. On campuses where WPAs direct well established FYC programs, it will mean reaching out to new writing center or WAC directors. On campuses with flourishing writing centers and experienced directors, it will mean inviting new directors of composition into partnerships. It also will mean thinking more broadly about formal preparation and continuing education for these varied WPA roles. One of the audiences for this handbook, for example, is the increasing number of students enrolled in writing program administration courses at both the MA and PhD levels. Such courses can help students look carefully both at the multiple possibilities WPA work offers as well as the ways those in the different roles can interact and support each other. The annual summer WPA conferences and workshops, of course, are other excellent ways of facilitating continuing education and networking, along with regular sessions and special interest groups at CCCC, NCTE, and MLA. In any enactment, however, this search for community rather than confinement, for collectives rather than isolated enclaves, will model postmodern composition theories that can contribute to healthy institutions, writing programs, faculty, staff, and students.

RESOURCES

Writing center staff have an increasingly rich selection of resources in terms of colleagues, associations, conferences, and print and online texts. The following listings cover some of the most visible resources, which, in turn, point to many others.

Organizations

Local, regional, national, and international organizations encourage collegiality beyond individual campuses. They also offer opportunities for both staff and consultants to present at conferences and to write for publication. These organizations are particularly committed to enacting collaborative models, so many undergraduate and graduate writing center consultants are full participants in these conferences. Their contributions add to programs and publications and boost students' confidence and commitments to academic work. Following is a representative list of these organizations:

International Writing Center Association (an NCTE affiliate)
CUNY Writing Center Association
East Central Writing Center Association
European Writing Center Association
MidAtlantic Writing Center Association
Midwest Writing Center Association
Northeastern Writing Center Association
Pacific Coast Writing Center Association
Rocky Mountain Writing Center Association
South Central Writing Center Association

Listserv

WCENTER (wcenter@acs.ttu.edu)

Publications

The Writing Center Journal: Joan Mullin and Albert C. DeCiccio, eds. (jmullin@uofto02.utoledo.edu)

The Writing Lab Newsletter: Muriel Harris, ed. (harrism@cc.purdue.edu)

National Writing Center Association Press, Byron Stay, ed. (stay@msmary.edu)

Barnett, Robert W. and Jacob S. Blumner, eds. *Writing Centers and Writing Across the Curriculum Programs.* Westport, CT: Greenwood P, 1999.

Briggs, Lynn Craigue, and Meg Woolbright, eds. *Stories from the Center: Connecting Narratives and Theory.* Urbana, IL: NCTE, 2000.

Buranen, Lise, and Alice M. Roy, eds. *Perspectives on Plagiarism and Intellectual Property in a Postmodern World.* Albany: State U of New York P, 1999.

Chapters of Writing Center Interest:

   Clark, Irene. "Writing Centers and Plagiarism." 155–67.

   Haviland, Carol Peterson, and Joan Mullin. "Writing Centers and Intellectual Property: Are Faculty Members and Students Differently Entitled?" 169–81.

   Shamoon, Linda, and Deborah H. Burns. "Plagiarism, Rhetorical Theory, and the Writing Center: New Approaches, New Locations." 183–92.

Capossela, Toni-Lee. *The Harcourt Brace Guide to Peer Tutoring.* Orlando: Harcourt, 1998.

Clark, Irene L. *Writing in the Center.* 3rd ed. Dubuque, IA: Kendall/Hunt, 1998.

Gillespie, Paula, and Neal Lerner. *The Allyn and Bacon Guide to Peer Tutoring.* Boston: Allyn and Bacon, 2000.

Grimm, Nancy Maloney. *Good Intentions.* Portsmouth, NH: Boynton/Cook, 1999.

Haviland, Carol Peterson, Maria Notarangelo, Lene Whitley-Putz, and Thia Wolf, eds. *Weaving Knowledge Together: Writing Centers and Collaboration.* Emmitsburg, MD: NWCA P, 1998.

Hobson, Eric. *Wiring the Center.* Logan, UT: Utah State UP, 1998.

Kinkead, Joyce A., and Jeanette G. Harris, eds. *Writing Centers in Context.* Urbana, IL: NCTE, 1993.

Mullin, Joan A., and Ray Wallace, eds. *Intersections: Theory-Practice in the Writing Center.* Urbana, IL: NCTE, 1994.

Murphy, Christina, and Steve Sherwood. eds. *The St. Martin's Sourcebook for Writing Tutors.* New York: St. Martin's, 1995.

Murphy, Christina, Joe Law, and Steve Sherwood, eds. *Writing Centers: An Annotated Bibliography.* Westport, CT: Greenwood P, 1996.

Myers-Breslin, Linda, ed. *Administrative Problem-Solving for Writing Programs and Writing Centers.* Urbana, IL: NCTE, 1999.

Chapters of Writing Center Interest:

   Dornsife, Robert S. "Initiating a Peer Tutoring Program in a University Writing Center."

   Harris, Muriel. "Selecting and Training Undergraduate and Graduate Staffs in a Writing Lab."

   Haviland, Carol Peterson and Edward M. White. "How Can Physical Space and Administrative Structure Shape Writing Programs, Writing Centers, and WAC Projects?"

   Healy, Dave. "Managing the Writing Center/Classroom Relationship."

   Houston, Linda S. "Budgeting and Politics: Keeping the Writing Center Alive."

   Kimball, Sara E. "Computers in the Writing Center."

Mullin, Joan. "Writing Across the Curriculum."

Myers-Breslin, Linda. "Running a Large Writing Program."

Nelson, Jane, and Kathy Evertz. *The Politics of Writing Centers*. Portsmouth, NH: Heinemann-Boynton/Cook, 2001.

Rafoth, Ben. ed. *A Tutor's Guide: Helping Writers One to One*. Portsmouth, NH: Boynton/Cook, 2000.

Ryan, Leigh. *The Bedford Guide for Writing Tutors*. 2nd ed. Boston: Bedford Books, 1998.

Silk, Bobbie. *Writing Center Manual*. Emmitsburg, MD: NWCA P, 1998.

ACKNOWLEDGMENTS

The authors would like to thank Libby Miles and Neal Lerner for their helpful readings of this chapter.

WORKS CITED

Bateson, Mary Catherine. *Peripheral Visions: Learning Along the Way*. New York: HarperCollins, 1994.

Boquet, Elizabeth H. "'Our Little Secret': A History of Writing Centers, Pre- to Post-Open Admissions." CCC 50 (Nov. 1998): 463–82.

Brannon, Lil, and Stephen M. North. "The Uses of the Margins." *The Writing Center Journal* 20 (Spring/Summer 2000): 7–12.

Colby, Richard, Carmen M. Fye, and Carol Peterson Haviland. "The Politics of Administrative and Physical Location." *The Politics of Writing Centers*. Ed. Jane Nelson and Kathy Evertz. Portsmouth, NH: Heinemann-Boynton/Cook, 2001: 85–98.

Delpit, Lisa D. "The Silenced Dialogue: Power and Pedagogy in Educating Other People's Children." *Harvard Educational Review* 58 (Aug. 1988): 280–98.

Ede, Lisa, and Andrea Lunsford. "Some Millennial Thoughts about the Future of Writing Centers." *The Writing Center Journal* 20 (Spring/Summer 2000): 33–38.

Grimm, Nancy. "The Regulatory Role of the Writing Center: Coming to Terms with a Loss of Innocence." *The Writing Center Journal* 17 (Fall 1996): 5–29.

Grimm, Nancy Maloney. "Rearticulating the Work of the Writing Center." CCC 47 (Dec. 1996): 523–48.

Haviland, Carol Peterson. "Writing Centers and Writing-Across-the-Curriculum: An Important Connection." *The Writing Center Journal* 5.2 and 6.1 (1985): 25–31.

Haviland, Carol Peterson, Maria Notarangelo, Lene Whitley-Putz, and Thia Wolf, eds. *Weaving Knowledge Together: Writing Centers and Collaboration*. Emmitsburg, MD: NWCA P, 1998.

Johnson-Shull, Lisa, Susan Wyche, and Brian Q. Griffith. "The 'Butterfly Effect': A Multiperspective Narrative of the Effects of Assessment on a Writing Center." *Weaving Knowledge Together: Writing Centers and Collaboration*. Ed. Carol Peterson Haviland et al., Emmitsburg, MD: NWCA P, 1998: 58–79.

Lerner, Neal. "Counting Beans and Making Beans Count." *Writing Lab Newsletter* 22 (Sept. 1997):1–4.

Lunsford, Andrea. "Collaboration, Control, and the Idea of a Writing Center." *The Writing Center Journal* 12 (Fall 1991): 3–10.

McLeod, Susan, and Elaine Maimon. "Clearing the Air: WAC Myths and Realities." *College English* 62 (May 2000): 573–83.

Reynolds, Nedra. "Composition's Imagined Geographies: The Politics of Space in the Frontier, City, and Cyberspace." CCC 50 (Sept. 1998): 12–35.

Simpson, Jeanne. "Re: Writing Centers in English Departments." Online posting. 4 Nov. 1997. In WCENTER archives <http://www.ttu.edu/wcenter/9712/msg00014.html>.

Sunstein, Bonnie S. "Moveable Feasts, Liminal Spaces: Writing Centers and the State of In-Betweenness." *The Writing Center Journal* 18 (Spring/Summer 1998): 6–16.

Waldo, Mark L. "What Should the Relationship between the Writing Center and Writing Program Be?" *The Writing Center Journal* 11.1 (1990): 73–81.

25

The GTA Experience: Grounding, Practicing, Evaluating, and Reflecting

✦ • ✦

Meg Morgan
University of North Carolina, Charlotte

A few days ago I received an email from a former graduate teaching assistant (GTA) in our MA-in-English program, now a doctoral student in women's studies at another university. She told me two things: that she won a university-wide teaching award and that she is now preparing masters and doctoral students to teach. She thanked me for all the energy and expertise I had invested in her education at UNC–Charlotte. In a very busy week for me, that note made, not only my day, but also my semester. I did not delete it; instead, I keep it on hand so when I do seem overwhelmed by the often unending and unjoyful tasks of a writing program administrator (WPA), I can remember what joy it is to work with graduate students—to see them become professionals, to care about what they do, and even to love it. And, in many cases, to become good at it.

Not all GTAs will do what my student did: join a doctoral program, work at teaching to the point where she wins a teaching award, and then work with prospective teachers. Some of our GTAs never set foot in the classroom again as teachers once they leave this university; yet, I am confident (and have some anecdotal evidence) that what they learn here—about preparation, about design, about responding—serves them well in most situations. As WPAs, then, we have the responsibility and privilege to bring to them a level of professionalism, both within and outside the teaching profession. Let me be very clear here: For several years as a WPA I envisioned that I was preparing GTAs for the profession of college teaching. Then I saw some of them quit teaching altogether to work in the corporate banks that dominate Charlotte. I saw others take positions in the high schools and some go on to doctoral studies—to undergo another GTA training program. I saw others just quit the assistantship and continue their graduate studies because they just didn't think they could make it in the classroom. So, I learned that preparation for college teaching was much too narrow and modified my position: I prepare my GTAs to teach in *this* program. However, I trust that their preparation as teachers is representative enough so that they are able to make any transitions to other careers they might need.

Although the preparation I provide is program-specific, it must pay attention to outside constraints, namely the regional accrediting agency. The Southern Association of College and Schools (SACS) mandates that graduate students working independently in a teaching situation must have earned eighteen graduate credit hours in the discipline in which they are teaching. Thus, because my department awards only a masters degree, our GTAs work in the writing center during their first year of two. Only in the second year can they teach in a classroom without a supervisor present. However, despite the short term of the classroom teaching, my English department commits time, money and energy to their training. In their first year, while they are working in the writing center, they take two graduate, three-credit courses: the first course teaches them how to tutor in the writing center and the second teaches them composition and reading theories, curriculum design, and teaching practice. (I teach this second course and have done so for eight years.) In their second year, they teach three sections of composition, usually one section in the fall semester and two in the spring.

This article is about getting GTAs ready to teach in the classroom. Although I describe what we do to get them ready to teach, in a larger context this article also describes the need to prepare them to be responsible professionals, to question and respond to what they do within an ethical context, and to look at the short- and long-range implications of their decisions. It is artificially divided into four parts: preparing the textual and logistical groundwork, preparing to practice, evaluating, and reflecting. Like the writing process itself, these four activities are recursive, redundant, interpenetrative. But their separation makes my explanation easier.

PREPARING THE TEXTUAL AND LOGISTICAL GROUNDWORK

Many GTAs come to an English department with no experience as college teachers. Most have only been college students. Before any teaching occurs, groundwork must be laid, an orientation that includes interpersonal, curricular/pedagogical, and managerial preparation.

Interpersonal

Many GTAs begin their GTA experience as strangers to this university: They don't know the faculty, the administration, and the resources available to them and to their students. They are unfamiliar with the student body, either in the individual or the aggregate. Many are unfamiliar with the political and power structures of the English department. My job as WPA/GTA supervisor demands that I spend some time discussing these issues with graduate students. Many GTAs are intimidated by a graduate faculty and I urge them, when possible, to talk one-on-one with their own teachers about teaching, about student performance expectations, and about resources available in the department. I urge them to introduce themselves to the Coordinator of the Graduate Program and to the Chair of the Department. I remind them that if they are interested in writing a thesis, they should find a faculty member with whom they can work, even informally. Outside the department, GTAs need to know someone in computing services, especially if they plan to teach in a computer classroom; they need to introduce themselves to a person in the Library who can speak for them, or to a counselor in the counseling center or nurse in the health center in case a student (or even a GTA) needs help.

Perhaps one of the more difficult topics to discuss with GTAs is the issue of authority. We do try to promote a student-centered classroom: We encourage group work at many levels, discourage unnecessary lecturing, encourage students to engage with each other in class discussion, and encourage one-on-one teaching when possible. So, when first-year students challenge the teacher or the teacher's policies, the tension between the teacher as an authority and the student as the center of the classroom often disables the teacher. Early in their training, I encourage the GTA to examine authority issues. I always encourage a cost/benefit analysis of engaging in a challenge with the undergraduate: Will the possible costs of responding to a challenge outweigh the possible benefits? However, issues of authority seem most problematic for GTAs *before* they enter the classroom. They worry about the disruptive student; they worry about not knowing the "right answer" to a question and what that may do to their authority. Often these worries disappear as they develop relationships with their students. I find it important that the GTA not depend on me or any other professor for authority. If there is an issue in the classroom, I encourage the GTA to try to resolve it instead of referring the student to a "higher" authority, an action that may deepen the GTAs insecurities and undermine her authority even more.

Curricular/Pedagogical

Curricular/pedagogical preparation means teaching the GTA the "what" and "how" of teaching in our particular program. In our student-centered, process-oriented curriculum, we teach rhetorically-initiated assignments, making them as real for the students as possible, in response to events and issues in the students' own political, social, and personal lives. For many GTAs, this kind of curriculum is most strange and unfamiliar: Many never enrolled in first-year writing or many enrolled in it at another university with a different curricular focus. For most of our GTAs, what a WPA might take for granted—concepts like *kairos*, invention, cohesion, revision, critical thinking—are unfamiliar. Pedagogical preparation includes how to begin and end a class effectively, how to set up classroom-based groups as well as project-based groups, how to make good decisions about classroom practice—whether to use lecture, large- or small-group discussion, modeling, demonstration, and so on.

Specifically, our curriculum is determined by the goals of our program. For the GTAs, these goals are non-negotiable, having been established through a departmental faculty committee. Probably the most important concept GTAs learn is that they are part of a program based on goals that were decided long before they entered it. Though goals may seem restricting, the GTAs learn that goals provide curricular consistency for students and that designing a curriculum is easier when they can look toward programmatic goals. For example, often they ask about the place of grammar and mechanics instruction in the curriculum. One of the six goals in our program states that students will be able to edit their own work. Clearly, some grammar instruction is necessary to meet the editing goal. However, that is only one of six goals—the others speak of how to use invention strategies, how to develop a discourse for an audience, and how to revise their own writing and help others revise. The GTA learns that by focusing on the teaching of grammar and mechanics, she cannot possibly accomplish the other stated goals. Things quickly get prioritized. Much of the curricular training is involved with reading composition theory, especially theory that affects how a course will be designed. For example, again, the Flower et al article "Detection, Diagnosis and the Strategies of Revision" is a standard in the curriculum. So are Berlin's "Rhetoric and Ideology in the Writing Class," Anson's "Response Styles and Ways of Knowing," and Fulkerson's *Teaching the Argument in Writing*. I also use *The New St. Martin's Guide to the Teaching of Writing* by Connors and Glenn. Although dated in many ways, its orientation matches the rhetorical emphasis in our program.

One of the curricular issues that GTAs must deal with is designing and sequencing assignments. We tend to follow the developmental sequence James Moffett describes in *Active Voice*, where writing proceeds according to a speaker (or writer) audience-based continuum: students write essays in which the distance between the writer and the audience grows wider throughout the semester. So, whereas the first essay may have as an audience the writer or persons close to the writer, the last essay is usually directed at the "general" audience. Although James Kinneavy in A *Theory of Discourse* describes a static model of discourse, we often apply his aims of writing to Moffet's continuum-based model, assigning an essay in the expressive aim, one or two in the persuasive, and the rest in the informative or referential. Finally, we adopt a rhetorical philosophy; though we don't teach Aristotle or Cicero, we certainly do emphasize some of the concerns of a classical rhetorical approach: invention, arrangement, style, and their relationships to real and fictionalized audiences. We also emphasize the role of rhetoric in constructing reality. In addition, the program also supports project-based assignments, in which students must write several documents (with different aims and audiences) within a single project. Several projects may be required throughout the semester, each one becoming increasingly challenging.

Although our GTAs learn something about responding to student writing in their first-year roles as tutors, they must also learn to respond to student writing in their roles as teachers in authority. We talk about response in several ways: through the reading of articles (Flower et al. and Anson, mentioned earlier), by examining individual assignments and student responses to those assignments, and also by examining the responses by teachers to student writing. We examine holistic scoring, often having a mini-holistic scoring session in class; we examine the use of analytic grading sheets as well marginal and end notes. Much of this is discussed in *The St. Martin's Guide to Teaching Writing*. However, we also ask rhetoricians on our faculty to give workshops to the GTAs on responding, who often discuss their own response styles. Finally, GTAs read folders of student work, collections of student writing that encompass the whole semester and, in that context, discuss the situated nature of responding and grading and the impossibility of ever being "objective," no matter what kind of grading rubric they might invent. During the semesters that they teach, GTAs show me high, medium, and low student essays, and we discuss them together, negotiating the best response.

Pedagogical discussions that deal with "how" students learn are closely tied to the curricular, not to teach GTAs to become novice psychologists, but to help them to understand the complexity of the student sitting before them. A quick introduction to learning styles, for example, is provided in Linda B. Nilson's text, *Teaching at Its Best*. Nilson outlines two learning styles, one based on David Kolb's process of learning and another based on sensory preferences. Nilson makes a good case for what she calls "multi-sensory teaching," a concept that makes good sense to the GTAs in my class who come to realize one mode of instruction may not do it for all of the twenty-two students in their classes. Instead, they must use lecture *and* overheads *and* small groups *and* large groups *and* physical manipulation of a text to have any chance of reaching their students. I also briefly talk about Howard Gardner's theory of multiple intelligences to make them aware of the many ways to understand their students. Athletes are not "dumb," but have "bodily-kinesthetic intelligence" more than "linguistic intelligence," for example. It helps. We obviously talk about other kinds of differences—racial, gender, class, and ethnicity—although many of my GTAs have worked in the writing center where they have seen firsthand how student writing is affected by this diversity. During their work in the writing center, they read articles on basic writers, second-language writers, and standard and nonstandard dialects.

Pedagogical discussion also includes, obviously, the design of the class teaching and learning. Inexperienced GTAs often do not understand how to design a fifty- or eighty-minute class. With good teaching, the design is invisible and the movements in the class effortless. But the movement takes a consciousness of planning and practice, which does not come easily for many graduate students. For example, I tend to think of a fifty-minute class divided into four chunks: five minutes for an opening ritual of some sort, twenty minutes for introducing new material, twenty minutes for practicing that material, and five minutes for the closing ritual. All chunks are tied together by the learning goals for that particular class. In the opening ritual, the teacher might take roll while the students perform an in-class writing connected to the goals of the day. So, if the goal of the day is to teach question-asking strategies for the researched project, while the teacher is taking roll, the students could be writing about when and how they find themselves asking questions, or could be given a topic related to the assignment and asked to generate questions about the topic. The next twenty minutes might be a lecture or discussion of the kinds of questions people ask, of the rhetorical context of question-asking, and of ways to evaluate "good" questions; the next twenty minutes might be a focused discussion of the in-class writing, using partners or small groups. The five-minute closing ritual might be the whole class reviewing what they learned about asking questions and comparing their initial questions to their ending questions. When GTAs learn that there are ways to segment the class to move the students from uncertainty or unknowing to a stage that is less uncertain and more knowing, they are often amazed. They see that in one class they can use several pedagogies that appeal to various student strengths and learning styles; that they can create an awareness of a gap in the students' knowledge, close the gap through demonstration or lecture, ask the students to practice new information, and then ask them again to demonstrate what they have learned.

Part of my need to teach students how to chunk classes comes from my own conviction that the ability to teach is not innate. Teaching is an art that can be learned, and one of the best ways to learn it is not only to take the risk with a new pedagogy but also to make the chance of failing less scary by balancing the pedagogies. If a GTA wants to use small discussion groups as a way to broaden students' knowledge of questioning strategies, but has never used small groups before, it certainly seems reasonable to use groups for only fifteen minutes of a class, not fifty. If the pedagogy fails, the recovery will be less traumatic for the GTA and for her students.

Segmenting the class gives a GTA the opportunity, thus, to practice with multiple pedagogies without making a huge investment in any one. It gives all GTAs opportunities to experience their own strengths as teachers and to give up the idea that teaching means standing at the front of the room lecturing. (Some of my worst experiences training GTAs have been exactly this situation—where the idea of teacher-as-pontificator is so deeply etched that the GTA cannot quite give it up.) It also provides opportunities to conceptualize the classroom activities in interesting ways: the students can move from individual learning experience (in-class writing and teacher demonstration) to social learning (small group and large group) back to individual learning, or whatever. I worked with a GTA once who always moved from individual, to small group, to large group, to individual within the class time. She varied the pedagogical activities from class to class, but the overall scheme was the same. I often thought of her teaching as symphonic.

Managerial

For many understandable reasons, new teachers, whether they are GTAs or not, fear the managerial. They fear the disruptive, unmotivated, or hostile student, the challenges to teaching such a student, and their making inappropriate or inadequate responses to the student. GTAs have a handle on what it means to plagiarize in the abstract, but they worry about what they might do when they encounter a case of plagiarism. They question their own attendance policies. In many cases, the managerial anxieties can be alleviated by pretty basic information. Most universities have policies on disruption and/or teaching centers with materials on how to handle it. Most GTAs will have the necessary human-relations skills to address such incidents in the classroom when they arise without damaging either the student or themselves. However, in case they don't, I provide scenarios in my graduate course to allow them to practice possible responses to incidents that might arise.

In some cases, student disruption can become the impetus for a "teachable moment." A student enters the classroom with an obscene picture on a sweatshirt; a young woman has shaved her head, pierced her nose, mouth, eyebrows, or whatever. The new teacher can open a conversation about the incidents, using the greatest classroom interpersonal tool, a sense of humor. Of course, some things aren't funny. Racist, sexist, homophobic comments or paraphernalia deserve a serious response and a serious discussion. Classroom comments made to provoke an incident might never become productive learning experiences, except in the negative: "I'll never do that again!" (See chap. 22, this volume.)

Though some managerial stuff is beyond our control—the incidents rise up spontaneously—others are perfectly predictable. GTAs ask me what to do when a student who has missed ten classes has to go home because his grandmother has cancer. The syllabus, the course "contract," always states the minimum and maximum numbers of absences, and I always tell the GTAs to consult the syllabus and then to refer the student to the same syllabus. GTAs ask me what to do if a student turns in a late paper or does not complete all the assignments. Although these contingencies are often explained on the syllabus, new teachers worry about them anyway. Of course, not everything can appear on the syllabus. Lately, for some reason, we have had a rash of parents calling to find out the progress of their sons or daughters in the course. Legally, we cannot tell the parent anything, and GTAs must be made aware of this law. GTAs must also be made aware of specific university policies that affect the student: what to do, for example, if a student plagiarizes; what to do if the GTA miscalculates the final grade; what to do if a student faints in class, or makes a sexual comment to the GTA, or says he or she is depressed and suicidal. The number and variety of potential managerial problems challenge this or any discussion of GTA training and will often preoccupy discussions with inexperienced teachers.

Preparing to Practice

Preparation is practice and practice is preparation. In some ways, even the most experienced teachers are always practicing, mainly because classes are never the same, that which makes teaching both continually frustrating and exciting. But GTAs who might never have taught at the college level need preactual experience practice, and any training program for them must get them into the habit of practicing. This need does not deny that all have been students and that status gives them some practice at being teachers: they've had to think like their teachers at times ("psych them out"); they've had to role play conversations with teachers; they've had to appeal to teachers; they've had to give oral reports before peers. Regardless, most of them have not had to teach: to "psych out" their students, to think like them, to role-play a class, to appeal to their needs.

There are many ways to afford the opportunity to practice. I use these three.

Observation

Faculty in the English department generously volunteer to be observed by one of the GTAs in the program. The GTA chooses a faculty member who is not currently teaching them. Together, they agree on the days of the observation. The GTA must observe the class for an entire project sequence. If the class is a writing class, the GTA might very well be observing the class for two or more weeks; if it is a literature class, it might be as long as the time it takes to read and discuss *Sense and Sensibility*. Before the observation, the faculty member and GTA meet to discuss the nature of the project; the GTA asks about learning goals, curriculum design, and pedagogy and, throughout the observation, tries to match the learning goals with the curriculum and the pedagogy. The GTA interviews the faculty member after the project is completed—sometimes even after each class, although I don't require it, and writes a short report for the class, a longer one for me, and makes an oral report.

Good things come out of this practice: (a) GTAs meet faculty members and interact on a collegial level—teacher to teacher; (b) they learn that many (but not all) teachers think through each class carefully—that the classes do not spring spontaneously from the head of the teacher; (c) they learn to match intent with outcome—sometimes the intention is great but the class fails anyway; (d) they learn to ask questions about teaching to an experienced teacher who wants to talk about teaching (I know of few good teachers who don't want to talk about teaching); (e) they learn that even a really good teacher can have a really bad day; (f) they learn about classroom practice— about asking questions, about giving clear directions, about treating students with respect, about challenging them, about how to solve some of the managerial problems that worry them. I have only one rule: when they report to the class orally and in writing, they can report only positive things. Only the GTA who has observed the class knows the negative.

Participating faculty members benefit as well. They can and often do request copies of the student reports, and I've seen these reports (which are very detailed) show up in merit salary files and even tenure/reappointment files. I have had revelatory conversations with faculty—who didn't know that they were doing (fill in the blank) in the classroom. Often faculty are taken back by the students' questions about goals, curriculum, and pedagogy because they had not thought about teaching in these terms. In some cases, a mentoring relationship emerges from the observation.

I have assigned this project for eight years, and only once, during the first year, did I have any problems, mostly with a GTA who could not or would not keep appointments with the faculty member.

In-Class Teaching Module

The second preparatory activity I use is the in-class teaching module. All GTAs must perform for 10 minutes before their peers, teaching an aspect of composition. The list, mostly based on the topics in *The New St. Martin's Guide to Teaching Writing*, includes: teaching an invention strategy, an arrangement pattern, a revision strategy, an aspect of style, an editing strategy. I also include teaching various reading strategies. The module must be complete from beginning to end; it must be in "real" time, and it must include at least two pedagogical strategies, such as discussion, small group work, or lecture. Students choose from the list, preparing a complete lesson plan (goals, curriculum, pedagogy). The graduate class usually pretends that it's a first-year writing or another undergraduate class. When possible, we tape the session, although we usually do not review the tape in class. After the 10 minutes, students take a few minutes to write their responses to the unit and then give (only positive) oral feedback. I invite GTAs to consult with me beforehand because I don't want to reinforce the notion that teaching occurs alone. (For a fuller description of this kind of practice, see Baker and Kinkead.)

I think the learning that occurs from this practice is substantial. They learn that nothing is worse than getting up in front of one's peers and pretending to do something that you are not sure of. They learn that the 10 minutes that seemed so long in the planning is a flash in the practice, and that no matter how uncomfortable they might feel, invariably they can get through it. This is a very painful experience for many students, full of anxiety and dread. Yet, in the eight years that I've taught this class, not one student has refused to go through with it. One student balked, but when she realized she would have to do it to pass the class, she went ahead and did a great job. Students have said that teaching a "real" class seemed much less scary after this experience. Perhaps most important, they also learn from each other and come to understand the interdependence that is part of the teaching experience. I realized an unexpected benefit several years ago. One graduating GTA was interviewing for a teaching position at the local community college. Part of the interview was a twenty-minute teaching unit she had to deliver before the recruiting committee. When she came to me in a panic, I reminded her that, in fact, she had already done a version of this in class. She stated that nothing could be worse than that experience, went off and did well for the community college people.

Syllabus

Designing a syllabus is an aspect of teaching practice that prospective teachers sometimes seem to take for granted. Seldom do they understand the choices a teacher must make in planning a course. So, I ask my GTAs to design a full-semester syllabus for their first-semester writing class, one that they must use the next fall. They work in groups of two or three (learning again that teaching is a collaborative act) and design guidelines, articulate policies, and plan a calendar for the class. They must choose a textbook from a list I give them and must also justify each assignment, its place in the semester, and how it will be evaluated within the context of the reading they have done in the graduate course. The experience is agonizing for many GTAs. They report that they might spend an entire evening deciding on an attendance policy or the exact learning goals for the second assignment. Each group turns in a draft to which the class and I respond, and, at the end of the project, each group makes a brief oral presentation to the class.

The learning benefits from this project seem obvious: they learn in most practical ways how to sequence course assignments; they must decide policies that will not harm their students. (Once a group of GTAs decided that they would accept no late first drafts and no final drafts without a first draft; one new teacher the next fall had a student who tried to hand in his first paper late, but the teacher would not accept it. The teacher was upset because she saw how such a policy could fail a student at the beginning of the semester. I believe she modified her policy that very day.) The GTAs have learned to negotiate something that will affect their very behavior. And, because they have consulted textbooks, experienced teachers, and old syllabi, they learn that teaching is an "ongoing conversation" in many English Departments. Practically, they have their syllabus for the next fall, a source of great relief for many.

EVALUATING

Given that the GTA has been prepared for the classroom through reading and discussion and that the preparation also has included opportunities for practice, it only seems reasonable that teaching should be evaluated based on that preparation. The process of evaluation can take many forms, but, like most evaluations, it is most comprehensive when it includes several and varied evaluative opportunities, including classroom observation, videotaping, paper-grading sessions, and student formative and summative critiques.

Perhaps the most obvious opportunity for evaluating GTA performance comes by observing the actual practice, which can be done either by the supervisor, usually the WPA, or by peers. Although procedures may vary depending on the needs of the program, observing more than once gives a better (but still not very complete) picture of the performance. At my university in our small program, I observe each GTA three times during the first semester. Each observation is preceded by a briefing and followed by a debriefing. During the briefing, the GTA tells me the learning objectives, the curricular matter to be taught, and the pedagogy to be used. Sound familiar? In addition, the GTA lets me know if there are any special circumstances I need to observe: discipline problems, high absenteeism, and lack of motivation. If a GTA has a problem designing a pedagogy, I will help; otherwise, I pretty much stay out of the picture. During the observation, I almost never participate in the class, although sometimes I will join a student group and may add a few words to help them. At the debriefing, I ask the GTA to discuss the specific strengths of the performance and areas for improvement.

Though I do not ask GTAs to observe each other, I know this is common practice in some schools. In fact, although our GTAs do not sit in on each other's classes, they do consult with each other about assignments, grading papers, and glitches and changes in the syllabus. In fact, one year, on their own initiative, the seven GTAs in the program wrote a common syllabus for the second semester course.

I also ask the GTAs to videotape themselves at least twice, once in the beginning of the semester and once near the end. I find much more resistance to the videotaping than to my observing, even though the department owns the videotaping machine and using it is pretty easy. The GTA arranges for the videotaping, keeps the videotape and then, at the end of the semester, chooses a brief segment to show to me and to the other GTAs. (Baker and Kinkead suggest videotaping the in-class teaching module; Brookfield also sees benefits to videotaping classes.)

As I noted earlier, I also look at student drafts of each assignment in the course. The GTA chooses a high, medium, and low essay from the class and before the GTA responds to the essay we go over the student writing. I am not trying to test the GTA in these meetings, but to make sure that there is a reasonable response to the student's writing.

I also ask the GTAs to distribute to their classes a variation of the Critical Incident Questionnaire found in *Becoming a Critically Reflective Teacher* by Stephen D. Brookfield. GTAs distribute the questions every Friday for a month beginning in the third or fourth week of the semester. They encourage their students to answer the questions fully, assuring them that their anonymous answers will be used to inform teaching practice. In class, on the next Monday, the GTAs go over the student responses and discuss any modifications they think should be made as a result of student input. The following questions come directly from the Brookfield text, yet I encourage the GTAs to make changes if they need to:

- At what moment in the class this week did you feel most engaged with what was happening?
- At what moment in the class this week did you feel most distanced from what was happening?
- What act that anyone (teacher or student) took in class this week did you find most affirming or helpful?
- What act that anyone (teacher or student) took in class this week did you find most puzzling or confusing?
- What about the class this week surprised you the most? (This could be something about your own reactions to what went on, or something that someone did, or anything else that occurs to you.) (115)

Because the GTAs teach student-centered classes, and because many of them interact with students in many ways, often the responses reveal nothing that the GTAs do not already guess. After the questionnaire, however, GTAs *know* students' attitudes towards small group work, peer response groups, the textbook. Sometimes students' messages are mixed, some liking group work, some hating it, and so on. Whatever, the GTAs have a written formative student assessment upon which they can act, if necessary.

Finally, at the end of the semester, summative student evaluations are administered to all faculty—full-time, part-time, and GTA. They have no choice about when the evaluations will be administered, who will administer them, and the questions students will be asked. None of us does. These are the evaluations of record, the ones that go into personnel files, a form of high stakes evaluation. However, no matter how couched this assessment might be in numbers or bubbles or factual-sounding statements, at no level are they "objective." The statements harbor assumptions about teaching that are usually not unpacked ("The teacher is organized": So what does that mean? Or the one that all students in the university have to answer, regardless of department: "This is the best teacher I've ever had." Who is the competition here, especially if we are administering the form to first-semester students: first-grade teachers, high school teachers, the basketball coach who led a student to a statewide championship?) GTAs, although they must be evaluated using this summative tool, learn to carefully assess its value to them.

However, the best thing about multiple and varied evaluation methods is that they are multiple and varied. It is only through the use of the observations, videotaping, consultation with the WPA, and Critical Incident Questionnaire results that improvement, not judgment, can be documented. From all this evaluation, GTAs learn that teaching is not a "natural" act, but rather a process of continual improvement. They learn that teaching can be messy, that students don't have a single, consistent point of view on what is good or bad teaching, on whether or not they have found the class "worthwhile." More than anything, they learn that students, peers, and supervisors are usually on their side.

REFLECTION

Reflection takes place in grounding, in practicing, in evaluating. In fact, the topical separation that I have proposed earlier in the article reaches its most absurd manifestation in this section. Reflection involves stepping back and challenging assumptions that inform all aspects of teaching. Because we are working with writing teachers, the reflection required of GTAs most often takes a written form. There are many possible kinds of reflection. In this section, I'll discuss two kinds of reflection that I actually do, and describe some that I or anyone else could do.

Reflection, according to Kathleen Yancey, involves looking both backward and forward, backward at where we have been or what we may know and forward to "goals we might attain" (6). Although she's writing mostly about student writing and reflection, students reflecting on their own writing

processes, there is no reason why the ideas she presents cannot be fully explored in the reflection upon teaching and the written articulation of teaching and learning theories, practices, and philosophies. Yancey presents three
kinds of reflection: reflection-in-action that focuses on a single composing
act; constructive reflection that focuses on looking at several composing acts
and theorizes from the particular, and reflection-in-presentation that focuses
on the presentation of learning and knowing. I use her constructive reflection
and reflection-in-presentation to prepare GTAs for teaching. I also use ideas
from Stephen Brookfield, again, as part of encouraging the GTAs to become
reflective practitioners.

Brookfield's book is a treasure house of ideas, including the Critical Incident
Questionnaire discussed previously. Mostly, he advises teachers to question assumptions about teaching, even those that seem noble on their face. He articulates clearly the power dimensions in the learning enterprise and warns
teachers to be aware of how they themselves can be used as instruments of
power in hidden, unexpected, and unacceptable-to -them ways. I use two of his
examples for discussion in my graduate curriculum design class. The first is his
discussion of the circle as a way of setting up desks in the classroom. Most
teachers assume that the circle is the perfect design for a student-centered
classroom, a "physical manifestation of democracy" (9). Brookfield reminds us
that whereas a circle may be democratic for those students who have learned
the culture of higher education, for those who are new to the academic enterprise, insecure, or self-conscious, the circle "can be a painful and humiliating
experience" (9). The second example I use involves the notion that teaching is
a vocation. This idea is often expressed in the "teaching philosophy" statements that I ask them to write (see next paragraph). Many GTAs wax eloquent
about their call to teach and the personal sacrifices that they are prepared to
make for their students. Brookfield warns however, that seeing teaching as a
vocation can work against them, that "[t]he concept of vocation serves the interests of those who want to run colleges efficiently and profitably while spending the least amount of money and employing the smallest number of staff that
they can get away with" (16). Needless to say, both these discussions result in
many GTAs feeling uncomfortable, rejecting these ideas, and attributing their
discomfort to my cynicism.

Within the contexts of reflection or "critical" reflection in Brookfield's case,
I ask my GTAs to construct two written documents that are overtly reflective
in nature. (The justification for the syllabus is reflective also, but in a different
way, I think.) I first ask them to write five teaching philosophy statements,
three spread through the semester during which they are enrolled in the curriculum design/pedagogy course, one at the end of the first semester they teach,
and one at the end of the spring (second) semester of classroom teaching.
Though I change the specific questions from year to year, for the first essay, they
always include the following:

- What does it mean to learn? What does it mean to learn in the discipline of English?
- Think of an experience in which you learned something quite easily. What made that learning easy for you?
- Think of an experience in which you had great difficulty learning something? How do you account for the difficulty and what did you have to do to accomplish the learning?
- Given your experiences and your beliefs about learning, what does it mean to teach well?

The GTAs seem to struggle with these questions and their answers. For the second essay, I continue to ask these questions and ask them to include discussions we've had in class about learning how to write into what they wrote previously. We are now getting into Yancey's notion of constructive reflection, in which writers begin to theorize themselves as writers by looking at several pieces of writing and constructing generalizations. Here, the GTAs begin to theorize themselves as teachers, by comparing what they imagine about learning and teaching with actual discussions, by looking both forward at what they must write and backward at what they have already written. The third essay asks them to continue to do the same. In the essays written after their experiences teaching in the composition class, I ask them to revisit their earlier statements, to reflect on what they wrote and then to reassess in the light of recent teaching experience. In the last two essays, the looking back includes reflecting on the actual classroom experience.

The fifth reflection combines both a constructive reflection and a reflection in presentation because I ask them to put together a teaching portfolio (See Peter Seldin for a detailed discussion of teaching portfolios and an example of one assembled by a graduate student.) Not only must they rethink the original statements made a year prior, but they must also explain how their materials and classroom practice enable or constrain their own teaching philosophies. With Brookfield in mind, I am asking them to challenge their assumptions about teaching and learning based on the training that they have accomplished over the past eighteen months.

Though I am pleased with the assignments I have designed, I believe more could be done to enhance the reflective practices of the GTAs. Yancey discusses something she calls "companion pieces" as part of reflection-in-action. In the companion pieces, students must comment on their own writing and well as on the comments they receive from the teacher. Asking undergraduate students to comment on their own writing as well as on the teachers' responses is a great idea; I often do it with my undergraduate writing students. This practice would be a solid addition to my or any GTA preparation program, giving prospective teachers opportunities to comment on their own ideas and to begin a dialogue with their teacher on teaching. Using teaching logs or learning journals and conducting what Brookfield calls "teacher learning audits" can all help to make new (and experienced) teachers step back from their practice (75).

CONCLUSION

For many WPAs, the best and most rewarding work we do is our work with prospective teachers. The best (and the least) we can do is prepare them for the professional (if not teaching) life that lies ahead. The training that I have outlined attempts to do so by giving them general tools, such as the framework of goals, curriculum, and pedagogy (which translates into general "where to," specific "what," and specific "how"), methods for understanding professional evaluation, and reflection. I also hope that I have taught them that few things are to be accepted uncritically, even the wonderful art of teaching. I also hope that they learn that teaching (and all work) is a social, interdependent experience, that although the practice is messy and unpredictable, it can be learned and that they have come a far piece into that learning.

ACKNOWLEDGMENTS

I would like to thank Laura Neff, a teaching intern, and Erin Pushman, a GTA, for their careful reading of this article and for their helpful comments.

WORKS CITED

Anson, Chris M. "Response Styles and Ways of Knowing." *Writing and Response: Theory, Practice and Response.* Ed. Chris M. Anson. Urbana, IL: NCTE, 1989. 332–66.

Baker, Mark A., and Joyce A. Kinkead. "Using Micro Teaching to Evaluate Teaching Assistants in a Writing Program." *Evaluating Teachers of Writing.* Ed. Christine A. Hult. Urbana, IL: NCTE, 1994. 108–19.

Berlin, James A. "Rhetoric and Ideology in the Writing Class." *College English* 50 (Sept. 1988): 477–94.

Brookfield, Stephen D. *Becoming a Critically Reflective Teacher.* San Francisco: Jossey-Bass, 1996.

Connors, Robert, and Cheryl Glenn. *The New St. Martin's Guide to Teaching Writing.* Boston: Bedford/St. Martin's, 1999.

Flower, Linda, et al. "Detection, Diagnosis, and the Strategies of Revision." *College Composition and Communication* 37.1 (1986): 16–55.

Fulkerson, Richard. *Teaching the Argument in Writing.* Urbana, IL: NCTE, 1996.

Gardner, Howard. *Frames of Mind: The Theory of Multiple Intelligences.* New York: Basic, 1983.

Kinneavy, James L. *A Theory of Discourse.* Englewood Cliffs, NJ: Prentice, 1971. Rpt. New York: Norton, 1980.

Moffett, James. *Active Voice: A Writing Program across the Curriculum.* Portsmouth, NH: Boynton/Cook, 1981.

Nilson, Linda B. *Teaching at Its Best.* Bolton, MA: Anker, 1998.

Seldin, Peter. *The Teaching Portfolio: A Practical Guide to Improved Performance and Promotion/Tenure Decisions.* 2nd ed. Bolton, MA: Anker, 1997.

Yancey, Kathleen Blake. *Reflection in the Writing Classroom.* Logan: Utah State UP, 1998.

26

GAT Training
in Collaborative Teaching
at the University of Arizona

Amanda Brobbel
Matt Hinojosa
Carol Nowotny-Young
Susan Penfield
D. R. Ransdell
Michael Robinson
Denise Scagliotta
Erec Toso
Tilly Warnock
Jocelyn D. White
University of Arizona

In their 1986 *WPA* article, "Creating the Profession: The GAT Training Program at the University of Arizona," Marvin Diogenes, Duane H. Roen, and C. Jan Swearingen contrast their view of training teaching assistants with "a traditional department's view that holds that graduate students are hired hands, duespayers on the lowest rung of the university ladder" (51). The authors propose instead to professionalize the teaching of composition by graduate assistants and associates in teaching (GATs) by welcoming them into the profession as "junior colleagues" (51). They advocate introducing GATs to "the strengths of the profession in the form of the best available scholarship, old and new" (51) and recommend that administrators "abandon a basic skill approach to training graduate students" and "empower graduate students by giving them access to rhetorical control in the classroom, a control born of a mastery of the elements of the teaching situation" (52).

We continue to follow these recommendations but with several revisions as more first-year GATs arrive with experience in teaching, writing, research; more enter with MA degrees in rhetoric; more graduate courses in all areas include theories of discourse, cultures, race, class, gender, and technologies; and as work in English departments changes across the country. One overall aim today is for GATs in English to understand teaching, and the teaching of writing particularly, as part of their graduate education, professional development, and future work.

English 591-1, Preceptorship, a four-credit required course, provides the initial and main site for training first-year GATs. This course includes weekly meetings on Thursdays from 3:30 p.m. to 5:30 p.m., a seven-day fall orientation, a two-day spring orientation, and attendance at the annual spring conference. The course is taught by eleven Teaching Advisors (TEADs), along with the faculty Course Director for English 101 in the fall, the Course Director for English 102 in the spring, and the Composition Director. Weekly Preceptorship includes typically a large group session followed by each TEAD meeting with a group of four to five GATs. (See "Preceptorship" on the Composition Program web page for the course syllabi: http://w3.arizona.edu/~comp.)

Each semester during a GAT's first year, a TEAD reviews a GAT's course materials, responds to questions and problems, visits two classes, reviews two sets of graded papers, collects a self-assessment, and writes an end-of-the-semester report. Support and supervision continue after the first-year, as each GAT has a TEAD who reviews course materials, responds to questions and problems, visits one class each semester, reviews one set of papers, and writes a semester report. (See the web page for forms to evaluate Preceptorship, Orientations, TEADs, and GATs.)

Three of the most important and variable influences on GAT training are the size of the UA Composition Program, variations in the teaching experience of first-year GATs, and research in rhetoric and composition. For example, during fall 2000, 44 first-year GATs and a total of 117 GATs taught composition. The program offered 264 sections of composition, 241 of these at the 100-level, for over 5,000 students. All first-year GATs teach English 101 in the fall and English 102 in the spring; after the first year they teach a range of composition courses from English 100 to advanced composition and business and technical writing. Most GATs teach a 2-2 load, but this year first-year GATs will teach a 2-1 load. There are some fellowships for GATs in their first year and for those working on their dissertations. Professional development opportunities also exist that expand GAT training and modify the 2-2 teaching load. GATs apply to teach in the Writing Center and general education courses, and to serve as editor of the *Student's Guide*, composition coordinator, computer coordinator, and intern, while teaching one course.

Because of the size of the program, we have faculty Course Directors who provide course goals, model syllabi and course materials, approved textbooks, standard policies, and processes for using alternative materials. In Preceptorship, we encourage GATs to develop their own courses within the program guidelines and with the assistance of their TEADs. (See the web page for course materials.)

Another significant influence on GAT training is that GATs are graduate students in the four graduate programs in English and the two interdisciplinary program connected to English: Creative Writing; English Language and Linguistics (ELL); Literature; Rhetoric, Composition, and the Teaching of English (RCTE); Comparative Literary and Cultural Studies (CCLS); and Second Language Acquisition and Teaching (SLAT). In fall 2000, twenty-one of the forty-four first-year GATs did not include teaching in their brief profiles, and most were new to graduate work, to Tucson, and to the University of Arizona. However, more GATs this fall than before were not first-year graduate students at UA. These continuing graduate students, therefore, had familiarity with the university and with graduate work, and some had assisted faculty in general education courses.

The 1986 article recommends that composition programs introduce GATs to "the best available scholarship, old and new." We do so now in a limited way, particularly during the first semester of Preceptorship when we focus explicitly on what and how to teach and only implicitly on why. We distribute articles, recommend readings, and offer workshops on specific issues, such as working with students with disabilities and using technology critically to teach writing. We also invite three national teacher/scholars in rhetoric and composition each spring to speak to and meet with GATs. Robert Connors, William Covino, and Shirley Brice Heath visited last spring; James Sosnoski, Patricia Harkin, Diane Freund, and Renato Rosaldo will present at the annual spring conference for GATs and other Arizona teachers in schools, community colleges, and universities. (See the web page for recommended readings, articles on electronic reserve, and information on Spring Conference 2001.) In addition, TEADs, Course Directors, and the Composition Director are active scholars in composition, rhetoric, and ESL.

Nevertheless, the development of experiential knowledge supersedes the teaching of theories in Preceptorship. We practice various theories, and we encourage GATs to teach from their strengths and incorporate knowledge from their graduate work into their composition classes. We consider it critical that GATs learn to assess theories and practices in order to use them for particular students and classes, but we do not fully teach GATs how to do this.

Also in keeping with the recommendations of the earlier authors, we teach GATs about rhetorical analysis, argument, research, and revision, all of which are informed by research in rhetoric and composition. But we now understand these actions, along with the following, as basic skills: close reading,

reading texts within broader contexts, and assessing authors' uses of persuasive strategies for particular purposes. In fact, we are currently trying to integrate more sentence-level instruction and editing into the curriculum. With
the support of TEADs and the program, GATs have primary responsibility of
their classes.

In the process of writing this article, Amanda Brobbel helped the authors
identify the current goal for first-year and experienced GAT training: to
teach "collaborative teaching." By "collaborative teaching" we mean that
GATs work with others on teaching, including their TEADs, other new and
experienced GATs, Course Directors, their Graduate Program Director, and
the Composition Director. Collaborative teaching promotes the kinds of interaction we foster in our writing classes; helps GATs understand their student writers within broader school, disciplinary, and work contexts; and
addresses work load issues to some extent; by making a large program and
university smaller, and by preparing them for future collaborative work as
members of programs, departments, and universities.

Because the TEAD/GAT small group interaction is the heart of GAT
training at UA, each of the following sections provides more specific information about how GATs learn to collaborate. Whereas we have created an extensive and expensive supervisory system, many individual elements of our
GAT training may be useful for programs of different sizes and structures.

Ten teachers coauthored this article to explain what we mean by "collaborative teaching," why we advocate it, and how it addresses tensions within a
large program in a large university. The authors include one small group of
GATs who worked together last year in Preceptorship and have continued to
collaborate during their second year of teaching: Amanda Brobbel in the Literature, Matt Hinojosa in RCTE, Denise Scagliotta in Creative Writing, and
Jocelyn White in Literature; five Teaching Advisors, Carol Nowotny-Young,
D. R. Ransdell, Michael Robinson, Erec Toso, and Susan Penfield; and Tilly
Warnock, currently Director of Composition.

TEACHING A CURRICULUM

Carol Nowotny-Young, TEAD: Teaching GATs involves negotiating the
usual institutional tensions—the university's expectations and requirements
versus the teachers' needs to design a syllabus that plays to their strengths
and expresses some of their own teaching philosophies. To balance these
needs, the TEAD must have a clear vision of the essential parts of the curriculum—that is, the required number of papers, the types of essays, the skills to
be learned—and must articulate these explicitly to the GATs. But teaching
advisors also help GATs find their own way into the curriculum. This second,
and most difficult, part involves "reading" the teacher and helping her discover her strengths and ideas about teaching. Many first-year GATs have

never taught before and don't know how to go about making a curriculum their own, or identify what "their own" curriculum might be like. Any GAT needs to know what he has to teach, and why he has to teach it. TEADs help GATs answer both questions and find the balance between institutional and teacher needs, and also respond if the GAT fails to realize the balance.

My experiences as both a graduate teaching assistant and a teaching advisor illustrate what this feat entails. When I first taught, as a graduate teaching assistant some twenty years ago, I learned a curriculum based on modes of development. Though I had certainly encountered mode-driven assignments during my twelve years in public schools and my four years as a college undergraduate, I had never taken a composition class. Thus, when my teaching advisors (we called them "supervisors" back then) mentioned the "process" and "definition" I would teach, I was bewildered. To make matters worse, the supervisors provided neither model syllabi nor sample assignment sheets, and their attitude during training discouraged shy new teachers such as myself from asking questions that might expose our ignorance. Apparently, the supervisors believed they shouldn't dictate a specific curriculum, that new teachers should "feel their own way in." However, the supervisors made clear that expectations existed by which they would evaluate us.

Somehow I muddled through that year. I don't think I taught very well, partly because I didn't feel comfortable creating a syllabus that expressed my own ideas about how the course should be taught. Instead, I patched together something I thought might satisfy my supervisor and the department, though it certainly satisfied neither my students nor me. But I came away with a clear idea of what not to do, should I ever be in a position to advise new teachers myself.

My chance came nine years later when the English department at the University of Arizona hired me as a teaching advisor. The curriculum had changed greatly from the one I learned as a graduate student, more process-oriented and student-friendly. We gave new teachers a detailed syllabus, complete down to the day-to-day activities and homework assignments. They could make small changes in reading assignments and daily activities, but they had to teach majority of the syllabus as written. My job as advisor was to make sure they understood and followed this syllabus.

As might be expected, the teaching assistants did not receive this rigidity well. That year, many were experienced teachers with their own ideas about how best to teach. In fact, one of the teaching assistants in my small group was a woman who had taught high school for many years and was returning to the university for a PhD in a midlife career change. She had a fully developed teaching philosophy and a repertoire of innovative methods, and she didn't think much of the syllabus we gave her. Her first act was to jettison all but the major writing requirements. I offered weak arguments about how all students in freshman composition needed to do exactly the same things at the same time. She countered that she could achieve the overall goals of the course just as well by her version of the curriculum and that she would teach better if allowed to work in her own way. In the end, we compromised: She would ensure that her students came out of the course with the same skills and knowledge as students in all the other English 101 classes; I would not interfere with her methods, provided they were reasonable and backed by solid pedagogy. It was a pretty good arrangement given that I was an insecure first-time TEAD and she was a determined rebel. But it worked out well. She eventually became one of the department's best teachers, and I kept my job.

Having experienced the two extremes—vagueness versus rigidity, too little curriculum definition versus too specific curriculum definition—I struggled during the next few years to find a happy medium (and learned that the right balance differs for every teacher-in-training). I learned to size up quickly the goals and main criteria of each new curriculum I taught. I learned to assess what I needed to make clear to all teachers and to identify who might need additional instruction and what kind. I also discovered that curriculum instruction came down to that original formula: What do teachers need to teach, and why do they need to teach it?

A few years ago, I agreed to chair a committee to review and revise the English 101 curriculum again. First we decided on the main goals of English 101. These included teaching critical thinking and reading, defining academic argument and how to construct one using both research and argumentative techniques, and, perhaps most important, showing how rhetorical situation determines the writer's choices. We then outlined a series of assignments to help achieve those goals. We decided to frame the course as an introduction to academic discourse, so the students would first choose an academic discipline they would be interested in exploring for the semester. This discipline could be one they had decided to major or minor in, but because many first-year students haven't yet selected a major, they could pick an area they wanted to explore. This discipline would provide a general focus for all of the writing assignments.

The first major assignment asks students to find an article written by someone in their chosen discipline and analyze how its rhetorical strategies work to persuade the intended audience and fulfill the author's purpose. The next unit focuses on creating an argument of the students' own and includes two writing assignments: an in-class essay in which they analyze a specific academic text for how it responds to the preceding discourse and contributes to the discussion and a documented argument addressing an issue of concern in the student's chosen discipline. The third unit offers students several options for taking a more personal view of themselves as writers and fledgling members of an academic discipline. They can (a) explore their work that semester and analyze its effect upon their future work, (b) describe their relationship to their discipline, narrating how they became interested in it and what they want to do in it (if anything) in the future, or (c) focus exclusively on them-selves as scholars and write a kind of literacy narrative. The final unit—the fi-nal exam—requires students to combine the skills they have developed in analysis, argumentation, and description/narration to develop an essay re-sponding to a work chosen by the department.

Individual teachers could choose their own approaches to these goals and tasks and develop their own sequences of reading and short activities, such as journals or research assignments, to supplement the major essays. In teaching this curriculum to new GATs, we needed to convey both the rigid skeleton and the areas of flexibility where the instructor could mold the flesh of his own course. I tried to accomplish this, in part, by designing the sample sylla-bus in week-by-week blocks, laying out the main requirements for each week but including options to help teachers think through how they might prepare their own syllabi. I also distributed the list of goals and outcomes that the cur-riculum committee identified for each unit. I intended these goals and out-comes to indicate to teachers how to think through the course without dictating what they should do. I also provided them with several model as-signments sheets, showing a variety of approaches to each assignment, which earlier teachers had developed. These methods met with limited success, mainly because the other important influences on curriculum develop-ment—such as conversations among teachers who had taught the course and teachers who were approaching it for the first time—could not yet take place. But here also the advising challenge arises. TEADs can show GATs what they must teach, but they can answer that "why" question—why something must be taught—only from an administrative perspective. Every time the curricu-lum is taught, a teacher must filter it through her own answers to that "why" question, based on her philosophy, ideologies, strengths, and experiences. Helping teachers find their own answers remains the most important aspect of teaching teachers to teach and the one with which the teaching advisor must work hardest.

CREATING ASSIGNMENTS

Jocelyn D. White, Literature: Working collaboratively is an excellent re-source for creating class assignments. Collaboration need not proscribe and of-fers a process that increases options by providing other perspectives on class-work and requirements. Collaboration is an aid that leaves room for indi-vidual teaching styles, personalities, and classrooms. Working together, GATs can produce more complete assignment sheets, use peers for feedback on stu-dent work and classroom activities, and tailor assignments for future courses.

When our group meets to create an assignment sheet, each of us comes to the meeting with different visions of the essay, often varying from rough ideas to a nearly completed assignment sheet. During the meeting, we discuss our different conceptions of the papers we want the students to complete and the problems we want to avoid. After this initial meeting, we have begun to turn our impressions of the essay into a concrete assignment sheet.

As each of us finishes parts of the assignment sheet, he or she e-mails them to other group members. Although we begin with the same idea (and usually choose similar requirements), we rarely create exactly the same product. Our electronic exchange of assignment sheets in varying stages of development allows us to choose parts of other group members' assignments (as easily as cutting and pasting from e-mail). This also provides a forum to continue discussions. From our shared ideas, each begins building, changing this or that to our own words, adapting requirements, or changing language to more closely match the language we use in our own classrooms. Even discussions on whether the outside source requirements are too stringent, or the page length appropriate, clarify each GAT's personal goals for the paper. A clear idea of the rationale behind my choices makes it easier to field the inevitable "Why?" questions from students and demonstrates to them that the assignment requirements are not random. When I clarify my goals for the assignment, I can more easily relay those goals to the class, and the quality of the papers increases.

The benefit of group collaboration in creating assignment sheets extends throughout the unit. Once we have the goal for the unit—the resulting essay—defined, each of us takes different steps to develop in students the necessary skills. A common background for the assignments provides other perspectives on the concepts necessary for the essay. When my class is struggling with a key idea, for instance, it helps to discover how other members of the group have explained the idea. Borrowing a handout or overhead from a group member may provide a clearer way of explaining a concept. Even without sharing such resources, simply talking over an issue and getting feedback from the group may uncover a different way of articulating.

In addition to using the group to explore options to address the writing task, group collaboration is a great asset when grading questions arise. As a TEAD group, we frequently norm a sample of essays from each class before each of us begins to grade. Thus we can discuss how the requirements of our essay assignment should actually appear in student writing. Though this exercise usually helps all new GATs, it has added benefits for a group teaching collaboratively. Because assignment sheets have similar requirements (and frequently deal with the same texts), the group becomes a resource for grading difficult papers. An objective reader acquainted with the ideas of the assignment helps to resolve grading dilemmas and creates a discussion of the paper's strengths and weaknesses.

Beyond its role as an idea generator, a resource for feedback, and a way to share a creative burden, collaboration serves as a tool that will make our future classes more effective. Because we plan to continue collaborating next semester, we can discuss how our different versions of the "same" class have worked: What assignments, activities, and resources were productive? Which didn't create the results we expected? We can plan the syllabus for next semester with confidence. Collaborative teaching certainly proves true the old adage—four heads are better than one.

GRADING RUBRICS AND DIFFICULTIES OF ASSESSMENT

Denise Scagliotta, Creative Writing: During my first week of GAT orientation, my mom thought it would be fun to mail me one of my old essays from my freshman year in college. I looked glowingly at the "A" at the top of the first page, but as I read on, I was disappointed to find myself reading a "C" paper. I then realized that I didn't really learn what an "A" paper was until my sophomore year when I got my first and only "C," along with extensive instructor commentary. I remember reading my teacher's suggestions and thinking to myself: "Oh, is that what you wanted? Why didn't you say so? I can do that." I was never exposed to peer reading or grading rubrics, so trial and error, for the most part, shaped my early college writing. After reading my old paper, I was immediately terrified that I would soon be responsible for grading fifty unsuspecting freshmen.

I felt much better when my TEAD introduced our small group to her use of rubrics to communicate grading standards to students. We all agreed that it would help to distribute rubrics to the class during revision and to include a copy with each graded paper, highlighting where the student's paper fell in areas of organization, content, expression, and mechanics. We used this method in the fall, but during the spring, we began to question the usefulness of rubrics in grading. After our new TEAD evaluated our first set of graded papers, she admitted that our rubrics lacked some clarity. Because of the complexity of evaluating written work, we had trouble getting students to understand how much weight each aspect of their papers carried. We didn't want them to see the grading scale as vague and subjective, but we also didn't want to make the rubric so "exact" that it would encourage them to count their comma splices. We wanted students to see how the rubric's general terms translated into the specific requirements of each assignment. Collaborating on assessment difficulties created an awareness of our own grading concerns and assumptions and helped us understand students' concerns and assumptions, an understanding essential to revising rubrics and finding common ground.

Wording the rubrics posed one of the biggest difficulties we encountered. We followed the general grading guidelines set up in Preceptorship, but because we each had a different approach, our rubrics reflected the vocabulary we used with our students. Some of us felt comfortable with the terms in the *Student's Guide* for English 101 and rhetorical analysis, and they carried that over into English 102. Others modified their approaches, but still managed to bridge the gap between the two courses. Although not all of us used the term *ethos* with our 102 classes, we all dealt in our rubrics with the presence of the writer's persona, voice, or authority. Whereas some members of our group described "A"-range topic sentences as "assertive," others stated that exceptional topic sentences "establish lines of reasoning." We respected that although we were evaluating the same features in our student work, we were most comfortable using the language that best fit our backgrounds and classroom agendas. Given the differences in terms between just the four of us, our difficulties communicating the terms successfully to fifty students made sense. All too often, characteristics of students' essays did not fall neatly into one category or another, and even if the terms "matched," it was still difficult to communicate how much weight each part of the rubric carried in the overall assessment.

In our meetings we discussed our grading methods and shared student responses to grades. After reviewing in our classrooms the standards of college writing, we were frustrated when a student turned in a "D" paper and insisted that it was an "A" paper, or when a student said, "I should get an 'A' on this paper because I worked really hard on it." We could not determine whether these responses were just wishful thinking or the students didn't fully understand the evaluation standards. When our group members brought up student comments such as these, it highlighted the difficulties students have with adapting to college writing. After all, we were adapting to these same standards. We found that grade distinctions were not always crystal clear.

Though we do not have all the answers, we agreed that rubrics give a student the big picture but are no substitute for margin and end comments. We thought that it might help students early in the semester if we devoted a class session to interpreting the grading rubric and allowed groups of students to work together evaluating sample essays. This exercise, along with peer reading, would familiarize students with the terminology of assessment, and it would help them understand the crucial distinction between general discussion and specific analysis. After collaborating as a small group of GATs, we had a fuller understanding of grading, and it seemed evident that a similar collaboration in the classroom would help student grasp the complexities of college writing.

OBJECTIVITY, SUBJECTIVITY, AND WORK LOAD TENSIONS: SCORING THE MIDTERM ESSAY EXAM HOLISTICALLY

Matt Hinojosa, RCTE: Having taught first-year composition for five years, I have participated in the ongoing conversation concerning the possible objectivity of grading student writing. Two sides are readily clear: Teachers cannot grade their own students' writing objectively, or they can grade objectively. Some contend that natural attachments form between teacher and student during the semester that might involve a particular student's struggle to overcome certain setbacks (both in class and out of class). These events in a student's progress may influence grades assigned, eliminating objectivity. Others suggest adhering to a grading rubric that spells out the criteria of the assignment. If a writer fails to meet the criteria, then a specific grade is assigned no matter what. The writing stands judged as it is. Aware of this grading tension, I will share some of my experiences with my GAT small group as we first taught English 101.

GAT work load pressures add to grading difficulties. During the first year, GATs normally take two seminars, teach two courses, and participate in Preceptorship and Colloquium. These requirements create pressures that increased collaboration on major assignments and even day-to-day lesson plans can help alleviate. Our small group realized quickly that working together on major assignments significantly reduced our individual work load. We saw no reason not to collaborate on writing and scoring the midterm essay exam, a requirement for all English 101 courses. With our teaching advisor's guidance, we developed our rationale for assigning the same midterm and, at my suggestion, scoring it holistically.

Because we had assigned the same or similar out-of-class essays already, we thought it practical to do so for the midterm. This collaboration proved extremely useful for two reasons. First, we better handled any problems with assignments that might have arisen because we were all doing the same thing. Second, by channeling our energy into generating just one assignment sheet, we reduced our individual work load. We believed we could duplicate this process for our midterm. Because the midterm came during the assignment on writing arguments, we made the midterm a persuasive essay in which the students made and defended a claim with reasons and a refutation. We had been teaching students to do this for their second out-of-class essay anyway, so dovetailing the midterm in this way reduced our work and forced students to draw upon previous class work. It made sense to us, then, to score it holistically. With the exception of our TEAD (who was not giving an exam because she was not teaching English 101), only I had prior holistic scoring experience. A week before we scored the midterm, our TEAD suggested that the five of us meet to norm the essays. At that meeting, we discussed the concept of holistic scoring, read five or six common exams, had some healthy debate, but largely agreed on what holistic score to assign to each essay. We talked at length about the objectivity that holistically scored essays bring to composition classrooms. Not reading our own students' essays made us feel much freer in scoring the essay. Suddenly, we didn't have an image of a specific student in mind; we had to evaluate the essay itself. For us, reading other students' writing and accepting the other readers' score as legitimate was the closest thing possible to objectively grading student writing.

After all of our students had taken the midterm, the five of us met for an afternoon to score the exams. Because there were only five of us reading and scoring two hundred essays, we worked out a system of who could read in order to evenly distribute the work load. Each essay needed two readings and the score could not be more than one number off; otherwise a third reading had to be done. There were the inevitable third readings but far fewer than expected. The scoring session consumed an afternoon, but by the time we were finished, the midterm exams had been graded—objectively and efficiently.

Assigning the same midterm to two hundred students in eight sections promoted consistency; our students had to meet the same level of proficiency to pass the midterm. Several voiced concern about having their midterm scored by someone unfamiliar with their work in the course, but English 101 attempts to get students to write for a wide variety of audiences, not just their instructors. Our experiment with the midterm exam was just a small contribution to the "real-world" audience situations we try to prepare our students for. This certainly provides a nice spin on the objectivity tension.

Collaboration and scoring essays holistically is nothing new in the composition world. Instead, I suggest that new and experienced GATs combine these practices more often. If nothing else, it offers a delightful change of pace, especially when conducted at midsemester.

WEB SITES AS A TOOL FOR TEACHING COLLABORATION

Amanda Brobbel, Literature: As Jocelyn mentioned earlier, our group found it useful to exchange ideas over e-mail. However, technology influenced our collaboration in other ways. The impetus for much of our spring semester collaboration came from our fall semester TEAD, who encouraged us not only to continue the collaboration we had found so beneficial in the fall but also to utilize the Project for On-Line Instructional Support (or POLIS) provided to instructors by the University of Arizona (http://www.u.arizona.edu/ic/polis). This resource allowed the strengths of each group member to be realized and used more effectively, building on lessons learned during Preceptorship and from our fall TEAD.

Initially, we considered designing a common Web site that would reflect the theme of our course; however, no one in the group had sufficient expertise to tackle the project. Because we all intended to use readings outside of the required anthology, *Writing as Revision,* our first-semester TEAD encouraged us to create a POLIS site for our students to connect to Electronic (or online) Reserves. Though their visual appeal may be low, POLIS pages contain full operating instructions and require no prior HTML code or specialized computer knowledge. These pages also allow instructors to instantly upload assignment sheets, messages, links to other Web sites, bibliographies, and journal or daily writing assignments. POLIS allowed each of us to create individual course homesites on which we could personalize content, particularly information pertaining only to our individual sections. Certainly, we found this convenient for students as well. Through this medium, they could access lost assignment sheets or journal activities missed or incorrectly recorded. Students can also contribute to various features of the course homesite, such as a bibliography for the required research paper. More important for our purposes here, POLIS allowed us to share material easily.

As with any group, each of us possessed certain strengths in the preparation of course material: Some had an easier time with assignment sheets, some excelled at generating handouts to help students understand assignments, and some had a gift for coming up with interesting daily journal assignments. By using POLIS, we could share without scheduling additional meetings (always a potential source of tension for GATs). Although during our weekly small group meetings we were encouraged to discuss the major assignment sheets, syllabi, and daily schedules, usually we lacked time to work out smaller details such as help sheets for the students or journal assignments. Because POLIS allows an instructor to post an assignment almost instantly, on any given day, only one group member need come up with a daily journal assignment. In fact, any assignment posted on a course homesite can be cut and pasted easily by other members of the group for use on their own homesites, especially using POLIS. During particularly busy moments of the semester, this was quite handy. Of course, this collaboration could work only because we kept to nearly identical schedules and material in our classes, a compromise that could create tensions in other groups. However, it reduced our work load and allowed us to share teaching ideas even currently.

SOME COMMENTS ON COMMENTING

D. R. Ransdell, TEAD: One of the more difficult activities for first-time composition teachers is commenting on essays. I trust my own experience is familiar: In high school AP papers came back with a single letter grade and occasionally a "good." In my fiction-writing classes, I received comments, but they addressed characterization and style. I was so underprepared to teach composition that my supervisor looked at my first set of comments in horror. "Don't you know how to do this?" he asked. "I don't even know what comments are supposed to look like," I confessed. Now, I'm convinced that we can best train new GATs by attacking head on the issue of commenting.

What do teachers need to know when they approach their first stack of essays? As Tilly Warnock, Director of the Composition Program, reminds us: Keep asking yourself what you're trying to teach and why. Even though student papers might have a myriad of problems, instructors need to prioritize to create reasonable goals. I attend first to issues of a clear thesis and deliberate organization. If the paper lacks a thesis, my comments try to guide the student toward creating one. If the thesis and organization work, I target analysis. Only on strong papers do I consider issues such as style, tone, or narrative hooks.

Many instructors use marginal comments to explain how specific paragraphs are working and end comments to sum up an essay's effectiveness, but grading styles differ. One distinction to make is between directive and facilitative comments. "Directive comments" tell students what to do: State your thesis, extend your analysis, use a topic sentence. Though some instructors argue that directive comments are too controlling, in some cases writers profit from hearing specific, strategic advice. "Facilitative comments" rely on questions: What did you want to stress in this paragraph? How else could you state your point? They attempt to help the students think through their ideas and discover directions for their own writing. On well-designed drafts, such comments are appropriate. New instructors should at least be aware of their choices and discuss their commenting with their students.

Because an essay should communicate rather than merely fulfill an assignment, instructors should respond to essays as readers as well as graders. (It's also useful to have other students read as "readers".) I ask GATs to comment on what interests them in their students' essays; usually it's possible to do so. This can pose a challenge, but part of our job should be to get students interested in, rather than intimidated by, writing. I ask GATs to balance negative with positive comments.

New instructors should realize the hard work and time involved in evaluating student writing. Before assigning grades to individual papers, instructors may need to read a set of essays, separate them into general A–D groupings, and then reread the papers against one another to distinguish finer differences, such as between a "B+" and a "B–." Through comparison, instructors can ground themselves and arrive at grades they feel confident about. Norming sessions can give instructors a sense of how the writing they assigned works for other readers. In sessions with new GATs, I ask each to bring copies of a student paper, especially one that troubles or confuses them. We read the papers and comment on them; the ensuing discussions give insight as to different ways to evaluate and appreciate student work. Most often GATs need to hear: "This essay is awful, give it a low grade," or, "Yes, this is what an 'A' paper should look like." They need to develop confidence in their judgment as readers. Instructors should be supportive, but the emphasis should be on "support," as you support a soccer team—there has to be a game in progress before you start cheering. Instructors shouldn't spend more time on a student's essays than the student does.

Grammar and mechanics *do* need to be addressed. Though most English instructors realize that standard grammar doesn't equal intelligence, students need to know that the world often reads nonstandard grammar as a sign of ignorance. As such, students need to be held accountable for using Standard Written English, but teachers disagree on how best to do so. New instructors need to consider how they will approach the subject. I scrutinize the grammar and language use on *one* page of an essay. If it appears that the writer probably knew better, I circle the mistakes. If I believe the writer cannot self-correct mistakes (especially true with international students), I make corrections myself. I invite students to use my office hours to help them edit other pages of their essays and allow them to submit revisions.

When they return papers, instructors should understand that many student believe their writing deserves high grades and will be angry and offended when their instructors don't agree. Students don't always understand how writing works, especially theirs, and instructors must find a way to talk to students about their grades, help them perceive what their writing has actually accomplished, and deflect adverse reactions. Instructors also need to realize that students may not be interested in their comments. I've seen students skip over my carefully prepared remarks to glance at their grade before stuffing their work into their backpacks on their way out the door. Although it's hard not to take such action as a personal affront, it's a reminder that the benefit of teacher comments is questionable. Though I believe comments help students, I have no proof that students actually benefit from my efforts.

Grading is a complicated, time-consuming, frustrating, interesting, inexact process. For new teachers, grading is necessarily a difficult aspect of teaching. Luckily, it's fascinating to see what students do when asked to commit ideas to paper. And in time (lots of time), responding to those ideas becomes a little easier.

GAT TRAINING FOR ESL COMPOSITION

Susan D. Penfield, TEAD and Course Director for ESL Sections: Working with experienced rather than first-year GATs in ESL composition represents a very different situation from those previously described for two reasons. Only GATs with at least one year of composition teaching here teach in the ESL courses, and ESL GATs come from the two graduate programs that accept only students with previous teaching experience: the MA ELL Program and the doctoral SLAT Program. These GATs are, therefore, very experienced.

Though the ELL and SLAT GATs are well trained, teaching ESL composition represents a new challenge for most of them. The syllabi for ESL composition, English 106, 107, and 108, parallels those for native English speakers in English 100, 101, and 102. Though we make adjustments to accommodate ESL students, we retain the major assignments described by Carol Nowotny-Young earlier. GATs in ESL composition sections have to balance carefully the goals for a composition class and the needs of ESL students.

Time is the biggest challenge and the key difference between teaching ESL composition sections and parallel sections. Grading takes longer since more focus goes to sentence-level correction and organization. Conferences typically take longer since more time is needed for explanation. In-class activities take longer; students often require training in American academic culture just to understand the nature of some class work. The GATs in ESL sections work together to find ways of managing time.

Ongoing GAT training relies heavily on collaboration. As Jocelyn White points out in an earlier section, "Collaboration is an aid that leaves room for individual teaching styles, personalities, and classrooms." Experienced teachers usually have a well-developed teaching persona, a sense of class-room management, and each brings past experience to bear on ESL composition sections. They need the freedom to implement what they are already comfortable with. Collaboration provides a medium to share the wealth of knowledge these already well trained professionals bring.

As a TEAD and the Course Director for the ESL sequence, I try to or-chestrate as much collaboration as possible. For instance, each semester, we schedule three workshops on problems that concern the GATs, such as grading, cross-cultural conflict, or syllabus design. GATs share ideas and collaborate by defining criteria needed for guidelines in the targeted area. We encourage all GATs to visit each other's classes. This particu-larly helps those new to ESL composition but really benefits everyone. The infusion of new teachers always brings new ideas, and the experi-ences offered by the teachers is a strong source of ongoing training. We maintain a listserv for ESL composition teachers designed as a quick source of support and an avenue for online discussions. Currently, a com-mittee of ESL GATs is compiling a teacher's guide specifically for these sections. It will contain assignment sheets, grading rubrics, syllabi, and supporting activities and materials. The ESL GATs will comment on how to use these materials.

Our continuing ESL GAT training seeks to address students' particular needs through shared efforts of the Course Director, graduate programs, TEADs, and GATs.

COMPOSING RELATIONSHIP: MENTORING AS REVISING

Erec Toso, TEAD: While reviewing student comments on course evalua-tions for first-year composition classes, I noticed a pattern of response. Stu-dents seemed particularly sensitive to whether they felt visible or heard by the teacher. And the degree to which they felt this affected their trust and openness to learning a new story about writing, revising, and researching. These patterns seemed not to be related to the texts read, the critical ap-proaches taken, themes of the course, or even the perceived difficulty of grading, but centered on the relationship students felt they had with the in-structor. In short, students who felt an instructor didn't care about their writ-ing, failed to hear challenges they were having with the writing, or wasn't available for real dialogue about the work tended to receive low marks from the students for overall effectiveness.

This underscores for me that, in addition to the content we convey, the outcomes we hope to achieve, and the methods we use, teachers need to be aware of the relationship we create in the classroom and how those relationships influence the willingness of students to revise their narratives of composing and shaping discourse. In short, teachers need to acknowledge that students bring stories of writing with them to the university and that these stories need to be recognized and affirmed before they can effectively be revised or adapted to better fit the demands of university writing.

This dynamic of affirming and shaping stories about writing and learning poses particular and substantial problems for TEADs. It gets to the heart of questions about my role as mentor and about the relationships GATs cultivate in their teaching, about relationship as practice and as content. What kind of relationship generates and contributes to learning, and how do the requirements, course policies, and bureaucratic realities fit in? To be sure, I have to fulfill certain professional responsibilities such as visiting classes, reviewing graded papers, and troubleshooting difficult class situations, but the matrix of these responsibilities and whether or not GATs feel they learn from our time together has as much to do with the relationship we cultivate as with any theory we discuss or bureaucratic errand we undertake. If I concentrate too heavily on my expertise, I may convey content to my GATs but may or may not be perceived as an effective mentor. I have to ask myself what characteristics of our relationship do I need to emphasize to reach the person. To do this most effectively, I feel a need to construct an "I" that is simultaneously self-reflective and aware of the limitations of subjectivity and perspective. This creates room for various perspectives to engage in a dynamic dialogue in which old ideas can connect to new information and new ways of seeing.

As a mentor, I believe in a paradoxical stance: one that receives and listens to outside ideas and offers guidance based on knowledge and experience when appropriate. Rather than advancing and enforcing a particular theory, methodology, or persona, I strive to invite new teachers to articulate and construct their perspectives, even as they collide with my own. An advantage of this is that no particular approach gets reified as the best or most effective. Instead, each semester, the GATs and I shape their teaching to best fit the changing demands of the classroom. The process of mentoring pushes all of us to reflect on what we do and why. I hope that they then transfer a form of this relationship to the classroom. When they do, it often shows up in course evaluations. "Rick," for example, built his course around a theme, brought in music, visuals, layered and textured his classes with activities, and met with students regularly outside of class, often on his own time. He received such responses on his course evaluations as "He never listened to me." And "He forced us to accept his ideas." He also received low ratings for overall effectiveness. "Laura," on the other hand, built her course around a theme, ran creative classes with varied activities, conferenced with students, and presented writing as a skill she was working on but had not yet mastered. The comments for the course again and again mentioned her receptivity to student ideas while engaging those ideas with her own strong, but unevangelical perspective, her availability for discussion and helpful commentary, and her tendency to include students in defining assignments. Students gave her exceedingly high marks in overall effectiveness.

This population of two is in no way intended to be conclusive, nor do I offer student perceptions of effectiveness as the sole criterion for evaluating a teacher. But these kinds of comments reflect students' tendency to respond to the kinds of relationship an instructor establishes in the classroom. Laura participates in and directs the endeavor of learning to write, owns her perspective but recognizes its limits, and invites students to articulate and shape their own ideas, all within the limitations of the course. Rick does all the right things but fails to create a learning relationship. The same principles apply, I think, to my mentoring relationship with GATs. That relationship is much more collegial and has slightly different goals, but ultimately is a container for learning. It is as a learner that I most like working with GATs. It is as a beginner that I am most receptive to learning. In that, we are never done revising.

If we want to teach students proficiency in academic discourse, we might remember how we stumbled and postured and despaired while doing so. This reflective humility levels the field to make us colleagues who are making it up as we go along, aware that students are doing the same self-fashioning. When students and GATs can see this as part of their work, a learning relationship is forged where we all start to connect the familiar and the known to the strange and the unknown.

WORKS CITED

Diogenes, Marvin, Duane Roen, and C. Jan Swearingen. "Creating the Profession: The GAT Training Program at the University of Arizona." *Writing Program Administration: Journal of the Council of Writing Program Administrators* 10 (Fall/Winter 1986): 51–60.

27

This Site Under Construction: Negotiating Space for WPA Work in the Community College

Victoria Holmsten
San Juan College

The story of the work of the writing program administrator (WPA) in the community college, I suspect, is that it is a story still being written by those of us who work in that space. Like spiders that spin real webs and web designers who spin the virtual ones, community college WPAs work in the world of connectivity and creativity. Our webs are constructed in and for our own contexts. The sites of our work are multiple, complex, and ever-changing. I boldly look for generalizations about community college contexts here, even as I acknowledge it may not be entirely possible to do so.

Putting a metaphor (a Web site) on top of another metaphor (the spider web) is a shaky business, but in this case seems appropriate as I attempt to think through another shaky business—the work of a WPA in the community college. As I map out ideas, I see links moving out in several directions. First, community college English departments do not house writing programs so much as they are writing programs, so this has important implications for WPA work in such an institution. Second, WPAs in community colleges work with both administrators and colleagues who may not understand the work of the WPA and it becomes part of our job to communicate this work to them. A third link in my web is that the role of the WPA in the complicated structure of the community college is constantly changing and potentially very broad in scope. The fourth link I identify here is that to my colleagues in the larger disciplinary context who may not understand the role or work of the community college WPA. My final link connects to an attempt to define a daily routine that seems to defy definition.

The written record of the WPA in the community college appears to be virtually non-existent. We do not have a long-standing tradition of writing program administration or writing programs in which to place our work. It is probable that this kind of work has not existed much in the relatively short history of the community college in this country. The first public junior college in this country was Joliet (Illinois) Junior College, established in 1901 (Vaughan 28). In the first quarter of the twentieth century, public junior colleges were established around the country, and they grew rapidly with the end of World War II as returning Americans took advantage of the GI Bill (Vaughan 31). It was also at this time that the term *community college* came into popular use (Vaughan 28), probably no accident as the public junior colleges grew and began to more closely define their missions and connections to community. Compared to the tradition of the university, the community college is a new institution.

In this newer institution that still seems to be in the process of defining itself, it is no surprise that as WPAs we are working to define our positions. In spite of the lack of a written record, it is possible that this work has existed, but has taken on different names and forms in the contexts of different institutions. From the WPA-L listserv, I have some clues that people who do work similar to mine in other community colleges might be called English department chairs, assessment coordinators, assistant deans, writing administrators, lead instructors, and more. I venture out on a slim tendril of the web as I attempt to describe a generalizable pattern for this work.

I begin with my own story in hopes of finding some pattern in these particulars. I have been the "writing program coordinator" at San Juan College in Farmington, New Mexico, for the past year and a half. This is my title because when the Vice President for Instruction asked me what I wanted to be called, this was my answer. His reply to me was a question, "Do we have a writing program?" This was a first lesson in constructing my own role in the institution. There was apparently a perceived need for this position in the upper administration of the school, but no one knew what to call me or what exactly I would be doing. This also helped me identify my biggest challenge—constructing a more public identity for what we do in our writing program.

San Juan College is a fast-growing comprehensive community college in the northwestern corner of New Mexico. Our district is San Juan County, which covers 5,514 square miles and a population that includes one corner of the Navajo Nation, several towns that are mostly Anglo, the northeastern side of the county that is more traditionally Hispanic, and miles of open space. We offer associate of arts degrees for transfer students and associate of applied science degrees and certificates for vocational students who do not plan to do further college work. Our student head count is currently over six thousand, which makes us pushing the limits of the "small school" category. Our English department is housed in the Division of Humanities, Social Sciences, and Fine Arts. We have a division dean who is a full-time administrator. Our English full-time faculty now numbers eleven, and we have approximately twenty adjunct instructors in any given semester.

As writing program coordinator, I am on a half-time teaching load. This means I teach fifteen credit hours per academic year, instead of fifteen credit hours per semester, our normal faculty load. I do not have dedicated clerical support or assigned work-study students. By an accident of growth and a turf battle, I landed in a larger-than-usual office, so I am able to maintain English department files, textbooks, and any thing else we think we need to store. These material conditions may seem appalling to WPAs from long-standing programs in universities, but they have represented a major breakthrough in institutional recognition of workload for my community college. Many of my colleagues on the Two Year College Writing Internet listserv (TYCwriting@yahoogroups.com) are still teaching the full load of fifteen credit hours per semester while valiantly working at many of the duties I've taken on as half-time writing program coordinator, so I am not willing to complain about difficult working conditions.

If I am pressed to explain why this position of writing program coordinator came about at San Juan College, I would point to two major factors. My guess is that both are not uncommon to other institutions. First was probably an attempt to manage growth. Our larger academic division, already glued together with an odd mixture of disciplines (not unlike what I see in many community colleges), was growing out of control. Upper level administrators decided our division dean, who was a social scientist, could use some assistance with the increasing pressure for more sections of English composition courses. The administrators were mostly concerned that I cover the major duties of schedule building and recruitment and hiring of adjunct faculty.

The second factor bringing about the creation of the writing program coordinator position was an increasing professionalism in our English faculty. As we worked together at SJC to define our values and assessment criteria, we developed a stronger professional identity and increasing impatience for allowing administrators from outside English studies to run our program. As we hired new faculty, we were able to recruit professionals trained in composition. Many of us took stronger interest in our own professional development and involvement as we worked together to rethink our English curriculum. We began to develop a sense of identity as an academic program. In short, we seem to have reached a sort of professional critical mass that moved us forward.

From these particulars, I begin to frame a pattern for what WPA work in the community college may resemble. Like all webs, it is fragile and malleable, but I hope the frame is strong enough to support a conversation about WPA work in two-year schools.

Link 1: Community College English Departments Are Mostly about Composition.   Composition is what we do. Most of our courses are composition courses. In the community college, we are not marginalized members of a department that is primarily focused on teaching literature to English majors. When our vice president asked me if we had a writing program, my answer should have been that we *are* a writing program. Perhaps it is due to my training in rhetoric and composition, but I think this goes deeper than a disciplinary prejudice—because we are a composition program, we are about teaching.

Community college students force us to focus on how they learn and how we need to be teaching. Our students come from very diverse backgrounds. I believe community colleges students represent a greater range of ages, classes, cultures, and abilities than do students in most colleges or universities. My observation has been documented in studies of community colleges and their students during the last three decades, many of them conducted by the American Association of Community Colleges (AACC). Cohen and Brawer offer a summary of findings in *The American Community College:* "The community college certainly serves a broader sector of the population than does any other higher education institution" (50). Those of us who teach in community colleges find no surprises in any of these demographic studies.

In my college classrooms over the years I have had everything from seventeen- to seventy-year-olds, and everything from a National Merit Scholar finalist to people who struggle to understand English sentence structure. Community college is the land of opportunity—we are there to break down many of the barriers students might find in more traditional academic settings. These students demand and deserve strong teaching, and they inspire us to become better teachers. Frank Madden writes that, "For most of us at two-year colleges, our multi-faceted role is defined by the needs of our students and vision of ourselves as transformative educators" (727). Many of us in community college teaching are there because we see that we can make a difference for students in our teaching.

One major difference between community college writing programs and university programs seems to be in the placement of developmental writing programs, perhaps even the existence of developmental courses. In community colleges, developmental education is usually defined as an essential part of our mission to meet community needs. New Mexico has legislated that all developmental education is the responsibility of community colleges. This appears to be happening in other states as well, and I know this is a much larger debate on a national level. Meanwhile, this presence of developmental education is an important part of how we define ourselves as a writing program.

Our basic writing courses, for example, do not set students off into the margins of our college, but they are an essential part of who we are as a writing program. More than half of our students take at least one developmental course when they come to college, and many of these courses are taught by full-time faculty. Because we are primarily a writing program, we are able to recruit and hire composition professionals. Every new full-time faculty member takes part in our developmental writing program, and through it we, as a faculty, have developed ourselves into stronger teachers. We have made teaching the focus of our collaboration, scholarship, and research. I extrapolate to other institutions that we are not an isolated case.

Frank Madden writes about this increasing professionalism in two-year college English faculty; he observes that many two-year college faculty are border crossers who are breaking down the traditional barriers between university faculty and community college faculty. "The evolution of two-year college faculty themselves is the most important enabler of border crossings—an evolution profoundly influenced by the working conditions, institutional expectations, and self-images of the faculty at each school" (723). Madden sees this increasing dedication to teaching, scholarship, and professional involvement as the future of the community college English faculty.

Another important structural difference in community college writing programs is the composition of the composition faculty. We do not, as a general rule, have graduate students teaching our composition courses. In an ideal world, most of our sections are taught by full-time faculty who understand that composition is the biggest piece of their work. Our adjunct faculty members (and yes, like many institutions we are over-dependent on adjuncts and take advantage of their good natures) tend to be more experienced teachers than typical twenty-something graduate teaching assistants. I do not wish to demean youthful enthusiasm in beginning grad assistant teachers, but I do wish to point out that community college teachers, on the whole, tend to be more experienced than grad assistant teachers most freshmen will meet in the research universities. Along with others in my aging baby-boom generation, I've come to understand that experience can be a good thing in a classroom.

In community college English departments, we teach writing, with a strong emphasis on the quality of the teaching. This is who we are and what we do.

Link 2: Our Administrators and Our Colleagues May Not Understand Who We Are or What We Are Doing. I think our job as community college WPAs is not only about constructing identities for our writing programs, but also about communicating what we think that identity means for our institutions. As I reported earlier, even the academic vice president who saw the need for this WPA position, did not know what to call it or even what it would entail. Every so often during my first year as writing program co-ordinator, the vice president would stop me and ask, "Now what is it exactly that you are doing with all this release time?" I do not really believe he thought I was sitting in my office and eating bonbons, but that is what it felt like to me when he kept asking. My colleagues often have displayed similar confusion as to what I have been doing with "all this release time." An important part of this job has been to convince others in the institution that this WPA position is a real and important job.

Patricia Bizzell's plenary address at the 2000 WPA Summer Conference offers insight and comfort. Her "memoirs" of her work as a "WPA without a program" at Holy Cross seem to have some strong parallels to community college WPA work. Her WPA work at Holy Cross has been a process of constructing the program and working on explaining it to administration and faculty colleagues. Bizzell observes that "the best writing programs emerge organically from their particular institutional contexts" (5), and that because she works in a small school, most of the parameters of traditional university writing programs do not apply to her situation. "I think these alternative types of writing programs can be found most often at small schools" (1). I would be so bold as to add that community colleges also have "alternative" types of writing programs where WPAs must find the "unique approaches to problems that afflict every writing program" (Bizzell 1), with the added challenges of constructing and explaining the program.

More of the written record on the small-school WPA seems to have strong parallels to my experience and probably to that of many community college WPAs. Of course there are many differences between small four-year schools and community colleges, but there appear to be some interesting commonalities. Thomas Amorose writes that a small-school WPA develops her influence with administrators and colleagues from an ability to accept and work within local "givens" rather than try to wield a power and authority that might not be available in a small-school context (97). "Power is not the primary instrument of her political success, and exertion of power in the small-school setting may often be counter-productive, leading to the erosion of the WPA's effectiveness" (Amorose 89). Amorose goes on to observe influence, that "relies on opportunities for persuading or convincing," is the "WPA's most effective tool" (95). Certainly, I have found this to be true in my own experience.

The issue of power can not be avoided in examining any kind of institutional context. There is plenty of interesting theory that dissects issues of power and relationships, but the bottom line in WPA work is how it plays out on Monday morning with our colleagues. My colleagues were nervous about the power issue when the vice president woke up one morning and decided to create my job position. I believe that my colleagues perceived that I had been suddenly elevated to some position of authority over them and their work.

And of course I had not. Unlike WPAs in universities who must have authority and power over a cadre of graduate assistants who are usually teachers-in-training, I am working with a faculty of my peers. There have been some tense moments as our collaborative faculty group has felt threatened by what they perceived as an instant rise to power on my part. Much of my time has been spent trying to emphasize the "coordinator" word in my title, and maintain our relationships of collegiality and collaboration. As Amorose observes, it is all about influence.

I believe that for my administrators, power and authority did not have anything to do with the position—their concerns are that I accomplish a certain number of lower-level administrative tasks. My job has been to find some middle ground, and I believe Amorose's description of the importance of influence comes closest to what my WPA work has been—working inside the community of the institution and the department, accepting the local "givens," and relying on my ability to persuade or convince colleagues and administrators that we do have a writing program. I have learned not to get upset when I am asked to account for my time; I have learned that an important part of my job is describing how I have constructed that time and how it involves them as my colleagues and administrators.

Link 3: Our Roles in Our Institutions May Be Constantly Shifting. The community college is a complicated institution. I can not offer an all-encompassing definition of *community college* because each institution is defined by its own community and the population represented there. As our communities grow (or shrink) and change, so must we. We are accountable to our state commission on higher education like all institutions of higher education in our state, but unlike our state universities, we are even more accountable to the community who surrounds and supports us. It is because of this need for local accountability that we must be ready to respond quickly to changing community needs. This heightened sense of flexibility is infused in the college philosophy and mission—we must be ready to grow and change as needed.

This extends to my role as WPA in my institution, and forces me to think outside the discipline of English studies. Howard Tinberg says this extra-disciplinary perspective is "a hallmark of those of us who work in community colleges: our mission is so complicated that it seems to transcend the disciplinary borders that characterize research institutions" (948). I am regularly called upon to fulfill roles in my institution that give me an opportunity to practice this. I have served as self-study coordinator and editor when the college went through our reaccreditation process several years ago; I was an active member on the college's student learning outcomes assessment committee for three years; I have been elected to vice president of our faculty and staff College Association government; I sponsored a student International Club for four years; I taught courses in the non-credit community learning division; and I have played the violin in several music department concerts.

In short, my role at the college requires that I look beyond the boundaries of the English department or the writing program. It is my strong suspicion that this is true for my colleagues who work in community college WPA roles. The complications of our institutions require us to lead complicated, and constantly shifting lives, in order to respond to the needs of our communities and to construct our roles as WPAs in our local contexts.

Link 4: Our Colleagues in the Larger Disciplinary Context May Not Understand Who We Are or What We Are Doing.   Community colleges are far more than the stereotypical high schools with ashtrays. Frank Madden writes convincingly about the "changing two-year college professoriate and an evolution in the relationship between two-year college English faculty and the profession at large. We have prepared ourselves to be and are legitimate members of the academy" (722). We are professionals who have dedicated ourselves to the scholarship of teaching and the importance of the first two years of undergraduate education. Many of us have the experience of attending national conferences and getting the deadening "Oh ..." response from our university colleagues when they hear that we are community college teachers. As community college WPAs we also own the task of negotiating our space in the larger WPA conversation. No—they don't know who we are and what we are doing, so we have to tell them.

I am fond of reminding my colleagues from the state universities that we in the two-year schools are teaching an increasing number of their first year writing students. In our college district, we are now enrolling more than half of our local high school graduates who choose to go on to college. This is true across our state of New Mexico: "Enrollment trends in New Mexico have shifted dramatically from the four-year to the two-year sector. The community colleges housed the majority of the higher education headcount enrollments for the first time in 1994 at 50.5%.... In addition, community colleges garner about 70% of the state's local undergraduate enrollment" (Renz 306). This is also a national trend. As reported by Vaughan in AACC's *The Community College Story,* "More than 50 percent of all first time college students in the United States attend a community college, and more than 45 percent of all minority students enrolled in higher education in America attend a community college" (2). These numbers appear to be growing as more entering college students see community colleges as their way into higher education.

If for no other reason than their own interests, WPAs from the larger transfer institutions need to take our work in the community colleges seriously. My experience on the WPA listserv (WPA-L) tells me that WPAs from these universities and other four-year institutions are very receptive to hearing from those of us who teach in community colleges. I believe there is increasing respect for our work in community college teaching, but it is up to us to communicate who we are to the larger academic community.

I make no pretense here of speaking for all of us who are working to negotiate WPA positions in community colleges. I hope more of us will add our experiences and insights to the general conversation so that we might have a broader picture of WPA work and college students learning to write across this country.

Link 5: The Daily Routine—Hard to Explain but Always Busy. Do we understand who we are and what we are doing as community college WPAs? In the postmodern terminology, we occupy multiple, contradictory subject positions. This is both a challenge and an opportunity. Perhaps no one really understands what I am working to construct as a WPA role in my institution, but this allows me room to negotiate parameters for that role that I believe to be important. On bad days it seems impossible; on good days it is a creative and intellectual challenge.

People reading this will probably identify with this fact—when I go home at the end of the day, I am hard-pressed to explain exactly what I did, although I know I was busy every minute my office door was open. In the concept of the college administration, I am building the English schedule; managing enrollment in English courses; recruiting, hiring, and mentoring adjunct faculty; coordinating assessment activities for English courses; coordinating English course articulation with local high schools; sitting on committees to represent English faculty as deemed necessary, chiefly hiring committees for new full-time faculty; and working as assistant to the division dean.

My colleagues in the English department have a slightly different take on my responsibilities. They see me as coordinator for departmental needs and backup for the support work they need to carry on with their very full teaching schedules. To them, I am also a liaison to the dean and other administrators. My colleagues expect me to call necessary meetings, deal with any disagreements with other faculty members and students, and make sure they get the teaching schedules they have requested. My colleagues in the larger faculty of the college are coming to identify me with "writing," and so I spend time talking to them about issues they have with students in their other-disciplinary courses. These conversations range from complaints about students who can't "do grammar" to questions about how to help students with writing tasks.

Yes, I do all those things. I also have a few ideas of my own as I work to negotiate this WPA work in my institution. I believe it is my job to encourage the development of a vision for the college writing program and become active in the construction of a more public identity for that program. I am working, with my colleagues in the English department, to establish a writing center. I would like to begin a writing-across-the-curriculum summer institute for college faculty. I feel responsible for maintaining connections to our community, our transfer institutions, and the discipline. I also understand that it is my role as the first writing program coordinator in my institution to negotiate the space for this work, and for those who will follow me in this position.

This has been a strong learning curve for me, and will continue to be one. If pressed for job requirements for a community college WPA, I would begin with this list: ability to listen and be nice to people; ability to multitask; tolerance for handling necessary grunt work, like collating and stapling, when necessary; ability to listen; strong sense of humor; willingness to take on tasks in larger institutional context that may not seem remotely connected to the writing program; ability to listen; ability to collaborate and share power/authority/influence as required by situation; bearing patience and learning not to take it personally; ability to listen; flexibility in daily work schedules and in tolerance of shifting job requirements; ability to listen.

The story of WPA work in the community college is under construction, and perhaps always will be because of the nature of the institutions where we place this work. There are many of us out there who take this work seriously. I issue an invitation to my colleagues at four-year schools and universities to talk to your local community college WPA. The need to articulate has never been greater and will continue to grow as our two-year schools expand. You have much to offer us, and I hope you will find we have more to offer you than you might have suspected. Clearly, we need each other.

We in the community colleges are part of a broader WPA tradition in our discipline. We are also inventors of a new tendril of the larger web as we work to invent ourselves and our WPA roles in community colleges.

WORKS CITED

Amorose, Thomas. "WPA Work at the Small College or University: Re-Imagining Power and Making the Small School Visible." *Writing Program Administration* 23 (Spring 2000): 85–103.

Bizzell, Patricia. "The WPA without a Program, or, Memoirs of a Local 'Writing Expert.'" Plenary Address. WPA Summer Conference. Charlotte Omni Ballroom, Charlotte, NC. 15 July 2000.

Cohen, Arthur M. and Florence B. Brawer. *The American Community College.* 2nd ed. San Francisco: Jossey-Bass, 1989.

Madden, Frank. "Crossing Borders: The Two-Year College." *College English* 61 (July 1999): 721–30.

Renz, Frank. "New Mexico." *Fifty State Systems of Community Colleges: Mission, Governance, Funding and Accountability.* Ed. Terrence A. Tollefson, Rick L. Garrett, William G. Ingram, and Associates. Johnson City, TN: Overmountain, 1999. 299–309.

Tinberg, Howard. "We Do Theory, Too: Community Colleges and the New Century" (Review). *College English* 57 (Dec. 1995): 945–49.

Vaughan, George B. *The Community College Story: A Tale of American Innovation.* Washington, DC: American Association of Community Colleges, 1995.

28

Writing Across the Curriculum

Martha A. Townsend
University of Missouri

All writing program administrators (WPAs), whether they have direct responsibility for writing-across-the-curriculum (WAC) or not, need an understanding of this thirty-year-old, vital subfield of composition. WAC
historian David Russell calls it "the most widespread and sustained reform
movement in cross-curricular writing instruction" in U.S. higher education
(*Writing* 272). Defining WAC, though, is easier said than done. A primary
characteristic of WAC is its idiosyncrasy. As Chris Thaiss points out, "Consciously or not, WAC theorists and program leaders have encouraged almost
unlimited variety in terms of what counts as writing and how it is evaluated.... [T]his lack of close definition is largely responsible for the growth of
WAC programs.... [a]llowing, even encouraging, different parts of a faculty
to maintain divergent, often conflicting goals ..." ("Theory in WAC,").

Susan McLeod and Elaine Maimon, pioneers in the field with more than
forty years of WAC experience between them, offer two definitions:

> From the teacher's point of view, *WAC is a pedagogical reform movement that presents an
> alternative to the "delivery of information" model of teaching in higher education, to lecture
> classes and to multiple-choice, true/false testing. In place of this model, WAC presents two
> ways of using writing in the classroom and the curriculum: writing to learn and learning to
> write in the disciplines (this latter may also be thought of as "writing to communicate")* (579
> emphasis in original);

and

From the WAC director's point of view, *WAC is a programmatic entity made up of several elements, all of them intertwined: faculty development, curricular components, student support, assessment, and an administrative structure and budget* (580 emphasis in original)

As a concept, WAC shares numerous precepts with first-year composition. It views writing as both a process and a product. It explores the relationship between writing, thinking, and learning. It is one response to the so-called "literacy crisis." It is informed by theories from composition and English studies and rhetoric. Beyond these shared precepts, though, WAC is more likely to be influenced by other disciplines such as communication, education, linguistics, philosophy, and psychology. Many involved with WAC would say their goal is to create a "culture of writing" on their campus.

In response to composition studies' growing interest in writing in the academic and professional disciplines, a 1984 survey of 404 colleges and universities generated nearly a 50 percent response and found these three premises underlying WAC efforts:

1. Writing skills must be practiced and reinforced throughout the curriculum, otherwise they will atrophy, no matter how well they were taught in the beginning.

2. To write is to learn.... [W]e are really talking about a new way of teaching and learning, in which students listen less and learn more.

3. Since written discourse is central to a university education, the responsibility for the quality of student writing is university-wide. (Griffin, 402–13)

For a concise overview of WAC for educated lay audiences, see Townsend, "Writing Across."

HISTORY AND EVOLUTION

Russell's research shows that cross-curricular writing instruction has occurred throughout American higher education. WAC, the most recent and most successful of these, dates to the early 1970s when the first faculty workshops were held within a short time of one another at Beaver College in Pennsylvania, conducted by Elaine Maimon, and at Central College in Pella, Iowa, conducted by Barbara Walvoord. Almost simultaneously, the Language-Across-the-Curriculum (LAC) movement developed in the United Kingdom, though at the precollegiate level. Leaders of the two movements read the same theorists and shared interest in one another's work. Although WAC is largely a pedagogically centered initiative, it does not typically take the form of a formal, "stand-alone" course like first-year composition. In the vast majority of programs, WAC's precepts are integrated into "content" courses in the disciplines, with instruction being offered by faculty in the disciplines. (See Models of Administration, later, for more on this.)

Early WAC programs received attention and considerable support from private philanthropic organizations including The Bush Foundation, Exxon, The Ford Foundation, General Motors, Lilly, and Mellon, and from public agencies including the National Endowment for the Humanities and the Fund for Improvement of Post-Secondary Education. But by the mid- to late 1980s, most external funding dwindled as philanthropists channeled grants toward newer initiatives. They considered WAC as having become "established" and expected institutions to carry forward programs on their own.

Despite the struggle to transition from external to internal funding, the WAC movement has not only survived but grown. Evidence of growth comes from several indicators. The National Network of WAC Programs, a directory of programs and directors maintained by Chris Thaiss at George Mason University, has increased from its initial listing of some thirty programs in 1981 to about five hundred in 1991, and further, to some six hundred fifty in 2000. The Network convenes a Special Interest Group annually at the Conference on College Composition, with newly interested WAC leaders attending each year. The biennial National WAC Conference hosted initially in South Carolina in 1993, 1995, and 1997, has moved on to Cornell in 1999 and to Indiana University in 2001. Attendance and interest is such that the conference will become an annual event in 2002. *Language and Learning across the Disciplines*, a professional journal devoted to interdisciplinarity, situated discourse communities, and WAC programs edited by Sharon Quiroz and Michael Pemberton has been published since 1995. A listserv, WAC-L, originated in 199? by Gail Hawisher, still operates, and the WPA-L, started by David Schwalm carries much WAC-based discussion.

WAC is still acquiring status as a subdiscipline in composition and English studies. But that status will no doubt be aided by the publication of an increasing number of research studies, articles, and books. (See "Research and Assessment," later, for more on this.)

THEORY

Two works, one from the US and one from the UK, are most frequently associated with WAC's beginnings: James Britton et al.'s *The Development of Writing Abilities (11–18) (1975)* and Janet Emig's "Writing as a Mode of Learning," in *College Composition and Communication* (1977). Of course, the dates of publication belie work that preceded their appearance. From 1966 to 1971, Britton and his colleagues undertook a study of some two thousand transcripts from students in all subject areas at sixty-five different schools in the UK. The British Schools Council project analyzes students' writing from two perspectives—function and audience—and concludes that students are not being exposed to the full range of options open to them. Emig's *The Composing Process of Twelfth Graders* (1971) is cited in Britton's work showing "some interesting parallels to our own work" (7). Other theorists influencing Britton's work include Bruner, Luria, Moffett, Piaget, Polanyi, Vygotsky. WAC workshops and curricula in the U.S. continue to draw on the theories Britton and his colleagues developed, especially with regard to audience (e.g., writing to the teacher as examiner vs. writing in a teacher-learner dialogue) and to function (e.g., expressive, or writing to discover; transactional, or writing to communicate; and poetic, or writing for its own sake).

Emig's "Writing as a Mode of Learning" is based on her earlier work in cognition. In this essay, Emig argues that "[w]riting serves learning uniquely because writing as process-and-product possesses a cluster of attributes that correspond uniquely to certain powerful learning strategies" (122). She cites Britton's *Language and Learning* (1971) in support of her notion that writing, "unlike talking, restrains dependence upon the actual situation" and thus slows down the learner so that connections can be made (127). Among other theorists influencing Emig's work include those also cited by Britton: Bruner, Luria, Moffett, Piaget, Polanyi, Vygotsky. It seems clear that Emig and Britton were responding both to one another and to a similar set of thinkers at the same time. Although WAC developed in the U.S. primarily in higher education and LAC in the U.K. primarily at the pre-collegiate level, that the two movements emerged more or less simultaneously and embody many correspondences is not surprising.

More recently, Chris Thaiss's bibliographic essay "Writing-across-the-Curriculum Theory" explores WAC as a programmatic concept. He attributes the rapid growth of WAC to practitioners' preference for inclusiveness and avoidance of narrow prescription. In his even later "Theory in WAC: Where Have We Been? Where Are We Going?" Thaiss focuses on "'first principles' ... the theories beneath the theories." He carefully puts "writing," "across," and "the curriculum" in historical context, both programmatically and pedagogically. Noting that "[w]hat most safely can be said is that 'writing' in 'writing across the curriculum' programs has been many things, not all of them compatible," he counts as "one of the failings of theory in recent years" scholars' propensity to stress the distinctions rather than the connections in WAC's lexicon. "Overall, what we mean by 'writing' and by 'learning to write' and 'writing to learn' varies from school to school, teacher to teacher, class to class, assignment to assignment, even from thought to thought within a teacher's response to a group of papers or to a single paper."

MODELS OF ADMINISTRATION

The absence of a unified theory of WAC, and the tolerance for multiple interpretations, is mirrored in the range of ways programs are conceived and organized. Many WAC programs designate specified courses as "writing-intensive," or "writing-enhanced," or the like; but many do not. (See Townsend, "Writing Intensive," for a discussion of the pros and cons of such labeling.) Most WAC programs are situated outside English departments, as a means of conveying wider institutional responsibility for writing; but not all. (See McLeod and Maimon for a discussion of the pros and cons of locating WAC in English departments.) How—and how well—programs are funded and to whom they report are also subject to wide variance. A few, such as Cornell University's John S. Knight Institute for Writing in the Disciplines and the University of Minnesota's CISW, enjoy multimillion-dollar endowments. More, such as the University of Missouri's Campus Writing Program and Indiana University's University Writing Program, are incorporated into their institution's annual budgets on a line-item basis, allowing them to achieve institutional mandates without undue focus on fiscal restraints. A too-large number scrape by year to year, uncertain about long-term funding and institutional commitment.

One way to think about administering WAC is to look at the relative emphasis put on the various components that comprise most WAC programs. Although most WAC programs will include most of these components, where the bulk of programmatic effort and resources go can be said to determine what "kind" of WAC program exists. A *student-centered* WAC program might feature, for example, a writing center where students may go for tutoring in many different types of writing assignments; high-stakes and/or barrier testing which students must pass to move, say, from lower-division to upper-division studies; and new opportunities for writing, for example, internships, mock conferences, and prizes for writing competitions. A *curriculum-centered* WAC program might feature graduation requirements, as in, say, two or three required writing-intensive or writing-emphasized courses, with a specified number of pages of writing per course, or a particular focus on writing throughout all of an institution's general education program. A *faculty-centered* WAC program would place heavy emphasis on faculty development through frequent workshops, follow-up consultation, periodic brown-bags, and various other kinds of programmatic support for their efforts. In this last model, the focus would be on changing pedagogical practices first, with improving student writing as a secondary outcome, even though that focus may not necessarily be foregrounded publicly. One way, then, to analyze or evaluate a program is to itemize where time and resources are placed and to ensure that resources are channeled toward the outcomes the institution desires.

PEDAGOGY

Throughout its thirty-year history, WAC has primarily been classroom oriented. Russell notes, "The WAC movement, unlike most of its predecessors, attempts to reform pedagogy more than curriculum.... It asks for a fundamental commitment to a radically different way of teaching, a way that requires personal sacrifices, given the structure of American education, and offers personal rather than institutional rewards" (*Writing* 295). This classroom orientation: (a) may be *generally, broadly situated in composition programs*—in "linked" courses; in "writing for the sciences," "writing for the social sciences," and "writing for the humanities" courses; in special text-based composition courses using, say, the popular *Writing and Reading Across the Curriculum,* by Laurence Behrens and Leonard J. Rosen published by HarperCollins in multiple editions; (b) may be *more narrowly situated in separate programs* that house "writing-intensive" or "writing-emphasis" courses in the disciplines, or within campuswide curricular reform efforts, most notably general education; or (c) may be *discipline-specific* in which case WAC becomes WID or writing in the disciplines.

Generally, the different ways of teaching that manifest themselves in WAC classrooms include some combination of writing-to-learn; learning-to-write; multiple, short writing assignments; multiple drafts and revisions; peer review; clarified evaluation criteria; and collaborative learning. Typically, WAC classrooms feature active learning techniques. They construe students as makers and discovers of meaning along with their instructors who are seen as coaches or colearners rather than traditional centers of authority. There is usually less lecturing and more class discussion. By far, the best resource for WAC faculty and for WPAs conducting WAC workshops is John Bean's *Engaging Ideas: The Professor's Guide to Integrating Writing, Critical Thinking, and Active Learning in the Classroom.* The book integrates the WAC and critical thinking movements in practical terms with an appropriate amount of theoretical foundation. All of the ways of teaching mentioned previously, and more, are described in easy-to-access language. One excellent, time-saving resource in addition to Bean is "Five Minute Workshops: Putting Writing Advice in Context" by Martha Davis Patton.

WAC is remarkably adaptable, as Thaiss has noted. In fact, Barbara Walvoord argues that in order for the movement to survive, "WAC, I believe, must dive in or die" (70). So, places she suggests linkages may be found are in teaching and learning centers, ethical thinking, critical thinking, assessment, and oral communication. Additional places where WAC finds likely intersections are with teachers of information technology, collaborative learning, general education (e.g., capstone, cluster courses), major-field education, service learning, distance learning, and international studies. On my campus, WAC is in the process of forming an alliance with the Center for Dispute Resolution.

SAMPLE SUCCESSFUL PROGRAMS

One measure of WAC's current influence in US higher education is that WAC is the criterion by which *Time/The Princeton Review* selected its 2001 "Colleges of the Year." Initially, the magazine's advisory panel for this annual issue intended to use technology as its focus for selection, but panelists "kept returning, however, to a fundamental challenge that is as important now as it was a century ago: the communication of ideas, whether in the sciences, humanities, engineering or mathematics, in college or the work force" (63). The panelists identified "schools that emphasize the role that writing plays in the development of critical thinking and problem-solving skills ... in all disciplines" (63). More than one hundred different schools in four categories were considered. The field was narrowed based on "important components of a good program. Is writing embedded throughout the curriculum? Does it affect nearly every student? Are the faculty given enough support to teach these writing-intensive courses? Does the campus have a writing center to which students can go for help and advice? And finally, for liberal-arts colleges, are students required to produce a major project during their senior year?" (63).

Higher education has ample cause for skepticism over the popular press's affinity for sound-bite journalism. And WAC leaders might well debate *Time/The Princeton Review*'s selection of particular WAC programs or its use of an educational movement for marketing purposes. Nonetheless, the focus on WAC is noteworthy for its calling to the public's attention a significant educational success. The magazine does claim not to rank the colleges and universities selected, but "to recognize those schools that are improving the education of their students—and setting examples for others ... they all teach their students how to use writing as a way to learn and think" (63).

What programs did the magazine feature, and why? A professor from Sarah Lawrence, representing the liberal arts college category, notes that her students' writing allows her to "teach better" (65). If writing assignments show that students are confused or passionate, for example, she focuses on that and class discussions improve. Cornell, representing private research universities, is noted for its program's emphasis on clear thinking, downplay of mechanics, and faculty's freedom to design syllabi in the language of their disciplines (68). Longview Community College in Kansas City, representing the two-year college sector, is cited in part because its director believes "the foremost purpose of the program is to teach students to use writing as a 'vehicle to explore ideas'" (70). And Clemson, representing public universities, is cited because not only writing is integrated into the curriculum but also oral, visual, and electronic communication as well—CAC, communication-across-the-curriculum (73).

Other programs mentioned in the article include Washington State, Arizona State–West Campus, Temple, Mount Holyoke, Tidewater Community College, Oregon's Reed College, Ohio's College of Wooster, and the Universities of Missouri, New Hampshire, and Chicago.

To this list of successful WAC programs, I would add Southern Connecticut State University, for its thoughtful, deliberate revivification of a previously dormant WAC program; Eastern Connecticut State University, which counters faculty resistance to teaching writing-intensive courses by keeping class size small in comparison to non-writing-intensive classes; George Mason University, where WAC has been a mainstay for two decades; and the University of Hawaii at Manoa where five writing-intensive classes have been required for some time now. For detailed descriptions of some of these programs and others, see *Programs That Work: Models and Methods for Writing across the Curriculum* by Toby Fulwiler and Art Young.

Finally, as the *Time/The Princeton Review* editors commented when they began their research on WAC, "[We found] a mother lode! … With so many excellent writing programs to choose from, we found the selection of individual colleges daunting" (63). Likewise, the programs mentioned here represent a fraction of the possible choices. A number of others could be referenced, and the omission of any is not meant to suggest lack of quality.

RESEARCH AND ASSESSMENT

With so many institutions claiming, via their WAC programs, to improve students' writing, thinking, and learning, what evidence is there that WAC "works"? For the justifiably hard-to-convince administrator who is asked to fund a WAC program, what compelling information can be offered? Given that WAC programs are highly individualized, and therefore notoriously difficult to compare with one another, criteria for evaluating programs and standards for evaluating individual students are also difficult to come by. This section offers a variety of ways to approach this challenging topic and several places to look for inspiration. Moreover, the disproportionate length of this section, relative to other sections in this chapter, is an indication of its importance and lack of coverage in other venues.

One could cite *How Writing Shapes Thinking: A Study of Teaching and Learning* by Judith Langer and Arthur Applebee. Although they studied students in secondary school classrooms (science, social studies, English, home economics), their findings are worth noting. Twenty-three teachers and five hundred sixty-six students participated in the multiyear project. The authors lived as observers in eight classrooms; examined instructional planning, classroom activities, and curriculum coverage; selected case-study informants; took field notes and observation schedules; interviewed teachers and students; analyzed writing samples; used think-aloud self-report techniques along with traditional tests; and conducted several experimental studies. When all was said and done, they concluded that "there is clear evidence that activities involving writing (*any* of the many sorts of writing we studied) [emphasis theirs] lead to better learning than activities involving reading and studying only" (135). They describe how particular kinds of writing affect different kinds of learning and suggest how teachers can use various kinds of assignments to help students achieve specific types of cognitive growth.

One could cite *The Harvard Assessment Seminars, First Report,* and *Second Report* by Richard J. Light, Professor of Education and Public Policy. One- to three-hour interviews were conducted with five hundred seventy undergraduate students. The *First Report* corroborates a number of pedagogies commonly employed in WAC. "A major finding ... is that modest, relatively simple and low-tech innovations can improve students' learning and active participation in class.... One example is the 'one-minute paper,' a simple idea that has spread quickly from a handful of innovators to many faculty members who now use it in their courses" (6). Finding C, "Characteristics of highly respected courses" reads:

Students have remarkably clear and coherent ideas about what kinds of courses they appreciate and respect most. When asked for specifics, students of all sorts (strong and not so strong, women and men, whites and minorities, freshmen and seniors) list three crucial features:

1.   Immediate and detailed feedback on both written and oral work.

2.   High demands and standards placed upon them, but with plentiful opportunities to revise and improve their work before it receives a grade, thereby learning from their mistakes in the process.

3.   Frequent checkpoints such as quizzes, tests, brief papers, or oral exams. The key idea is that most students feel they learn best when they receive frequent evaluation, combined with the opportunity to revise their work and improve it over time. (8–9)

The *Second Report* goes even further to corroborate WAC pedagogies. Finding B, "Students value strong writing skills" reads:

Of all skills students say they want to strengthen, writing is mentioned three times more than any other. When asked how they in fact work on their writing, students who improve the most describe an intense process. They work with a professor, or with a writing teacher, or with a small study group of fellow students who meet regularly to critique one another's writing. The longer this work-related engagement lasts, the greater the improvement. (8–9)

In a detailed breakdown on the importance of writing, three hundred sixty-five undergraduates were asked about the courses they were taking: What is your total time commitment to each? What level of intellectual challenge does each pose? What is your level of personal engagement for each? And, how much writing is required for each?

The results are stunning. The relationship between the amount of writing for a course and students' level of engagement—whether engagement is measured by time spent on the course, or the intellectual challenge it presents, or students' self-reported level of interest in it—*is stronger than any relationship we found between student engagement and any other course characteristic* [emphasis in original]. It is stronger than the relations between student engagement and class size. It is far stronger than the relationship between level of engagement and *why* a student chooses a course (required versus elective; major field versus not in the major field). The simple correlation between the amount of writing required in a course and students' overall commitment to it tells a lot about the importance of writing. (25–26)

In another detailed breakdown, sixty graduating seniors were asked, "How—in what context—is writing instruction most helpful?" Their answers are nearly unanimous. "They believe they learn most *effectively when writing instruction is organized around a substantive discipline* [emphasis in original].... Students urge more writing instruction in a substantive context. Their ideal is to combine writing instruction with actual writing assignments in a particular discipline" (35).

One could also cite research conducted at UCLA's Higher Education Research Institute by director Alexander Astin. After studying the academic and cognitive development of more than 20,000 students at 200 institutions, Astin reports, "Some of the most fascinating results concern the partial correlations of self-reported growth measures with involvement measures" (243). Though he warns that interpretations must be cautious, they are nonetheless "highly suggestive":

> For example, the number of courses taken that emphasize the development of writing skills is positively associated with self-reported growth, not only in most of the academic or cognitive areas (general Overall Academic Development, critical thinking, writing, general knowledge, preparation for graduate school) but also in several affective areas: public speaking, leadership, and interpersonal skills. *This pattern certainly reinforces the idea that the current emphasis on "writing across the curriculum" is a positive force in undergraduate education today* [emphasis added]. A closely related involvement measure is "having class papers critiqued by instructors." This measure, which implies not only that students are being given writing assignments but also that they are receiving direct feedback from faculty, has positive partial correlations (beyond the effect of number of writing-skills courses taken) with most academic outcomes: general knowledge, knowledge of a field or discipline, analytical and problem-solving skills, writing skills, preparation for graduate or professional school, and Overall Academic Development. (243)

Although the work of Langer, Appleby, Light, and Astin offers excellent backing for WAC programming, few compositionists or WPAs are prepared to undertake such large-scale research. After relying on such sources to make the case for WAC, what assessment can be accomplished on the local level? WAC literature is appropriately cautious about relying on positivistic studies, and some specific examples are worth mentioning. Ed White notes that the nature of writing and writing programs seems ill suited for empirical inquiry, which requires relatively uncomplicated and clear phenomena. "Our primary job, in program evaluation as in many other aspects of our work," he says, "is to help others see the complexity and importance of writing, to distinguish between the simple and the not so simple, to be willing to accept the evidence of many kinds of serious inquiry into the nature of creative thought" (205–6). Among a list of seven reasons Toby Fulwiler gives that make WAC difficult to evaluate, the one that highlights the complexity of the task is:

> Successful WAC programs run deep into the center of the curriculum.... [They] are more comprehensive than the label alone suggests; they are really language, learning, and teaching programs, involving students and faculty from diverse disciplines. They take place over extended periods of time with sometimes subtle treatments, practice, and activities being the only noticeable changes.... This may mean that it is as difficult to 'prove' that WAC works as it is to 'prove' that students are liberally educated after four years of undergraduate instruction. (64)

David Russell notes that "Qualitative studies have predominated in recent years because the early attempts to perform quantitative experimental studies yielded confusing results" ("Where Do?").

Still, WAC research abounds, with the trend toward mixed methodological studies that are highly contextualized. Russell reports, "One of the most significant developments in writing research over the last fifteen years has been the large number of naturalistic studies of college-level writing in the disciplines, over 100, inspired by the WAC movement" ("Where Do?"). His useful review of a number of these studies is organized in reverse chronological order, starting with writing in professional workplaces, then writing in graduate education, intermediate courses for majors, and finally general or liberal education courses. Furthermore, he says:

> The most striking thing about the qualitative WAC/WID research literature is that it suggests over and over that when writing mediates further involvement with the activity—the social life—of the discipline, it is more successful, both for inviting students to go further intellectually and personally and for selection (helping them and other stakeholders make informed decisions about their future involvements). The literature suggests that for students to get the kind of involvement necessary to write some new genre successfully, they need four things: motivation ... identity ... tools ... [and] processes. ("Where Do?")

This body of research, Russell suggests, is that those designing writing experiences must consider not merely what we want students to *know*, but what we want them to be able to *do* with the material they are learning.

For a compendium of ways that long-time WAC practitioners have relied on, *Assessing Writing across the Curriculum: Diverse Approaches and Practices* (1997) edited by Kathleen Blake Yancey and Brian Huot is both helpful and broad. The editors offer five "grounding assumptions" about WAC program assessment: it focuses on the big picture; it is similar to research in that it typically relies on a question or set of guiding questions that motivate inquiry; it begins with an explicit understanding about the nature of writing; it relies on diverse methods; and it focuses on learning and teaching and on how the two interact so as to chart that interaction in order to understand how to enhance it (8–11). The theorists referenced most frequently throughout all of the studies in the book are Egon Guba and Yvonna Lincoln, pioneers in naturalistic research; cited most often is their *Fourth General Evaluation* (1989). Topics in the fourteen chapters include the role of faculty in WAC assessment, the use of portfolios in WAC assessment, the links between research and assessment, audiences for assessment, formal program reviews and self-studies, and documenting excellence in teaching and learning.

Also useful is *Thinking and Writing in College: A Naturalistic Study of Students in Four Disciplines* by Barbara Walvoord and Lucille McCarthy. Written in collaboration with four teachers whose classrooms and students they studied (in business, history, social science, biology), the book examines teaching methods and students' strategies and concludes with nine principles for "reshaping our teaching in response to what we learned about our students' thinking and writing" (238). Lincoln and Guba's work figures prominently here, too. The book also contains an excellent chapter on the research theory and methodology guiding the study.

The old assessment saw "multiple measures, over time" is worth repeating here as a reminder that virtually all WAC research, and especially program assessment, is multimodal and continuously ongoing. WAC WPAs should expect to play a significant role in contributing to this already substantial body of literature. A good place to begin is by reading *The Writing Program Administrator as Researcher* edited by Shirley Rose and Irwin Weiser. "As we become more professionalized as a group," they note, "we are also becoming more interested in defining the nature of our work and setting standards for its evaluation" (x). WAC WPAs, with their rich affiliations across the disciplines, have much to offer.

TIPS FOR WAC WPAs— ## AND THE PEOPLE THEY REPORT TO

Several good sources are available on starting new WAC programs. *Writing across the Curriculum: A Guide to Developing Programs* by Susan McLeod and Margot Soven is concise but comprehensive. Although *Developing Successful College Writing Programs* by Ed White isn't particular to WAC, it contains much that WAC WPAs will find useful. The following bits of advice may seem self-evident, but coming from experienced WAC developers as they do, they are shared with conviction that is earned via success and failure, trial and error, experimentation, testing, and perseverance:

- Go slowly, and don't fret the definitions—good WAC programs take years to develop; you'll work out the details as you go along.

- Secure both top-down and bottom-up support—it takes *both* adminis-trative *and* faculty cooperation to make WAC successful; one without the other will not be effective.
- Administrators need to be supportive not just philosophically, but fis-cally, too; no good WAC program has developed on the cheap.
- Faculty need to have policymaking power ("ownership") over the WAC program; teaching, learning, curriculum, and faculty development are their purview.
- Remember that WAC is highly individualized; every institution must work within its own milieu to craft a program that works for it.
- Tie WAC to your institution's mission statement; there isn't a college or university that doesn't promote good thinking and clear communication.
- Tie WAC to campus assessment; WAC's qualitative, multimodal mea-sures can help your institution establish its accountability.
- Be willing to change with times and circumstances; WAC's inclusive-ness and adaptability allow for adjustments as you learn what works.
- Pay attention to your campus's reward structure and work to affect it if necessary; WAC calls for radical changes for some faculty and they will rightly expect to have their efforts valued.
- Rely on testimony from successful alumnae about the value of writing and thinking in their careers; use their expertise to influence on-cam-pus constituencies.

WORKS CITED

Anson, Chris M., ed. *Writing Making Learning: Cross-Curricular Scenes for Reflection and Faculty Development*. Oxford UP, forthcoming.

Astin, Alexander W. *What Matters in College? Four Critical Years Revisited*. San Fran-cisco: Jossey-Bass, 1993.

John C. Bean. *Engaging Ideas: The Professor's Guide to Integrating Writing, Critical Thinking, and Active Learning in the Classroom*. San Francisco: Jossey-Bass, 1996.

Britton, James. *Language and Learning*. Baltimore: Penguin, 1971.

Britton, James, et al. *The Development of Writing Abilities (11–18)*. London: Macmillan Education, 1975.

Emig, Janet. *The Composing Process of Twelfth Graders*. NCTE Research Rpt. No. 13. Urbana, IL: NCTE, 1971.

—. "Writing as a Mode of Learning," *College Composition and Communication* 28 (May 1977): 122–28.

Fulwiler, Toby. "Evaluating Writing across the Curriculum Programs." *Strengthening Programs for Writing across the Curriculum*. Ed. Susan H. McLeod. San Francisco: Jossey-Bass, 1988. 61–75.

Fulwiler, Toby, and Art Young, eds. *Programs That Work: Models and Methods for Writ-ing across the Curriculum*. Portsmouth, NH: Boynton/Cook, 1990.

Griffin, C. W. "Programs for Writing across the Curriculum" 36.4 (Dec. 1985): 398–403.

Guba, Egon, and Yvonna Lincoln. *Fourth Generation Evaluation*. Newbury Park, CA: Sage, 1989.

Langer, Judith A., and Arthur N. Applebee. *How Writing Shapes Thinking: A Study of Teaching and Learning*. NCTE Research Rpt. No. 22. Urbana, IL: NCTE, 1987.

Light, Richard J. *The Harvard Assessment Seminars, First Report*. Cambridge, MA: Harvard University Graduate School of Education and Kennedy School of Government, 1990.

—. *The Harvard Assessment Seminars, Second Report*. Cambridge, MA: Harvard University Graduate School of Education and Kennedy School of Government, 1992.

McLeod, Susan, and Elaine Maimon, "Clearing the Air: WAC Myths and Realities." *College English*. 62 (May 2000): 573–83.

McLeod, Susan, and Margot Soven. *Writing across the Curriculum: A Guide to Developing Programs*. Newbury Park, CA: Sage, 1992.

Patton, Martha D. "Five-Minute Workshops: Putting Writing Advice in Context," *Best Practices in Composition*. Ed. Cindy Moore and Peggy O'Neil. Urbana, IL: NCTE, forthcoming.

Rose, Shirley K., and Irwin Weiser. *The Writing Program Administrator as Researcher*. Portsmouth, NH: Boynton/Cook, 1999.

Russell, David R. "Where Do the Naturalistic Studies of WAC/WID Point? A Research Review." *WAC for the New Millennium: Strategies of/for Continuing WAC Programs*. Ed. Susan McLeod, Eric Miraglia, Margot Soven, and Christopher Thaiss. Urbana, IL: NCTE, 2001. 259–298.

—. *Writing in the Academic Disciplines, 1870–1990: A Curricular History*. Carbondale: Southern Illinois UP, 1991.

Thaiss, Christopher, "Theory in WAC: Where Have We Been? Where Are We Going?" *WAC for the New Millennium: Strategies of/for Continuing WAC Programs*. Ed. Susan McLeod, Eric Miraglia, Margot Soven, and Christopher Thaiss. Urbana, IL: NCTE, 2001. 299–325.

—. "Writing-across-the-Curriculum Theory." *Theorizing Composition: A Critical Sourcebook of Theory and Scholarship*. Ed. Mary Lynch Kennedy. Westport, CT: Greenwood, 1998. 356–64.

Time/The Princeton Review. "But Can They Write?" 2001, 63–74.

Townsend, Martha A. "Writing across the Curriculum." *Encyclopedia of English Studies and Language Arts: A Project of the NCTE*. Ed. Alan C. Purves. New York: Scholastic, 1994. 1299–1302.

—. "Writing Intensive Courses and WAC." *WAC for the New Millennium: Strategies of/for Continuing WAC Programs*. Ed. Susan McLeod, Eric Miraglia, Margot Soven, and Christopher Thaiss. Urbana, IL: NCTE, 2001. 233–258.

Yancey, Kathleen Blake, and Brian Huot, eds. *Assessing Writing across the Curriculum: Diverse Approaches and Practices*. Greenwich, CT: Ablex, 1997.

Walvoord, Barbara E. "The Future of WAC." *College English* 58 (Jan. 1996): 58–79.

Walvoord, Barbara E., and Lucille P. McCarthy. *Thinking and Writing in College: A Naturalistic Study of Students in Four Disciplines*. Urbana IL: NCTE, 1990.

White, Edward M. *Developing Successful College Writing Programs*. San Francisco: Jossey-Bass, 1989.

29

More Than a Room of Our Own: Building an Independent Department of Writing

Barry M. Maid
Arizona State University East

Becoming a writing program administrator (WPA) is most often a faculty member's first administrative position. As a result, new WPAs often look at their first year on the job with many mixed emotions—including some trepidations. Then, discovering the program they are about to lead is being considered to be moved outside of the English Department can multiply the new WPA's anxiety level tremendously. In reality, standing outside of an English Department can be both an exhilarating or a frightening moment for a WPA. Whereas some might fear the lack of security which comes with being safely tucked inside an English Department (usually the largest academic unit on a campus), many others will feel the excitement of having more control over their program's destiny. As I have recently detailed the different manifestations of Writing Units outside of English Departments ("Working Outside of English Departments: Understanding and Negotiating Administrative Reporting Lines"), I would like to take this opportunity to present more of a "fantasy scenario." Because we already know some of the ways independent writing units can be structured, what I'd like to answer here is what might be the best way to organize a unit.

One of the first phrases fledgling administrators will hear, and one they need to pay close attention to, is "institutional context." This phrase covers a multiplicity of issues covering such wide-ranging topics as geographical location, demographics of the student body, history, and Carnegie status. Perhaps from the perspective of creating an independent writing unit, the most important institutional context is that of mission. A powerful argument for creating a new unit is that the writing program can better meet the needs of the institution's mission by standing outside of English.

Before moving on, I do want to make a cautionary note. Most of this discussion is primarily relevant to four-year institutions. However, I have recently been engaged in an ongoing conversation with a faculty member from a community college in a metropolitan area who is discussing with his administration the idea of moving the large writing program out of the humanities division into a separate writing division.

With that caveat I'd like to progress in the following way. First of all I plan to look at institutional issues which concern the creation of independent writing departments. Then, I'll discuss faculty issues covering teaching/curriculum issues, service, and scholarship—especially as it relates to WPAs. Of course all of this plays a role in helping to determine the all-important issue of promotion and tenure. Finally, I'll turn to the problem of budgets.

LOCATION, LOCATION, LOCATION

Though we have multiple options before us, I will state unequivocally that until the inherent structure of American academic institutions changes significantly, the ideal Independent Writing Unit will be a full-fledged department offering programs which lead to degrees. Academic departments located in colleges seem to be the most secure, though a department's security may depend on which college it is housed in. For example, a unit I helped to create, my former department, the Department of Rhetoric and Writing at the University of Arkansas at Little Rock, seems very secure. However, even secure programs can have problems. Although they were not full-fledged departments, the recent history of the English Composition Board at the University of Michigan and the Program in Composition and Communication at the University of Minnesota show us that. In fact, in *A History of Professional Writing Instruction in American Colleges*, Katherine Adams tells us that there were a number of independent writing programs and departments that were created at the beginning of the twentieth century. Almost all of them were subsumed by English Departments. The ones that have maintained their independence, interestingly enough, were those in colleges of engineering and agriculture. The Department of Rhetoric, now in the College of Agriculture, Food, and Environmental Sciences at the University of Minnesota, dates from 1909. The Department of Technical Communication in the College of Engineering at the University of Washington has a history taking it back to between the two world wars (Russell 122).

So, then, given a choice, where do we want our newly-minted writing department to reside? If your university has a College of Professional Studies, that may be your best new home. The reason for this is that programs in such a college are, by definition, applied in nature. They connect with industry and government. In fact, they tend to do what we do. Colleagues in other programs which may reside in a College of Professional Studies are more likely to understand the kind of work we do because their work is similar. Their publications are likely to be multiauthored. They do real public service like consulting and industry training. Their programs stress internships. Their programs look more like ours than do programs found in traditional Colleges of Liberal Arts. Having colleagues throughout the college who understand the nature of your work can be an incredible advantage when working on collegewide curriculum issues and college promotion and tenure committees. Oh, yes, it also doesn't seem to hurt that the salary scales of faculty in Colleges of Professional Studies also tend to be higher than the scales in Colleges of Liberal Arts.

If your university doesn't have a Professional College, there can be other interesting options. The Department of Writing and Rhetoric at the University of Central Arkansas is housed within the College of Fine Arts and Communication. For this particular program which features not only rhetoric and composition but creative writing as well, it's a very nice fit. The work of the rhetoric and composition faculty is understandable to other communications faculty whereas the creative work of the creative writing faculty is equivalent to the creative endeavors of the other fine arts faculty.

One last suggestion is to look for where the Department of Journalism is located at your institution (assuming it is a separate department and not represented by part of a faculty line in English). Journalism presents us with an interesting model. On one hand, we can see it (I think accurately) as a small subset of Writing Studies. It is after all, a highly specialized and contextualized form of applied writing. On the other hand, Journalism Departments are not viewed as anomalies. In fact, Journalism accredits its programs and mandates both class size and instructor load.

WHAT'S IN A NAME?

One of the problems we face is that most of the population—especially those outside the academy—expect us to be in an English Department. There's no good reason for that except they just know everything that has to do with language, reading, and writing, is called "English." (Although the study of language, reading and writing may not necessarily have to be called "English," Thomas P. Miller's *The Formation of College English* tells us how it came to be.) If we're given the choice to choose our own name, I think there are several factors to consider—some of which will be driven by the composition of the unit. In terms of academic capital, there are few words as powerful as *rhetoric*.

I'm a firm believer that if you can somehow use the word *rhetoric* in your unit title, it will help establish academic credibility. That's important. Be prepared for some debate from some colleagues across campus. The faculty of Speech Communication might feel they have a vested interest in Rhetoric. And they do. In fact, if they hadn't broken off from English themselves in 1914, we might still have them within our units (Parker 4). You might get opposition from English. Even though English, unlike Speech Communication, may have a weak argument in laying claim to the word *rhetoric*, they may attempt it anyway. However, at the same time, be prepared to explain what rhetoric means and why you use it to your external constituents. They are likely to be uncomfortable with the word and might see it as pejorative.

We've already seen some units emerge with the word *rhetoric* in their name: Rhetoric and Composition (University of Texas at Austin), Rhetoric and Writing (University of Arkansas at Little Rock), Rhetoric and Writing Studies (San Diego State University). Other programs simply use the word *writing*, such as the Department of Writing and Linguistics at Georgia Southern University. If the unit also has a program in technical communication (something which is becoming the norm), the question also arises as to whether that emphasis needs to be in the unit name. Do we want to use "Technical Writing"? "Technical Communication?" "Technical and Scientific Communication" (James Madison University)? The phrase I happen to prefer, but that no one else seems to like, is simply "Applied Writing." I happen to think that almost all kinds of writing, except what academics call Creative Writing, is subsumed under the rubric of "applied." Even academic writing is a kind of applied writing. The problem remains, however, how do we name a unit with a title that is truly descriptive of who we are and what we do and has the intended impact on all audiences. It is most likely an impossible task.

WHO DO WE INCLUDE OR EXCLUDE?

Maybe talking about naming the new unit was a bit premature. Perhaps we should have considered what faculty will be housed in the unit before we think of the name. Clearly, if you include certain words like *linguistics* in your unit name you are making a statement about what faculty will help to comprise the new unit. On the other hand, not including the word linguistics doesn't necessarily mean linguistics won't be taught or that linguists won't belong to the unit. Generic names may work for unit names, but there are very few generic faculty.

Who gets included in this new Writing Department poses some interesting and challenging questions. Should all the faculty be PhD's and tenure track? The fantasy answer is "of course." In the present American academy, tenure track PhD faculty have more status than non-tenure-track, non-PhD faculty. If the new writing department is going to compete on a level playing field with the rest of the university, it needs to be staffed like the rest of the university. That being said, this isn't going to happen. First of all, tenure track faculty are expensive. Second, I'm not sure there are enough of them to go around. There aren't many institutions that now have sufficient writing faculty to staff a department—especially a department that might be expected to have a reasonable number of majors, staff a first-year program, provide support for writing across the curriculum (WAC), English Ed/Writing Project, and so on. When you think about it, there aren't enough tenure line faculty on most campuses to simply staff the needed number of administrative posts writing programs seem to generate. Part of the reason for this is because when new or replacement lines become available in English Departments, writing is viewed as only one specialty among many. And since it has lower departmental status, it often gets slighted or ignored. However, once writing moves outside of English the competition for the new or replacement lines is more likely to take place with Deans who are more inclined to make decisions based on student demand rather than on filling an esoteric program niche.

In the ultimate fantasy then, all the faculty in the unit will hold appropriate terminal degrees and be tenured or tenure track. (Note I purposely used the phrase "terminal degree" not PhD's. Many well-established people in rhetoric and composition don't have PhD's. Some have EdD's, some DA's. If the unit is going to include creative writers then MFA's are the appropriate terminal degree. Likewise, a large writing unit might want a specialist in legal writing. In that instance, a JD might be the appropriate terminal degree.) The reality is that most units won't be completely comprised of tenure-track faculty. Does that mean that a writing department will be doomed to have tiers of faculty? I think the answer to that is "yes." I suspect this is not as horrible as many think—especially if the roles and rewards of the different tiers are clearly articulated and adhered to. Doing so is especially important at yearly evaluation and promotion and tenure time. That brings us to the issue of full-time non-tenure-track faculty. It's a thorny issue, and I've detailed how I handled its reality elsewhere ("Non-Tenure Track Instructors at UALR: Breaking Rules").

There are multiple reasons programs might use adjuncts. The typical assumption is that the institution can't possibly hire enough tenure track faculty to cover first-year composition (FYC). Just having a department of writing isn't going to change the reality. However, it's possible that the culture which grows within an independent writing department might just change the nature of who is an adjunct in FYC. This is not the place to argue for or against the whole issue of the quality of adjuncts or how institutions treat adjuncts, but, I do think it is appropriate to think about what qualities and credentials are necessary to teach FYC (the course most often taught by adjuncts). If a doctoral degree in rhetoric and composition is necessary to teach FYC, then almost every institution in the country is guilty of academic fraud in whom it places in the composition classroom. What we can say, I think, is that minimum requirements for teaching FYC be training in rhetoric and composition and continuing professional development. That means the many institutions who staff their FYC courses with teaching assistants (TAs) can breathe a bit easier, if and only if, those institutions demand their TAs not only engage in training prior to their teaching apprenticeship but also engage in continued professional development in the teaching of writing during their teaching experience. I think the same holds true for adjuncts. A wide variety of people with differing experiences, degrees, and expertise might be very appropriate to adjunct in FYC; however, they do need to have training and continued professional development opportunities.

An independent unit might also successfully hire adjuncts who are elsewhere employed in writing, editing, or similar positions to staff the unit's technical writing or workplace writing courses. Bringing their workplace expertise into the classroom adds an ethos to the program that students recognize and appreciate. It also helps tie the program to local industry. However, I'd still stress that even working professionals need professional development opportunities. Those opportunities can be as varied as attending local workshops on pedagogy or getting financial support to attend national conferences such as CCCC.

A MAJOR QUESTION

If an independent writing program is going to be a real academic department, it needs a major. Numbers of majors (and especially majors who receive degrees) are part of how administrators measure success in academic units. Without majors, a unit isn't even in the game. The exact nature of the major will vary considerably from institution to institution depending much on mission of the institution and the expertise of the faculty in the unit. The major which is offered in the writing department of Small Liberal Arts College needs to be different from the major offered by the writing department at Whatever Institute of Technology. I'd expect that Small Liberal Arts College would offer a program that emphasized rhetoric and expository writing. Courses might include history of rhetoric and creative non-fiction; however, I wouldn't be surprised to see options in creative writing or technical and professional writing. At Whatever Institute of Technology the focus is more likely to be on technical and professional writing; yet, I would still expect some courses in rhetoric with some electives in expository and creative writing. If we then look at a potential major at One Size Fits All State University, we're likely to see a major that has tracks (because one size never fits all). There might be a core curriculum including some rhetoric, and perhaps one course in nonfiction, one in technical writing, and the like. Students could then track in a technical/professional way, an expository way, or perhaps a pedagogical way appropriate for students interested in education.

I would also strongly recommend that writing departments offer a minor or concentration. Many other academic units are more than happy to recommend writing as a minor to go along with their major. It makes sense. Good communication skills are at a premium. When we get students who become content specialists in their major and then gain good communication skills by minoring in writing, we end up with students that become very desirable at hiring time. A minor in writing can, therefore, be an important add-on to other degrees. This connection through a minor also goes a long way in helping the writing department establish good working relationships across the campus. Such relationships not only help in establishing and maintaining a WAC program but also when faced with many other campus issues—including general education curriculum.

WHAT'S WRONG WITH SERVICE?

In many ways, service is the most misunderstand concept in the American academy. From the turn of the twentieth century, the idea of service became, along with teaching and research, one of the three prime responsibilities of the American academician. However, initially service meant real professional service, using one's professional expertise to help external constituencies: industry, agriculture, government. In fact, what we call that kind of service today is "consulting." What most faculty now term service is what I'd prefer to call *citizenship*. It means working within one's institution as a good citizen. Interestingly, even being a good citizen is often looked upon as low work. I've said many times that the American professoriate is a service profession in denial. All faculty really do is provide service. I think that's all right. Physicians, attorneys, investment counselors are all service professions and have no problem admitting so. Yet, most faculty feel they are "too good to engage in service." I not only think there is something sad about that, I feel it is inherently counterproductive. Because service, at all levels, is denigrated by faculty, the worst kind of teaching is, of course, the service course.

Once service courses are demonized, FYC wears a bull's-eye. No matter where it is placed, when the concept of service caries a stigma, FYC will be seen as a problem rather than an opportunity. Clearly the mere formation of an independent department of writing will not change an institution for the better, but I do think that certain actions taken by an independent writing department can significantly help to move institutions towards rethinking the idea of service. The reality is that on more and more campuses FYC is no longer the only "service" provided by writing faculty. It's only the largest and the most visible. Interestingly enough the other service functions of writing faculty tie in more closely with their colleagues' own professional interests and are, as a result, often looked upon more favorably by all concerned. We can see this emerge in growing numbers of required classes (not necessarily general education but within majors) for an advanced course in technical writing or professional writing. Indeed, we see these same requirements or strong suggestions made by graduate programs. We only have to look at the graduate seminar Michael Keene has taught for years at the University of Tennessee, which is a course for PhD candidates in other disciplines in how to write a dissertation. Though working with a different population, Keene's course is no less a service course than is FYC

If as members of our own degree granting unit, that is as true peers, not as a subset of some über-discipline we actively engage in service teaching for our colleagues' majors and graduate students—and admit to doing service—perhaps we can in some small way help to reestablish the credibility of service within our institutions. If not, the worst that can happen, if we are in our own degree granting department, is that FYC becomes something that all faculty do just as faculty in other general education areas do. Part of the stigma attached to FYC is that it has become something that is taught only by those too junior to avoid it or whose academic specialty requires it. Far too many faculty in English Departments think that specializing in rhetoric and composition means specializing in First Year students.

I'M A WPA, YOU'RE A WPA, WE'RE ALL WPAs

There was a time when being a WPA meant tending to a FYC program and nothing else. However, the last twenty years have seen a wide range of programs that writing faculty might direct. First of all, I think it needs to be clear the Chair of an Independent Writing Department is a WPA. Department Chairs clearly have a different set of peers, both on campus and across institutions, than do directors of FYC, but the disciplinary issues that are at the root of the best WPA work are the same for writing department chairs. Likewise, each unit will likely have a writing center director, perhaps a director of WAC, maybe a writing project/secondary ed director, and finally any program offering a degree will have another WPA who coordinates either the graduate and/or undergraduate curriculum. Oh, yes, let's not forget the director of FYC. At any one time, then, there may be as many as seven different faculty doing program related administrative work. This fact has both positive and negative effects on the unit. Negatively, what this means is that if each of these program administrators receive a one-half release for their administrative responsibilities (a reasonable average), then seven FTE (full-time equivalent) faculty automatically become 3.5 FTE faculty. This fact clearly has a significant impact on the unit's ability to deliver classes. However, the positive side to the fact that writing units are administratively intensive is that more faculty get the opportunity to do administrative work. When faculty do so, especially with the right kind of departmental support, they necessarily learn much more about how their institution works. They acquire an institutional knowledge that most faculty never attain. Indeed, it is institutional knowledge of this nature which makes more and more WPAs candidates for higher level administrative positions. Even when all of the faculty stay within the unit, it means almost the entire faculty is savvy to institutional ways. All of us who have sat on university wide committees understand just how important that is for almost all the faculty in one unit to have that ability.

Of course, not every faculty member needs to do or should do administrative work. Some faculty are happiest and most productive as teachers and scholars when they never do administrative work. Again, this is one of the advantages of an independent department. When there are three rhetoric/comp or tech comm specialists in an English Department of, say thirty, then all three are likely to spend their entire careers trading off being Director of First Year Composition, Writing Center Director, and WAC Director. (It may also mean that there is an "unofficial rule" that none of them can ever serve as Chair because then who would hold the third WPA position?) There is never any chance for respite from administrative work. Aside from the frustration and sometimes tenure and promotion problems such a situation might engender, it's just a bad model for faculty development. All faculty need the opportunity to have different options in their careers. Sometimes those options might entail holding a variety of administrative positions; sometimes the options might mean serving as a faculty member—teaching and exploring new areas.

Only in English studies is it assumed that those who study specific academic specialties, rhetoric and composition or technical communication, are de facto administrators. Though not everyone in a writing department needs to serve some time doing administrative work, the fact that a good number of the faculty will do administrative work during their career helps the entire faculty to understand the nature of program-based administrative work. Work of this nature, once understood, can be valued and appropriately considered within the unit in matters of yearly evaluation and promotion and tenure. It is highly unlikely that WPAs in Writing Departments, who through their program development, their presentations at CCCC and WPA, their articles in journals like WPA have obtained national recognition and respect from their peers, will be doomed to permanent Associate Professor status because they fail to ever write a single-authored monograph. It is perhaps the single-most compelling reason for having a department of our own. Once in a Writing Department, we are evaluated by peers who understand our work because they do similar work. We are seen as a norm—not an anomaly. In a writing department, documents like Christine Hult's, "The Scholarship of Administration" or the WPA's "Evaluating the Intellectual Work of Writing Program Administrators," will not have to be appended to promotion and tenure applications because they are already an acknowledged part of the disciplinary knowledge. To put it bluntly, faculty in departments of writing write promotion and tenure guidelines that are based on the kinds of teaching, scholarship, service, and program-based administration that writing faculty—not English faculty—really do. The Writing Program at Syracuse University and the Department of Rhetoric and Writing at the University of Arkansas at Little Rock are just two units that have already produced such documents.

FINALLY, IT'S ABOUT MONEY ...

For those countless directors of FYC, writing center directors, and other program directors who have had to beg Department Chairs, Deans, and Provosts for pennies to hire more teachers, more tutors, make more copies for class, or the like, the thought of having a department with its own budget seems too good to be true. Even if the Chair still needs to be approached, surely the Chair of the Department of Writing will understood our needs. I suspect such a Chair will understand the needs. I also suspect that Chair will not have the kinds of funds to support the unit as it needs to be supported. That seems to be a truism of academic life. Even cheap programs—and writing programs are cheap programs—are expensive. If an academic unit like a Writing Department, which is necessarily going to have legitimate fiscal demands from multiple programs is going to survive, it is going to have to significantly change the way it thinks about getting funding. Yes, the traditional proposal to the dean and provost needs to be continued; however, that mode of increasing funding needs to begin to be viewed as a path of last resort. Departments of Writing simply must look for alternative ways of finding funding. Fortunately, I think what we do in Departments of Writing situates us quite nicely once we acknowledge we need to be aggressive in looking for funding and understand that we must operate on a long-term "investment model" rather than the short-term "quick-kill model."

First of all, I'd recommend that we look at each of our programs and determine who their constituency is. I'd then look at the faculty and determine their unique expertise—understanding that not everyone is expert in everything. I'd then decide which programs might be capable of finding increased funding within existing institutional structures and which programs need to start thinking about looking for external funds. Again, it's important to note that all institutions have local constraints that make them all unique. It's imperative to understand and work within those local constraints. However, I will offer the following suggestions.

Programs that are clearly student centered, such as writing centers, are well-positioned for asking for internal funding through direct student fees. I am well aware of all of the problems inherent in increasing student fees. It's, frankly, an ugly way to finance anything. And with Boards trying to hold down tuition increases, it's become a "silent tuition increase." Still, it is a viable and a relatively inexpensive (to students) way to considerably increase program revenues. One of the best examples of how this can be implemented is at the University of Texas at Austin where the Undergraduate Writing Center (housed in the independent Division of Rhetoric and Composition) brings in a significant amount of money every year when the modest fee is multiplied by their huge undergraduate population.

WAC programs need to acknowledge that what they do is faculty development. Once that occurs, they become eligible for a variety of internal and external faculty development funding opportunities. In fact, good WAC work can serve as a model for all kinds of faculty development work across a campus. As a result, it's possible for WAC programs to partner with other campus-based faculty development programs.

Finally, there is the possibility of external funding. It's both seductive and dangerous, but, I think, might just yield the most productive results. When most humanities faculty think of external funding, they most often think of grants. The fact is that the number of grants available for writing programs is relatively small. However, it is possible and sometimes quite productive to partner with colleagues from other disciplines. The important thing to remember about grants is that you can't expect to sustain a program on a grant. A Writing Department is much more likely to receive money for something innovative—for start-up. That means that even if you get that start-up money, you're going to have to come up with a means for sustaining the program. Another reality to face is don't expect grants to take the place of day-to-day funding needs. A grant might fund a new computer for a faculty member working on the grant, but don't expect a grant to buy computers for all the faculty or to build a new computer classroom.

Beyond grants, there is development. Everyone is now looking for a rich person or organization to donate money to sustain their program. There are, again, several realities to keep in mind. First, philanthropic organizations don't just give huge amounts of money to someone just because they ask for it—not even if they have a tremendous need. People and organizations donate money when they have long-term, well-established relationships with academic units. Departments that develop relationships with local industries, relationships which are mutual and not one-sided, are the ones most likely to benefit, in the long term, from development dollars. Local industries who have regularly used your students as interns and have hired your graduates may become the best candidates.

I would also suggest that units that have a strong technical-communication element in their faculty think about creating a faculty-consulting consortium. A simple model for such a consortium would be that clients would contract with the consortium for professional expertise which might be anything from technical editing, to training workshops, to a variety of other services. The client would then pay the consortium (a unit of the university).

The consortium would keep a percentage of the fee, perhaps 15%, and the faculty member would then receive the rest. Although this would cost the individual faculty members a small percentage of their usual consulting fee, I'd suggest that a consortium approach is more likely to generate more work than will an individual.

Finally, it may make sense for all of these external programs to be coordinated by one more administrative position. This final position would, ideally, be a senior faculty member who has experience working with external constituencies. I would envision this person not only helping to develop and continue relationships with local businesses but also working with the director of the writing project in relationships with public schools and state departments of education, working with the director of FYC on service-learning opportunities, and maybe even helping to steer faculty members towards appropriate grant opportunities. I'd also expect this person to be the department's contact with its alumni organization.

THE FINAL REALITY

I'm aware there will probably be no institution that will ever follow my plan. Every institution is guided by its own local context. An institution's mission, culture, budgetary realities, as well as other factors will all come into play as an independent writing department is formed and develops. I think the most important thing to remember when faced with the challenge of forming a new department is that past experiences, especially those formed in English departments based on English department culture, are not the only models in the academy. Those who are forming new units need to look not only to other independent writing departments but also to other departments at their own institution, perhaps in other colleges, whose mission is more akin to their own. While never surrendering the value of scholarship, writing departments are more likely to also truly value teaching and real service. New units must commit to the importance of teaching and service by codifying it in their evaluation and promotion and tenure documents. The roles and rewards of faculty in a Department of Writing must emphasize the commitment to teaching. To do so will align most Departments of Writing more closely with their university's mission. To do even some of this will create an academic home for us that is very different from the one most of us experienced in graduate school and very different from the home many of us knew if we started our professional careers in English Departments.

CODA

In most areas of study, it's relatively easy to present an established canon of texts. This is not the case with Independent Writing Programs. Except for some work that is presently in the publication process, most of the information needs to be gleaned tangentially. Any good historical account of rhetoric, writing, or composition programs in the American academy is a good start. I've already mentioned the books by Kate Adams and Tom Miller. I've cited David Russell's *Writing in the Academic Disciplines, 1870–1990*, James Berlin's *Rhetoric and Reality*, and John Brereton's *The Origins of Composition Studies in the American College, 1875–1925* also provide interesting information.

In terms of understanding the nature of faculty roles and rewards and how those fit into writing programs and departments, Ernest Boyer's *Scholarship Reconsidered* and Glassick, Huber, and Maeroff's *Scholarship Assessed* are necessary starting places. It then becomes possible to focus specifically on writing faculty and look at Chris Hult's, "The Scholarship of Administration" as well as the WPA's "Evaluating the Intellectual Work of Writing Program Administrators."

As far as work that only deals with issues concerning independent writing units, I have already referred to my piece that appears in the *Allyn and Bacon Sourcebook for Writing Program Administrators*. Probably what looks like it will be the most important work in the area to date is the collection, *A Field of Dreams*, being edited by Peggy O'Neill, Angela Crow, and Larry Burton. It will include not only chapters about independent programs but also comments by leading composition scholars about the consequences of independence.

WORKS CITED

Adams, Katherine H. *A History of Professional Writing Instruction in American Colleges: Years of Acceptance, Growth, and Doubt*. Dallas: Southern Methodist UP, 1993.

Berlin, James A. *Rhetoric and Reality: Writing Instruction in American Colleges, 1900–1985*. Carbondale: Southern Illinois UP, 1987.

Boyer, Ernest. *Scholarship Reconsidered: Priorities of the Professoriate*. Princeton: Carnegie Foundation for the Advancement of Teaching, 1990.

Brereton, John C., ed. *The Origins of Composition Studies in the American College, 1875–1925: A Documentary History*. Pittsburgh: U. of Pittsburgh P, 1995.

Glassick, Charles E., Mary Taylor Huber, and Gene I. Maeroff. *Scholarship Assessed: Evaluation of the Professoriate*. San Francisco: Jossey-Bass, 1997.

Hult, Christine. "The Scholarship of Administration." *Resituating Writing: Constructing and Administering Writing Programs*. Ed. Joseph Janangelo and Kristine Hansen. Portsmouth, NH: Boynton/Cook, 1995. 119–31.

Maid, Barry M. "Non-Tenure Track Instructors at UALR: Breaking Rules." *Moving a Mountain: Transforming the Role of Contingent Faculty in Composition Studies and Higher Education*. Ed. Eileen E. Schell and Patricia Lambert Stock. Urbana, IL: NCTE, 2000, 76–90.

—. "Working Outside of English Departments: Understanding and Negotiating Administrative Reporting Lines." *The Allyn and Bacon Sourcebook for Writing Program Administrators*. Ed. Irene Ward and William Carpenter. Needham Heights, MA: Allyn and Bacon, forthcoming. 34–46.

Miller, Thomas P. *The Formation of College English: Rhetoric and Belles Lettres in the British Cultural Provinces.* Pittsburgh: U. of Pittsburgh P, 1997.

O'Neill, Peggy, Angela Crow, and Larry Burton. *A Field of Dreams: Independent Writing Programs and the Future of Composition Studies.* Logan, UT: Utah State UP, forthcoming.

Parker, William Riley. "Where Do English Departments Come From?" *College English* 28 (Feb. 1967): 339–51. Rpt. in *The Writing Teacher's Sourcebook.* Ed. Gary Tate and Edward P. J. Corbett. 2nd ed. New York: Oxford UP, 1988. 3–15.

Russell, David R. *Writing in the Academic Disciplines, 1870–1990: A Curricular History.* Carbondale: Southern Illinois UP, 1991.

WPA Executive Committee. "Evaluating the Intellectual Work of Writing Program Administrators: A Draft." *WPA: Writing Program Administration* 20 (Fall/Winter 1996): 92–103.

30

Issues in Writing Program Administration: A Select Annotated Bibliography

Rebecca Jackson
Southwest Texas State University

Patricia Wojahn
New Mexico State University

In her introduction to *Kitchen Cooks, Plate Twirlers, and Troubadours*, Diana George uses the metaphor of plate twirling to describe the lives of writing program administrators (WPAs)—"on stage, trying to sustain the illusion of perpetual motion, worried over how to end the show without losing control as those plates go crashing onto the stage floor" (xi). George's description may be tongue in cheek, but we suspect that many WPAs have felt like plate spinners from time to time, working hard to create movement and balance amidst a "host of constraints" (Bizzell ix). The essays in this collection certainly reflect this view. We see WPAs developing and revising curricula; mediating conflicts; advocating for and advising students; training and evaluating graduate student teachers, adjunct instructors, and full-time writing faculty; managing budgets; conducting research; coordinating or contributing to writing-across-the-curriculum (WAC) programs; developing assessment tools; administering writing centers; staying abreast of conversations and controversies in a number of disciplines; evaluating programs; serving as a liaison among students, faculty, and administrators from across the institution; and investigating and

467

selecting technologies. Of course, most WPAs are also teaching a range of courses, sitting on various institutional committees and boards, maintaining an active research agenda, and publishing in their area of specialization. The list goes on.

To keep these plates twirling, WPAs must draw on everything they know (Bizzell viii). WPAs must also be able to locate information about issues and situations they *don't* know much about. This bibliography is designed to assist WPAs in this process, to help them answer two important questions about the range of activities and subjects of concern that make up their professional lives and work: (a) what key perspectives have emerged from disciplinary conversations about particular subjects? and (b) how have WPAs, in particular, responded to these subjects? Put another way, the bibliography is designed to provide WPAs quick and easy access to articles, bibliographies, professional statements, collections, and books that (a) map the contours of those conversations most relevant and important to WPAs—the controversies surrounding first-year writing, for example, and (b) offer WPA perspectives on the subjects of these conversations.

We have divided the bibliography itself into sections that address particular aspects of WPA work. Section headings are designed to reflect the range and nature of materials included within particular sections:

- Writing Programs: Histories, Curricula, Reform.
- Writing Program Administration: Models and Methods.
- WPA as Researcher and Scholar.
- Teacher Education, Professional Development, and Evaluation.
- Writing Assessment.
- Computers and Writing.
- Writing Across the Curriculum.
- Writing Centers.
- Promotion, Tenure, and Professional Issues.
- Legal Issues in Writing Program Administration.

The annotations we provide of materials within sections are descriptive only. We do not attempt to evaluate how persuasive or valuable a particular work is, although we recognize, of course, that selecting some materials for inclusion in a bibliography—and excluding others—is itself an evaluative act. In choosing which materials to keep and which to cut, an extremely difficult process, we relied heavily on "disciplinary consensus"—reflected in consistent and frequent references to particular works—and our own commitment to including materials that reflect the range and tenor of conversations important to WPAs. We follow the last section of the annotated bibliography— Legal Issues in Writing Program Administration—with a list of previously published bibliographies relevant to writing program administration, as well as a list of position statements drafted by the Conference on College Composition and Communication and the Council of Writing Program Administrators .

WORKS CITED

Bizzell, Patricia. Foreword. *Kitchen Cooks, Plate Twirlers, and Troubadours.* Ed. Diana George. Portsmouth, NH: Boynton/Cook, 1999. vii–ix.

George, Diana. Introduction. *Kitchen Cooks, Plate Twirlers, and Troubadours.* Ed. Diana George. Portsmouth, NH: Boynton/Cook, 1999. xi–xiv.

WRITING PROGRAMS: HISTORIES, CURRICULA, REFORM

General

Bloom, Lynn A., Donald Daiker, and Edward M. White. *Composition in the Twenty-First Century: Crisis and Change.* Newbury Park, CA: Sage, 1992. Comprised of papers and talks delivered at the Conference on Composition in the 21st Century: Crisis and Change on the "new geography of composition." Includes essays exploring new sites and forms of writing instruction; predictions about future assessment practices; possibilities for research on writing programs and program administration; possible directions in writing research; and the impact of political social issues on the teaching of writing.

Bullock, Richard, and John Trimbur, eds. *The Politics of Writing Instruction: Postsecondary.* Portsmouth, NH: Boynton/Cook, 1991. Provides a range of perspectives on the state of our discipline and addresses key issues related to the status and complications of writing instruction in higher education. Covers such issues as the status of adjunct faculty, the relationship between literature and composition, and the application of feminist and "radical" pedagogies in the writing classroom, all in an effort to consider the place—and potential power and status—of writing instruction in the academy.

Buranen, Lise, and Alice M. Roy, eds. *Perspectives on Plagiarism.* Albany: State U of New York P, 1999. A collection of theoretical and practical essays exploring a range of perspectives on plagiarism. Includes discussions of plagiarism and the "new abolitionism"; plagiarism and writing centers; plagiarism in peer writing groups; and other essays of potential interest to WPAs.

Guba, Evon G., and Yvonna S. Lincoln. *Fourth Generation Evaluation.* Newbury Park, CA: Sage, 1989. Outlines a constructivist approach to program evaluation emphasizing collaboration between stakeholders and program evaluators. Details the advantages of evaluation that arises from negotiation.

Hartzog, Carol P. *Composition and the Academy: A Study of Writing Program Administration.* New York: MLA, 1986. Reports findings from a survey of forty-four writing programs in a variety of institutional settings. Covers programmatic changes and reasons for change; administrative structures; information about program directors; writing program design and curricula; information about writing faculty and teaching assistants; attitudes about and opinions of writing programs; and future plans. Concludes with case studies of writing programs at University of North Carolina–Chapel Hill, Harvard, and the University of Pennsylvania.

Hilgers, Thomas, and Joy Marsella. *Making Your Writing Program Work: A Guide to Good Practices.* Newbury Park, CA: Sage, 1992. Offers strategies for building, sustaining, and revising effective writing programs. Includes chapters on developing curriculum, hiring and training faculty and staff, managing a budget, conducting program and evaluation research, administering a writing center, revising existing programs, and preparing for the future.

Janangelo, Joseph, and Kristine Hansen. *Resituating Writing: Constructing and Administering Writing Programs.* Portsmouth, NH: Heinemann-Boynton/Cook, 1995. A collection of essays exploring what makes writing programs unique or "different"—what distinguishes them from other academic programs. Seeks to educate a number of different audiences about writing program administration, begin conversations about writing program work, and bring writing programs in from institutional and departmental margins. Groups essays into sections covering philosophical issues and institutional identities; the WPA within and across departments; and professional and scholarly identities. Includes discussions of working conditions and part-time faculty; reforming writing curriculum to include various technologies; professional development programs; writing centers; writing across the curriculum; program evaluation; writing program administration as scholarship; WPA as scholar/researcher.

McLeod, Susan. "The Disabled Student and the Writing Program: A Guide for Administrators." *Writing Program Administration* 13.1-2 (1989): 45–51. Asserts that WPAs must develop plans and establish guidelines designed to address the needs of disabled students in the writing classroom. Suggests that a strong relationship between the WPA and the administrator in charge of student services is key to developing and implementing guidelines. Includes Washington State University's guidelines for accommodating students with disabilities.

—. "Evaluating Writing Programs: Paradigms, Problems, Possibilities." *Journal of Advanced Composition* 12.3 (1992): 373–82. Stresses that WPAs must understand the value and importance of program evaluation for program design, revision, and accountability, as well as the difficulty of developing a rigorous and appropriate evaluation design. Describes and contrasts quantitative and qualitative research methods for program evaluation, illuminating advantages and disadvantages of each. Emphasizes tailoring program evaluation methods to audience needs.

White, Edward M. *Developing Successful College Writing Programs.* San Francisco: Jossey-Bass, 1989. Outlines a strategic approach to the development and administration of writing programs founded upon research, planning, and evaluation. Includes chapters on ways to improve the status of writing on campus; the role of research in establishing a writing program and developing curricula; the purposes of writing assessment; the support and evaluation of writing faculty; and issues in writing program evaluation.

Witte, Stephen, and Lester Faigley. *Evaluating College Writing Programs.* Carbondale: Southern Illinois UP, 1983. Describes and discusses weaknesses of the two predominant models of writing program evaluation—the "expert-opinion" model and the quantitative model. Presents a theoretical framework for valid evaluations of writing programs founded upon knowledge of "necessary components" of evaluation—cultural and social context, institutional context, program structure and administration, curriculum, and instruction—and an understanding of the interconnected nature of these components.

Histories

Berlin, James. *Rhetoric and Reality: Writing Instruction in American Colleges, 1900–1985.* Carbondale: Southern Illinois UP, 1987. Covers the landscape of writing instruction throughout much of the twentieth century, with a focus on rhetorical theories and approaches positioned in light of historical, educational progression. Pairs the overview of rhetoric as a discipline with a discussion of corresponding advances in literary studies. Justifies the place of writing instruction in the college curriculum.

Connors, Robert. *Composition-Rhetoric: Backgrounds, Theory, and Pedagogy.* Pittsburgh: U of Pittsburgh P, 1997. Traces the history of writing instruction in America since the nineteenth century. Classifies "periods" within this time frame: "Early American Composition-Rhetoric" (1800–1865); "Postwar Composition-Rhetoric" (1865–1885); "Consolidation Composition-Rhetoric" (1885–1910); and "Modern Composition-Rhetoric" (1910–1960s). Examines the relationship between writing instruction and various "concurrent cultural trends."

Goggin, Maureen Daly. *Authoring a Discipline: Scholarly Journals and the Post-World War II Emergence of Rhetoric and Composition.* Mahwah, NJ: Erlbaum, 2000. Provides a comprehensive view of the development of the discipline of rhetoric and composition through scholarly journals and oral accounts. Presents the discipline as a social construct, evolving through political, intellectual, and material struggles.

Basic/Developmental Writing

Baker, Tracey and Peggy Jolly. "The 'Hard Evidence': Documenting the Effectiveness of a Basic Writing Program." *Journal of Basic Writing* 18.1 (1999): 27–99. Reports on retention rates of students in a basic writing program in an inner-city, open admissions university. Argues for more research and documentation on the impact and efficacy of basic writing pedagogies.

Gleason, Barbara. "Evaluating Writing Programs in Real Time: The Politics of Remediation." *CCC* 51.4 (2000): 560–88. Shares findings of a case study examining a three-year pilot program in which basic writers were mainstreamed at the college level. Discusses the importance of considering and assessing the impact of context when designing and studying such projects.

Greenberg, Karen L. "The Politics of Basic Writing." *Journal of Basic Writing* 12.1 (1993): 64–71. Argues against assertions that basic writing programs marginalize students, obstruct student progress, attempt to make students conform, or ineffectively place students in such programs. Discusses how many basic writing programs instead focus on many students' "right-to-succeed."

Harrington, Susanmarie, and Linda Adler-Kassner. "'The Dilemma That Still Counts': Basic Writing at a Political Crossroads." *Journal of Basic Writing* 17.2 (1998): 3–24.

Overviews how basic writing has been defined in the past two decades to explore roots of political battles related to basic writing. Discusses possible future directions for exploration of the position of basic writing programs in academic institutions.

Horner, Bruce. "Discoursing Basic Writing." CCC 47.2 (1996): 199–222. Calls for a renewed look at the positive motivations underlying the design of early basic writing courses, including the "insights of open admissions" that problematized the "social and political role of educational institutions." Analyzes assumptions evident in public debate about open admissions that deny how the material, social, and political challenge those working and learning in marginalized basic writing courses and that carry important implications for the teaching of writing in general.

Soliday, Mary. "From the Margins to the Mainstream: Reconceiving Remediation." CCC 47 (1996): 85–100. Shares a detailed account of the experience of a student enrolled in a "mainstreaming" effort that circumvented test scores for placement and instead offered an enriched writing course designed to meet many of the challenges of open admissions. Positions this effort as a "progressive alternative" to "traditional remediation."

First-Year Writing

Bamberg, Betty. "Alternative Models of First-Year Composition: Possibilities and Problems." WPA: Writing Program Administration 21.1 (1997): 7–18. Summarizes the New Abolitionists' objections to first-year composition. Uses the WPAs' perspectives, roles, duties, and interests to assess various alternative models of first-year composition—writing-intensive courses, freshman writing seminars, linked writing courses, and focused content writing courses. Argues that WPAs must weigh a variety of factors before developing and implementing a particular type of first-year writing course, including students' levels of writing proficiency and availability of resources and support.

Chase, Geoffrey. "Redefining Composition, Managing Change, and the Role of the WPA." Writing Program Administration 21.1 (1997) 46–54. Argues that administrators seeking to reform or abolish first-year writing must recognize that composition programs are complex systems, that changes to one facet of a program will alter other facets of the program. Advocates a "holistic" approach to potential change, one grounded in a keen understanding of local conditions, an evaluation of a program's internal coherence, and assessment of a program's external relevance. Concludes that program changes should reflect understanding of and attention to these issues.

Crowley, Sharon. Composition in the University: Historical and Polemical Essays. Pittsburgh: U of Pittsburgh P, 1998. Critiques problems in the humanities, with a focus on a composition and its current position within English departments. Provides historical analyses to comment on the state of the discipline.

David, Denise, Barbara Gordon, and Rita Pollard. "Seeking Common Ground: Guiding Assumptions for Writing Courses." CCC 46.4 (1995): 522–32. Argues the need to identify and articulate those traits that make a writing course a writing course. Proposes three primary traits as a point of departure—development of writing ability as the primary object; focus on students' texts; establishment of writing as the subject of the course.

Petraglia, Joseph, ed. *Reconceiving Writing, Rethinking Writing Instruction*. Hillsdale, NJ: Erlbaum, 1995. A collection of essays exploring, in general, the "weak relationship" between research on and theories of writing and "general writing skills instruction"—perhaps best known as first-year writing. Includes historical, theoretical, and practical considerations of the subject. Concludes with essays on possible alternative approaches to writing instruction.

Silva, Tony. "An Examination of Writing Program Administrator's Options for the Placement of ESL Students in First-Year Writing Classes." *Writing Program Administration* 18.1-2 (1994): 37–43. Synthesizes scholarship comparing L1 (first language) and L2 (second language) writing. Discusses four placement options arising from this scholarship: mainstreaming L2 writers, placing L2 writers in basic or developmental writing courses; placing students in credit-bearing first year writing courses designed specifically for L2 writers; placing equal numbers of L1 and L2 students in "cross cultural" composition classes. Suggests that the best approach may be to offer L2 students all of these options.

Trimbur, John. "Towards Programs of Study in Writing." *Writing Program Administration* 22.3 (1999): 9–30. Suggests that we have overburdened first-year writing with multiple theories, expectations, and purposes. Proposes a sequence of writing courses—tailored to the institutional context—that would extend writing beyond the first-year course. Suggests that such programs might enable us to flesh out various theoretical approaches to the teaching of writing.

Service Learning

Adler-Kassner, Linda, Robert Crooks, and Ann Watters, eds. *Writing the Community: Concepts and Models for Service-Learning in Composition*. Washington, DC: American Association for Higher Education, 1997. Includes essays addressing where the field of composition and the pedagogical use of service learning have been, are, and might go. Discusses administrative, logistical, and organizational considerations critical to the success of service learning. Addresses the need to report and research existing service learning models and the impact of this approach on students, faculty, administration, as well as the community.

Herzberg, Bruce. "Community Service and Critical Teaching." CCC 45.3 (1994): 307–19. Cautions against assuming that by being involved in service learning, students will automatically adopt a "social imagination" or learn to question systemic realities that lead to community problems. Rather, students are more likely to attribute problems to individuals, to personal problems. This suggests the need for courses in which service learning is adopted to address explicitly questions of "social structures, ideology, and social justice." Uses a case in which this approach is used to show that although the resulting learning and social awareness ideally should be more encompassing than taking the view of problems as attributable solely to the individual, it remains difficult for students to see problems originating in existing social/power systems and to locate solutions in more broad social action.

Jacoby, Barbara. *Service Learning in Higher Education*. San Francisco: Jossey-Bass, 1996. Presents an overview of what service learning is, along with key principles and theories related to service learning approaches. Addresses benefits to students, the academy, and the community and provides concrete examples illustrating all of the aforementioned. Also discusses implications for administrators and policymaking.

Rhoads, Robert, and Jeffrey P. F. Howard, eds. *Academic Service Learning: A Pedagogy of Action and Reflection.* New Directions for Teaching and Learning. San Francisco: Jossey-Bass, 1998. Discusses service learning as a movement with great potential for serving, first, as a pedagogical model allowing for learning; second, as a model requiring substantial intentionality and planning; third, as a model connecting service with learning as well as theory; fourth, as relevant to the course and topic in which it is applied. Individual chapters address various forms of service learning as well as a range of issues critical to this pedagogy, including how service learning fits the academic culture and ways to understand practical considerations and theoretical underpinnings of service learning. Includes key resources in the form of books, articles, and Web sites.

Schutz, Aaron, and Anne Ruggles Gere. "Service Learning and English Studies: Rethinking 'Public' Service." *College English* 60 (1998): 129–48. Problematizes service learning and its role and purposes in academic, private, and public spheres. Calls for more critical exploration before adopting and promoting service learning and suggests the need to proceed with clear theoretical and pedagogical goals to step out of the easy path that leads to reinforcing the status quo and ignoring the complexities underlying the issues service learning experiences raise.

WRITING PROGRAM ADMINISTRATION: MODELS AND METHODS

Amarose, Thomas. "WPA Work at the Small College or University: Re-Imagining Power and Making the Small School Visible." *Writing Program Administration* 23.3-4 (2000): 85–103. Argues that focused disciplinary emphasis on WPA power in larger institutions ignores the realities of WPAs in small colleges and universities where the wielding of power is often less important—and more risky—than other "political instruments." Argues that authority is often the most available and influence the most necessary.

Aronson, Anne, and Craig Hansen. "Doubling Our Chances: Co-Directing a Writing Program." *Writing Program Administration* 21.2-3 (1998): 23–32. Argues that codirecting/cochairing a writing program may be one way to ameliorate and/or overcome the "political and professional pitfalls" that most WPAs face. Emphasizes that comentoring allows directors to share and shift responsibilities to accommodate personal and professional realities, focuses attention on the department rather than the administrators, and enables a more equitable model of leadership.

Corbett, Edward P. J. "A History of Writing Program Administration." *Learning from the Histories of Rhetoric: Essays in Honor of Winifred Bryan Horner.* Ed. Theresa Enos. Carbondale: Southern Illinois UP, 1993. Traces the history of writing instruction, writing program administration, and the professionalization of writing teachers and the discipline from the late nineteenth century to the present. Predicts that present and future records of writing instruction and writing program administration will be rich and complex.

Dickson, Marcia. "Directing without Power: Adventures in Constructing a Model of Feminist Writing Program Administration." *Writing Ourselves into the Story: Unheard Voices from Composition Studies.* Ed. Sheryl I. Fontaine and Susan Hunter. Carbondale: Southern Illinois UP, 1993. 140–53. Argues that a "feminist model" of writing program administration would emphasize collaborative decision making and shared power, while recognizing that fitting models to real programs is difficult, if not impossible. Proposes, instead, seven key characteristics of feminist administrative structures, including collaborative processes, an emphasis on experimentation, support, and mentoring, and a system of rewards.

George, Diana, ed. *Kitchen Cooks, Plate Twirlers, and Troubadours.* Portsmouth, NH: Boynton/Cook, 1999. Presents WPAs' stories of entering the profession and "becoming" WPAs, working in writing programs, and working and collaborating across disciplinary boundaries. Essays explore the intersections of personal and professional lives; the political, institutional, and economic realities of WPA work; the joys and challenges of working with others; and the experience of juggling a multitude of different tasks.

Goodburn, Amy, and Carrie Shively Leverenz. "Feminist Writing Program Administration: Resisting the Bureaucrat Within." *Feminism and Composition Studies: In Other Words.* New York: MLA, 1998. 276-90. Discusses the authors' resistance to and conflicts with the nonhierarchical administrative structure they initially advocated and sought to enact. Proposes that such conflicts arise because we have internalized and are shaped by bureaucratic and patriarchal administrative models. Concludes that successful feminist writing program administration rests not only on our ability to change administrative structures, but on our willingness to talk about and reflect upon the resistance we feel during the process.

Gunner, Jeanne. "Decentering the WPA." *Writing Program Administration* 18.1-2 (1994): 8–15. Argues that the pervasive "WPA-centric" administrative model is "anti-democratic"—ignores the realities, rights, and needs of writing instructors—and, as such, hinders the move to professionalize the WPA position and the discipline at large. Recommends a "decentered" administrative structure for writing programs, one that emphasizes shared authority and influence.

—. "Identity and Location: A Study of WPA Models, Memberships, and Agendas." *Writing Program Administration* 22.3 (1999): 31–54. Uses examples from published scholarship to trace the evolution of WPA self-representation—from the "unitary WPA" model to the "post-unitary WPA" model. Describes the "unitary" model as hierarchical and inflexible, the "post-unitary" as collaborative and fluid.

—. "Politicizing the Portland Resolution." *Writing Program Administration* 20.3 (1997): 23–30. Argues that the Portland Resolution is an essentially conservative document, one that fails to address the calls for change in working conditions and treatment of adjunct faculty advanced in its predecessor document, the Wyoming Resolution. Addresses the importance of viewing the document as a space for and site of dissensus.

Harrington, Susanmarie, Steve Fox, and Tere Molinder Hogue. "Power, Partnership, and Negotiations: The Limits of Collaboration." *Writing Program Administration*

21.2-3 (1998): 52–64. Explores the conflicts faced by three members of a writing program committee. Argues that a fully theorized model of collaborative administration must (a) address the reality of faculty status and hierarchy across the institution, (b) recognize the inevitability of conflict and the necessity of conflict management, and (c) acknowledge administrators' and collaborators' multiple allegiances.

Holton, Susan A., ed. *Mending the Cracks in the Ivory Tower: Strategies for Conflict Management in Higher Education*. Bolton, MA: Anker, 1998. Observes that although conflict is an inevitable aspect of administrative and institutional life, it can be managed effectively. Includes essays on conflict in academia, conflict between administrators and faculty, chairs and deans, faculty and faculty, faculty and student, student and student. Concludes with a discussion of the "Holton model" for conflict management.

Hult, Christine. "Politics Redux: The Organization and Administration of Writing Programs." *Writing Program Administration* 18.3 (1995): 44–52. Compares the organization and administration of writing programs to various political systems—monarchy, dictatorship, oligarchy, anarchy, constitutional government. Outlines conditions necessary for achieving a "utopian ideal."

Kinkead, Joyce, and Jeanne Simpson. "The Administrative Audience: A Rhetorical Problem." *Writing Program Administration* 23.3 (2000): 71. Stresses that WPAs must understand administrative culture and rhetoric in order to achieve goals and effect programmatic change. Provides definitions of key administrative terms (*retention, attrition, credit hours, FTEs, productivity, mission statement, assessment,* and *accountability*), and offers additional strategies for "shap[ing] and reshap[ing] institutions."

McLeod, Susan H. "Requesting a Consultant-Evaluation Visit." *Writing Program Administration* 14.3 (1991): 73–77. Discusses the advantages of bringing in trained consultants to evaluate a writing program. Provides typical reasons for requesting such an evaluation and encourages WPAs to consider the value of this form of assessment.

Meeks, Lynn, and Christine Hult. "A Co-Mentoring Model of Administration." *Writing Program Administration* 21.2-3 (1998): 9–22. Describes and discusses a comentoring model of writing program administration emphasizing equal contributions, power sharing, and strategic shifting of roles. Argues that a comentoring administrative model "transforms" rather than "dilutes" power.

Miller, Hildy. "Postmasculinist Directions in Writing Program Administration." *Writing Program Administration* 20.1-2 (1996): 49–65. Suggests that whereas feminist approaches to teaching have been instantiated and examined in academic settings for quite some time, conflicts over feminist approaches to administration have been little explored. Presents what feminist approaches to administration might look like, how and why they might conflict with masculinist ideology and practice, and how aspects of the two might be productively employed into a "postmasculinist" approach.

Rhodes, Keith. "Marketing Composition for the 21st Century." *Writing Program Administration* 20.3 (2000): 51–69. Discusses the ways in which principles and practices of Total Quality Management might help WPAs address social and institutional threats to writing programs. Contends that better marketing of composition may help to diminish such threats and increase the status of writing.

—. "Who's the Boss? The Possibilities and Pitfalls of Collaborative Administration of Untenured WPAs." *Writing Program Administration* 21.2-3 (1998): 65–80. Challenges prevailing "utopian" views of collaborative writing program administration. Discusses how pressures to publish, competing allegiances and responsibilities, and constant criticism of programs affected one particular collaborative administration. Calls for case studies that examine both the possibilities and challenges of collaborative writing program work.

White, Edward M. "Use It or Lose It: Power and the WPA." *Writing Program Administration* 15.1-2 (1991): 3–12. Contends WPAs must recognize and use their power in strategic ways. Identifies several sources of power and concludes that one of the best ways to protect our writing programs is to fight for them.

WPA AS RESEARCHER AND SCHOLAR

Rose, Shirley K. and Irwin Weiser, eds. *The Writing Program Administrator as Researcher: Inquiry in Action and Reflection.* Portsmouth, NH: Boynton/Cook, 1999. A collection of essays exploring the nature and scope of WPA research with emphasis on the following questions: On what sites do WPAs focus their research? What kinds of research questions do WPAs ask? What research methods best help them address these question? What values guide WPA inquiry? Who are the stakeholders in WPA research? To what ends do WPAs conduct research? And how might WPA research be evaluated? Includes, among others, essays discussing such diverse topics as writing center research methods; assessment of teacher-training programs; the potential role of feminist research methods in WPA inquiry; historical/archival methods in writing program research; and survey research and curriculum development.

WRITING ASSESSMENT

General

Belanoff, Patricia. "The Myths of Assessment." *Journal of Basic Writing* 10.1 (1991): 65–66. Challenges various notions related to assessment including the idea that (a) we know the purposes and standards of our assessments, what they should be, and why; (b) we know what our assessments truly measure; (c) we can agree on criteria of effective writing and how to consistently identify and weigh these criteria through our assessments; and (d) we believe in an "absolute standard" that can be applied "uniformly." Argues that the variety of assessment at various institutions is in fact a positive and that assessment can best serve its purpose by being developed and situated in each particular environment.

Elbow, Peter. "Taking Time Out from Grading and Evaluating While Working in a Conventional System." *Assessing Writing* 4.1 (1997): 5–27. Reports on "pedagogy and practice" surrounding grading and evaluating, based on experience. Discusses problems with conventional grading systems and approaches and provides a range of alternatives, including the option of not grading all assignments, the use of port-folios, and the adoption of grading contracts. Provides rationale for adopting each alternative.

Haswell, Richard. "Minimal Marking." *College English* 45.6 (1983): 600–04. Pro-motes a prompt method for addressing the lower-level problems in students' writ-ing in a way that can facilitate and bridge multiple revisions in a manner that "shortens, gladdens, and improves" the marking of papers, all while giving stu-dents agency in identifying and fixing their own errors.

Haswell, Richard, and Susan Wyche-Smith. "Adventuring into Writing Assess-ment." CCC 45.2 (1994): 220–36. Shares the process of creating assessment ma-terials for placement at one institution to support the argument that the local conditions should be the "major shaping force." Encourages others to create and implement their own assessment instruments so that external forces do not dic-tate outside ideals on a given program and its goals.

Huot, Brian. "A Survey of College and University Writing Placement Practices." *Writing Program Administration* 17.3 (1994): 49–67. Reports results of a survey of writing placement practices and types of writing courses offered at two- and four-year colleges and universities. Discusses the importance of designing a place-ment program within the context of each given institution. Finds many institu-tions measuring writing through direct methods (such as writing samples) rather than traditional methods of assessment (such as multiple choice). Argues that we need to learn more about assessment as well as placement.

—. "Toward a New Theory of Writing Assessment." CCC 47 (1996): 549–66. Argues the importance of taking the lead in assessment so that external others do not have that power. Offers principles for a new theory and practice of writing assess-ment, one that may be site based, locally controlled, context-sensitive, rhetori-cally based, as well as accessible to writers whose work is being assessed.

Tchudi, Stephen. *Alternatives to Grading Student Writing.* Urbana, IL: NCTE, 1997. Distinguishes among "response," "assessment," "evaluation," and "grading" to ar-gue, in particular, the value of response to writing rather than maintaining grading practices that provide students with judgments rather than with coaching. Essays in this collection provide a range of alternatives to grading as well as discussions of types of grading that seem to prove more valuable than others.

White, Edward M. *Assigning, Responding, Evaluating: A Writing Teacher's Guide.* 3rd ed. New York: St. Martin's, 1995. Based on writing and reading theory, focuses on evaluation designed to help students learn as opposed to evaluation designed for administrative purposes. Provides teachers with useful background on various practical strategies for creating effective writing assignments, evaluating to essay tests, using various types of diagnostic tests, developing placement and certifica-tion measures, responding to student texts, and employing portfolios.

White, Edward M., William D. Lutz, and Sandra Kamusikiri, eds. *Assessment of Writ-ing: Politics, Policies, Practices.* New York: MLA, 1996. Portrays the complex nature of writing assessment in the field of writing. Chapters address such topics as politi-cal and legal issues, equity issues, various models of writing assessment, reliability and validity, as well as more recent issues such as portfolio of computer-assisted evaluation.

Williamson, Michael, and Brian Huot, eds. *Validating Holistic Scoring for Writing Assessment*. Cresskill, NJ: Hampton, 1993. Suggests that writing assessment must evolve with our changing notions and models of writing itself. Provides a series of essays addressing trends and continued complexities in writing assessment, with a focus on widely used holistic scoring methods.

Wolcott, Willa, and Sue M. Legg. *An Overview of Writing Assessment: Theory, Research, and Practice*. Urbana, IL: NCTE, 1998. Begins with an overview of current issues on writing assessment in the context of assessment in general. Then focuses on key topics such as assessing writing directly, designing topics for writing assessment, using portfolios for assessment, training, scoring holistically, using primary trait and analytic scoring. Addresses issues of reliability and validity, issues of equity, issues related to assessing writing in the disciplines, and future directions of assessment.

Portfolio Evaluation

Hamp-Lyons, Liz, and William Condon. *Assessing the Portfolio: Principles for Practice, Theory, and Research*. Cresskill, NJ: Hampton, 2000. Provides, through a series of essays, an overview of recent efforts in portfolio assessment. Discusses the theoretical underpinnings of this form of writing assessment, complications of using and evaluating portfolios, as well as recent research on the use of portfolios in assessment.

Nystrand, Martin, Allen Cohen, and Nora Dowling. "Addressing Reliability Problems in the Portfolio Assessment of College Writing. *Educational Assessment* 1.1 (1993): 53–70. Discusses results of a study of reliability in portfolio assessment. Results suggest that the variations in types of texts included in the portfolio present significant difficulties for reliably assigning a single score to a portfolio. In the study, reliability improved to acceptable rates when evaluators rated individual pieces within the portfolio. The latter practice also is less likely to privilege students who happen to be strong in the documents requested for the portfolio over those students whose strengths lie in other types of writing.

Yancey, Kathleen Blake, and Irwin Weiser, eds. *Situating Portfolios: Four Perspectives*. Logan: Utah State UP, 1997. A collection of over thirty writing teachers—at various levels and at different types of institutions—all sharing their experience and positions on the multiple uses, challenges, and potentials of portfolios. Provides insights about the historical use of portfolios, findings from qualitative studies of the use of portfolios, suggestions about what we can learn about students and the curriculum by reading portfolios, what students can learn through their portfolios, what models of portfolios can reveal about what portfolios can and cannot achieve, and relevant theoretical and political issues related to portfolios.

COMPUTERS AND WRITING

Anson, Chris M. "Distant Voices: Teaching Writing in a Culture of Technology." *College English* 61.3 (1999): 261–80. Considers ways in which writing teachers—and their students—may be drawn to "rapidly developing technologies" and the corresponding implications for our classrooms. Suggests that we use caution when adopting new technologies and that we instead consider the ways in which their use supports our pedagogical theories. Also recommends interrogating the motivation behind some of the technological advances so that our writing advances are in our control, not the other way around.

Condon, William. "Selecting Computer Software for Writing Instruction: Some Considerations." *Computers and Composition* 10.1 (1992): 53–56. Discusses the difficulty of selecting the best software for writing instruction and student writers. Shares several key aspects to consider when selecting such software, including the purpose(s) for which the software is needed, the range of purposes the software might be used for, and user-friendliness. Suggests that writing instructors also consider creating their own software for desired purposes.

Harris, J., George, D., Hult, C., & Killingsworth, J. "Computers in the Composition Curriculum: Looking Ahead." *WPA: Writing Program Administration* 13.1-2 (1989): 35–43. Discusses the need for WPAs to shape the way computers are used to teach writing rather than letting the computer shape writing instruction. Focuses on ways that computers can affect the teaching of writing. Specifically, computers and computer-based classrooms are (a) allowing for more dialogue, collaboration, and student-centered pedagogies, (b) providing easier access to more information, and (c) changing the ways we view and create texts.

Hawisher, Gail, and Sidney I. Dobrin. *Evolving Perspectives on Computers and Composition.* Urbana, IL: NCTE, 1990. Identifies important questions that computers and composition teachers and researchers face as they consider and use technology and its role in pedagogy and the practice of writing. Essays in this collection address changes in research and scholarship, changes in the classroom, changes in instructional media, and changes in the politics surrounding computers.

Hawisher, Gail, and Paul LeBlanc, eds. *Re-imagining Computers and Composition: Teaching and Research in the Virtual Age.* Portsmouth, NH: Boynton/Cook, 1992. Discusses how our notions of literacy change as our teaching and our learning occur online rather than in print. Essays in this collection address how writing and the way writing is taught also change as the medium used to share our words changes.

Holdstein, Deborah. "A Politics of Composition and Technology: Institutions and the Hazards of Making New." *Writing Program Administration* 20.1-2 (1996): 19–31. Offers scenarios pointing to the complex issues related to academic rewards and the potential risks of those who work on "technologies of literacy" and embrace the "new" when institutions may continue to view scholarship and pedagogy in ways that devalue such efforts.

Holdstein, Deborah, and Cynthia L. Selfe. *Computers and Writing: Theory, Research, Practice.* New York: MLA, 1990. Offers a range of issues designed more for consideration within the discipline of writing than for pragmatic, "how-to" purposes. Essays in this collection address complications, controversies, and implications of evolving technologies for writers, from examining the professional role of an English department's "computer person" to the question of who profits from the development of courseware.

Huot, Brian. "Computers and Assessment: Understanding Two Technologies." *Computers and Composition* 13.2 (1996): 231–43. Posits a cautionary argument against the tendency to view computers and assessment as transparent or objective. Suggests that rather than considering computers and assessment acontextually, we assess, understand, and intentionally combine strengths of each with human assessment based on needs in specific contexts.

Kemp, Fred. "Who Programmed This? Examining the Instructional Attitudes of Writing-Support Software." *Computers and Composition* 10.1 (1992): 9–24. Addresses the "ideological dimensions of software" in the context of the equipment available; the pedagogy employed; and the instructor making informed, considered decisions about all of the aforementioned. Argues that using computers only for word processing limits instructional potential. Provides a brief, historical overview of and commentary on various types of software used for specific classroom purposes and encourages instructors to make decisions about the software based on informed, pedagogical goals.

Logie, John. "Champing at the Bits: Computers, Copyright, and the Composition Classroom." *Computers and Composition* 15.2 (1998): 201–14. Provides a brief, historical overview of copyright laws, with a special focus on "fair use" exemptions and the more recent laws most relevant to the composition classroom and to the increasing use of multimedia and online materials. Concludes with an annotated list of online resources focused on intellectual property issues.

Self, Cynthia L. *Technology and Literacy in the Twenty-First Century: The Importance of Paying Attention* (Studies in Writing & Rhetoric). Carbondale: Southern Illinois UP, 1999. Calls for writing teachers to take a considered and active role in shaping the way our culture views literacy. Specifically critiques the Technology Literacy Challenge, a literacy project sponsored by the federal government, which in effect fosters continued inequities in our society. Offers alternative to this agenda for positively shaping literacy and a more equitable society.

Selfe, Cynthia, and Susan Hilligoss, eds. *Literacy and Computers: The Complications of Teaching and Learning with Technology.* New York: MLA, 1994. Describes the potentials and complications of teaching and learning with technology. Chapters in this collection focus on a range of issues related to computing, from politics and economics to social implications and the nature of reading and writing.

Taylor, Paul. "Evaluating Software: What Thoreau Said to the Designer." *Computers and Composition* 10.1 (1992): 45–52. Discusses various aspects to consider when selecting software, including the theoretical underpinnings of the software, the actions allowed and encouraged by the software, the consistency of the interface, the connectivity of the program with other programs, the provision of feedback, as well as the software's customizability. Argues, however, that the way the software is integrated into the curriculum is ultimately more critical than usability issues.

Taylor, Todd. "Computers in the Composition Curriculum: An Update." *Writing Program Administration* 20.1-2 (1996): 7–18. Provides an update on hardware, software, synchronous and asynchronous online communication, and the World Wide Web to allow WPAs to make informed decisions about technology as it continues to evolve. Encourages similar, more frequent overviews because technology for writing and communicating will continue to change rapidly, and WPAs are already charged with decisions about this and so many other elements critical to writing programs.

TENURE, PROMOTION, AND PROFESSIONAL ISSUES

Barr-Ebest, Sally. "Gender Differences in Writing Program Administration." *Writing Program Administration* (1995): 53–73. Reports findings from a study comparing the status and progress of male and female WPAs. Concludes that despite similar training, experience, and job responsibilities, male WPAs earn higher salaries, publish more, and are more likely to be tenured than are female WPAs. Recommends steps female WPAs can take to protect and promote themselves.

Boyer, Ernest. *Scholarship Reconsidered: Priorities of the Professoriate*. Princeton: Carnegie Foundation, 1990. Calls for an expanded definition of "scholarship," one that moves beyond traditional notions of research and publishing. Advances, describes, and discusses four types of scholarship: scholarship of discovery, of integration, of application, and of teaching.

Gebhardt, Richard, and Barbara Genelle Smith Gebhardt, eds. *Academic Advancement in Composition Studies: Scholarship, Publication, Promotion, Tenure*. Mahwah, NJ: Erlbaum, 1997. Explores the nature of the work of composition faculty and WPAs and how that work may be productively viewed and evaluated. Essays in the collection focus on such topics as promotion, tenure, mentoring, external reviews, as well as writing administration—and a range of academic practices—as scholarship and teaching.

Hult, Christine, et al. "'The Portland Resolution': Guidelines for Writing Program Administrator Positions." *Writing Program Administration* 16.1-2 (1992): 88–94. Provides a statement of professional standards written and supported by the WPA organization. Addresses various audiences, with a particular focus on WPAs and those with whom they work, as well as those to whom they report. Presents job descriptions, suggestions for evaluation WPAs, resources that should be available to those in the WPA position, general guidelines for preparing to be an effective WPA, and diverse responsibilities that might be expected in a WPA position.

Janangelo, Joseph. "Somewhere between Disparity and Despair: Writing Program Administrators, Image Problems, and *The MLA Job Information List*." *Writing Program Administration* 15.1-2 (1991): 60–66. Argues that advertisements for WPA positions in the *JIL* undermine WPA status and professionalization. Suggests specific ways of addressing the situation, including establishing guidelines for WPA job descriptions, advertising in *Writing Program Administration*, and opening discussion with department heads about the complexities of writing program administration.

TEACHER EDUCATION, PROFESSIONAL DEVELOPMENT, AND EVALUATION

Anson, Chris, et al. *Scenarios for Teaching Writing: Contexts for Discussion and Reflective Practice*. Urbana, IL: NCTE, 1993. Asserts that teachers of writing, novice teachers in particular, benefit from exploring, responding to, and reflecting upon the experiences of seasoned writing instructors. Offers complex scenarios developed from actual events in various writing programs to stimulate thinking and discussion about the work involved in teaching writing—developing effective writing assignments; using readings in writing courses, responding to student writing; teaching grammar, usage, and style; negotiating interaction in classes, conferences, and writing groups; and designing future writing courses

Anson, Chris M., ed. *Writing and Response: Theory, Practice, and Research*. Urbana, IL: NCTE, 1989. Essays in this collection address the complex relationship between response to student writing and development of writing ability. Includes essays on theories of response, essays discussing new insights on and approaches to response, and reports of research on response in various classroom contexts.

Barr-Ebest, Sally. "The Next Generation of WPAs: A Study of Graduate Students in Composition/Rhetoric." *Writing Program Administration* 22.3 (1999): 65–84. Reports findings of a survey of the nature and focus of graduate preparation for teaching, research, and administration in rhetoric and composition. Concludes that preparation for teaching is strong, whereas preparation for conducting research, publishing research, and administering programs is generally weak. Discusses options for addressing weakness in these areas: course work in research methods; practice in developing, conducting, and writing about research projects; internships; and course work in various facets of administration.

Centra, John A. *Reflective Faculty Evaluation*. San Francisco: Jossey-Bass, 1993. Offers innovative ways to evaluate innovative teaching, including portfolios and self-reports. Suggests ways to include faculty in evaluating and improving teaching effectiveness and ways to productively make use of student evaluations. Also addresses legal issues related to faculty evaluation.

Cogie, Jane. "Theory Made Visible: How Tutoring May Affect Development of Student-Centered Teachers." *Writing Program Administration* 21.1 (1997): 76–84. Reports on a qualitative study of the effects of writing center tutoring on graduate assistant teachers' classroom teaching. Concludes that writing center tutoring had overwhelmingly positive effects. Tutoring gave teachers a window on individual writing processes, allowed them to experiment with different strategies for helping writers, and solidified their commitment to student-centered teaching.

Corbett, Edward P. J., Nancy Myers, and Gary Tate. *The Writing Teacher's Sourcebook*. 4th ed. New York: Oxford UP, 1999. A collection of essays exploring (a) the "contexts of teaching"—theoretical perspectives, teacher roles and experiences, student roles and experiences, sites of teaching, curricular approaches; and (b) issues in the teaching of writing—assigning writing, responding to and assessing writing, composing and revising, teaching audience and style.

Fontaine, Sheryl I. "Revising Administrative Models and Questioning the Value of Appointing Graduate Student WPAs." *Foregrounding Ethical Awareness in Composition and English Studies*. Ed. Sheryl I Fontaine and Susan Hunter. Portsmouth, NH: Boynton/Cook, 1998. 83–92. Encourages a critical and ethical examination of appointing graduate students to various WPA positions. Argues that this kind of administrative model encourages values—competition and exploitation, for example—at odds with those advanced in the profession. Argues for a revised model of administration that emphasizes the active participation of all graduate students.

Hult, Christina. *Evaluating Teachers of Writing*. Urbana, IL: NCTE, 1994. Addresses the formative and summative evaluation of writing teachers. Offers a series of essays on political, ideological, pedagogical, and practical issues that make writing teacher evaluations particularly complex. Provides a range of evaluation methods as well as suggestions for evaluating specific groups of teachers, such as adjunct and tenure-track faculty.

Latterell, Catherine. "Training the Workforce: An Overview of GTA Education Curricula." *Writing Program Administration* 19.3 (1996): 7–23. Surveys and critiques required graduate-level courses in composition designed for graduate teaching assistants (GTAs). Approaches to GTA preparation vary widely—apprenticeships, "practica" courses, teaching methods courses, and theory seminars—although "practica" courses are most common. Argues that "practica" courses, though useful, may not be the best GTA preparation model. Advocates a "teaching community" model of GTA preparation, one that will introduce GTAs to writing theory and pedagogy from a variety of perspectives.

Long, Mark, Jennifer Holberg, and Marcy Taylor. "Beyond Apprenticeship: Graduate Students, Professional Development Programs and the Future(s) of English Studies." *Writing Program Administration* 20.1-2 (1996): 66–78. Questions current models of training graduate assistants as teachers and researchers and proposes instead training that not just additionally prepares students for careers as future administrators but also acknowledges students' potential roles in reconfiguring the "status of teaching, program service, and administrative work." Further argues for promoting graduate students' roles in decentralizing writing program administration and in envisioning a more collaborative administrative structure.

Myers-Breslin, Linda, ed. *Administrative Problem Solving for Writing Programs and Writing Centers: Scenarios in Effective Program Management.* Urbana, IL: NCTE, 1999. Presents the experiences and challenges faced by actual writing program and writing center administrators as case studies for discussion and problem solving. Each scenario places readers in the role of administrative problem solvers, establishing a context for the particular challenge faced, and offering a statement or list of key challenges for consideration. Scenarios conclude with authors' comments about how they approached and dealt with the administrative challenge described.

Rose, Shirley K., and Margaret J. Finders. "Learning from Experience: Using Situated Performances in Writing Teacher Development." *Writing Program Administration* 22.1-2 (1998): 33–52. Advocates the use of highly contextualized role-playing activities ("situated performances") in educating novice teachers of writing. Argues that situated performance activities foster experiential learning, self-conscious reflection, and awareness of multiple contexts and perspectives.

Tate, Gary, Amy Rupiper, and Kurt Schick, eds. *A Guide to Composition Pedagogies.* New York: Oxford UP, 2001. Includes twelve essays, each discussing one of the most influential and significant theoretical and pedagogical approaches to the teaching of writing: process pedagogy, expressive pedagogy, rhetorical pedagogy, collaborative pedagogy, cultural studies approach, critical pedagogy, feminist pedagogy, community-service pedagogy, pedagogy of writing across the curriculum, writing center pedagogy, basic writing pedagogy, and pedagogies involving technology.

Thomas, Trudelle. "The Graduate Student as Apprentice WPA: Experiencing the Future." *Writing Program Administration* 14.3 (1991): 41–52. Argues the importance of preparing graduate students in rhetoric and composition for work in administration. Identifies qualities of successful graduate student WPAs—willingness to "advocate" for students and writing teachers; creative vision; ability to work with people across the power continuum. Suggests ways departments might help aspiring WPAs acquire the experience they need: creating WPA apprenticeships; providing service opportunities in the department and university; offering varied teaching opportunities; involving aspiring WPAs in training and professional development programs; and giving them experience with assessment.

Yancey, Kathleen Blake. *Reflection in the Writing Classroom*. Logan: Utah State UP, 1998. Applies Donald Schön's work on reflective practice to three kinds of reflection relevant to the writing classroom—reflection-in-action, constructive reflection, and reflection-in-presentation—and argues that each is integral to the development of students' writing abilities and identities as writers. Asserts that when students reflect on their writing during the composing process they are reflecting-in-action; that when they reflect on their writing between writing events they are engaged in constructive reflection; and that when they reflect on a body of completed work for a specific audience (a portfolio, for example) they are reflecting-in-presentation.

Zimmerman, Ray, and Ellen Strenski. "Using the World Wide Web for Instruction Development: Writing Program Home Pages, On-Line Course Manuals, and Web-Archived Staff Listservs. *WPA: Writing Program Administration* 20.3 (1997): 91–101. Uses examples from UC–Irvine's Composition Program to explore the role various kinds of electronic resources might play in training and supporting teachers of writing. Examines uses of writing program home pages, course Web sites with information and material for both instructors and students, and staff listservs. Concludes with ten advantages of on-line training and three challenges (construction, maintenance, and access to technology).

WRITING ACROSS THE CURRICULUM

Bean, John C. *Engaging Ideas: The Professor's Guide to Integrating Writing, Critical Thinking, and Active Learning Theory in the Classroom*. San Francisco: Jossey-Bass, 1996. Blends ideas from two higher education movements: WAC and critical thinking. Argues, for instance, that one of teachers' primary roles is to design interesting problems that allow students to engage with ideas actively rather than passively, for instance, through processes enabling students to understand how members of a discipline ask questions, conduct research, as well as construct knowledge and arguments. Integrates theory and research within a broad range of practical ideas for teaching critical thinking in various settings.

Herrington, Anne, and Charles Moran, eds. *Writing, Teaching, and Learning in the Disciplines*. New York: MLA, 1992. Depicts a history of the writing-in-the-disciplines (WID) movement in higher education. Chapters in this collection discuss a range of issues, from the intellectual and political to the pedagogical.

Kirscht, Judy, Rhonda Levine, and John Reiff. "Evolving Paradigms: WAC and the Rhetoric of Inquiry." CCC 45.3 (1994): 369–80. Addresses the conflict between using writing to learn as opposed to discourse and discipline-specific conventions as a foundation for writing across the curriculum. Positions social construction theory and the "rhetoric of inquiry" as means to usefully bridge the two poles.

Malinowitz, Harriet. "A Feminist Critique of Writing-in-the-Disciplines." *Feminism and Composition Studies: In Other Words.* Ed. Susan Jarratt and Lynn Worsham. New York: MLA, 1998. Expresses concern that WAC, as it currently exists, re-creates the university and the disciplines rather than interrogating, deconstructing, or seeking to transform the disciplines. Asks that we consider a feminist education model in which students are encouraged to explore, for instance, what creates disciplinary boundaries, whose interests are being served, and how the underpinnings of the construction of knowledge in various disciplines privileges or excludes. Admits that a move against blind assimilation into the disciplines can by risky and suspect among multidisciplinary peers.

McLeod, Susan, and Elaine Maimon. "Clearing the Air: WAC Myths and Realities." *College English* 62.5 (2000): 573–83. Provides an overview of issues related to what WAC is, does, and could be. Examines a series of notions about WAC argued here as myths, including the notions that WAC is actually a reductive "grammar across the curriculum"; that WAC and WID are in opposition to one another, with WAC's writing-to-learn approaches seen as more rigorous; and that WAC theory promotes rather than challenges the status quo.

McLeod, Susan H., and Margot Soven, eds. *Writing across the Curriculum: A Guide to Developing Programs.* Ed. Newbury Park, CA: Sage, 1992. A collection of essays discussing the development and administration of WAC programs, as well as strategies for integrating WAC into department and university programs. Includes chapters on starting a WAC program; conducting faculty workshops; creating writing intensive courses and writing fellows programs; and involving the writing center in WAC initiatives.

Miraglia, Erica, and Susan McLeod. "Whither WAC? Interpreting the Stories/Histories of Enduring WAC Programs." *Writing Program Administration* 20.3 (1997): 46–65. Uses information from a past and more current survey of WAC programs to track challenges of the WAC movement. Reports on three factors that emerged as common to enduring programs: (a) administrative/funding support, (b) grassroots/faculty support; and (c) strong and consistent leadership.

Walvoord, Barbara. "The Future of WAC." *College English* 58.1 (1996): 58–79. Applies as a framework the view of WAC as a social movement to interpret WAC's past and to envision the future. Calls for WAC to function as a "mature reform organization" to meet a range of challenges such as defining its relationship to institutional administration, technology, and assessment.

Yancey, Kathleen Blake, ed. *Assessing Writing across the Curriculum.* Geenwich, CT: Ablex, 1997. Includes a series of essays on integrating and evaluating writing across the curriculum. Addresses writing assessment in a wide range of contexts and for a students with varied learning styles and disciplinary backgrounds.

WRITING CENTERS

Barnett, Robert J., and Jacob Blumner, eds. *Writing Centers and Writing Across the Curriculum Programs.* Westport, CT: Greenwood, 1999. A collection of essays using institution-specific examples to explore the promises and challenges of evolving relationships between writing centers and WAC programs. Includes discussions about writing center-WAC partnerships; the role of writing centers and tutors in furthering WAC initiatives; the role of writing centers in institutions with no formally constituted WAC program; the impact of organizational change—a constant—on writing center-WAC partnerships; and others.

Brooks, Jeff. "Minimalist Tutoring: Making the Student Do All the Work." *Writing Lab Newsletter* 15.6 (1991): 1–4. Reiterates North's claim that the goal of tutoring is learning, not flawless documents. Offers specific strategies for encouraging writers to accept ownership and responsibility for their learning and work.

Clark, Irene L., and Dave Healy. "Are Writing Centers Ethical?" *Writing Program Administration* 20.1-2 (1996): 32–48. Explores the question of writing center tutoring as suspect or inappropriate, and its effects as potentially leading to charges of plagiarism. Contends that typical responses to such charges have led to "noninterventionist" approaches to tutoring but argues that such approaches may themselves be ineffectual and themselves unethical. Calls for a "new ethic" that can address the "theoretical, pedagogical, and political facts of life" and allow writing centers to be a changing force in the academic landscape.

Grimm, Nancy. "The Regulatory Role of the Writing Center." *The Writing Center Journal* 17.1 (1996): 5–29. Challenges the uncritical acceptance of writing center work as politically neutral, even liberatory. Argues that writing centers often serve to regulate literacy, to enforce institutional standards of literate practice. Contends that writing centers are potential sites of critique and transformation, places where tutors and students might uncover the values implicit in institutionally sanctioned literacies and work to alter them as well.

Harris, Muriel. "Solutions and Tradeoffs in Writing Center Administration." *The Writing Center Journal* 12.1 (1991): 63–79. Identifies several common writing center scenarios and the multiple ways writing center directors might respond to these situations. Emphasizes that every possible solution embodies trade-offs. Encourages writing center directors to use these scenarios to develop their abilities to think creatively and critically about the issues they face.

—. "Talking in the Middle: Why Writers Need Writing Tutors." *College English* 57.1 (1995): 27–42. Argues that writing center tutorials offer writers a kind of help and knowledge about writing that writing classrooms and other forms of instruction cannot. Discusses the unique benefits of tutorial interaction: one-to-one interaction facilitates the writer's independence; helps writers better understand the "hows" of writing—how to brainstorm, how to ask questions that will spark revision, and so on; provides writers with opportunities to voice affective concerns; assists students in understanding disciplinary and academic discourse.

Healy, Dave. "Writing Center Directors: An Emerging Portrait of the Profession." *Writing Program Administration* 18.3 (1995): 26–43. Reports findings from a survey of writing center directors about their titles, their gender, their education, and their attitudes about writing center administration. Observes that the survey results confirm established perceptions about writing center directors: Most are female working in non-tenure-line positions for relatively low salaries. Notes that despite such discouraging trends, respondents felt that their work with tutors and students was greatly rewarding.

Hobson, Eric, ed. *Wiring the Writing Center.* Logan: Utah State UP, 1998. Essays by WPAs and researchers explore the possibilities of and potential problems with technology in writing center settings. Includes descriptions and discussions of asynchronous online writing center conferences; online tutor training; online outreach to teachers across the disciplines; web design; usability testing; online writing centers in high school and community college settings; computer-writing center history; administrative and professional repercussions; and other issues.

Kinkead, Joyce, and Jeanette Harris, eds. *Writing Centers in Context.* Urbana, IL: NCTE, 1993. Offers case studies of twelve writing centers in various institutional settings, from community and liberal arts colleges to private and public comprehensive and research universities. Each case study includes information about the profiled writing center's mission, services, clientele, tutor training, outreach, evaluation, and future directions.

Lunsford, Andrea. "Collaboration, Control, and the Idea of a Writing Center." *The Writing Center Journal* 12.1 (1991): 3–10. Asserts that social constructionist theory—embodied in collaborative practices—threatens widely accepted writing center models: the writing center as "storehouse" and the writing center as "garret." Describes the storehouse as skills focused, locating knowledge outside of us, in the world. Describes the garret as writer focused, locating knowledge within the individual. Proposes the "Burkean" parlour as an alternative model, one founded upon the theory that knowledge is socially constructed—negotiated in and through conversation.

North, Stephen. "The Idea of a Writing Center." *College English* 46 (1984): 433–46. Identifies and discusses common misperceptions about the role of writing center. Contends that writing centers are not and should not be viewed as "skills centers," grammar "fix-it" shops, or sites of remediation. Writing centers reflect the "two most powerful contemporary perspectives on teaching writing": Writing is a process; and the most effective writing instruction is student centered. Introduces the axiom "our job is to produce better writers, not better writing."

Silk, Bobbie Bayless, ed. *The Writing Center Resource Manual.* Emmitsburg: National Writing Centers Association Press, 1998. Includes essays by writing center administrators on starting a writing center, managing a writing center, and addressing "special needs and opportunities." Specific topics include establishing a writing center identity; assessing needs and developing funding proposals; keeping records; training and evaluating tutors; evaluating writing center services; managing a budget; working with ESL students; working with faculty from across the disciplines; and conducting writing center research.

Shamoon, Linda K., and Deborah H. Burns. "A Critique of Pure Tutoring." *The Writing Center Journal* 15.2 (1995): 134–51. Challenges the "orthodoxy" of nondirective, student-centered writing center practices. Argues that directive tutoring, in many cases, is an equally effective instructional method. Concludes that an ideal model of writing center practice includes both directive and nondirective methods.

Waldo, Mark. "What Should the Relationship between the Writing Center and the Writing Program Be?" *The Writing Center Journal* 11.1 (1990): 73–80. Asserts that writing centers should not be viewed or used as service components of the writing program. Argues, instead, that writing programs and writing centers should be equal and complementary, sharing common theoretical and pedagogical approaches, and working to achieve similar goals. Concludes that a "symbiotic" relationship between writing programs and writing centers helps raise the status of writing on campus, making writing programs and writing centers central to the mission of the university.

Olson, Gary A., ed. *Writing Centers: Theory and Administration.* Urbana, IL: NCTE, 1984. Brings together previously published and new articles on writing center theory and administration. Includes discussions on developing and overseeing budgets; developing, keeping, and using records; staff training; developing tutoring programs; and developing tutor handbooks.

LEGAL ISSUES IN WRITING PROGRAM ADMINISTRATION

Goonen, Norma M., and Rachel Blechman. *Higher Education Administration: A Guide to Legal, Ethical, and Practical Issues.* Westport, CT: Greenwood, 1999. Explores legal, ethical, and practical facets of the kinds of decisions higher education administrators are called upon to make. Includes chapters on hiring, compensation and employment, promotion and tenure, terminations and nonrenewals, academic freedom, student disputes on academic matters, and transcripts and degrees.

Hollandar, Patricia A., D. Parker Young, and Donald D. Gehring. *A Practical Guide to Legal Issues Affecting College Teachers.* Asheville, NC: College Administration Publications, 1995. Provides an overview of legal issues relevant to higher education faculty. Discusses legal relationships, legal distinctions between public and private institutions, academic affairs, student rights and responsibilities, employment, liability, and risk management. Includes brief descriptions of relevant federal statutes.

Lang, Susan. "Who Owns the Course? Online Composition Courses in an Era of Changing Intellectual Property Policies." *Computers and Composition* 15.2 (1998): 215–28. Demonstrates the complications of copyright law and its application to online resources and information, particularly with respect to ownership of online courses developed by composition instructors and other academics.

BIBLIOGRAPHIES

Anson, Chris M., John E. Schwiebert, and Michael M. Williamson. *Writing across the Curriculum: An Annotated Bibliography.* Westport, CT: Greenwood, 1993.

Bizzell, Patricia, Bruce Herzberg, and Nedra Reynolds, eds. *Bedford Bibliography for Teachers of Writing.* 5th ed. New York. Bedford, 2000 www.bedfordbooks.com/bb/.

Catalano, Timothy, et al. "TA Training in English: An Annotated Bibliography." *Writing Program Administration* 19.3 (1996): 36–54.

Murphy, Christina, and Steve Sherwood, eds. *Writing Centers: An Annotated Bibliography.* Westport, CT: Greenwood, 1999.

Strickland, James. "An Annotated Bibliography of Representative Software for Writers." *Computers and Composition* 10.1 (1992): 25–35.

POSITION STATEMENTS

CCCC Position Statements: <http://ncte.org/ccc/ex.html>.

- Students' Right to Their Own Language
- The National Language Policy
- Scholarship in Composition
- Statement of Professional Guidance
- Writing Assessment: A Position Statement
- CCCC Statement on Ebonics
- Promotion and Tenure Guidelines for Work with Technology
- CCCC Statement on Second-Language Writing and Writers
- Drafts of Statements under development

Evaluating the Work of Writing Program Administration: <http://www.cas.ilstu.edu/ english/hesse/intellec.htm>.

NCTE Position Statements: <http://ncte.org/positions>.

- Guidelines for Workload of College English Teachers
- Expanding Opportunities: Academic Success for Cultural and Linguistically Diverse Students
- Additional Statements related to K–12 Teaching

The Portland Resolution: <www.cas.ilstu.edu/english/hesse/policy.htm>.

Statement on Intellectual Work and the WPA: <www.cas.ilstu.edu/english/hesse/policy.htm>.

ADDITIONAL RESOURCES

"CompPile: An Ongoing Inventory of Publications in Post-Secondary Composition and Rhetoric, 1939–1999." Ed. Rich Haswell. <http://www.comppile.tamucc.edu>.
"Writing Program Home Pages." <www.its.uidaho.edu/comp/programhomes.html>.
Consultant-Evaluation Services: <www.cas.ilstu.edu/english/hesse/consult.htm>.

Appendix A

PORTLAND RESOLUTION

Guidelines for Writing Program Administrator Positions

Adopted by the Council of Writing Program Administrators, 1992

Published in WPA: Writing Program Administration 16.1/2 (Fall/Winter 1992): 88–94.

Christine Hult and the Portland Resolution Committee: David Joliffe, Kathleen Kelly, Dana Mead, Charles Schuster

Background

The theme of the 1990 Council of Writing Program Administrators Conference was "Status, Standards, and Quality: The Challenge of Wyoming." Christine Hult, editor of WPA: Writing Program Administration, presented a paper at the conference that essentially called for extending the challenge of the Wyoming Resolution—and the subsequent Conference of College Composition and Communication (CCCC's) "Statement of Principles and Standards for the Postsecondary Teaching of Writing"—to WPAs. In "On Being a Writing Program Administrator," she invited WPAs to begin a dialogue toward the formulation of a statement of professional standards by the WPA organization. Such a statement would outline prerequisites for effective administration of writing programs as well as equitable treatment of WPAs. At the pre-conference workshop, participants were working on similar document, which they dubbed the "Portland Resolution." A representative committee was commissioned by the WPA Executive Committee to draft a document; their combined work was presented at the 1991 summer conference and also sent to WPA members in WPA News to solicit comments toward revision of the document. This final version of the Portland Resolution, accepted by the Executive Committee at their 1992 CCCC meeting, is intended to help both Writing Program Administrators and those with whom they work and to whom they report develop quality writing programs in their institutions.

Guidelines for Writing Program Administrator Positions

I. Working Conditions Necessary for Quality Writing Program Administration

Many WPAs at colleges and universities, and department or division chairs at community colleges, find themselves in untenable job situations, being asked to complete unrealistic expectations with little tangible recognition or remuneration, and with few resources. The CCCC statement points out the exploitation of writing teachers at all levels, including program administrators: "The teaching, research, and service contributions of tenure-line composition faculty are often misunderstood or undervalued. At some postsecondary institutions, such faculty members are given administrative duties without the authority needed to discharge them; at others, they are asked to meet publication standards without support for the kind of research that their discipline requires." The following guidelines are intended to improve working conditions for more effective administration of writing programs.

1. Writing job descriptions for WPAs. Each institution is responsible for providing clear job descriptions or role statements for its WPAs (See Part II below). Such descriptions should be flexible enough for WPAs and the institution—and open to negotiation, especially when hiring a new WPA or starting a new writing program. The institution is responsible for providing a clear formula for determining "equivalence" for a WPA: What responsibilities are equivalent to teaching a full load (as determined by that institution)? What release time will be given for administration and staff development? What administrative work will be counted as "scholarship" in tenure and promotion decisions?

In addition, WPA positions should be situated within a clearly defined administrative structure so that the WPA knows to whom he or she is responsible and whom he or she supervises. A WPA should not be assigned to direct a program against her or his will or without appropriate training in rhetoric and composition and commensurate workplace experience. If a WPA needs specialized training in any area outside the usual purview of rhetoric and composition studies, the institution must be prepared to provide for and fund that training.

2. Evaluating WPAs. The institution is responsible for setting forth informed guidelines for assessing the work of a WPA fairly and for determining how administrative work is to be compared to traditional definitions of teaching, research, and service in decisions involving salary increases, retention, promotion, and tenure. Assessment of a WPA should consider the important scholarly contribution each WPA makes by virtue of designing, developing, and implementing a writing program.

3. Job security. WPA positions should carry sufficient stability and continuity to allow for the development of sound educational programs and planning. The WPA should be a regular, full-time, tenured faculty member or a full-time administrator with a recognizable title that delineates the scope of the position (e.g., Director of Writing, Coordinator of Composition, Division or Department Chair). WPAs should have travel funds equivalent to those provided for other faculty and administrators and should receive a salary commensurate with their considerable responsibilities and workload (including summer stipends). Requirements for retention, promotion, and tenure should be clearly defined and should consider the unique administrative demands of the position.

4. Access. WPAs should have access to those individuals and units that influence their programs—English department chairs or heads, deans, the Faculty Senate, Humanities directors, budget officers, people in admissions and in the registrar's office, and those who have anything to do with hiring, class sizes, placement. WPAs should have ample opportunities and release time to work in close consultation with colleagues in related fields and departments—Writing Center Directors, freshman advisors and freshman affairs officers, basic skills or developmental writing faculty, English-as-a-Second-Language Specialists, student counseling services, committees on student issues such as retention or admissions standards.

5. Resources and Budget. WPAs should have the power to request, receive, and allocate funds sufficient for the running of the program. Resources include, but should not be limited to, adequate work space, supplies, clerical support, research support, travel funds, and release time. WPAs should be provided with administrative support—e.g., clerical help, computer time, duplicating services—equal in quality to that available to other program directors and administrators.

II. Guidelines for Developing WPA Job Descriptions Each institution should carefully consider the role statements or job descriptions for its WPAs. Depending upon the size and scope of the writing program, the amount of administrative work expected of each WPA will vary considerably. Typically, however, WPAs have been exploited in these positions: given unrealistic workload expectations with little credit for administrative work. At large institutions with diverse programs staffed by numerous faculty or graduate assistants, several WPAs may be needed (e.g., Director and Associate Director of Writing, Writing Center Director, Basic Writing Director, Computer Writing Lab Director, Director for Writing Across the Curriculum, and so on). At smaller institutions with fewer faculty and less diverse programs, fewer writing program administrators may be needed. It is also desirable to provide advanced graduate students with administrative experience in the form of internships or assistantships to the WPAs.

The following outline suggests both the scope of preparation needed to be an effective WPA and the diverse duties that WPAs at various institutions may perform. This list is illustrative of the kinds of duties WPAs typically are engaged in: it is not descriptive of an "ideal" WPA. Nor do we wish to imply that each WPA should be assigned all of these duties. On the contrary, the workload of each WPA should be carefully negotiated with the administration annually in the form of a role statement or job description to which all parties can agree.

1. Preparation for a WPA should include knowledge of or experience with the following:
   - teaching composition and rhetoric
   - theories of writing and learning
   - research methods, evaluation methods, and teaching methods
   - language and literacy development
   - Various MLA, NCTE, and CCCC guidelines and position statements

- local and national developments in writing instruction
- writing, publishing, and presenting at conferences

2. Desirable supplemental preparation may include knowledge of or experience with the following areas:

Business
- accounting
- business administration
- grant writing
- information systems and computers
- personnel management
- records management
- public relations

Education
- curriculum design

- English as a Second Language

- testing and evaluation

- psychology of learning

- developmental or basic writing

3. As a particular institution negotiates job descriptions with each WPA, the responsibilities of the WPAs may be selected from among the following comprehensive list:

Scholarship of Administration:
- remain cognizant of current developments in teaching, research, and scholarship in rhetoric, composition, and program administration
- pursue scholarship of teaching and curriculum design as part of the essential work of the WPA Faculty Development and Other Teaching:
- teaching a for-credit graduate course in the teaching of writing
- designing or teaching faculty development seminars
- training tutors
- supervising teaching assistants and writing staff
- evaluating teaching performance: observing and evaluating TAs and adjunct faculty in class; reviewing syllabuses and course policy statements; reviewing comments on student essays and grading practices

- preparing workshops and materials, conducting workshops, and conducting follow-up meetings
- Undergraduate writing, reading, language, teaching, courses, etc.

Writing Program Development:
- designing curricula and course syllabi
- standardizing and monitoring course content
- serving on or chairing departmental committees on writing
- initiating or overseeing WAC programs
- developing teaching resource materials/library
- interviewing and hiring new faculty and staff
- selecting and evaluating textbooks (which may include establishing and supervising a textbook committee; maintaining a liaison with the bookstore; ensuring that orders are properly placed)

Writing Assessment, Writing Program Assessment, and Accountability:
- coordinating assessment and placement of students in appropriate writing courses
- administering writing placement exams and diagnostics (this may include creating and testing an appropriate instrument, acting as second reader for instructors, notifying the Registrar and instructors of any change in placements)
- administering competency, equivalency or challenge exams
- creating, or having access to, a database of information on enrollments, faculty and student performance
- administering student evaluations of teachers
- evaluating data on student retention, grade distribution, grade inflation, enrollment trends
- reporting to supervisors, chairs, deans, etc.
- conducting program reviews and self-studies

Registration and Scheduling:
- determining numbers of sections to be offered
- evaluating enrollment trends
- staffing courses
- monitoring registration

Office Management:
- supervising writing program office and secretary and staff

- supervising maintenance of office equipment and supplies
- (managing computer lab & staff)*
- (managing writing center staff)*
(*may be separate positions)

Counseling and Advising:

- arbitrating grade disputes and resolving teacher and student complaints, such as placement, plagiarism, grade appeals, scheduling problems (which may include acting as liaison with the appropriate office)
- writing letters of recommendation for graduate students, adjuncts, and tutors

Articulation:

- coordinating writing courses and instruction with other academic support services (e.g., study skills center)

- coordinating with English as a Second Language programs

- coordinating with remedial/developmental programs
- coordinating with high school (AP, CLEP, concurrent enrollment) programs
- coordinating with English Education programs
- revising and updating any publications of the writing program
- discussing the writing program with administrators, publishers' representatives, parents, prospective students

Appendix B

Evaluating the Intellectual Work of Writing Administration

Council of Writing Program Administrators

History and Background of this Statement

Preamble

It is clear within departments of English that research and teaching are generally regarded as intellectual, professional activities worthy of tenure and promotion. But administration—including leadership of first-year writing courses, WAC programs, writing centers, and the many other manifestations of writing administration—has for the most part been treated as a management activity that does not produce new knowledge and that neither requires nor demonstrates scholarly expertise and disciplinary knowledge. While there are certainly arguments to be made for academic administration, in general, as intellectual work, that is not our aim here. Instead, our concern in this document is to present a framework by which writing administration can be seen as scholarly work and therefore subject to the same kinds of evaluation as other forms of disciplinary production, such as books, articles, and reviews. More significantly, by refiguring writing administration as scholarly and intellectual work, we argue that it is worthy of tenure and promotion when it advances and enacts disciplinary knowledge within the field of Rhetoric and Composition.

1. Introduction: Three Cases

A Literary Scholar: Rewarding the Production of Knowledge

In her fourth year as a tenure-track assistant professor at a land-grant university, Mary C. came to her current position after teaching for two years at a private university where she had established a good reputation for both her scholarship and her teaching. Her present department places considerable emphasis on teaching, at least for a research university, and her colleagues have taken special note of her pedagogical skills in their annual evaluations, recognizing that teaching quality will play some role for both the dean and the provost in decisions on tenure and promotion. Nonetheless, Mary has wisely concentrated on publishing refereed articles, poems in magazines with good literary reputations, and a book with a major university press. After all, the format for promotion and tenure at her university identifies these as "categories of effort" that weigh heavily in the awarding of tenure and in promotion to higher rank. The guidelines also emphasize the importance of quality in scholarly efforts as measured not just by the judgment of her departmental colleagues but also by outside evaluators who provide an estimate of the currency and value of her scholarship as well as the prestige and visibility of the outlets in which her work appears.

By describing Mary's achievements in this familiar manner, we may be able readily to understand why she is likely to be promoted—and why her chances for advancement differ markedly from other instructors within the broad field of English literature and composition, particularly those who work as writing administrators. To do this, we need to view her work, despite its undeniably humanistic content, as the production of specific commodities—albeit scholarly commodities—with a clear exchange value, perhaps not on the general market but certainly in academic institutions. While Mary's colleagues and others who read her work can appreciate it for its uses—for the personal value of her insights into literary works or as poetry worth sharing with friends and students—the institution assigns it positive importance because the work assumes recognizable and conventional forms to which value can be readily assigned, and the valuations are likely to be recognized and accepted by most colleagues and academic departments. Because Mary's work takes conventional forms and has a recognized exchange value, her institution uses it as a basis for justifying its decision to award her with tenure and promotion—a justification it owes to the university community, to the board of regents, and to the academic community in general.

A Composition Teacher/Scholar: Rewarding Pedagogy and Pedagogical Knowledge

Twenty years ago Doug R. might have been an uncertain candidate for tenure and promotion. An assistant professor at a regional state university with a large composition program, Doug has published a number of articles in highly regarded journals in rhetoric and composition studies, though his publication record is by no means extensive. Doug's institution, however, has a well-developed system for student and departmental teaching evaluations, and Doug scores especially high on his classroom performance in both student questionnaires and on the frequent faculty observations filed by a variety of senior colleagues within the department, including the chairperson and the writing program director. Moreover, both by contract and by informal agreement, both the department and the administration at Doug's institution are required to take into account demonstrated excellence in teaching when evaluating faculty for tenure and promotion. It helps as well that Doug's specialty is composition, an academic specialty that is viewed by the administration as central to the university's undergraduate mission.

Doug's academic achievements, especially as a classroom teacher, have made it likely that he will be tenured and promoted. His pedagogical efforts take forms recognized by his colleagues and his institution and they are assigned value by accepted procedures. In combination with his published scholarship (and typical departmental committee service), Doug's teaching—which has been evaluated and quantified and made visible—becomes a strong factor in his promotion. Doug is also an innovative teacher who has shared his contributions to curricular design and pedagogy through workshops at his own institution and through presentations at national conferences. Besides having value for his colleagues and for students, these efforts appear on his vita: they constitute an important part of his reputation as a professional.

A Writing Administrator: A Problematic Case

Cheryl W. has been working hard as an assistant professor and writing director at a medium-sized university, a position for which she was hired after taking a Ph.D. in rhetoric and composition and teaching for two years (ABD) at a college with a nationally known WAC program. Cheryl has a teaching load of only One/Two, but her responsibilities are overwhelming: supervision and curriculum design for a large first-year composition program, TA training, design and administration of an emerging WAC program (with faculty workshops and publicity), many hours in the office dealing with student issues and writing reports, and an occasional graduate course in composition theory. In addition, Cheryl has guided development of five upper-level writing courses for both English majors and students in other fields, in the process greatly expanding the writing program. Cheryl's department and her institution support the growth of her program, perhaps because she has carried it out both diplomatically and professionally.

Unfortunately, Cheryl has published only a handful of refereed articles, far below the expected level for candidates for tenure and promotion at her institution. Moreover, because she has a relatively light teaching load, she has not been able to develop as thorough and far-reaching a reputation as a teacher as have most of her colleagues, and she has to face the expectation, held by her university faculty generally, that anyone with such a light teaching load should have published much more. This expectation is not the result of any hostility towards rhetoric and composition as a field; indeed, two of her colleagues, one of whom works in rhetoric and technical communication and the other of whom specializes in composition research and teacher training, have published a good deal and are considered prime candidates for tenure and promotion. Cheryl and her supporters suspect, in fact, that the productivity of these other two writing specialists may become an argument for denying her tenure and hiring someone who will be productive in ways that the department and the institution can readily recognize and value.

While many members of Cheryl's department agree that she has been working hard, they are not sure that she has been doing "real work." Others, who think her efforts have been valuable to the department, have difficulty specifying her accomplishments other than stating that "she has done an excellent job running the writing program." The problem is particularly clear to one of Cheryl's colleagues, the former director of the writing program, who recognizes the specific tasks involved in activities like supervising teaching assistants and who also recognizes that Cheryl has accomplished these tasks with energy, vision, and expertise. This colleague sums up the problem facing Cheryl and her supporters this way: "First you have to be able to specify exactly what it is that you do as a WPA; then you have to convince people that your work is intellectual work, grounded in disciplinary knowledge, demanding expertise, and producing knowledge or other valued ends, not simply busy work or administrivia that anyone with a reasonable intelligence could do; and finally you have to demonstrate that your work has been both professional and creative—worthy of recognition and reward." Unless Cheryl can do these things, her efforts will not have value within her own institution, nor will they have exchange value when she applies for another position, unless, of course, that institution has already developed a clear definition of the intellectual work of a writing administrator and can evaluate Cheryl's work within these terms. Right now, however, Cheryl will have to list her administrative categories in the small box labeled "Service" on her institution's tenure/promotion form, a category distinguished by its lack of clear definition in contrast to the detailed subcategories under "Research" (books, articles, chapters, reviews, presentations, and grants) and "Teaching" (student evaluations, supervisory reports, curriculum development, presentations and publications). Unless there is a way to demonstrate the intellectual value of her work, Cheryl is unlikely to be rewarded for her administrative work and will be denied tenure and promotion.

2. The Production of Knowledge and the Problem of Assigning Value to Academic Work

Terms like "exchange value" and "use value" and the concepts they embody help lay bare the system of academic judgments and rewards we are all familiar with, a system that lies behind the three cases described in the previous section. Academic institutions grant tenure and promotion (and hire) because they share the same understandings and values. Although departments of English, and institutions of higher education generally, may differ substantially as to the particularities of what they value—teaching, book publication, scholarly articles, local publishing, community outreach, etc.—there is considerable congruence among them concerning the ways they quantify academic work.

We use the term "quantify" advisedly. Tenure and promotion are granted on the basis of criteria that might be said to be objective. They are too familiar to rehearse here, but they might be generally described with the phrase "professional accomplishment" as measured and indicated by books, articles, conference presentations, teaching evaluations, etc. These accomplishments are concrete and can be evaluated; they can be counted, weighed, analyzed, and held forward for public review. In most departments of English, for example, to have a book accepted by Oxford, Yale, or Harvard University Press is to be assured of tenure and promotion. In colleges that place a primary value on undergraduate instruction, a faculty member whose teaching evaluations place her in the top three percent is similarly likely to be tenured and promoted. Perhaps more important than their quantifiable nature, these accomplishments are largely familiar to faculty and administrators; they are exactly the kinds of accomplishments that have been considered by universities for years in cases of tenure and promotion. Familiarity breeds ease of use; university machinery works most smoothly and efficiently when there is little or no quarrel about the means by which decisions are made. Indeed, in the case of scholarship, many of us might agree that the all-too-prevalent tendency to prefer quantity over quality is a clear sign of intellectual work turned into a quantifiable commodity. What this tells us, however, is that academic systems of evaluation and reward have for a long time assigned clear exchange values to scholarship and are now on the way to doing so with teaching.

Activities other than research and teaching, however, have little exchange value, no matter how highly they might be valued on an individual basis by fellow faculty, by administrators, or society. Only when such activities lead to a move outside faculty ranks, to a deanship, perhaps, do they take on exchange value. Otherwise, they generally appear under the ill-defined and seldom-rewarded category of "service" in promotion and tenure evaluations, a category to which the work of writing administrators is too often relegated.

In academe, work that long has been categorized as "service" occupies a wide spectrum and has proven extremely difficult to describe and evaluate. The 1996 report of the MLA Commission on Professional Service "Making Faculty Work Visible: Reinterpreting Professional Service, Teaching, and Research in the Fields of Language and Literature" states the problem clearly:

Service has functioned in the past as a kind of grab-bag for all professional work that was not clearly classroom teaching, research, or scholarship. As a result, recent efforts to define it more precisely (as "professional service") have tended to select out one subset of these activities and fail to account for all the clearly professional work previously lumped together under this rubric. ... Yet it is hard to come up with a principled definition based on common features or family resemblances among all these activities and to avoid confusions with the concept of citizenship. (184)

We do not expect to resolve the problem completely in this document. The MLA report provides useful information with its distinctions between applied work and institutional service (see 184-188). It also challenges the traditional view of service as a separate category of faculty work by identifying service, teaching, and scholarship as sites of both "intellectual work" and "professional citizenship" (162-63, 173)—an approach which means that "research is no longer the exclusive site of intellectual work" (177) and that service "can also entail substantive intellectual labor" (178).

Another helpful perspective is found in Ernest Boyer's Scholarship Reconsidered: Priorities of the Professioriate. Boyer argues that scholarship is not one category but is rather distributed over four somewhat distinguishable categories:

Discovery, Integration, Application, and Teaching. The one that concerns us here is Application. Boyer makes clear that "Colleges and universities have recently rejected service as serious scholarship, partly because its meaning is so vague and often disconnected from serious intellectual work" (22). More importantly, Boyer argues that:

> a sharp distinction must be drawn between citizenship activities and projects that relate to scholarship itself. To be sure, there are meritorious social and civic functions to be performed, and faculty should be appropriately recognized for such work. But all too frequently, service means not doing scholarship but doing good. To be considered scholarship, service activities must be tied directly to one's special field of knowledge and relate to, and flow directly out of, this professional activity. Such service is serious, demanding work, requiring the rigor-and the accountability-traditionally associated with research activities. (22)

Let us emphasize the main point here: "To be considered scholarship, service activities must be tied directly to one's special field of knowledge and relate to, and flow directly out of, this professional activity. Such service is serious, demanding work, requiring the rigor-and the accountability-traditionally associated with research activities." What Boyer is arguing is not that all service should count; rather, service can be considered as part of scholarship if it derives from and is reinforced by scholarly knowledge and disciplinary understanding.

As Boyer makes clear, in work of this sort, "theory and practice vitally interact, and one renews the other" (23).

Clearly there are many service activities that support and enhance departmental and university structures. Service on departmental and college-level committees is one of the clearest examples. Serving as the director or coordinator of an academic program may be another. Such service is considered a form of scholarship, however, only if it flows from and contributes to the scholarship of the field. In our terms, such work is intellectual: it requires specific expertise, training, and an understanding of disciplinary knowledge.

An example may be in order. Let us presume that the director of a first-year writing course is designing an in-house placement procedure so that students new to the college can be placed into the appropriate course in the first-year composition sequence. She will need to decide whether to use direct or indirect measures of writing ability; will need to assess the implications that the placement procedure will have on high school curriculum; will want to consult research on such things as the nature of writing prompts, whether an objective test and a writing test should be used together, and the optimal amount of time for the exam. Thus what some see as a simple decision (place students according to an ACT score) is, in reality, complex intellectual work involving disciplinary knowledge, empirical research, and histories of practice.

An additional dimension of this kind of intellectual work is that it neither derives from nor produces simplistic products or services. Rather, it draws upon historical and contemporary knowledge, and it contributes to the formation of new knowledge and improved decision making. These kinds of practices lead to new knowledge and innovative educational programs, and contribute to thoughtful and invigorated teaching.

3. Evaluating The Work Of Writing Administration

What this document is arguing is that a definition of writing administration as intellectual work in colleges and universities must take into account the paradigm established by research and scholarship. At its highest level, this means the production of new knowledge (what Scholarship Reconsidered calls the "scholarship of discovery"). But the contemporary scholarly paradigm embraces a much broader spectrum of intellectual work. For instance, The Disciplines Speak, the report of a national working group of representatives from sixteen different professional associations (including CCCC and MLA), indicates that scholarly activity can be demonstrated in ways as diverse as "publishing the results of one's scholarly research, developing a new course, writing an innovative textbook, implementing an outreach program for the community ... or assisting in a K-12 curriculum project" (Diamond and Adam 13). And the MLA's "Making Faculty Work Visible" offers this list of some of the "projects and enterprises of knowledge and learning" in English studies:

- creating new questions, problems, information, interpretations, designs, products, frameworks of understanding, etc., through inquiry (e.g., empirical, textual, historical, theoretical, technological, artistic, practical);

- clarifying, critically examining, weighing, and revising the knowledge claims, beliefs, or understanding of others and oneself;

- connecting knowledge to other knowledge;

- preserving ... and reinterpreting past knowledge;

- applying aesthetic, political, and ethical values to make judgments about knowledge and its uses;

- arguing knowledge claims in order to invite criticism and revision;

- making specialized knowledge broadly accessible and usable, e.g., to young learners, to nonspecialists in other disciplines, to the public;

- helping new generations to become active knowers themselves, preparing them for lifelong learning and discovery;

- applying knowledge to practical problems in significant or innovative ways;

- creating insight and communicating forms of experience through artistic works or performance. (175-76)

Within this contemporary scholarly paradigm, writing administration may be considered intellectual work when it meets two tests. First, it needs to advance knowledge—its production, clarification, connection, reinterpretation, or application. Second, it results in products or activities that can be evaluated by others—for instance, against this list of qualities which, according to The Disciplines Speak, "seem to characterize that work that most disciplines would consider 'scholarly' or 'professional'":

- the activity requires a high level of discipline-related expertise.

- the activity ... is innovative.

- the activity can be replicated or elaborated.

- the work and its results can be documented.

- the work and its results can be peer-reviewed.

- the activity has significance or impact. (14)

In order to be regarded as intellectual work, therefore, writing administration must be viewed as a form of inquiry which advances knowledge and which has formalized outcomes that are subject to peer review and disciplinary evaluation. Just as the articles, stories, poems, books, committee work, classroom performance, and other evidence of tenure and promotion can be critiqued and evaluated by internal and external reviewers, so can the accomplishments, products, innovations, and contributions of writing administrators. Indeed, such review must be central to the evaluation of writing administration as scholarly and intellectual work

Defining and evaluating the work of writing administrators is a process that needs to be made explicit so that those who do this work—and they are often beginning faculty who are over-worked, over-stressed, and untenured—stand a real chance of succeeding professionally within departmental and institutional contexts. On a national level, this process not only can provide guidelines to help institutions and faculty understand and properly evaluate the work of writing administrators, but also produce some degree of empirical data that can create an exchange value for administrative accomplishments parallel to that already in place for research and teaching.

The remainder of this document will suggest guidelines which we hope will prove useful to individuals, committees, and departments working to develop materials and policies for evaluating writing administrators ("WPAs," as they are often called). First, Section 4 will propose five descriptive categories within which the intellectual work of a WPA can be best considered. Then, in Section 5, we will suggest several evaluative criteria by which merit pay increases as well as tenure and promotion decisions can be made fairly and thoughtfully in terms of the quality and the quantity of intellectual work achieved by a writing administrator. Finally, Section 6 will provide a framework that can be used to organize the accomplishments—and to help in the evaluation—of individuals devoted to writing administration.

4. Five Categories Of Intellectual Work

Although writing administration, like the work of any other administrative figure on campus, is subject to a variety of different interpretations, we propose that much of it can be understood as falling within one or more of these categories:

Program Creation, Curricular Design, Faculty Development, Program Assessment, and Program-Related Textual Production.

Program Creation

Whatever the specific focus of administration (first-year course, WAC program, writing center, etc.), one of the primary scholarly accomplishments of writing administration is the creation of a program. By creation, we mean those specific activities that reconceive the philosophy, goals, purposes, and institutional definition of the specific writing program. Program creation is not something that every writing administrator does or should do; if a WPA inherits a well-designed program that is generally viewed positively by students, faculty, and campus administrators, then it is likely that the program will be maintained. Even in such cases, however, a person engaged in the intellectual work of writing administration can add, modify, or otherwise develop a significant new emphasis or supplementary support system. For example, a writing administrator might create a Writing Center to support and enhance undergraduate instruction; or the he might revise the emphasis of second-semester composition by altering the programmatic goals from a traditional research paper to shorter essays emphasizing academic discourse or cultural studies.

Our point here is that program creation is a strong indication of intellectual work, since successful programs are grounded in significant disciplinary knowledge, a national perspective that takes into account the successes and failures of other composition programs, and a combined practical and theoretical understanding of learning theory, the composing process, the philosophy of composition, rhetorical theory, etc. An obvious corollary is that writing programs that fail, other than when attacked on the basis of budget and ideology, often do so because they lack this scholarly foundation.

Curricular Design

Although closely related to program creation, curricular design is a somewhat differentiated use of scholarly knowledge that is still strongly representative of intellectual work. Indeed, although we separate the categories for the sake of elaboration, they greatly overlap. Curricular design is the overall articulation of the administrative unit: the establishment of a programmatic architecture that structures and maintains the various components of the composition program being evaluated. Curricular design does not inevitably depend on or illustrate scholarly knowledge; in combination with program creation, however, it is strongly indicative of intellectual work.

Once a WPA has engaged in program creation, for example by developing an innovative curricular emphasis for English 101, the next step is to integrate that new emphasis within the curriculum. That is likely to mean reconfiguring course requirements, altering curricular emphases, choosing new textbooks that more fully endorse the new vision, etc. Another example can be drawn from Writing Across the Curriculum (WAC), a program that is often independent of any specific department but whose director must often be promoted and tenured within English. Program design for a WAC director might include the articulation of requirements and standards by which the program includes some courses and excludes others, the development of criteria for evaluating the success of specific courses, the creation of well-articulated expectations so that faculty across the disciplines include writing in their courses with some degree of commonality. Curricular design is not a purely technical matter; it requires an understanding of the conceptual, a grounding in composition history, theory, and pedagogy. This is inevitably the case since its chief goal is to lead the writing program toward a coherent and explicit philosophy.

Faculty Development

Whether working with faculty, teaching assistants, lecturers, adjunct faculty, or undergraduate peer tutors, it is clear that no writing program can succeed unless its staff is well trained and generally in accord with the overall programmatic goals and methodologies. Thus one of a writing administrator's chief responsibilities is to maintain a strong staff development program. The chief responsibilities, here, are to: develop and implement training programs for new and experienced staff; communicate current pedagogical approaches and current research in rhetoric and composition; provide logistical, intellectual, and financial support for staff activities in course design, pedagogical development, and research; maintain an atmosphere of openness and support for the development and sharing of effective teaching ideas and curricular emphases; maintain open lines of communication among administrators, support staff, and faculty; etc.

Although it is often overlooked, faculty and staff development depends primarily on one factor: the degree to which those being administered value and respect the writing administrator. Staff development cannot be accomplished by fiat. Instructors cannot simply be ordered and coerced, no matter how subordinate their position within the university. Thus faculty development, when it truly accomplishes its purpose of improving teaching and maintaining the highest classroom standards, is one of the most salient examples of intellectual work carried out within an administrative sphere. To be an effective administrative leader, a WPA must be able to incorporate current research and theory into the training and must demonstrate that knowledge through both word and deed.

Program Assessment and Evaluation

Accountability is one of the over-riding concepts in higher education generally, and in writing administration specifically. No single method or paradigm exists that is appropriate for all composition programs; on the contrary, each writing administrator must develop site-specific measures for the assessment and evaluation of the goals, pedagogy, and overall effectiveness of the composition program. In a composition program, that assessment may take the form of portfolios; in that case, the scholarly expertise of the WPA takes the form of designing the portfolios, creating a rigorous and meaningful assessment procedure by which the portfolios can be evaluated, etc. In a WAC program, the writing administrator would likely need to develop assessment measures in order to demonstrate that writing-enhanced classes are indeed consolidating the knowledge of majors across campus and producing undergraduate students that have achieved a genuine measure of compositional ability.

In order to achieve meaningful assessment (by which we mean overall determination of programmatic effectiveness) and meaningful evaluation (that is, specific determination of students and instructors), writing administrators must bring to bear scholarly knowledge concerning holistic scoring, primary trait scoring, descriptive analysis, scoring rubrics, and other information that spans various disciplines. This knowledge and its application are essential if the program is to demonstrate its value and be assured of continuing funding.

Program-Related Textual Production

By this category, we mean the production of written materials in addition to conference papers, articles in refereed journals, scholarly books, textbooks, and similar products that would be evaluated the same whether produced by a WPA or any other faculty member. (Textbooks are a special case. Clearly, not every textbook offers evidence of intellectual work; a grammar work book that asks students to fill in the blanks or a reading anthology that is highly derivative and lacking in substantive pedagogical apparatus may not meet national and departmental definitions of intellectual work. Many textbooks, however, represent significant advances in instruction, both locally and nationally, and are, therefore, important ways for compositionists to demonstrate their scholarly expertise.)

Besides such products, numerous other texts must be considered as part of the writing administrator's resume of scholarly production. These include such things as innovative course syllabi which articulate the WPA's curricular design; local, state, and national funding proposals for the enhancement of instruction; statements of teaching philosophy for the composition curriculum; original materials for instructional workshops; evaluations of teaching that explicitly articulate and promote overall programmatic goals; resource materials for the training of staff as well as for the use of students in classrooms, writing centers, and other programs. Clearly boundaries must be set; not every memo, descriptive comment, or teaching evaluation embodies the concept of intellectual work. But any responsible system of evaluation needs to acknowledge that individuals engaged in the intellectual work of administration concretize their knowledge—and build a reviewable record—through the authorship of a body of textual materials related to program creation, curricular design, faculty development, and program assessment.

5. Evaluative Criteria

Writing administrators provide leadership for many different kinds of programs—such as first-year courses, writing-across-the-disciplines programs, writing centers, and law programs—and they work in a wide variety of institutional settings—among them, two-year colleges, private four-year colleges, and large universities with an array of doctoral offerings. So it is it not possible to establish a fixed set of criteria by which to evaluate writing administrators. It is possible, however, to offer general guidelines and suggestions which WPAs, personnel committees, department chairs, and others can use as they prepare materials and develop personnel policies that fit specific institutional contexts.

Guideline One

The first guideline is based on the previous section, which describes five broad areas in which the intellectual work of writing administration occurs. We urge that materials and policies for the evaluation of WPAs focus on the following areas:

- Program Creation
- Curricular Design
- Faculty Development
- Program Assessment and Evaluation
- Program-Related Textual Production.

Guideline Two

The second guideline attempts to clarify what sort of activities and products within the five categories should be considered "intellectual work." We suggest that a particular product or activity of a WPA is intellectual work when it meets one or more of these four criteria:

- It generates, clarifies, connects, reinterprets, or applies knowledge based on research, theory, and sound pedagogical practice;

- It requires disciplinary knowledge available only to an expert trained in or conversant with a particular field;

- It requires highly developed analytical or problem solving skills derived from specific expertise, training, or research derived from scholarly knowledge;

- It results in products or activities that can be evaluated by peers (e.g., publication, internal and outside evaluation, participant responses) as the contribution of the individual's insight, research, and disciplinary knowledge.

Guideline Three

The third guideline suggests more specific criteria that can be used to evaluate the quality of a product or activity reflecting a writing administrator's intellectual work:

- Innovation: The writing administrator creates one or more new programs, curricular emphases, assessment measures, etc.

- Improvement/Refinement: The WPA makes changes and alterations that distinctly and concretely lead to better teaching, sounder classroom practices, etc.

- Dissemination: The WPA, through workshops, colloquia, staff meetings, and other forums, is able to communicate curricular goals, methodologies, and overall programmatic philosophy in such a way as to lead to positive and productive results for students, instructors, and school.

- Empirical Results: The WPA is able to present concrete evidence of accomplishments; that evidence may take the form of pre- and post-evaluative measures, written testimonials from students and staff, teaching evaluations, etc.

That list, of course, is far from comprehensive. Indeed, as "Making Faculty Work Visible" puts it, "[i]ntellectual work in a postsecondary setting may excel in various ways," among them, "skill, care, rigor, and intellectual honesty; a heuristic passion for knowledge; originality; relevance and aptness; coherence, consistency, and development within a body of work; diversity and versatility of contribution; thorough knowledge and constructive use of important work by others; the habit of self-critical examination and openness to criticism and revision; sustained productivity over time; high impact and value to a local academic community like the department; relevance and significance to societal issues and problems; effective communication and dissemination" (177).

Guideline Four

The fourth guideline emphasizes the centrality of peer evaluation to describing and judging the intellectual work of writing administration. The Council of Writing Program Administrators encourages the use of peer review in evaluating the intellectual work of WPAs. This will likely require the WPA to create a portfolio that reflects her or his scholarly and intellectual accomplishments as an administrator; this portfolio would be reviewed by outside evaluators selected by the department in consultation with the person being evaluated.

6. Implementation

The Council of Writing Program Administrators is convinced that WPAs can be evaluated on the basis of their administrative work and that the four guidelines sketched above can help in the process by providing clear categories to organize the work of the writing administrator and by providing meaningful criteria by which to review that work.

Implicit in the guidelines of Section 5 is a framework that can be used to organize accomplishments—and to help in the evaluation—of faculty who are involved in writing administration:

A. *The Work of Writing Administration*

Description of activities and products organized by the five categories in Guideline One. (As the final paragraphs of Section 5 indicate, evaluation could include a wide range of program-related written materials "in addition to conference papers, articles in refereed journals, scholarly books, textbooks, and similar products that would be evaluated the same whether produced by a WPA or any other faculty member.")

B. *Evidence of Intellectual Work*

Representative activities and products with evidence relating to Guideline Two.

C. *Quality of Intellectual Work*

Representative activities and products with evidence relating to Guideline Three.

D. *Peer Review*

Reports from scholars and writing administrators qualified to evaluate the materials against broad professional standards.

That general framework could serve as an heuristic for writing administrators preparing personnel materials and as an organization for their portfolios, and it might work to guide reviews of portfolios by the institution. Given the wide range of duties possible for a given writing administrator—and the wide range of institutions within which WPAs work—that framework can also serve as a starting point for revision and refinement by writing administrators, personnel committees, department chairs, and others working so that the evaluation of writing administrators fits distinctive local conditions.

If you are engaged in such work, the Council of Writing Program Administrators hopes you find this document a useful source of ideas about the intellectual work of writing administration and how this work can be evaluated. There are, of course, many other resources that you can turn to as you develop responsible means to evaluate writing program administrators. Here is a brief list of reports, articles, and books (the first several of which were quoted in this document):

Ernest L. Boyer. Scholarship Reconsidered:

Priorities for the Professoriate. Princeton:

Carnegie Foundation for the Advancement of Teaching, 1990.

Robert M. Diamond and Bronwyn E. Adam, eds. The Disciplines Speak: Rewarding the Scholarly, Professional, and Creative Work of Faculty. Washington: American Association for Higher Education, 1995.

MLA Commission on Professional Service. "Making Faculty Work Visible: Reinterpreting Professional Service, Teaching, and Research in the Fields of Language and Literature." Profession 1996. New York: MLA, 1996. 161-216.

Offprints are available from the MLA.

Works Cited

"ADE Statement of Good Practice: Teaching, Evaluation, and Scholarship."

ADE Bulletin No. 105 (Fall 1993): 43-45.

Lynn Z. Bloom. "The Importance of External Reviews in Composition Studies." Academic Advancement in Composition Studies. Eds. Richard C. Gebhardt and Barbara Genelle Smith Gebhardt. Mahwah: Lawrence Erlbaum, 1997.

Council of Writing Program Administrators. "Guidelines for Self Study to Precede a Writing Program Evaluation." Teaching and Assessing Writing. Edward M. White. San Francisco: Jossey-Bass, 1994.

———. "Guidelines for Writing Program Administrator (WPA) Positions." WPA: Writing Program Administration 16.1-2 (Fall-Winter 1992): 89-94.

Christine Hult. "The Scholarship of Administration." Theorizing and Enacting Difference: Resituating Writing Programs within the Academy. Eds. Joseph Janangelo and Christine Hansen. Portsmouth: Boynton/Cook-Heinemann, 1997.

"Report of the Commission on Writing and Literature." Profession 88. New York: MLA, 1988. 70-76.

Duane H. Roen. "Writing Administration as Scholarship and Teaching." Academic Advancement in Composition Studies. Eds. Richard C. Gebhardt and Barbara Genelle Smith Gebhardt. Mahwah: Lawrence Erlbaum, 1997.

History of this Document

Evaluating the Intellectual Work of Writing Administration" evolved over several years since the WPA Executive Committee began developing an "intellectual work document" on the scholarly and professional activities of writing administrators. Robert Schwegler, Gail Stygall, Judy Pearce, and Charles Schuster—consulting with Executive Committee members and others—developed approaches which Charles Schuster drafted into the version published in the Fall/Winter 1996 issue of WPA as a way to solicit additional response. Following discussion of that draft and various responses at the July 1997 Executive Committee meeting, Richard Gebhardt coordinated a revision effort and drafted versions discussed, modified, and approved by the Executive Committee during its meetings in 1998. The Council of Writing Program Administrators recommends this document a source of ideas about the intellectual work of writing administration and about how this work can be evaluated responsibly and professionally.

Appendix C

WPA Outcomes Statement for First-Year Composition

Adopted by the Council of Writing Program Administrators (WPA), April 2000

For further information about the development of the Outcomes Statement, please see http://www.mwsc.edu/~outcomes/

For further information about the Council of Writing Program Administrators, please see http://www.cas.ilstu.edu/english/hesse/ wpawelcome.htm

A version of this statement was published in WPA: Writing Program Administration 23.1/2 (fall/winter 1999): 59-66.

Introduction

This statement describes the common knowledge, skills, and attitudes sought by first-year composition programs in American postsecondary education. To some extent, we seek to regularize what can be expected to be taught in first-year composition; to this end the document is not merely a compilation or summary of what currently takes place. Rather, the following statement articulates what composition teachers nationwide have learned from practice, research, and theory. This document intentionally defines only "outcomes," or types of results, and not "standards," or precise levels of achievement. The setting of standards should be left to specific institutions or specific groups of institutions.

Learning to write is a complex process, both individual and social, that takes place over time with continued practice and informed guidance. Therefore, it is important that teachers, administrators, and a concerned public do not imagine that these outcomes can be taught in reduced or simple ways. Helping students demonstrate these outcomes requires expert understanding of how students actually learn to write. For this reason we expect the primary audience for this document to be well-prepared college writing teachers and college writing program administrators. In some places, we have chosen to write in their professional language. Among such readers, terms such as "rhetorical" and "genre" convey a rich meaning that is not easily simplified. While we have also aimed at writing a document that the general public can understand, in limited cases we have aimed first at communicating effectively with expert writing teachers and writing program administrators.

These statements describe only what we expect to find at the end of first-year composition, at most schools a required general education course or sequence of courses. As writers move beyond first-year composition, their writing abilities do not merely improve. Rather, students' abilities not only diversify along disciplinary and professional lines but also move into whole new levels where expected outcomes expand, multiply, and diverge. For this reason, each statement of outcomes for first-year composition is followed by suggestions for further work that builds on these outcomes.

RHETORICAL KNOWLEDGE

By the end of first year composition, students should

- Focus on a purpose
- Respond to the needs of different audiences
- Respond appropriately to different kinds of rhetorical situations
- Use conventions of format and structure appropriate to the rhetorical situation
- Adopt appropriate voice, tone, and level of formality
- Understand how genres shape reading and writing

- Write in several genres

Faculty in all programs and departments can build on this preparation by helping students learn

- The main features of writing in their fields
- The main uses of writing in their fields
- The expectations of readers in their fields

CRITICAL THINKING, READING, AND WRITING

By the end of first year composition, students should

- Use writing and reading for inquiry, learning, thinking, and communicating Understand a writing assignment as a series of tasks, including finding, evaluating, analyzing, and synthesizing appropriate
- primary and secondary sources
- Integrate their own ideas with those of others
- Understand the relationships among language, knowledge, and power

Faculty in all programs and departments can build on this preparation by helping students learn

- The uses of writing as a critical thinking method
- The interactions among critical thinking, critical reading, and writing
- The relationships among language, knowledge, and power in their fields

PROCESSES

By the end of first year composition, students should

- Be aware that it usually takes multiple drafts to create and complete a successful text
- Develop flexible strategies for generating, revising, editing, and proof-reading
- Understand writing as an open process that permits writers to use later invention and re-thinking to revise their work

- Understand the collaborative and social aspects of writing processes

- Learn to critique their own and others' works

- Learn to balance the advantages of relying on others with the responsibility of doing their part

- Use a variety of technologies to address a range of audiences

Faculty in all programs and departments can build on this preparation by helping students learn

- To build final results in stages

- To review work-in-progress in collaborative peer groups for purposes other than editing

- To save extensive editing for later parts of the writing process

- To apply the technologies commonly used to research and communicate within their fields

KNOWLEDGE OF CONVENTIONS

By the end of first year composition, students should

- Learn common formats for different kinds of texts

- Develop knowledge of genre conventions ranging from structure and paragraphing to tone and mechanics

- Practice appropriate means of documenting their work

- Control such surface features as syntax, grammar, punctuation, and spelling.

Faculty in all programs and departments can build on this preparation by helping students learn

- The conventions of usage, specialized vocabulary, format, and documentation in their fields

- Strategies through which better control of conventions can be achieved

Author Index

Subject Index

A

AACC. *see* American Association of Community Colleges

AAC&U. *see* American Association of Colleges and Universities

AAHE. *see* American Association of Higher Education

Abolitionist strategy, 192–194, 214, 219–230

Access
 to computers, 347–351
 types of, 349

ACE. *see* American Council on Education

Activity system, 18

ADE. *see* Association of Departments of English

Adjunct instructors, 181–201

Administration. *see also* Writing program administration
 advancement in, 113–135
  motivations for, 114–116
  versus certification, 81t–82t
 collaborative, 253–262
 in community colleges, 433–435
 and computing, 351–357
 definition of, 20
 preparation for, 118–122
 styles of, 43
 virtues of, 26
 of WAC programs, models of, 442–443

Administrators, characteristics of, 127–130, 128t

AEE. *see* Alternative Educational Environments

Agency
 and assessment, 309–312
 and ethical decision making, 159

Aggressive behavior, approaches to
 direct, 338–339
 indirect, 336–338

Alliance building, outreach and, 317–318

Alternative Educational Environments (AEE), 373

Amateurism, 75–76

American Association of Colleges and Universities (AAC&U), website, 8

American Association of Community Colleges (AACC), 432

American Association of Higher Education (AAHE)
 on faculty roles and rewards, 9
 formation of, 74
 website, 8

American Association of School Administrators, 151

American Association of University Administrators, 151

American Association of University Professors, 151
 website, 23

American College Personnel Association, 151

American Council on Education (ACE)
 Fellows Program, 6
 website, 121

Application, 12

Archivists
 documentation strategies for, 281–283
 mind-set of, 276–277
 rationale for, 279–281
 WPAs as, 275–290

Articulation, 315–330
 and assessment, 303–314

Assessment, 303–314
 bibliography on, 477–479
 computing and, 352–354
 versus evaluation, 303–304
 and outreach, 326
 and TA training, 419–420
 of WAC programs, 446–450

Assignments, designing and sequencing, TAs and, 396–397, 417–419

Association of Departments of English (ADE), 121

Attendance, and aggressive behavior, 336–337

Authority issues, 13, 15
 contrapower harassment, 331–339
 decentering, 25
 responsibility without authority, 130
 TAs and, 395

B

Bard College, 328

Beauty, centers and, 28

531